Teaching Law
and Literature

Modern Language Association of America
Options for Teaching

For a complete listing of titles,
see the last pages of this book

Teaching Law and Literature

Edited by
Austin Sarat,
Cathrine O. Frank,
and Matthew Anderson

The Modern Language Association of America
New York   2011

© 2011 by The Modern Language Association of America
All rights reserved. Printed in the United States of America

MLA and MODERN LANGUAGE ASSOCIATION are trademarks
owned by the Modern Language Association of America. For information
about obtaining permission to reprint material from MLA book publications,
send your request by mail (see address below), e-mail (permissions@mla.org),
or fax (646 458-0030).

Library of Congress Cataloging-in-Publication Data

Teaching law and literature / edited by Austin Sarat, Cathrine O. Frank and
Matthew Anderson.
        p. cm. — (Modern Language Association of America options for
teaching)
    Includes bibliographical references and index.
    ISBN 978-1-60329-092-0 (hardcover : alk. paper)
    ISBN 978-1-60329-093-7 (pbk. : alk. paper)
  1. Law and literature—Study and teaching—United States. 2. Law—Study
and teaching—United States. 3. Law and literature.   I. Sarat, Austin.
II. Frank, Cathrine O.   III. Anderson, Matthew Daniel.
    KF277.L38T43 2011
    340.071'173—dc22   2010052290

Options for Teaching 32
ISSN 1079-2562

Cover illustration of the paperback edition: *Rights o' Man*, a limited edition
letterpress print by Peter Chasseaud, © Peter Chasseaud 2010. Poster for a new
production of Benjamin Britten's *Billy Budd* at Glyndebourne

Published by The Modern Language Association of America
26 Broadway, New York, NY 10004-1789
www.mla.org

Contents

Part III: Texts

Austin Sarat, Cathrine O. Frank, and Matthew Anderson

Introduction

We begin with the simple observation that, while there is a large body of scholarship *about* law and literature and there are many scholars "doing" law and literature (i.e., invoking one discipline to illuminate something about the other), there is a surprising absence of guidance about how to bring this research into the classroom—no sense, in other words, of how to *teach* law and literature. Although this volume is intended to begin filling that gap, we hope that the essays collected here will inform and prompt other projects geared to what we do as teachers. Most important, we hope that these essays will inspire innovative teaching.

This book provides a resource for teachers interested in learning about the field of law and literature and how to bring its insights to bear in their classrooms, both in the liberal arts and in law schools. Our goal was to put together a volume that is as ecumenical as possible. A teacher new to law and literature will find here an introduction to the field's history, critical approaches, and seminal texts, along with advice about how to design courses, syllabi, and assignments; how to organize and shape class discussions; and how to find supporting materials. Those already familiar with the field will see connections with their own practices, suggestive possibilities for new work, and opportunities for collaboration. We hope that

1

newcomers and veterans alike will find in this volume an inviting sense of community and shared enterprise.

Newcomers will be introduced to the field's key terms, beginning with "law and literature" and its counterpart, "law as literature." At once a set of historical terms, marking out phases of the movement, and a rubric for conceptualizing the relation between two discourses, these phrases continue to provide a shorthand for, respectively, the literary representation of legal ideas, forms, and persons alongside the study of narrative, rhetorical, and interpretive practices of law.

Part of this book's purpose is to shift the field's center from law schools, where it originated, to the undergraduate liberal arts curriculum. One barely speaks of "law and" without imagining "law as." Therefore, by referring to literature and law, we also invoke the possibility of thinking about literature as law, or the idea, suggested by Robin West in her contribution to the volume, that cultural forms can assume the force of law. In this sense, "law and" and "law as" offer a foundational nomenclature that has become useful, both in its export and in its deconstruction, for conceptualizing other law and humanities fields.

Newcomers will see in the history of law and literature important parallels to the larger movements in academic thought (e.g., the focus on literary theory and hermeneutics in the 1980s, the rise of new historicism and cultural studies in the 1990s), but the field's development has also been motivated by specific tendencies in legal education and legal thought.

As important as the theoretical and historical background is, however, prospective teachers want to know what others have done in classrooms and what they can do to capture their students' imagination. Our contributors have outlined model courses and detailed their approach to specific texts, including staple literary and legal texts (novels and trial reports) as well as new ones that redefine both what counts as literature (film, music, digital media) and what counts as law (ceremonies, blawgs). The essays collected here are thus a resource in an immediate sense: readers can use this book to create a course, integrate new readings into an existing syllabus, and learn how to negotiate the challenges of interdisciplinary teaching by seeing what has worked, as well as what hasn't, for our contributors.

Experienced teachers of law and literature may ask, How is the field different from what it was in the 1970s and 1980s? Have its aims changed? Does it still make sense to speak of law and literature? What difficulties has the field overcome, and what new opportunities exist to refresh or expand existing approaches? The volume provides a retrospective survey of the field, written by several of its founders. But the juxtaposition of these sometimes asymmetrical histories can reveal paths for new scholarship and teaching.

Our emphasis on teaching might strike veteran readers as nostalgic. Today's field of law and literature seems less focused on educating lawyers and judges than on extensions of literary theory to questions of legal interpretation. Instead, we have classes in the undergraduate curriculum—and, of particular interest here, in the undergraduate curriculum of literature departments—where students' encounters with plays and novels are enriched by a new interest in legal culture, by the comparison of legal and literary responses to questions of representation and justice, and by the comparison of the formation of legal and literary subjectivity. At the same time, today's law and literature syllabus may include pop cultural forms, like hip-hop or new digital media, as much as statutes and novels.

There is also greater circumspection now about arguing that literature can save law from the lawyers and the lawyers from themselves. If reading literature doesn't necessarily make us better people, then why read it, let alone encourage law students to take courses in it? One response to this skepticism is that if reading literature is not a sure path to human improvement, there is still value in pairing law with other ways of knowing. Albeit less invested than it once was in the dichotomies of moral versus economic or affective versus rational knowledge (distinctions that informed the creation in 1988 of the *Yale Journal of Law and the Humanities*, for example), the field of law and literature today remains committed to opening law and legal practices to the kinds of critique that are standard in literary and humanistic studies: Why does this form emerge in this place at this time and in this way? What are the cultural conditions that make law possible? How do law's processes compare with those of other rhetorical modes and canons of interpretation? How might looking at a familiar text through other disciplinary eyes change one's understanding of it?

Another way of responding to questions about the educational value of law and literature is to consider whether the field is a strictly textual phenomenon. Some essays in this volume situate legal and literary studies in a broader cultural context and incorporate nonliterary texts, such as Native American ceremony and hip-hop, and noncanonical texts, such as prison literature, alongside digitally cloned performances. But aren't these other ways of knowing at work in other forms and outside the academy? The emergence of truth and reconciliation commissions, for example, or the inclusion at sentencing of victim impact statements suggests that the work of law and literature already has moved both outside the classroom and off the written page. The emphasis on telling one's own story or on speaking to power and countering official narratives, which has been central to law and literature, has brought the lived stories of law's subjects to the fore, thereby shifting law and literature's attention away from the classroom. Indeed, in connection with the question of what constitutes a legal or a literary text, practitioners of law and literature are now asking how to trouble what counts as both legal and literary knowledge.

As Julie Stone Peters asks in her contribution to this volume, does it still make sense to speak of law and literature? In the move toward non-literary and even nontextual forms, the phrase may no longer represent the range of work done in its name. At a time when scholars across the humanities are increasingly uniting with literary scholars and legal scholars in their recognition of the need for a more self-consciously and program-matically coherent humanistic approach to law, a strict focus on literature and law may seem narrow and dated, out of step with the opening to a broader rubric of law and the humanities. It may read as a failure to ac-knowledge ways of thinking about texts and their audiences that recognize that globalization has changed the nation-state—and, with it, the idea of national literature on which traditional literary studies rests—and that the proliferation of new media may signal the end of print culture.

Nonetheless, law and literature remains a meaningful and important pairing, not least because it asks us to consider why literature, or the study of literature, has seemed so relevant to law. The law and literature move-ment, as it is often characterized (particularly with reference to its energy and cohesiveness in legal studies in the 1970s and 1980s), addressed this question from its inception, as the essays in part 1 make clear. Robert Weisberg's experiment suggests, for example, that other pairings just don't seem to generate the same productive friction. Yet is literature everywhere indeed relevant to law everywhere? Do they exist in the same relation to each other the world over? Our approach relies on a deepening sense of the interpenetrations of literature and legal culture, that is, on a sense of the specific, contingent ways in which literary texts emerge from and en-gage with particular traditions—for example, legal and religious traditions of textual interpretation—at discrete historical moments.

Such an engagement requires specific disciplinary knowledge, both of law and of literature. Whatever new institutional or disciplinary configura-tions emerge from the foregrounding of culture in the age of globalization and new media, there will continue to be a need for the specialized knowl-edge of genre, period, and tradition and for the sensitivity to language, rhetoric, and the strictures of form that are among the hallmarks of the study of literature.

One of the field's underexplored questions is the influence of its Anglo-American roots. Globalizing the study of law and literature will require transliterating its rubrics: the creation of an approximate study that would have meaning precisely because it remains open to cultural difference and the contingencies of history. Why has law and literature been a predominantly Anglo-American phenomenon? The English and American traditions, though they share common law, are more different than alike in key respects.

A few of these differences play a role in the elaboration of American legal consciousness: for example, the contact between European and indigenous culture during the early colonial period, the influence of the Puritan imagination, the experience of slavery and the constitutional framework that sanctioned it, the idea of the frontier, and the impact of immigration. Perhaps the most salient difference, however, lies in the conception of sovereignty and the reverence for the idea of the rule of law that emerged in the American political imagination during the revolutionary period and that acquired institutional force with the Supreme Court's decision in *Marbury v. Madison*. As Thomas Paine famously proclaimed, "in America the law is king" (279).

The point here isn't to celebrate the singularity of American legal consciousness but to describe its contours as a way of framing an understanding of the impetus behind law and literature. There are good reasons to be restrained in praise for the American constitutional model—the Dred Scott decision, for example: the American Constitution recognized slavery as lawful. Its treatment of women and indigenous peoples was not exemplary. Still, there is something vital in John Adams's celebrated dictum that America's is a government of laws, not people (*Massachusetts Constitution*). Indeed, as the American legal scholar Paul Kahn has argued, attachment to the idea of the rule of law is such an article of faith in American law schools and legal studies that it is difficult for legal scholars today to create the critical distance necessary to see and describe it as an article of faith. Kahn compares the project and challenge of a cultural study of law in America with those of a cultural study of Christianity faced by Western scholars of religion before the twentieth century:

> [T]he study of Christianity was not an intellectual discipline. It was, instead, a part of religious practice. Its aim was the progressive realization of a Christian order in the world—reform within the Christian community, and conversion abroad. Only when the theological project

became capable of suspending belief in the object of its study could a real discipline of religious study emerge. . . . The scholar of religion should not be asked whether Christ is God or what is the correct belief about the Trinity. Similarly, the scholar of law's rule should not be asked whether law is the expression of the will of the sovereign and thus a form of self-government. These are propositions internal to the systems of belief. A scholarly discipline of the cultural form approaches these propositions not from the perspective of their validity, but from the perspective of the meaning they have for the individual within the community of belief. . . . Distance from one's own beliefs is a necessary condition of such scholarship, yet that distance is not easily obtained. (2–3)

The point to be taken from Kahn is that while a major strain of law and literature scholarship has been motivated by a trope of rescue—the idea that literature can humanize the law anew—the mission would not have the same impetus if investment in the idea of the rule of law weren't so strong. In our view, this is the chief reason why law and literature hasn't taken hold the same way in other national traditions. Where there have been signs of interest in it (e.g., Italy and France), one finds a rhetoric of liberty and equality and often a stronger conception of the state, but nothing like the American reverence for the rule of law.

In America the interplay of law and literature is part of a triad, religion being the third term. The work of Robert Ferguson, a literaray scholar, is indispensable here, especially for an understanding of the recalibration that occurs during the early republican period and the way it finds expression in American law and letters. As Ferguson indicates, a striking aspect of the transition from the colonial to the republican period is the rivalry between law and religion and how the former displaces the latter. "The abrupt removal of religious voices from controlling political discourse in the post-Revolutionary era remains one of the neglected stories in American history," he writes (*Reading* 54). "[R]eligious discourse had much less to do with civic identity in the early republic than it did in the colonial period, and it fell increasingly under the rhetorical sway of natural legal rights." This displacement of religion by law in the aftermath of the revolution—the constitutional separation of church and state—presents scholars with two challenges:

The proficiency with which the law superseded religion in republican formations has created a conceptual divide in the history of ideas. On the one hand, religious displacement from civic discourse has made it harder to determine how early Americans actually thought about the public sphere. On the other hand, the ease with which the law supplanted its philosophical rival has made it just as difficult to differentiate what remains from what has been displaced in public understandings. (57)

Ferguson reminds us that the interaction between legal and religious sources does not end with the early republican period but rather persists (he notes in *Law and Letters*, for example, that Lincoln contemplated an amendment that would insert God into the Constitution [313]) in the mode of a dialectic, about which there are questions to be raised:

> The recognition that religious explanation joins legal explanation in the construction of American liberty leaves many questions unanswered. If the religious sources of liberty are powerful and significant, *why* did they disappear from civil discourse so rapidly in the early republic? *Where*, in the continuing dialectic, are the religious contributions to civil and political liberty in American life? *How* did religious and legal sources of liberty interact to produce a distinct American understanding? *What*, if anything, does a closer look at religious explanation restore to a balanced understanding of American liberty? (*Reading* 53–54)

Ferguson's attentiveness to the interplay of law and religion is part of his broader interest in the entwinement of "law and letters" and, more specifically, in the centrality of the figure of the lawyer-writer in the founding articulations of an American understanding of liberty and the rule of law. He is keenly aware of the perils, ideological and otherwise, of nostalgia for the period of the founding as a putative golden age populated by statesmen who were men of letters. Yet he does not want this skepticism to lead us to minimize the significance of the belletrist sensibilities and commitments of many of the key figures of the early republic, who considered themselves to be part of a transcontinental community of letters.

If Ferguson teaches us to become close readers of the language and texts that attend the emergence of the American experiment in constitutional government and to pay heed in particular to the resonances of the religious imagination even as it is displaced by a secular discourse of natural law, Kahn calls our attention to how this displacement simply shifts the forms and longings of religious belief onto the legal imagination and its institutions. In this he follows and develops Carl Schmitt's claim that "[a]ll significant concepts of the modern theory of the state are secularized theological concepts" (Kahn 147n15). Ferguson and Kahn both help us understand what Kahn calls the "genealogy" and "architecture" of the contemporary American belief in the rule of law—that is, they help us see it as a cultural belief system.

With respect to the trope of rescue that frames much of the scholarship of the law and literature movement, the idea of law must be invested with enough power and significance to motivate the rescue in the first place. But what is the role of literature? In different yet complementary ways, Ferguson and Kahn point to an answer that connects the American and British traditions and brings us up to the present moment. Literature is to be read in the context of the broader turn to culture, outlined by Matthew Arnold in *Culture and Anarchy* (1869), as a salve to counter the effects of democracy and industrialization. Arnold, the poet of "Dover Beach," makes visible what culture is asked to provide the antidote to and argues that culture needs to be understood as the corollary of another signal transition of the nineteenth century in the West, the death of God:

> The Sea of Faith
> Was once, too, at the full, and round earth's shore
> Lay like the folds of a bright girdle furled.
> But now I only hear
> Its melancholy, long, withdrawing roar,
> Retreating, to the breath
> Of the night-wind, down the vast edges drear
> And naked shingles of the world.   (lines 21–28)

Arnold leaves unsaid but demonstrates through the writing of the poem itself that culture—especially literature—is called on to fill the vacuum left by the displacement of religion. Even as the sea of faith recedes, drawn out by the tidal pull of emergent secularism, the poem performatively reassures us that literature will be able to supply a language as textured, purposive, and meaningful as the one that is being lost. Whether that hope in the reach of literature is justified is very much an open question and at the heart of the law and literature enterprise.

In its closing strophe, the poem ends with what in retrospect reads as an uncanny intimation of the horrors of World War I and the trenches— the war that would shatter the West's confidence in the coherence and integrity of its cultural resources:

> Ah, love, let us be true
> To one another! for the world, which seems
> To lie before us like a land of dreams,

So various, so beautiful, so new,
Hath really neither joy, nor love, nor light,
Nor certitude, nor peace, nor help for pain;
And we are here as on a darkling plain
Swept with confused alarms of struggle and flight,
Where ignorant armies clash by night.   (29–37)

There is a line of descent, a kind of apostolic succession, running from Arnold's *Culture and Anarchy*, through Lionel Trilling's *The Liberal Imagination* (1950), to James Boyd White's seminal law and literature text *The Legal Imagination* (Sarat, Anderson, and Frank 6). To the extent that law and literature draws inspiration from Arnold, its project is not a narrow subfield of legal or literary studies but rather a conjoining of two of the most powerful currents of belief in the West, the belief in law and the belief in literature, both of which need to be read against the backdrop of the rise of secularism.

In this account, literature offers the necessary corrective to a liberalism that can too easily become dogmatic and triumphalistic. This corrective works on two levels. First, literature can help make visible some of law's blind spots and expand the compass of the liberal imagination to include people whose lives and experiences traditionally do not appear before the law. Second, a literary sensibility can keep the language of the liberal state — the language of law — from becoming merely instrumental, a vehicle for the unmediated, unself-conscious exercise of power. Literature has much to offer in the training of lawyers because it helps us remain alive to law's force and aware of the unsettling but inescapable ambiguities and uncertainties that accompany acts of legal judgment.

In *The Legal Imagination* (1973), White sees the law and literature project as essentially pedagogical: his goal for law students is that they will have something to say, mean what they say, and be capable of saying it in writing. That he identifies the study of literature as a touchstone and template undoubtedly shows, as he himself observes in this volume, the influence of the New Criticism, which was the lingua franca in his days as an undergraduate. That the study of literature cultivates a tolerance for and appreciation of ambiguity is certainly one claim that many New Critics would recognize. Present-day commitments to cultural studies would seem to run counter to White's more traditional, canonical investments, yet to the extent that his interest lies centrally with helping students cultivate critical thinking and fluent, effective, and meaningful writing in preparation for life as active, constituent members of a self-legislating polity, all these years he has been encouraging liberal education tout court, not simply the education of lawyers or justices.

White articulates a vision of legal study in which teachers in the under-graduate classroom cultivate imagination, inspiration, and a tolerance for complexity and contradiction. This work has been intrinsic to the poetics of law and literature. To the extent that the field connects with current efforts to open the study of law as a discipline of the liberal arts unto itself, its success will depend on how effectively it inspires teachers and administrators alike with a sense of its extraordinary promise as a field of humanistic scholarship and a subject of study for students.

Instead of replicating disciplinary division in separate law and literature sections, we organized this volume as one might approach a syllabus for a course with three sections: the field's description, thematic approaches, and texts. Each section includes contributions from both legal and literary scholar-teachers in a dialogue that points to new directions for the study of law and literature.

Theory and History of the Movement

Part 1 of our volume contains essays by many of the leading scholars in the field. Its structure is loosely chronological: it begins with the work of White and ends with an essay by Robin West, who connects theorizations about the cultural life of the law with a dramatic, recent instance of the interplay of literature and law.

White takes the project of this volume as an occasion to return to his *The Legal Imagination* and reflect on the context from which it arose and on the text's continued relevance. He reviews what he assumed the law to be, what he thought the teaching of law should involve, what he thought literature was, and why he thought a turn to literary texts might offer an important way of thinking about and teaching the law. Though he looks back here, his commitment to a vision of legal education as an extension of the liberal arts is as timely today as it was thirty years ago.

White describes the fears and assumptions circulating in the middle of the twentieth century that drew law away from its historical connection to the humanities and toward the social sciences. One assumption was that disciplines like psychology, sociology, and economics "could produce knowledge of a sort that the humanities could not" and that this knowl-edge would be the preferred "foundation of law." This diminishment of the humanities led to the neglect of "literary and rhetorical" skills that informed legal practice, skills that included close reading and clear writing. But for White, legal practice repeatedly required lawyers and judges to confront "a literary moment," one "in which the very question [they were] addressing was one of meaning."

The meanings that legal professionals had to construe ultimately affected decisions about people's lives. In contrast, to become a literary scholar, as White initially set out to do, was to engage in a profession that rarefied literature and set it apart from the political and ethical questions ordinary life routinely raised. The attraction of law school for White, then, lay in its connection to the real, even if law seemed "sui generis, its own unique cultural form," having no foundational ties to other cultural forms. His project became one of consciousness-raising: to make law students and practitioners of law see what was implicit in their practice and ought to be explicit in their education; to make them see that law, being a language with its own ways of conceptualizing and ordering the world, had "something to learn from other arts of language and culture"; that law, using a "language of power," needed literature just as much as "the study of 'literature' had needed law." The close study of how literary texts enabled multiple interpretations and the requirement it placed on readers to weigh and judge those meanings could prepare law students to think about their own competencies when confronting "a real problem in the world." It is precisely because the law is a language of power that students need to resist its ability to overcome their own unique expression (in speech and in writing) and reduce it to forms and rules that originate from law rather than from a thinking and feeling, human center.

The ethics of thought and expression that *The Legal Imagination* sought to inculcate in students was informed by the belief that, for good or ill, things could be done through legal language that other languages could neither make possible nor prevent. Richard H. Weisberg elaborated on but also critiqued this argument in his groundbreaking study of the resentful reader, *The Failure of the Word* (1984). Working in a vein sympathetic to White's, Weisberg has consistently argued that law and literature is about reunifying two fields of narrative activity that until recently in Western culture were conjoined. He locates this division between law and letters in the post-Auschwitz, deconstructive distrust of all authoritative codes and in the "naive" or "misguided" faith of law's emerging "human rights community" in a language that unifies law and justice. In his contribution to this volume, Weisberg, like White, revisits the intellectual and cultural climate out of which the law and literature movement emerged.

Weisberg reconsiders the tension, after Auschwitz, between disavow-
ing and directly confronting "all pretensions to knowledge and all attempts
to formulate a grammar of understanding." Charting the history of his
thinking in what amounts to a major reassessment of the field, he brings
readers to the moment when he decided that it was necessary to "seek out
and speak directly of the *nature and causes* of the *specific* 'authoritarian
absoluteness' whose horror had recalendered our imaginations." He characterizes the history of the movement as an effort to provide a "corrected
ethical syllogism," a textually based ethics, one that would allow for the
specificity of narrative and the possibility that the directness of story could
counterbalance the "obliqueness" of theory.

At a time when theory dominated literary scholarship and departments
were peopled by scholars "avoiding their canonical surrounding," practitioners of law and literature were the radicals, he explains, because they
wanted to read stories and were more open to the possibility that stories
(especially those of "law, justice, alterity, hermeneutic distortion, comparative theology") could inform our direct response. He sees the movement
as a survivor because of its search for an "empathic code"—the return
of a Ciceronian unity in contemporary poethics—which recognizes the
existence of good and bad codes as well as resentful and ethical readers.
Weisberg shows how such readers interact with and interpret these codes
to produce radically different results.

As Peter Brooks puts it in his essay, the law is "compounded of narrative"; "it is all about competing stories," which do not simply convey
facts but weave them into powerful representations of reality to be judged.
Where the stakes of such decision making are dramatic (culminating in the
loss of life, property, status), Brooks urges a thoroughgoing appreciation
for and development of analytic, narratological tools in the "world of law"
(especially the law school curriculum), which "does not overtly recognize
narrative as a category in the process of legal adjudication." As routinely
as law turns to stories, it just as often seeks to "deny," "tame," "interrupt," and "suppress" them in an effort to preserve its rational authority
and control.

Brooks is interested in restoring the connection between law and literature, coaxing law to reintegrate its repressed rhetorical self. If he is less
immediately concerned than White with what White refers to as "the best
works of our literary tradition," Brooks hopes, like him, that law students
can become more self-conscious about their rhetorical practices. The professionalized American legal academy must relax its autonomy so as to

become more open to the hermeneutic insights of literary scholarship or "more closely responsible to other social and cultural creations of meaning" generally. Brooks writes:

> The law-and-literature movement has arisen in large part from those who believe that law needs to be accountable to more than itself. . . . It needs to be tested against a realm of human value to which literature speaks—not in any simple sense of moral uplift but in its address to the human condition.

Law students must learn not just to tell stories in court but to use narratological tools to understand how stories work, which in turn means that the legal academy must acknowledge and integrate narrative into its thinking about adjudication.

Brooks also discusses what students of literature can learn through contact with law and how they can develop their own poethical reading strategies. For him as for White and Weisberg, the student trained in close reading and possessing mature interpretive skills can read any text. But for Brooks, the "textual corpus" should show law and literature confronting each other with their differing constructions of reality. Literature students reading case law, for example, learn to value the stakes of interpretation that "has consequences in the real world—where rhetoric and narrative are not 'merely' possible world games but issues on which people may lose their liberty and even their lives."

In Brooks's assessment, the challenge that law and literature faces at present is to destabilize dominant paradigms of law and legal education and make significant inroads into the core conceptualizations of what law is and how it should be taught. The insights that literary studies offer—notably, "a questioning of law's internal definitions of some of its terms of art, of the languages it deploys in talking about human agency, of its unproblematic understandings of narrative and rhetoric"—are still viewed by most legal scholars as peripheral.

The problems of cohesion experienced by law and literature may be symptomatic of many interdisciplinary pairings that experience an inherent, post-Freudian *concordia discors*: a union based on the attraction of opposites may not lead to methodological innovation—to a new, synthesized discipline—but the tension between them can be productive. Peters introduces the maxim that "all interdisciplinarity . . . is disciplinary symptom" and, in her contribution to this volume, focuses on the "collective longing" for that perfect, balancing opposite whose existence reveals something about each desiring partner. In law and literature, this longing has stimulated the enterprise up to now.

But the enterprise was bound to deconstruct itself, suggests Peters. In the "narrative of historical rupture" of the two disciplines lay the impetus for the nascent field's project of reunification, but "in disseminating this narrative, the subdiscipline in some sense produced the conceptual separation it claimed to be combating." Literature came to accept "the inconsequence of the aesthetic" when it ceded political effectiveness to law, just as law internalized an image of soulless mechanism when it made literature the locus of humanism. Each field overcompensated for its perceived shortcomings and thereby undermined the possibility of reunification.

A previous generation of law and literature scholars may have expressed anxiety that their respective legal or literary disciplines lacked authenticity, but the future of the movement, as for the humanities in general, Peters argues, will be characterized by a broad-based mode of cultural inquiry that is more relaxed about the made-upness of the real. Echoing Elaine Scarry, she asks, "Why should exposure of the fact that things"—that is, human creations such as law, science, gender, and childhood—"were once created necessarily downgrade their authority?" If the terms of the field of law and literature and the interdisciplinary longings they encode now seem "vaguely quaint, [the movement's] contents overflowing its narrow dual disciplinary signifiers," then the disciplinary turn toward culture might lead to better descriptions of "how things became real and what their realness consists in." It might further augur a return to an appreciation of the "value of the illusions about authenticity" more generally that underlie not just traditional disciplinary boundaries but a widely shared sensibility regarding the integrity of the real.

Like Peters, Robert Weisberg examines the particular appeal of law and literature from among the many possible combinations of academic disciplines. If the point of interdisciplinarity is to bring together disciplines that are sufficiently similar to bear comparison but sufficiently different to produce creative tension, then other combinations would be as interesting. For Weisberg, "the law-literature connection remains almost uniquely compelling, perhaps precisely because of its odd asymmetry." He describes the many points where law and literature seem to converge, only to reveal further vectors of difference that some students and scholars disregard or manipulate in order to achieve coherence. For Weisberg, a more productive approach is less categorical. The recognition of "useful sublinkages as they arise in interesting patterns" or the pursuit of "partial commonalities" helps us resist the totalizing tendencies of forced symmetry.

Taking the "diagnostic" route, the way "to imagine a unified culture" that ends neither in utopia nor dystopia, Weisberg situates the rise of law and literature in the context of the modern debate over judicial review and of resistance by some to "the dominance of microeconomic utilitarianism in the development of law as an academic study." In keeping with his interest in the specific cultural history of the field, he argues that literature and literary criticism are of greatest use to legal scholarship when they highlight "the political and moral and economic contingencies of legal institutions" and help us see "the Kantian liberal model of the individual as a complex figure of social self-definition." This view that the study of literature can cultivate an understanding of the contingencies of historical experience and of legal judgment has many points of contact with the views articulated by White and Richard Weisberg.

If the new cultural attitude that Peters discerns can be thought of proleptically, as a dialectical response to the ambivalence between "celebration and lament" that Robert Weisberg diagnoses in his essay, West reminds us that the category difference between the real and the made real is still meaningful and that the consequences of the erosion of that difference can be serious. She concludes part 1 of this volume by offering an account of law and literature that brings us to the present and makes visible the value of the cultural criticism of law, by revealing some of the pitfalls that await a legal imaginary that frames and experiences the real in terms of a literary precedent. Her essay illuminates both the potentials and the limitations of the law-culture nexus through the lens of a comparison between Tom Wolfe's *I Am Charlotte Simmons* and "a still unfolding legal drama and its aftermath—a now thoroughly discredited allegation of rape, made in the spring of 2006 by a young woman in Durham, North Carolina, against three Duke lacrosse student-athletes." As her reading of this interplay of the fictive and the real makes plain, the dissolution or forgetting of the boundaries that separate a literary imagination from reality sometimes results in a loss of fidelity to an actual experience of suffering and injustice.

West rehearses the history of the field as part evolution, part revolution. Like Peters, she sees culture and its texts as the new vanguard of "law and" studies, but her history makes clear that cultural analyses of law have followed patterns introduced by law and literature. Detailing the literary, jurisprudential, and hermeneutic modes of the field, she observes that there is no cultural project fully analogous to the literary one of "reading literature to the end of appreciating its substantive insights regarding the nature of law." She believes that we miss opportunities to understand law differently when we fail to consider the cultural texts or products that carry the moral authority of law. We also risk distorting the meaning of cultural realities by applying a different model of law than the one that obtains in that particular time and place.

Her reading of the case at Duke raises related questions: What were the cultural texts functioning as law in Durham that spring? What could we have learned if we had paid attention to them? More broadly, what insight into the nature of law does the case at Duke open up and contribute to jurisprudential debate? As she explains, "[W]e truly cannot understand the 'law' that framed the allegation in Durham—indeed we cannot make sense of the allegation itself—without broadening our definitional understanding of what law is, to include its constituent cultural parts." For West, the media coverage of the case reveals the way that pop culture (Wolfe's novel) came to function as evidence of the truth of the allegation. The novel "*was reported as presenting* the back story" of the events at Duke and schools like it. In other words, the book became part of media culture, which in turn created the "cultural narrative of Duke undergraduate life" that made the allegation believable. The media reading—or, more accurately, misreading—of Charlotte Simmons's fictional assault produced a cultural context in which the rape allegation, albeit false, was nonetheless read as true.

It is tempting, West suggests, to blame Wolfe and his character for contributing to the scandal that erupted, but to do so requires ignoring the novel, in which Charlotte Simmons is complicit in (or, at least, is so situated as to be unable to avoid becoming complicit in) those harms: "By not understanding, not experiencing, and not resisting this sex she did not want, welcome or enjoy, as *assaultive*, and responding accordingly, Charlotte compounded her own injury" and "undermined her integrity." By conflating this unread text with the publicized narrative of rape provided by the Durham prosecutrix, the media obfuscated what could have been a strong cultural insight into the nature of law and rape law. As West explains, consensual but unwelcome sex is not a crime subject to the law's scrutiny, but cultural texts like Wolfe's novel can communicate the subjectivity of the women and men who experience it.

All the essays in part 1 address three issues: the value of the real as a category of being and experience; the constitution of cultural forms; and the role of narrative in framing, organizing, and otherwise giving shape both to the real and to cultural forms. White's preference for the law's connectedness to the politics and ethics of ordinary life, Richard Weisberg's rueful characterization of the difference in the post-Shoah world between doing something in law and doing nothing in literature, and Brooks's concern with the impact on people of arguments and judgments that begin with—and can only be critiqued through—strong interpretive practices express the sense of insufficiency and consequent longing in literature for power and relevance that Peters diagnoses as an "interdisciplinary illusion." We might also see law's yearning for something human and cultural in West's continued sensitivity to literary as well as to cultural representations of experience that allow us to hear and empathize with a broader range of voices and stories.

In her analysis, West includes cultural products that are not textual (i.e., visual, televisual, oral) but that, with literature, contribute to the creation of cultural realities that function as law. She calls on her readers to recognize how these realities are generated to determine the kinds of stories that can be told, by whom, and how they are understood. Her turn toward culture is also a return to the book: a call for responsible, close reading that resonates with the work of White and Richard Weisberg. There is a cultural literacy at work both in White's idea of the civic-minded professional trained in classical and canonical works of literature and in Weisberg's closing analysis of Cicero that West, mindful of those people who are not part of the "textual community" as well as of the nontextual ways communities may be founded, calls on us to redefine. Looked at from West's point of view, the notion of cultural unity exemplified in the Ciceronian model—a model Robert Weisberg asks us to approach with caution and that Richard Weisberg's account of theory's preference for the particular over the universal would seem to undermine—raises questions about which stories constitute this shared cultural heritage and the costs of not being conversant with them. To combat or compensate for this narrowness, the unity of law and literature must either be configured differently or its study must proceed on the assumption that contemporary audiences have strong interpretive abilities or literary skills. So we come back to the idea of a liberal arts education and to the study of law within it.

West's shift from the literary as law to culture as law, from analysis of the book to the dissection of cultural forms more broadly, is consonant with the projects of expanding the kinds of narrative that frame particular communities and of making us better readers. Her analysis of the Duke case enacts the kind of interpretive, descriptive performance that Peters's disillusionment calls for. That is, if we are meant to realize that the law-literature enterprise is essentially a performance, and if we are meant to become more comfortable with the idea that the real has always already been the made real, then we must develop better descriptions of the real and how it came to be. West's excavation of cultural assumptions buried in the layered narratives of Duke undergraduate life describes precisely how a specific allegation could be so viscerally believed, so powerfully "made real," and yet be false.

This narrative analysis exemplifies Robert Weisberg's proposed approach to law and literature, in which organically occurring points of overlap between the two fields are described as they arise instead of through a deductive (and too often reductive) application of principles to texts. Those concerned that law and literature in this guise lacks the political urgency that informed its origins should recall that *descriptive* is not the same as *neutral*. As Brooks reminds us in his essay, facts are elements in competing stories: how we tell and interpret them affects the world, either by heightening our awareness of the made-upness of legal realities or by increasing our sensitivity to how those realities nonetheless do their work. Neither of these projects is diminished when the text of those stories is literary or cultural.

Teachers in the various disciplines of the humanities seek to acquaint their students with the students' place in human history, to expand their sense of how that history is told, and to connect students to the values of liberal learning through which they may become, like Cicero's audience, skilled interpreters of their many rhetorical worlds.

Model Courses: Themes and Pragmatic Challenges

Teachers interested in creating a course in law and literature or in adding a law-lit perspective to an existing course will find part 2 of this volume especially helpful. The model courses described here are presented chronologically—from a course that considers the generic indebtedness to medieval law of *The Canterbury Tales* to one that shows the influence of digital technology on the legal status of performance—and bring together authors, genres, legal concepts, shared themes, canonical texts, and emergent issues. The essays apply the ideas raised in part 1, such as the representation of law in literature, the literariness of legal documents, law's place in the domain of culture, and the challenges and rewards of interdisciplinary study.

Ayelet Ben-Yishai asks why the nineteenth-century novel was obsessed with law. One consequence of this obsession has been the dominance of the novel in law and literature. In the nineteenth century, a period of legal reform and intensified professionalization of legal practice, the novel's establishment influenced some of the earliest formal acknowledgments of the overlap of law and literature (see Wigmore, "List of Legal Novels"). It became the focal point of the field's foundational arguments. In other words, the study of law in literature has often meant the study of law and the novel.

Diane Hoeveler, Lisa Rodensky, Ben-Yishai, and Caleb Smith all deal with the relation of the techniques of the novel to changing legal contexts. Hoeveler looks at how the conventions of the gothic novel—for example, the need for there to be a damsel threatened by a figure of aristocratic or religious corruption—cause the novel's presentation of legal themes to appear "rationalistic and utilitarian," even though the genre otherwise evinces a yearning for providence and authority that characterized the premodern legal system. In all gothic texts, this split between progress and nostalgia becomes the focus of the course's examination of the uneven shift toward a secular, print-based, rationalistic understanding of legality as well as the novel's relocation of authority from the judge to the popular reader. Rodensky, sharing Hoeveler's interest in the conventions of genre, shows how the Victorian novel circumvented the problem of determining criminal intention through its omniscient narrators. In her survey of novels from Dickens to Hardy, Rodensky offers a legal vocabulary, information about pertinent case law, and basic legal principles. She discusses how crime and criminality intersect with questions of realism and genre as well as with more general themes, such as personal agency, of interest to all areas of the humanities.

Ben-Yishai's course Legal Realism extends interest in the British realist tradition to French and American novels. Her examination of omniscience in Balzac reveals literary differences that arise from differences in each country's legal system—here, French civil law's reliance on Roman law and the syllogism versus the English preference for precedent and common law. By considering law reports and case law, Ben-Yishai demonstrates the importance of specifying legal culture when legal and literary conventions intersect. Smith extends the work of both Hoeveler and Ben-Yishai by turning to the gothic novel in America. Like Hoeveler, he acknowledges conventional readings of the gothic novel and Romanticism generally as flights from Enlightenment rationality. But his seminar situates the novel in a legal and social history—the rise of the penitentiary and the application of legal fictions such as civil death—that allows a critique of legal concepts that ultimately connects a convict's civil death to a slave's social death.

These courses remind us that the novel was the central text of a nascent law and literature movement, but the essays collected here respond to the dominance of the novel in two ways. First, they apply law and literature's initial preoccupation with this genre to other genres and other periods. Second, they show that law is literature: legal texts—a piece of legislation, a constitution, a trial—can be read for their own rhetorical value. Mary Flowers Braswell's course on Chaucer reveals that *The Canterbury Tales* derives its framework partly from the manor courts in which Chaucer worked. Even his characterizations depended on contextualizing pilgrims through specific examples of legislation. Law defines literature even as Chaucer's literary sensibility allowed Chaucer to see the stories embedded in law. Peter Herman uses the ancient constitution as a crucial lens for reinterpreting early modern poetry and drama. The balance of power between king and Parliament established by the constitution shows how law could condone the literary rebellions of Milton's Satan while criticizing Richard II's pretension to absolute power in Shakespeare's play. In both courses, the legal text is not merely the context for but also a part of the production of literary form as well as civic values. Similarly, Victoria Myers asks students in her course on Romantic drama to consider how certainty can be attained in judgments and how persons or institutions acquire the authority to judge. By focusing on reforms that made the trial a drama, thereby linking legal practice with dramaturgy, she shows how the Romantic drama participated in debates about the authority of legal institutions.

Other essays provide less an alternative to the novel than an evolution of the uses of narrative. Discussion of particular narrative structures—both as a common denominator in law and in literature and for their joint function, in Robert Cover's terms, of *paideia* or world creating ("Nomos" 105)—forms a bridge to essays about the kinds of narratives told, by whom, and about which subjects. These contributions indicate new directions to be pursued in a cultural critique of both law and literature. Alex Feerst and D. Quentin Miller both address an understanding of legislation, social policy, and judicial decision as rhetorical abstractions that nonetheless possess the very real authority to render people, in Miller's terms, embodiments of "law's consequences." Feerst describes a series of United States immigration policies and relates the personal narratives of immigrant individuals transformed by them; Miller looks at literature by prisoners as well as literature that imagines or documents the prison experience. The personal stories that they offer as evidence of the way law makes subjects is of particular interest in Patricia D. Watkins's course The Law in African

American Literature. Applying critical race theory, Watkins surveys African American literature and explains how texts as apparently different as Frederick Douglass's *Narrative* and Anita Hill's accusations against Clarence Thomas are nevertheless united through their explicit subversion of the dominant narratives about blacks and about American justice.

These authors are interested in the way law affects the formation of individual and group subjectivity, in the way its texts imagine and enforce particular subject positions. Alyce Miller and coauthors Cristine Soliz and Harold Joseph widen the relevance of this dynamic while testing the limits of the kinds of texts that authorize it. Miller combines readings in animal literature, case law, law review articles, and critical essays to explore how animals are used and represented in literature and law and the relation with human beings these uses entail—for example, how speciesism connects with discourses of racism and sexism. Soliz and Joseph historicize contemporary conflicts between United States law and Native American ceremony over the control of tribal lands as the conflict between their differing views of the function of law and its role in the fashioning of identity. The American legal system's current failure to understand Native American ceremony as valid law, they argue, is a major factor in the environmental contest over developing natural resources. More fundamentally, it overrides a collective Native American imaginary by imposing a United States legal, religious, and literary one.

The rights issues and property laws that these essays address are integral to any discussion of the contours of subjectivity. Philip Auslander and coauthors Hilary Schor and Nomi Stolzenberg focus these discussions further in their respective essays on intellectual freedom and intellectual property. In a team-taught course on the law and literature of the First Amendment, Schor and Stolzenberg explore the historical relation between free speech and free love and ask the provocative question of how both legal and literary narratives work to shape our "seemingly innate desires." Auslander asks whether a live performance can or should have the status of intellectual property. Focusing on synthespians, the digital clones derived from human performance and capable of future digital manipulation (with or without the actors' consent), he shows how new technologies are changing the relation between performer and performance and raising new ontological questions of who the performer is and who has a right in the performance.

Part 2 of this volume also addresses difficulties that teachers of law and literature encounter and offers practical advice for handling them. Simon Stern, who like many of our contributors and a growing number of scholars in the field holds both a PhD in literature and a JD, addresses the methodological blind spots that literature students and law students bring to their respective law-lit classrooms. Literature students tend not to understand the way a legal opinion is shaped and bound by precedent; law students typically underappreciate how law, as narrative, is shaped by linguistic conventions that are not merely matters of genre and style. Brook Thomas's "lawterature" course provides examples of different ways in which law and literature interact—for instance, law's effect on literature, literary responses to a legal controversy—while respecting their disciplinary differences. In contrast to this structural approach, Valerie Karno's studies of incarceration and of property and contract depend on viewing law and literature as mutually influential cultural artifacts and on reading their texts in tandem.

These courses show the tendency of "law and" courses to address themselves to fairly specific audiences. Thomas's course, for example, is designed for English majors and students taking the humanities and law minor at the University of California, Irvine. Noting this trend and the institutional exigency of required courses, Bridget Marshall develops a "lite" version that exemplifies ways that the integration of legal issues, texts, and readings of literature enhance the general education and English survey courses she teaches. Viewing literature in a legal context helps students connect early American literature to the world around them; in-class "trials" sharpen their skills in argumentation.

From the medieval to contemporary period, from legal texts such as United States Indian treaties to the First Amendment, from literary genres such as the gothic novel to protest literature, and from general education to graduate work, the courses that appear in this part draw on materials familiar to the teacher of law and literature. Yet new issues and changing canons are emerging as the field moves past its groundings and disciplinary separations. Therefore this part includes courses that view law and literature equally as culturally produced discourses and that redefine what counts as legal text.

Texts

Just as "Model Courses" provides a variety of templates for teaching the theoretical issues introduced in part 1, "Texts" further specifies the law and literature project by turning to particular legal and literary works while keeping in mind the divergent needs of new and practiced teachers.

In the seventeen essays of part 3, contributors address many genres: the Hebrew Bible, a modern saga of Albania, an English-Algonkian lexicon, an eighteenth-century libel trial, documentary theater. Canonical works by Shakespeare, Dickens, Dostoevsky, and Kafka are joined by new texts, such as gay memoir, hip-hop, and other pop culture media that expand the law and literature canon beyond the traditional domains of literature and legislation. The three main areas of legal and literary teaching dealt with are canonical texts and authors, alternative literary responses to them, and new forms of cultural engagement with the law that destabilize both law and literature as discourses, practices, and fields of inquiry. In this way, part 3 introduces teachers new to the field to some of its foundational texts while demonstrating for more experienced practitioners both new approaches to familiar material and innovative approaches taking place in the classroom.

Essays by Elliott Visconsi, Kieran Dolin, Florence Dore, Theodore Ziolkowski, and Harriet Murav offer new readings of Shakespeare, Dickens, Dreiser, Kafka, and Dostoevsky—major authors in any canon but ones who have been especially prominent in the study of law and literature. Visconsi sets *Measure for Measure* against the backdrop of Jacobean England and reads the play as "a sustained piece of legal thinking, an anthropology of the rule of law in all its social, political, moral, and cultural dimensions." Dolin adds to existing readings of *Bleak House* as legal satire through his analysis of the novel's female narrator, whose otherwise normative voice instigates a "symbolic revolution" that supplements England's nineteenth-century legal reform movement. Dore looks to Freud's *Dora* and United States obscenity laws to demonstrate how *Sister Carrie* offers "a novelistic account of the failure to achieve a feminine sexual identity outside censorship." Ziolkowski resituates *The Trial* in terms of Austrian law and Kafka's career of more than twenty years as a lawyer to highlight the novel's specific representation of competing legal systems and its role in an evolving conception of guilt. Murav recovers a complex, chiastic perspective on the relation between law and literature in Dostoevsky's writings by calling attention to the influence of his legal journalism. Whereas in novels such as *Crime and Punishment* and *The Brothers Karamazov*, Dostoevsky offers representations that are critical of law and expose its vulnerability to the indeterminacy of meaning, in his legal journalism he marshals his rhetorical and imaginative skills as a writer to effect determinate outcomes. In the Kornilova case, for example, he uses his art to help secure the acquittal of a person already convicted. These essays provide an introduction to some of the staple texts of law and literature's literary side, texts that echo the interests of the field's early humanist phase as well as more current, more historically situated leanings.

With Chaya Halberstam and with David H. Fisher, we step back from the modern period and connect, respectively, with a sacred religious textual tradition and with the world of saga culture. Halberstam, writing from the perspective of religious studies, offers a view of law and literature as the next iteration of the Bible as literature movement. Her aim is not so much to secularize a sacred text as to reconsider how we conceive of and read the relation between literature and law in the Hebrew Bible or Old Testament. She suggests that the legal codes in the Torah are characterized by an essential literariness. She proposes that we introduce students to a way of reading that foregrounds the interconnectedness of law, narrative, and poetry in the "normative universe" of that textual tradition. Fisher bridges the worlds of saga Iceland and early-twentieth-century northern Albania through a reading of *Njal's Saga* (a thousand-year-old text) and *Broken April* (1990). He describes how this comparative approach makes palpable for students the climate and deleterious consequences of an ethos of revenge in shame-honor cultures—an ethos that many students are soon able to identify as still obtaining in the West. But as they learn of the cultural exhaustion that accompanies the endless blood feuds and cycles of revenge, students also develop an appreciation for the wisdom the texts encode about the usefulness of law. Susan Sage Heinzelman's reading of Delarivier Manley's 1714 fictional autobiography *The Adventures of Rivella* not only positions it as the centerpiece of a reconceptualization of law and literature's gendered history but also uses it to approach unfamiliar texts generally and thereby expand the law-lit canon. Similarly, Nancy Marder discusses a series of novels (by Zora Neale Hurston, Toni Morrison, Gloria Naylor, and Cristina García) that mark the development of feminist legal theory and its extension of the canon in terms of gender, class, ethnicity, and sexual orientation. Heinzelman and Marder call us to situate literary and legal texts in their cultural contexts in such a way that we see the marginalization of women writers as part and parcel of a forgetting of history. In this view, canonicity—literary or legal—is part of a broader, ideological project of portraying historical experience as univocal; of stripping history of its internal contests, contradictions, and structures of oppression; of writing a history that appears rhetorically disinterested and ideologically neutral. Ravit Reichman juxtaposes a story by Joseph Conrad, "The Tale," and a United States Supreme Court decision to open a discussion of the concept of neutrality. The legal narrative produced by the Supreme Court reveals a neutrality marked not by absence of feeling but by the power to decide which version of an emotion is legally appropriate and which is not. Greg Pingree offers a comparative reading of several judicial opinions that address homosexuality and several gay memoirs from the past few decades to show how a powerful rhetorical device—what he calls the moral syllogism—shapes the structure of legal and literary texts alike.

Nan Goodman, Linda Myrsiades, and Jacqueline O'Connor in their essays on American law and literature uncover the historical contingencies of law; law is seen as an evolving, contested compound of multiple and variegated voices, traditions, and interests. Each writer considers the cultural specificity and resonances of particular moments in American legal and literary writing. Goodman makes audible the underappreciated presence and significance of indigenous voices in the colloquy of early American literature and law. Myrsiades reconstructs the cultural scene of a famous eighteenth-century trial, *Rush v. Cobbett*, and through its example reminds us of why it is appropriate to think of law more as a discourse than as doctrine. O'Connor focuses on documentary theater, a growing subgenre of twentieth-century drama that has produced remarkable plays that "transform legal texts into literary texts and legal proceedings into theatrical performances"; the plays therefore "highlight the performative aspects of the law." These essays demonstrate the granularity of specific historical moments and thus contribute to a thicker account of American literary and legal history, from the early colonial period to the present.

The textual readings these scholars outline open up a traditional understanding of literature and law to include a more representative range of voices, texts, and subject positions, in an effort not simply to expand the literary and legal canons but also to restore or cultivate a sense of the texture of the present. Put differently, they are interested in the relation between culture and tradition. On one level, they call us to revise or reclaim traditions of literature and law; on another, they draw our attention to ways in which the lived, historical complexities of culture can become reified by the authority of tradition.

Richard Schur is interested in hip-hop not just because it offers an important critique of law but also because he hears that critique as internal to traditional law, integral to the law's cultural life and therefore not an extralegal text. Lenora Ledwon reviews a list of texts drawn from popular culture that she has introduced in her classrooms, texts valuable for the views of law that they inscribe. She notes the sensibility that citizens bring to the exercise of their civic duty as jurors is far more likely to have been shaped by representations of law in popular culture than by professional training in the law. Zoe Trodd asks students to think of the tradition of alternative constitutions—for example, John Brown's "Provisional Constitution" and the Black Panthers' Constitutional Convention of 1970—as a tradition of protest literature and to connect that tradition with the Declaration of Independence and the Constitution. She models a way of reading the literary and legal traditions together that gives a sense of liberal democracy as a radical project.

The contributions to this volume provide rich and varied perspectives on the field of law and literature: from its origins as a movement to its establishment as a field; from the novel's dominance of that field to the ceremonies, dramas, and other performances that take us beyond the worlds of text; from conventionally legal texts, practices, and ways of thinking to new, cultural forms of law. These perspectives are historical in nature but also attuned to the present, to what we define as our contemporary objects of study and to the need to create a critical distance from our assumptions and practices. Because the organization of this volume is schematic, it opens to other constellations of essays (e.g., on race, gender, class, period, genre), which in turn can make visible opportunities for new work. As literature and law branches out into the domains of culture, we hope our readers will also look forward, using this volume to explore the interrelations between law and world literature, lyric poetry, music, and art as well as the implications of new media and posthuman studies on the way we conceptualize legal and literary studies and why.

Part I

Theory and History
of the Movement

James Boyd White

The Cultural Background
of *The Legal Imagination*

I want to speak in this essay about one aspect of the origins of what is often called the law and literature movement in the United States,[1] namely, how it got going. I shall do this by explaining the aims and assumptions of my own early contribution to it in the form of *The Legal Imagination* (first published in 1973). What I say will thus have some of the features of autobiography, but I hope it will be plain that this story is not really about me but about the state of the culture in which modern law and literature emerged.

At the time this book was written there was very little that connected the law with the literary humanities in a self-conscious way. But any claim that law and humanities began in 1973 would obviously be ludicrous, for the connections between law and the arts of language go all the way back to the beginnings of law in European history. The lawyer was, for the Greek and Roman alike, in large measure a rhetorician. Rhetoric was the center of European education until at least the seventeenth century, and long after that it was believed that a good education in the humanistic past was essential to excellence in law. The institution of the university began with schools of law, in Bologna and elsewhere, and law was seen to be naturally connected to philosophy, history, philology, and theology (e.g., see Gilmore).

In the nineteenth and much of the twentieth century, it would have been obvious to most lawyers that they were speakers and writers by occupation, that law itself was a branch of the larger culture (see Ferguson, *Law*). One need look no further than Justice Frankfurter's famous advice to a twelve-year-old boy who wished to become a lawyer:

> My dear Paul:
>
> No one can be a truly competent lawyer unless he is a cultivated man. If I were you, I would forget all about any technical preparation for the law. The best way to prepare for the law is to come to the study of the law as a well-read person. Thus alone can one acquire the capacity to use the English language on paper and in speech and with the habits of clear thinking which only a truly liberal education can give. No less important for a lawyer is the cultivation of the imaginative faculties by reading poetry, seeing great paintings, in the original or in easily available reproductions, and listening to great music. Stock your mind with the deposit of much good reading, and widen and deepen your feelings by experiencing vicariously as much as possible the wonderful mysteries of the universe, and forget all about your future career.
>
> > With good wishes,
> > Sincerely yours,
> > [*signed*] Felix Frankfurter
> > (qtd. in E. London, *Law* 725)

It is really only in the rather odd intellectual climate of the mid–twentieth century and beyond that it would have been possible to think that the law had no connection with the other arts of language and disciplines of thought we normally think of as constituting the humanities. In my view, this blindness to the obvious was produced by a convergence of a set of influences: in philosophy, the kind of logical positivism that wanted to reduce meaning to the empirically testable; the more general view that science simply eclipses the value of other forms of thought (and with it the desire to claim the status of "science" for the study of social, political, and economic phenomena); a widespread desire at a time of international peril to affirm the masculinity of science against the perceived femininity of the humanities; and the self-conscious turn to what is called social science in the law, first in the form of sociology and psychology, then of economics. The assumptions here were that these fields could produce knowledge of a sort that the humanities could not; that this knowledge was testable; and that it could be the foundation of law—law based upon social realities that were accurately represented by disciplines that shared the name, and hoped to share the prestige, of science. The idea that law could be seen as one of the social sciences became prevalent in the 1930s, under the rubric of legal realism, and it has since grown more intense.

I will return to this way of thinking in just a moment. My point now is a simpler one, that when I and others began to think of connecting the law with the world of humanities and literature, what we were doing was not something new and shocking, though that is how some saw it and perhaps how it felt to us, but something very old-fashioned indeed. We were seeking to make conscious a tradition that went back to the beginnings of legal thought in the West. But this was a tradition that took itself largely for granted, and there was very little that addressed it directly. By the time I was in law school in the early 1960s, for example, there were only a scattering of contemporary pieces explicitly about the connections between law and literature: an essay by Justice Cardozo ("*Law*" 3–52); a fine article on judicial style by Walker Gibson; a popular anthology compiled by Ephraim London (*World*); and important work by Owen Barfield (see Tennyson 56), an English lawyer (of whose work at the time I was unfortunately not aware). But it is fair to say that there was no widespread drive to connect the activities of law with what could be learned from our humanistic past. Thus to look at the law, as I wished to do, as an art of thought and language, with its own characteristic concerns and methods, was simultaneously old-fashioned and newfangled, surprising to almost everyone.

I was often asked—as you may want to ask—What can literature possibly have to do with law? This question, repeated over and over again as I began my work, and indeed since then too, reflects in my view a deep misunderstanding of the nature of both literature and law, sometimes on the part of those who profess one or the other.[2]

In order to speak about the way in which connections between these two fields of activity can be drawn, by showing how they were in fact drawn in my own early work, I shall need to speak about my own education, in law school and before. For my ways of imagining the law and the literature that I was interested in connecting were to a large degree shaped by the ways in which I was taught these things both at the university and in the practice of law. My vision of law and literature, that is, was based upon a particular idea of what *law* is, or can be, as well as a certain idea of what *literature* is, and what can be learned from it. I shall begin by trying to explain these two ideas, tracing them out in terms of my education—an education that made it both surprising to connect these apparently different things and at the same time, by a sort of paradox, quite a natural thing to do.

I shall begin with what "literature" meant to one educated as I was. In college I studied mainly Greek and English literature. Greek exposed me to the wonderful works that are available only in that language—Homer, Plato, Euripides, and Sophocles—and introduced me to the reality of language difference itself. One does not and cannot think the same way in Greek and in English. In each of these languages one can do and say things that one cannot in the other, for each expresses its own culture—its own values, its own sense of what should count as reason, its own way of imagining or constituting the social and natural worlds. The study of other languages has always been central to the humanities, and for good reason: it teaches us that the ways we think, our ways of imagining ourselves and the world we inhabit, are not the only ways. The study of other languages puts into question our own language and the assumptions implicit in it; in doing so, it makes possible a certain kind of cultural criticism, one that holds out the possibility of growth beyond the taken-for-granteds of our own world.[3] For me the study of Greek held this kind of promise, and when I turned to law, it was natural for me to regard law as a language too, as one way among many of doing things with words.

As for the study of English literature, I was trained in the close reading of literary texts, especially poems, a kind of reading sometimes spoken of as the New Criticism. The main idea of this kind of work is that what happens in language, especially in artful language like that of the best poems, can be enormously complex and important, and this in several dimensions simultaneously: aesthetically, intellectually, emotionally, ethically, even politically. We learned that the meaning of a literary expression is not statable in the form of a proposition or an idea but lies in the complex experience of engagement with it, an experience that has its own shape and significance and that can be apprehended only by a mind and imagination trained to observe and respond to such things.[4] We believed that understanding a literary expression of the best kind requires the highest and most complete intelligence. In this sense, learning to read and judge the best literature was thought to be an education of the whole mind, and a worthy goal for a whole life.

Built into this process was the activity of judgment. We would argue endlessly about the merits of a poem or novel or the style of a prose writer. Is this a really good poem or story or sentence, or is it flawed, defective, weak? Is it somehow great despite its flaws — or even because of them? This judgment was not merely an aesthetic one: the question mainly had to do with the quality of thought and imagination, its comprehensiveness and truthfulness, its openness to contrasting truths, its capacity for new and living speech, and this on the most important of human topics: war and death, love and art, truth and knowledge, meaning and meaninglessness.[5] The literary judgment was thus also an ethical one, sometimes a political one.

It was a premise of our work that to read well required one to write well. The quality of our own expressions mattered supremely, we were taught, for it is in the quality of one's expression that one demonstrates, for good or ill, the quality of one's mind, of one's imagination, of one's education; this is where one shows how far one has realized, or failed to realize, the possibilities for meaning that distinguish human life.

In this way we came to see that literature was not to be regarded merely as an item of high consumption, like fine wine, or as an elegance of life, but lay at the center of our own imaginative and expressive lives: for we, like the writers we read, could collapse into empty clichés, sentimental slogans, or the vices of advertising or propaganda; or, like them, we could try to find ways to use our language to say things worthy of respect. This sense of the danger and power of language was to be of great help to me when it came to the study of law.

I loved this kind of engagement with language and literature, but when I went to graduate school, with the idea of becoming a professor of English, I found that there (unlike my college) literature was seen as a field of activity set apart from ordinary life, and from politics and ethics as well. To put it in a word, the reading of literature was professionalized, and for me that threatened its value. So I decided not to make my life simply as a reader of literature but to go to law school instead, with the object of becoming a lawyer. I naturally imagined the legal education I sought as learning to read and write well the language of the law, which was of course a language of power. Without quite knowing it, I was discovering that the study of literature needed the law, just as I was soon to discover that the law needed literature.

As you can see, I already had an idea of what the law was — an activity of mind and language — and it was not one widely shared in the general culture. It was and is common for nonlawyers and new law students alike to think of the law simply as a system of rules, sometimes cast in rather technical and arcane terms. On such a view, a legal education consists mainly of learning the rules, including where necessary the special meaning of the terms of art in which they are expressed. The application of the rules is thought to be simple enough: one looks at the world to see whether the rule applies or does not, then makes one's commonsense judgment. What sets the lawyer apart from other people is his or her knowledge of the rules and where to find them. Of course there may be problems in interpretation and application, but these are not very interesting and can be handled by rough common sense. What matters on this view is the system of law itself; its purposes and its coherence, matters that can be thought about largely in terms established by sociology or political science or even economics.

In an American law school of my era much energy was devoted to upsetting this simplistic vision of law. Of course rules can be applied in a nonproblematic way a good bit of the time, we were taught, but that is not where lawyers and judges spend their time. They focus on problems of meaning, and these are constantly before us. In any legal case that gets very far, it will be possible to make competing and contrasting arguments about the meaning both of the facts and of the law, arguments that are rational, coherent, and have persuasive force. The defendant and plaintiff will maintain opposing views, with considerable power; judges will concur and dissent, again often with good reasons on both sides.

The world of law—I speak especially of American law—is thus not a world of authoritarian clarity, not a world in which a system works itself out automatically, but a world of deep uncertainty and openness, of tension and conflict and argument, a world where reasons do not harmonize but oppose one another. This means that it is a world of learning and invention, where a great premium is placed on one's ability to make sense of an immense body of material as it bears on a particular case.

To learn to "think like a lawyer" was said to be the aim of law school. This activity was imagined as highly complex, comprehensive, exploratory and tentative, open to alternatives, subtle, and mature. Learning to think well in this mode was regarded as a proper object of an education, indeed of a life—just as at college I had been taught that learning to think well about literary texts, in literary ways, could be the object of a life. In both cases it was the quality of one's thought and expression that mattered above all.

This is what my legal education was to be like. But, as I suggest earlier, no one seemed to be consciously aware that this education was fundamentally literary and rhetorical in kind, with something to learn from other arts of language and culture. The law was seen as sui generis, its own unique cultural form with its own inherent intellectual and ethical merits.[6]

Much to my surprise, then, my literary training was of real and practical value both in the study of law and, later on, in the practice of law. I was used to the close reading of texts; used to seeing in one composition or expression a range of possible meanings; used to arguing for one reading as dominant, against the reality of other possibilities; and, perhaps above all, used to seeing both in written and oral expressions performances of mind and imagination that could be done well or badly. In other words, there was from the beginning a natural point of connection for me between these two forms of activity and life, the reading of literary texts and the practices of law.[7]

I was prepared too, as I say above, to make judgments, both intellectual and ethical in nature, about what people said or wrote. Just as a poem might be condemned as sentimental and a history as a string of received ideas, so a legal argument might be dismissed as conclusory or a judicial opinion as simply the unexamined reiteration of platitudes. Just as in literature we were trained to judge quality in a poem or novel, in law school we were being trained to see the vast differences between the good lawyer and the poor one, the good judge and the poor one—differences that made themselves apparent especially in what these people said, in the ways in which they thought and spoke, in the texts they produced.

This view of things was borne out by my experience in law practice, where I was faced directly with the questions, What is excellence in the practice of law? How can I best try to attain it? In thinking about these matters I found myself attending, over and over, to what the best lawyers in our firm did and said with language, trying to understand what they were doing and why. The secret of their intellectual and professional quality to a large degree lay there, I thought, in what they found it possible to say, if only I could learn to see it.

It seemed to me that the lawyer was asked again and again to address what I would call a literary moment, a moment in which the very question he or she was addressing was one of meaning: the meaning of the experience of a client or witness or opposing party; the meaning of a piece of testimony; the meaning of a word or phrase in a statute or contract; and behind all these things the meaning of the fluctuating and uncertain mass of documents, principles, understandings, and conventions we call the law. To a very large degree it was the lawyer who was given the task of making that meaning and doing it well.

For me, then, the law was above all an activity of mind and language, with all that involved, an activity that invited comparison with other such activities, especially with the best works of our literary tradition, where we might find examples of the most important kinds of success. The center of legal education, as I saw it, was the opportunity it afforded to strive for excellence of thought and expression alike. The good lawyer, the good judge, were marked by a capacity for a kind of whole-minded attention and thought, one object of which was to transform oneself into a wiser and more acute intelligence.

One of the premises of law as I learned it was that good and decent people can respectably and respectfully disagree about the outcome properly required by the law. What this means is that excellence, for lawyer and judge alike, is not to be confused with choosing the right result; it lies instead in the process of thought and imagination by which one articulates one's questions and thinks one's way through to one's conclusions. One could admire greatly a judge with whom one habitually disagreed and have deep contempt for one who normally voted like oneself.[8]

How then are we to think about the set of activities of mind and language the lawyer and judge must master? The answer of the law school in which I grew up was, simply by learning to do them. This was a kind of craft teaching. It was perhaps not thought necessary or even interesting to find a more explicit way of thinking about what we were doing,[9] but that was what I wanted to do and tried to do in *The Legal Imagination*. My hope in this book was to develop a way of thinking about the activities of mind and imagination that lie at the heart of law—at what happens when a lawyer or judge is faced with a real problem in the world, a loss or conflict, and seeks to bring to bear upon it the language of the law.[10]

My method was to use a series of questions and writing assignments to ask the student to function both as a lawyer, speaking the language of the law, and in the other ways in which he or she had competence by education and experience. In the class we then looked at what the student produced with the eyes of the sort of legal and literary critic I had been trained to be, asking questions about the nature and limits of the language used, the ways in which it has been replicated or transformed, the quality of mind revealed in the activity of thought and writing, and the ethical perils and opportunities it represented.

One persistent question had to do with the language of the law, which the student must as a lawyer both speak and write: is it necessarily dead, formulaic, mechanical, empty (as it surely is in some hands); or is it—can it by art be made to be—alive, full of meaning and significance? To achieve this, the student must make his or her language the object of thought and attention, accept the responsibility for the use and transformation of it, and resist the human desire to collapse uncritically into its forms.

The idea of the book is in this way to set up an internal dialogue in the student's head between the "law" the student is learning and whatever else he or she knows and is. As a way into these tensions I use both literature and ordinary language, but it could be anything of which the student has command, from music to mathematics to baseball or farming.

Using this method, the book considers a range of questions and problems. How in a general way can one compare legal and literary expressions? How does the law work as a system of meaning and social construction? How does the lawyer's argument—the language, the way of thinking—change as he or she addresses different audiences? How should statutes be composed and interpreted? How should the law talk about human beings, especially in the insanity defense, in sentencing judgments, in institutions of various kinds, and in the language of race? How is the law used, for good or ill, to build human relations over time, to structure social expectations, to instill values that will guide discretion? How do judges and lawyers reason, and how should we decide whether a particular act of legal reasoning is good or bad? How can we understand and criticize the form of literature we call the judicial opinion? At the end, I shift emphasis, asking the student to think of the law itself in a metaphorical way: Is it a kind of poetry, of rhetoric, of history? Here the students have to find their own ways of talking.

In all of this the student has been asked to think of legal language and legal education as dangers: of legal language as potentially narrow and technical and dull, as excluding from consideration virtually everything that matters, and as founded on a form, the rule, in which the truth can never be said; and of legal education as habituating the student to this language, making his or her mind the servant of the language rather than the other way round. These are real problems, and worth thinking about. My hope was that as the student came to see that the life of the lawyer is a life of writing and speech, of expression, of the arts of language, he or she would come to see it also as presenting opportunities of a unique kind—for what can be done with legal language cannot be done with anything else—and to recognize that the life it offers can be one full of interest and importance and value, at least if he or she can make it so.

Notes

Another version of this essay appears in longer form in *Teaching Law in the Mirror of Literature*, edited by Barbara Pozzo (2010).

1. I need to say that this name is itself in question: sometimes people speak of "law and the humanities," sometimes of "law and language," sometimes of "law, culture, and humanities." Whatever term is used, the kinds of work being done under this general rubric vary greatly in genre and intention alike. There is no organized program here, no commitment to an ideology, no plan of conquest. Rather, as is consistent with the nature of literature itself, and of the humanities, the idea is that many flowers may bloom, different in shape and color. This means, among other things, that we cannot talk meaningfully about the promise or limits of something called "law and literature" as if it were a program based on a set of shared assumptions that necessarily shaped its productions. The kind of criticism called for here is not in that sense theoretical, not a global affirmation or rejection, but, like the work in question itself, particular in nature.

2. Richard A. Posner's *Law and Literature: A Misunderstood Relation* seems to me in particular to misunderstand both law and literature. Posner finds that he can learn nothing from his reading of Homer, Shakespeare, and the rest except tricks for manipulating others through language, an unfortunate consequence of his own habits of reading that in my view says nothing about the works with which he finds he cannot valuably engage. See my review of this book, "What Can a Lawyer Learn from Literature?"

3. The view of language and culture I sketch here is elaborated in my book *When Words Lose Their Meaning*. The point about language difference, and the art of reading and translation it requires, is developed in my *Justice as Translation*.

4. For a classic statement of this thesis, see C. Brooks.

5. The common idea that literature is somehow merely aesthetic in character, as though there were no substantive concerns in our greatest literature, is demonstrably wrong. The *Iliad* and *Aeneid* are about war, Dante's *Commedia* and Milton's *Paradise Lost* about the justice of God, Keats's "On a Grecian Urn" about art and time, Herbert's "Pulley" about the creation of man, Dickens's *Bleak House* about social injustice, Austen's *Mansfield Park* about human morality, and so on. What *is* true is that these works have their own ways of treating their subject, which is not that of the modern academic book or article, but in fact far harder to achieve and of far greater significance.

6. How about social science? We were told that social science had much to offer the law, mainly in the form of reliable findings about the world. The idea was that, up until the moment at which modern social science made something else

possible, the law had had to rely on necessarily intuitive judgments about human behavior and motivation, on tradition and culture. Now psychology, sociology, and economics could provide a kind of scientific knowledge of the world on which legislatures and courts could rely in the formulation of rules and judgments. This was, and is, in my view completely unobjectionable. Of course the law should learn what it can about the world, from whatever reliable source. This is no threat to law, because law will in the end be the forum in which the reliability of the findings of social science will be debated and determined, just as is the case with other forms of expert testimony. The law will translate what can be said in these other ways into its own discourse and use them for its own purposes.

7. Let me add a point. To a certain kind of mind, the question in reading is simply to ask what is the main idea. But in law, as in poetry and other forms of literature, the main idea is usually rather simply stated and it is not the real point. The poet is saying I am in love or full of grief or in despair; the First Amendment says speech is a good thing, the Fourth Amendment says people are to be protected against searches, and so on. But you could write a book, or teach a whole course, about the significance of *the ways in which* Shakespeare says in his sonnets that he is in love or despair; likewise, you could write a book or teach a whole course about *the ways in which* speech is protected under the First Amendment. Life and quality are in the style, not imagined simply as a form of elegance, but as all that matters most when one uses language.

8. Contemporary interest in the quality of legal thought is well expressed in the preface to the first volume of the distinguished journal the *Supreme Court Review*: "In many recent comments on the Court and its critics, the point has been made that, in the words of Professor Henry Hart, 'neither at the bar nor among the faculties of law schools is there an adequate tradition of sustained, disinterested, and competent criticism of the professional qualities of the Court's opinions.' It is believed that one of the reasons for this deficiency has been the absence of a publication devoted exclusively to the presentation of such criticism. This annual, then, proposes to fill the gap by providing a forum in which the best minds in the field will be encouraged freely to express their critical judgments. Over and over again, justices of the Supreme Court have announced the desirability of, indeed the necessity for, such critiques of their work. It is hoped that *The Supreme Court Review* will meet that need" (Preface).

9. One important effort to be self-conscious about the law was the fine course taught by Albert Sacks and Henry Hart, The Legal Process. Their materials have since been published by Foundation Press.

10. For more recent reflections on teaching law, see my *From Expectation to Experience*.

Richard H. Weisberg

Law and Literature as Survivor

Thinking and Doing after Auschwitz: The Way We Were

The Hartman Reader Was Leader ...

> *Every generalization leaves a hollow feeling in the pit of my stomach.*
> —Hartman, "Night Thoughts after Auschwitz"

Everything connected to our literary environment had been in disarray. Narratives were distrusted, the grammar of the single sentence made fearsome, the urge to generalize trumped by "interpretive flexibility" (Hartman, *Minor Prophecies* 91).[1] The single vision, the idea itself of the originating creative source, the devotion to the story as carrying within it some small or major truth—none of this any longer passed for our currency. We continued to read, read closely and sometimes well. Where a text, however, posed the slightest risk of proposing a vision—say, a vision of justice—it was outsourced (lawyers got the job, at least in part). Discarding all narrative authorities, we substituted several high theoretical ones. These were wonderful and dense and different one from the other, but each managed to disdain all pretensions to structure.

We were thus busy for some years sloughing off various earlier impulses toward a uniformity of narrative vision, abjuring the sense of unity discoverable in many traditions, be they Hebraic, Aristotelian, Romantic, structuralist, or (especially) high literary. We were engaged in the game of destabilization; perhaps insufficiently cognizant of how old and tired that game had become, we hopped onto a new cycle of programmatic deconstruction. Thinking ourselves forwardly placed, we instead rolled backward, toward those who had set up the disunifying rules, men whose brilliance two thousand years ago instantiated the hermeneutic chaos we believed we were inaugurating. Like the early Christians, we rejected all codes.[2]

We had our reasons. Perhaps the most salient of them only gradually emerged: like most thoughtful communities, we were affected by—if as yet unable to deal with—the ways in which our discourse had been co-opted, in the very heartlands of European culture, and reduced across the Continent to the simplistic albeit highly effective end of genocide. Hitler had used the totalizing rhetoric we now wished, in our every rhetorical performance, to avoid. A way of reasoning arose that tended to conflate and devalue *all* authoritative discourse.

A critical distance to power and the simplistic rhetoric undergirding it struck us as a radical if temporary solution to what Geoffrey Hartman was calling in a general way "the question of our speech" ("Question") and what he and I together framed as "the problem of our discourse after the Holocaust" (our project so entitled involved joint residencies at the Rockefeller Foundation center in Bellagio during the late spring and early summer of 1996). In a powerful and complex formulation of this anxiety, Hartman first proposed "that the calendar itself should undergo a revision, at least in our internal reckonings. Thus 1997 could be re-dated as 52 after Auschwitz or 55 after the Coordination of the Final Solution at the Wannsee Conference" (*Fateful Question* 99). Our speech, too, needed to be recalibrated. The sublime, whether on the macro level of grand narrative or the micro level of the directly referential utterance, could no longer enter our discourse:

> You cannot get rid of the sublime, yet there is no possibility of a specifically postmodern sublime because of the way spiritual values have, in the past, imbued ideals with violence, or a deadly, authoritarian absoluteness. "No word intoned from high," Adorno writes, "not even a theological one, can be justified, untransformed, after Auschwitz." (118)

This remarkable passage might stand, and did for many of us, as the ultimate caution regarding our own practices, be they discursive, hermeneutic, or literary-critical. "How to speak, or how not to speak, has thus become an acute and self-conscious decision. . . . As a sinister double of the sublime, the non-integratability of Auschwitz is part of our present misery" (102, 118).

For Hartman, the alteration in our understanding of language after Auschwitz led with uncertain logic to a negative answer to the epistemological challenge (playing on a now inappropriate Kantian idealism), "dare [we] to know the Holocaust?" (103). No ordered system of discourse would help us find such knowledge or even guide us toward or away from the search itself. The philosophers of the past used a language foreign to us now; and those more ready to hand were either reconfigured to suit our sense of imbalance (Nietzsche) or judged as culpable, for "if Heidegger's is a work of philosophy that stands for greatness in its field, and Heidegger ignores the Shoah, what can be concluded about Heidegger?" (104).

Hartman, whose writing always provoked thought through exactly such paradoxes, now suggested of the Shoah both that any writer who "ignores" it would somehow be off the mark and that it had rendered fatefully problematic the very idea of directing discourse toward a mark. But for the community I have been describing, there eventually arose from his elegantly complex ruminations the fateful question of deconstruction. Why of all modes of thought did this one so occupy the space of the longest shadow of the later twentieth century? In what way after the Shoah was it fitting for us — or perhaps on the contrary (as I have suggested both in conversations with Hartman spanning four decades and in some of my own writing ["Paul"]) somehow inadvisable — to slip away from all pretensions to knowledge and all attempts to formulate a grammar of understanding? Might we not have chosen, even in Year One after Auschwitz, but certainly as reflection matured and discourse reemerged from the victims themselves, to seek out and speak directly of the nature and causes of the specific "infinity" whose horror had recalendered our imaginations (Hartman and O'Hara 447)? To what extent, in other words, might the "generalization leav[ing] a hollow feeling in the pit" of our stomachs (Hartman, "Is an Aesthetic Ethos" 139) be precisely what we needed to formulate, precisely the "poetics after the Shoah" (Hartman and O'Hara 446) that compels and terrorizes us?

While the Maddening (or Mad?) Others Did Their Work in the World

L'instant de la decision est une folie, dit Kierkegaard.

—Derrida, "Force de loi"

The instant of decision is a madness, says Kierkegaard.

What language, given the Shoah, was appropriate for (and appropriated to) us? While we were struggling with the authority of all narrative traditions, some of us also finding in our blanket rejection of grammatical structure a critical distance we managed to associate with political radicalism, other kinds of people, who had other ways of understanding narratives, brought about real change in the post-Shoah world. Some of these others were lawyers, men and women similarly devoted to the study of how language works, of how it means, of how it confuses, of how it affects its various audiences.[3] Lawyers endeavored at Nuremberg—in the Hartmanesque Year One after Auschwitz!—to establish codes that would prevent future genocides. Unlike our postmodern community, they did not sense the aporia of law, the inevitability, as we came to see it, of a disjunction between law and justice. They have not as yet achieved their goals, but their efforts assumed and continue to assume the possibility of codifying, and then interpreting faithfully, a grammar of goodness or at least betterness for the world.[4]

We may have admired their efforts, but we decided instead to theorize our skepticism about such grammars and especially about their implementation through interpretive performance. Where Nietzsche had called for vitalistic, nonresentful action that might lead to just codes of law (Weisberg, "Nietzsche's Hermeneutics"),[5] we ignored such suggestions, instead recasting that careful philologist as the guru of indeterminacy.[6] Paul de Man, in a very un-Nietzschean passage on codes in *Allegories of Reading*, established for us—without in any way proving—that the performance of any codified grammar entails interpretive subversiveness:

> The indifference of the text with regard to its referential meaning is what allows the legal text to proliferate, exactly as the preordained, coded repetition of a specific gesture or set of gestures allows Helen to weave the story of the war into the epic. . . . The system of relationships that generates the text and that functions independently of its referential meaning is its grammar. To the extent that a text is grammatical, it is a logical code or a machine. . . . There can be no text without grammar; the logic of grammar generates texts only in the absence of

referential meaning, but every text generates a referent that subverts
the grammatical principle to which it owes its constitution. (268–69)

De Man separated the code as a constitutive thing from the interpretation of it as performance. The text of the law, described as "the preordained, coded repetition of a specific gesture or set of gestures," presented
itself as a nondesiring grammar that had the consistency of "a logical code
or a machine." Without much demonstration, the interpreter was not only
absolved from any grounded allegiance to that grammar but also enjoined
to undermine it: "[E]very text generates a referent that subverts the grammatical principle to which it owes its constitution." We took this to mean
that the legal code—but why more so than a nonlinguistic machine, such as
a truck or toaster?—compels a performance that disequilibrates its outward
presentation. In other words, the difficult task of producing through legal
language a codified grammar of justness would founder on the shoals of an
inevitable undermining of the code through performative subversion.

The conclusion of this stunning passage reverses the Nietzschean assertion (in *The Genealogy of Morals* [*Zur Genealogie*] but also elsewhere)
that a just legal code may in fact be faithfully followed by a less subjective
("unpersönlichere") interpreter (307), one committed, to the extent possible, to follow the code's grammar. Nietzsche's evaluation of any code
depended, of course, on the values of its codifier; no code deserved any
allegiance unless it was positively valued, free of all *ressentiment,* and likely
to work gradually, slowly, toward the result of justice (Weisberg, *Failure,*
pt. 1). Nietzsche might have admired the post-Nuremberg effort to codify
a better world; he would not have relished our deconstructively universal
reactivity, our unwillingness to choose, whether among codes, texts, narratives, or even authoritative grammars.

Our skepticism about codified law as a means to the end of justice
emerged from the same set of tragic events that had motivated those active
others at Nuremberg and has been motivating them in courts and legislatures ever since. (De Man, for example, might in part have traced code
skepticism to his own wartime experiences.)[7] For the lawyers, genocide
provoked linguistic answers through an internationalized human rights
law. For us, though, Hitler's Europe meant the end of all codes. To seek
the world's improvement through linguistic norms set down in law struck
us, at best, as naive.[8] Had not Jacques Derrida so informed us in his most
elaborated ruminations on the inevitable distinction (at least he saw it as
inevitable) between justice and law? Using exactly this text's pronoun to

describe these active others, he wrote with a kind of regretful—perhaps sarcastic—distance:

> They respond, it seems to me, to the most radical programs of a deconstruction that would like, in order to be consistent with itself [pour être conséquente avec elle-même], not to remain enclosed in purely speculative, theoretical, academic discourses but rather (with all due respect to Stanley Fish) to aspire to something more consequential, to *change* things and to intervene in an efficient and responsible, though always, of course, very mediated way, not only in the profession but in what one calls the *cite*, the *polis* and more generally the world. Not, doubtless [sic] to change things in the rather *naive* sense of calculated, deliberate and strategically controlled intervention, but in the sense of maximum transformation in progress, in the name of neither a simple symptom nor a simple cause. . . . ("Force de loi" 960; "Force of Law" [Cornell, Rosenfeld, and Carlson] 8–9; all emphases are in the original except for *"naive"*)[9]

The passage's assumptions, particularly about law and law-related activism, we preferred not to challenge. Surely workers in our sibling narrative discipline, whose rhetorical performances were so connected to ours in the humanities (J. White, *Legal Imagination*), must have shared our view that there was something naive about their focused legal activities in the polis and in the wider world! So we preferred not to look to any formulation, least of all to the kinds of direct naming through referential grammar we associated with law, to reform the still inchoate set of issues (if, after Auschwitz, we might even locate discrete issues) produced by people's words and deeds all over Europe during World War II.

Our radical insistence on the unsettling (to Hartman) if not even misguided (to Derrida) nature of all generalizations, particularly legal ones,[10] took the place of a realistic and challenging discourse in the polis, designed to effectuate situated, strategic change. Meanwhile, our siblings on the front lines of language and meaning, many of them human rights lawyers fighting real battles on the world stage, held fast to the notion that the grammar of an effectively drafted and politicized legal code might help constrain the violence of local leaders and, in the long run, cabin if not eliminate the human impulse toward genocidal behavior.

If philosophy had failed, we believed, law surely could provide no answer. Instead, an uneasy relationship came to exist between us humanists and the human rights community. Hartman suggested that the post-Auschwitz sensitivity had "opened our eyes to atrocities in the gulag, and, nearer to the present, in Cambodia, Guatemala, Bosnia, and Rwanda" (*Fateful Question* 100). Still, we exhibited a barely disguised disdain for those who were codifying and performing law in these areas, those who stubbornly resisted Derrida's dictum that "no existing, coded rule [*aucune règle existante ou codée*] can or ought to guarantee absolutely" a determination of what is just, that "each decision is different and requires an absolutely unique interpretation" ("Force of Law" 23).[11]

As Domna C. Stanton put it, less hyperbolically, in her thoughtful foreword to the recent *PMLA* symposium "The Humanities in Human Rights":

> [H]uman rights and the humanities have been grappling, less or more self-consciously, with some of the same issues in the last two decades — first and foremost, perhaps, the tensions between the universal and the particular, the local, the culturally relative. Human rights discourse openly embraces the universal ("the Universal Declaration of Human Rights"), though it is far from clear what the term specifically means in covenants and charters and, most especially, in practice. . . . Still, by contrast, the humanities' rejection of Enlightenment master narratives has led to the focus on the local, not only as the site of the political ("all politics is local") or of intellectual work (Foucault's "specific" intellectual . . .) but also as a way of rejecting the imperialistic posture of speaking and acting "for" or "in lieu of" silenced others. (1519–20)

Whether part of a Derridean fighting faith or less dramatically distributing some cautionary advice, we tended to launch our code-skeptical barbs at an activist agenda, which was in part dependent on, and sometimes quite proud of, its belief in a grammar of codified law. Contemporaneously, however, we who study literature recognized both the appropriateness of post-Shoah longings for a better world and more generally the "pursuit of ethics" that has recently reinvigorated our own literary work (Buell).

The Fateful Error of Our Totalizing Syllogism

Again, Hartman stands as our theorist of what he calls "a non-transcendent ethics" (*Minor Prophecies* 144). In praise (and defense) of de Man, he paradoxically finds in his former colleague's work both a rigorous ethic based on the inalterable premise that, to quote de Man, "the text *knows* what it is doing" (*Allegories* 144) and a rejection of "every tendency to totalize literature or language" (qtd. in Kimball 43). Can any ethics, however, avoid all totalizing impulses? Hartman does not shy away from the conundrum: "deconstructive reading no longer aims to establish a master-code but undoes every totalizing perspective"; yet "its largest effort is to see Western tradition as a totality, one that has erroneously promoted the closure of the commentary process by reifying canon and book" (*Minor Prophecies* 106).

It seemed OK, as a matter of theory, to be ethical, as long as the totalizing impulse in the ethical system sought to do away with all (other) totalities. Such an ethic was born of the experience of the Shoah—whether Hartman's or Derrida's experience, as among the victims, or de Man's, as among the perpetrators (de Man playing a youthful and quite minor role). It gave rise to a syllogism whose underpinning proved to have greater ethical than logical weight. The major premise is unproblematic: to convey their dreadful programs, Hitler and his cronies almost always employed a totalizing grammar,[12] epitomized in what Hartman called the "master-code." The minor premise, which founders on historical studies of the causes of the Shoah, holds that such discourse brought about in a fairly direct way the obedience of masses of Europeans to the will of the grotesque codifier. The conclusion is that every master code, every grammar of direct referentiality, every totalizing language is thus to be rejected. Along with master narratives, there fell all idealisms, all canons, and especially all generalizing codes. At a high level of ethical thought, we came to see the avoidance of directness as the debt we owed to those who had paid the genocidal price for the brutal discourse of both the leaders and the followers in Hitler's Europe.

We have been learning more and more about the varying discourses of the wartime years. The minor premise of our fateful syllogism has not held its ground. The most significant communities in Hitler's Europe, legal and religious, came around to his programs not through knee-jerk submissiveness to his totalizing rhetoric but instead through a gradual and quite nuanced abandonment of traditional values, an abandonment produced largely through complex professional discourse. Only the programmatic destabilization of their own prior codes permitted communities to abjure long traditions they knew were being violated by their leaders' debased and bizarre rhetoric. Their interpretive convolutions have been increasingly studied, particularly regarding Vichy France (Drapac 15–30; Weisberg, *Vichy Law*, chs. 2 and 10; Weisberg, "Differing Ways")[13] and the Third Reich itself (Mueller 193–94; Littell 45–55).[14] In general, these studies tend to show that a simple reaffirmation of religious and legal principles

might have changed the history of more than one European country.[15] Instead, the communities did the work for their leaders; they deconstructed
their finest "trained intuitions" (Cardozo, *Selected Writings* 226).[16]

A post-Shoah way of responding to what we know of the fatal complexities of wartime discourse thus might better have opted for directness
and choice instead of obliqueness and avoidance. The corrected ethical
syllogism might have pitted the good code against the bad code instead
of programmatically destabilizing all codes. Its logic might have run as
follows: in the face of a totalizing discourse we receive as unacceptable or
wrong, we respond not with an equivocal discourse that leaves us open
to an avoidance or even an acceptance of what we thought bizarre but
instead with a straightforward resistance and a strong reaffirmation of the
values that the unacceptable discourse had offended.

With such or similar thoughts in mind, a small subgrouping of us in
the humanities sustained "the very idea of law and literature."[17]

Text into Theory: How Law and Literature Survived

> *It is probably even more difficult in America than it is in Europe to
> plead for the reconstructive role that the humanities can play in the
> highly threatened social and political realm such as we experience it
> today, differently, but in a similar manner, throughout the world. . . .
> It is important . . . to make our case heard in the public spheres by
> participating courageously and appropriately in this "democracy of
> opinion" that our modern society of the spectacle has become.*
> —Julia Kristeva

Preserving, without Fetishizing, the Material Text

In her recent, evocative ruminations on the field of law and literature, Julie
Stone Peters imagines an interdisciplinary colloquium during which the
literary scholars fantasize about being activists while the lawyers in their
midst pretend to be poetic ("Law").[18] She suggests, there and elsewhere,
a set of unidisciplinary yearnings that were in part satisfied by each field's
dream of cohabiting with the other.[19] In a response to her, I emphasized
the eventual possibility of what I called a cyclical return to the unity of law
and literature ("Law and Literature in Dialogue").

Furthermore, I offered a very different portrait of those early law and
literature confrontations. At the origins of the contemporary law and literature movement, I perceived a yearning on the part of the literature

professors less to be out there in the world than to be free of the classics. At the *Billy Budd* conference whose proceedings later became the first number of *Cardozo Studies in Law and Literature*, the law professors and judges dutifully brought into the symposium classroom their marked-up copies of the tale, while the specialists in American literature, Melville, and nineteenth-century fiction declined to sully their hands with a copy of the actual story.[20] For these theorizing humanists there was no text in that class.[21] The lawyers wanted to grasp, in all senses, stories about justice.

Still, the movement from the very beginning was largely informed by its literary side. In fact, the theoretical environment, while antipathetic to close readings of stories, surely helped law and literature through its uneasiness with all bounded structures, including disciplinary ones. More valuable, however, was the participation of prominent scholars in literature departments, the substantial special-session gatherings at MLA meetings,[22] the production of a scholarly corpus motivated by an impulse Lawrence Buell sees revived today as "the first and most longstanding of those [ethical] strands . . . the moral commitments of literary texts and their implied authors" (7).

Law and literature thought ethically, but it thought out of the box. Its ethics endeavored to counter the quite different ethical impulse I examined above. Its approach was textually based. It was more confident than many postmodernists in the possibility of responding to the world discursively, directly, and with the help of stories that addressed worldly questions: law, justice, alterity, hermeneutic distortion, comparative theology, the foibles of authoritative discourse if not of the underlying structures it pretended to support.

Law and literature scholars insisted that the best insights into how to read and understand the world emerged from stories. Reversing the position Christopher Norris correctly imputes to de Man (136–37), we suggested—particularly regarding certain procedural novels—that "many texts display a discernible desire to be understood a certain way" (Weisberg, "Text" 980). Text preceded theory. The seemingly radical practice among the literature scholars of avoiding their canonical surroundings was contradicted by law and literature's careful readings of plays, novels, and poems.[23] Law and literature produced fine, sometimes sharply innovative literary-critical work during the years of high deconstruction. Sometimes, as in James Boyd White's seminal work, the radical element consisted of the mere juxtaposition of poetry with the seemingly banal language of the law (*Legal Imagination*, ch. 6). Elsewhere, previously received textual meanings were overturned.[24]

Textual analysis centered on works in all genres that spoke to questions of law and justice. For some, such as my colleague Peter Goodrich, these stories provided a broad-based deconstruction, *avant la lettre* and without further theorizing, of the law. Fiction rendered overt the law's unstated assumptions, and the story became a unique source of jurisprudence:

> A literary analysis, in short, promises eventually to collapse both the modernity and the unitary identity of law, it promises to tear down the absolute pretension of law, to destroy the idols of legal form, to deconstruct or cast aside that character, identity, or fate which claims for law a superiority or truth which neither logic nor science can ever fully impose. Literature, as a genre in relation with law, threatens the end of law through the very fact of that relationship between the literary canons and the norms, the canons, of law. ("Of Law" 199)

In this view, whose only fault is that it proves too much, the material text of the story stands as the surest signpost to the law's pretensions. No theory questioning the institution or concept of law is needed, if only the seeker after wisdom appeals to the ultimate directness of literature's iconoclastic proposals about the law.[25]

But Goodrich goes too far. As we proceeded to modify and vary the corpus of fictions about law (Weisberg, *Poethics,* ch. 4), it emerged that storytellers usually preserve the possibility of law as a means toward justice while more centrally unmasking the character and interpretive approach of the story's lawdoer (a term I prefer to Rousseau's "lawgiver," that "impostor" described by de Man [*Allegories* 274]). Storytellers tend to mark out a positive space for at least some legal codes and procedures—if performed faithfully instead of subversively. Stories about legal error signal with considerable narrative precision the hermeneutic distortion of misguided, mischievous, or malicious legal actors (Holdheim; Weisberg, "Law in and as Literature"). Justice is disrupted less by the underlying law than by the resentful interpretations of authoritative lawgivers (Weisberg, *Failure*).

The Corpus of Stories and the Preservation of Law

> [D]er letzte Boden, der vom Geiste der Gerechtigkeit erobert wird, ist der Boden des reaktiven Gefuehls! . . . Der aktive, der angreifende, uebergreifende Mensch ist immer noch der Gerechtigkeit hundert Schritte naeher gestellt als der reaktive. . . .
>   In welcher Sphaere ist denn bisher ueberhaupt die ganze Handhabung des Rechts, auch das eigentliche Beduerfnis nach Rechtauf

Erden heimisch gewesen? Etwa in der Sphaere reaktiven Menschen?
Ganz und gar nicht. . . . Der Entscheidenste aber, was die oberste
Gewalt gegen die Uebermacht der Gegen- und Nachgefuehle tut
und durchsetzt—sie tut es immer, sobald sie irgendwie stark genug
dazu ist—, ist die Aufrichtung des Gesetzes, die imperativische Erk-
laerung darueber, was ueberhaupt unter ihren Augen als erlaubt,
als recht, was als verboten, als unrecht zu gelten habe; . . . von nun
an wird das Auge fuer einer immer unpersoenlichere Abshaetzung
der Tat eingeuebt, sogar das Auge des Geschaedigten selbst (obschon
dies am allerletzten).

—Nietzsche

The ground of reactive feeling [ressentiment] is the last ground oc-
cupied by the spirit of justice [Geiste der Gerechtigkeit]! The active,
attacking, encroaching man is still a hundred paces closer to justice
than his reactive counterpart. . . . To what sphere is the basic man-
agement of law, indeed the entire drive toward law, most connected?
In the sphere of reactive people? Absolutely not. Much more so in the
realm of the active, strong, spontaneous, aggressive. Historically un-
derstood, the place of law is situated as a battle against the reactive
emotions, a war waged by means of that active and aggressive power
that here uses a part of its strength to quiet the ceaseless rumblings
of ressentiment and to enforce a settlement. The most decisive move,
made by the higher power against the predomination of grudge and
spite, is the establishment of the law, *the imperial elucidation of*
what counts in [the founding actor's] eyes as permitted, as just, and
what counts as forbidden and unjust. . . . From then on, the eye will
seek an increasingly impersonal evaluation of the deed, even the eye
of the victim itself, although this will be the last to do so.

The corpus of law and literature works tends in two distinct ways to re-
construct rather than deconstruct law. First, stories provide a constant and
increasingly necessary goad to the performance of democracy. At the turn
of the twentieth century, John Henry Wigmore, then dean of the Northwestern Law School, insisted that lawyers, judges, and law students read
certain kinds of novels throughout their legal careers. The fictional works
he recommended in a series of published articles all concerned law, lawyers,
legal reasoning, and the individual's search for justice through law.[26] For
both disciplines, seen autonomously, the impulse for such a directed set
of readings was peculiarly American (although it has quite recently been
reinvigorated by the French [see Simonin]), and it remains thoroughly
democratic. For the lawyer and judge, novels representing law in action
uniquely expand their sensitivities to the speech, ambitions, and feelings

of those their work so deeply affects. According to Wigmore, solely these lifelong excursions into the *comédie humaine*—and he includes on his otherwise largely Anglo-American list Balzac, Dostoevsky, Dumas, Hugo, Octave Thanet, and other Continentals—would permit their ears to open to the multiplicity of voices otherwise kept dumb by an elitist and too often cruel approach to justice.

Meanwhile, a democratizing impulse might equally but differently inspire the lay reader of such legal novels. If Wigmore's list stood a chance of opening the ears of lawyers and judges to the voice of laypersons, the latter needed to open *their* ears to the potential abuses of legal players, particularly of legal interpreters bent on distorting the law to support wealth, government, majoritarian religion, or other powerful interests. Again, in an era when the texts of the law have become more and more specialized and arcane (Ferguson, *Law* 290), the alert critic of legal authority in a democracy needs to rely on literary (or popular culture) representations of how judges speak (Weisberg, "How Judges Speak").

Law and literature, against the grain of these recent years, has seasoned its own many skepticisms about law with a healthy sprinkling of confidence in the possibility of the good code. Nietzsche, whose "actual position," according to Robert C. Holub, "is different—sometimes substantially different—from the position most contemporary critics associate with him" (262; see also Holub n15), points to such a code; the potential exists for justice through laws, through a coolly interpreted code whose values are sound. We are surrounded by good and bad codes, good and bad interpreters. Choice is all.

There are always four possible Nietzschean variations on the hermeneutics of law: a good code, retained through the cool interpretations of nonresentful readers; a good code, undermined by resentful readers; a bad code, preserved by resentful readers; a bad code, undermined by the active and aggressive energies of the healthy will to power. The taxonomy includes the possibility of justice on earth, and stories subtend this possibility.

The good code performed by the just individual? Hardly what we postmoderns would expect from real life, much less stories! Yet, as the French scholar Gerard Gengembre argued during one of France's first law and literature colloquia, all of *La comédie humaine*, and certainly its soundest lawyer, Derville, demonstrates a generally positive mapping of Napoleonic Code onto human ambition and desire (see also Kornstein). Balzac's slightly older contemporary, Stendhal, went so far as to read three pages of the Napoleonic Code every day for inspiration. In *Le rouge et le noir*, Julien Sorel coolly interprets that code correctly, even against his own self-interest, hence almost perfectly exemplifying the highest-order Nietzschean paradigm in Nietzsche's *Genealogy* (2.11). Julien consistently imposes on himself what he calls a duty or "devoir"—mediated by various heroic models (Girard, ch. 5), primary among which are Napoleon and the code that bears that name, both of which are referenced some twenty-five times in the novel. When Julien is arrested for the attempt on Mme de Renal's life, which he at first believes to have succeeded, he announces to the examining magistrate, "I caused death with premeditation. . . . I bought the pistols from the gunsmith, and had him load them. Article 1342 of the Penal Code is explicit. I deserve death, and I am ready for it" (470). Julien's reverence for a sound code—and note his assurance that the "Penal Code is explicit," that is, that its grammar is accessible and applicable to his particular case—trumps his self-interest in avoiding punishment.

In *Billy Budd, Sailor*, on the other hand, a resentful interpreter (Captain Vere) undermines a code that, had it been faithfully followed, would have saved Billy's life instead of destroying it. In employing his interpretive and rhetorical brilliance to subvert a good code, Captain Vere must answer to the skepticism of Billy's fellow crewmen at the trial, who know the articles of war and wonder, both privately and publicly, why he strays so far from the safeguards that the code seems to extend to defendants such as Billy (Weisberg, *Failure*, chs. 8 and 9).

Meanwhile, it is the resentful control over bad codes that increasingly predominates in nineteenth- and twentieth-century stories, partly explaining, as Wolfgang Holdheim first observed, the frequency of judicial errors in these tales, as well of course as the near-universal disdain lawyers inspire in readers of mainstream fiction. If Continental criminal procedure liberates hermeneutic excesses that violate a hard-won narrative truth (Weisberg, *Failure*, chs. 3 and 4), English and American law is attacked by novelists from Dickens to Doctorow as encouraging directly the corrupt preservation of wealth and power (Weisberg, *Poethics*, pt. 2).

Nietzsche's fourth variation, the intentional undermining by just individuals of resentful codes, also has its place in stories. Although lawyers bent on the preservation of justice appear far less frequently in mainstream fiction than they do in Hollywood films (Weisberg, "Verdict"), there are a few edifying examples in narratives; Derville in Honoré de Balzac's *Le colonel Chabert*, Bibikov in Bernard Malamud's *The Fixer*, and Sir Thomas More in Robert Bolt's *A Man for All Seasons*. Usually, though, this class of courageous individuals consists not of lawyers but of outsiders. Zarathustra-like, they escape the resentful mainstream to find a new way, which is always already there, a justice that needs only a new speaker. The powerless voice quietly overcomes the entrenched acceptance of the status quo among established lawyers (R. West, *Caring,* introd. and ch. 4). So, in Susan Glaspell's "A Jury of Her Peers," two women find themselves together in the kitchen of a neighbor who has just been arrested on suspicion of murdering her husband. As the altogether unpleasant county attorney and both women's husbands look for evidence elsewhere in the house, the women manage to piece together, from what they sensitively observe as neighbors, the real motive for the suspect's actions: a pattern of violence wreaked on her, and on what was precious to her, by her husband. As outsiders to the law's pretense of rationality, they are able to find a truth unavailable to the three authorities, who dismiss their insights and indeed their very attempt to judge accurately instead of formalistically. As often happens in such stories, the outsiders manage to take control, and a narratively marked just outcome ensues.

All such narratives eventually clarify for their audiences the rightness or wrongness of the operative legal code and thus of the interpretive strategies adopted toward it by various players. Nietzsche, an admirer of Stendhal, believed with the fictional Julien Sorel that the morality of the code will emerge if the interpreter wishes to discover it. Glaspell's women subvert the debased practices of myopic lawdoers, performing instead an empathic code that the reader comes to see as appropriate.

A Coda on Helen of Troy and Medea:
De Man versus Cicero and Cardozo

> *For Cicero, it may be said, was the one man, above all others, who made the Romans feel how great a charm eloquence lends to what is good, and how invincible justice is if it be well-spoken; and that it is necessary for him who would dexterously govern a commonwealth, in actions, always to prefer that which is honest before that which is popular, and in speaking, to free the right and useful measure from every thing that may occasion offence.*

> —Plutarch

A Ciceronian unity of law and letters seems closer today than it was when that twentieth-century Cicero, Benjamin N. Cardozo, bemoaned modern lawyers' loss of their traditional ties to literature (*Selected Writings* 339). Citing Stendhal's daily readings of the Napoleonic Code, Cardozo consistently unified the two narrative enterprises that so influence and bind communities. If Stendhal finds inspiration in the codes, the judge, as exemplar of public discourse designed to work toward justice, seeks it in literary art:

> We find a kindred phenomenon in literature, alike in poetry and prose. The search is for the just word, the happy phrase, that will give expression to the thought, but somehow the thought itself is transfigured by the phrase when found. There is emancipation in our very bonds. The restraints of rhyme or meter, the exigencies of period or balance, liberate at times the thought which they confine, and in balancing release. (225)

In his judicial work, Cardozo struggled to find a linguistic structure for justice. He saw as literary this process of translating sound judgment into words.[27]

While in the tradition of Cicero and Stendhal on the perceived unity of good thought and good narrative form, Cardozo stopped short in his judicial writing of directly invoking stories or poems. Although many judges have done so through the years,[28] he doubted the readiness of his audiences for the subtle appreciation of literature's place in the doing of justice. Cicero had no such qualms. In perhaps his most famous speech, he urges the Roman assembly to choose Gnaeus Pompeius for command in the continuing struggle against Mithridates. During the prior command of Lucullus, Mithridates had evaded capture. Evoking this recent incident, Cicero refines the assembly's powers of judgment by retelling a much older story:

> [T]he way in which Mithridates escaped from his kingdom is reminiscent of the flight in which Medea, according to the myth, once betook herself from this selfsame country of Pontus. As she fled, the story goes, she scattered the limbs of her brother along the route where her father was likely to follow, with the intention that his pursuit should be slowed down and delayed by fatherly sorrow, as he collected each piece of his son's body in one place after another. That is very much what Mithridates did. As he went, he left behind him in Pontus an enormous quantity of gold and silver and all the beautiful things which he had inherited from his ancestors and which he himself during the earlier war had plundered from all parts of Asia and accumulated in his own kingdom. Our soldiers were too intent upon picking all this up; and meanwhile the king slipped through their hands. Medea's father Aeetes had been delayed by grief—but our men were slowed down by more pleasurable experiences. And so the terrified fugitive found asylum with

Tigranes, the king of Armenia, who comforted his desperate guest and gave him new strength and life when all seemed lost. (45–46)

In evoking the story, Cicero could rely on the assembly's knowledge of such "mythological tales in which there is reason to believe . . . that a substratum of truth exists, though overlaid by a mass of fiction" (Bulfinch 109).[29] Medea's dismemberment of her brother had been recounted early in Euripides's play (lines 160–740). But mapping the myth onto the political lesson Cicero was teaching the assembly assumed their ability to interpret it along common lines of understanding. Two fugitives from Pontus have succeeded by anticipating the frailties of their pursuers. The earlier story ended in horrors still felt by audiences centuries later; the present political crisis may end as badly unless correct choices are made now. To ease the assembly into that choice, the orator artfully associates the fleeing Medea with the enemy Mithridates and the Roman soldiers with the fully sympathetic Aeetes. These pairings spark the response Cicero wants: if the assembly picks Pompeius, history will see not only that the enemy (Mithridates-Medea) was vanquished but also that the honor of the military was redeemed from its recent avarice to the side of the good (Pompeius-Aeetes).

The multilayered discourse of a Cicero exulted in the literary sophistication of its audience and worked with a set of communal understandings grounded in stories. De Man, without the exaltation, makes similar assumptions about his audience when he refers to Helen of Troy in the midst of the passage on codes given above:

> The indifference of the text with regard to its referential meaning is what allows the legal text to proliferate, exactly as the preordained, coded repetition of a specific gesture or set of gestures allows Helen to weave the story of the war into the epic. . . .

I cannot improve on the attempts of those fine de Manians Samuel Weber and Neil Hertz to clarify this puzzling reference (Weber 244, 255n49). I only suggest that, perhaps against himself, de Man desires here a reunification of law and literature. Like Cicero, he summons an old story to support a new claim. But where Cicero relished the very possibility of referential meaning that moves him to speak the Medea story to the assembly, de Man's reference ironically denies that possibility.

De Man insists, unlike Cicero, that each interpretive move, whether legal or literary, resists through falsification any prior judgment or story. I have tried to show the blindness of that claim. But requiring us to imagine, Helen's creative link to a code, he hints at the theoretical insight so far unachieved except in stories.

Notes

This essay first appeared, 1 March 2008, as working paper 221 for the Jacob Burns Institute for Advanced Legal Studies at the Benjamin N. Cardozo School of Law. Translations are mine, unless otherwise indicated.

1. The context links contemporary theory back to the appeal made by I. A. Richards for an "interpretive mobility" (from Hartman, qtd. in Hartman and O'Hara 259), an early appeal to that intertextual density that avoids the conclusion, the single meaning, the generalization.

2. See, among recent ponderers on the strong differences between Christian and Jewish allegiances to texts and codes, Bloom 80–84; Weisberg, "Twenty Years"; and Waldron.

3. For the classic formulation of what every lawyer knows about the subject, see Chafee.

4. For a sixtieth-anniversary perspective on Nuremberg, including the remarks of three then-young assistant prosecutors reflecting on the promise and potential of Nuremberg principles, see "Symposium."

5. For an analysis of Nietzsche along similar grounds, see Birus.

6. Derrida accomplished this feat most famously in *Éperons* (*Spurs*). In "Force of Law," he manages to avoid Nietzsche on law, a pragmatic necessity, given Nietzsche's diametrically opposed approach to that subject.

7. As a student of de Man and admirer of his work, I was flagging these issues long before—and continue to think of them quite apart from—the "scandal" ("De Man Missing").

8. The word *naive* appears tellingly in Frank Lentricchia's description of de Man, as reported and analyzed by Christopher Norris: "As Lentricchia reads it, de Man's is currently the most 'advanced' form of this desire to neutralize political activity by showing it to rest on hopelessly naive ideas about mind, language, and reality" (3).

9. The allusion to Fish seems to read him (as I have in a relevant context) to question exactly that activist professional potential that Derrida here sees as "particularly true of 'law schools.'" For an exchange between Fish and me on the subject of the Shoah that engages some of the issues discussed in this essay, see Fish, "Holocaust Denial" and my "Fish."

10. For my more extended take on Derrida's antinomianism, see "Twenty Years."

11. I do not include Hartman in my "we." His considerable interest in the interweaving of legal rhetoric and the Holocaust is everywhere clear (e.g., his chapter "The Voice of Vichy" in *Longest Shadow*). While he does not systematically analyze the possibility of law's offering answers to genocide, he is thoroughly committed to the inquiry connecting law to literature in a manner that differs from other postmodernist border crossings. In his chapter "Midrash as Law and

Literature" in *Longest Shadow*, he writes: "Of course, literary commentaries and midrashic ones have their differences [that may] make Jewish scholars more zealous to avoid contamination. There is fear that the motive for Midrash will be mistakenly reduced from Everything is in the text, and what the text says signifies its relevance to the actions and thoughts of the interpretive community, to Everything is text, and the text is a structure of imaginary relations, a tissue without issue" (209). By means of this distinction, developed throughout the chapter, Hartman's careful interweaving of the midrashic "interpretive bounty" (Hartman and O'Hara 208) into some deconstructionist approaches marks off the idea of what I am calling the code from the "tissue without issue."

12. Brutal as the Nazi regime was, though, its words needed to be fashioned for various audiences. Trial balloons of various sorts had to be floated, particularly but not only during the first years of the regime, on such questions as euthanasia and "resettlement to the East" (Davidowicz 83). At the beginning of the Third Reich, but also well into the war itself, words like "resettlement" and "to the East" masked harsh realities that would have upset too many people if directly expressed.

13. See also Fraser, *Law* ("The Case against Vichy") and *Jews* ("Aryanization: The Discourse of Legalized Evil").

14. Given the German judiciary's strongly authoritarian traditions, the occasional instance of complexity and even of protest during the Third Reich become all the more interesting. Like lawyers and judges, religious figures too would display through discursive strategies, albeit rarely and less openly, their uneasiness with Hitler's programs. See Phayer 67–110.

15. Examples of a straightforward response by lawyers to what they deemed unacceptable to their professional traditions include that of Jacques Maury to the racial laws of Vichy France (see Weisberg, *Vichy Law* 54–55) and Dr. Lothar Kreyssig, who publicly and frontally criticized Hitler's euthanasia laws (Mueller 193–94). There were depressingly few religious figures who protested unambiguously. Those professionals who avoided a direct appeal to their finer traditions did so by their own choice and by means of their own rhetorical deviousness. No writer has better analyzed the loss of discursive simplicity during the Holocaust than Franklin H. Littell: "But what of the Christians? What of the smooth churchmen who made their peace with the Adversary, retreating into the pre-history of their pre-baptismal condition, even while they found a form of words to cover with pious phrases their loss of human face?" (56–57).

16. In Justice Cardozo's phrase, lawyers are at once free to develop their professional practice yet also constrained by their finer traditions.

17. The phrase is from the title of an early review of my *Failure of the Word*, by John D. Ayer. Ayer, reflecting a largely superannuated general skepticism at the outset of the movement, now (along with some two hundred other law professors in North America alone) prefers to be included.

18. See the different and thoughtful response of Peter Brooks to her piece ("Law and Literature"), which became part of an exchange to which I later contributed.

19. Peters elaborates: "For literary theorists working on human rights, there is a peculiar idealization of political and economic victimhood, as if these could somehow authenticate the project of the humanities generally. For human rights theorists, there is an idealization of 'narrative' or 'story,' which somehow has access to an underlying reality from which more traditional forms of legal analysis are excluded" ("'Literature'").

20. For the ensuing articles, see the inaugural issue, especially Dan Tritter's preface to *Cardozo Studies in Law and Literature*.

21. I am referring of course to Stanley Fish's *Is There a Text in This Class?*

22. In three successive years, 1976–78, the annual meetings of the MLA sponsored a special session on law and literature. Increasingly large gatherings (peaking at eighty or so in 1978) heard joining with the lawyers such literary scholars as Jean-Pierre Barricelli, Jerry Frese, David Grossvogel, Wolfgang Holdheim, Richard Jacobson, W. Nicholas Knight, and Blair Rouse; the proceedings of the first session were expeditiously published in the *University of Hartford Studies in Literature*.

23. An excellent bibliography of scholarship relating to all genres has been compiled by Daniel Solove for the Law and Humanities Institute, available on the Internet. For a superb appraisal of some of this scholarship, see Gaakeer.

24. Readings of well-worked texts made a difference in their respective interpretive communities, even in those communities uninterested in law and literature as a field. For the field of comparative literature, an example of a pathbreaking inquiry that was also seminal for law and literature is Holdheim's *Justizirrtum*, as were perhaps the textual readings that Jean-Pierre Barricelli and I presented in *Interrelations of Literature* (Weisberg and Barricelli). The movement's readings of *The Merchant of Venice* and *Billy Budd, Sailor* have had at least some effect on traditional scholarship about those well-worked texts; see my appraisal of these effects in *Poethics* (ch. 3 and n34 to that chapter). Brook Thomas's readings of Melville, but also of Stowe, Cooper, and Hawthorne, have influenced the specific interpretive communities dealing with those writers; see his *Cross-Examinations of Law and Literature*. Some of the work on Dostoevsky in my *Failure of the Word* has found a second home in ensuing critical editions of *Notes from Underground* and *Crime and Punishment*. Finally, scholars in the movement have contributed to an understanding of Shakespeare's technical language in the sonnets—see Cormack.

25. Goodrich shares my view, in an ongoing debate that continues to energize law and literature practitioners: we believe that, with the greatest sensitivity to a story's many complexities, to the many voices in stories, and to the deliberate byways to meaning set up by almost all storytellers, there is in the end at least the possibility of a narrative judgment about characters, values, and institutions represented in fictional works. Instead of law's being seen as the place for judgment (and closure), while literature exults in ambiguity and endless openness, this view reverses that assumption and finds closure on many issues (in the quoted passage, the pretensions of law) to reside more frequently in stories than in legal discourse. See Goodrich, "Response."

26. The seminal law and literature story is told, and the list further theorized and expanded, in Weisberg, "Wigmore's 'Legal Novels.'"

27. Cardozo would have found quite strange, as have I, de Man's denial that "[n]on-verbal acts, if such a thing were to be conceivable . . . can ever be separated from the attempt at understanding, from the interpretation, that necessarily accompanies and falsifies it" (*Allegories* 127–28). Cardozo believed that the act of judgment is not entirely verbal and, more important, that translating that act into language entails no necessary falsification.

28. For a recent survey of judicial invocations of stories, see DeStafano.

29. The account of these events is described in *Bulfinch's Mythology.*

Peter Brooks

Law, Literature: Where Are We?

Law and Literature: So Far

It's no secret that law and literature became something of a movement: not quite what you would call a school but nonetheless a set of perspectives, an agenda for research, an aspiration to cross-disciplinary understanding. The movement arose, it seems, in reaction to a growing predominance of law and economics as the paradigm in legal education. It responded to a rumor, increasingly audible since the late 1970s, that there was something of interest going on in the interpretive humanities that might be germane to legal studies. The transfer of a number of graduate students from the humanities, where job prospects looked bleak, to law schools no doubt acted as a vector in the transmission of ideas. In the 1980s and 1990s, law and literature spawned conferences, essays, anthologies, and then histories and critiques of the enterprise. I understand there is a recently published textbook on the subject—designed for law school courses—whereas others have written the obituary of a movement that seems to have run out of breath. In my own view, the movement has more often than not strayed from its most productive paths of inquiry but remains of crucial importance, perhaps now more than ever. We (meaning in this instance citizens of the United States) have witnessed in the past few years the greatest divorce between law and humanism in our nation's history.

The law and literature rubric has since its inception covered a range of understandings of that *and*. The phrase can mean "law in literature," as when one studies representations of the law in literary works (e.g., Aeschylus's *The Oresteia*, Dickens's *Bleak House*, Melville's *Billy Budd*, or Kafka's *The Trial*). Such a study is not a negligible enterprise, since literature is often profoundly about discovery of the law; tragedy, especially, may always be about an encounter with the Law, discovered in the moment of its infraction. Or the phrase may mean "literature in the law": summoning legal scholars and practitioners, including judges, to read literature to become more sensitive to the human consequences of legal actions. More subtly, the *and* can call for a confrontation and debate between two fields that overlap in ways that require a dialogue. All these understandings respond to a desire to bring legal and humanistic thought together—or back together again, since there is reason to believe they once were more closely connected than they have become in American legal ideology and education.

The most dramatic claim of law and literature has resulted from the deliberate invasion of law by literature, on the argument that interpretive methods and theories elaborated in literary studies can and should be imported into legal study. Literary theory in the late twentieth century gained a certain prestige, or notoriety, from its flamboyant and well-publicized debates on questions of interpretation, the nature of the linguistic sign, and the ways in which meaning is created and decoded. It became an export commodity, forced on the attention of scholars in other fields. Since American law is highly textual—eventuating, as one rises in the hierarchy of courts, in extensive written opinions that often turn on issues of interpreting other written documents, including the Constitution—theories and practices derived from fields that had long thought about what it means to read and to interpret seemed to make good sense. A number of legal scholars turned, with enthusiasm or bemusement, to issues raised by hermeneutics and various forms of poststructuralism. They asked, for instance, Are the grounds of legal interpretation as stable as they traditionally have been claimed to be? Are there any grounds of interpretation that do not derive from the practice of interpretation—that is, from the rhetoric of the law itself? Legal scholarship here has been abetted—or perhaps goaded—by the work of literary scholars and theorists who saw in law a nexus of textuality and worldly power, hence a field in which their tools might be of some real use in the world.

Judges, lawyers, and legal scholars have tended to treat the language of the law as if it were fully hermetic, to be judged only within the texts and traditions of the law. They have often assumed that interpretation in the law may proceed on unchallenged assumptions about intention and meaning, how each lines up with the other, how they are to be determined. One result of the infiltration of literary-critical thinking into the legal domain has been a questioning of how law defines its terms of art, of the languages it deploys in talking about human agency, of its unproblematic understandings of narrative and rhetoric. Yet the most widely read book on law and literature, Judge Richard A. Posner's *Law and Literature: A Misunderstood Relation*, takes the position that the two domains should be insulated from each other: literary criticism should be free to construe texts in a New Critical manner, according to textual implications alone, free from constraints of intention or context; whereas legal interpretation must always be intentionalist and contextualist, attentive to the explicit or implicit original intent of the Constitution, of statutes, and of prior decision making.

The question then is, Should Posner's cordon sanitaire around the law and its language be maintained? Even more: Can it be maintained, even if we wish it to be? An era of suspicion has been inaugurated, and it may prove impossible to keep legal language from the contamination brought by literary-critical thinking. At stake here is the autonomy of the law, as practice and as intellectual discipline: can the law stand alone? And a derivative question: Should legal studies be so intent to isolate themselves from other interpretive disciplines in the university?

What's at Stake?

In their first law school class, students typically are told that they must learn to think like a lawyer, and this lesson will have been repeated frequently by the time the JD is delivered. Thinking like a lawyer involves divesting yourself of your preconceptions about the rights and wrongs of a case, divesting yourself of your instinctive sense of where justice lies or how fair play should be exercised, in order to learn to analyze human actions in their intersections with law. The hypothetical cases presented on law school exams are intentionally baroque, with a plethora of ornament and potentially misleading byways. Students learning to think like a lawyer must sort it all out according to identifiable and pertinent law, precedent, and legal doctrine. How is this case like and unlike *x* number of cases that fall into the same general category? How, indeed, do you know to what category a particular case belongs? To the uninitiated, such issues are formidably difficult: the legal savvy just isn't there. The uninitiated reader of such material may be led to reflect on how a long American tradition, before the coming of law schools, made learning the law a matter of hands-on apprenticeship to a practicing attorney. The law is above all a praxis, a way of doing things, a language of shared references and intentions, and an enterprise very much directed to an outcome: some form of adjudication, with winners, losers, settlements, sentences.

So lawyers in training must learn to read and argue within the constraints of the law and its traditions. The downside to this approach is the claim that legal culture stands apart from other social practices and cultural understandings. Law, after all, lies embedded in most of our ways of living in an ordered society, so there might be something to gain in holding law more closely responsible to other social and cultural creations of meaning. It may be valuable to challenge the implicit claim that legal terms of art—for instance, the language of intent or the will—are self-definitional and therefore off-limits to nonlegal questioners. Is the notion of human agency implicit in much legal language true to contemporary understandings of how people behave? Does it matter? Do legal opinions obscure something of importance in describing confessions under interrogation as the product of a "free and rational will"? Consider, as an extreme example of the law's attempt to keep its language to itself, the now infamous torture memo of 1 August 2002, which has constant recourse to the dictionary—to various dictionaries, in fact—to produce definitions of *torture* so bizarre that even our administration was reluctantly forced to repudiate them (see Bybee; P. Brooks, "Plain Meaning"). The common reader has the right to say, No, this cannot be right, not even in the law.

From early in history, law was closely allied to a rhetorical practice. Rhetoric in ancient Athens was mainly about helping you make your case in courts of law or other public assemblies. In the early history of the United States, the practice of law was closely tied to a rhetorical tradition embodied in public oratory, very much taught in American high schools and fostered through public debate and oratorical contest. But the law eventually suppressed its rhetorical origins in favor of a claim to professional autonomy and a professionally hermetic language. Perhaps the process of disciplinary professionalization, represented by the rise of the law school and its increasing autonomy in the university, always entails a repression of rhetorical origins, which come to seem scarcely avowable as a foundation. While legal studies, like courts of law, sometimes need to listen to testimony from fields outside, law nonetheless constantly asks, Is this relevant to the law? In what terms can the law use it? The law assigns its actors various gatekeeping functions in order to preserve its nature and autonomy.

Hidden in all our disciplinary formations lies some residue of what was repressed over the course of their history. This residue might have a half-life that could let it still make a difference. What if legal studies were to rediscover the role of rhetoric and narrative in legal decision making, for instance? What if learning to think like a lawyer was thought to require more questioning of what that really means? If legal knowledge necessarily relates to a pragmatic horizon—what the knowledge is needed for—it might nonetheless ask if that horizon is too narrowly drawn. At the outside limit, legal studies should pay more attention to those critics, reaching back at least to Jean-Jacques Rousseau, who have claimed that law is founded on an act of violent usurpation and deceit. A similar claim has been urged by Robert Cover, and others have noted with him that the exercise of the law is a field of violence, suffering, dispossession, and even death. Is the awareness of such a claim totally useless for the student or even the practitioner of law?

I would put in this manner what is at stake in the encounter of law and literature. What if law and literature were not separate entities but rather twins separated at birth and seeking, with something of the melodrama such searches involve, to reunite? That is, what if literature and its study (and the interpretive humanities in general) harbored a kind of *impensé* of the law—an unrealized potential—that had been suppressed, or repressed, in the course of its evolution? In educational and institutional terms, this thesis argues for a more active dialogue between legal and humanistic interpretive communities. The law and literature movement has arisen in large part from those who believe that law needs to be accountable to more than itself: to more than the legal institution, its languages and rituals. It needs to be tested against a realm of human value to which literature speaks—not in any simple sense of moral uplift but in its address to the human condition.

A Teaching Example

Let us leave such transcendent abstractions and talk more concretely about teaching law and literature. There are of course many possible approaches. Some are thematic. Studying marriage in its legal and imaginative representations offers a good example since our understanding of marriage, even of its legal parameters, derives as much from literary dramatizations as from legal pronouncements.[1] Current debates about whether to institute same-sex marriage, for instance, call on a rhetoric about marriage that derives from cultural (and religious) sources more than from legal ones, and an analysis of that rhetoric can be helpful in understanding the conflicting ideologies of marriage now in contention.

The most probative and compelling courses may be those that confront directly the ways in which the two disciplines go about interpreting their texts and describing their conceptions of reality. In recent versions of such a course that I devised, we opened with what Chief Justice William Rehnquist wrote about the plain meaning of statutes (in *Leocal v. Ashcroft*) and what can happen to this plainness in strong instances of interpretation, ranging from the 1 August 2002 memorandum from the Office of Legal Counsel at the Justice Department on the definition of torture to Humpty Dumpty's theory of interpretation in Lewis Carroll's *Through the Looking-Glass* (123).[2] Then we looked at Justice Antonin Scalia's claim that constitutional interpretation needs to be founded on the "original understanding" of the Constitution (as garnered from the Federalist Papers, the ratification debates, etc.)—a position Scalia sees as an improvement on interpretation based on the "original intent" of the framers, though it in fact gets him into trouble, since—as we literary critics understand—any recourse to how a document was understood in historical time at once opens up the prospect of a changing, evolving horizon of meaning. To radicalize the issue, I set against Scalia a short and accessible essay by Paul de Man, "The Return to Philology," an apologia for (very) close reading that argues that literature should be taught "as a rhetoric and a poetics prior to being taught as a hermeneutics and a history" (25–26). What if one were to apply such a program of reading to the law, setting aside the usual, quasi-theological presumptions about what a given legal text should mean? The next step is to study some instances of the law's attempting to interpret in slippery circumstances: for instance, as to whether the display of a Christmastime crèche on public property in Pawtucket, Rhode Island, violates the doctrine of separation of church and state. The Supreme Court—in this case, *Lynch v. Donnelly*, in the person of Justice Sandra Day O'Connor—found itself forced to offer a theory of how we interpret symbols, one that any critic nourished on Roman Jakobson and other analysts of communication will find distressingly thin and naive.

The idea here is not to score points on those who are required to adjudicate difficult social issues involving communication but rather to show that there are other disciplines and interpretive cultures that have developed some expertise that might be relevant to the adjudication. The law is a decision-making process. Common law is the sum of the decisions made in the past, which need to be read and interpreted in order to know how a present case resembles and differs from the tradition in which it stands. The law—whether common law or statutory or constitutional interpretation—is inherently intertextual, and the ways in which it reads precursor texts in order to arrive at the creation of a new text, a new legal opinion, has close analogies in literary history. So it is that a number of classic texts on how to read literature—from William Wimsatt's "What to Say about a Poem" to Stanley Fish's "Is There a Text in This Class?," from Mikhail Bakhtin on dialogism to Roland Barthes on classical rhetoric—prove helpful in thinking about problems of legal interpretation in ways that judges rarely articulate. Legal rhetoric is not simply transparent; the choice of an Oliver Wendell Holmesian plain style is itself a rhetorical choice that has decisional consequences. The audiences to which legal rhetorics are addressed—whether other judges, juries, legislatures, police precincts, or the public at large—play a constitutive role in shaping the law. When, in one of the most dramatic instances in American history, the Supreme Court sought to end school segregation by its fiat in *Brown v. Board of Education*, it had to find a rhetoric of both force and accommodation (the famous, nearly oxymoronic phrase "all deliberate speed," for instance), and when the governor of Arkansas defied the fiat, the Court (in *Cooper v. Aaron*) had to reach for a rhetoric of adamant determination and extremity, foregrounding in particular the Court's time-honored right to say what the law is.

In my courses in law and literature, questions of narrative assume a large place—inevitably, given my scholarly concerns over the years. A riveting public trial—O. J. Simpson, the Rodney King case—often serves to remind us how much the law is compounded of narrative. It is all about competing stories, from those presented at the trial court, elicited from witnesses, rewoven into different plausibilities by prosecution and defense, submitted to the critical judgment of the jury; to their retelling at the appellate level, which must pay particular attention to the rules of storytelling, the conformity of narratives to norms of telling and listening; on up to the Supreme Court, which must tress together the story of the case at hand and the history of constitutional interpretation, according to the conventions of stare decisis and the rules of precedent, though often, since dissents are allowed, presenting two different tellings of the story, with different outcomes.

Trial lawyers know that they need to tell stories, that the evidence they present in court must be bound together and unfolded in narrative form, and law school clinics in courtroom advocacy pay attention to story-telling skills as part of the art of persuasion. Yet the law rarely speaks in a doctrinal or analytic way about its narrative dimension. On the contrary, it seems to want to deny the importance of story, to tame it by legal rule, to interrupt it by cross-questioning, to suppress it through the equation of story with the emotional, the irrational, the dangerous wild card in a discourse committed to reason and syllogism. The analytic tools of narratology, including questions of point of view, voice, implied audience, and the fundamental distinction between story and narrative discourse (*fabula* and *syuzhet*, in the fundamental Russian formalist distinction), almost never are found in the law, even in those cases that seem urgently to call for such attention.

I have worked with students on a well-known rape case from Maryland, *Rusk v. State* and *State of Maryland v. Rusk*. Edward Rusk was convicted at trial; the conviction was reversed in the first appellate court, then reinstated in the highest state court. In the decisions on each level, there was a majority and a minority opinion starkly opposed to each other. Thus we have four different retellings of what we know is the same story of what happened between a man and a woman one night in Baltimore. The story was constructed at trial, then rewritten at the appellate levels—with dramatically different results, sending Rusk to prison for seven years or else releasing him. How could these four stories, based on the same facts—and none of the principal events of what happened that night was in dispute—have had different outcomes? The answer is that the narrative "glue" was different: the way incidents and events are made to combine in a meaningful story, one that can be called consensual sex on the one hand and rape on the other. The blanks of intention and meaning were filled in by the judges' differing narrative discourses and presuppositions. Often, one detects, at issue is a judge's sense of how a woman is supposed to behave in certain circumstances, a set of unexamined cultural doxas (as Barthes would have said) that work toward our everyday construal of narratives. The differing outcomes in the retellings of the *Rusk* cases offer a dramatic instance of how narratives take on design, intention, and meaning. They do not simply recount happenings; they give them shape, give them a point, argue their import, proclaim their results.

It is also instructive to work with students on how cases are presented on appeal. A petition to reopen a case decided at trial must find a way to retell the story in a striking and immediate way, from the first sentence forward, that has some chance of convincing a judge (or, more probably, a judge's law clerk) that something is truly amiss and demands remedy. Only a narrative discourse that can recast the story that won out at trial in such a way as to show its fault lines, or its nonconformity to the rules governing storytelling at law, has any chance of a new hearing. The "cert. petition" (petition for a writ of certiorari) of a person condemned to execution offers the most dramatic instance of how the way a story is told can become a matter of life and death. At such stakes, the more refined our analytic tools for analyzing how stories are told, the better.

Anthony Amsterdam and Jerome Bruner (lawyer and psychologist, respectively) argue that the traditional notion that adjudication proceeds by "examining free-standing factual data selected on grounds of their logical pertinency" must give way to the realization that "increasingly we are coming to recognize that both the questions and the answers in such matters of 'fact' depend largely upon one's choice (considered or unconsidered) of some overall narrative as best describing *what happened* or *how the world works*" (111). These assertions seem unimpeachable to literary narratologists, who have long argued that narrative is one of the large categories in which we order and construct reality. Yet they remain heretical in the world of the law, which does not overtly recognize narrative as a category in the process of legal adjudication. A dialogue that brings such narratologists as Boris Tomachevsky, Tzvetan Todorov, Barthes, Gérard Genette, and Shlomith Rimmon-Kenan to bear on the shape and intent of literary narratives can be useful in showing how they work on their listeners and readers, how their formal designs make designs on their audience. Narrative is never innocent; it always intends. In the law, the way that intention is decoded—the kind of conviction produced by a given narrative—has much to do with whether or not the outcome is conviction in the penal sense.

So the courses I have taught focus on narrative and rhetorical transactions: the ways in which stories and arguments at the law are made effective, made operative, and the need for an analytic, even a suspicious attention toward the ways in which narrative and rhetoric work on us. "A syllogism is not a story," writes Justice David Souter in *Old Chief v. United States* (189), the only Supreme Court opinion I know of that actually discusses the possible import of narrative in the law. Syllogisms may mask stories, however; and stories may imply syllogisms. The literary critic's sense of genre and how it works seems a useful part of the legal actor's and the legal analyst's tool kit. It can provide real insight into evidentiary stories—for instance, narratives of search and seizure and the possible legality of what they uncover—and the confessional stories on which so many convictions depend.

I could pile on more examples of how the engagement of law and literature can work productively. What I have said is mainly couched, I realize, in terms of what literary disciplines can bring to the study of law; my main audience in this teaching has been law students. I hope that one can detect the implications in the other direction as well: the benefit to students of literature in engaging a textual corpus whose interpretation has consequences in the real world, where rhetoric and narrative are not merely possible world games but issues on which people may lose their liberty and even their lives.

For the past several decades we have talked much about interdisciplinarity and practiced it with varying degrees of success. It seems to me that the law and literature movement offers an instance of where disciplined, responsible interdisciplinary study can really matter. The study can be frustrating, to be sure, since disciplines, especially in the context of professional schools intent on qualifying students for the practice of a métier, tend to reject transplants into their internal systems. To breach the autonomy of a professional discipline is not easy. To convince that discipline that it needs to think about what it has repressed, cast out of consciousness, is difficult indeed. Nonetheless, students are there and willing to listen.

Notes

1. The course Marriage in Law, Culture, and the Imagination was cotaught by Kerry Abrams and me at Virginia Law School in the spring of 2006.

2. Versions of Law and Humanities: Reading and Interpretation were taught by Daniel Ortiz and me at Virginia Law School in the fall of 2005 and by Robert Post and me at Yale Law School in the spring of 2008.

Julie Stone Peters

Law, Literature, and the Vanishing Real: On the Future of an Interdisciplinary Illusion

I begin with a story: some never-to-be-untangled amalgamation of history, caricature, and the truer than true that is fiction. A little over a decade ago, at a great and august university, a group of professors met to talk about law and literature. The law professors had been reading Adorno and Althusser; Barthes, Benjamin, and Butler; Deleuze and Derrida. The literature professors had been reading critical legal studies and Amnesty International reports. The law professors were worried that narratology and postcolonial theory might already be passé. The literature professors were concerned, as a matter of principle.

The professors went around the room identifying themselves and their hopes for the seminar. "My project involves *thinking* the law via Althusser," said one professor. "I'm working on Joyce and Proust as legal visionaries, using Foucault, Barthes, and Derrida to show them implicitly proposing, *avant la lettre*, every single doctrinal innovation in trial law of the postwar era," said another. "My project," said a third, "is to recognize the power of legal narrative as a tool of liberation for women and people of color, because listening, *really* listening to them telling their own stories in the courtroom might just allow us to begin the transformation we so urgently need, from an ethic of justice to an ethic of care." Finally it was the turn of the literature professor who had initiated the seminar. "I'd like to use law to end poverty, racism, and war," he exclaimed. "I'd like all you lawyers to help me bring a case that would get them declared illegal by the Supreme Court!" A great roar of applause arose from the literature professors. "That's ridiculous," blurted out the law professor who was the seminar's cohost. "That's the most reductive and naive idea of law I've ever heard." There was a brief silence in the room. "Well," said the literature professor, his face turning purple, "we clearly have the wrong kind of lawyers!" And he stormed out of the room.

The law professors were gravely disappointed. Why did the literature professors have such a reductive idea of the law? Why did they think that to call legal rules indeterminate was to get halfway to revolution, when any two-bit lawyer knew, for better or worse, that you could argue a legal point any way you wanted? And why, at the same time, did they seem to leave their poststructuralist insights at the door when they took up the law as a cudgel? What was this compulsion to pursue some vague, naive, and undertheorized notion of justice? It was clear that the literature professors needed to go to law school.

The literature professors were also gravely disappointed. Why weren't the law professors interested in using law as that great tool of revolutionary power it had the potential to be? And what was this business of stories as somehow truer than law, as if once you called something a story, it was exempt from ideology critique, as if narrative were ever free from the coercions of generic convention, the feints of rhetoric, its own multiplicity and contradictoriness? It was clear that the law professors needed to go to grad school.

Calling on Benjamin Cardozo's 1925 essay "Law and Literature," scholars writing in post–World War II academia periodically attempted to outline a program for the study of law as a rhetorical and literary art (e.g., E. London, *Law*; Reich, "Toward the Humanistic Study"). But not until the 1970s did the conjunction of law and literature become institutionalized, producing conferences, special sessions at annual meetings, bibliographies, course rubrics, institutes—becoming, that is, a distinct subdisciplinary formation.[1] In 1980, Kenneth Abraham could still refer to law and literature as "an unlikely pair" (676). But by the mid-1980s, the study of law and literature had become a movement and, by the 1990s, a subdiscipline. Each of law and literature's major projects—humanism (dominant in the 1970s and early 1980s and focusing largely on literary texts), hermeneutics (dominant throughout the 1980s and focusing largely on literary theory), and narrative (dominant in the late 1980s and 1990s and focusing largely on legal cases)[2]—used different kinds of texts, had different kinds of goals, and worked toward these goals with different kinds of interpretive strategies. Despite these differences, one might trace a set of shared preoccupations and recurrent aspirations tied to specific institutional changes and historical events[3] but also (taking a broader view) expressing more general anxieties about the function and meaning of the humanities and human sciences in the last quarter of the twentieth century. In this, law and literature might be thought of as an exemplary case of the interdisciplinary struggles of the past few decades.

Humanism

The defining feature of law and literature in its earliest formal incarnations was its commitment to the human as an ethical corrective to the scientific and technocratic visions of law that had prevailed in most of the twentieth century. As J. Allen Smith wrote in "The Coming Renaissance in Law and Literature," "Fundamentally, our problem arises from our failure to . . . ground ourselves securely on the humanistic tradition, of which literature is a chief expression and from which the profession should draw nourishment and direction" (85). The work that came to be seen as the founding scripture of law and literature as a joint disciplinary project was James Boyd White's textbook *The Legal Imagination* (1973), intended to give law students a literary and rhetorical education that would stave off the administrative statism of the bureaucratic 1970s. White invited law students to "imagine as fully as possible how it might be said that law is not a science—at least not the 'social science' some would call it—but an art" (xxxiv–xxxv). Literature, as the most human of the humane arts, could teach the law "humanistic judgment" (Weisberg and Barricelli 150) by reminding us of the rich humanity that lay behind judicial decisions; by offering reflections on the human meaning of law's central concepts; and by offering models of rhetorical excellence, reuniting legal practice with the great tradition of forensic oratory on which it was founded.

At the center of this humanist vision was the notion that literature could somehow bring the real to law. If earlier in the century legal realism had attempted, with the help of the social sciences, to bring social reality to law as an antidote to legal formalism, the humanist realism of law and literature was to serve as an antidote to the sterile technicality of the social sciences. The renaissance in law and literature that Smith announced could redress the "cleavage between law and reality" ("Coming Renaissance" 85). As Richard Weisberg argued, using the example of *The Brothers Karamazov*, literature could offer "a critique par excellence of the way the law twists reality into a false codified form" (Rev. of *The Legal Imagination* 330). Weisberg, probably the person most responsible for galvanizing law and literature as a subdiscipline from the late 1970s on, would later complain of the way in which "postmodernist criticism and 'free market' microeconomics" had "attracted masses of [legal] practitioners away from . . . the passions, the hopes, the reality of the world around them" (*Poethics* xiv). Literature had offered from the outset to reclaim that reality for law and, out of it, to forge a new legal ethics, what Weisberg came to call "poethics": the use of literature to fill "the ethical void in which legal thought and practice now exist" (4).

In the process, literature, through its affiliation with law, would also attain a new reality. Scholars could discard the "elitist, superficial view of literature as essentially a civilizing influence to render lawyers fit for life in polite society," explained Harold Suretsky in 1979. Literature could instead be seen as "a source of truth which can help to analyze and criticize the law" (728). Humanistic discussion of the law constituted, as Peter d'Errico explained in a 1975 essay, "a search which is a praxis," in which "reflection is merged with activity so that we are neither academics separated from the 'real' world, nor 'activists' cut off from the process of inquiry and education" (58). Law could, thanks to literature, recall its lost humanity. At the same time, speaking truth to power, literature could at last do something real.

Hermeneutics

While legal humanism seemed a powerful antidote to the bureaucratic state in the 1970s, it was out of alignment with the theoretical debates at the center of literary study in the late 1970s and early 1980s, which were preoccupied with challenges to the identity of the human subject presumed by traditional humanism and to the identity of the humanist text as the central agent of human meaning. With the very concept of the author pronounced dead by French theory and the text pronounced dizzyingly indeterminate, to seek ethical reality in authors and texts seemed a naively idealist enterprise. As important, the genteel liberal humanism that lay behind law and literature in the 1970s seemed an inadequate response to the overwhelming victory of the right in 1980 and the newfound power of what was to become the Rehnquist court. If literature had something to offer law, it was not a return to an outmoded humanism but instead an interventionist hermeneutics that could demolish the originalist and textualist theories that sustained the rulings of an increasingly reactionary court.

Literary hermeneutics promised liberation of the law from its bondage to an archaic text and the dead white men who continued to haunt it. But it also threatened to unmoor law from its traditional interpretive bases. Responding to this threat in a 1982 essay, the constitutional scholar Owen Fiss made an impassioned protest against literary deconstruction, which he characterized as "the new nihilism" (740–41). "This nihilism . . . is the deepest and darkest of all nihilisms," he wrote, not only threatening "our social existence and the nature of public life as we know it in America" but unmooring "reality" itself and "demean[ing] our lives" (763, 740). From this sense of ontological panic emerged such right-wing backlash texts as Judge Richard Posner's famous 1988 diabtribe against law and literature (*Law*). But the hermeneutic turn also created angst on the left. One felt, explained Sanford Levinson, "a pervasive anxiety," a loss of "confidence in one's ability to ground description or analysis in a purported reality" (377).

But if literary hermeneutics could stir fear about the accessibility of the real, it could also offer models for salvaging the real. "Lawyers would do well to study literary . . . interpretation," wrote Ronald Dworkin firmly in 1982, explaining that the plethora of interpretive options offered by literary criticism could show law the way through poststructuralist uncertainty to a more realist legal hermeneutics ("Law" 182). Stanley Fish's notion of interpretive communities, elaborated in *Is There a Text in This Class?* (1980), became a touchstone for the discussion, cited by critics right, left, and center (and debated most energetically by Fish himself), standing for the proposition that, as Abraham put it,

> the objects, texts, and facts with which this and every other enterprise works are real in the only way that anything is real . . . by virtue of [their] acceptance within a community of interpretation whose existence is a prerequisite to the production of knowledge itself. (694)

If literature could thus help law shore up its stability, law could in exchange respond to literature's own sense of destabilization. In his introduction to *The Politics of Interpretation* (an essay collection emerging from the 1981 conference in which many of the claims about law and literature's shared hermeneutic project were first aired), W. J. T. Mitchell spoke of the intensified longing that literature as a discipline, deprived of its traditional humanist and interpretive authority, felt for "the 'real world' of social and institutional power," the world of "state power and real social change" (iv–v). Both a profession of this longing and a critique, Edward Said's contribution to the collection repeatedly invoked the opposition between the ideal world of literature and philosophy and the real world of law and politics. Literary criticism, and in particular literary Marxism, wrote Said, exists in "cloistral seclusion from the inhospitable world of real politics. [Real] politics is mainly what the literary critic talks about long-ingly and hopelessly" (16).[4]

Law offered literary theorists a way out of longing and hopelessness through what appeared to be a concrete role in legal politics. In the wake of the hermeneutic debates, literary critics could attempt to do "real politics" through constitutional interpretation—the kind of virtuoso interpreta-tion performed, for instance, by Elaine Scarry's lengthy law review article ("War and the Social Contract") arguing that the Second Amendment prohibits nuclear stockpiling. As Peter Brooks explained, with a shade of autobiographical irony, law presented itself to literary critics as the site of "an exceptional intersection of textuality and social power":

> Literary critics—who often harbor a bad conscience about their pro-fession—have displayed a desire to break out of the realm of fictions, to engage large cultural issues: to make their interpretive techniques work on something closer to "reality." ("Law as Narrative" 15)

Narrative

The interpretive framework that seemed best suited to join the legal vision of the truth of literature to the literary vision of the reality of law in the late 1980s was feminist theory. As the literary scholar Carolyn Heilbrun and the legal scholar Judith Resnik explained, feminist scholarship was dedicated to uncovering "the realities of women's lives" through the re-covery of women's "long unheard voices," "their own language and their own narratives" (1919, 1931, 1934). For Heilbrun, bringing the realities of women's lives into the reality of the legal arena offered a cure for what Said and Brooks had characterized as the literary critic's desire, longing, and hopelessness. Asked to deliver a paper at a law school workshop, "with that suddenness that we think of as connected only with falling in love, but which equally marks intellectual passions," she instantly realized that "here was a context in which real changes in the language and stories of women might be enacted" (1920).

This proposition—that listening to the stories of those regularly excluded from power could enact "real changes"—became the center of "narrative jurisprudence" or, in its more folksy moments, "the legal storytelling movement." Influenced by the poststructuralist critique of master narratives, feminist and critical race theory, the rapid proliferation of truth commissions, and psychotherapeutic claims for the healing power of telling one's story, narrative jurisprudence had a definite political program. In a 1988 letter, Richard Delgado, one of narrative jurisprudence's leading proponents, proclaimed:

> The main cause of Black and brown subordination is not so much poorly crafted or enforced laws or judicial decisions. Rather, it is the prevailing mindset through which members of the majority race justify the world as it is. . . . The cure is storytelling, . . . counterhegemonic [storytelling to] quicken and engage conscience.
> (qtd. in Scheppele 2075)

If narrative was cure, it was cure through its access to a reality that was previously inaccessible but that oppositional storytelling could uncover. Stories could "uniquely bridg[e] the gap between law and reality," explained one review of Delgado's work. "[P]opulated by real people," taking place "in real time," "[s]tories . . . are 'real' whether they are offered as fact or fantasy, myth or matter of fact." Stories produced an alternative "epistemological accuracy," founded on the "plural truths of lived experience" rather than on "objective" reality (Hayman and Levit 398–99, 436).

Many legal and literary scholars writing about narrative jurisprudence were critical of presuppositions about the inherent truth, exemplarity, or ethics of stories.[5] But legal storytelling appealingly clothed its truth claims in a humanist rhetoric revived and rendered palatable through its transfer to the sphere of oppositional politics. In Delgado's words, the ultimate goal of narrative jurisprudence's brand of "counter-reality" was to "humanize us" ("Storytelling" 2412, 2440). It was no longer Shakespeare who was to be the guide to ethical value or Cicero who was to serve as a model humanist rhetorician but the marginalized, victimized, voiceless other. Narrative jurisprudence could thus show law a way out of its poststructuralist impasses by offering a postcritical return not simply to the real but to the *humanist* real. We must ask ourselves, wrote Robin West in 1993, "whether . . . the laws we enact . . . serve our best understanding of our *true* human needs, our true human aspirations, or our true social and individual potential, as gleaned from the stories we tell about ourselves and each other" (*Narrative* 7). Habitually fixated on "economic man," alienated from "literary woman," law could reclaim human feeling through a return to empathy, love, and (in West's pervasive metonymy) the heart. *Brown v. Board of Education*, she explained, was exemplary, not only as a "sympathetic . . . response to a cry of pain" but also because it "speaks to our real need for fraternity rather than our expressed xenophobia; it taps our real potential for an enlarged community and an enlarged conception of self rather than our expressed fear of differences" (175–76). The xenophobia and fear that the law expressed were untrue to our nature. The virtues embodied by the literary were what, in the end, was most real in us.

The Disciplinary Hall of Mirrors

This skewed and partial history, perhaps more caricature than history, doubtless obscures the impressive work that has emerged from law and literature over the past thirty or so years, but it does so in an attempt to reveal instead the particular nexus of disciplinary projections that were essential to its formation. That is, I've attempted not to display the collective contribution of law and literature but to uncover its collective longing (a project that is not merely institutional diagnosis but, I admit, also autobiographical confession).

All interdisciplinarity, one might argue, is disciplinary symptom: somatization, in the disciplinary body, of some invisible pain, thwarted desire being acted out as neurosis. Interdisciplinarity might be thought of as hysteria, in the ancient Greek sense, in which the wandering of the uterus from its proper home was thought to produce histrionic symptoms in the patient, publicly theatricalizing the patient's interior dislocation. In this sense, law and literature might be seen as having symptomatized each discipline's secret interior wound: literature's wounded sense of its insignificance, its inability to achieve some ever-imagined but ever-receding praxis; law's guilty sense of its collaborationism, its tainted complicity with the state apparatus, its alienation from alienation itself. Each in some way fantasized its union with the other: law would give literature praxis; literature would give law humanity and critical edge. Behind both these instantiations of "discipline envy" (in Marjorie Garber's phrase) lay a view of the other discipline as somehow possessing the real. Law seemed, to the literary scholar longing for the political real, a sphere in which language could make things happen. Literature seemed, to the legal scholar longing for the critical-humanist real, a sphere in which language could stand outside the oppressive state, speaking truth to law's obfuscations and subterfuges.

As in all interdisciplinary adventures, these hypostasized versions of the disciplinary other spoke to preexisting disciplinary identities. Literature had become itself—a separate aesthetic field in the late eighteenth century and a discipline in the nineteenth century—precisely because of its claim on the humanist tradition in the face of utilitarianism and academic scientism.[6] Law and literature scholars have often understood the two domains as, in Brooks's self-consciously melodramatic terms, "twins separated at birth" ("Law and Literature" 1645).[7] Lawyers, they stress, were historically trained in Ciceronian oratory; the humanist tradition was central to modes of legal argument. According to this narrative, law and literature were artificially sundered somewhere between the eighteenth and twentieth centuries—through disciplinary specialization, the corollary of industrial specialization, and through the concomitant attempt to rid the utilitarian sphere of the irrational aesthetic and, in parallel formation, to rid the aesthetic sphere of the crudely utilitarian. The legal sphere, once a place of humanist reflection, became increasingly autonomous and formalist, hermetically sealed off from the humanity it was meant to serve. At the same time, the literary sphere, once a place of political and ethical advocacy, became increasingly alienated from "the ethical implications of writing and reading" (1646). In this light, the late-twentieth-century project of rejoining law and literature defied both the apolitical aestheticism that had overtaken literature and the scientific formalism that had overtaken law, attempting to return power to art and meaning to power.

One might contest this history, with its implicit narrative of a golden past in which law was harmonious with broader traditions of rhetoric. True, in the sixteenth century, Cicero and Quintilian stood as ideal guides to forensic oratory, schools of rhetoric were revived as legal training grounds, and in the English Inns of Court future lawyers were steeped in the humanist dramatic tradition. Yet at the same time Renaissance legal practice was characterized by what we would consider extreme formalism, using a professional language incomprehensible to the uninitiated and requiring precise Latin formulas in every complaint. The notion that law became a formalist enterprise in the nineteenth century, sealed off from the natural law, narrative, and rhetorical traditions that had always informed it, is equally questionable. During this period, Hugh Blair's 1782 *Lectures on Rhetoric and Belles Lettres* (published in dozens of editions) was an indispensable text for aspiring lawyers. The case method, first introduced into United States law schools in the 1870s by Christopher Columbus Langdell, exemplar of formalism, was a self-consciously narrative method—law and literature *avant la lettre*—intended to teach students through compelling stories rather than through bland codifications of doctrine. Twentieth-century American legal thought has in fact been dominated by the anti-Langdellian critique of formalism, most notably that of the legal realists, though always in dialogue with a resurgent formalism.

But if law and literature were never really separate, the narrative of historical rupture was necessary for the law and literature field to lay claim to its mission of reuniting the two disciplines. However, in disseminating this narrative, the subdiscipline in some sense produced the conceptual separation it claimed to be combating. As law and literature developed, this separation was intensified by each discipline's splitting and transfer of disciplinary desire: to project the humanist real onto literature was implicitly to accept the law as a system of utilitarian calculus; to project the political real onto law was implicitly to acknowledge the inconsequence of the aesthetic. Thus interdisciplinarity exaggerated disciplinarity, caricaturing disciplinary difference through each discipline's longing for something it imagined the other to possess. From the interstices of crossed desire arose a kind of Cain-and-Abel division, in which literature was cast as good twin, law as evil twin. As Jane Baron puts it, the law and literature movement

> defined out of the category "law" almost everything worth having; beauty, sensitivity, emotions, moral lessons—all these and so much more [were] the province of literature. The province of law [was] barren of everything but rules, an empty domain of raw power.
> ("Interdisciplinary Legal Scholarship" 45)

Literature was offered as a cure for law; sadly, law was incurable. At the same time, literature was disabled by its very virtue: law (masculine, powerful, nasty) could do things; literature (feminine, weak, sensitive) was helpless.

In this sense, the interdisciplinarity of law and literature enacted a double movement that ran counter to its own project. It sought to break down disciplinary boundaries, but, through its imaginary projection of each discipline's difference, it exaggerated those very boundaries. Literature came to see itself not only through its lack (in relation to a hypostatized ideal of law) but also through law's idealist understanding of literature. Law came to see itself not only through its lack (in relation to a hypostatized ideal of literature) but also through literature's idealist understanding of law. In the disciplinary hall of mirrors, they met in the shared space of mutual projection, in work that acted out both sets of anxieties while repressing some of the most important insights of each discipline.

This disciplinary acting out produced a set of characteristic contradictions. Law became the great political redeemer, realizing through the courts the dreams of a more revolutionary moment. At the same time, abstracted from particular cases, it became the univocally ugly hegemon, the force of monolithic evil, an immovable power against which the Cassandra-like voice of literature would eternally, but with tragic futility, assert the value of the human spirit. Literature as a field attempted to preserve its hermeneutics of suspicion (in Paul Ricoeur's famous formulation), in which literary works were to be read as documents not of the human spirit but of barbarism, ultimately and tragically expressions of false consciousness (32–35). At the same time, it attempted to embrace the vision of law and literature, in which literature, abstracted from particular works, had become the voice of truth, an abiding ethical guide.

The Always Already Real and the End of Interdisciplinarity

The persistent, if sometimes embarrassed, vision of the real at the center of each of law and literature's major projects—a real aspiring to ethical authenticity, ontological certainty, narrative honesty—emerged from the center of postmodern skepticism as a kind of return of the repressed. Clothed in scare quotes, enveloped in equivocation, the real signaled a yearning that, in ordinary critical discourse, dared not speak its name. As law and literature became a movement, the real came to stand in for the political and ethical aspirations that its achievement would supposedly bring to pass. While the language of the real tended to emerge unconsciously or apologetically, the claims for the eventual good that would emerge from it were brazen: revolutionize the law with literature; make the literary life one worth living. As the object of a movement, the real became a surrogate for the good and was made to bear the weight of its demands.

This was, perhaps, too much to ask. But one might nonetheless see in the search for the ever-receding real a productive force, necessary to the tremendous disciplinary changes that both law and literature as fields underwent during the last quarter of the twentieth century. Literature came to embrace cultural studies as an essential part of a discipline whose interpretive techniques could now be applied legitimately to the great array of social texts. Law became something like a full-fledged academic field, not merely a professional training ground but a discipline whose object of study—law as a historical, social, and linguistic entity—was subject to the analytic techniques of the humanities and social sciences. Insofar as we take law and literature to exemplify the broader disciplinary restlessness of the late twentieth century, to recognize the value of its search for the real is to recognize more generally the value of the illusions about authenticity that may have lain beneath the past few decades' interdisciplinary adventures.

In an evocative essay, "The Made-Up and the Made-Real," Scarry offers an analysis of the particularly late-modern form of skepticism in which anxieties about the solidity of the real came into being, describing the breakdown of the analytic separation between the made up (aesthetic objects that retain their fictional quality) and the made real (human creations such as law, science, gender, and childhood that inhabit the world without bearing the marker of their creation). She asks why this breakdown entails persistently hostile challenges to things made real as nasty delusions (the oppressive product of "sinister plots and 'hegemonic' enactments" [216]). Why must exposure of the fact that things were once created downgrade their authority? Why should the realization that aesthetic things have something in common with other created things lessen the prestige of the aesthetic generally? Scarry suggests that the future of the humanities lies in a redirection of our energies: from the attack on things for feigning realness to the "generation of accurate descriptions" (215)—descriptions telling us how things became real and what their realness consists in.

As we seem more willing to embrace the fact that the made real is, after all, really real, claims for the revolutionary power of the ever-receding real have disappeared. We seem to recognize, consciously or unconsciously, that the demand that the real revolutionize the law or make the literary life worth living was a demand for something that was, after all, always already there. The demand for the real was, in other words, superfluous. At the same time, it was insufficient to the claims of revolution or meaningfulness. Well on the other side of the millennium, we have perhaps at last exhausted our sense of crisis and doubt about the real, recognizing that to expose the made-upness of something is not necessarily to dim its prestige, let alone to do away with it. Conversely, to say that the made real is really real is not to say that it can't be changed. With the receding of postmodern epistemological and ontological questions may come an end to the hermeneutics of suspicion proudly, if not arrogantly, embraced in the last quarter of the twentieth century. Perhaps we are beginning to move from disenchantment to reenchantment (always underrated), unhobbled by fears of enchantment's unreality or by fantasies of some ever-receding real on the other side of disciplinary paradise.

Arguably, law and literature depended on its own antidisciplinarity. If as a subdiscipline it helped each field work through its fantasies about the other, to some extent those fantasies could no longer survive in disciplines that had naturalized each other instead of each viewing the other as a foreign import—that is, in disciplines that had come to seem always already interdisciplinary. Even as a journal like *Law and Literature* became an independent entity (liberated in 2002 from its affiliation with Cardozo Law School), its title began to seem vaguely quaint, its contents overflowing its narrow dual disciplinary signifiers. The proliferation of essays over the past decade or so looking back at law and literature as a phenomenon might be taken as a sign that we are moving beyond it as a cognizable interdisciplinary formation: millennialism, perhaps, but also signifying law and literature's transformation into something bigger and necessarily more amorphous.[8] That Guyora Binder and Robert Weisberg's exhaustive *Literary Criticisms of Law* (2000), offering a 544-page assessment of the past thirty years of work, ultimately rejects the critical modes most closely associated with literature and ends with a celebration of "cultural criticisms of law" (462–539) may indicate something of the future of law and literature. Like literature itself as a discipline, embarrassed by too narrow an association with the strictly literary, law and literature is beginning to shed its second term and meld into "law, culture, and the humanities" (the title of the scholarly organization that seems now to serve as home for the discipline-formerly-known-as-law-and-literature), erasing "literature" with a new lexicon ("culture," "the humanities"), that raises a new set of anxieties for a (still) new millennium.

One of the sleights-of-hand of interdisciplinarity is that it deludes us into the belief that we've escaped our disciplinary boundaries. But that delusion also allows us freedom from interdisciplinary longing. Such freedom is well suited to the spatial and geographic paradigms we currently inhabit. We think of ourselves as global: rather than defy boundaries, we leap over them—less disciplined, perhaps, but also less frustrated by imaginary constraints. Worrying less about how to find something real on the other side of the disciplinary divide, we have more room to think about the consequences of disciplinary tourism, to ponder the new terms we've erected as touchstones of our common project, and to offer richer readings of those real (sometimes hyperreal) objects of our teaching. If law and literature per se does not survive the assimilation of disciplinary multiplicity as an inherent part of its respective disciplines, in its end may be its beginning.

Notes

This essay appeared in a longer and somewhat different version in *PMLA* 120.2 (2005): 442–53.

1. The first MLA special session on law and literature took place in 1976, and sessions have followed regularly thereafter. On law and literature courses in the 1970s, see J. Smith, "Coming Renaissance" 91. On the field generally during this period, see Danzig and Weisberg; Kretschman and Weisberg; J. Smith, "Aspects"; and Suretsky.

2. I follow here Jane Baron's taxonomy in "Law" (1063–66). For alternative taxonomies, see Binder and Weisberg; Julius.

3. A partial list of the changes in literary studies might include the accession to tenured positions of the civil rights and Vietnam-era generations, inspired by the memory of civil rights battles won in the courts; the political frustrations of high theory and the felt need to inject the metaphysical politics of deconstruction with more concrete institutional politics; the perceived failure of the shrinking Marxist project as a mode of political criticism and a turn toward the insider politics of law. A parallel list in legal studies might include the shrinking of the humanities academic job market in the 1970s, leading humanities PhDs eventually toward legal academia (see J. Smith, "Coming Renaissance" 88; Suretsky 727); the slow deprofessionalization of legal study, from the 1970s on, in the attempt to establish law as an academic field comparable to other fields (see Edwards; Posner "Deprofessionalization"); the demand for sophisticated theories of constitutional interpretation to sustain the achievements of the civil rights movement (see Binder and Weisberg 28–111); the felt need for a humanist counterforce to law and economics and to the textual conservatism of the Reagan-era Supreme Court.

4. Said's specific object here is literary Marxism, particularly as exemplified in Jameson's *The Political Unconscious,* but his comments apply to the profession more generally.

5. See, e.g., Coughlin; Farber and Sherry; P. Brooks, "Law as Narrative" 16; Gates, "Let Them Talk" 37, 47.

6. For a summary of the scholarship on the rise of literature, see Peters, "'Literature'" 257–74.

7. For a brief but eloquent version of this argument, see P. Brooks's response to the original version of this essay ("Law and Literature in Dialogue").

8. For recent historical assessments of law and literature, see most notably Binder and Weisberg; see also Freeman and Lewis, especially Julius's introduction and Weisberg's contribution ("Literature's Twenty-Year Crossing").

Robert Weisberg

Law, Literature, and Cultural Unity: Between Celebration and Lament

The enthusiastic curiosity of a law or literature professor (or student) about exploring the relation between law and literature is understandable. But a perennial issue is why this particular intellectual linkage is both so tempting and so vexing and why the exploration raises so many basic questions about the purposes or consequences of the endeavor.

Is the relation between law and literature one of identity? of a partial but significant common denominator that creates some mutual reenforcement? of symmetrical opposition (possibly including some intersection) of a sort that creates mutual challenge? Or does the relation, once carefully examined, turn out to be asymmetric or even orthogonal? These conceptions of the relation help capture both the anxiety and attendant intellectual energy of this scholarly movement.

Viewing the relation as one of identity can begin with the undeniable and banal: both law and literature are roughly the names of academic disciplines—although in the United States that identity exists only at the graduate level.

But superficial identity invites the implication of at least partial opposition and creative tension. The intrigue of the idea of a law-literature identity is that law and literature would seem to pull in contrary directions.

86

Hence the common oppositions in our intuitive notions of law and literature—respectively, reason/passion, abstraction/particularity, or, more provocatively, timeless category / temporal contingency, cold utility / emotive empathy. Moreover, to think of the relation as a mix of identity and creative opposition implies some aspiration of an immanent deeper harmony, if not ultimately restored unity.

This set of possible relations between two academic disciplines raises the question of why law and literature are the chosen pair. If the purpose of pairing disciplines to explore partial identity or creative tension were to cause students to confront the opposing challenges of reason and passion, wouldn't we expect to see symposia on, for example, the linkage of mathematics and poetry? Except for the possibility of highly esoteric inquiries into symbolology, that linkage is manifest in the academy only in the uninteresting concept of the curricular distribution requirement. More interesting for examining a dynamic creative pull—let us say between two sets of explanations for human motivation—would be a pairing of economics and psychology. We do in fact now see the emergence of a new field of behavioral economics. But even it is a mildly modified version of a primary host field (economics modified by cognitive heuristics).

The law-literature connection remains almost uniquely compelling and vexatious, perhaps precisely because of its odd asymmetry. It combines a worldly vocational discipline, partly operating as a field of liberal learning and somewhat fitfully assimilated into a liberal arts curricular structure, with a revered form of art studied largely through the lens of an analytic methodology and generating a professional academic vocation.

The very reference to academic literature underscores another asymmetry of this pairing. We face the heterogeneity of roles in the legal system—judge, jury, advocate, legislator, and so on—while we face a different heterogeneity on the literary side, one that is simpler but more significant: artist versus critic. Still another troublesome asymmetry emerges. Students and teachers of literature do not assume they have much knowledge of law; they probably understand that there is a difference between their general impression of law from popular culture and the formal education in law that only law school offers. Indeed they are tempted to look into law's connections to literature in part because they respect law as an esoteric alternate world that they might, were they to undergo some modest legal learning, come to appreciate. But law students—and lawyers and law professors—generally assume they have a fair baseline knowledge of literature as a result of their undergraduate education or general cultural upbringing.

Even if people on the law side would disavow knowledge of the high intellectual technology of modern literary theory, they view literature as part of common experience, not professional exotica.

This asymmetry may have strong if unpredictable effects, depending on how students or scholars recognize their asymmetric limits. Some people coming from the literature side are honestly humble about their limited knowledge of law and try not to make narrowing assumptions about law, though they may do so inadvertently. Some law people may assume that they know literature and are therefore unconsciously prey to their own predispositions or superficial ideas about it. Both insecurity about and overvaluation of one's knowledge of another discipline can lead to distortions that confound the exploration of the law and literature link.

The distortions can take myriad forms, but here are two obvious ones. Law students may know that they do not know literary theory but may be confident that they know literature in general and believe that it is inherently and mainly about emotive expression. Literature students, modest about how much they can understand of law, play it safe by assuming that law is inherently and mainly about rules, and so they underappreciate the political contingencies and interpretive freedom of legal thinking and practice.

The distortions can have different effects. One effect we do *not* see these days in the academy is the normative inference that law exhibits a valuable objectivity that embarrasses literature by exposing its indulgence in narcissistic subjectivity or chaotic meaninglessness. The two most obvious distortive effects plaguing law and literature studies look in the opposite direction: one is the inference that literature embarrasses law by offering the desirable alternatives of empathy, particularity, and individuality to law's presumed opposites thereof (Binder and Weisberg 3–4, 16). The mechanism for this embarrassment is often the law and literature approach of reading in parallel legal and literary texts with overlapping subject matter, but sometimes it is the law as literature approach of analyzing legal discourse for its subtle techniques of deploying subliminal verbal imagery or narrative framing to suppress passion and particularity.

The other distortive effect is the inference that literature embarrasses law by exposing as false law's pretense of being platonically or scientifically objective. The mechanism for this embarrassment is usually the law as literature approach of demonstrating that declarations, explanations, or applications of legal authority manifest aesthetic inventions or contestable social judgments that undermine law's claim of authority (Binder and Weisberg 17).

Some law-literature commentators have avoided these distortions by changing their starting point, finding identity in a more supple category: a common trope is to proclaim that law and literature are both forms of discourse. Now *discourse* is a vague, elusive term, and its use reminds us of another risk of distortion here: announcing a law-literature linkage can become a performative act of self-presentation. Commentators who claim to discover the discourse overlap publicize their talent for perceiving emanations of language beyond its ostensible purposes, demonstrating that they are shrewd observers of culture who can evocatively express the notion that distinct forms of language or thought participate in some cultural action of wider or more pervasive significance.

But a virtue of this kind of more impressionistic generality is that it can point us toward some useful commonalities between law and literature and thereby help us avoid distortive binaries and forced symmetries. Much of the best scholarship about the law-literature relation is happily unconcerned with finding categorical coherence in it. Instead, scholars find useful sublinkages as they arise in interesting patterns. Law and literature both involve interpretation of texts and contexts. It benefits a lawyer to deploy a resilient situational pragmatism, an ability to bridge the calls of law and equity. Literature can keep the lawyer's mind nimbly able to appreciate the plurality and dynamism of meaning. Conversely, some knowledge of law can help the literary person appreciate how the practical arts of regulation and government can resonate with the aesthetic and provide rich topics or narrative lines for fiction and drama. At its common-law core, the art of judging is a matter of reading the zeitgeist—a partly aesthetic, partly pragmatic apprehension of social experience.

The pursuit of commonalities and symmetries can be subdivided into such components as rhetoric, narrative, interpretation, and other modes of literary criticism of law. But the appeal of this pursuit may lie in something only implied by, or unconscious in, its practitioners. That appeal lies in the vision, often the dream, of a unified culture. The linkage of law and literature suggests a dissatisfaction with the cultural separation of powers we associate with the modern liberal state. Perhaps art and government share a metaforce called cultural discourse, and perhaps its forms—legal, political, scientific—overlap and interact. This vision may be a platonic ideal or, more modestly, a worthy sentiment—that is, there may be moral and philosophical value in imagining a less atomistic society. Even modern secularists who decry the blurring of church and state might empathize with the desire to unite spirit and law, and indeed certain communitarian movements complicate any easy left-right distinction along these lines. On the other hand, the dream can be a nightmare: the notion of the organic state has troubling historical roots, and some of the most worrisome modern versions of it come from literary figures of modernity (especially the T. S. Eliot of *Notes toward the Definition of Culture* or, worse yet, *After Strange Gods*) whose genius in capturing the spiritual agonies and longings of the world of secular rationalism led them down some politically frightening paths.

To imagine a unified culture may be neither utopian nor dystopian; it may simply be diagnostic, the broadest way of conceiving interdisciplinary studies. The diagnoses of unity can be quite varied. There is the benignly diagnostic social history associated with the cliometric history of Ferdinand Braudel, admonishing us that grand movements in political and military history can also be read through ground-level microtrends in daily life—as a complementary, not an alternate world. There is a subversive version in Michel Foucault (*The Order of Things*), suggesting that certain supposedly circumscribed and separate instruments of authority in society might come to be part of a network of subtler and more pervasive forces, so that culture begins to look like a political conspiracy.

The early scholars of the contemporary law and literature movement had clear, if implicit, goals in establishing—or, in the view of many, restoring—the link between the two fields. One specific goal motivated some of the founding practitioners of law-literature scholarship: to defend judicial discretion as a legitimate and necessary response to majoritarian politics. This goal entailed viewing the modern judge as the descendant of the neoclassical civic figure of law and letters as well as a quietly charismatic figure of moral inspiration (J. White, "Law as Rhetoric" 684–86). As a corollary, these writers sought to infuse the judicial task with a generous commitment to Kantian liberal values, and they extended this aspiration to all lawmakers and all lawyers. Opening their hearts and imaginations to the world of literature could fortify judges in their ability to confidently justify their constitutional discretion; it could also redeem legal practice from the limitations of crass utilitarianism or thoughtless rule-boundedness (J. White, *Heracles' Bow* 240–41).

Another theme of the early law-literature movement shows up in the work of a more diffuse set of commentators and has a very different, if not quite opposite, motivation. This theme is less concerned with solving a legal and historical problem about constitutional law and the profession, and more concerned with resistance to the dominance of microeconomic utilitarianism in the development of law as an academic study (Weisberg, *Poethics* 8–9). These two motives reflect the two sources of literary mode, classical and Romantic.

Among nonspecialists in literature there may be some these days who associate it with postmodernism, deconstruction, and so on, but in the minds of most American lawyers and most American university students not specializing in literature, a conventional Romanticism remains the dominant model. This model conceives the individual heart and imagination as superior faculties of knowledge, the work of literature as the medium of creative innovation and emotional sublimity, and art generally as a source of transformative and revolutionary spiritualism.

This literary predicate naturally, if not always happily, encourages in those interested in law and literature a redemptive or corrective view of the role of literature for law, a project of restoring the affective and the spiritual to the instrumental and objective. Of course in theory this Romantic predicate could spin law the other way, rereading law as itself affective expression and imaginative transcendence. But clearly that is not how things have played out in our intellectual history. No one has told the story of the Fourteenth Amendment or the Sherman Act in Whitmanesque terms.

The alternative provenance of the law-literature movement, classical or neoclassical, has far stronger roots. The American generalist student of literature does not know or well appreciate the older model of literature as continuous with philosophy and either mimetic or normative, not expressive. This model is rooted in a classical rhetoric and interested in emotion chiefly for educative or other instrumental purposes. From Sidney to Pope, poetry is about moral education in perennial vices and virtues or scientific representation of the natural state of things (Binder and Weisberg 7). This better-credentialed literary model certainly was known to the lawyer-leaders in early American history. The iconic legal figure in our founding story is the Ciceronian ideal of lawyer and cultural statesperson (Ferguson, *Law* 11–33). This figure is not a myth but an accurate description of a working political and cultural model well into the nineteenth century, the statesperson of law and letters. Though susceptible to the charge of golden-ageism, the model extends into the twentieth century as well, in the legal profession's persistent belief in the lawyer as generalist statesperson of wisdom and donor of that wisdom to statecraft and civic morality (Gordon, "Legal Profession" 307–14).

This model is manifested in Victorian England in the Arnoldian concept of the cultural statesperson who shapes a liberal education, which includes imaginative literature. The educational goal was neither to analyze literature's complexities nor to indulge its passions; it was to appreciate literature for its civilizing value as a component of social discipline and character building. Literature's opposition to the utilitarian operated mainly in the sense of enhancing a civility that could mitigate the worst excesses of market capitalism, a civic-minded sensibility that could check bigotry and extremism and redeem mere self-interested preference. Literature was a medium of cultural leadership in responsible, not revolutionary, terms. Indeed, the modern American university student does not realize that the availability of literature in the curriculum is far more the result of the kind of legacy of Matthew Arnold, through such figures as Lionel Trilling, than of any institutional commitment to Shelleyan freedom or Byronic sublimity. Trilling's deep and often agonized project of sustaining a sensibility of cultured civility against the forces of materialism—capitalist, Marxist, and Freudian—is a more historically accurate pedigree of modern academic literature than either high-tech literary theory or Romantic expressionism.

The Romantic-classical distinction in literary models is itself crudely binary—as the nuanced balance of Wordsworthian desire to recollect sublime emotion in tranquillity reminds us. The particulars of American history complicate things further: our nineteenth-century Romanticism is infused with an eighteenth-century Protestantism, our transcendentalism with evangelical moral uplift. But the distinction between these conceptual sources for the literary side of the law-literature equation helps as we consider some of the specific forms the equation has taken.

The credentials of the classical model of literature should enhance the project of the rhetorical criticism of law. That is, both normatively and analytically, we can view the lawmaker and law applier as continuing the tradition of the cultural rhetorician who deploys the language arts to induce virtuous commitment to civic values. Indeed, that model continues to embarrass—and occasionally motivate—political liberals because of a double ambivalence that plagues them. While liberals remain devoted to judicial review, they often have a somewhat guilty conscience about disrespecting majoritarian will, while they also are philosophically uncomfortable about invoking any abstract principles that sound too close to natural law jurisprudence. The classical-rhetorical model suggests an attractive way out of this dilemma.

The attraction of the model became apparent in the recent legal scholarship that emerged under the civic republican movement in constitutional law. This movement was inspired by J. G. A. Pocock's famous work on the republican tradition in Renaissance Europe, seventeenth-century England, and the early American colonies (*Machiavellian Moment*). Optimistically drawing on the quaint country ideology of older, aristocratic lawyer-leadership, modern legal academics sought to address the problem of objective grounding for constitutional adjudication by reference to an idealist value of process. If modern liberalism resisted announcing timeless deontological principles of virtue, it could substitute principled deliberation or disinterested rational dialogue about the common good as the core values of citizenship (Michelman; Sunstein). This project faced the inherent difficulty of finessing process/substance distinctions. Constitutional scholars drawing on the law and literature movement have attempted to envision the modern judge as a judicial artist who uses interpretive art, in a notoriously ambiguous phrase, to "give meaning and expression to public values" (Fiss 753). The challenge to liberals posed by this classical tradition remains salutary; it also provides an excellent analytic model for depicting literature that can help us see the representations of sensibility and character as mechanisms for lawmaking.

Narrative criticism, more than other forms of literary criticism of law, is prone to the distortions of categorical thinking about the relation of law and literature. Commentaries about narrative in law are prone to utter general pronouncements: how law, coldly reductive and suppressing underlying human narrative, can be redeemed by narrative; that deep insights about law necessarily follow from the realization that narrative accounts of an event compete in their perspective and selectivity; that discerning narrative in law undermines law's supposed claims to certitude or perfect logic (Binder and Weisberg 201–91). Some suggest that narrative offers natural or authentic experience as a challenge to law or that narrative is particularly the realm of subordinated peoples or constituencies, so that bringing narrative to bear on legal analysis is politically liberating.[1]

These general declarations about law and narrative are, in various combinations, true, obvious, misleading, or wrong. The strength of narrative criticism of law lies in specific treatments about how it operates. Lawmakers and law appliers deploy narrative to achieve their practical goals, and specific readings of these strategies can illuminate how they achieve those goals. The analyst may discover subtle interactions between a trial and a narrative or dramatic technique (Binder, "Representing"; Ferguson, "Story"). Some good narrative criticisms take on the broader scope of viewing narrative as part of the cultural mythmaking embedded in many legal systems (W. Miller, *Bloodtaking*). All law has some kind of founding myth or provenance to justify authority and obligation. So narrative in law is neither a matter of authenticity liberated nor subjectivity exposed. It is not a major revelation that narrative is intrinsic to law. Narrative is part of the apparatus by which law, like every other institution, explains its power, reinforces its authority, and performs its tasks. Narrative is one of the major ways we order collective life.

Many law and literature commentaries focus on the common denominator of interpretation. As with narrative, pronouncements at a high level of generality—as that law and literature are essentially about the problematic nature of interpretation—are not especially significant. The important question is whether either law or literature is illuminated by the comparison in interpretive methods or problems. At the heart of much of this commentary is a sense of crisis involving both ambivalence about popular will and fear of indeterminacy. The relation between these two concerns helps us understand how a literary perspective can illuminate the interpretation problem in law.

The perceived interpretive crisis in law focuses on the modern figure of the judge, especially in constitutional and statutory cases. The anxiety is that sometimes judges fall from a transparent realm of legal authority into a painful struggle to determine what they owe to popular will, to overcome the opaqueness of language and intent, and to identify counter-majoritarian criteria more objectively grounded than their own preferences. Analysts of legal interpretation tend to associate this crisis with the legacy of slavery and the Civil War, often viewing it as a long-delayed aftershock to the enactment of the Civil War amendments. Some also trace it to the rise of academic formalist legal doctrine associated with the Langdellian era.

Construed more broadly, interpretation has always been a part of American law, and there was plenty of legal interpretation done in the early nineteenth century. It was largely common-law interpretation, and as such it did not present a conceptual or political intrusion into law but simply the normal work of law. The real interpretive project of common law was to use legal wisdom to construe social experience and thereby identify the custom that constituted the common law. This exercise raised questions about popular will, but it was left to wise judges to determine when social practice had emerged as true custom. There was creative tension in the task, between construing versus improving majority sentiment. But intellectual intention was in play, not institutional agony, and antebellum American lawyers had a healthy sense of the rhetorical art of mediating between volatile popular will and institutional stability. The challenge may have been greater for judges confronting statutory or constitutional texts, but they drew on their common-law skills to put textual commands to discernible social purposes.

To draw a rough historical line, later in the nineteenth century a new scientism about determining the public good made it more challenging for judges to evaluate social interest and purpose, and interpretation became more an instrument than a constituent of law. But obviously the more important factor was that the Civil War devastatingly complicated the question of judges' obligation to respect popular will, making legal interpretation an intellectual problem it had never quite been before. Judges vacillated among the roles of scientific empiricist, authoritative reader of social value, and quiescent servant of majority will, and such intellectual and political forces as progressivism and scientism competed over the proper balance of free markets and social regulation. But even if interpretation had become a contested practice, it was not yet a metaphysical or epistemological dilemma. That phase in law's self-consciousness about interpretation came only with the modern civil rights revolution.

It was with the emergence of the Warren Court that interpretation became so roiling a problem as to call for the help of literary theory. The unavoidable and distinctly American dilemma of reconciling a once constitutionally mandated legacy of slavery with modern notions of liberty and equality and the peculiar, if not unique, problem of judicial review in a popular democracy—these challenges led many legal scholars to seek aid and comfort in literature. Some found technical assistance in principles of reader-response theory to justify the interpretive freedom that judges might enjoy in the face of apparently resistant popular will or limiting text (Fish, *Is There a Text* 21–67). Some, most notably Ronald Dworkin, found less technical and more creative literary models whereby judges could identify and expose Kantian ideals inherent in American legal principles without violating popular will (*Law's Empire*). Some assisted judicial independence by emphasizing an antiempiricist concept of language. By this concept, neither the intentions of authors nor language itself could fix meaning, but judges were a particularly advantaged example of an "interpretive community" operating under consensus and "disciplinary rules," through which legitimate meaning emerged (Fiss 745).

The turn to literary models was often salutary in helping judges find—and justify—the pragmatic creativity that they honestly believed was delegated to them when their assigned function in our legal system required them to adapt vague constitutional commands and either overly vague or overly rigid legislative commands to perceived social needs. The danger in using literature lay in the attractiveness of literary theory and in the frequent conclusion that literature taught lawyers that interpretation was a philosophical problem about indeterminacy (Peller). The better lesson is that the problem for modern judges has not been about epistemology or ontology, because law raises such foundational problems of language and meaning no more or less than any other institution. American history has produced some very specific problems of interpretation, and recurrence to literary interpretation can supply some useful tools in solving those nonmetaphysical problems.

In this regard, deconstruction-based criticism is not a productive avenue for law. It provides a misleading analytic apprehension of law; worse yet, it morphs into a faux ethical criticism of law for the alleged felony of essentialism. Too many lawyers have been entranced by the notion that all signification is false consciousness, that all language is literary creation, that all representation is inherently inauthentic. However useful deconstruction may be as an abstract philosophy of law, its premises are too categorical to be treated as part of law-literature studies, though they have perhaps been indirectly useful as a creative goad to writers in such allied fields as critical race theory.

In sum, the literary apprehension of society is not an extrinsic perspective that can either redeem or debunk law. Aesthetic creation plays a role in much of law, and aesthetic understanding can help in the analysis or criticism of law as a way of seeing the political, moral, and economic conflicts and contingencies of legal institutions. Literature can indeed enhance Kantian values in law. But it does so best when it helps us see the Kantian liberal model of the individual as a complex figure of social self-definition, in such varying roles as citizen, bureaucrat, expert, merchant, consumer, fiduciary, employee, spouse, debtor, creditor—the whole panoply of legal roles in our social dramas. Similarly, a general and regular immersion in, and sometimes a very targeted reference to, fiction and drama can help us appreciate the cultural contests and rituals by which authority gets contested and allocated, through such social and legal phenomena as injunctions, promises, indictments, consents, interests, expectations, purposes, and privileges. The partial and often conflicting commonalties can be celebrated or lamented or decried at general and theoretical levels, but best of all they can be observed and opportunistically recruited in the study of important legal issues.

Note

1. Everyone knows that trial lawyers try to persuade or even manipulate fact finders with creative narrative framings of the facts. Some commentators wrongly believe that this awareness is a significant insight. Others point out that sometimes the criminal defense story tries to destroy the appearance of narrative coherence in the facts of a case to create reasonable doubt (Dershowitz, "Life").

Robin West

Literature, Culture, and Law at Duke University

What is the relation of law and literature? Why study literature, or study about literature, in law school? Participants in the law and literature movement of the last quarter of the twentieth century explored three logically possible relations, each of which grounded a different pedagogical as well as scholarly project. First, law might sometimes be the subject matter of great literature; when it is, literature should be read for the value of its insights into the nature of law. Second, literature might sometimes have the force of law or might in the past have had that force or might have it in the future; if so, then in order to know the law as it is, once was, or could be, we need to know its literary narrative root. There may not be a firm distinction, in other words, between the law that is, was, or could be and the various products of our literary imagination. Third, law might be enough like literature that we can better understand how we glean meaning from legal texts if we attempt a better understanding of how literature is read and interpreted. These quite different interdisciplinary projects—which I call, respectively, the literary, the jurisprudential, and the hermeneutic—constitute what we typically refer to in law schools as the law and literature movement. It is still thriving, but it was at its most robust in the 1970s and 1980s.

In the last fifteen years or so, the law and literature movement has been increasingly overshadowed, at least in the legal academy, by the law and culture movement. Some of the initial theorists of the new movement presented it as a critical response to, and perhaps an alternative to, the old movement (e.g., Binder and Weisberg). Despite this initial adversarial relation, however, the law and culture movement now seems more an outgrowth of the law and literature movement than a critical alternative to it. Legal-cultural scholars have for the most part embraced the various possibilities canvassed above; they have simply expanded them to reference culture, defined capaciously, rather than just imaginative literature. Thus law is sometimes the subject matter of culture (and culture sometimes the subject matter of law); culture might sometimes have (or have had in the past or have in the future) the political and normative force of legal authority; and law might itself be best understood as a culture and therefore best studied in the same way one would study culture. With one notable exception, the contemporary law and culture movement in law schools consists of the scholarly projects premised on these three possibilities. To the degree that culture encompasses literature, this development is obviously an overdue and welcome expansion of the law and literature movement.

One stark difference between the movements cuts the other way. One of the central scholarly and pedagogical projects of the law and literature movement—to read literature for its substantive contribution to our understanding of law—has no real analogue in cultural-legal studies, at least to date.[1] The law and culture movement seeks enriched descriptive understanding of the various relations of the two fields so as to better understand law and its dissemination and reception. Cultural-legal theorists do not, for the most part, examine the products of culture to unearth and then reflect on truths they may contain regarding the nature of the law. This lack is unfortunate. As our focus in humanistic studies of law shifts and broadens from literature to culture, we should be careful not to lose our attentiveness to the critical perspectives contained in imaginative literature and culture both, no matter how those terms are defined.

In this essay, I survey these two interdisciplinary movements by expanding a bit on their definitional relations, highlighting their continuities and discontinuities with each other. I also venture a brief explanation for the relative marginalization of what I call the literary project, both in law and literature and in law and culture. Then I look at a recent legal drama and its aftermath, a now thoroughly discredited allegation of rape made in the spring of 2006 by a young woman in Durham, North Carolina, against three Duke lacrosse student athletes. The African American woman who brought the charge (the prosecutrix) had been hired as a stripper by the students to perform at a lacrosse team party, and it was during the party, she initially alleged, that the gang rape occurred. This allegation—it has since been contradicted by the prosecutrix herself, and the charges brought pursuant to it were dropped—triggered a bout of both soul-searching and incrimination at Duke and in Durham, among and between the various town-and-gown communities implicated by the accusation. I suggest that both interdisciplinary projects, cultural-legal and literary-legal analysis, may have something to offer our understanding of what did and did not happen at Duke.

Law/Literature

In the law and literature movement, the first posited relation between the disciplines is the most commonsensical: literature and law are distinct enterprises, but literature does often treat law as its subject matter.[2] We should attend to the depictions of law we find in imaginative literature, for the simple reason that literature may contain truths about law that are not easily found in nonnarrative jurisprudence. Sometimes literature's treatment of law or the rule of law is unabashedly celebratory—*A Man for All Seasons* (Bolt) or To *Kill a Mockingbird* (H. Lee) are examples. Some-times our canonical literary authors have been harshly critical of law—think of Mark Twain's compromised lawyer-protagonist in *Pudd'nhead Wilson*; Herman Melville's depictions of vindictive, *ressentiment*-driven adjudication in *Billy Budd, Sailor* or his account of nineteenth-century law and equity in "Bartleby the Scrivener"; Toni Morrison's accounting of the Fugitive Slave Act in *Beloved*; Susan Glaspell's rendition, in "A Jury of Her Peers," of legally sanctioned patriarchy at the turn of the century; or even Aeschylus's at best ambiguous endorsement of the rule of law over clan or family justice in *The Oresteia*.[3] All this narrative, imaginative literature tells us something that law itself cannot and that other forms of legal scholarship likewise do not, about the meanings of law in the lives of its subjects, its agents, and its adjudicators and the meanings of law in the lives of those whom law willfully ignores, subjugates, marginalizes, or excludes. The reason to read and study such literature, especially what are sometimes called legal novels, in law school is straightforward: literature contains insights into the nature of law not readily found elsewhere. Those insights are not, however, either obvious or uncontested, and their unearthing requires serious scholarship as well as pedagogy.

The second possible relation between the disciplines assumed or argued by some law-lit scholarship is quite different and in tension with the first. Literature might sometimes be law, and law might sometimes be literature. This claim needs immediate qualification: it is generally understood that at least today there is a great difference between positive law, enacted by sovereigns in accordance with a rule of recognition, and imaginative, narrative fiction. Literature doesn't have law's political power, whatever its normative force. It cannot command. Nevertheless, one of the earliest and most significant lessons to be learned from the law and literature studies of the 1970s and 1980s is that this difference is only a contingent truth about the law and literature of our times, not a truth about the essence of either. The distinctions that seem clear and intuitive to us between law and literature were not always so clear and might not always be so in the future.

Let me give an example of how the seemingly clear jurisprudential distinction between law and literature has been fruitfully questioned. In his award-winning *Law and Letters in American Culture* (1984), Robert Ferguson, of Columbia University, argued that in the Jeffersonian and preformalist era of American law, elite lawyers viewed law as part of a seamless web of cultural authority. This web included not only Blackstone, common law, and the emerging jurisprudence of the Supreme Court but also the literary, religious, political, and even scientific classics of the Western canonical tradition. The man of law and letters, Ferguson showed, in the century before Christopher Langdell attempted to and largely did sever the connection between law and letters and before the realists sought to replace it with ties to the social sciences, viewed legal authority (*Blackstone's Commentaries*, the United States Constitution) as of a piece with other authorities (the Bible, the Greek tragedies, authoritative histories). The common-law cases of property and tort, standard legal treaties, and the emerging opinions from the state courts and United States Supreme Court could and should sit side by side, in a well-educated lawyer's library, with Sophocles's *Antigone*, Aristotle's *Politics*, Shakespeare's tragedies, the King James Bible, and the wisdom of Ptolemy and Copernicus regarding the natural laws of planetary motion. The law should and did, at least for elite lawyers, contain the laws of nature, society, rhetoric, poetry, and philosophy as well as the positive law of consideration, contract, and the negligence rule. The law contained the classics of Western thought, and the classics contained the wisdom necessary to the decent governance of the young republic. A lawyer who truly knew the law—though there were only a handful of them—had studied all this. Knowledge of high culture should be imparted as a seamless part of our law to an elite class of men, who could then be trusted, as lawyers, with the reins of governance.

The "man of law and letters" exists as an important historical counter-example to our contemporary insistence that law and literature are separate spheres and that some sort of interdisciplinary bridge is required to connect them. Political authority and intellectual, moral, and cultural authority have not always been so separate, nor need they be in the future.[4]

Finally, in the third relation, law might be sufficiently like literature that we can profitably view both as exemplars of something still larger. Of what? One answer suggested by hermeneutic scholars, literary critics, literary theorists, and eventually interpretation theorists in American law schools is that both law and literature inhabit the world of texts.[5] If law is textual, it requires interpretation. And, for there to be interpretation, there must be a community of interpreters. Positive law of all forms—statutory, common, and constitutional—and imaginative literature share enough of a to-be-interpreted textual essence that it is fruitful to think of them as two aspects of the same thing. Whatever we might know or posit about the nature of interpreting literature might therefore be usefully applied to the task of understanding the interpretation of law, and whatever might be true of the relations among author, reader, and text in literature might likewise be true of the relations among author (whether contract drafter, constitution writer, opinion writer, or legislator), reader, and text in law.

What is to be learned from the comparison? Primarily, what legal scholars gleaned from critical theory of the late twentieth century was that the task of interpreting a text to discern its meaning cannot be a matter of simply delving into the mental state of the text's author. The meaning of a text—any text, from *Moby-Dick* to a Pepsi commercial to a contract to a judicial opinion—cannot be equated to its author's intention. But how then does one ascertain the meaning of a text? From the various schools of hermeneutics, interpretation, and related inquiries in literature departments, legal scholars borrowed capaciously and eventually incorporated into their own studies a plethora of alternatives: the meaning of a text, in law as elsewhere, is to be found not in an author's mental state and not in the text itself but in the community of readers that generates the meaning, or in the reader's mind, or in some holistic or interactive process between text and the interpretive community. The process of generating meaning, according to the new wisdom, is governed not by restraining conditions implied by the author's corporeal and historical being but rather by the interpretive community's norms and principles.

Those were the three major projects of law and literature at the end of the century. It is clear, in retrospect, that by the end of the 1980s what was sometimes called the law and interpretation wing of the movement had almost entirely supplanted the literary and historical wings. By 1990 or so, attention had turned decisively away from the content of the legal novels and away from either the historical or utopian possibility of litera-ture's having legal or political force; it was lavished instead on hermeneu-tics. The process of interpretation became the primary subject of inquiry for law-lit scholars.

It's worth noting a more local, more overtly political explanation for the interpretive turn in law schools and legal studies: it served the needs of the liberal legal academy of the 1970s and 1980s. The turn essentially suggested that the meaning of a text cannot reside either in its plain mean-ing or in its author's intentions. Constitutional scholars conversant with or participating in law and literature studies quickly drew the inference: the meaning of the Constitution likewise is not—cannot be—simply identi-fied with what its language apparently demands or what the framers in-tended. Taken seriously, the turn freed not only the liberal constitutional lawyer, theorist, and visionary but also the Constitution's authoritative liberal readers, the Warren and Burger Courts, from the Constitution's lit-eral language—a language that says a great deal about protecting property, contract, and commerce and nothing at all about privacy, contraception, homosexuality, or integrated schools. The turn also freed constitutional theory from the authoritarianism embedded in originalist constitutional interpretation.

This move from author or plain meaning to living community as the source of meaning of texts was of more than academic interest. The United States Supreme Court, in interpreting the text of the Constitution in *Brown v. Board of Education*, had famously declined to decide the case by investi-gating whether the framers of the Fourteenth Amendment did or did not intend to cover the specific instance of state-sponsored school segrega-tion. By declaring that history is irrelevant with respect to constitutional meaning, they set off a long interpretive and even constitutional crisis. Over the decade that followed the *Brown* decision, it became increasingly apparent to commentators and courts both that either the Constitution meant something other than what its framers meant or *Brown* was wrongly decided. Neither alternative seemed palatable: *Brown* was decided unanimously and in a way that justice and the country clearly required; yet, if the Constitution's meaning was unhinged from its framers' intent, could the Constitution mean anything at all and hence have the constraining force of law? If *Brown* was right, it was lawless. The interpretive turn promised to resolve this crisis. The Constitution indeed means something other than what its framers intended, but not in the service of crass politics. It means something other for the basic reason that it is, after all, a text, and all texts have meanings untethered from their authors' intentions. Intentionalism, discredited everywhere as a theory of meaning, is likewise discredited with respect to the Constitution.

What did the sudden prominence of the interpretive turn mean for law-literature studies generally?[6] If the relation between law and literature is best described by reference to their shared textuality or their shared status as objects of interpretation, then the striking and nonobvious relevance of the study of literature to law is not the criticism it may hold but rather its value as a case study: if we want to understand the processes of interpretation, we might profit from understanding literary interpretation. What the law and literature participant should learn from literature is therefore not substantive but methodological. One then takes that methodological knowledge and applies it to law.

Law and Culture

What is the relation of culture and law? What projects does that relation imply, and what justifications does it suggest, for the study of culture in law schools? Over the past decade, scholars of law and culture have begun to develop a theoretical apparatus with which to explore their relations and hence the ways in which cultural studies might inform our understanding of law. The three possibilities that have emerged as most salient roughly parallel the three relations of law and literature discussed above, but with this difference: the study of culture yields no substantive insight into the nature of law.

As two distinctly different phenomena, culture and law might exist in any number of relations to each other. They might be oppositional: law does sometimes seek to contain, minimize, censor, or neutralize culture—particularly a culture that threatens mainstream values, such as violent television and video games aimed at children, pornography, goth clothing styles, or head scarves signifying religious difference. At the other end of the spectrum, law might seek to accommodate cultures or subcultures that we value, by protecting them against the machinery of ordinary law, carving exceptions to general rules so as to protect the insularity and identity of a preferred group, such as the Amish, or not applying antitrust regulation to professional baseball. But whether law seeks to oppose or accommodate, it does so as an outsider: the law that censors, minimizes, counters, or accommodates culture is not itself culture. And culture, whatever it is, is not law. Sometimes culture, either popular or high-brow, acts as the color commentator to the legal world of action. Television shows and movies undoubtedly convey legal norms to law's subjects. Studying culture, then, can give us a window into the popular acceptance or rejection of legal norms.[7] Culture may disseminate law, convey its norms, or challenge those norms, and in the process it may pervert its meaning.

The second possibility we might call the Geertzian turn, a critical rejection of the first: rather than view law and culture as different social forms, law is profitably understood as a culture, and in a way that directly parallels and quite explicitly expands on the claims of the interpretation theorists regarding the relation of law and literature. Law is text, the interpretation theorists pointed out, and therefore whatever we know about interpreting literary texts is germane to the issue of how we ought to interpret legal texts. But in a post-Geertzian anthropological world, texts are not just what is identifiably literary and not just what is written. Cultural texts need not be narrative or written. Law, partly written, partly a practice, is an example. Therefore whatever we have learned about culture should be applicable to law as well. Likewise, if legal culture is a subculture, then to understand it we need to understand the relation of subcultures and dominant cultures—an inquiry that cultural studies should assist.

The third and I believe most promising suggestion to emerge from law and culture studies to date is that culture might sometimes be law or profitably understood or read as law. In an influential article specifying a possible set of foundational claims for the law and culture movement, Naomi Mezey argues for this third relation. Neither the first nor second relation captures the full interrelatedness of law and culture: both miss the degree to which culture can be law and law culture. The equation that culture sometimes is law clearly requires lawyers and legal scholars to engage in cultural-legal analysis. Law's very positive commands cannot be fully

understood unless we include in our understanding of what law is a substantial space for its cultural reality. Likewise, we cannot fully understand
what culture is without including the law that partly constitutes it.

Mezey's claim is a quite profound echo of the literature-as-law view
attributed by Ferguson to the Jeffersonian man of law and letters, but
with this difference. It is not the society's high-cultural texts that make the
seamless web of communal authority with the high positive law (such as the
Constitution), which in turn regulates the lives of an elite class of republican citizens in a civic empire. It is not Sophocles's *Antigone*, Aristotle's
Politics, Shakespeare's *Merchant of Venice*, *Blackstone's Commentaries*, and
so on that form the web of cultural authority that can have the force
of law. It is rather culture of all descriptions, high, low-brow, and mid-
brow—*Law and Order, Perry Mason, LA Law, CSI, Ally McBeal*, and so
on—that constitutes an irreducible if often ignored or unseen part of our
law. By *law*, I mean all our law, not just the higher law of constitutions or
the common law of antiquity, law that exists—from Miranda warnings to
speeding limits to gun rights—often against the command of conventionally marked legal texts. The content of the law that truly emanates from
the people can be understood only by reference to the culture that law
incorporates—the law and order shows in which Miranda rights are firmly
embedded, the car culture of the open plains that makes discretionary
Montana's speed standard, the felt entitlement to weapons in an individu-
alistic and somewhat lawless subculture, and so on. The culture is a part of
the law, and the law cannot be understood or known apart from it; the law
in turn generates a culture that incorporates its dictates.

As law is democratized, fragmented, popularized, and simply multi-
plied from the Jeffersonian period to our own, so is the culture with which
the law is connected. Not *Antigone* but *Ally McBeal*, not *The Oresteia*
but *The Sopranos*, not high culture but high school culture explains the
contours of our criminal and family laws of violence, murderous revenge,
and intrafamilial or intertribal feuds, spats, and gang wars. The seamless
web that was the object of the study of the man of law and letters remains
—but the webbing consists of culture, not high literature, while the law
is that which we squabble over and enact, not that which we inherit to
maintain our ties with ancestors as we act out our lives in a heterogeneous
and populist democracy.

Thus the law and culture movement has developed fruitful analogues
to the law-as-literature and literature-as-law projects: law might be read as
a form of culture, or culture might sometimes be read as law. There has

appeared no cultural analogue to the law-in-literature project described above. There has been no systematic treatment, of which I'm aware, of the possibility that cultural products, no matter how defined or conceived, might actually contain insights into the nature of law that influence jurisprudential debates. No one has advanced the claim that we should turn to culture, not only because culture disseminates legal ideas and is heavily informed by and informs law but also because the products of culture can deepen our understanding of law. We have not had the cultural equivalent of the call to return to the text that Richard Weisberg issued several years back, urging law and literature participants to examine literature for its jurisprudential content rather than for the nature of the interpretive enterprise by which we ascertain its meaning ("Text"). That is unfortunate.

Law, Culture, and Literature at Duke, Durham, and Dupont

As discerning journalists, bloggers, and essayists discovered, the allegation of rape and its aftermath in Durham, North Carolina, in spring 2006 occurred in a maelstrom of competing cultures: the cultures of Duke University, including the academic, athletic, sexual, and feminist subcultures, and their sometimes warring conceptions of the value or harm of recreational sex; the competing cultures of town and gown, including the relatively privileged economic culture of the Duke students and the underprivileged economic culture of the students at other local colleges; the black culture, with its distrust of the legal system, and the white culture, with its own fears; the strippers' culture and its relation to its white and black clientele; the culture of the women's health and rape crisis center in the community, with its own presuppositions about sex and rape; the medical culture; and so on.[8]

It is entirely appropriate, given this cultural proliferation, to study the Duke episode as an instance of law as culture in all sorts of configurations: legal culture was sometimes in competition with, sometimes in cooperation with, and sometimes in cooptation with these other cultures. The contrast between local culture and legal culture was stark. When the rape allegation was first made — and widely believed — the norms of legal culture, including law's insistence on individualized stories of agency, responsibility, and action, seemed to oppose the grand cultural narratives of race, sex, and class responsibility that dictated so much of the community's initial responses to the allegation. The legal culture embraced a conception of sex as criminal and wrong when nonconsensual, in tension with the sexual culture's embrace at Duke University of a more permissive ethic. In the most romanticized understanding of legal culture, the law and its representatives in Durham imposed a rule of equal treatment of all regardless of race or class, in the face of the economic and racial privilege of Durham's various elites. Thus the charge against the white male athletes of nonconsensual intercourse was heard, then aggressively pursued, although their innocence was presumed—while competing subcultures either countenanced rape and privileged wealth, whiteness, and masculinity or assumed both individual and collective guilt.

As the allegation became less believable, the story of the relation between legal and local culture changed dramatically. A prosecutor up for reelection had allowed legal consideration of individual responsibility to be swamped by cultural narratives of racial oppression and gendered harm. He lacked the backbone or the detachment to resist the pull of the cultural instead of listening to the individual narrative. The bar association eventually brought an ethics charge against him for failing to comply with the norms of prosecutorial behavior. A law school committee investigated the university's athletic culture and, applying ordinary legal and social scientific methods, found it not nearly so debased, racist, and misogynist as the community's immediate response to the rape accusation had led the rest of us to believe. The moral? Law in Durham was not something distinct from culture; it was itself a culture, interacting with others.

The Duke case also supports Mezey's more radical claim that sometimes culture *is* law. We truly cannot understand the law that framed the allegation in Durham—indeed, we cannot make sense of the allegation itself—without broadening our definition of what law is to include its constituent cultural parts. A hundred years ago, the charge of rape could not and would not have been brought, no matter how strong the evidence: it would have been unthinkable that a white man could rape a black woman, because her consent would have been presumed and her lack of consent would have been considered irrelevant. Even thirty years ago, the charge could not have been brought: it would have been unthinkable that a man could rape a woman of any color who had consensually entered a private home for the purpose of stripping, fully intending to sexually excite men. Regardless of her color, the sex worker's consent to sex would have been presumed from the moment she entered the house. These presumptions about rape law were fully embedded, whether or not articulated, in the law. They were understood and acted upon by everyone—prosecutors, police, men, women, strippers, lacrosse-playing university students, white and black citizens all. They formed part of the definition of rape and hence of the law that criminalized it. Thus knowledge of both culture and cultural change is as essential as North Carolina's criminal code to understand the law that formed the content and context of the rape allegation.

A grasp of culture is also essential to understand why this charge was so widely believed. Why was the claim that these young men raped this woman so instantly credible and to so many people? Other women—sex workers, dates, girlfriends, acquaintances—making claims of sexual assault in private homes or hotel rooms by their johns, boyfriends, or customers, even where the possibility of a crime is admitted, instantly lack credibility. Recall the dismissive reaction to Juanita Broaddrick's claim in the 1990s that Bill Clinton had raped her back in 1978. The credibility of the Duke claim was dependent not only on the existence of a culture in which it was possible to believe an allegation that a group of white student athletes indeed raped a black stripper. It was also dependent on the existence of a culture in which it would make an intelligible narrative: that the students wanted to do this and were capable of disregarding the woman's lack of consent—were sociopathic, in essence.

The allegation becomes believable if in that culture unleashed sex, including sexual violence, is accepted; if, at Duke, barriers against rape have been eroded, at least with respect to high-status white men and low-status black women. It becomes believable if the culture has degenerated to accept sexual conquest as a natural entitlement of social or athletic success, if male athletes are thought better of if they rape women. It becomes believable in a culture where women, not just young women, subordinate women, women of color, and women who are sex workers but all women—are dehumanized in the minds of male student athletes, male students, all men. Only then is it possible that these successful athlete-scholars so disregarded this woman's humanity as to gang-rape her in a bathroom.

And so, *was* there such a culture? The media reporting on the Duke allegation coalesced remarkably quickly around the claim that indeed there was a rape-positive culture at Duke, with virtually all the attributes recited above, and proceeded to mount the evidence for it. First, there was the evidence presented by the student athletes themselves: an obscenely violent, misogynist, and threatening e-mail message sent by one of the players shortly after the alleged rape (Reitman; Peter Boyer). There was also the athletes' arrest histories of drunken and boorish behavior. More broadly, there was the evidence presented consciously or willy-nilly by the Duke student body. In interviews, Duke students divided on whether the sexual culture was liberatory or oppressive for women, but remarkably they agreed that there was a culture that tolerated or celebrated sexual conquest and that had contempt for constraints on conquest, be those constraints feminist or puritanical. Academically, a queer-theoretical analytic had developed at Duke that blurred the distinction between consensual and nonconsensual sex—as had radical feminism before it, but this time toward a different end: whereas radical feminists had restricted the scope of acceptable sex to what women welcomed, queer theorists extended the scope to include sex that once was seen as harassing or debasing. Social life, seemingly, followed suit. Constraints on sex—from traditional moralism to sex harassment laws, from religious conservatism to radical feminism—had to go. In such a culture, a rape allegation was both intelligible and credible. The spring 2006 allegation of rape in Durham, in short, does not simply invite cultural-legal analysis. The intelligibility and credibility of the crime require it.

Rape at Dupont: Popular Literature as Culture as Law

The most telling evidence of the debased sex culture at Duke, however, at least for some culturally inclined journalists reporting out of Durham, was Tom Wolfe's best-selling novel *I Am Charlotte Simmons*. Set at a fictionalized version of Duke, it tells the story of a virginal scholarship student from Appalachia trying to gain social approval in the midst of a debauched, sexually unbounded, undergraduate social scene at Dupont University, an internationally ranked institution also known for its world-class basketball team, excellence in lacrosse, economically privileged students, and raucous student parties. Charlotte is ultimately successful in her social climb—by the end of the book, she has managed to secure the affections or at least the attention of a high-status basketball player—although her success comes at the cost of her integrity, her academic career, and her self-possession. Along the way, she is pressured by a particularly boorish lacrosse student into painful, unwanted, and unwelcome sexual intercourse. The scene, which takes place at a drunken party celebrating the team's success, is told from her point of view. The reader feels her pain and sees that she is the victim of an undergraduate culture that both glorifies a man's athleticism and disregards her humanity.

The parallels between Wolfe's novel and the allegation at Durham immediately captured the attention of journalists.[9] Wolfe had researched his book thoroughly; his daughter had attended Duke while he was writing it; and in many ways he seemed to have down cold the lacrosse culture, the athletic culture, and the undergraduate university culture at Duke and other athletic powerhouses. The novel—and even his protagonist's name, Charlotte Simmons—became a shorthand reference, in some of the media reporting on the rape allegation, to the rape-positive culture of Duke University or at least of the athletic subculture at Duke. The novel, in effect, was reported as presenting the backstory of the morally degraded climate at schools like Duke, thus explaining how the rape of a black woman and mother from a local college, employed as a stripper by a group of lacrosse players, could have been committed. Wolfe's book, and the book's fictional world of undergraduates, became a part of the media culture that in turn produced the narrative of Duke undergraduate life in which the rape allegation was heard. The fictional sexual assault of Charlotte Simmons made more credible the nonfictional charge of rape in Durham.

In the sex panic that resulted from a community's overly credulous acceptance of a rape charge, Wolfe's novel provides an example of a bit of culture production in which the culture became a bit of law. The novel supplied evidence to the community at Durham and elsewhere of a rape that never happened.

Where Is Charlotte Simmons Now? Pop Lit as Critique

There is a problem with this indictment of Wolfe and Charlotte Simmons for their participation in the creation of a sex panic in Durham: focused on the novel's reception, it elides the novel itself. The sex in Wolfe's book actually bears little resemblance to the alleged rape in Durham. First, Charlotte Simmons was not raped. She did not say no, did not resist to the utmost, did not communicate a lack of consent, and it is not clear that her partner believed her to have withheld consent or even that he was aware of her discomfort and pain (*I Am* 518–23). Second, Charlotte did not experience the sex as an assault. She also realized, rightly, that claiming that it was would have jeopardized her social ascent. During this sex that wasn't rape, she basically alienated her socially striving self from her injured self and prioritized the interests of the former over the latter.

(She wants to tell her partner to stop but thinks, "What would it look like if she said no — *now?*" [520].) In other words, she saw her social success as dependent on her acceptance of this physical intrusion. By not resisting, she compounded the injury: she undermined not only her academic career but also, Wolfe makes clear, her moral character. At Durham, the woman reported an assault and claimed it was rape. If she undermined her integrity and credibility by reporting a crime that did not happen, the fictional Charlotte undermined her integrity by not naming, claiming, or blaming; by not resisting the assault; and by being complicit in the subsequent denial of it.

The injury that the fictional character sustained may be more prevalent, and far less visible, in the real world we inhabit than the violent rape falsely alleged at Duke. Charlotte Simmons suffered oppressive and unwelcome sex with a partner who felt no imperative, moral or legal, to respect her. So why didn't she resist? Likely, from her need for status and recognition at any cost. She came to Dupont an immature young woman, lacking in character; in Wolfe's signature misanthropic style, she is not an antihero but unpleasant and unlikable from the start. She comes out of Dupont, four years later, much diminished. The sex to which she submitted without resistance was a big part of the reason why.

The contribution of this novel is that it renders a full description of the experience of intrusive, unpleasurable, and undesired — but consensual — sex and the harm it can cause to one's character and emotional life. Wolfe's novel is and should be read as a critique of potent and harmful but nevertheless legal sex and of the culture that legitimates, honors, and encourages it. It is not a critique that one will easily find, in our various scholarly treatments of rape and rape law, feminist and otherwise, or in legal literature.

By conflating the painful and undesired sex that Charlotte undergoes with rape, we misdescribe both. By pairing Wolfe's book with the events in Durham, whether to explain the rape-positive culture or the sex panic, we misdescribe it. Wolfe's subject was neither rape nor a rape-positive culture but the harms of undesired sex.

Without downplaying the significance of a cultural-legal analysis of the events in Durham and the role of Wolfe's novel in those events, I suggest that treating the novel only as a part of a culture that produces legal understanding obscures the critique the novel makes regarding consensual but unwanted sex on college campuses and more broadly. We can and should read the book as a part of a popular culture that created a context in which a false rape allegation was heard, interpreted, assimilated into preexisting narratives, and widely believed. But it is also a critique of sex.

What is true of Wolfe, Durham, Duke, and Dupont might also be true of popular culture across the board and its relation to law. If we wish to understand our law, its value in our lives, and the harm it can do, we should read both canonical and popular literature about law for its content and not only as evidence of our perceptions of law or of the quality or potency of the culture that literature is producing or is produced by it. Popular narrative fiction, television shows, and films, no less than canonical literature, may have something to teach us about law, life, and sex.

Notes

1. One exception is Richard Sherwin's fine article on jurisprudence in film in the *UCLA Law Review*.

2. Literature is also often the subject of law, such as copyright law or contract law.

3. See Weisberg, *Failure* 131–76; Luban 283–334; B. Thomas, *Cross-Examinations* 164–82; Angel; Ball, *Word*; R. West, "Authority."

4. There are other ways in which the distinction between law and literature might be blurred. It might make sense, for example, to regard a lawyer's task as akin to a narrator's. Legal analysis has an explanatory structure that is in part narrative and can and should be separately studied as such. Also, the legal arts might be fruitfully studied, and practiced, as a literary form, having a distinctively literary set of ethical and aesthetic norms. James Boyd White and Martha Nussbaum both explore these and related themes. See White's *Legal Imagination*, Nussbaum's "Cultivating Humanity."

5. Fish, *Doing*; Fiss; Dworkin, *Matter*; Levinson and Mailloux.

6. I have criticized the interpretive turn in law and literature studies more generally and on other grounds. See "Are There Nothing but Texts" and "Adjudication."

7. For an example of this sort of cultural analysis of law, see Mezey and Niles.

8. Of the many journalistic treatments of the many conflicting cultures that were affected by and that affected the rape case, perhaps the most thorough was Janet Reitman's. See also Peter Boyer.

9. See Reitman; Peter Boyer. In the face of the scores of articles and blogs linking Charlotte Simmons with the Duke case, Wolfe gave an interview to deny that Duke University was the model for his fictional Dupont.

Part II

Model Courses

Diane Hoeveler

Where the Evidence Leads: Teaching Gothic Novels and the Law

Every year I teach courses on the gothic novel at both the graduate and undergraduate levels. Whether I am teaching majors (as I obviously am in the graduate course) or nonmajors, I have found it useful to be explicit about the theoretical approaches that one brings to a text. Hence, I have developed a style of teaching that helps students see the differences between four dominant schools of theory: formalist, historicist, ideological, and psychoanalytic. Increasingly, I have focused on the topic of law as both a major historical and ideological component of the gothic novel.

This essay examines how to teach the British gothic novel as an exploration of a number of contested legal issues during the late eighteenth and early nineteenth centuries. As Michael Scrivener has observed, one of the dominant concerns in legal evolution during this period was the reform of what was referred to as the premodern Bloody Code, a legal system that listed two hundred capital crimes, most of them offences against property. The Bloody Code was also infamous for revealing the upper-class domination of the legal system. Like the many depictions of aristocratic divorce or adultery trials that were printed and widely circulated in popular pamphlets, the Bloody Code as well as these sensational adultery trials had the effect of showing the aristocracy to be corrupt and immoral and thereby abusing the advantages it had been accorded by this same legal system (Scrivener 128). As Leon Radzinowicz's study makes clear, by the 1830s and 1840s legal reforms had occurred because of the utilitarian and ratio-nalistic approaches proposed by Jeremy Bentham, James Mill, and their followers, but the gothic novel's popularity straddles the divide between the earlier, class-based approach to law and the later utilitarian reforms. We see in gothics (as in other Romantic texts) an ideological bifurcation between what Jürgen Habermas refers to as the premodern, paternalistic, providential, divine-right approach to law versus modernity's utilitarian, rationalistic replacement of the divine and authoritarian with the human and the secular ("Modernity").

I focus on the legal palimpsest that emerges in contested form in one gothic novel after another: the oral versus written testimony debate that was central to the evolution of a modernized, secularized, print-based cul-ture; the anxiety that emerges in textuality when a providential, divine-rights legal system symbolized by a judge is replaced by novels that examine more real-life legal issues and by criminal cases decided by a jury of one's peers; and the continued contest between providential and aristocratic-authoritarian appeals to legality and the emerging rationalistic and utilitar-ian approach (the way that law replaces religion as "the main ideological cement of society," as J. A. Sharpe has noted [145]).

To see the growing importance of the written document as proof in legal trials, one need only think of Ann Radcliffe's *The Romance of the Forest* (1791). The dead body of Adeline's father is found in a trunk after Adeline finds the diary he kept while being held prisoner by his diabolical brother. Both the body and the diary are necessary to prove conclusively that he was murdered for his property: the body without the diary would not signify, and Radcliffe and her readers know this. Although the gothic novel began as an essentially conservative genre, with strong aristocratic sympathies, it quickly evolved into a middle-class discourse system as more bourgeois authors began to claim the genre for their own interests. What James Watt refers to as the earlier, "Loyalist" strain of the gothic novel anticipated the threats on the French monarchy and encoded in its fictions an adherence to the rights of primogeniture, birthright, and class-based virtue (42–69). Horace Walpole's *The Castle of Otranto* (1764) and Clara Reeve's *Old English Baron* (1778) are the most blatant and earliest ex-amples of the "Loyalist" gothic in the British tradition. But this strain of gothic (heavily invested in a providential discourse as well) continued to live on in even pulp gothics, such as the anonymous *The Animated Skeleton*

(1798), suggesting that even lower- and middle-class audiences still found pleasure and escape in what I would call class-based nostalgia by reading texts that no longer presented their social, political, and historical realities.

I try to get students to see that the evolution of legal issues in the gothic novel reflects the process by which a print-based culture replaced an earlier and anachronistic oral-based culture. For instance, in many gothic novels the claims of written documentation generally trump oral testimony, unless a royal or authoritarian arbiter appears in a civil trial case or a monk or clergyman in an Inquisition trial. One can recall the attempt by Monçada in Charles Maturin's *Melmoth the Wanderer* (1820) to renounce his clerical vows by appearing in a civil court:

> "Wretch," said the Superior, "when have such papers as those profaned the convent before? When, till your unhallowed entrance, were we insulted with the memoirs of legal advocates? How comes it that you have dared to—" "Do what, my father?" "Reclaim your vows, and expose us to all the scandal of a civil court and its proceedings." (138–39)

Legal vestiges of the ancien régime continue to appear in gothic novels—for instance, the notorious lettre de cachet, auto-da-fé scenes, varieties of torture, or anonymous letters to the authority accusing an enemy of crimes against the state. The demonizing of these outmoded and European-Catholic strategies allows British bourgeois gothic authors and their readers to measure approvingly the distance they have moved in modernizing and secularizing Britain.

The gothic, of course, also questions the authority of civil law itself, and hence one continues to see in gothic novels the presence and power of ecclesiastical courts vying with civil courts in rendering decisions and passing judgments over people. For instance, students can be reminded here of the notorious trial of Justine Moritz in Mary Shelley's *Frankenstein*, who confesses to a crime she did not commit and who is convicted on the most circumstantial of evidence:

> The person to whom I addressed myself added that Justine had already confessed her guilt. "That evidence," he observed, "was hardly required in so glaring a case, but I am glad of it; and, indeed, none of our judges like to condemn a criminal upon circumstantial evidence, be it ever so decisive." (83)

Finally, one of the central issues facing this culture was what Habermas has called the invention of a "public bourgeois sphere" ("Public Sphere"

49) in which the growing middle class could operate in an increasingly professionalized arena where written discourse and a print culture dominated over oral testimony. As John Richetti has noted, there was an increased investment in imagining the legal system as monolithic, while the emergence of the new public sphere was dependent in part on an understanding of the law in which it was "conceived of as an embodiment of permanent and universal norms rather than as an imposition by the sovereign for securing order and power" (115). The growing divide between the public and private spheres, and the concomitant dispute between dynastic-political and personal-individual concerns, can be seen by examining the evolution of the early gothic novel. Whereas the earliest, such as *The Castle of Otranto* and *The Old English Baron,* concern the unlawful usurpation of thrones and duchies (however small), the later increasingly focus on besieged families or the threats to a father's or mother's power in the household (e.g., Radcliffe's *A Sicilian Romance* [1791] or *The Italian* [1797]).

Perhaps one of the most blatant examples of the unjust nature of European justice can be found in Radcliffe's *Mysteries of Udolpho* (1794), when Count Morano is arrested shortly after returning to Venice:

> [H]e had been arrested by order of the Senate, and, without knowing of what he was suspected, was conveyed to a place of confinement, whither the most strenuous enquiries of his friends had been unable to trace him. Who the enemy was, that had occasioned him this calamity, he had not been able to guess, unless, indeed, it was Montoni, on whom his suspicions rested, and not only with much apparent probability, but with justice. (422)

Montoni apparently suspected Morano of trying to poison him but was unable to obtain the evidence he needed to bring a charge against him.

A major issue in the gothic universe is the relative reliability of oral versus written testimony, or what Toni Wein calls the lack of any "simple correspondence between oral/human and written/text" (297). Anachronistic markers of orality riddle the trial scenes in *The Castle of Otranto* and *The Old English Baron*: snatches of remembered conversations, bits of clothing and jewelry that are said to belong to the murdered ruler, or summarized speeches presented by the narrator. (I provide on handouts for my students a summary of the major positions taken by critics like Leslie Moran, David Punter, Beth Swan, and Kathryn Temple on the topic of the gothic and law. I also post them on the *Desire2Learn* site I maintain for the course.)

In my courses, I begin my more detailed survey of teaching the theme of law in gothic novels at the beginning, with Walpole's inaugural gothic, *The Castle of Otranto*, almost a case study of anxious aristocratic concerns. In its focus on a dispute over lawful title to the principality of Otranto and the legality of an older male seeking to divorce his aged wife for a young bride who can provide him with a male heir, we see writ large the historical romance and antiromances of King Henry VIII. Like Henry, Manfred alleges that his marriage to Hippolita is incestuous, and he wants a divorce in order to marry Isabella, the fiancée of his dead son, Conrad. Like Henry, whose brother was married to Catherine of Aragon very briefly before that elder brother died, Manfred also searches Scripture for some way out of his marriage. He tells his confessor:

> But alas! father, you know not the bitterest of my pangs! It is some time that I have had scruples on the legality of our union: Hippolita is related to me in the fourth degree— It is true, we had a dispensation; but I have been informed that she had also been contracted to another. This it is that sits heavy at my heart: to this state of unlawful wedlock I impute the . . . death of Conrad!— Ease my conscience of this burden; dissolve our marriage. (49)

Manfred in fact earlier "contracted a marriage for his son with the marquis of Vicenza's daughter, Isabella; and she had already been delivered . . . into the hands of Manfred, that he might celebrate the wedding as soon as Conrad's infirm state of health would permit" (15). But on the verge of the wedding, Conrad is mysteriously killed and Manfred is suddenly without a male heir. Manfred loses no time in offering himself as the groom:

> "[I]n short, Isabella, since I cannot give you my son, I offer you myself."— "Heavens!" cried Isabella . . . "what do I hear! You, my lord! You! My father in law! the father of Conrad! the husband of the virtuous Hippolita!"— "I tell you," said Manfred imperiously, "Hippolita is no longer my wife; I divorce her from this hour. Too long has she cursed me by her unfruitfulness: my fate depends on having sons." (23)

In addition to attempting to divorce his wife by a simple oral declaration of dissatisfaction (a crime in the private sphere), Manfred is guilty of living as a usurper of the principality of Otranto from the rightful heir,

Lord Frederic and his son Theodore (58). Their claim is disputed by Manfred, who continues to assert his right to the land and the bride:

> You come, sir knight, . . . to re-demand the lady Isabella his daughter,
> who has been contracted in the face of holy church to my son, by
> the consent of her legal guardians; and to require me to resign my
> dominions to your lord, who gives himself for the nearest of blood to
> Prince Alfonso. . . . I shall speak to the latter article of your demands
> first. You must know, your lord knows, that I enjoy the principality
> of Otranto from my father Don Manuel, as he received it from his
> father Don Ricardo. Alfonso, their predecessor, dying childless in the
> Holy Land, bequeathed his estates to my grandfather Don Ricardo,
> in consideration of his faithful services. . . . But Frederic, your lord, is
> nearest in blood—I have consented to put my title to the issue of the
> sword—does that imply a vitious title? (64)

Notice that Manfred's claim and counterclaim are made verbally and
that the dispute is to be settled by the sword, both relics of a medieval,
premodern chivalric code of conduct, both strategies essential to the loyalist, antimodern agenda of a beleaguered aristocrat like Walpole.

In a similarly anachronistic manner, *The Old English Baron* concerns
a dynastic dispute as well as the murder of the rightful ruler, this time re-
playing the saga of Richard III as the historical ghost haunting this gothic
tale. These two early gothic novels position themselves as retellings of
Shakespearean narratives, their sympathies clearly on the side of inherited wealth, class privilege, and innate aristocratic virtue. Lord Lovel and
his wife have both been murdered by his kinsman Sir Walter Lovel, who
usurps the property and title, thinking that he has also disposed of their
heir, Edmund. But Edmund has been raised by a village couple who reluctantly reveal the truth by swearing on a bible to Edmund and Father
Oswald, his advocate, that Edmund is indeed the son of the murdered
Lord and Lady Lovel. When this information is brought to Sir Philip Har-
clay, he exclaims:

> What shall be done with this treacherous kinsman! This inhuman mon-
> ster! This assassin of his nearest relation? I will risk my life and fortune
> to bring him to justice. Shall I go to court, and demand justice of
> the King? Or shall I accuse him of the murder and make him stand a
> public trial? If I treat him as a Baron of the realm, he must be tried by
> his peers; if as a commoner, he must be tried at the county assize. But
> we must show reason why he should be degraded from his title. . . . I
> will challenge the traitor to meet me in the field; and, if he has spirit

enough to answer my call, I will there bring him to justice; if not, I will bring him to a public trial. (181)

Resorting to a duel again reifies the early gothic's loyalist posture, suggesting that the shame of a public trial is more than an aristocrat should or could bear, even if he is an assassin. The public-private split here, with the aristocrat inhabiting a secretive private realm where his crimes are concealed from public view by his peers, would appear to be viewed with nostalgia by Reeve and, one assumes, her readers.

By the time Radcliffe published *The Mysteries of Udolpho* in 1794, the emphasis in the gothic had shifted to legal issues that could be located in the private realm of marriage settlements and the inheritance of houses. As Amy Louise Erickson has argued, women's property rights were actually better protected under the earlier system of equity, chancery, and ecclesiastical law (operating approximately until the seventeenth century) than under the new common law (codified by Sir William Blackstone in his *Commentaries on the Laws of England* [1765–69]). As she notes, common law did not recognize contracts made by a woman before her marriage, while under ecclesiastical law a family's land could descend to daughters in the event that there were no sons. By the early eighteenth century, however, provisos in common law limited a woman's right to inherit land, while new statutes were added to ecclesiastical law that reduced a woman's rights to her husband's or father's goods. Further, the practice of dividing an estate equally among all surviving children was ended. Students begin to see anxiety over the effects of this later legal development in a number of gothic novels (culminating perhaps best in Emily Brontë's *Wuthering Heights*). Women begin to use the legal technologies of wills and codicils in order to maintain their property rights even after marriage. Female novelists begin to depict heroines who will do almost anything to resist being what Blackstone referred to as femes covert.

In *The Mysteries of Udolpho*, St. Aubert, the heroine's father, is financially ruined and yet extracts a promise from his daughter Emily, "that you will never, whatever may be your future circumstances, *sell* the chateau." St. Aubert even enjoins her, whenever she might marry, "to make it an article in the contract, that the chateau should always be hers" (78). The villain in the piece, Montoni, schemes to possess La Vallée and marries Emily's aunt, Madame Cheron, as the first part of his strategy:

> But Montoni, who had been allured by the seeming wealth of Madame Cheron, was now severely disappointed by her comparative poverty. . . .

> He had been deceived in an affair, wherein he meant to be the deceiver;
> out-witted by the superior cunning of a woman. . . . Madame Montoni
> had contrived to have the greatest part of what she really did possess,
> settled upon herself. (190)

In addition to issues of wills, inheritance, and property settlements, dramatic court trial became a gothic staple by the end of the eighteenth century. As Jonathan Grossman notes, William Godwin's politico-gothic *Things as They Are; or, The Adventures of Caleb Williams* (1794) was among the first novels to feature "a newly juridical conception of character and narrative form" (37). In *Caleb Williams*, we find a number of trial scenes, as well as scenes where Caleb, accused as a criminal, encounters pamphlets and broadsheets depicting him and describing the history of his various supposed misdeeds. Godwin was not merely, as Grossman suggests, "present[ing] a historic struggle between criminal biography and the novel" and pursuing "radical aims" of legal reform in *Caleb Williams* (38); his emphasis on legal narratives and apparatus in the novel also served to appeal to the reading public's fascination with the law and sensational crimes and trials.

After *Caleb Williams*, students see a much greater prevalence of criminal trials in gothic fiction; in fact, it is as though readers, so accustomed by this time to seeing criminals tried for their crimes and punished on the gallows, demanded the same theme in popular fiction. Earlier gothic fiction generally ended with the villain's extrajudicial death or religious repentance. For example, in *The Castle of Otranto*, "Manfred signed his abdication of the principality, with the approbation of Hippolita, and each took on them the habit of religion in the neighbouring convents" (110). In *The Mysteries of Udolpho*, the villain Montoni, after many years and several hundred pages of villainy, dies almost in passing, so that an inattentive reader might miss it: "[B]eing considered by the senate as a very dangerous person, [Montoni] was, for other reasons, ordered again into confinement, where, it was said, he had died in a doubtful and mysterious manner" (567). Throughout the 1790s, as the minor gothic writers imitated Radcliffe and Walpole, we find similar dispositions of villains' fates, as in Richard Sickelmore's *Edgar; or, The Phantom of the Castle* (1798), where the evil Bernardine and the avaricious Armine both die peacefully, despite their many horrid crimes, after having repented of their sins.

By the first and second decades of the nineteenth century, it becomes clear that readers expected the gothic villain to be punished by judicial means after a trial in a civil or sometimes ecclesiastical court. For example, Percy Bysshe Shelley's first attempt at a gothic novel, *Zastrozzi* (1810), concludes with the trial of the titular villain and his accomplice, Matilda, for their long careers of crime. The trial is ostensibly conducted by the Inquisition, although it appears to be public, which reflects nineteenth-century judicial practices more accurately than sixteenth-century ones.

As an instructor, I would like to be able to trace a neat progression in the gothic, charting for my students an increasing investment in the rationalistic worldview taken by reforms in the law and a decline in anachronistic, premodern, providential narratives. But in fact, later gothic novels continue to present vehemently providential narratives and use anachronistic legal codes to prop up their adherence to a chivalric code of conduct. One need only think of *Melmoth the Wanderer*, James Hogg's *Private Memoirs and Confessions of a Justified Sinner* (1824), or Charlotte Brontë's *Jane Eyre* (1847). Gothic fictions are split in their presentations of flawed juries that hear murder cases (as in *Frankenstein*) and of the continued and preferred power of judges to function as dei ex machina, substitutes for an omniscient God. There is a deep nostalgia in gothic works, a mourning for the premodern, oral, providential universe and for all its outmoded class privileges and corruptions. It might be more accurate for us to say that the gothic is hopelessly split in its presentation of the law because it is constrained by the power of its conventions. It needs, according to the rules of genre, to present a damsel in distress and an oppressive count or corrupt monk, and yet such devices cause its use of legal themes to be seen as rationalistic and utilitarian (liberal) rather than conservative. Gothic novels are similarly ideologically bifurcated on the issue of the court system, some works seeing the court as almost godlike in its power, others presenting the legal system as class-based, unjust, and inhumane in its execution of inequitable laws. By introducing students to the topic of the law as both a historical and an ideological issue in the gothic novel, instructors can help them better understand the role that literature plays in shaping the larger environment we inhabit. Our laws and our rights have not always been in place or uncontested; indeed, they were issues of public debate, and a large part of that discussion occurred in novels. By seeing how the law has evolved, students come to appreciate the continuously shifting interaction between literature and the law.

Lisa Rodensky

Making Crime Pay
in the Victorian Novel
Survey Course

There are plenty of crimes in Victorian novels and as many different ways to integrate discussions of them into an undergraduate survey course. Long and multiplotted affairs, Victorian novels inspire wide-ranging discussions in undergraduate courses. Crime and, more specifically, criminal responsibility can be among the major topics of discussion, and they usefully intersect with other, more general themes—for instance, those that concern agency and personality. Discussions that focus on criminal responsibility can also help students attend to the novel as a genre and consider more fully and consequentially its freedom to enter into a character's mind through the third-person narrator.

In this essay, I outline approaches to introducing representations of criminal responsibility into classroom discussions of three canonical Victorian novels that often turn up in an undergraduate Victorian novel survey course: *Oliver Twist*, *Middlemarch*, and *Tess of the d'Urbervilles*. This approach invites students to investigate how these novels enact the relation between mental state and action, the two elements that define a crime. Criminal responsibility depends on the existence of and the relations between these elements, and Charles Dickens, George Eliot, and Thomas Hardy all explore and at times exploit the complications at work in and between these elements. The explorations illuminate both the novel's treatment of cultural assumptions about criminal responsibility and the novel's special power to represent the contradictions and confusions often at work in those assumptions. Analyses of criminal responsibility help students grasp the complex interplay between the Victorian novel and its culture.[1]

Oliver Twist is a good place to start a course in which the instructor wants to introduce questions about criminal law. Students readily understand that Dickens challenges the Victorian reformist discourses that produce inhumane conditions for the poor in the guise of improvement; they see that the children in the workhouse, on the baby farm, or apprenticed to the likes of Gamfield or even Sowerberry are in danger of losing both their souls and their lives. The debates concerning the formation of character (pitting environment against nature) that Dickens explicitly introduces in his prefaces inevitably give rise to questions about responsibility and especially criminal responsibility. His eponymous hero prompts students to consider how the novel depicts individual responsibility in a criminal law context. In the first or second class on *Oliver Twist*, students find themselves in Fagin's den with Oliver, but, unlike Oliver, they know that Fagin is a fence and that the boys are thieves. One way to approach this first third of the novel is to ask students to consider Dickens's descriptions of Oliver's agency, the limits of Oliver's knowledge and of his ability to act on that knowledge. In his pre-Fagin life, Oliver seems to know more and can act on his intentions (he beats up Noah for insulting his mum, for instance), but when he gets to the thieves' den and his knowledge would implicate him in the criminal activities that the boys undertake for Fagin, Dickens shields him from such knowledge. An instructor might ask students why Oliver at once witnesses and sleeps through Fagin's inventory taking and incriminating mutterings as Fagin looks over his stolen goods. The passage in which Dickens describes Oliver in a state of aware-unawareness often gets students talking about this important ambiguity, and this discussion may move them to think harder about representations of responsibility.

Oliver perceives Fagin's actions but as part of a dream or, later on, as a game with the other boys. Only when Oliver finally recognizes Charley Bates's attempts to rob Brownlow at the bookstall does Dickens allow Oliver to register criminality: Oliver's face burns, and he feels he'll be damned. Obviously Oliver had no intention of participating in this robbery—how could he, given that he didn't know a crime was about to take place? We know his state of mind through a third-person narrator, and we know for a certainty what Oliver knows and intends. Because criminal intention is an essential element in the commission of a crime, Dickens arranges Oliver's participation so that Oliver becomes part of the gang without incurring any responsibility for having done so. Zeroing in on the importance of criminal states of mind allows students to recognize the line Dickens walks in his representation of Oliver here and elsewhere in the text. Students can see that Dickens keeps him from acquiring a criminal record, a criminal past, even as Oliver lives among criminals, and this observation might point to ways that Dickens uses the principles of criminal law to protect Oliver. Without acquiring knowledge, Oliver can have no intention to commit a crime, no matter what he does (e.g., going to the bookstall with the Dodger and Bates).

Questions of criminal responsibility animate *Oliver Twist* from beginning to end but nowhere more potently than in the last third of the novel, in which we confront Nancy's murder, Sikes's death, and Fagin's being tried as an accessory before the fact. Usually the last class on *Oliver Twist* focuses on Fagin's trial and last night in jail — thrilling scenes — but beyond and behind their dramatic force is the fact of Fagin's crime. Students probably don't know exactly what it means to be an accessory before the fact, and Dickens mentions it only once. Since it's easy to miss, it's worth asking students if they can name the charge brought against Fagin and explain what it means. To be an accessory before the fact meant in the nineteenth century (and means now in the twenty-first) to be indirectly involved in a crime in such a way that one is party to that crime and responsible for it. An accessory before the fact aids, abets, counsels, or commands another to commit a crime. In an important sense, an accessory doesn't himself commit a crime, though he is a party to the commission of a crime and therefore becomes criminally responsible for that crime.[2] Clearly Fagin does not murder Nancy with his own hands, yet he is tried for that murder (although during the trial scene no one identifies the charge against him) and hangs for it.[3] Dickens takes advantage of a category from criminal law that attaches responsibility to a specific intent but not a specific act. Sikes acts out Fagin's intention, which is exposed after the spying Morris Bolter (the former Noah Claypole) reports back to Fagin about Nancy's meeting with Brownlow and Rose Maylie. Asking students to attend to the moment when Fagin works himself up into a fury over what he thinks is Nancy's betrayal of him as "every evil thought and blackest purpose lay working at this heart" (318) puts them in touch with the intensity ("every," "blackest") and clarity of Fagin's intentions ("purpose"). But what, students might ask, does Fagin do?

Fagin's criminality emanates from what he is, not from what he does, since compared with those who work for him, he does little. Like a Mafia don, he is the figure who evades responsibility because others act for him, but both Dickens and the criminal law find their way to him through a category that makes a bad intention do the work of a direct criminal act. Students might be asked to consider and discuss how much more damning Fagin's thoughts are just before Nancy's murder than the words he speaks to Sikes. A good paper topic might be to compare Fagin's thoughts to his words. When Dickens dramatizes the dialogue between Sikes and Fagin just before the murder, it isn't so clear what Fagin is aiding or abetting, because what he tells Sikes to do is anything but clear, and students can productively identify such ambiguities.[4]

To enrich students' understanding of the tensions in the text with respect to criminal liability, instructors might help students recognize not only how Dickens takes advantage of the charge of accessory before the fact (and so aligns himself with the criminal law) but also how he exposes the dangers of the widening net of criminality, which creates guilt by association. These are tensions at work in the culture as a whole. Oliver appears to be an associate of some very unsavory figures, and when representatives of the law come in contact with him—whether it's the menacing magistrate Fang or the Bow Street runners—they pass judgment on him for the company he keeps. He is, after all, present at not one but two attempted robberies. Here (and elsewhere) Dickens asserts the superiority of the novel's narrative voice to the law it depicts. Whatever story Oliver's actions might appear to tell, the truth emerges from Dickens's representations of his inner life.

It's a giant leap from the urban squalor of Dickens's *Oliver Twist* to the provincial respectability of Eliot's *Middlemarch*, and while crime is a topic of Dickens's novel, it is not in *Middlemarch*. Questions of moral judgment are everywhere in the text, but crime itself and questions of criminal responsibility enter most explicitly and specifically in the last third of the novel, when the banker Nicholas Bulstrode takes over the care of the ailing blackmailer Raffles. As different as *Middlemarch* is from *Oliver Twist*, students are able to see that like Dickens, Eliot is thinking about the relation between intention and action and also situating that relation in a criminal context (though not only a criminal context). They are usually quick to point out that Eliot in this later text is more invested in representing complex mental states than is Dickens. This observation allows an instructor to introduce Eliot's interest in the developing Victorian discipline of psychology more generally and puts students in touch with the interconnections among psychology, criminal law, and the nineteenth-century novel.

New developments in psychology and physiology promised to provide more information about the relation between mental state and behavior, between intention and action, and those developments entered and were tested not only in the courtroom (often in connection with a diminished-capacity defense) but in the novel as well. One class session might focus on Eliot's representation of Bulstrode's state of mind in the passages leading up to the moment when Bulstrode passes the liquor cabinet key to Mrs. Abel. Taking students through Eliot's moment-by-moment account of Bulstrode's crisis can lead to a discussion about the vocabulary used to portray the mind (both in the Bulstrode chapters and elsewhere) and about whether Bulstrode knows his own mind (as Fagin does; and if students have read *North and South*, they can compare how Elizabeth Gaskell represents Margaret Hale's complicated relation to her intentions when Hale intervenes during the riot scene). Does Eliot show Bulstrode as being in control of his thoughts and feelings? as the agent of his own mental activity? as the agent of the muscular movements caused by that mental activity? He is and he isn't. Instructors might take the class back to the strange case of Madame Laure, the object of the young Lydgate's desire while Lydgate is studying in Paris. Trying to explain how it came to pass that Laure stabbed her husband, Lydgate can admit only two possibilities—accident or premeditation—but Laure explains the act as an intentional accident ("My foot slipped . . . I meant to do it" [151]). What neither we nor Eliot can or will determine is whether the act is one or the other. It is both. Through this ambiguity Eliot complicates our judgment of responsibility.

Taking notice of the vocabulary Eliot uses in these pages (*desire, intention, motive, impulse*) could generate a discussion about the differences among these terms. Instructors might ask students how the detailed and complex descriptions of Bulstrode's state of mind influence our judgment of Bulstrode. Eliot's narrator poses the question hypothetically:

> A man vows, and yet will not cast away the means of breaking his vow.
> Is it that he distinctly means to break it? Not at all; but the desires

which tend to break it are at work within him dimly, and make their
way into his imagination, and relax his muscles in the very moments
when he is telling himself over again the reasons for his vow. (695–96)

This is a particularly good passage to move through with a class, because
it allows students to see Eliot making the "desires" the force that tends
to break the vow. The "he" becomes the figure worked upon. The third-
person narrator has access not only to Bulstrode's conscious mind but
also to the semiconscious desires that affect his bodily functions ("relax
his muscles"), and this special knowledge reveals the blurred boundaries
between voluntary intention and involuntary desires and bodily motions.
Instructors might note that the narrator allows readers to see the workings
of a mind before an act takes place in a way that is obviously not possible
in life. Bulstrode's state of mind lacks the clarity of Fagin's, but it is clear
that Bulstrode wants Raffles to die.

In *Middlemarch*, descriptions of mental states and acts bring us into an
exploration of the distinctions between moral and legal responsibility—a
fertile topic for class discussion. Instructors could suggest that moral guilt
involves bad thoughts in and of themselves while the law requires an act.
Bulstrode, students will quickly add, does more than wish. Why, an instructor might ask, isn't the wish enough for us to condemn him? Does
it make a difference to our judgment of him that he finally does act (he
passes the key to Mrs. Abel)? Students might want to talk about how Eliot portrays that passing of the key (in the passive voice). One of the first
Middlemarch reviewers, Sidney Colvin, refers to Bulstrode's crime as a
"passive murder" (333), and students might take up what moves Colvin
to use this language.

Although Eliot uses her narrator's powers to give readers access they
would not have in life, that access doesn't determine Bulstrode's responsibility. In the end, she asks readers to consider what can't be known about
Bulstrode's mind, even by the third-person narrator. What Bulstrode *does*
is known: he passes the key to Mrs. Abel, although Lydgate advised him
not to give Raffles alcohol. The act reasserts itself as a way of assessing both
moral and legal responsibility, but because of the ambiguities of causation
(many Middlemarch doctors would have prescribed alcohol for a man in
Raffles's condition), the lawyer Hawley fails in his attempt to mount a
legal case against Bulstrode. In the notebook she kept for *Middlemarch*,
Eliot made clear that Bulstrode would not be tried or convicted for Raffles's death: "The idea which governs the plot of Bulstrode is, that there

is nothing which the law can lay hold of to make him responsible for" (*Quarry* 54). Her direct statement illuminates the importance of action to moral responsibility, for if Bulstrode's act, giving the key, cannot be laid hold of as a legally culpable element, then it looks more like a necessary element of our judgment of Bulstrode as morally culpable, even if he slips through the fingers of the law. Fagin does not slip through the law's fingers, even though he has arguably done less than Bulstrode; but, then, Dickens makes Fagin's intentions clearer to us when Fagin contemplates Nancy's seeming betrayal. Students can consider, and perhaps write about, the complexities of Eliot's representations of states of mind and compare some passages in the Bulstrode chapters with passages in *Oliver Twist*. If the workings of the mind in *Middlemarch* frustrate the reader's desire for clarity in assessing criminal responsibility, then students may come to see why the external act remains an important element in assessing responsibility—even in a novel, which has the power to go where no court can go.

Although the law cannot reach Bulstrode, it surely and tragically reaches Hardy's Tess. *Tess of the d'Urbervilles*, a work that often completes a Victorian novel survey and begins a course on the modern novel, both insistently introduces questions about criminal responsibility and makes them beside the point. Given this tension, instructors might ask students to consider how Hardy more aggressively draws readers' attention to their assumptions about agency than does Dickens or Eliot. One way into the thinking about this difference is to focus on moments when Hardy exposes agency as a fiction that the realist novel has buttressed. Hardy's own summation of Tess reflects his self-consciousness about the question of agency and, by extension, responsibility. He remarked in an interview with Raymond Blathwayt in 1892:

> I still maintain that her innate purity remained intact to the very last; though I frankly own a certain outward purity left her on her last fall. I regarded her then as being in the hands of circumstances, not morally responsible, a mere corpse drifting with the current to her end. (*Thomas Hardy* 40)[5]

The implicit and explicit tensions at work in this comment—between the inward and the outward, agency and its absence, moral and legal responsibility—shape the novel as a whole, particularly the two scenes that generate the most challenging class discussions: the rape and the murder.

Of course, with respect to the rape scene, we aren't weighing Tess's criminality but Alec's. Yet Alec's depends on Hardy's representation of her role in the act. Students readily recognize the ambiguities Hardy creates in the scene. Questions then necessarily arise about how those ambiguities interfere with our ability to make a judgment about the act and Tess's participation in it. Students might be directed to several essays that address this question, one that continues to be central to the text (Brady; W. Davis; Rooney; Sutherland 202–10; M. Williams, " 'Is Alec' " and " 'Sensitive' "). These questions return students to an analysis of the novel's third-person narrator introduced in discussions of *Oliver Twist* and continued in *Middlemarch*. Why doesn't the narrator tell us what happened? Why don't we enter Tess's mind during these crucial moments in the scene? One possibility is that the physically and emotionally exhausted Tess is asleep. If asleep, she is effectively absent during the act. Here students might make connections between this scene and the scenes in *Oliver Twist* in which the unconscious Oliver finds himself in compromising situations. Critics have put this scene in the context of leading Victorian rape cases, in particular *R. v. Young* (1878), which made it clear that a victim could not consent to sexual intercourse if she was asleep (W. Davis; see also M. Williams, " 'Sensitive' " and "Is Alec' "). While students recognize that Hardy provides evidence that the sleeping Tess is a victim of a crime (having had the "coarse pattern" "traced" on her, this "beautiful feminine tissue, sensitive as gossamer, and practically blank as snow" [77]—the passive voice in the description enacting her passivity), they might wonder about the weird way he turns her into a mist. Hardy insists on "obscurity" and puts Tess as a "pale nebulousness at [Alec's] feet" (76). Can one victimize a "pale nebulousness"? To read the case in legal terms may seem inadequate or inapt. Does moral and legal language (*victim, perpetrator*) have a place in this text that explicitly rejects Victorian morality and by extension the legal principles based on that morality?

To make the most of Hardy's late-century representations of criminal responsibility in *Tess*, one class might be spent on the murder scene. Tess stabs Alec with a carving knife—about that fact there is no doubt—yet Hardy complicates the reader's assessment of her guilt as we come to see the deed from Angel Clare's point of view. To begin with, students might take up Angel's responses to Tess just before she returns to Alec on that eventful morning. Having had his epiphany in Brazil, Angel can finally see beyond his own conventional standards of morality and blames not Tess but himself for the situation she finds herself in. "Ah—it is my fault!" he exclaims. As readers, we've long wanted Angel to see things this way, yet his acceptance of responsibility seems irrelevant, as indeed the narrator suggests when he intervenes to note that "speech was as inexpressive as silence" (366). Having put aside blame, Angel can only gaze at this wife, and the narrator tells us that Angel "had a vague consciousness of one thing, though it was not clear to him till later; that his original Tess had spiritually ceased to recognize the body before him as hers—allowing it to drift, like a corpse upon the current, in a direction disassociated from its living will" (366). Students could be asked here to think back to *Oliver Twist* and recall the moments when Dickens makes Oliver an object dragged from place to place. The language in *Tess* is echoed in Hardy's comment in the interview cited above, and it is clear that at this point in the novel Hardy means to disconnect her body from her will. She still has a "living will," but it has nothing to do with what her body does. This dissociation makes the murder all the more challenging to assess.

From here students might be asked to tell how Hardy describes the murder. They might notice, for instance, that we see Tess confront Alec from the point of view of the landlady, Mrs. Brooks, who is spying on them through the keyhole of their door. We have no more access to the scene than Mrs. Brooks does, no access to Tess's mind during the murder; we have just her description of it to Angel after the fact. We hear Tess's voice, though mostly not sentences, only "fragments" and a "murmur" (368). As Tess leaves the boardinghouse, Mrs. Brooks sees "the form of Tess" (369), and when Angel first sees Tess coming toward him on the road, she is again a form. Her own description of the deed—"I have done it—I don't know how" (372)—underlines the dissociation of the act from specific knowledge of it.

Instructors can use the dissociations in *Tess* to demonstrate Hardy's challenge to Eliot's idea of personality, an idea that offers character as a "process and an unfolding" (*Middlemarch* 141). They might also link this disconnection of Tess's body from her will to the ways Hardy represents Tess's discontinuities elsewhere (Tess is famously "the same, but not the same" after the birth of Sorrow [95]). With these ideas in mind, students might write about how Hardy's resistance to earlier conceptions of character also questions the foundations of our assumptions about criminal responsibility. After Tess declares that she has killed Alec, Angel thinks to himself, "It was very terrible, if true: if a temporary hallucination, sad. But anyhow here was this deserted wife of his" (373). If Angel is pushing aside the question of her guilt, are we invited to do the same? Angel makes the answer to his question beside the point. Does Hardy prepare readers to accept this conclusion by showing that the assumptions about agency that they hold dear don't apply to Tess? Or does Hardy ask us to understand that Angel is shirking his responsibility to judge Tess because of the guilt he himself feels? Students could write an essay that considers these questions and explores more fully the ambiguities in Hardy's representation of the stabbing.

Taking up questions of criminal responsibility in these Victorian novels gives students a very specific way into thinking about elements, both formal and thematic, central to the texts. When students register the tensions between different approaches to criminal responsibility, they can more readily identify other rich complexities at work in these richly complex novels.

Notes

1. I take up these questions more fully in my *Crime in Mind*.

2. Different nineteenth-century cases used different language to define accessory liability. The charge was notoriously hard to pin down.

3. Students interested in this problem might read John Sutherland's recent treatment of it in "Why Is Fagin Hanged and Why Isn't Pip Prosecuted?" in his *Can Jane Eyre Be Happy?* The essay is short, accessible, and provocative.

4. If students want to pursue this problem in actual Victorian cases, an instructor might direct them to two that take up accessory liability: *Rex v. Murphy* (1833) and *R. v. Coney, Gilliam, and Tully* (1883)—the latter can be accessed through the *LexisNexis* database and the former is described in the latter. Though these cases take up the problem of the principle in the secondary degree (another kind of indirect liability), they are really getting to the heart of difficult issues raised by accessory liability. Students might write an essay in which they use *R. v. Coney* to analyze how Dickens represents Fagin's responsibility for Nancy's murder. Since the judges' opinions in *Coney* reveal how much accessory liability depends on assumptions about who the accused is, this discussion might readily open up into a larger exploration of Dickensian anti-Semitism.

5. The interview as a whole ("A Chat with the Author of *Tess*") is worth reading. Hardy's ambiguous tone as he discusses Tess's responsibility suggests that he recognizes and both satisfies and undermines his readers' expectations with respect to responsibility.

Ayelet Ben-Yishai

Teaching Legal Realism:
A Senior Seminar on
the Realist Novel and the Law

In recent years, much of the innovative work in the field of law and literature has been focused on the Victorian novel. Remarkably, and not coincidentally, interdisciplinary scholarship in the Victorian period is frequently
of the law-and-lit variety. Two main points can explain this interesting
phenomenon. The first and most obvious reason is the law's potential
for narrative exploration. Where better to locate this interdisciplinary endeavor than in the British nineteenth century, which, by virtue of its realist
novels, has long been a privileged site for narrative inquiry? The second
reason, more historically motivated (and more implicit in current scholarship), pertains to the common law's role in preserving and maintaining
the idea of Englishness itself, an idea that was crucial to the political and
social reform characterizing much of the era's concerns. It is thus no wonder that Victorian novelists who were concerned with political and social
change were obsessed with the law, and no wonder that Victorianists, especially those who attach supreme importance to context, are fascinated
by the striking similarities and telling differences between law and literature of the nineteenth century.

My senior seminar inquired into the British realist novel's so-called
obsession with the law. The seminar was taught at the University of Haifa,

to English majors who were all seniors and whose first language was Arabic, Hebrew, Russian, or English. The goal was to examine such legal concepts as status, property, objectivity, contract, precedent, and evidence and their role in structuring novelistic concerns. The course adopted an interdisciplinary and comparative approach, reading novels of three major realist traditions — British, French, and American — alongside legal texts. Our close textual investigation examined the way both legal and fictional texts represent and concomitantly shape the culture in which they are created. Our comparative readings enabled us to discuss what is specifically British and what might be more general about this obsession. Through our readings and discussions, we not only gained knowledge and understanding of important concepts and processes in law and literary realism but also considered the concept of a historically specific legal culture. Finally, we gained experience with both the payoffs and pitfalls of comparative and interdisciplinary work.

After a theoretical and historical introduction, most of the course was devoted to reading five novels and accompanying critical articles and some historical writing. (Reading five novels was considered a heavy assignment by my students, most of whom were not native English speakers.) Each novel brought up specific themes and legal issues; each ultimately had its own conception of the relation between law and literature, which allowed us to elicit a particular engagement between narrative form and its social, political, and cultural context.

The Novels

My selection of novels was influenced by both their thematic and their formal characteristics. I first considered the extent to which the law figured in the construction of the plot and how central it was to the novel. I suggest choosing novels that vary in the roles played by the law. Novels that have famous and important trial scenes or that have lawyers as protagonists or antagonists are of course staple offerings of such courses, as are novels that involve questions of justice or consider major moral and ethical dilemmas.[1] Equally important are novels that raise questions of law in its wider sense — that is, the relation between might and right, between class and status. Also important are questions of authority and authorship, of the regulation of gender and sexuality and of commerce and contract. In fact, a large part of class discussion is geared toward pointing out the legal culture of the novel rather than the specific legal practices represented in it. In this seminar, we read in a legal light themes hitherto not connected with law and read patently legal moments as cultural phenomena. For example, we referred repeatedly to the ways in which the novels exhibited an English and British identity that was created and reinforced by the common law—how common-law doctrine, rhetoric, and practices all worked to create a sense of history since "time immemorial," as Edward Coke would have it (qtd. in Pocock, *Ancient Constitution* 35). The sense of Englishness fostered by the common law through precedent, obligation, and propriety is thus shared even by those who have no experience of legal practice, as by novels that have only an oblique engagement with the law.

The course was as much about the realist novel as it was about the law. It related formal aspects of the novel to developments in the legal culture of the period. I thus suggest choosing novels that are formally diverse. I chose Walter Scott's mélange of realism and romance (*Guy Mannering*), Honoré de Balzac's and George Eliot's high realism (*Père Goriot* and *The Mill on the Floss*), William Dean Howells's American realism (*The Rise of Silas Lapham*), and Wilkie Collins's sensationalism (*The Woman in White*).

Critical Articles

Critical articles assigned in tandem with the novels brought up, explicitly or implicitly, questions concerning a novel's participation in its legal culture. These articles provide not only insights into the novels but also examples of interdisciplinary work that the students may use as models. In addition to discussing the critics' insights into the novels, we thus paid attention to their methodology. I assigned readings from seminal works on the history of literary realism (Watt) and its form (Levine), British legal history (Baker), as well as sections from Henry Maine's *Ancient Law*, all of which gave the students knowledge of canonical critical texts that have become touchstones of the two disciplines. In order to raise the question of interdisciplinarity, I assigned Julie Stone Peters's article "Law, Literature, and the Vanishing Real: On the Future of an Interdisciplinary Illusion."[2]

Legal Texts

My original intention was to teach the legal context through readings in British (and American and French, when appropriate) legal history and through primary sources consisting of legal documents (law reports, contracts, treatises.) This plan was almost immediately discarded. The students' nonexistent background in the law in general and in the common law in particular made the reading of legal documents an exercise in futility. I realized that it was too much to expect them to read primary sources in law as well as in literature; the long and complex novels and articles that they read were more than enough to challenge them. This of course is a compromise. Ideally students should have a firsthand experience reading legal documents. Training them to do this would have taken time and effort at the expense of the novels and articles I wanted to teach. I thus provided, through lectures, the legal context for the debates that came up in class, explaining contract theory, the history of the jury trial, the formal structure of a law report, the promulgation of the statute, and so on. The only disciplinarily legal texts the students read were selections from Baker and from Maine.

We opened the course by asking its most obvious question: Why study law and literature? Peters's article helped us contextualize our course in current academic discourse and consider the payoffs and pitfalls of interdisciplinary work more generally. What was at stake for each discipline at each stage? Peters argues that each discipline imagines the other as having a better purchase on the real. She shows how the union of law and literature was powerful but problematic in that it reinforced a limited and limiting view of each discipline, thus resurrecting and reinforcing disciplinary boundaries (449). Interestingly, these views were shared by my students, who had trouble shaking their conviction that law was dry and narrow but belonging more to the real world and therefore important, while fiction allowed for a more comprehensive representation of emotions and subjectivity and was therefore more humane, if less real and significant to the world.

Peters proposes an examination of the real, of how some discourses and concepts have become more real than others (451). But if we want to understand how the real became real, what better place to look than in the realist novel? I thus ended the discussion of Peters's article by introducing the raison d'être of this course: historicizing and contextualizing many of the questions that have been asked by the law and literature movement in recent years. My contention is that the perceived impasse of the movement stems from a tendency in earlier scholarship to regard both disciplines in terms of abstract universals ("law is coercive," "literature allows for emotional complexity") rather than specific practices, such as the shift from eyewitness testimony to circumstantial evidence and its implications for narrative forms (Welsh, "Stories"). Some of the most interesting recent works in the field (largely unmentioned in Peters's article) are analyses of the intersection of law and literature at specific historical and cultural junctures (in our context, analyses by Dolin; Grossman; Schmidgen; Schramm; Tucker; Welsh, "Stories"). Both law and literature consist of diverse practices and deserve to be studied as such.[3]

The concept of a historically specific legal culture has been gaining currency in recent scholarship in the study of law and society. I believe it can prove productive for the law and literature movement. The premise of my course is that law and literature were two important ways in which literate people of the nineteenth century made sense of their lives and changing national culture. Understanding how these discourses participated in the meaning-making venture means understanding more about Victorian culture.

History of the Common Law

I began the course with an introduction to the history of the common law's basic tenets, while relating them to general concerns in British history—the spread of the common law, colonialism, class, industrialization, commerce. I differentiated among legal theory, doctrine, and practice and showed how they have depended on one another. I also showed their historical contingency.

Five key principles of the common law in this introduction were that it is nonstatutory, that it is based on precedent, that judges and judgments are central to its determination, that it is casuistic (case-based), and that the process of its deliberation is adversarial. I also stressed that each of these components, whether doctrinal or practical, has a history of its own and that the relation among these components and their importance in the legal system and in society as a whole were constantly shifting.

A good way to explain the principles of the common law is to contrast them to and differentiate them from other systems or practices.[4] In my introduction, I

> contrasted the British common law to Continental civil law. Civil law is code-based and precedential; it is also not adversarial but inquisitorial.
> contrasted case-based and code-based lawmaking. The first is central to the common law, but I explained that no modern legal system is purely one or the other and that all systems tend toward a mix of the two.

differentiated between common-law courts (based on general legal
rights) and Chancery or equity courts (based on individual judicial
discretion). I elaborated on the history of equity and its relation
with the common law until the abolition of Chancery in 1875 and
the transferral of equity to the realm of the common law.

distinguised, in the common-law system, between criminal and civil
law and, in civil law, between torts and contracts.

I ended my introduction by describing briefly some of the key issues
and conflicts in Victorian legal culture. I stressed the idea (and ideology)
of reform at the center of this culture, a reform that not only is electoral
and legislative but also encompasses property rights, women's issues, and
the court system.

Sir Walter Scott's *Guy Mannering*

We examined the novel along two parallel axes, the one formal (romance
to realism), the other legal and thematic (status to contract). Using Northrop Frye's definition of *romance* and Ian Watt's account of formal realism, we traced the ways both these genres play out in the novel, trying to
locate *Guy Mannering* on what has often been regarded as a trajectory
from romance to realism. We moved on to chapter 5 of Maine's work
of legal history and anthropology, *Ancient Law.* Maine argues that law
and society developed from traditional societies in which individuals were
bound by status, to modern ones, in which individuals are viewed as autonomous, free to make contracts, and thus bound by their own actions and
associations. We traced this development from status to contract in *Guy
Mannering*, especially as it is manifested in the characters and actions of
Guy Mannering and Harry Bertram. Our close historical readings showed
that both axes of development were predicated on the ascendance and
abeyance of empirical thought, rationalism, industrialism, and urbanization.

Both the realist novel and nineteenth-century jurisprudence grappled
with a similar concern: whether to judge according to who one is or according to what one does. With this idea, we returned to the romance/
realism question and noted Ian Duncan's argument that the natural order
of representation in *Guy Mannering* is articulated on a plot that is pro-
digiously unnatural—that is, artificial, contrived. We thus replaced the
simple trajectory from romance to realism with a nuanced and dialectical

relation between them. We also forsook the binary opposition between status and contract set up by Maine. Close readings of the novel helped us recognize the inextricability of status from contract in the novel. We thus ended up tracing a double dialectic: that between status and contract and that between romance and realism, both of which are expressed through the legal thematics of the novel and its form.

Honoré de Balzac's *Père Goriot*

Balzac's novel, read in English translation, prompted discussions of authority, surveillance, authorial power, and the importance of detail. Nineteenth-century France is characterized by an unprecedented number of changes in political regimes and forms of government. Retaining and maintaining a sense of stability in this context was the arduous task facing the French legal system.[5] Questions of authority, stability, and authenticity have also been pivotal in critical writing on the French realist novel. The literary critic Christopher Prendergast argues that by means of authoritative narration Balzac tries to reestablish order in a world devoid of it. The students were interested in the various systems of rules and laws presented in the novel: societies' law, codes of honor, the criminal code, and the criminals' code, among others. I pointed out that another system of rules, the conventions of realist representation, also governed the novel and participated in its legal culture. French civil law is characterized by a unidirectional move: the law is applied to a particular case, but its outcome has no impact on the law itself. This attribute is associated with egalitarianism and French republicanism: the law is objective and the same for all. However, it also creates an effect of arbitrariness, rigidity, and control. Significantly, these attributes have been linked to the French realist novel, especially to its so-called omniscient narration.

George Eliot's *The Mill on the Floss*

The common law has its own way of ensuring stability and control—precedent. Our discussion of *The Mill on the Floss* opened with a close reading of a prominent legal metaphor in the novel: passing judgment. Noting how the characters needed a precedent to be able to make sense of a particular situation, even to recognize it as a situation requiring a judgment or response, we turned to a discussion of the doctrine of legal precedent and its shifting importance in the history of the common law. Legal precedent not only provides the details of specific cases that can be compared with the ones at hand; it also espouses a way of thinking and reasoning, one that has had an immense influence on English culture and the cultivation of Englishness.

Precedential reasoning, like cultural forms, brings the past seamlessly into the present. In the chapter "St. Oggs Passes Judgement," the gossips of the town can imagine only two possible stories: a successful love story in the form of a potboiler romance and a melodrama, the story of the fallen woman (Loesberg). Generic expectations (literary precedents) determine the characters' ability to read the situation and pass judgment on Maggie. The narrative in this chapter presents only two generic precedents (romance and melodrama), but the *Mill on the Floss* as a novel presents yet another: literary realism. Guided by the conventions of realism, the readers of the novel know better than the gossips of St. Oggs; they know to trust the information given them by the narrator. Many of the students now got the point of the course; although precedent and precedential reasoning are legal concepts and practices, they have valence in the larger culture. Not only the Victorian legal system but also the residents of St. Oggs and the readers of the novel were concerned about the preservation of stability and continuity in the face of rapid change.

The second part of our discussion was based on Melissa Ganz's article "Binding the Will," in which Ganz explores Eliot's interest in contract as a structure for social relations. I elaborated on nineteenth-century developments in contract doctrine. Since a contract is an enforceable promise or obligation, changes in contract law reveal the obligations society deems important at a given point in time, what values it wants to uphold and what it wants to regulate publicly. Though most obligations in *The Mill on the Floss* are not contracts, we recognized, following Ganz's arguments, that Eliot is concerned with the same social and epistemological questions faced by the jurists who were framing the debates on contract theory.

William Dean Howells's *The Rise of Silas Lapham*

Contract theory provided a useful segue into Howells's *The Rise of Silas Lapham*. United States and British contract law doctrine in the nineteenth century was similar but not identical. Despite the similarities, Howells's novel reveals a legal culture of contract that is very different from Eliot's.

In Eliot, contract is a way of thinking about obligation; contract in Howells stands in for responsibility, a weaker and more poorly defined form of accountability for one's actions. Many of the differences reflect the distinction between contract in a society on the verge of capitalism and one in its throes (B. Thomas, "*Rise*"). Our comparison also raised questions of private and public realms and consequently questions of gender. In Eliot, almost all business is family business; the private and public are inextricable. In Howells, however, an economic model of contract seeps into the private realm. Marriage is presented as a contract first and foremost, even as the epitome of all contracts. The laws governing the public sphere—"economies" in the parlance of the novel—are used to regulate interpersonal and emotional relationships, as in Mr. Sewell's "economy of pain" (241).

The move from a discussion of contract law and theory in *The Mill on the Floss* to that in *Silas Lapham* was a turning point in the course. Even those students who had earlier been unsure or wary of the idea of a legal culture and its relevance to literary study began to see how it all came together. They understood that even though both novels were dealing with contract, doing so in a different social-political context changed the nature of the questions being asked—for example, about familial and community obligations in Eliot, about the limitations of economic models of responsibility and liability in Howells.

Wilkie Collins's *The Woman in White*

Collins's novel is an obvious example of the influence of a legal form on literature. *The Woman in White* is a compilation of narratives that individually are witness (subjective) accounts but together form what Alexander Welsh has called "strong representations," that is, "carefully managed narratives of circumstantial evidence" encompassing more than can ever be experienced at first hand (*Strong Representations* ix). But the representation is too strong. The narrative is pat, almost glib; everything fits too well. Readers of *The Woman in White* are ostensibly put in the place of the judge, but the judging, as D. A. Miller argues, has already been done for them.[6]

Moreover, the legal result at the end of the novel is the one desired by its compiler and main narrator, Walter Hartright. Why does he then feel the need to write a competing legal narrative, as he declares at the outset? Having exposed Sir Percival as illegitimate and Count Fosco as a spy and traitor and having restored his wife's legitimate identity and place, Hartright needs to legitimize his undeserved new position, that of the former drawing master and now father of the Heir of Limmeridge. This position, unthinkable at the outset of the story in the eyes of all concerned, becomes a reality at its end, threatening to undermine Hartright's enterprise.

The narrative of *The Woman in White* thus reveals a convoluted relation between law and legitimacy, a mélange of two epistemologies: first is an empirical mode, which is invested in the ability of facts to determine a case and verify a truth; second is the communal mode of truth making that values social status and a community's approbation.

Returning to the question of status and contract first raised by *Guy Mannering*, we were able to reconsider the historical and cultural intersections of law and literature in each of these five novels. We were also able to reconsider the way the form of these realist novels used legal thematics and structures to convey and construct a sense of the real.

The students' papers combined research into their chosen novel's historical and legal background with close formal readings of its text.[7] Even the most basic papers on the legal themes or figures in the text had that combination. For example, several students noted the repeated and diverse acts of judging in Eliot's novel: one took the thematic tension between nature and society in *The Mill on the Floss* as a comment on Victorian debates between natural and positive law; another analyzed Tom's judgmental role in terms of Eliot's philosophical preoccupation with determinism. One student argued that *Pere Goriot*'s Rastignac, although he leaves law school for Parisian society, actually does function as a lawyer; the novel is in fact a collection of evidence he gathers for the purpose of indicting a corrupt French society and a powerless legal system. Transposing our class discussions of contract law in the British and American contexts to that of Restoration France, and connecting it to our theoretical discussions of realism, the student concluded that even though *Père Goriot* is filled with broken promises and unmet obligations, these help the novel keep it generic promise to its readers: a truthful representation of reality. Another paper showed not only how Scott uses law as a marker of Western logic and individualism against an orientalist supernatural but also how that binary opposition is deconstructed through *Guy Mannering*'s deployment of character.

At the end of the course, the students admitted that they had initially thought the relation between law and literature was forced, a contrived or trendy new angle on literature. They agreed that this relation had opened new ways not only of regarding literature but also of thinking about the engagement of literature in the cultural, social, and political world in which it is written and read.

Notes

1. For a long list of possible novels (many of them now sadly out of print), see Wigmore, "List of Legal Novels" and "List of One Hundred Legal Novels."

2. The Peters essay in this volume is an updated version of her 2005 *PMLA* essay. An additional bibliography of Victorian law and literature criticism, including texts by Kieran Dolin, Jonathan Grossman, Jan-Melissa Schramm, Irene Tucker, and Alexander Welsh ("Stories"), was put on reserve for the course. I made sure to mention these texts and integrate their approaches and arguments in our class discussion, in part so that the students could make use of them in their research for the seminar paper.

3. Of course, any analysis requires abstracting specific practices into a general legal culture. The point is to locate a historically contingent generalization rather than a universal abstraction.

4. This is also a good moment to discuss again with the students the usefulness of comparative analysis.

5. For additional background material on French civil law and postrevolutionary legal culture, see D. Kelley; Hilaire; Merryman; Youngs; Halperin.

6. Miller shows how this sensational novel disciplines readers to value intuition over empirical proof. Instead of weighing the evidence, as readers are led to believe they are doing, they assent to what has already been decided for them.

7. Students were required to create an annotated bibliography to document their research in preparation for the final paper. This bibliography needed to include an article about the novel or writer on which or whom they had chosen to focus, an article about a formal or thematic issue they found remarkable, an article that deals with the historical or legal contexts or concepts in which they were interested. After citing the article properly, students had to summarize its main points. In a second paragraph, they had to explain how the article was or was not relevant to their work or how they expected to use it in their paper.

Caleb Smith

American Undead:
Teaching the Cultural Life
of Civil Death

But, fated to a living tomb,
For years on years in woe to brood
Upon the past, the captive's doom
Is galling chains and solitude.

> —Harry Hawser, Eastern State Penitentiary,
> Philadelphia, 1841

Anyone who teaches antebellum American literature knows that it is haunted by shades, ghosts, and the living dead. For those who wish, as I do, to teach these works of the imagination in relation to history, such monsters can cause trouble. The gothic creatures of Edgar Allan Poe and the talking corpses of Emily Dickinson, for example, often seem to be so many nightmarish fantasies, flights from the real world of power, money, and law. Indeed, many of our students come to us with learned prejudices about the gothic, even about Romanticism in general, as a kind of irrational escapism from the serious business of enlightened modernity. Recently, thanks especially to Toni Morrison's influential *Playing in the Dark*, that old account of the antebellum imagination has begun to lose its hold, and we regularly connect the gothic to the history of slavery—the dark reality

147

of torture and inhumanity, social death and zombie life in the circum-Atlantic world. In this essay I present a course unit that invites students to historicize the literary undead in relation to another kind of legal and car-ceral mortification, the civil death of the convict in the penitentiary. Here, some study of law and criminal justice encourages us to think of literary ghosts as apparitions of a deeply important, but almost forgotten, part of the antebellum world.

Most of my undergraduates are surprised to learn that the prison sys-tem has a moment of origin at all, that there was a time before imprison-ment became the standard sentence for almost every serious crime. They seem to share Nathaniel Hawthorne's sense that "[t]he founders of a new colony, whatever Utopia of human virtue and happiness they might origi-nally project," must eventually build a prison (45). It is a nice defamil-iarizing gesture, then, to show students how some great figures of the American Revolution—Thomas Jefferson, Benjamin Franklin, Benjamin Rush—were also architects of another kind of social experiment, the peni-tentiary. Suddenly, it seems necessary to reconsider the complex relation between enlightened civil society and the darkness of the prison interior. Preparing the way for this conversation, we begin with Alexis de Tocque-ville's visit to America in the early 1830s.

Tocqueville received a commission from the French government to travel with another young aristocrat, Gustave de Beaumont, for the pur-pose of studying the famous model penitentiaries of Pennsylvania and New York. The two ambassadors entered the imposing gates, looked into the solitary confinement cells, and interviewed inmates and wardens. Their thoughts are recorded in their *Report on the Penitentiary System in the United States, and Its Application in France* (Beaumont and Tocqueville; the nineteenth-century translation by the German American reformer Francis Lieber is in print). Beaumont and Tocqueville were impressed by the re-formed system of punishment, which substituted incarceration for hang-ing and mutilation, promising to turn criminals into obedient subjects:

> [W]hen, in his solitary cell, in the midst of the pains of a stinging con-science, and the agitations of his soul, [the prisoner] has fallen into a dejection of mind, and has sought in labor a relief from his griefs; from that moment he is tamed, and forever submissive. . . . (72)

Modern, enlightened discipline would aim not at the offending body but at the redeemable soul.

As they traveled, Beaumont and Tocqueville were observing more than just prisons. Tocqueville in particular was making the notes that would eventually become his sweeping account of Jacksonian politics and culture, *Democracy in America*. In Tocqueville's larger work, incarceration and criminal law were of relatively minor importance—but, as some recent critics have observed, his theory of democracy seems haunted, at times, by the penitentiary (Dumm 134). A few choice excerpts from *Democracy in America* can open the conversation about prisons and the world at large. Describing the difference between the sovereign use of force in the old regime and the "tyranny of the majority" in America, for instance, Tocqueville writes:

> Princes made violence a physical thing, but our contemporary demo-
> cratic republics have turned it into something as intellectual as the hu-
> man will it is intended to constrain. Under the absolute government of
> a single man, despotism, to reach the soul, clumsily struck at the body,
> and the soul, escaping from such blows, rose gloriously above it; but in
> democratic republics that is not at all how tyranny behaves; it leaves the
> body alone and goes straight for the soul. The master no longer says:
> "Think like me or you die." He does say: "You are free not to think as
> I do; you can keep your life and property and all; but from this day you
> are a stranger among us. . . . You will remain among men, but you will
> lose your rights to count as one. When you approach your fellows, they
> will shun you as an impure being. . . . Go in peace. I have given you
> your life, but it is a life worse than death." (255–56)

The mutilated body seemed, to Tocqueville, to be disappearing from the historical scene; in its place arose an "impure being," a ghostly exile condemned to "a life worse than death."

Tocqueville's "impure being" is an intriguing metaphor for the estranged self in the modern world, but some consideration of the institutions where Tocqueville had been spending his time suggests that it was more than a metaphor. Here we turn to a second set of readings, introducing the legal fiction of civil death. With origins in ancient penal codes and medieval monastic rituals, civil death has a long, curious history. To give students a sense of what the term means in antebellum America, two sources are useful: the open letters on prison policy exchanged by Stephen Allen and William Roscoe (Allen; Roscoe) and relevant sections of John Bouvier's monumental *Institutes of American Law* (1851). (All are available online.) Allen, an inspector at New York's Auburn Prison, saw the penitentiary as a substitute for capital punishment, imposing a virtual death:

> [W]hat are the natural and political rights of a criminal convicted of
> rape, highway robbery, burglary, sodomy, maiming, forging public

securities, &c. the punishment of which is death by the laws of England; and in this state, imprisonment for life? Are they not *dead in law*, and consequently without rights, natural or political?
(4; emphasis added)

Thus at least one of the great model penitentiaries, according to those who oversaw its operations, was a scene of living death where convicts were excommunicated from the body politic and divested of legal rights. Elam Lynds, the legendary warden of Auburn and Sing Sing interviewed by Beaumont and Tocqueville, called his inmates "coarse beings, who have had no education, and who perceive with difficulty ideas, and often even sensations" (164). Such figures, Lynds suggested, were literally dulled to the world; they could be controlled only by the whip and an atmosphere of terror.

Bouvier's text, not as immediately involved in the problem of prison discipline, nonetheless defines the rights of the citizen against the mere "natural life" of the convict condemned to civil death: "The enjoyment of civil rights is attached to the quality of citizen of the United States. This quality is subject to be lost by abdication or renunciation of the rights of citizen, or by civil death" (94). Bouvier goes on to define the term: "Civil death is the state of a person who, though possessing natural life, has lost all his civil rights by a judicial condemnation, and is, as to them, considered dead" (95). Here, students may begin to reflect on the complex relation between the discourse of rights and the institutions of law. To what extent are human rights an effect, rather than a foundation, of modern codes of citizenship?

Once students have a grasp of civil death as a legal fiction with real consequences—exposing convicts to discretionary violence and excluding them from the circle of the fully human—we move to narratives that describe the prison as a kind of tomb. Beaumont and Tocqueville's *Report*, despite its measured approval of the corrective designs of the penitentiary, also refers to it as a scene where inmates are "dead to the world" (84). The figure of speech recurs throughout the many pamphlets and legislative documents of the prison reform movement. Perhaps the richest source is Charles Dickens's account, in *American Notes*, of his visit to Eastern State Penitentiary in 1841. His narrative is full of gothic horror and sentimental tears. Dickens describes the prisoner's initiation to solitary confinement as a kind of ritualized death:

Over the head and face of every prisoner who comes into this melancholy house a black hood is drawn; and in this dark shroud, an emblem of the curtain dropped between him and the living world, he is led to the cell from which he never again comes forth until his whole term of imprisonment has expired. He never hears of wife or children; home or friends; the life or death of any single creature. He sees the prison officers, but, with that exception, he never looks upon a human countenance, or hears a human voice. He is a man buried alive; to be dug out in the slow round of years; and in the meantime dead to everything but torturing anxieties and horrible despair. ("Philadelphia" 91)

The prison seems to enact, almost theatrically, the legal fiction of civil death. (For graduate students and advanced undergraduates, instructors might pair Dickens with Erving Goffman's account, in *Asylums*, of "mortification" in total institutions.) Dickens goes on to describe a series of inmates, each with a touch of morbidity. One is a "helpless, crushed, and broken man"; another "look[s] as wan and unearthly as if he had been summoned from the grave"; another has built a flowerbed that "look[s], bye-the-bye, like a grave" (93, 94, 95). Dickens's text mediates between the legal and the literary; it prepares students to see how the gothic dungeons and tombs of antebellum literature addressed some major legal and institutional problems of the time.

The antebellum novel most readily associated with the question of punishment is, of course, Hawthorne's *The Scarlet Letter*. Often, students have encountered Hawthorne in high school or in first-year surveys; they remember a descendant of Puritans whose fiction critiqued the rigidity of colonial American moral life. Having learned something about nineteenth-century law and prison reform, however, they can begin to understand how *The Scarlet Letter* interrogates not only a deep American past but also the disciplinary transformations of Hawthorne's own moment. They might see, for instance, the shift from public to private punishment—from spectacle to the self-discipline of the penitentiary—mapped onto the differences between Hester Prynne's humiliation at the scaffold and Arthur Dimmesdale's secret misery. Hester achieves a "lurid triumph" over those who have attempted to mark her body with a symbol of their authority, but Dimmesdale, suffering in solitude, is more profoundly and thoroughly destroyed. Supervised by the modern man of science, Roger Chillingworth, and made "to die daily a living death" (149), he wastes away, becoming a "ghost" (132). In his case, "power," in Tocqueville's terms, "goes straight for the soul." One way to teach *The Scarlet Letter*, then, is as a novel about how a modernizing American body politic discovers the ineffectiveness of public punishment and, by contrast, the power of a penitential regime of solitude and living death. Such a reading works especially well when the novel is brought into conversation with Rush's famous essay on public punishments (*Essays* 79–94).

Once we have detached Hawthorne's great novel of punishment from his family history and antiquarian interests, we begin to see how a vision of a carceral living death looms in the literary imagination of his contemporaries, too. Take, for instance, the haunted mind of Poe. In "The Cask of Amontillado," a narrator, wishing to "punish with impunity," walls his rival up inside a catacomb, among abandoned bones. In "The Pit and the Pendulum," a prisoner is "unstrung" by his confinement, "becom[ing] in every respect a fitting subject for the species of torture which awaited [him]" (*Complete Tales* 250). "The Premature Burial" and "The Fall of the House of Usher" also concern the nightmare of a living entombment. Joan Dayan has suggested that the architecture of Poe's dungeons may have been inspired by the Philadelphia prison; we can understand, as well, how his animate corpses embody the legal black magic of civil death.

If Poe's stories are terrified of solitude, Dickinsons's poems provide a more ambivalent case. Many students are familiar with Dickinson's legend—the nun of Amherst who withdrew from the public world, discovering in seclusion her unique poetic voice. Again, careful teaching can help dispel the myth, reconnecting Dickinson to her world. I offer students a selection of texts concerned with solitude, but also with law (the Dickinson household was full of lawyers) and with prisons. Poem 412, "I read my sentence—steadily—," seems to be a meditation on the composition and revision of poetry, but it turns into something else when the speaker reads "God have mercy . . . ," the conventional last lines of a death sentence. Elsewhere, Dickinson seems at once drawn to and repulsed by the condition of solitary confinement; she writes that "A Prison gets to be a friend" (652) but also that "Doom is the House without the Door" (475). Finally, the curious poems in which the speaker is already dead—where "The Feet, mechanical, go round" and "The Nerves sit ceremonious, like Tombs" (341)—can be understood as reflections on the estrangement that Tocqueville calls "a life worse than death."

Thus our study of the cultural life of civil death moves across several spheres—law, journalism, and works of the literary imagination—and brings them into a conversation about the deathlike status of persons divested of rights and excluded from the human community. In my experience, this interdisciplinary constellation of documents provokes rich, sophisticated undergraduate papers. Many students are drawn to the idea of subversion, arguing that literary works undermine the social order imposed by the law. They look, for instance, to the craftiness of Poe's narrators or the fine artistry of Dickinson's poems for evidence that some subtle human intelligence has endured legal and carceral mortification. Others take a more skeptical view, arguing that the gothic is a kind of propaganda reinforcing legal and journalistic ideas about criminals' inhumanity. Perhaps the most illuminating papers—and, to the teacher, the most satisfying ones—turn the interrogation around, showing not only how literary works engage the law but also how legal tropes such as civil death have a kind of literary character. They begin to see the law the way James Boyd White saw it, decades ago, as a "system of meaning" ("Making Sense"). We have done more than place literary works in context; we have seen how law and literature can illuminate each other and, beneath artificial disciplinary boundaries, how the tropes of a kind of literary imagination help constitute history itself.

Beyond the walls of the penitentiary, we can connect the cultural life of civil death to other images, other contexts. In a sophomore seminar on antebellum literature, Savages, Witches, Prisoners, and Slaves, I invited students to consider the ghostly prisoner in relation to what Orlando Patterson famously called the slave's "social death." Accounts of the mortification of slaves in narratives by Frederick Douglass (*Narrative*) and Harriet Jacobs are richly resonant with literary depictions of the prison interior. Antebellum writing also includes some fantastic examples of subversion, such as Harriet Beecher Stowe's Cassy, the slave who terrorizes her master by pretending to be a ghost. In many ways, the antebellum penitentiary, with its rehabilitation programs and its attention to the soul, defined itself against the brutal violence of the plantation; however, focusing on civil death and dehumanization exposes some surprising connections and may help explain why, after the Civil War, prisons became such powerful instruments for the renewed oppression of African Americans.

Finally, some teachers may wish to reflect on the afterlife of civil death today. If we accept conventional accounts of the penitentiary developed by Michel Foucault (*Discipline*), David Rothman (*Discovery* and "Perfecting"), and others, the institution seems to be obsolete. Its reformed system of penitence and correction seems to have devolved into the sprawling network of war prisons, warehouses, private detention centers, and other institutions that critics call the "prison-industrial complex" (Schlosser). However, if we shift our focus away from surveillance and rehabilitation, toward the violent divestments of civil death and mortification, we begin to see more continuity than rupture. Without warping the past to fit the political imperatives of the present, we might begin to consider, in con-versation with our students, what happens when the law removes certain offenders from the living circle of rights-bearing humanity. What might the ghosts of nineteenth-century prisons teach us about the illegal alien, the enemy combatant, and other figures emerging to haunt the American legal and imaginative landscape now?

Mary Flowers Braswell

Teaching Legal Fiction:
Law and *The Canterbury Tales*

Every statute or ordinance creates a fictive world.

—L. H. Larue

Students knowledgeable of crime scene investigation techniques, gleaned from movies, board games, and television, fill the desks of my Chaucer classes. Acquainted with acoustic reflectometry probes, chronographs, and alternative light sources, they understand the necessity of careful scrutiny, of examining witnesses, processing all the evidence, preserving the chain of command, and maintaining objectivity. Yet these same students balk at the task of close reading a literary text, at searching for hidden meanings and ferreting out unexplored allusions. Despite repeated instruction and varied handouts from me, they remain unaware of what they should look for and write. Thus I use two, not disparate but similar, disciplines—literature and law—to build each other. Each requires a fixed regard for evidence, a multidisciplinary approach, and meticulous observation. Each calls for inductive and deductive reasoning and for an application of such reasoning to the facts. Crime scenes contain multiple voices, some living, some dead, some false, some true. Nothing can be overlooked; nothing can be disturbed (Byrd 1–2; Christianson 34–55). Geoffrey Chaucer's *Canterbury*

Tales, like the works of Charles Dickens, profits from a crime scene analysis and, because both men spent so much time in the courts and because their most complex characters are crooks, from an examination of contemporary law (Braswell 13–20). Law can help us understand where Chaucer acquired the framework for his most famous work and why his characters, unlike those of other contemporary poets, contain such breadth and depth.

The students in this Chaucer class are seniors and graduate students at an urban university, and they have a wide range of abilities. They are largely English or history majors, and some will go on to attend law school. They come to the course with little knowledge of the Middle Ages but with much knowledge of popular culture. Although this unit provides an interpretation of aspects of Chaucer's poetry, its main purpose is to teach students to apply skills they have already mastered—without pain, I might add—to difficult academic texts. When studied in the context of literature, Chaucer's works echo Dante, Jean de Meun, and Ovid, but when seen against a background of medieval law, they reflect the customals, letter books, medieval manor courts, and plea and memoranda rolls. Many of his stories—The Shipman's Tale, The Franklin's Tale, The Miller's Tale, and the framework to *The Canterbury Tales*, for example—reveal the generic qualities in a variety of laws, bills, complaints, quitclaims, and writs (Braswell 17–20). Chaucer's plotlines often mirror issues current in medieval courts. His trademark ambiguity echoes the guilty-innocent atmosphere of the courtroom, where facts can be made to seem first one thing and then another, as though one were saying, "Here is a text; in how many ways can it have meaning" (Gopen 334). With literature as with the law, the answer often depends on the nature of the evidence one has and on the talents of the individual best able to argue it.

There is no question that Chaucer knew the law. For centuries he was reputed to have been a lawyer. One 1396 record even refers to him inexplicably as an "attorney" aiding Gregory Ballard in the legal possession of a manor (*Chaucer Life-Records* 510). The poet was believed to have studied at the Inns of Court, though we have no evidence that he in fact did. Still, as justice of the peace, justice *ad Inquirendum*, and member of parliament, he would have tried cases and administered law. He would later fictionalize such laws in *The Canterbury Tales*.

The General Prologue is about law. But because it is about so much more than that (and because this is a literature class) we begin with a rundown of the literary precedents and techniques at Chaucer's disposal. First we review Boccaccio's *Decameron*, commonly believed to be the source for the framework, and then the *Novelle* of Giovanni Sercambi. Students are initially satisfied with superficial similarities: collections of tales by a variety of narrators (*Decameron*) or stories told while traveling along the road (*Novelle*). Chaucer's characters, uniquely drawn from various walks of life, are often modeled on estates satire (lampoons of the social classes) or influenced by individuals the poet might have known. The students are struck by the fact that, even though the journey to Canterbury is made for an ostensibly religious reason, almost all the pilgrims are sinners, unrepentant ones at that. Most seem to violate the rules that govern their professions. Although we are told that the Monk is worthy to have been an abbot (line 165) and that the Shipman was a "good fellow" (395), we cannot take that at face value, especially since the Monk also eschews the required manuscript copying and the Shipman forces his victims to walk the plank. Like the accused and the guilty in a court of law, Chaucer's characters are more ambiguous and complex than they initially seem.

After several weeks of dissecting The General Prologue through literary antecedents, feudal hierarchy, codes of dress, ecclesiastical positions, rules of weights and measures, and battle tactics, I present the class with several singular fourteenth-century texts: *The Court Baron, Leet Jurisdiction in the City of Norwich during the Eighteenth and Nineteenth Centuries,* and the *Fleta*. Students are initially frustrated and puzzled: they have no idea what a "leet" is or a "court baron," and they know nothing about the concept of manor law. I believe that in order for them to understand what Chaucer is truly about, they must expand their horizons and pursue the poet from the viewpoint of a different field.

Both *The Court Baron* and *Leet Jurisdiction*, as well as passages from the *Fleta*, can be found in the publications of the Selden Society, of which the library at the University of Alabama, Birmingham, is fortunate to have a complete run. These volumes, published in 1890, 1891, and 1955 respectively, are in the public domain, and I digitize parts for my students. They contain the original Latin records (I run off a few pages) with the translation on the facing pages. The section from *The Court Baron* runs twenty or so pages; *Leet Jurisdiction* contains twenty-four documents, beginning in the early thirteenth century, so I pick the later fourteenth-century selections I want to use; and I reproduce the first twenty pages of the *Fleta*. These sections are designed to clarify procedure for legal assemblies. They present a group of offenders gathered before a bailiff, who calls on them to tell their "tales," which often stem from their professions or trade. The court ends with a judgment and a feast.

Rather than lecture the class on what they can expect to find in these pages, I charge the students to discover for themselves by exercising critical thinking. I provide them with the following very basic handout, and, because it is easy and quick, I instruct them to do research on *Google* as necessary to answer the questions:

1. Read the document carefully without reading any critical material. Write a paragraph describing its purpose.
2. Read the definition of a leet court in *Wikipedia*. Write a paragraph in your own words.
3. Read carefully pages 244 and 246 of the *Fleta*. Exactly when is the manor court scheduled and why?
4. Look carefully at the beginnings of any of the court documents. The court is conducted by a bailiff or "bailee." What exactly does a bailiff do?
5. In the *Court Baron*, certain individuals are called up before the court. Although their particulars differ, in general, they are foregrounded for one reason. What is that reason?
6. Why would the characters be introduced to the court in terms of their professions?
7. In the Middle Ages each of the offenders before the court would tell a brief "tale" of his or her alleged wrongdoing; these people were then referred to as "narrators." Briefly recount three of the tales they tell. Are these tales related to their professions? Why? Are these tales refuted? By whom and why?
8. Who is writing up the record? Not the bailiff or the tale tellers. Where do you think this person might be located physically? What would have been his charge?
9. This is a course on *The Canterbury Tales*. Why do you think you were given an assignment about leet courts? (Note: the answer to this is not an easy one.)

Students are required to write out complete answers to all the questions before they come back to class and to be prepared to discuss their papers in groups of three.

I am careful to monitor the students and to give them only the time they actually need so they will not simply converse at loose ends. Some groups will immediately focus on "April" when "all things are opening," for the manor court's appointed assemblage (line 246); the "bailiff" (Harry Bailly?) as the judge for the tales and tellers; and the professions—goldsmiths and fishmongers, but also millers, reeves, and cooks—as the raison d' être for the stories to be told. These students will begin speculating on larger issues. Others will be such literal thinkers that they will be stuck on the dissimilarities; sometimes, even hints from me will not help.

The class then turns to the text of The General Prologue. Chaucer's story begins in April, when Harry Bailly convenes an assorted group of pilgrims at the Tabard Inn and proposes a contest for the trip to Becket's shrine. (The real Harry Bailly seems to have been a justice of the peace.) The rules are thus: each pilgrim will narrate two tales of mirth and solace, both going and returning; Bailly himself will determine which is best, and anyone who "be rebel to [his] juggement / Shal paye" for a supper to be held at journey's end (833–34). To keep a record of the process, Chaucer the pilgrim becomes the scribe, or "narrator" (a legal as well as a literary term), swearing to record every utterance exactly as it is stated and revealing an acute awareness of both the spoken and the written word. These lines spoken by the pilgrim, as the students learn later, are freighted with legal nuance: "charge," "untrew [untrue]," "feyne [fain]," and "writ" (lines 733, 735, 736, 739). The pilgrims traveling to Canterbury, like the participants in the leet, are introduced by their professions; it is often the laws they have broken in pursuance of their trades that Chaucer foregrounds, and most of these transgressions are the same as those from the manor court. The miller in both the court records and the *Tales* measures out grain with false weights; both cooks sell "pastees" that have been warmed up twice: "twies hoot and twies coold" (CkT 4348). Chaucer's language and that of the court records are often the same. Students are left with two distinct but parallel texts, one literary, one legal, containing similar plots, characters, and themes.

Before launching into an old-fashioned lecture, I direct the class to Mark Allen's *Chaucer Bibliography Online* (http://uchaucer.utsa.edu), with which they are not familiar. The materials in this database date back to 1975. Reading the titles gives students a chance to see that law is a legitimate subject and to see how many others have broached it. I explain to them that they must take this step before writing their own papers. The search for "law" under "Expert Keyword" turns up more than three hundred entries; for "legal," seventy. The materials are briefly annotated, and I have the students take notes on their findings and discuss those findings in class.

At this point, I instruct the students on Chaucer's probable association with the manor court system. As early as 1941, the historian Margaret

Galway speculated that from 1385 to 1389, when the poet was living in Kent, he was in service to the king and queen and acted as overseer to one of Richard's estates—probably Eltham in Kent or Sheen in Surrey. Chaucer knew this court as justice of the peace: he observed its litigants and read its laws, and he may have witnessed it firsthand. He clearly realized its potential as a literary genre. Underneath the literary characters of *The Canterbury Tales* one finds a judge, a scribe, and squabbling narrators who tell tales to promote their self-interests and debase their peers. The manor court seems to have influenced Chaucer's narrative structure more than did either the *Decameron* or the *Novelle.*

Can we go further than this? Is there more evidence to gather? another link to connect? I direct the students back to the legal texts and ask them to look carefully at the individuals who appear before the court. Are these people guilty or not? Are they simply misunderstood? Can we ever know? In *The Court Baron* one finds William Long, accused of grinding his grain at the lord's mill and leaving without paying his toll, clearly a malicious act. William counters, however, that he acted in "forgetfulness and negligence," not from evil intent. Is he a criminal or simply confused? Thomas the Fishmonger is accused of knowingly selling "stinking fish" that made the people gravely ill (50, 51). But Thomas responds that he bought the fish for new and without corruption and that is how he sold it. Is this an act of premeditated malice or not? Even though the anonymous scribe of the *Court Baron* tells us no more and we never know the fate of William or Thomas, we can assume that the individual who could accumulate the most facts and was most persuasive to the judge had the best chance to win the case.

Although the scribe is not a poet, we can clearly hear the two sides of the charge as related by the court. Ambiguity is buried deep inside the accused; to clarify it,"one must be able to perceive as many of the latent [meanings] in words and phrases as possible. Then by defining away the ambiguities one can limit the possibilities of accidental or intentional misinterpretation by others" (Gopen 341). Thus when examining Chaucer's characters, students must search for word nuances—"hairs" and "fibers," as it were—and use every tool at their disposal to demystify the text. Chaucer's Cook obeys the laws of a trade in which he excels. He is considered a master chef and skilled in the use of England's best spices. But he is accused of recycling his pastries, and his shop is full of flies. He is employed by the guildsmen to whom appearance is all; but that the sore on his shin is syphilitic implies unwholesome behavior. Is he culpable or not? One text is presented, positing certain narrative facts; another text follows that distracts readers (Braswell 75). They were swayed by the positive description, but now they have to account for the negative one. How will they decide? Does the Knight practice or not practice the precepts of feudal law? Does the Sergeant of the Law conduct his dealings to the advantage or disadvantage of his clients? Chaucer the poet, writing for a literary audience that included actual lawyers, supplies more evidence for us to ponder, more clues to investigate than any advocate in a medieval court record.

At the end of this unit, the members of the class, like a team of CSI investigators, conduct a walk-through, retracing their steps and determining what they have accomplished. The work has been basic; I have set it up so that the students will not fail, but they have been exposed to new skills and a new perspective, which they will be able to use when dissecting a more daunting text. In a more advanced course the students will track down manuscripts, identify scribal hands, and check for interpolations and corrupt passages. They will search for missing evidence, chase false leads, and acknowledge with reluctance that some cases remain "cold." Such is the province of the medieval knowledge seeker and the world of the medieval sleuth.

Peter C. Herman

Teaching Early Modern Literature through the Ancient Constitution

I begin with a truism: law shapes interpretation—that is to say, one understands the meaning of a literary text through one's understanding of the era's fundamental laws. Analyzing how an early modern author treats the question of gender, for example, will be guided by the laws concerning gender in the early modern period, and this principle holds especially in works dealing with England's political structure. For many years, literary critics of both old- and new-historicist stripes have assumed that the English monarchy was an absolutist institution. The monarch was, as the phrase goes, God's lieutenant on earth, accountable only to God and superior to the law. Disobeying the sovereign was the same as disobeying God, and rebellion inevitably brought with it failure and misery.

One finds these concepts handily summarized in the widely available "Homily against Disobedience and Willful Rebellion" (first published in 1570 in the wake of the Northern Rebellion and the pope's releasing Catholic subjects from their oath of allegiance to Elizabeth).[1] According to this document, the subject owes the monarch unquestioned political and financial obedience:

it is the will of GOD . . . that you be in subjection to your head and king. This is GOD'S ordinance, GOD'S commandement, and GOD'S holy will, that the whole body of every Realm, and all the members and parts of the same, shall be subject to their head, their king, and that (as S. Peter writeth) for the Lord's sake: and (as S. Paul writeth) for conscience sake, and not for fear only. Thus we learn by the word of GOD, to yield to our king, that is due to our king: that is, honour, obedience, payments of due taxes, customs, tributes, subsidies, love and fear. (*Homily* 1.10.3.346–54)[2]

"Such," Lily Campbell wrote in 1947, "was the Tudor philosophy" (215). Such is the conception of order, wrote E. M. W. Tillyard, that "everyone believed in Elizabeth's days" (20). To be sure, Campbell and Tillyard had good reason for thinking so, as one can find this view frequently repeated elsewhere, such as the 1559 *Mirror for Magistrates*, Thomas Elyot's *The Book of the Governor*, and the political works and speeches of King James VI and I.[3]

But while many nails have been driven into Tillyard's coffin for mistaking *an* Elizabethan world picture for *the* Elizabethan world picture (e.g., Dollimore 5–6) and while some critics recognized the variety of views of kingship circulating in early modern England (see W. Carroll; Robin Wells), a surprising number of contemporary scholars have followed Campbell and Tillyard in assuming that the Tudor polity was a fundamentally absolutist institution, guided by the Justinian principle "what pleases the prince has the force of law" and holding that the monarch is above the law and accountable only to God. David Scott Kastan, for example, proposes that in *Macbeth*, "the orthodox moral position is at odds with the orthodox political position [i.e., absolutism and the unqualified rejection of rebellion]" (177).[4]

Obviously, this position has very significant pedagogical implications. First, there are local interpretations. By placing Shakespeare's second tetralogy, sometimes known as the Henriad (*Richard II*, the two parts of *Henry IV*, and *Henry V*), which deals with Henry IV's deposition of Richard II, next to the "Homily," one can readily get students to accept that John of Gaunt's refusal to do anything about Richard II's ordering the murder of his brother would have been received by Shakespeare's audience with nodding heads and murmurs of approval:

God's is the quarrel, for God's substitute,
His deputy anointed in His sight,

Hath caus'd his death, the which if wrongfully,
Let heaven revenge, for I may never lift
An angry arm against His minister. (1.2.37–41)

Conversely, when Christopher Marlowe's Tamburlaine asked his low-born followers, "What say my other friends? Will you be kings?" (2.5.67), or when Thomas Deloney's Jack of Newbury overtly criticized Henry VIII for privileging military adventures in France over protecting his realm from invasion (asked why he will not abandon the anthill he guards and visit the king, Jack responds, "[W]hile I am away, our enemies might come and put my people in hazard as the Scots did *England*, while our King was in *France*" [36]), Elizabethans were horrified at these departures from the homily's emphasis on hierarchy and strict obedience. Law thus determines interpretation.

However, absolutism and the concept of authority enshrined in the homily never constituted the orthodox political position of early modern England.[5] That position was the "ancient constitution," a term coined during the 1640s that refers to four overlapping principles enshrined in English common law and political practice: monarchy's human rather than divine origin; the necessity of the monarch's ruling in concert with Parliament (also known as "mixed monarchy"); the monarch's inability to alter the nation's laws without Parliament's explicit consent; and the principle that the monarch is subject to the law.

In *De Republica Anglorum* (1582), Sir Thomas Smith declares, "The most high and absolute power of the realm of England, is in the Parliament," not in the monarch alone, and the legitimacy of the laws produced by Parliament derives from the joint approval of both parties, not one or the other:

> and upon mature deliberation every bill or law being thrice read and disputed upon in either house . . . and after the Prince himself in presence of both the parties doeth consent unto and alloweth. That is the Prince's and whole realm's deed: whereupon justly no man can complain, but must accommodate himselfe to find it good and obey it. (78)

Even further, English legal authorities consistently reiterated that the law reigned over both the king and Parliament. To quote Edward Coke's paraphrase of Bracton: "The King is under no man; but only God and the law, for the law makes the King: Therefore let the King attribute that to the law, which from the law he hath received, to wit power and dominion" (102).

The ancient constitution received its fullest articulation in Sir John Fortescue's highly influential *De Laudibus Legum Angliae* (*In Praise of the Laws of England*), a dialogue written in the late fifteenth century (frequently republished).[6] In this work, Fortescue contrasts royal rule, which he overtly associates with civic law and France, with the distinctly English institution of political rule, the fundamental difference being the amount of power allotted to the monarch:

> For the king of England is not able to change the laws of his kingdom at pleasure, for he rules his people with a government not only royal but also political. If he were to rule over them with a power only royal, he could be able to change the laws of the realm, and also impose on them tallages [taxes] and other burdens without consulting them; this is the sort of dominion which the civil laws indicate when they state that "what pleased the prince has the force of law." But it is far otherwise with the king ruling his people politically, because he himself is not able to change the laws without the assent of his subjects nor to burden an unwilling people with strange impositions, so that, ruled by laws that they themselves desire, they freely enjoy their goods, and are despoiled neither by their own king nor any other. (17)

Fortescue is even more explicit when his prince raises the question of the civil law maxim "what pleased the prince has the force of law": "The laws of England do not sanction any such maxim, since the king of that land rules his people not only royally but also politically, and so he is bound by oath at his coronation to the observance of his law" (48).

Fortescue does not specifically address what happens if a monarch breaks his oath and rules by will, not law, but others were more forthcoming. As John Selden puts it in his *Table-Talk*, "Though there be no written law for it [deposition], yet there is Custom which is the best Law of the Kingdom; for in England they have always done it" (137). The historical Richard II, for example, was not violently deposed but removed from power by process of law (although he was murdered shortly thereafter). As Edward Hall writes (and his account is reproduced almost verbatim in *Holinshed's Chronicles*), Richard's enemies put before Parliament ".xxxv. solempne [solemn] articles" to prove that he "was an unjust and unprofitable Prince and a tyrant over his subjects, and worthy to be deposed" (Hall 9; *Holinshed* 3: 859).[7] Of particular interest is item 16: "[Richard] said that the laws of the realm were in his head, and some time in his breast, by reason of which fantastical opinion, he destroyed noble men and impoverished the poor commons" (10; 860). Therefore, this document concludes, "king Richard was worthy to be deposed of all honor, rule and Princely governance" (11; 861). Sir John Hayward also reproduces the articles of deposition in his *Life and Reign of King Henry IV* (135), and while the size and cost of Hall and *Holinshed's Chronicles* necessarily limited their circulation, Hayward's controversial book enjoyed tremendous popularity: "No book ever sold better," claimed John Wolfe, the publisher (Manning 2).

Focusing a course on the ancient constitution allows both teachers and students to revisit some of the best-known works of the canon, in particular those dealing with the problems of rule, law, dissent, and rebellion, from a fresh perspective.[8] To demonstrate, I give three examples from the beginning, middle, and end of the Tudor-Stuart era: Sir Thomas More's serioludic masterpiece *Utopia* (1516), Shakespeare's Henriad (1596–99), and John Milton's *Paradise Lost* (1667). Each provides multiple perspectives on questions of law and rule instead of endorsing one position or another. Their purpose is not to solve problems but to create them.

Scholars have largely situated More's book in the context of humanism's revival of classical antiquity (in this case, Plato's *Republic*) and More's own ambivalence about entering the service of Henry VIII. More was a lawyer, from a family of lawyers, and steeped in the common law (Ackroyd 53–64). *Utopia* therefore benefits from being taught in the context of the ancient constitution and Henry VIII's intention, evident from the very start of his reign, to increase the scope of monarchic power.[9] Significantly, More designs the political structure to exemplify the "regime of consent" prescribed by Fortescue and the ancient constitution (Sacks 124). Thus More gives his best state a government in which each rank is chosen by the one below:

> Every thirty families choose annually an official whom in their ancient language they call a syphogrant but in their newer a phylarch. Over ten syphogrants with their families is set a person once called a tranibor but now a protophylarch. The whole body of syphogrants, in number two hundred, having sworn to choose the man whom they judge most useful, by secret balloting appoint a governor, specifically one of the four candidates named to them by the people. . . . (67)

According to Fortescue, the English are "ruled by laws that they themselves desire" (17), and More imports this principle into Utopia as well:

> Therefore whatever is considered important is laid before the assembly of the syphogrants who, after informing their groups of families, take

counsel together and report their decision to the senate. Sometimes the matter is laid before the council of the whole island. (68)

As for deposition, like the English monarch, the governor holds "office for life" but can be ousted "on suspicion of aiming at a tyranny" (67).

And yet, as numerous scholars have pointed out, More habitually undercuts his supposedly ideal Utopians (see G. Logan 221–29), and the same may apply to his treatment of Utopian politics. Is mere "suspicion" of tyranny sufficient cause for ousting? or should the governor have to commit tyranny first? Remarkably, More does not give his imaginary republic a king. Is this choice an implicit attack on the institution of monarchy? or an invitation to view Utopian politics as skeptically as their pacifism, given how many reasons they give to justify war?[10] With Fortescue and the ancient constitution in mind, students may want to investigate further the relation between the "Dialogue of Counsel" in book 1 (in which More's narrator, Hythlodaeus, debates with More's representation of himself the usefulness of entering court service, the latter asserting that "what you cannot turn to good you must at least make as little bad as you can," the former arguing that service entails sharing "the madness of others as I tried to cure their lunacy" [50]) and the polity More creates in book 2. Students and teachers may also want to compare More's treatment of Utopian law with his habit of implicitly inviting a skeptical view of his supposedly ideal state (see G. Logan). Is More anticipating the expansion of treason in the 1534 Treason Act from requiring evidence of an "open deed" to mere speech (Lemon 6–9)? And if so, should Utopian governance be included among the "customs and laws" the narrator finds "very absurdly established" (151)?

The ancient constitution also provides an important pedagogical tool for helping students understand the legal contexts for Shakespeare's Henriad. Set against selected passages from Fortescue and from Smith (as well as selected passages from the various chronicle sources), John of Gaunt's embrace of absolutism (quoted above), Richard's own view of monarchy (e.g., "The breath of worldly men cannot depose / The deputy elected by the Lord" [3.2.56–57]), and the Bishop of Carlisle's condemnation of Henry's ascension to the throne in terms that reject royal accountability to anyone other than God ("What subject can give sentence on his king? / And who sits here that is not Richard's subject?" [4.1.121–22]) suddenly appear to run counter to the basics of English legal culture. Instead of confirming Shakespeare's adherence to a providentialist understanding of history that posits the War of the Roses as divine punishment for Richard's deposition, the play seems to justify his removal on the grounds that Richard and his allies adhered to a fundamentally un-English view of monarchy and its prerogatives.

Furthermore, the emphasis in the ancient constitution on the monarch's subservience to the law, because it is the law that creates the monarch, brings into stark relief how Shakespeare's Richard threatens the fundamental structure of England's polity through his irresponsible, and illegal, seizure of John of Gaunt's assets after his death. English law, as Fortescue writes, ensures that everyone may "freely enjoy their goods, and are despoiled neither by their own king nor any other" (17). It is exactly this principle that Richard violates when he says that he will "seize to us / The plate, coin, revenues, and moveables / Whereof our uncle Gaunt did stand possess'd" (2.1.160–62) to fund the Irish wars, and, as York immediately points out, violating the sanctity of inheritance undermines the foundations of Richard's legitimacy:

> Take Hereford's rights away, and take from Time
> His charters and his customary rights;
> Let not to-morrow then ensue to-day;
> Be not thyself, for how art thou a king
> But by fair sequence and succession? (2.1.195–99)

Yet the matter is more complicated, for if the ancient constitution provides the justification for Richard's removal, the rest of the Henriad dramatizes a descent into moral chaos and civil war. If the first play in Shakespeare's trilogy (or quadrilogy, depending on how one counts *Henry IV, Part 2*) justifies Richard's removal for his offenses against the ancient constitution, the rest of the cycle seems to justify the absolutist claim that rebellion leads to, in that wonderful phrase from the homily, "Babylonical confusion" (1.10.1.31). Even Henry V, who earlier dismissed his father's worries about legitimacy ("You won it [the crown], wore it, kept it, gave it to me; / Then plain and right must my possession be" [*2H4* 4.5.221–22]), before the Battle of Agincourt begs God to excuse his father's crime: "O, not to-day, think not upon the fault / My father made in compassing the crown!" (*H5* 4.1.293–94). The point to stress to students is that Shakespeare is writing not a constitutionalist brief but a play dramatizing multiple points of view, each qualifying the other. By reproducing the arguments of both absolutism and the ancient constitution, he creates, as Rebecca Lemon writes, "a meditation on rulership itself, engaging with questions of rule through imaginative expression and inventive conceit" (54).[11]

Finally, the ancient constitution provides an important lens for reinterpreting the problem of rebellion and Satan's fall in *Paradise Lost*. Milton's knowledge of this tradition cannot be doubted. The ancient constitution lies behind the justifications for the English Civil War; Milton explicitly invokes it in his 1649 defense of Charles's execution, *The Tenure of Kings and Magistrates* ("Whence doubtless our Ancestors who were not ignorant with what rights either Nature or ancient Constitution had endow'd them . . . thought it no way illegal to depose and put to death their tyrannous Kings" [1062]). The ancient constitution's emphasis on the consent of the governed underscores Milton's proposals in *The Ready and Easy Way to Establish a Free Commonwealth* (1660): "The happiness of a nation must needs be firmest and certainest in a full and free Council of their own electing, where no single person, but reason only sways" (1139).

Significantly, Milton echoes the language of the ancient constitution throughout *Paradise Lost*, thereby destabilizing any easy interpretation of Satan as unqualifiedly evil and God as unqualifiedly good. When Satan speaks in terms of freedom constituting the native right of all angels, who are, if not equal, "yet free / Equally free" (7.591–92), his words echo the emphasis on freedom repeated in virtually all the constitutionalist arguments of this period. Similarly, when Satan speaks of casting off yokes and when Mammon sneeringly invokes the "splendid vassalage" of Heaven (2.252), they summon up the widespread sense that slavery is fundamentally antithetical to the liberties guaranteed the English subject by the ancient constitution (Herman, *Destabilizing* 90). Concomitantly, Milton casts God as an absolute monarch who demands—and receives—exactly the fawning, cringing, servile adoration Milton condemns in *The Ready and Easy Way* (*Paradise Lost* 4.957–60; *Ready and Easy Way* 1139; Herman, *Destabilizing* 98) and whose sudden alteration of Heaven's political structure, his transfer of power to the Son (Worden 236), results in civil strife. Finally, Satan's depiction of God's actions as "new laws" and "new counsels" (5.679–81) echoes Charles's search for new means of ruling and the resistance occasioned by his perceived novelties. In sum, using the ancient constitution allows students to understand the full range of Milton's complexities, to view *Paradise Lost* as arising from and engaging England's legal culture. Like More and Shakespeare, Milton uses the ancient constitution to create problems rather than solve them.

To conclude, there are two major advantages to centering a course in early modern literature on the ancient constitution. First, it provides a more accurate view of early modern culture, one that takes into account the full range of legal ideologies, not just absolutism. Second, it grants students the opportunity to understand the close connections between the early modern period and our own, since the ancient constitution is the foundation for the American Constitution. The fundamentals of early modern English legal culture, in other words, are the fundamentals of our own.

Notes

1. I have silently modernized all early modern spellings.

2. While the full text is available online from the University of Toronto, Wootton includes a redacted version in *Divine Right and Democracy*.

3. James's *The True Law of Free Monarchies* (1598), *Basilokon Doron* (1599), and speeches to Parliament are frequently excerpted and anthologized. For a handy paperback collection of these works and others, see his *Political Writings*.

4. Two other examples: Richard Helgerson declared, "The intense national self-consciousness of the younger Elizabethans arose under the aegis of Tudor absolutism" (9); Russ McDonald unqualifiedly stated, "England was an absolutist state in Shakespeare's day and would remain so until the middle of the seventeenth century" (298). Nonetheless, some literary critics have noted the error of this view (D. Hamilton; Norbrook), and the ancient constitution has increasingly become central to historical interpretations of early modern literature (e.g., W. Carroll; Jordan; Lemon; and C. Perry).

5. See W. Carroll for a good survey of the various theories of kingship circulating in early modern England.

6. According to the *Early English Books Online* database, editions of Fortescue's text appeared in 1543, 1567, 1573, 1599, 1620, 1660, and 1672.

7. On the shaping presence of the ancient constitution in *Holinshed's Chronicles*, see A. Patterson; on the ancient constitution in earlier Tudor historical writing, see Herman, "Rastell's *Pastyme*."

8. Other texts that work well in the classroom are Thomas More's *History of Richard III*, Shakespeare's Henry VI plays, *Thomas of Woodstock*, Sir Philip Sidney's *Old Arcadia*, Thomas Dekker's *The Shoemaker's Holiday*, Thomas Heywood's *The First and Second Parts of King Edward IV*, Fulke Greville's "A Dedication to Sir Philip Sidney" and *Mustapha*, Ben Jonson's *Catiline*, George Chapman's *Bussy D'Ambois*, James Shirley's masque *The Triumph of Peace* and its Royalist answer in Thomas Carew and Inigo Jones's *Coelum Britannicum*, the Putney debates, tracts by Gerrard Winstanley and by the English Levellers (Sharp), Andrew Marvell's "An Horatian Ode," and Milton's *Paradise Regained* and *Samson Agonistes*.

9. Before his coronation, Henry VIII tried to alter the coronation oath by adding clauses that would severely weaken the checks on monarchic power. See Herman, "*Macbeth*" 231n73.

10. Although the Utopians regard war with "utter loathing" (118), they will go to war to drive out an invading enemy; to drive out an enemy who has invaded an ally; "in pity for a people oppressed by tyranny"; to avenge "injuries" done to their friends; to avenge "unjust persecution under the color of justice in any other

country, either on the pretext of laws in themselves unjust or by the distortion of laws in themselves good"; or to drive out the natives of a territory they wish to colonize (76, 118–19).

11. On Shakespeare's problematic treatment of the ancient constitution in *Macbeth*, see Herman, "*Macbeth*."

Victoria Myers

Law and Drama in the Romantic Era: A Model Course

The British Romantic era provides an especially rich context in which to study the relation between law and drama. The era saw the beginning of numerous changes in legal practices, including the greater participation of lawyers in the courtroom, the use of forensic expert witnesses, the extension of jury rights, and (through print) the increased public knowledge of trials. Although often debarred from making direct political statements, dramas frequently incorporated elaborate allusions to notorious trials as a way of participating in debates about the authority of legal institutions. In the course described in this essay, students study this relation, scrutinizing legal proof, trial practices, and the role of the jury in legal reform on the one hand and dramaturgy, dramatic belief (or suspension of disbelief), and the civic function of drama on the other.

Although this array of concepts sounds formidable, the course works well in an undergraduate class of mixed English majors and nonmajors taking a university-required upper-division literature course. Undergraduates find questions of what can be known, believed, and acted on particularly interesting, especially when these are coupled with questions about the grounds for trusting individuals and institutions. Onstage conflicts and real-life trials render such questions specific and immediate. Over the course of the term, students learn how legal thinking and issues permeate Romantic-era drama and how dramatists help form lay understanding of legal culture and can even intervene in debates about the judicial system.

To give our work focus and direction, I organize our study into units, each addressing a problem that derives from law but also applies to drama:

> Can we classify acts by different persons as the same? What counts as an act? a motive? a consequence?
>
> What counts as responsibility? What exacerbates or mitigates responsibility?
>
> How can we attain certainty in our judgments of innocence and guilt? Is there guilt that the law cannot reach?
>
> What gives a person or an institution authority over the behavior of others?
>
> Can we act justly without preserving institutions? Can we preserve institutions without acting justly?

In each unit, we usually begin with a modern-day theoretical statement—for example, from Joseph Raz on authority—and an open discussion that elicits students' previously formed assumptions and reasoning on the question. Using rhetorical analysis, we then read one of the dramas to see how the playwright would solve the problem. Usually we end up with only a tentative solution and with a desire to consult the historical-legal context. At this point we discuss relevant documents, which we analyze for their premises and reasoning but also as rhetorical performances aimed at specific audiences. Brief lecture supplies the context for the documents. We then return to the drama to discover how these specific matters appear in the language and dramatic action. Several units conclude with the students' writing an argumentative essay defending their interpretation of the play in light of the legal theory and historical evidence.

This approach, besides addressing students' relative lack of training in either literary analysis or legal reasoning, also relates law and literature through their common ground in rhetorical argument. Such argument, while not opposed to reason, functions well in situations that demand less than demonstrative reasoning; it responds to a context of tradition and accepted practices as well as to contingencies in the political and social environment. Wendy Olmsted sketches a rationale for discovering and using this common ground by addressing a major stumbling block: that indeterminacy and ambiguity, which appear so desirable in literary analysis, appear foreign to legal reasoning. In all rhetorical situations, she argues, indeterminacy functions in relation to determinacy; "[t]erms and distinctions that are used to inform decisions about matters that can be otherwise are at once relatively determinate and relatively indeterminate" (238). She illustrates how in case law (and, by extension, in common law) indeterminacy meets determinacy by using argument by example and analogy. These important forms of rhetorical argument function "within an adversary system . . . designed to facilitate the doing of what is just by ensuring that differences as well as similarities are urged and that competing examples are presented" (243). The relation describes legal reasoning, but it also captures the preoccupation of Romantic-era dramatists with motifs of ambiguity, open-endedness, and skepticism, expressed in their representation of legal institutions and trials.

To examine these motifs and discover their function in producing the play's meaning, students learn a rhetorical analysis of drama that exhibits connections (though not identity) with legal reasoning. They attend to scenic structure, stage action, thematic repetitions, and rhetorical argument in the dialogue — the playwright's persuasive tools. Structuring scenes around arguments that have analogical relations to each other is characteristic of much canonical Romantic drama. Samuel Taylor Coleridge, for example, constructs *Remorse* in a pattern that calls for comparisons between different cases of concealment and deception, some of them defensible, others reprehensible, even criminal. Students discover how the playwright develops his interpretive standards and rules in a way similar to the analogical reasoning described by Edward Levi (secs. 1 and 2) and by Steven Burton (chs. 1 and 2). A writing assignment for unit 1 grows from this discussion along the following lines:

> Putting yourself in Coleridge's place, write a rule that defines the form of deception that you believe is criminal. Discuss which cases of deception in the play would come under this rule and which ones would not. Discuss problematical cases, arguing the pros and cons for bringing them under this rule and discussing what point there might be for the playwright to make them problematical. Are there some ways in which the drama exceeds the bounds of legal reasoning?

Students hone their vocabulary and contextualize their discussion by studying concepts of action, intentionality, consciousness, motives, and moral liberty as expressed in passages from Thomas Reid (essay 4, chs. 1–4) and from Jeremy Bentham (chs. 7–11). These readings help them see how drama responds to moral categories and premises that also enter into legal reasoning; they lay the ground for the question, raised later, whether laws are the same as moral norms.

While unit 1 explores analogical reasoning in law and drama, unit 2 develops students' understanding of deductive argument. By formulating definitions of responsibility and thinking about the connection of responsibility to moral premises, they discover ideological underpinnings of such reasoning. We read from John Rawls's *A Theory of Justice*, useful because Rawls situates his issue in a deductive argument (connecting a community's justice with its citizens' stable desire to act justly) and describes a manner of acquiring the moral sentiments that ideally ground legal rules and limit indeterminacy (67–94). This thesis helps students understand key sections of the "Introductory Discourse" to the *Plays on the Passions*, in which Joanna Baillie argues that her plays serve a civic function by providing moral training in recognizing pathological passions in their earliest stages of growth. In her tragedy *De Monfort*, students analyze how community-held standards of behavior function as premises for approbation and disapprobation in the characters' various arguments and debate why these arguments fail to prevent De Monfort from committing murder.

Students' reactions to De Monfort's act raises the question of how De Monfort would have been treated in the legal structure of Baillie's England. Common norms direct moral deductions, students learn, but statutes and common law direct legal deductions. We use William Blackstone's *Commentaries on the Laws of England* for the statement of the law classifying acts of killing and try to determine why De Monfort's act would be murder rather than justifiable or excusable homicide (4: 179–202). Applying these rules to his acts and motives allows students to test how (and how far) legal deductions from statutes or common law limits indeterminacy still left in place by moral norms. They experience little difficulty in determining De Monfort's deed to be murder under these rules, but they also discuss the acts and motives of other characters, who inadvertently impel the murder. Having to decide how dramatically induced sympathy can affect judgment, students begin to discover the differences between determinacy aimed at by legal rules and determinacy aimed at by moral rules. Baillie's civic concerns also show that legal decisions must remain permeable to community knowledge. From Joel Peter Eigen's *Witnessing Insanity* students learn how the court in Baillie's century attempted to deal with violent passions as constraints on an individual's will and gradually admitted expert testimony in order to gain some control over subjective definitions of insanity (ch. 1).[1]

By the time we reach unit 3, students have studied two kinds of legal reasoning and their similarities to dramatic technique. These skills are important to the students' understanding of the texts, but they also provide a way of talking about the focus of the course: Romantic dramatists' incorporation of legal issues in the rhetoric of drama and their contribution thereby to the lay public's understanding of legal issues and practices. On a more subtle level, they are beginning to appreciate that determinacy and indeterminacy are relative and to raise questions about law's relation to morality.

The thematic coherence of the course around the relation between determinacy and indeterminacy sometimes depends on a complex interplay among modern legal theory, historical context, and dramatic text. Unit 3 constructs this interplay by exploring two kinds of potential skepticism in the law, fact skepticism and rule skepticism. Students have already encountered them in dealing with deception (*Remorse*) and murder (*De Monfort*). To gain some personal and historical anchor for the question of how we can attain certainty of someone's innocence or guilt, we read an excerpt from book 10 of William Wordsworth's *Prelude*, in which the poet imagines himself "plead[ing] / Before unjust tribunals" (lines 376–77) in France during the Reign of Terror, when the stability that Rawls talks about has been severely undermined. The opening chapter in Barbara Shapiro's historical study *"Beyond Reasonable Doubt" and "Probable Cause,"* read along with a brief excerpt from Sir Geoffrey Gilbert's influential early treatise *The Law of Evidence* (1: 1–5), helps students consider limitations on absolute certainty about matters of fact and on conclusions drawn from such evidence; it also shows them how English law by the eighteenth century had developed rules for evaluating evidence in view of epistemological limitations. In reading act 1 of Wordsworth's *The Borderers*, we consider how the playwright gives us clues, which the protagonist, Marmaduke, lacks, for interpreting the appearances of Herbert's guilt.[2] Students read act 1 in the earlier version of the play, where many of these clues are absent, to experience the condition of Marmaduke's mind and figure out what Marmaduke needs to come to a just conclusion. To see how fact skepticism operating in drama can mirror and comment on fact skepticism in law, we discuss statements from several critics of the era concerning an audience's suspension of disbelief. Henry Home, Lord Kames (1: 104–27); Alexander Gerard (47–52); Samuel Johnson (430–32); and Coleridge (*Biographia* 2: 5–7, 132–34) all consider whether an audience believes the reality of the representation on stage while it is watching. In discussing later acts, we ask how Marmaduke functions as an audience-jury for Oswald's representations and whether and why he suspends disbelief.

To move from fact to rule skepticism, we read an excerpt from H. L. A. Hart's *The Concept of Law*. Although it presents some difficulties for undergraduates, they can understand the distinction between primary and secondary rules by discussing how these rules arise from or relate to what Rawls calls moral sentiments. They can perceive the structure of rule recognition by contrast with the breakdown of institutions Wordsworth observes in the French Revolution. They can grasp Hart's discussion of the indeterminacy of examples or the open texture of legislated rules and precedents by reference to the discussion of analogical and deductive reasoning in the first two units. Hart captures the dilemma of a society that needs "certain rules" to apply deductively to cases yet is also inclined to leave some issues open to be settled in specific cases (130). By describing the legal system's techniques for circumscribing judicial decisions, Hart emphasizes that the system has some degree of consistency and thus can maintain confidence in its justness. This understanding forms the backdrop for students' reading the rest of *The Borderers*, where the villain, Oswald, appears as a rule skeptic and prevents Marmaduke from bringing his accusation against Herbert into anything resembling a court of justice, where procedures for coming to a decision would satisfy his need for community validation.

With *The Borderers*, we turn to one of the trials that influenced Wordsworth's rhetorical construction of the play and much of its language, the trial of Thomas Hardy for treason in 1794. Using excerpts from the opening speeches, we discuss Thomas Erskine's accusation that the attorney general flouts legal probability and fosters rule skepticism (*Speeches* 2: 283–89, 300–17; 3: 12–21, 41–45, 72–79). If we have time, we also discuss the speeches of Saint-Just and Condorcet in the trial of Louis XVI, another influence on Wordsworth's play, which provides startling evidence of the breakdown of accepted norms (Walzer, *Regicide* 120–27, 139–58). With this context, students can understand the play as an intervention in what Wordsworth sees as his government's destruction of belief in the British legal system's adherence to justice. In their discussion, students notice that Wordsworth makes analogies between Marmaduke and Oswald and establishes analogies between his drama and external trials. These multiple parallels, which students variously interpret in their essays, illustrate vital relations between determinacy and indeterminacy.

Students' interest in the drama-trial nexus intensifies in unit 4, with Percy Bysshe Shelley's severe challenge to legal authority in *The Cenci*. The question of what gives a person or institution authority over others takes us to the heart of legal debates in the Romantic era. In the provocative essay "The Obligation to Obey the Law," Raz argues that there is no obligation to obey the law, distinguishes among reasons for obedience (prudence, morality), and suggests that obedience arises from adherence to extralegal imperatives (233–49). Though the instructor must supplement with some explanation of Raz's concept of exclusionary reasons and legal normativity, his concepts provide a useful framework for discussing authority and autonomy in Shelley's play. Studying the rhetorical structure of *The Cenci*, students uncover the analogies among paternal, religious, and political authority, often found in traditional justifications of legal forms in the monarchical state. The dilemma of Beatrice, who believes that religious and legal institutions provide no redress for her father's raping her, is to find ground to authorize his murder.

Shelley has incorporated the language and issues of two contemporary trials — those of Daniel Isaac Eaton ("Proceedings") and William Hone — for blasphemous libel, in which the prosecutors argued that the authority of law is rendered ineffectual by attacks on religious authority, which they likened to the authority of parents. By insisting on the jury's right to consider law as well as evidence, Eaton and Hone both demonstrate the dependence of legal authority on a public that can endorse countertraditions of religion and literature. Analogy becomes parody in their demonstration of the open texture of the law, a rhetorical tactic that in Shelley's play characterizes acts of subversion. Shelley's "A Philosophical View of Reform" helps students interpret Beatrice's murder as a response to legal oppression. Is violent reform ever justified? Can the oppressed individual morally rise above her historical circumstances?[3]

The final unit, comparing the integrity of law as an institution with the moral integrity of an individual, brings the dilemma to a head in George Gordon Lord Byron's *The Two Foscari*, raising the question of whether we can act justly without preserving institutions and preserve institutions without acting justly. By the end of the course, relating determinacy and indeterminacy has become for students not only a mode of arguing in literature as well as law but also a goal of Romantic-era thinking and finally a site on which its drama interprets legal issues and forms a lay legal culture.

Notes

1. The applications of William Blackstone's *Commentaries* and of Joel Eigen's *Witnessing Insanity* are made in Myers, "Joanna Baillie."

2. See my analysis of the early version of *The Borderers* ("Justice").

3. The relation between Shelley's play and the trials of Eaton and Hone is developed in Myers, "Blasphemy Trials."

Alex Feerst

Immigration, Law, and American Literature

In 2005, immigrants constituted 12.4% of the American population, numbering about 35.7 million, according to the Census Bureau (Paral). As a century ago, they remain concentrated along the east, west, and south coasts, but increasingly and strikingly they live throughout the nation. On 7 June and again on 28 June 2007, cloture motions that would have ended debate on Senate Bill 1348, the Comprehensive Immigration Reform Act of 2007, failed by fifteen and seven votes, respectively, representing the bill's collapse. On 10 August 2007, the Bush administration set out to accomplish through regulation what had failed in legislation. The Department of Homeland Security announced a series of new immigration rules that featured increased penalties for employers of undocumented workers. Absent from the new enforcement-oriented regulations were the guest worker and "earned citizenship" provisions featured in S. 1348.

Current immigration policy decisions stand to profoundly change future American realities. Teaching undergraduates the political and historical underpinnings of immigration in the United States may help ensure that it is an informed electorate that shapes the nation's demographic destiny. This essay presents five brief examples, drawn from an undergraduate course I taught at Macalester College, of approaches to the literature of American immigration from a legal perspective. Following the method taken by Lisa Lowe and others of reading legal and cultural texts as mutually illuminating contexts, the overall goals of this course were to foster a general engagement by students with historical and contemporary issues surrounding immigration, to consider how various literary imaginations have engaged with immigration, and to explore how the social realities created by legal texts may structure the content and form of literary texts.[1]

Some Practical Concerns

Many literary texts represent experiences or consequences of immigration. Trying to categorize or qualify them leads quickly to questions of how texts relate to the focal point of immigration and about the usefulness of this organizing principle. In practice, I need to direct students' attention, without unduly restricting or predetermining discussion of not so reducible literary elements, to how each text engaged with the issue of immigration. I found that constructing *immigrant* as a literary element was itself part of the inquiry of a course that provides opportunities for discussing and reflecting upon such key concepts as canonicity, ethnicity, citizenship, multiculturalism, and cosmopolitanism.

Here are some things to consider. If we apply the terms of individual citizenship to literary texts, what follows from considering a text the product of the first, second, third, or other generation? Second-generation American authors, for example, may return to and stylize their parents' first-generation experience, in texts such as Pietro di Donato's *Christ in Concrete*, written from a temporal standpoint that lingers over and reworks inherited experience. The generation concept quickly breaks down under scrutiny and leads to questions of how exactly one constitutes the core events of immigration and regards its individual, familial, and communal afterlives.

Immigrant texts may be written by a native speaker of English, as with Andrew Carnegie's autobiography, or by someone who came to English after childhood, as with Michael Pupin's autobiography, or by someone who belongs in neither category.[2] Authors such as Abraham Cahan who come to English later in life as a second or third language bring up questions of the ways in which second-language expression creates linguistic and literary phantom limbs. Considering work by nonnative English speakers also leads to the largely dormant archive of non-English-language American writing and to questions about how American literature in translation may fit into the broader field.[3]

Considerations of native language lead to the tracing of proliferating networks of literary pedigree. Cahan's *The Rise of David Levinsky*, in which the protagonist has taken pains to master English, is sprinkled with a catalog of canonical British, rather than Yiddish or Russian, writers as its title character's favorites and as its own implicit model. Like *Levinsky*, Carlos Bulosan's *America Is in the Heart* foregrounds the influence of canonical English letters but also gestures to the novels of Jose Rizal. Jamaica Kincaid's *Lucy* brings the postcolonial condition of Caribbean school memories filled with English poems about European flora one has never seen to a snowy New York landscape, where this rub is submerged and largely beside the point.

Immigrant writing includes first-person and third-person accounts, genre fiction and modernist and postmodernist experiments, fictionalized memoir and autobiographical fiction. These several axes provide a preliminary vocabulary for situating texts—for example, Cahan's *Levinsky* as a first-generation, first-person fiction written in English as a second language by an Eastern European new immigrant in early-twentieth-century New York; di Donato's *Christ in Concrete* as a second-generation, third-person, loosely autobiographical fiction in a native speaker's English; and Bulosan's *America Is in the Heart* as a memoir in acquired English and Ramón Pérez's *Diary of an Undocumented Immigrant* as a memoir in English translation.

Legal texts including statutes, judicial opinions, and legal scholarship may usefully be read alongside literary texts as context or counterpoint. For example, the legal background of Chinese exclusion may be pieced together from California State statutes along with opinions from the cases *Chae Chan Ping v. US*, *Fong Yue Ting v. US*, *Wong Wing v. US*, and *US v. Wong Kim Ark*.[4]

One could fairly describe this course as a law-oriented, newhistoricist approach to immigration texts. The major writing assignment of the course flowed from this idea: students chose and researched a legal or policy issue—for example, a set of statutes, a series of judicial opinions, a government program, a topic of significant public debate, or some combination of the above—as an interpretive context for developing a reading of one or several of the course's required or supplemental texts.

This type of course could engage more directly with legal hermeneutics to ask how legal interpretive practices might in turn influence literary approaches. But my focus was on the content and effects of immigration policy, and so interdisciplinary interpretive questions, as they arose, were secondary concerns.[5]

Literary and Legal Properties

Disparities between New York and California property law regimes with respect to immigrants around the beginning of the twentieth century suggest the influence a state's prerogative to experiment with policy in response to local issues may have on literary form. The California Alien Land Law of 1913 prohibited aliens ineligible for citizenship from owning land or real property; they could obtain leases for no more than three years. This law affected primarily Chinese, Indian, Japanese, and Korean farmers in California. The constitutionality of the prohibition on American citizenship for East and South Asians, on which California property ownership rested, was challenged in the cases *Takao Ozawa v. United States* and *United States v. Bhagat Singh Thind*. The Magnuson Act of 1943 further undermined this exclusion predicated on citizenship eligibility. After the Supreme Court found in *Oyama v. California* that the 1913 and 1920 California Alien Land Laws did abridge Fourteenth Amendment due process rights, the Supreme Court of California, in *Sei Fujii v. State of California*, found the alien land laws unconstitutional. The state repealed the laws a few years later, in 1956.

This prohibition correlates with the episodic, migratory form of California immigrant texts like Bulosan's memoir, which takes place in Filipino gathering spots and Chinatowns up and down the West Coast. *Levinsky*, by contrast, is a rags-to-riches narrative, in which David, in New York, bootstraps with various forms of capital, including a factory, to achieve his ascent; it is difficult to imagine an analogous rise for an Asian immigrant in California. The ambulatory structure of Bulosan's text may flow from many factors, such as the agricultural base of West Coast immigrant labor as opposed to light industry in New York. But the legal prohibition against owning real property in California must be a significant cause of the text's restless movement and episodic form. This type of comparative analysis asks students to develop a general approach to interpreting structural differences. Focusing on how factors that influence regionalism in literary texts are also related to a given state's legal environment allows students an expanded context for thinking about the role of federalism in American culture.

Domestic Policy, International Diplomacy

If immigration law is sometimes foreign policy by other means, the response of various texts to this fact often explicitly puts quotidian experience in a broader diplomatic context. In *Tokyo Life, New York Dreams*, Mitziko Sawada documents the methods used in concert by the Japanese and American governments to manage emigration in symbiosis with domestic and international political developments in the early twentieth century. To this end, Japan created two categories by which citizens of Japan could emigrate: *imin*, meaning "migrant," and *hi-imin*, "nonmigrant," to distinguish students and professionals from laborers. This categorization was followed by the Gentleman's Agreement of 1907, in which the Japanese government agreed to stop issuing laborer-level, *imin* passports in exchange for certain United States concessions, such as allowing continued immigration to unite families and preventing discrimination against Japanese children through segregation in American schools (xx). This agreement between governments in engineering the makeup of the immigrant population is a striking example of the inextricability of domestic and foreign policy. It also points to the Japanese government's interest in polishing its image in the West and to the aftereffects of its military victory over Russia.

The varied experiences of the largely Asian population that passed through Angel Island, off the coast of San Francisco, from 1910 to 1940, embodied such shifting international power relations. The recently unearthed and translated protomanga by Henry Kiyama, published in the United States as *The Four Immigrants Manga*, depicts the ways a cohort of four Japanese immigrants to the United States navigated engagement with Euro-American culture as subjects of a modernizing imperial Japan. Among other things, Kiyama explores through his protagonists' comic misadventures the forms of difference between classes of Japanese migrants and nonmigrants, as well as Chinese immigrants, staging the arrival of four young men who are quickly released from Angel Island ("Don't worry," one reminds the others, "we're from Imperial Japan. They have a consulate here" [30]). Other noteworthy scenes are the young Japanese city boy who refuses to address a peasant Japanese boss with an honorific because "America is a democratic country" (79); the two companions who are so ashamed of being associated with entering Japanese laborers that one gnaws a lamppost in frustration until consoled by learning that the 1907 ban on immigrants from Hawai'i will eliminate the problem (85); a couple that plans to have as many children as possible because "luckier than most. . . . We can transfer title to our children who were born here" (126); and the departure for Japan of a still-single entrepreneur who sees no way to have a family after the 1924 ban on further immigration.

The perspectives of Chinese immigrants on the same social reality is reflected in the translations of poems etched into Angel Island walls by detainees, published in the collection *Island* (Lai, Lim, and Yung). Along with disenchantment and frustration from having to wait in sometimes years-long quarantine before they could enter San Francisco, many almost-immigrants ruminate on the place of China in the world and its inability to command better treatment for its recent emigrants: "One should know that when the country is / weak, the people's spirit dies" (88). Some de-scribe the concentric lack of family and national power that decided their fate: "For what reason must I sit in Jail? / It is only because my country is weak and my family poor" (84). Others lament the folly of disadvanta-geous economic relations with Western nations: "Our country's wealth is being drained by / foreigners, causing us to suffer national / humiliations" (92). Still others anticipate the day when American power might be subor-dinated to China's ascent, and some plot revenge on a personal scale ("If there comes a day when I will have attained my ambition and become suc-cessful, / I will certainly behead the barbarians and spare not a single blade of grass" [84]) and a national scale ("They will build many battleships and come to / The U.S. territory, / Vowing never to stop till the white men are / completely annihilated" [90]). Directing students to the layered fil-tration process put in place by the Japanese–United States Gentleman's Agreement, the Chinese Exclusion Acts, and the practice of quarantine asks them to consider the bigger picture of domestic policy, in this case how the push-and-pull forces of immigration may be manipulated for the sake of foreign relations and how they may yield subjective responses that resonate on a global scale.

Braceros, Wetbacks, and Guest Workers

Pérez begins his diary by explaining his village's tradition of migrating to work in the United States and recounting the mythology of an earlier generation of bracero veterans who returned with American dollars. From Pérez's perspective, the Bracero Program, under which more than 4.5 mil-lion Mexicans worked in the United States over a period of twenty-two years (1942–64), once discontinued, segued into an illegal "emigrant stream" that picked up the economic slack left by the dissolution of the

United States–Mexico contract (Craig ix). For the men of Pérez's village, legal shifts may affect the tradition's details, but the continuity of migrant memory Pérez taps into suggests a pragmatic understanding of economic and labor relations, notwithstanding enforcement practices.

Pérez's migrant labor picaresque ends when Pérez learns of the Simpson-Rodino Bill, which would become the United States Immigration Reform and Control Act of 1986. It offered amnesty for undocumented residents who could prove continuous presence in the United States since 1 January 1982 and tightened control of illegal labor indirectly by imposing sanctions on employers of illegal workers. Faced with this carrot-and-stick choice between greater commitment or separation from the United States, Pérez decides to return for Mexico. For him, this policy shift complicates a relation that had enjoyed an economic and cultural equilibrium. His return to Mexico closes his diary with repudiation of the United States as unfit for permanent residence; he rejects the classically ingratiating immigrant narrative whose end point is assimilation.

The failed Comprehensive Immigration Reform Act of 2007 included provisions resembling the contractual labor system of the Bracero Program and the amnesty provisions of the Immigration Reform and Control Act. As a supplement to these policies, Pérez's narrative relates the human practices, such as crossing methods and tactics for circumventing detection by the Immigraion and Naturalization Service (INS), and the resulting critiques of American materialism that arise from the historal relation of partly disavowed cross-border interdependence.[6]

Rotating Credit Associations and Native Speakers

In Chang-Rae Lee's *Native Speaker*, John Kwang, the ethnic pol under Henry Park's observation, is brought down by the revelation of his rotating credit society (*ggeh* in Lee's rendering of the Korean).[7] After Kwang's unlucky car accident, Park learns that the federal government has used Kwang's *ggeh* to find and round up undocumented immigrants who participated. If the novel's central metaphor is that of assimilated immigrant identity as a form of spying disloyal to all, Kwang's panethnic rotating credit association is the linchpin of the book's mystery plot, held together by a collaborative IRS-INS sting operation, in which illegal immigrants are collaterally ensnared by the investigation and prosecution of unregulated banking and tax fraud. In creating a panethnic rotating credit association in which trust among immigrants as kin in general supersedes specific nation-of-origin loyalty, Kwang has cast over his followers a net of economic solidarity that is exploited by the INS. This collaborative sting on Kwang's *ggeh* not only illustrates the general precariousness of the immigrant's position but also underscores how federal immigration policy may ambiguously interact with other aspects of the law in ways that may not be fully articulated or justified.[8]

The Reenfranchisement of Piri Thomas

Nearly a third of Piri Thomas's *Down These Mean Streets* takes place in prison. The memoir concludes with Thomas's release and return to his neighborhood, and his determination to move forward with his life. Outside the text, under New York election law of the time, Thomas lost his right to vote and assiduously pursued its reinstatement, corresponding with Senators Jacob Javits and Robert Kennedy and Governor Nelson Rockefeller (P. Thomas, "Piri's Journey"). He eventually received an executive order restoring his right to vote and, a separate requirement, establishing his citizenship. Thomas lost his vote in the events that constitute *Mean Streets* but later leveraged his reenfranchisement, in part through connections made possible by his status, after the publication of *Mean Streets*, as an advocate for Puerto Rican youth. His cultural spokesmanship, cemented by his memoir, eventually served to alter his legal status.

At the individual level, the cultural and racial concerns through which Thomas finds his identity as a Nuyorican in the text are anchored and complemented by his real-world petition for the reinstatement of the franchise. More broadly, felon disenfranchisement and its disparate impact by race connect the cultural politics of immigration, ethnicity, and race with the concrete practice of electoral politics and the importance of intervention in state voting laws, especially resonant since the 2000 presidential election, which determine how citizenship is exercised.[9]

The above examples suggest how focusing on the nexus of law and literature with respect to immigration may provide opportunities for undergraduates to engage with the social, cultural, legal, and political questions presented by immigration policy; confront in detail the various human realities created by immigration policy; and consider how the shaping of immigrant individuals and communities affects cultural production.

Notes

1. Lowe describes her project as a "materialist critique of the institution of American citizenship" that proceeds by bringing together the legal discourse that "most literally governs citizenship" and texts of "national culture" that "powerfully shape who the citizenry is" (ix, 2).

2. "Native speaker" as an explanatory concept has been problematized but still serves as a rough heuristic. See Davies; Paikeday, *The Native Speaker Is Dead!*

3. Many non-English American literature resources have recently become available through the efforts of the Longfellow Institute at Harvard University.

4. These statutes and opinions are analyzed in scholarly accounts in David A. Martin and Peter H. Schuck's collection *Immigration Stories.*

5. The course was introductory, for majors and nonmajors. A more advanced version of it could fruitfully take up hermeneutic issues more appropriate for English majors experienced with prevalent interpretive practices.

6. In 2003, the INS was merged into Immigration and Customs Enforcement (ICE), an agency under the Department of Homeland Security.

7. Names for this ubiquitous practice vary, including *susu, tontine, tanda,* and *hui.* Anthropologists use the general term "rotating credit and savings associations," abbreviated as ROSCAs. See Geertz; Ardener; Low.

8. A notable example of state intervention in immigration policy enforcement is the Illegal Immigration Relief Act Ordinance (IIRA) of Hazleton, Pennsylvania, which fines landlords for renting to undocumented immigrants. The ordinance was struck down as unconstitutional on 26 July 2007. See Illegal Immigration Relief Act; *Lozano v. City of Hazleton.*

9. Under §152 of New York Election Law in force at the time of Thomas's conviction, a person convicted of a felony lost the right to register and vote unless pardoned or restored to the rights of citizenship. The law was amended in 1976 and is now NY Election Law §5-106 (2), under which New York currently prohibits voting by incarcerated felons and ex-felon parolees. This prohibition was challenged in *Hayden v. Pataki.* For background data and discussion of the topic, see Manza and Uggen.

D. Quentin Miller

Vital Visions: On Teaching Prison Literature

It is ironic that prisoners, who make up a larger percentage of the United States population than they ever have, are virtually invisible. Our contemporary judicial and penal system makes it easy to overlook prisoners: it removes them from sight and keeps them in a carefully controlled environment, where they remain until, presumably, they are ready to reintegrate into society. Yet the prisoner's perspective is important, even crucial, to an understanding of one's society and culture. It is also crucial to an understanding of American literature, and certainly to any inquiry connecting literature to the law, for imprisonment is a possible outcome of legal decisions. A thorough inquiry into literature and the law should not end with the way public policy, law enforcement, or courtroom deliberations affect stories. Peter Brooks writes, "The law fascinates the literary critic in part because people go to jail, even to execution, because of the well-formedness and force of the winning story" ("Law as Narrative" 18). The well-formed narratives of courtroom deliberations are not the end of the story, though: imprisonment, regardless of the crime, of the circumstances of its occurrence, or even of the actual guilt or innocence of the incarcerated individual, constitutes its own set of narratives. In much prison literature, the

189

moment of arrest or courtroom sentencing is only the beginning of the story.

Canonical American authors such as Henry David Thoreau and James Baldwin learned something essential during their brief stays in jail. In "Resistance to Civil Government," Thoreau speaks of his time behind bars with the same exuberance he uses to describe his cabin at Walden Pond; he marvels at the "wholly new and rare experience" he has, and observes, "It was a closer view of my native town. I was fairly inside of it. I never had seen its institutions before. . . . I began to comprehend what its inhabitants were about" ("Civil Disobedience" 218). Baldwin, who endured an absurd stint in a Paris jail after a friend left a stolen hotel sheet in his room, reflects on the laughter directed at him after he tells his story in a French court: "In some deep, black, stony, and liberating way, my life, in my own eyes, began during that first year in Paris, when it was borne in on me that this laughter is universal and never can be stilled" (*Notes* 158). Both authors describe their prison experience in terms of a vision change. Because the vast majority of Americans will never spend time in jail, or even enter a jail, they can best experience a similar vision change by reading prison literature—that is, literature written by prisoners or literature that imagines the prison experience. In his book *Brothers and Keepers*, John Edgar Wideman describes himself in relation to his incarcerated brother this way: "Robby was talking to me, but I was still on the outside, looking in" (76). This is the condition of most readers of prison literature: literature written on the inside is almost always directed toward readers on the outside, and a distance remains between the incarcerated subject and the reader, but "looking in" is the first step to understanding.

The prisoner's vision is vital to an understanding of literature and the law. For one thing, the law is something more than an intellectual abstraction to the prisoner. For another, prisoners embody the law's consequences. Their voices help articulate a broad and deep vision of the place of the law in literature. Finally, prison literature is a corrective to prison images framed by Hollywood and by the news media, most of which sensationalize the prison experience or lead the viewer to easy moral conclusions about prisoners, condemning them rather than humanizing them.

I have argued elsewhere that many great works of American literature have included the prison experience ("Behind the Wall" and *Prose* 1–11). Nathaniel Hawthorne's *The Scarlet Letter* begins outside a prison; Herman Melville's "Bartleby, the Scrivener" ends in one; and a host of other works— "Resistance to Civil Government," Rebecca Harding Davis's "Life in the

Iron-Mills," Theodore Dreiser's *Sister Carrie*, Baldwin's "Sonny's Blues," and "Letter from Birmingham Jail," by Martin Luther King, Jr., to name just a few—have the prison experience at their core. Scholars of other nations' literary traditions can no doubt come up with a host of examples of classic literature that center on imprisonment.

Regardless of the body of literature one selects for a prison literature course, the first step toward analysis is likely to be classification. The subject of imprisonment is, after all, based on the fundamental judgment of the juror, the impulse to place the accused into one of two basic categories: guilty or innocent. Literature, like the law, tends to complicate stories so that such dichotomies are too simple. One way to approach prison literature is to devise ways to classify it that resist a binary system based solely on judgment. It is natural to classify prison literature according to the circumstances of the incarcerated: political prisoners, prisoners of conscience, the wrongfully imprisoned, prisoners who are reformed, prisoners who become embittered because of their incarceration, and so on. This classification should be an opportunity to fulfill what are for me the three goals of any course on prison literature: a deep understanding of the meaning of incarceration in a narrative; a willingness on the part of the reader to see the world of the prison that has been hidden, distorted, sensationalized, or rendered separate by popular misconceptions of the social function of incarceration; and an understanding of the effects incarceration has on society as a whole.

I have taught versions of a course on contemporary United States prison literature for the past decade. My university, Suffolk University in Boston, was founded as a law school a century ago, and many of our undergraduates pursue a career in law or criminal justice. Our department offers only undergraduate courses in the context of a traditional liberal arts curriculum, but the course I am describing could be adapted easily to a graduate program. I have focused on classification in order to enhance our institutional mission of encouraging critical thought in a liberal arts context. Extending the motif of vision, I have used a relatively simple system to organize my prison literature syllabi based on narrative perspective: inside, outside, or in-between.

Texts that take the inside perspective are written in the voice of or from the point of view of prisoners, and the examples are myriad. A good place to begin is with an anthology of writings by prisoners in writing programs, such as Bell Gale Chevigny's collection *Doing Time*.[1] Since my course focuses on American literature of the past half century, my inside texts have included John Cheever's *Falconer*, King's "Letter from Birmingham Jail," and Leonard Peltier's *Prison Writings*. A range of rhetorical situations can be seen in this selection: Cheever's novel invites sympathy and pathos; King's invites outrage at injustice; Peltier's argues vehemently for the author's innocence. Farragut in Cheever's novel regards prison as redemptive: he kicks his drug addiction and establishes himself in a community by the end. Peltier's prison experience is the opposite: he is deprived of necessary medical attention in prison and records his bodily degeneration, though his spiritual strength endures.[2] King focuses less on the physical prison than on the social circumstances that led to his incarceration. In short, each inside perspective leads to a different interpretive outcome, and that difference helps achieve the goal of understanding the complex meaning of incarceration in a narrative.

The outside perspective, a view of prison from outside its walls, also presents a range of interpretive possibilities. Truman Capote's *In Cold Blood* and Norman Mailer's *The Executioner's Song* are perhaps the most familiar examples: these are narratives of an outsider's attempt to understand the life of the imprisoned. The reader shares the author's sense of alienation from this world and, with the author, undergoes the process of penetrating and discovering that world. (This perspective is also common in the many narratives of writers who enter prison to teach, such as Wally Lamb in his introduction to *Couldn't Keep It to Myself* or Mark Salzman in his memoir *True Notebooks*.) These are narratives of encounter and self-examination. Attitudes toward crime, criminals, and incarceration are both reinforced and challenged by narratives with an outside perspective, which rarely have a uniformly cynical or uniformly affirmative response to crime and punishment. Because these narratives tend to reveal a perspective that changes over time with regard to incarceration, they help readers revise their distorted or incomplete vision of it.

To achieve my third goal—to demonstrate the effects of incarceration on society as a whole—I focus on the in-between perspective. These narratives center around contact between prisoners and the outside world through the liminal space of the visiting room, and they are illustrated most poignantly through a narrative from a family member. I use two major works in my course that introduce the perspective of a family member: Wideman's *Brothers and Keepers* and Baldwin's *If Beale Street Could Talk*. Both narratives are actually composed of hybrid perspectives: the bulk of Baldwin's novel is narrated by Tish, whose lover, Fonny, has been wrongfully imprisoned. Yet Baldwin gives voice to Fonny's private experience in the book's final pages, and Tish's perspective temporarily vanishes, even though she is the novel's first-person narrator. Similarly, Wideman allows his brother, Robby, to tell his own story in his own words. Wideman's book (which critics have found difficult to classify, given its unique blend of biography and autobiography, structured by a novelist) switches narrators and thus perspectives throughout and sometimes even within the same sentence. Both books originate on the outside, but their narratives are fluid between outside and inside perspectives, thus showing that the prison wall is a more permeable barrier than it appears.

The three goals I have advanced here are all ways to work against the chief pragmatic challenge to instructors of prison literature—namely, that students have been inundated with Hollywood and television representations of prison that impair their ability to read prison literature with clear eyes. In the popular imagination, prisons are places that inspire fear because they consist of codes, hierarchies, and language controlled by the criminals who inhabit them. Based on films such as *The Shawshank Redemption*, *American History X*, or *American Me* or the long-running HBO series *Oz*, prison is a lawless but self-contained world in which the uninitiated are constantly subject to extortion, rape, and murder and must defend themselves to survive. These stereotypical images might have some basis in reality but are so dramatic that most readers cannot enter the world of the prison and assess it according to the standards dictated by the literature itself (e.g., an appeal to read with sympathy). The concrete wall topped by barbed wire and razor ribbon is, in this regard, a metaphor for the reader's limitations, and the wall originates outside the world of the book.

A second, related pragmatic challenge is that a reader's response to the literature can be excessively emotional and insufficiently analytic. Like any social issue, incarceration invites instinctive reactions, ranging from the desire to abolish prisons altogether to the belief that all criminals deserve harder punishment than they receive. Complicating this dynamic in the classroom is the fact that one in thirty-two adults in the United States has done time, which means that statistically one student in a typical classroom has spent or will spend time in prison. This statistic may not apply to most colleges and universities in the United States because of social class and related issues, but it is likely that more than one student in a class is connected to someone behind bars. This circumstance makes the subject of incarceration personal, whether students are in favor of prison reform or not. That an increasing percentage of United States citizens have experienced incarceration makes it more difficult for a group of student readers to stereotype prisoners. It also makes it more difficult to approach prison literature analytically. Theoretical or critical secondary material can be useful here. Michel Foucault's study *Discipline and Punish* is especially effective in this regard.

Foucault is rich fare to serve to undergraduates in more than small portions, but I have found that *Discipline and Punish*, worked through slowly, forms a critical basis for the literature we read in prison literature courses and offers an important historical perspective that students may otherwise lack. Many students cannot imagine that there is or has ever been an alternative to our current prison system. Like any institution, the modern prison obscures its own history and makes its existence seem inevitable. The prison, according to Foucault, emerged in the eighteenth century as a kinder way to punish criminals, without the public spectacle of torture and execution. As democracy replaces monarchy, the criminal—who had been an enemy of the king—is now an enemy of the people. This observation raises a number of crucial questions about the relation between society and the criminal and asks the readers to consider the role of the prison in this relation. Foucault can help students articulate the ostensible aim of prison as opposed to its real effects. The modern penitentiary, according to him, has had seven "universal maxims": the transformation of the individual's behavior; the distribution or classification of convicts according to their crime and age; the possibility to modulate sentences (e.g., parole, time off for good behavior); socialization through work; education; technical supervision; and finally transition back into society (269–70). Foucault asserts that prisons fail to achieve these seven maxims regardless of prison reform; moreover, prisons are structured to fail; "prison, and no doubt punishment in general, is not intended to eliminate offences, but rather to distinguish them, to distribute them, to use them" (272). His argument leads outward from the prison into the broad social consideration of how power is distributed and maintained.

A host of questions about the purpose of the modern prison are raised by Foucault's work, and I suggest that they be discussed in conjunction with any inquiry into prison literature. The fundamental question raised by the practices of the modern penal system has to do with its intent. Do prisons exist to deter crime, to reform criminals, or to make society safer for law-abiding citizens? Is contemporary society truly concerned with and knowledgeable about the increasingly mechanical, efficient, and impersonal prison system? Foucault's argument leads toward a deeper understanding of social class and political power as part of the logic behind the modern prison.

One alternative to the prison is deportation, according to Foucault, an observation that should prompt valuable discussion of the rights of prisoners and their status in society. Recent detentions by the United States government and the military in Iraq and Guantanamo Bay, Cuba—military prisons in the heart of enemy country—should point to the relevance of such discussion. Using Foucault to raise such probing questions about incarceration prior to an encounter with prison literature will clarify the importance of narrative perspective in prison literature.

Like Foucault's work, my syllabus goes well beyond the disciplines of both law and literature. Reading literature in the way I am describing could easily lead students to questions addressed in other disciplines, such as history, sociology, psychology, and government. I have cotaught a version of this course with a colleague from the sociology department, and our sometimes divergent perspectives facilitated a richer experience for our students, who are unaccustomed to approaching a subject from different angles. One benefit of studying prison literature is that it is easily expanded, not narrowed, by the fusion of more than one discipline.

But the greatest benefit of studying prison literature is that it leads naturally to ethical examination. It catalyzes students, makes them confront their culture's nightmares and the darkest shadows of human experience. Ancient Greece, birthplace of both literature and democracy, invented drama to help its citizens work through in a public forum the fundamental difficulties of social existence. Prison literature similarly dramatizes a landscape created by policy makers and reimagined by writers; it fuses the rational and artistic poles of law and literature. That it is increasingly legitimized in the academy allows students to contemplate, again in a public forum, a part of their world that has been invisible. Once they have begun to see prisoners in their society and in their curricula, they are in a position to revise the way they see themselves, which should be the goal of any educational endeavor.

Notes

1. H. Bruce Franklin's anthology *Prison Writing in Twentieth-Century America* is another excellent collection, but it goes beyond the chronological scope of my course. Judith Scheffler's anthology *Wall Tappings* and Wally Lamb's anthology *Couldn't Keep It to Myself* both contain work only by women inmates. There are also a host of works by smaller presses that have published prison writing, such as Robert Ellis Gordon's *The Funhouse Mirror* or *"The Crying Wall,"* by Victor

Hassine, Robert Johnson, and Ania Dobrzanska. Individual prisons or state prison systems occasionally publish works from their writing programs, and the PEN Freedom to Write committee is another good source for this material.

2. Mumia Abu-Jamal's *Live from Death Row* is another popular text in prison literature courses that discusses a controversial case from the perspective of the convicted inmate.

Patricia D. Watkins

Using Critical Race Theory to Teach African American Literature

The following are some little-known facts that students can learn from the laws named and legal issues raised in the assigned texts in my literature course African American Novels and the Law, which I teach to an ethnically diverse class. In 1850, Congress passed a law awarding hearing officers in fugitive slave cases five dollars if they ruled that a person was not a fugitive slave and ten dollars if they ruled that the person was a fugitive slave. During World War I, the United States military issued a document ("Secret Information concerning Black American Troops") requesting French soldiers not to salute black American officers. During World War II, America received and interned over two thousand Latin Americans of Japanese descent. In 1943, American sailors entered Los Angeles barrios and stripped the clothing from Latino civilians while white policemen ignored the sailors and charged the victims with rioting and vagrancy. In 1950, Congress passed a law to detain subversives and established six detention camps in the United States (Nixon). In 1980, the Department of Justice concluded that in 1965, FBI Director J. Edgar Hoover had blocked the prosecution of the men responsible for killing four black girls in a 1963 Birmingham, Alabama, church bombing (Barber). In 1988, a study commissioned by the Dallas *Times Herald* found that the average prison sentence for convicted rapists was ten years if the victim was white, five years if the victim was Hispanic, and two years if the victim was black (Kennedy 73).[1]

From the antebellum period to the present, African American writers have used facts like these to challenge the dominant narrative of American liberty, equality, justice, and innocence. I have taught this course to expose students to such counternarratives. I taught it to examine some of the connections between law, on the one hand, and narrative and fiction, on the other—much of the fiction being fabrications that students had been taught since they entered elementary school.[2] Finally, I taught the course to expose students to a contemporary movement that connects literature and the law, critical race theory (CRT).

I used CRT in the course for two reasons. First, like many critical race theorists (criticalists), the authors on my syllabus wrote narratives and counternarratives that demonstrate that the American law practiced in their time failed to guarantee justice for black Americans. (By "American law," I mean the statutes, judicial decisions, orders, trials, procedures, and other methods by which the federal, state, and local governments significantly affect blacks' lives.) Second, I used CRT because its theories illuminate authors' narratives in ways that other methodologies do not. For example, in John A. Williams's 1967 novel *The Man Who Cried I Am*, the president of the United States has appointed the black protagonist and many other black Americans to important positions in his administration in clear response to Russia's cold-war propaganda about America's mistreatment of blacks. The president's action resonates with criticalist Derrick Bell's theory of "interest-convergence," the belief that "white elites will tolerate or encourage racial advances for blacks only when they also promote white self-interest" (Delgado, *Critical Race Theory* xiv). By analyzing the nuances of Bell's theory, a literature student may discover meaning in Williams's novel that otherwise would go unnoticed.

In the first class, I introduced CRT and provided information about the legal research that students would have to do in the course. I briefly explained how the authors on the syllabus and criticalists are alike. A general belief of criticalists, arrived at in the 1970s, is that traditional methods of seeking blacks' civil rights (e.g., litigation) no longer work or work too slowly and that new methods of seeking justice (e.g., storytelling and counterstorytelling) must be found (xiii). Storytelling and counterstorytelling demonstrate how the practice of American law has been unresponsive and sometimes even hostile to legal justice for black Americans. To gain such justice, both criticalists and the authors on my syllabus wrote narratives and counternarratives that "[construct] social reality in ways that promote [blacks'] self-interest" (xiv). I left the introduction of other CRT beliefs for discussion as they became relevant throughout the semester and moved on to the research that each student had to do in order to discuss a legal issue in an oral report, short documented essay, and long research paper.

I told students that if they could not find a legal issue on their own, they should not feel embarrassed to ask me for assistance, because I know from personal experience that students attend law school for three years learning how to recognize legal issues. I told them that I would not require them to read cases, because I did not want us to spend as much class time explaining the cases as discussing the literary texts. I told them that they could learn about courts' opinions secondhand by reading summaries and analyses of them in scholarly texts like those listed in the selected bibliography on the course syllabus. For straightforward legal history and analysis, I highlighted such texts as A. Leon Higginbotham's *In the Matter of Color* (providing a black liberal's analysis of American law) and Randall Kennedy's *Race, Crime, and the Law* (providing a black conservative's analysis of American law). For legal analysis and interpretation by criticalists, I highlighted Richard Delgado's *Critical Race Theory* (for its introduction to CRT and its essays that both exemplify and critique CRT), and I highlighted Patricia J. Williams's "Spirit-Murdering the Messenger" (for a definition of her concept of the "spirit injury"). Not by my design, all the texts in the selected bibliography—CRT and not—reveal American law's historic enmity to blacks. That enmity has shown itself in the existence of constitutionally sanctioned slavery; in local, state, and federal blind eyes to lynching; and in drug-sentencing guidelines that effectively have disfavored blacks. I told students that even if a legal document relevant to our assigned narratives was old or obscure—for example, the Fugitive Slave Act of 1793—they could find it online by entering keywords into a search engine like *Google*.

In the first few weeks of class, students asked for my assistance in finding legal issues so that they could do the research for their oral reports, but by the seventh week they began to experience as much satisfaction in finding legal issues in the novels as law students experience finding legal issues in fact patterns and cases. For the lesson on *The Man Who Cried I Am*, a student reported on the issue of governmental abridgments of constitutional rights, pointing to the McCarran Internal Security Act (passed by

Congress in 1950) as a real-life precedent for the King Alfred Plan in the novel, the major part of the federal government's final solution for disposing of all black people if they began a rebellion. For the lesson on Stephen L. Carter's *The Emperor of Ocean Park*, a student noticed the issue of law enforcement's failure to investigate fully the murders of blacks, which in the novel is tied to two or three major homicides. As a real-life equivalent, the student pointed to what she claimed was law enforcement's settling on identifying Wayne Williams as the lone murderer of Atlanta children between 1979 and 1981 even though evidence pointed to Klansmen's involvement in some of the murders. The student reporter on the last novel of the semester, Octavia Butler's *Parable of the Sower*, a work of science fiction set in the years 2024 to 2027, also showed proficiency in spotting legal issues. In Butler's future, the CRT-identified "property right in 'whiteness'" (Bell 7) has been lost because business corporations run America and make America's laws, while the poor and middle classes of all races are becoming "debt slaves" as a result (Butler 264). The student reported on the issue of slavery, pointing to convict labor laws and to the black codes of 1865 and 1866 as real-life legal precedents to support the novel's vision of the legal status of blacks and others in a future America.

Before students began making oral reports in week 4, I modeled the reports in weeks 2 and 3, when we studied Frederick Douglass's *Narrative* and Harriet Jacobs's *Incidents in the Life of a Slave Girl*. I showed students that they should begin by making the narrative provide the context for the legal issue in their report. They should then explain a law, a case, or statistics, for example, that they found relevant to the legal issue they had chosen. Finally, they should explain how the narrative constructs the law or how the law clarifies the narrative.

I encouraged students to distribute a handout of at least one page before beginning their oral reports. Among the handouts students eventually distributed were copies of federal statutes, Jim Crow laws, crime statistics, and summaries of court decisions on a single issue (e.g., restrictive housing covenants). These handouts proved valuable in two ways. First, they allowed students to see how terms were spelled and to absorb the names of people and cases as the reporters talked. Second, they recorded information that many students used in their essays for the closed-book final examination. While reading the final examinations, I was pleased that students identified major laws and cases by name.

Although our focus in the course was novels, I began with Douglass's *Narrative* and Jacobs's *Incidents* because these two slave narratives provide a historical and legal foundation for understanding major themes and legal issues in the novels, such as the physical abuse of black men and the sexual abuse of black women. To begin our analysis of the narratives, the students and I discussed some of the racist ideology that allowed Douglass's masters to treat him, as he says, like a brute, and that allowed Jacobs's de facto master to start making sexual advances to her when she turned fifteen. To provide examples clarifying the racist ideology, I distributed a handout quoting Thomas Jefferson's suggestion in *Notes on the State of Virginia* that African women and orangutans copulated. I also distributed quotations from David Hume in "Of National Characters" (1742), Immanuel Kant in "On National Characteristics" (1764), and Georges Leopold Cuvier in "Varieties of Human Species" (1797). These three men, in addition to Jefferson, either stated or suggested that Africans were innately inferior to whites. All the quotations explained to students—at least in part, because nothing can fully explain it—the existence of slavery in a land that declared its independence from England by stating "that all men are created equal, that they are endowed by their Creator with certain unalienable Rights, [and] that among these are Life, Liberty and the pursuit of Happiness" (*Declaration*). After my students and I discussed the racist ideology represented by the four quotations, I modeled the oral reports, discussing the United States Constitution for the Douglass lesson and court cases like *State of Missouri v. Celia, a Slave* (1855) for the Jacobs lesson. In week 4, the students began their own oral reports on the nine novels that we analyzed in the course.

In the twelfth class of the semester, analysis of Toni Morrison's *Song of Solomon* allowed my students and me to discuss a kind of law that we had not previously analyzed, community law—that is, the law that blacks use among themselves to identify, as Morrison puts it, "what was legal in the community as opposed to what was legal outside it" ("Language" 121) and who the outlaws were "by our definition, not by somebody else's" ("One out of Sequence" 71).

As usual, we started the Morrison lesson with two student reports. The first student discussed the killings of Emmett Till in 1955 and the four girls who died in a Birmingham, Alabama, church bombing in 1963. The student distributed time lines for both cases, showing that the killers of Till died in 1980 and 1990, never having been found guilty of his death, and that the last murderer of the girls was found guilty in 2002. The second student reported on possible sexual abuse in *Song of Solomon*, choosing this legal issue because the protagonist's mother nurses him until he is old enough for his feet to touch the floor while he sits on her lap. After students responded to the two reports, I asked them to share other comments and questions about the novel.

I told students that Morrison distinguishes between the laws and out-laws of the black community and the white community. I asked them to tell me what the black communities in *Song of Solomon* think about sexual relations between close family members and about white-on-black, black-on-white, and black-on-black homicides. We tried to account for the dif-ferences between the fictional black communities' laws on these issues and actual state laws and African customary law, which is the law of Africans uninfluenced by Islam or Christianity. I showed students a statement made by Antony Allott in his discussion of African customary law: "on the whole a system of law reflects a way of life; it represents an adjustment to life in a particular society and particular environment" (56). Based on Allott's statement and Morrison's fictional communities, the class concluded that the nonconforming law in those communities is an adaptation made by people who are neither African nor white American to an environment that is neither Africa nor the America that whites experience. The commu-nities' laws are an adjustment to their own unique environment.

The major challenge for me as an English teacher of my course Afri-can American Novels and the Law was not to let a focus on the law keep the class from seeing the narratives as literature. In large part, I solved the problem by discussing how the literary genre to which each text belongs is intrinsically suited to analyzing the law. Douglass's *Narrative* and Jacobs's *Incidents* belong to the genre of antebellum slave narratives, which had the purpose of showing the lawful horrors of slavery in order to speed its end. *Clotel*, an antebellum novel written by a fugitive slave, had the same purpose (W. Brown). *Iola Leroy*, which shows blacks' separate and unequal suffering under the law of the post-Reconstruction period, is a counter-narrative to and signifies on the antiblack novels then being written by members of the plantation tradition of American literature (F. Harper). *The Street* (Petry) and *If He Hollers Let Him Go* (Himes) are naturalistic novels — specifically, of the Richard Wright school of naturalism, which had as its thesis, "In an unwholesome environment the Negro is doomed to meet disaster in America" (Hughes 86). *The Man Who Cried I Am* can be discussed as a black arts novel, *Song of Solomon* as a black aesthetic novel, and *A Visitation of Spirits* as a black gay aesthetic novel (Kenan) — all three genres contemplating defiance of the law. Finally, *The Emperor of Ocean Park* can be discussed as a detective novel that is set in motion when someone breaks the law and *Parable of the Sower* as a science fiction novel that contemplates the future of the law. Each narrative belongs to a literary genre that intrinsically lends itself to a critique of American law. I connected the author's presentation and representation of the law in each text with the conventions of the respective genre.

The next time I teach African American Novels and the Law, I plan to take advantage of a final opportunity to put the assigned texts in a literary context at the end of the course. I will ask my students if they now understand why W. E. B. DuBois, sounding like a criticalist, wrote in 1926:

> I stand in utter shamelessness and say that whatever art I have for writing has been used always for propaganda for gaining the right of black folk to love and enjoy. I do not care a damn for any art that is not used for propaganda. But I do care when propaganda is confined to one side while the other is stripped and silent. (986)

The students need not agree with DuBois's statement, but I hope that they respond, having read literary representations of American law and having studied CRT, American law, and the administration of that law from the colonial period to the present, "We understand."

I selected the texts for the course on the basis of three criteria. First, each text had to invite discussion of a legal issue that was current when the text was written or published, thus reflecting the author's contemporaneous reaction to blacks' treatment by the law. Second, each text had to contribute at least one different legal issue toward a chronological survey of African Americans' experience of American law. Third, the texts as a group had to represent a variety of literary genres so that students could see the variety of African American literature. I list these texts in the order we read and discussed them, noting some of the literary motifs; laws, cases, and legal issues; and CRT concerns.

1. *Narrative of the Life of Frederick Douglass* (1845), by Frederick Douglass. Horrors of American slavery: US Constitution, slave codes, plantation law. CRT: spirit injury.
2. *Incidents in the Life of a Slave Girl* (1860), by Harriet Jacobs. Vulnerability of black women to sexual assault: *State of Missouri v. Celia, a Slave* (1855), *George (a Slave) v. State* (Mississippi, 1859), *Grandison (a Slave) v. State* (Tennessee, 1841). Running from the law: Fugitive Slave Acts of 1793 and 1850, *Scott v. Sandford* (1857). CRT: underprotection of black women, intersectionality, spirit injury.

3. *Clotel* (1853), by William Wells Brown. Indignities of slavery: anti-miscegenation laws, *Loving v. Virginia* (1967). Race and color consciousness: early variations in state laws, the one-drop rule. CRT: intersectionality, unequal protection, spirit injury.

4. *Iola Leroy* (1892), by Frances E. W. Harper. Unfulfilled promises of equality: the Fourteenth Amendment, Jim Crow laws, Civil Rights Act of 1875, "Civil Rights Cases" (1883), *Plessy v. Ferguson* (1896). Voting rights: the Fifteenth and Twenty-Fourth Amendments, Voting Rights Act of 1965, *Harper v. Virginia State Board of Elections* (1966). CRT: unequal protection, spirit injury.

5. *The Street* (1946), by Ann Petry. Vulnerability of black women to sexual assault. Housing discrimination: restrictive housing covenants, *Shelley v. Kraemer* (1948). Employment discrimination: state and city laws. CRT: intersectionality, unequal protection, spirit injury.

6. *If He Hollers Let Him Go* (1945), by Chester Himes. Vulnerability of black men to white women's accusations of rape: lynch law, Senate's apology for not passing antilynching legislation (2005). Legal lynching: the Scottsboro Boys (1931), *Coker v. Georgia* (1976). Employment discrimination: Executive Order 8802 prohibiting discrimination in the defense industry (1941). Police contributions to violence against blacks and other people of color: the Red Summer of 1919, Detroit riots of 1943, Zoot Suit Riots of 1943. What modern America has done to people of color: Executive Order 9066 to intern Japanese Americans (1944), *Korematsu v. United States* (1944), World War II internment of Japanese Latinos. CRT: unequal protection, jury studies, convergence of interests, spirit injury.

7. *The Man Who Cried I Am* (1967), by John A. Williams. Injustices to black soldiers in and out of the military: "War Department General Order 143: Creation of the U.S. Colored Troops" (1863), "Secret Information concerning Black American Troops" (1918). Federal surveillance of and violence against blacks: COINTELPRO, Emergency Detention Act of 1950 (McCarran, secs. 811–26). CRT: convergence of interests.

8. *Song of Solomon* (1977), by Toni Morrison. Absence of justice for black victims of violence: Emmett Till (1955), four black girls killed in church bombing (1963). Blacks' laws and outlaws: slaves' laws, free blacks' laws, Morrison's "village law." CRT: unequal protection of blacks, jury studies, lawbreakers and outlaws in the black community.

9. *A Visitation of Spirits* (1989), by Randall Kenan. Black homophobia: biblical law. CRT: outlaws in the black community, legal protection of lesbians and gay men, spirit injury.

10. *The Emperor of Ocean Park* (2002), by Stephen L. Carter. Federal government's inadequate responses to blacks' civil rights movements. CRT: affirmative action, inadequacy of liberal reform.

11. *Parable of the Sower* (1993), by Octavia Butler. Drug use in the black community. Police violence against the poor and blacks. CRT: black outlaws, "property right in 'whiteness.'"

Notes

1. My university reflects the diversity of the city where it is located, Los Angeles. Thus, when an assigned text in any African American literature course that I teach refers to or makes relevant a current or historical event in which the government harms any people of color or homosexuals, I mention the event not only because of its intrinsic significance but also because Asian Americans, Arab Americans, Latinos, blacks, gays, lesbians, and other others (as well as whites) regularly enroll in my African American literature classes.

2. In one semester of legal shocks, nothing seemed to stun my students more than a statement written by Supreme Court Justice Clarence Thomas in the case *Lawrence et al. v. Texas*: "I can find [neither in the Bill of Rights nor any other part of the Constitution a] general right of privacy" (605–06). Thomas's statement shattered for my students the fiction of Americans' unquestionable right to privacy—in this particular case, sexual privacy between consenting adults. Sharing a judge's awareness of such fictions is crucial to those seeking social justice.

Alyce Miller

The Legal and Literary Animal

The burgeoning pet industry; the vast amount of current interdisciplinary scholarship that examines and rethinks our moral and ethical obligations as understanding of animal intelligence, cognition, and emotion evolves;[1] the rise of a growing field of law known as animal law,[2] which encompasses both welfarist and rightist approaches in developing legal theories for litigating and legislating animal issues—all these developments make it evident that interest in the animal is at an all-time high.[3]

A university literature course that places nonhuman animals at the center and engages with the implications, both legal and literary, of that centering offers possibilities for exploring the complexity engendered by shifting notions of what constitutes animal and examining the many facets of our relationships with nonhuman animal friends. That animals have intrinsic value and are worthy of our moral consideration has only recently begun to seriously challenge the long-held belief that animals are inferior and therefore consumable and disposable. Law can be a useful critical tool for examining literary texts; it can also be a tool for effecting social change. A course on the legal and literary animal can help lay the groundwork and provide an occasion for activist engagement.

In the eyes of United States law, nonhuman animals are still considered property, things, and this conceptualization accounts for the fact that animals have neither subject position nor agency in it. Many involved in the field of animal law point to ongoing changes in the legal status of animals in other countries like Germany and Austria (where animals have been given, at least in writing, constitutional protection). Both rightists and welfarists argue that those with dominion over animals, ranging from pet owners to corporate farmers raising animals for food to medical researchers engaged in experimentation with animal subjects, have responsibilities for them. Yet laws pertaining to animals have typically considered only human protection and convenience and the more extreme kinds of animal cruelty.

In literature, nonhuman animals appear as important symbols, characters, and even protagonists, sometimes allegorized, sometimes personified. In more realistic works, they are sometimes sentimentalized, sometimes demonized. Though ever-present throughout children's literature, animals are appearing more and more in works for adults, such as Mr. Bones, the dog protagonist in Paul Auster's *Timbuktu*, or nonfiction works like Carolyn Knapp's observant *Pack of Two*. In the last few years, there has been a surge in memoirs about writers' relationships with pets. In much literature about animals lie implicit questions about the connections and relationships between human and nonhuman animals and how they are represented. This literature offers a perfect starting point for examining our perceptions of animal consciousness; the contradictions inherent in our treatment of animals; the choice of which we cherish and privilege, which we choose to see as needing protection, which we consume, and which we eradicate.

Courses in law and literature typically focus on connections between law-related fictions (representations of law in works of literature, like courtroom dramas) and actual legal documents (case law, testimony, confession, etc.) as literature. A course on animal law and literature takes a slightly different approach, since nonhuman animals are neither featured in literature as subjects of litigation proceedings nor engaged in activities normally associated with legal literature: the confession, the testimonial, and so on. Because animals are not yet recognized as having standing in courts of law, they may not be parties in legal proceedings that affect them.[4]

A law and literature course about animals could easily be adapted for a graduate seminar or a broader undergraduate audience, but a logical constituency would be upper-division English or humanities majors. Such a course is also useful for law students, but the literature component might be a hard sell, because law and literature classes are generally electives in law school and treated as less significant. While some humanities majors may feel frustration when first encountering case law, my experience has been that with a little basic preparation and a quick tour of concepts like issue spotting and holding, students are quickly able to apply their analytic skills to work through the arguments and issues in complicated cases as well as judicial opinions.

Rationale for the Class

Combining the subject of animals with narrative and law offers a multilayered critical lens for exploring relationships between human and nonhuman animals and the ways in which nonhuman animals are viewed, represented, portrayed, and used. There is a lot at stake here; how we think about, represent, and see nonhuman animals through cultural and social narratives has great impact on animals. Though the Cartesian precept that animals are simply automata has clearly been discounted, animals remain disposable and dispensable, and their value is typically determined through a market economy. Still, a number of animal law scholars and some lower-court judges (especially in cases involving companion animals like dogs and cats) have made inroads in disrupting conventional notions about animals as things, even suggesting that some animals, notably primates, have a right to extended protection that verges on self-determination. For example, Angela Campbell recently argued in the *Animal Law Review* that a chimpanzee may meet the basic requirements for appearing as a witness in a court of law under evidence rule 501. Emerging evidence that nonhuman animals think, problem-solve, and lead emotional lives has led many zoos to include animal enrichment programs and respond more appropriately to animals' social needs. For example, because elephants function in complex social groups, they should not be separated. Recent recognition that nonhuman animals use tools has challenged tool use as the dividing line between human and nonhuman animals. But how do we avoid hierarchical thinking? Are dogs deserving of better treatment than rabbits or chickens? Should we honor the primacy given to primates by thinkers and legal scholars like Steven Wise or the privileges accorded to the animals we choose as companions?[5] As we learn more about nonhuman animals, the question becomes, How do our notions of the animal change and shift?

What are the implications of such shifts for science, law and legislation, medicine, corporate farming, animals in research, zoos, pets, humanism, and so forth?

Whether animals are represented in legal cases or in literature, good starting questions are, What does it mean for them to speak, and who speaks for them? When animals are voiced, as they often are in poems and fiction, what do they sound like? Do they simply speak like four-legged versions of people? When advocates and nonadvocates alike, engaged in legislation and litigation, speak for them, what is being said and how? What are the consequences? What are the connections between discourses of speciesism and discourses of racism and sexism? What might we make of the fact that black dogs are the most likely to be euthanized? How do we interpret the well-established connections between animals and women, between animal abuse and domestic violence?

A course on animal law and literature could engage many of these and other questions along the spectrum of animal welfarism and animal rights and draw on a provocative reading list combining animal literature, case law, law review articles, and critical essays. The following four sample units lay a conceptual foundation for teaching a course on literary and legal animals. Moving from the question of what constitutes the animal to relationships between human and nonhuman animals and some of the ways nonhuman animals are represented and voiced in law and literature, these units suggest texts and methods that teachers might either integrate into already established courses or develop into thematically oriented special-topics courses. Some general suggestions and an abbreviated reading list are provided in the conclusion.

Sample Units

Unit 1: What Is an Animal?

We begin by considering how the law identifies and defines *animal*, and we take into account the implications of categories. Animal advocates often use the term *nonhuman animal* instead of *animal*, though the law does not. Is an insect an animal? a goldfish? A useful entry point is to look at several cases in animal law that take up this issue, such as *Knox v. Massachusetts SPCA*, then examine how the definition of *animal* affects who is covered by anticruelty statutes, for example. Under the Animal Welfare Act, rabbits were recently reclassified as poultry and thereby exempted from certain slaughterhouse protections. Legal designations of domestic versus wild carry similarly serious implications for the way in which animals are perceived and treated. Readings in literature by writers who directly address difficult and even disturbing human interactions with animals can be blended with legal texts. In Ernest Gaines's short story "The Sky Is Gray," the young boy protagonist, accustomed to eating certain kinds of birds, is horrified when he observes the brutal killing of the beautiful redbird his mother has trapped for food. When she insists that he kill a second redbird, he refuses and is punished. How we distinguish between animals we wish to protect and the animals we consume is deeply connected to how we perceive ourselves. What does it mean to privilege some animals over others? In his book *Rattling the Cage: Toward Legal Rights for Animals*, Wise, a lawyer and animal activist, makes a compelling case for extending the legal status of personhood to bonobos and chimpanzees, whom he singles out as being more closely related to human animals, sharing, according to some researchers, as much as 98.3% of DNA (132). Is closer to human the criterion by which we then assign nonhuman animals legal protections and status?

This question leads us back across the dividing line to a discussion of our own animal nature. For a more sophisticated group of students, the Canadian writer Marian Engel's controversial, award-winning novel *Bear*, in which a lonely woman researcher begins an erotic relationship with a captive bear, might serve as a provocative platform for looking at often distorted and mythic perceptions of wild animals endemic to our culture. It might also open the door to considering wild animals as spectacle, other, feminine, sexualized. An interesting contrast to this portrayal is the feral child. An obvious text is François Truffaut's 1970 film *L'enfant sauvage*, which can prompt an interesting conversation on what we believe it means to be human.

Unit 2: Animal as Property: Rights, Standing, and Dominion versus Stewardship

Animal studies troubles the boundary between human and nonhuman. Unit 2 considers the significance of categorizing any sentient creature as property. The problem of viewing animals as property might be initially addressed by examining other rights movements that have responded to oppression and issues of personhood (for slaves, women, children). An entire course could examine and compare legal discourses and case law on slavery and women with current discourses and case law on animals—not analogizing experience, of course, which is a common misconception, but examining systems of oppression and similarities in the structures of arguments. Another interesting and useful approach is to focus on the specific parallels between children's and animal rights movements, as rights afforded to children and nonhuman animals are often held on their behalf by others (parents, pet owners, etc.). There are also historical and legal convergences, such as the story of Mary Ellen Wilson, the abused child in the nineteenth century who was rescued by the SPCA before there were child protection services.

The protection model offers an important connection not only to the children's rights movement but also to the larger question of how human beings perceive their relationship to nonhuman animals and to which of them. Is protection paternalistic, or might we imagine it as the portal to autonomy? In much of his work, the ethicist and religious scholar Andrew Linzey (author of *Animal Gospel* and *Animal Theology*) explores the tension between Judeo-Christian notions of dominion and the concept of stewardship or caretaking. If we conceive of animals as creatures over whom we have dominion and therefore relegate them to the category of property, with which we can do whatever we choose, we take a very different direction from that of the animal rights movement, which argues for animals' autonomy, subjectivity, and happiness. The concept of protection is at work, at least on the books, in federal statutes like the Endangered Species Act and the Marine Mammal Protection Act, as well as in state statutes that are intended to protect native species. Small shifts in legally expressed attitudes toward animals considered pets can be found in some lower-court decisions and opinions—namely, in cases of wrongful death or injury suits of companion animals. Traditionally, the most an animal owner could recover in such a situation would be the monetary value of the animal. But in the case of injury or death by negligence of certain companion animals, mostly dogs and cats, some courts have allowed the possibility for recovering noneconomic damages for emotional distress and the equivalent of loss of consortium.[6] In addition, the wills and trusts code has for some years recognized pet trusts (not all states do), and some courts have overseen custody disputes in divorce cases as to who keeps the family dog.[7] Changes in the language of some city and state ordinances from *pet owner* to *guardian* and from *pet* to *companion animal* carry more than symbolic weight. The linguistic shift, already taking place in communities around the country, paves the way for perceptual and behavioral shifts to the advantage of the nonhuman animals in our lives.[8]

Unit 3: Animal Voices: Representations of Animals in Literature

The way we speak about animals influences the way we make them speak in a variety of fictional and nonfictional modes. Nonhuman animals have long figured in literature, whether as the allegorical figures in Aesop's fables and George Orwell's *Animal Farm,* as the sentimentalized figure of the red pony in John Steinbeck's realist novella by that title; or as the unsentimental and brutal portrayal of a dog in Jack London's gripping short story "Bâtard." Animals have been cuted up and personified as detectives and travel companions. They have also been treated as serious protagonists, as in Auster's *Timbuktu,* and as actual narrators, as in Dave Eggers's short story "After I Was Thrown in the River and Before I Drowned." An entire collection of poems about dogs and from the point of view of dogs by writers who live with dogs was gathered under the title *Unleashed* (Hempel and Shepard); it examines everything from animal cruelty to imaginings of happy dog speakers.

Representations of animals in literature often reflect cultural and social attitudes of particular times and places. An interesting pairing of works written at opposite ends of the twentieth century might be Thomas Mann's thinly fictionalized essay, translated as "A Man and His Dog," about his relationship with Bashan, a spirited dog with whom he forges a bond but can never fully comprehend, and Knapp's contemporary *Pack of Two,* in which Lucille, a companion dog, offers Knapp a kind of hard-won salvation after Knapp recovers from alcoholism. A number of recent story collections have used animals as tropes throughout, such as Brad Watson's *Last Days of the Dog-Men,* in which a literal dog plays a role in each story, and Jill McCorkle's *Creatures of Habit,* in which the animal-titled stories ("Monkeys," "Snakes," etc.) play along a blurred line of what it means to be animal.

Unit 4: The Unsentimentalized Animal in Literature

Where the readings in unit 3 promote discussion of how cultural and historic differences create different animals, unit 4 raises the question of what we need animals to be and assumes that studying our relationship to them can tell us about both them and ourselves. Writers have long celebrated the joys of interspecies companionship, but the realities of loving animals and understanding them present very real limits. In his essays "Calliope Times" ("Personal History") and "Circus Music," Edward Hoagland makes tragic observations on the real lives and suffering of circus animals. In "Dog Trouble," Cathleen Schine poignantly details her relationship with a violent, aggressive dog she adores and eventually has to euthanize. "Hawk," by Joy Williams, tells of the day the narrator's beloved dog makes a vicious, unprovoked attack on her. These four essays provide an excellent foundation for probing such legal issues as breed bans (the most common one focuses on dogs known by the general category of pit bulls) and commercial uses of animals in zoos and circuses. In addition, a unit on the unsentimentalized animal opens a window into animal abuse as well as general domestic violence. Four readings in this vein are Jim Grimsley's excruciating and beautifully written novel *Winter Birds*, which portrays and confronts the horrors of domestic violence, and three poems that expose very different and nuanced aspects of the cruelty born of ignorance or greed: "The Puppy," by Wesley McNair; "Tormenting the Cat," by Charles Harper Webb; and "Commerce," by Michael Waters.

A course on animal law and literature could be easily organized around any of the above units for an entire semester. Additional topics are animals in entertainment and animals and children. Books like *Beautiful Joe* (Saunders), narrated by an abused dog who ends up loved and triumphant, or the brave rescues by the eternal heroine Lassie (Rosemary Wells) might serve to examine the ways in which animals are represented in children's literature in particular. Film clips might include classics like *That Darn Cat!* and *One Hundred and One Dalmations*, as well as the more recent spate of films with talking, personified, and self-actualizing animals, such as the nonhuman characters in *Babe*. A course unit on animals and crime might begin with Edgar Allan Poe's famous locked-room detective tale "Murders in the Rue Morgue," which conceives of a beast (actually an orangutan) who is uncovered as the perpetrator of hideous and inexplicable violence. This othering of what is now a familiar primate demonstrates the emotional and aesthetic attitude toward animals that was commonplace before the twentieth century and made it possible, perhaps even acceptable, to decimate large populations of wild animals that were seen as threats. In the thirteenth century, a murderous pig was publicly tried and burned for killing a child, and a sow clothed in a man's garb was put on trial in the fourteenth century for maiming a child—the sow was tortured and hanged (animal cries of pain were often determined to be confessions of guilt). E. P. Evans's *The Criminal Prosecution and Capital Punishment of Animals* explores numerous historical court cases in which all sorts of animals—rats, insects, dogs, and horses—were prosecuted for crimes. A film clip from Daniel Mann's *Willard* or Phil Karlson's sequel, *Ben*, would lead to an exploration of the traditional demonization of certain animals like rats. Animals perceived as witches' familiars might also be of interest, like the role of Puss, the Money Cat, in Ann Petry's young-adult novel *Tituba of Salem Village*. A unit like this could naturally segue into animals and gender, animals and speciesism, and animals and race, using J. M. Coetzee's controversial novels *Disgrace* and *The Lives of Animals* as centerpieces.

There might also be a unit on the half-human, half-animal figure that has permeated myth, literature, and film. Examining some of those representations, including actual human animals who chose to become animal, like the man known as Lizard Man (whose interest was aesthetic) and the man who called himself Cat Man, might lead to interesting discussions about use of this transgressive figure in such films as *The Fly*, *Cat People*, and *Silence of the Lambs*. In his heart-breaking poem "The Sheep Child," James Dickey gives voice to the product of an animal and human coupling that produces a monster. In "The Metamorphosis," Franz Kafka opens his story with the conceit that Gregor Samsa, a normal man, has awakened one day to find he has turned into a bug. Are such meldings simply a form of spectacle, played either for comic or horrific effect, or do they begin to trouble the line between human and nonhuman animals?

The sharp divisions between human and nonhuman animals are already being challenged by new scientific information, and yet the law, sadly, has lagged behind. Law can be a tool for social change, but it has also been used to reinforce the status quo. No matter how much we debate the status of animals from ethical and moral positions, the real action lies in changes in the law. Yet what changes are appropriate? What is the proper legal status for animals? Does the category of property offer protection, as some legal scholars have argued? What kinds of laws will best help nonhuman animals? Which kinds might inadvertently or intentionally cause further harm? How do we conceive of legal rights for animals? Our often conflicted and puzzling attitudes toward nonhuman animals can be readily explored in the cultural stories we tell ourselves about them in our literature and the narratives we rely on to formulate laws and doctrines regarding them. The blending of legal and literary stories offers more nuanced and complex approaches than simply focusing on one or the other. Reading literature through the lens of law, and law through the lens of literary narratives, opens up a more imaginative way of thinking about legal and literary animals that might also enhance the ways teachers approach other subjects, such as children's literature or crime literature.

Notes

1. This scholarship includes work by ethologists like Marc Bekoff (*The Emotional Lives of Animals*) and Jonathan Balcombe (*Pleasurable Kingdom*), cultural studies scholars like Cary Wolfe (*Animal Rites*), primatologists like Jane Goodall (*My Life with the Chimpanzees*), feminists like Carol Adams (*The Sexual Politics of Meat*), essayists like the writer and activist Alice Walker (her essay "Am I Blue?"), fiction writers like J. M. Coetzee (*Elizabeth Costello*), the dog trainer and philosopher Vicki Hearne (*Animal Happiness*), the feminist-scientist Donna Haraway (*When Species Meet*), and the religious scholar Andrew Linzey (*Animal Gospel*). Each year the number of national and international conferences devoted to scholarship on animals grows significantly.

2. Animal law courses and programs now exist at about eighty law schools around the country, including Harvard, Rutgers, Northwestern, UCLA, Stanford, Columbia, the University of Michigan, and the University of Arizona. Current articles that explore legal issues and changes in the law can be found in law journals such as *Animal Law Review* (Lewis and Clark Law School) and *Journal of Animal Law* (Michigan State University Law School) and in the publications of the Animal Legal Defense Fund (ALDF). The seminal work for the animal rights movement is Peter Singer's now classic *Animal Liberation: A New Ethics for Our Treatment of Animals*, first published in 1975, in which Singer argues for moral standing for animals. Other important books on the legal status of animals are Steven Wise's *Rattling the Cage* (which focuses on the great apes) and Gary Francione's *Introduction to Animal Rights: Your Child or Your Dog?* (which argues that animals should not be considered property).

3. Welfarists work to improve conditions for the animals we use and consume ("better cages"); rightist, much more like abolitionists, would like to see an end to all exploitation of animals ("empty cages").

4. Animals do not meet the requirements, as outlined in article 3 of the United States Constitution, for standing and therefore do not, on their own, have access to redressing wrongs in our legal system. Standing is a legal concept in which a party must demonstrate ample connection to an injury or harm before being allowed to press a claim in a court of law. Under certain circumstances, and with sufficient proof of connection, a third party (e.g., a trade union, someone with interchangeable economic connections, or someone who is representing a class action suit) may be given standing to proceed in a court of law. For an important case that addresses standing for animals on these issues, see *Lujan v. Defenders of Wildlife*.

5. Anticruelty statutes vary from state to state, but farm animals and hunted animals are often exempt from them.

6. Traditionally, because of their status as property, the value of a nonhuman animal has been determined by the market. In other words, if you paid $50 for your dog at the shelter, that is the value of the dog. In the last few years, tort law has seen a good deal of activity in case law and in evolving legal theories that take into account the bond between animals and people and the reality of emotional distress and loss of companionship experienced by a pet owner if an animal is killed or injured. The state of Tennessee is the first to authorize noneconomic damages in wrongful death suits for companion animals. See *La Porte v. Assoc. Independents Inc.*

7. A particularly high-profile divorce case involved custody of a California dog named Gigi and her wealthy owners, Stanley Perkins and Linda Perkins. The case drew attention, in part, because of the huge sums of money spent and because of the videotape ("A Day in the Life of Gigi") submitted into evidence as proof that Gigi belonged with Mrs. Perkins.

8. An intriguing and thorny debate takes up the question of whether non-human animals have better protections available (ironically) as property than if stripped of their property status, which some argue would leave them in legal limbo. Therefore, some other status has to take its place, and the legal scholar David Favre has suggested an idea called equitable self-ownership.

Cristine Soliz and Harold Joseph

Native American Literature, Ceremony, and Law

Our model course was designed around themes relevant to ceremony and law in American Indian literature taught by Cristine Soliz in ethnic studies and American Indian studies at the University of Washington and at Colorado State University, Pueblo. In 2003, Soliz reworked the themes at Diné College, the tribal college at Tuba City, with Harold Joseph (then its director) for a sophomore Native American literature class.

The classroom contexts range from sizable, multicultural classes at a research university in Seattle; to a class of Chicano students at a mainly undergraduate campus in Pueblo, Colorado; and finally to classes of twenty to thirty Native American students at a tribal college in a rural town on the Navajo reservation. Diné College was the first tribally controlled college and has been operating since 1968. It is a branch of the main campus at Tsaile, Arizona, and one of seven satellites maintained as distance learning centers. All, including the main campus, are in rural areas and remote from amenities. Tuba City is the largest town on the reservation and is adjacent to a Hopi town, Moencopi, and not far from a small Paiute community. There are twenty-one tribes in Arizona and nineteen in New Mexico, so it is not unusual for a class in Tuba City to have a student or two from any of the nearby tribes or even Pueblos who maintain ties with the Hopis.

We began discussing ceremony at Tuba City because students and employees regularly ask for time off to attend ceremonies: kachina dances for the Hopi, squaw dances or others for the Navajo. The enactment of ceremony can require participants to stay awake for several nights, but this practice is not understood from a Euro-Western view. In white-run schools in Hopi land, for example, this failure to understand discourages students from investing time in ceremonies. As recently as the 1990s, Navajo high schools in Tuba City experienced a similar problem: even when a curriculum to help preserve the culture was being set, several Navajo teachers asked whether Navajo culture had anything worth saving. These examples make it clear that the epistemology of and rationale for ceremonies are being lost. The original intent in establishing tribal colleges, however, was to rectify damages caused by Western pedagogy by allowing the colleges to set their own curriculum "without assimilation" (*Tribal Colleges* A-2). We felt that a course on ceremony could lead to calendars planned around ceremonies rather than around Euro-Western structures.

In different institutional settings, rhetorical warrants for class discussions also differ, even though students may equally lack background information. For example, although many students have never heard of Indian removal or extermination, the reaction of Native Americans to this information in a tribal context (where students have some knowledge of their tribal histories) differs from the reaction of those in a multicultural setting: Native American students experience a bonding with other tribes and a reconnection to their own cultures, while other students' reactions range from white guilt to personal trauma. So sensitivity is requisite when planning teaching strategies.

Ceremony is a ritual way of organizing and conceptualizing our physical and spiritual relation both to space and to all life-forms. From our perspective, American Indian ceremony is thus law and is as central to Native identity and culture as written law is to United States culture. However, the historic conflicts between American Indian ceremony and United States law, especially in the way land is conceptualized, have obscured ceremony's significance. (United States law organizes land from a monetary perspective as property and real estate, whereas Hopi ceremonial law, for example, approaches it in the interests of balance and conservation: land is alive and meant to be protected—not owned—for the survival of future generations. Focusing on Native American literature about ceremony, our course frames ceremony as law and thus expands definitions of what counts as law. It offers a way for Native Americans to reconnect to their historic identities and traditions (in addition to promoting respect between Native and non-Native communities), and it provides alternative ideas about how to restructure our ties to the land.

Our course thus explored ceremony as it intersects with philosophies and systems of law that have different ways of comprehending the reality of America and of claiming legitimacy for notions of governance in America. We wanted the course to lead students to appreciate ceremony's importance and to challenge them to think critically about environmental and civic issues in their own reservation experience as well as in the larger Southwest community. Through both efferent and aesthetic readings, students looked at Native American literature in relation to three kinds of legal texts: ceremony, Indian treaties, and federal law.

American Indian Ceremony

Native American literature is often about sustainability, both of the environment and of Native cultures themselves. Its orientation to the environment specifically contrasts the way Native ceremony looks at land and the way United States law looks at land. Native traditions and texts thus offer readers an epistemological alternative to how human beings currently relate to the earth, an alternative that answers the global appeal of the United Nations to people to alter their practices toward earth, one another, and all life-forms (Annan). Threats to the environment are also threats to Native American ways of life, which Leslie Marmon Silko outlines in an essay referencing the 1981 federal report "A Continuing Quest for Survival." According to Silko, Native American culture suffers in direct relation to the continued extraction of resources, ranging from water to oil, from Native American land ("America's Debt" 617). Current examples corroborate her prediction: the Desert Rock coal plant in New Mexico reportedly will cause only ten percent less pollution than old plants (Kraker), and Southwest tribes battled in court an Arizona ski resort's venture on the San Francisco Peaks to make snow from treated sewage. The power of mountains as a life source is central to indigenous thought, and for centuries the Peaks have had unbroken ties to Hopi ceremonies to sustain life on earth. At Tuba City we studied ceremony as environmental law in the artificial snow case, using the United Nations sustainability text and William D. Ruckelshaus's "Toward a Sustainable World." (Additional works that access environmental issues are James Welch's *The Indian Lawyer* and Silko's *Almanac of the Dead*.) The students readily connect to ceremony and see it as a valid way of regulating harmonious ties to the land.

In a scene in *Wynema: Child of the Forest* (1891), by the Muscogee author Alice Callahan, a white teacher and a missionary discuss an after-burial ceremony in which Indians dismount at a creek and walk into the water, some immersing themselves and others splashing their faces or heads, then walk out backward. The missionary does likewise and tells Genevieve, the teacher:

> "[T]he Indians believe that the water will keep off the disease, and they have an inkling of the truth . . . [because] it is declared in Holy Writ that 'Cleanliness is next to godliness,' and truly a clean body is proof against disease."
>
> "But don't you think that by participating in . . . strange ceremonies, you . . . encourage the Indians to keep up their barbaric customs?" Genevieve asked. (27)

While the missionary reads this ceremony symbolically as Christian canon, the ceremony shows Muscogee knowledge of physiopsychic principles: the power of the human psyche to release things that twist a mind after a death and interment. The release is both physical and spiritual. You don't verbalize them on a psychiatrist's couch, because your body and mind left them with the earth at that place where the water washed them away. By treating disease as only physical, the psychic and spiritual economy of suffering and loss become abandoned. What can we say about those who immersed themselves totally in the river? How deep was their grief? Students are asked what kind of power they think was made manifest at that place. They are asked to think about how they release their fears or anger when a loved one dies. The ceremony operated as law in maintaining an orderly existence. What would happen to these people in the story if this "barbaric custom" were forbidden? Or if the creek were polluted by a paper mill upstream? What knowledge would subsequently be lost to us?

Reading ceremony through fiction, however, raises questions about the possibility that the textualized representation of a ceremony will detract from its potency. What if readers can't step outside European frameworks of law and literature? What if the approach to literature and its aesthetics does not include oral stories or performance? Students might consider that ceremony's place in some fictional texts parallels the way ritual ceremonies themselves remain circumscribed in the real world of law—that is, in a world that cannot see law except in law's texts. We respond to the rationale of the ceremony, not to appropriate it from the tribes but to recognize its power both in the text and in the real world.

Christopher Ronwanien:te Jocks, a Native scholar in religion, notes the complex relation Indian ceremony has "with other domains, including economics and politics" (425), as did Gary Witherspoon in his study of Navajo ceremonial language. These domains are often obscured by religion, which is taken to be the only means of interpreting ceremony, as we note in the artificial snow case. Whereas European ceremony has been authorized by law, Native ceremony establishes and enacts law and normalizes behavior in a harmonious way (Vattel 48). It is founded on the human link to the workings of the natural world. In *Wynema,* the Muscogee mourners interact with that world to be healed. Native American students recognize this complexity in their final essays when they express the urgent wish to recover ceremonies and the knowledge that goes with them.

Reading ceremony in this way introduces three problems, which can be addressed directly in classroom discussion. First, in United States–Indian relations there has never been an equal exchange of power. As Jocks points out, the "sharing of spiritual practices" can occur only "among equals . . . with the permission of both parties" (416). How then do we read ceremony against a long history of cultural and spiritual appropriation? How can we share a practice that isn't recognized as law? Second, the historic suppression of ceremony, ranging in form from torture to the later Indian Religious Crimes Code from 1883 to 1932 (Talbot 9; Price), has resulted in the loss of information. How can we recover ceremony and its lessons? Third, the written nature of law and literature seems to preclude Native ceremony or at least makes it hard to reconcile that ceremony with European textual and historical traditions and institutions. How can we hear a ceremony in this culture of print?

With these questions in mind, a thoughtful study of ceremony in Native American literature can offer a comparative way of understanding law. Higher-level courses might address the legal categories and networks that legitimate our practices. If Native American ceremony lacks an apparatus of law enforcement, what are the consent mechanisms for a community that values choice over force? Native Americans are active participants in their system, perhaps because ceremonies appeal to the human need for interaction and play; they encourage participation by their festive nature and involve important pedagogical practices, such as storytelling, songs, games, and giveaways (Paul Boyer). If physical laws form the foundation of ceremony as law—sustaining the harmonious interdependence of existence and ensuring human conformity—how foundational is ceremony for other Native American laws, such as those regarding visibility, autonomy, and the right of grievance as the means of keeping harmony and promoting happiness in the human community? Ceremony recognizes the diversity and interdependence of all life, so that human beings and the natural world remain in balance (Deloria 69). In Hopi, nature is the center of law and controls everything people do in their ceremonies. Ceremony's aesthetic forms interact with living and natural forces so that life can continue. For the Hopi, this path is the Sun Trail. For the Navajo, it is the Beauty Way, a house made of dawn and corn pollen. So our course reads ceremony as a productive text in a framework whose center is not human, a text that includes coyote and badger stories and implicity recognizes the need to moderate human power.

Indian Treaties

Early treaties bridge the gap between ceremony and European law. Lawrence Wroth suggested in 1928 that they are the first American literature. Students at Tuba City analyze his description of an interchange between the Onondawa and the colonists in the Lancaster Treaty of 1744 that suggests conflicting views of council fire and treaty (327). Why do the colonists want more council fires, yet some Indians feel that a past one is still in effect? In learning teams, we locate online a speech by Canassatego and identify the ceremonial aspects of council fires in the treaty.

Notwithstanding the importance of treaty rights, the centrality of treaties, particularly regarding the environment, has been overdetermined precisely because ceremony is not taken as a valid perspective on America—even though it provides an older view of America and is therefore fundamental to the American imaginary. The long-term consequences for white Americans of having excluded Natives—the opportunities for misunderstanding created by their disconnection from Native communities—became apparent in the Makah whale hunt of 1999, which evoked an astonishingly violent reaction from the Seattle public and Greenpeace (W. Johnson). Students at the University of Washington, including several Makah enrolled in the class, studied this hunt as events unfolded. The tribe had voluntarily deferred their hunting rights when whales became endangered because of overhunting by others, but when whale runs were up again, the Makah resumed their ceremony. Public focus on treaty as the ground of contest eclipsed the priority of Makah ceremony as a vital law of harmony. As with the case of the artificial snow, the focus on religion may be seen as a departure from the rational base of environmental law, since religion, for some, is irrational.

Students in the course are required to select a treaty to study throughout the term and be able to cite its narratives. A helpful article, "Teaching the Narrative Power of the Law," paraphrases Peter Brooks: "Essentially everything a lawyer produces is a story . . . that a reader must interpret. . . . It's not a work of fiction . . . but the writer is making choices that tell a story about that reality . . . [for example] what . . . devices drive those choices?" (Couch). This approach helps us read the narratives in a treaty— particularly in later treaties, which are devoid of ceremonial language and Native rhetorical styles—and discuss the significance of this rhetorical exclusion of Indians in the later treaties.

Federal Indian Law

Indian treaties and Native American literature are circumscribed by federal Indian law. Some scholars argue that the curriculum of Indian studies should be grounded in federal law, specifically in the Supreme Court's Marshall trilogy, a group of decisions led by Chief Justice John Marshall in the 1800s that adversely affected Indians (Cheyfitz 95, 6). But we see ceremony as a fundamentally different and prior form of law. One text we studied (both at CSU-Pueblo and Tuba City) to contrast federal Indian law and ceremony is Albert Yava's letter to the government. Yava wrote during the Dawes Act period (from the General Allotment Act of 1887, effective to 1934) to explain why building fences would harm Hopi way. One reason he gave is that because fierce winds carry the soil to new places each season, Hopis contracted the planting with those whose land had the soil (564). Amid the dances for planting, the ceremonial contracts with the families whose land had the soil were no doubt an exciting part of the process. We ask students to consider how the Hopi systems of economics and negotiation changed with the imposition of United States law. Students at Pueblo saw this imposition as oppressive government, whereas at Tuba City students were more interested in the insights into their identities and traditions that discussion of these issues provided.

Another reason Yava gave is that women controlled the land. A theme we studied at Pueblo, "Identity Formation and Indian Women," used Yava's letter and Virgina Woolf's *A Room of One's Own* to analyze differing senses of legal power as a factor in shaping identity. We focused on the role of private property in determining one's status as savage or civilized. How, for example, did white, Christian males who owned property, women, and slaves compare with nonwhite, non-Christian males whose wives owned the property? How does the choice not to possess others shape identity in Indian culture? Yava's letter suggests that because women control the land, Old World criteria for being civilized were not those of Indians.

Federal law's reliance on notions of property that differed categorically from those of Native Americans is an important factor in the failure to see ceremony as law. William Robertson's *History of the Discovery and Settlement of North America* (published in London in 1777 and popular during Indian removal) argued, for example, that law was based on property and so because Indians were "strangers to property," they didn't have law (Konkle 12). In the same vein, Marshall's 1823 opinion in *Johnson v. McIntosh*, which Eric Cheyfitz discusses in his work on Indian literature and law, endues "certain chiefs" with the right to trade land. Cheyfitz says Marshall situated Indians "on the model of a Western corporation or joint-stock company" that appoints a chief as a "CEO of sorts" in the matter of trading land (50). We recently analyzed Marshall's representation of Indians and compared the enactment of ceremony with the enactment and performance of United States law over Indians.

Our course Native American Literature, Ceremony, and Law would meet the mission of a tribal college and general education requirements, fit into courses on federal and Indian relations, and ground Native American or ethnic studies students who enter law studies. Again, the overarching aim of the course is to frame ceremony as law. In settings ranging widely, from a tribal college on a Navajo reservation to a sizable class at a research university in a major metropolitan area, this framework, which ceremony governs, makes it possible for students not only to establish a connection with a vital indigenous tradition but also to think critically about what counts as law.

Hilary Schor and Nomi Stolzenberg

Free Speech and Free Love: The Law and Literature of the First Amendment

We write this essay as professors, respectively, of literature and law, who have over the years come up with several intriguing (for which, read "eccentric") ideas of ways to teach what is often a tired conjunction, law and literature. To us, the most exciting and productive of these ampersand courses are those that seem to arise out of a mere, if alluring, coincidence. For can it be only a coincidence that two canonical figures in the history of free speech also penned some of the earliest and most powerful calls for freedom and self-expression in the domains of love, sex, and marriage? John Milton, the great seventeenth-century poet who established himself as the father of free speech in his "Areopagitica," the first serious polemic against government censorship, wrote another political pamphlet, "The Doctrine and Discipline of Divorce," in which he argued, movingly, in favor of the right to divorce—an argument astonishingly ahead of its time even as it harked back to the Hebrew bible as the source for its authority. Similarly, John Stuart Mill, the writer of *On Liberty*, still the seminal statement of the value of nonconformism and freedom of belief in the English-speaking world, subsequently wrote "The Subjection of Women." "Subjection" is, like Milton's divorce tract, a trenchant and surprisingly prescient analysis of the relations between the sexes; unlike Milton's, it is also one of the earliest feminist tracts, championing both the general principle of sexual equality and more-specific individual rights, including the right to freedom of choice (and the freedom to err) in matters of romantic love and marriage. For both Mill and Milton, the marriage question — the idea that the legal institution of marriage constitutes both a form of oppression and the possibility of social reform — loomed large in their thinking about the larger cause of personal freedom. Yet their writings on love, marriage, and the sexes are rarely considered together with their writings on freedom of thought, freedom of speech, and freedom of belief.

Our law and literature seminar is organized as an investigation of the basic question, Where are the deep connections, and where the possible tensions and conflicts, between these two sets of ideas? The history of the idea of free speech in the West is usually cordoned off from accounts of evolving notions of romantic love and sexual freedom. Yet the culture wars that rage over liberalism today are plainly impossible to separate from the liberalization of sexual mores that culminated in the last century in the sexual revolution of the 1960s, the divorce revolution of the 1970s, and the movements for women's and gay rights. The rights of freedom of speech, freedom of the press, and freedom of religious belief — the so-called intellectual freedoms — are enshrined in the First Amendment as our most fundamental constitutional values. Rights to individual freedom in the emotional domains of love, sex, and marriage have a much less secure legal footing, as is made clear by the ongoing debate over *Roe v. Wade*'s doctrine of family privacy and reproductive choice and by the never-ending backlash against liberal sexual mores. By focusing our attention on their common doctrinal foundations as well as on the intellectual and cultural legacy that they share, this seminar invites students to consider the parallels, links, and conflicts that exist between the ideas about freedom of choice in matters of religious faith, political opinion, and intellectual thought that we customarily summarize as free speech and ideas about freedom of choice in matters of sexuality, romantic attachment, and family relations — what constitutional law refers to dryly as the doctrine of privacy or what, earlier, more adventurous and more romantic generations imagined as free love.

The students in our graduate seminar come from literature departments and the law school, and we work together with them to forge a common language between literature and law. The class is at once like and unlike any they might get in the individual programs or schools from which they emerge. From the standpoint of the law school, the seminar looks less like the typical law and literature seminar that adorns many a law school curriculum than like the seminars on the theory and history of the First Amendment offered occasionally in more theoretically ambitious JD programs. (Stanley Fish and Vincent Blasi's jointly taught seminar at Columbia and Virginia in the 1990s is a good example.) Indeed, it might best be regarded as a revisionist version of the First Amendment seminar. In addition to the usual suspects who inhabit such courses—Milton and Mill on censorship; John Locke, James Madison, and Thomas Jefferson on religious freedom; and Oliver Wendell Holmes and Louis Brandeis as the architects of the modern legal doctrines of privacy and free speech—we fold in literary material on philosophical libertinism, Puritanism, Freudianism, first- and second-generation feminism, and anarchism, represented by the likes of Emma Goldman. (Not coincidentally, political anarchists were advocates of free love and also the chief targets of the government suppression that gave rise to modern First Amendment doctrine in the early twentieth century).[1] Our version of the First Amendment course is further distinguished from the usual law school seminar by the fact that we combine political theory and constitutional doctrine with short novels (we vowed not to assign any text longer than roughly one hundred pages—only Sade violated that stricture). Works like Leo Tolstoy's "Kreutzer Sonata" and Philip Roth's *The Dying Animal* contain surprisingly cogent political commentary on the proper relations among law, liberty, and love, breaking down the distinction between the genres of literary fiction and legal and political theory and helping us see the problematics of liberalism more clearly.

From the standpoint of an English curriculum, our seminar can perhaps best be seen as a reframing of the standard exploration of the marriage and adultery plot and of the role of law in it. By joining literature's customary focus on the marriage question to the analysis of case law, legal doctrine, and theories of the First Amendment, we enlarge the inquiry to encompass new questions and relations between new terms, bringing into focus the predicament that continually besets liberalism as it tries to navigate between the shoals of libertinism and anarchism, on one side, and puritanism, on the other. Whereas a free-speech seminar at a law school might find itself moving easily from Milton to Locke to Mill, with long meditations over debates in American constitutional law, a traditional literature class would move from the Puritans to the libertines to contemporary feminism, with a long pause over the nineteenth-century novel—most likely Nathaniel Hawthorne's *The Scarlet Letter* or Tolstoy's

Anna Karenina—with consideration of Tony Tanner's brilliant *Adultery and the Novel* and of its nagging interlocutors Michel Foucault and the feminists. We attempt to frame the adultery question much more widely, noting its ceaseless efforts to distinguish itself from both libertinism and puritanism ("liberty, not license" and "no legislation of morality" being liberal theory's constant, and constantly conflicting, refrains). The debates we would track in the law seminar also haunt the literature seminar, displacing it from its usual orbit.

Our pedagogical challenge is to take a group of students with very different skills and backgrounds, who generally share the defiant prejudice of self-constituting desire, which is the common plot of nineteenth-century fiction, and to move them to recognize a far more complicated dynamic of freedom, choice, and error. In creating this class around the debates over the relation between sexual and political liberty, particularly as they meet in the marriage question, we bring to bear different understandings of how to read legal texts in addition to questions about the role of narrative itself in shaping our seemingly innate desires.

We begin the seminar with the assumption that all the students have some basic knowledge of First Amendment law and that most have read a nineteenth-century novel. (Interestingly, when we asked who had read the assigned literary works before, only one student—a law student who had done his undergraduate work at an evangelical Christian college— answered in the affirmative.) We lay the groundwork by beginning with Milton's "Areopagitica" and Mill's *On Liberty*, the classic free-speech texts, in order to prepare the students to question the relation between free speech and free love. Perhaps what is more novel in our approach is the choice to plunge into the possibilities and limits of free love through a less familiar pairing of Tolstoy's breathtaking tale of a jealous husband driven to murder, "The Kreutzer Sonata," and Roth's exhumation of male sexual jealousy, one of his late meditations on marriage and mortality, *The Dying Animal*. Among the many parallels between the two works, the most striking is that each contains a sustained and well-argued diatribe against marriage. The two texts form a fascinating dialogue. Their differences are obvious: Roth's antimarriage polemic is easily read as a sexual libertine's critique; Tolstoy's protagonist assails libertinism as well as marriage (which he regards as nothing but licensed libertinism or licensed sex) in the name of true (Christian) love. The students are asked to consider whether the distinction between Roth's libertine and Tolstoy's antilibertine really holds up. They are asked to consider the possibility that Roth's and Tolstoy's critiques of marriage, and the affirmative ideals of personal liberty espoused by each, bear some relation to the liberal ideas about freedom from censorship and conformism explored in the first week's readings. The ferocity of the speakers in both texts and their seeming misogyny, even misanthropy, undermine some of our easy assumptions. If this is what the full expression and ambivalence of freedom sound like, how much freedom can any person bear?

In the third pair of readings, presented in the following week — Milton's "Doctrine and Discipline of Divorce" and Mill's "The Subjection of Women" — we are able to lay out some of our central questions, as both Milton and Mill posit the freedom to choose in romantic love, the freedom to move from marriage to divorce, as constitutive of the modern political subject. Where Tolstoy and Roth might be read as merely ranting, and Mill's and Milton's formulations of the right to freedom of expression might be seen as merely theoretical, here sexual and political freedom come together absolutely. Mill's statement that "the principle of freedom cannot require that [a person] should be free not to be free," that "it is not freedom, to be allowed to alienate [one's] freedom," becomes the manifesto of not only civil liberty but also romantic choice (On Liberty 103). Milton argues that "those words of God in the institution [of marriage], promising a meet help against loneliness . . . were not spoken in vain" (*Doctrine*). Milton, the Christian, articulates a decidedly romantic ideal of marriage (and divorce), which is interestingly juxtaposed against the critical perspective of the very secular Mill, who claims that under current English law, a wife "is the actual bondservant of her husband" who "is held to . . . a lifelong obedience to him . . . through her life by law" ("Subjection" 147). From this conjunction the students must draw out the question of our course: how the plot of romantic love and the theory of political freedom inform and challenge each other to enhance our understanding of both.

Students are surprised that Milton argues that "to grind in the mill of an undelighted and servile copulation must be the only forced work of a Christian marriage . . . [from which one] mourns to be free" (*Doctrine* 712) or that Mill claims that "all women of spirit and capacity" in Victorian England would prefer doing "almost anything else, not in their own eyes degrading, rather than marry, when marrying is giving themselves a master" ("Subjection" 145). This conjunction prepares them for the larger issues we wish to raise: What is the relation between romanticism and liberalism? between Christianity and liberalism? between liberalism and libertinism—and antilibertinism? Does a person have a right to a change of heart? If so, what are the theoretical foundations of that right? What is the proper relation of love to law, of liberty to law, and liberty to love? Does liberal freedom, which encompasses freedom of thought, freedom of speech, and freedom of belief, extend to desire, and if so, where might be the limits to desire? How are romantic and sexual freedom linked to the intellectual freedoms? If free love and free speech are not linked, what keeps them apart?

We needed to offer a historical approach that was neither reductive nor idiosyncratic and to keep the students focused on the skills of close reading and interpretation, which are central to any intelligent pursuit of either literature or law. As in any interdisciplinary course, we needed to show how a few central issues emerged in interesting dynamics as the course progressed. We describe three of these briefly.

The first is the question of puritanism, desire, and the law. We juxtapose *The Scarlet Letter* with long excerpts from Milton's *Paradise Lost*. Hester Prynne's challenge to Puritanism, that "what we did had a consecration of its own" (195), usually rings in such a course as a challenge to repressive puritan ideology; but paired first with *Paradise Lost* ("I made him just and right / sufficient to have stood, though free to fall" [3.98–99]) and then with Locke's and Madison's essays on toleration, Hester's plea has a more ambivalent resonance. Far from being opposed to Puritanism, her antinomian language draws on the Puritan tradition of the inner spirit, of the higher law any individual can find in biblical text and injunction—as Milton found and used to ground his pleas both for toleration of speech and freedom to divorce. We try to increase students' awareness of the tension in Puritanism between repressive and antinomian impulses by pointing to the unexpected lightening of the law that Hawthorne depicts—that is, the Puritan community's decision not to exact the letter of the punishment by killing Hester for adultery but to allow the spirit of the scarlet letter to carry out its office.

The second unexpected landing place in our inquiry into the relation between freedom of belief and freedom of desire lies in the space between feminism and libertinism, which we explore through the conjunction of the Marquis de Sade and Angela Carter and through a more general discussion of anarchism. Early-twentieth-century anarchists, such as Goldman, drew on the texts of previous anarchist writers like Tolstoy, seeming enemies to feminism and liberty. Their common concern with the woman question, sexual freedom, and critiques of marriage was prefigured by the eighteenth-century libertines. Carter's emphasis on Sade as a potentially "moral pornographer" and her idea that one

> might use pornography as a critique of current relations between the sexes . . . [whose] business would be the total demystification of the flesh and the subsequent revelation, through the infinite modulations of the sexual act, of the real relations of man and his kind. (19–20)

in turn prefigure the radical feminist legal theory of Catharine MacKinnon, who challenged the idea that a free marketplace of ideas offers real freedom to women (itself an echo of ideas put forward by Tolstoy in his "Kreutzer Sonata").[2] Highlighting the ambivalence in Sade's "Philosophy in the Bedroom" between the words "prescribe" and "proscribe," Carter anticipates the question of narrative and law that would obsess feminist legal theory of the 1980s. Is Sade, like so many libertine writers, using literature and the imagination to open up a path to freedom, or is he reminding us of the dangers of utter and violent lawlessness, which includes the lawlessness of an unlicensed and uncensored press?

A similar ambivalence haunts the third of our more unusual pairings: second-wave feminists and current debates among Freudian, Marxist, and feminist critics. Our earlier section on anarchism and free-love feminists like Goldman approached feminism initially through traditional liberal critiques of law—including Mary Wollstonecraft's *Vindication of the Rights of Woman*, an attempt to create an Enlightenment for women. But our first encounters with feminist thought also included George Eliot's scathing critique of women readers, "Silly Novels by Lady Novelists," which suggests that it is fictions of desire, as much as facts of law, that trap us in dangerously illusory narratives of freedom. Later in the course, we pursue this thread through 1970s feminism—for example, in Alix Kates Shulman's brilliant novel *Memoirs of an Ex-Prom Queen*. We also look at returns to liberal models of the freely contracting individual, such as *Ms. Magazine*'s famous marriage contract, which has clear roots in Mill.[3]

Finally, in this section, we look at the critiques of 1970s women's lib and liberal feminism that later emerged through the lens of both radical feminist legal theory (e.g., MacKinnon) and, less predictably, Esther Freud's novel of the post-1970s generation, *Hideous Kinky*, which raises the question that Roth queried in *The Dying Animal*: Whose freedom, and whose choice, will truly matter? Who will speak for the children, the next generation, the victims of an unleashed or an all-too-free desire? Both the child narrator of Freud's *Hideous Kinky* and the aggrieved son of Roth's narcissistic narrator (who, like Milton's Satan, gets all the best lines), stand as exemplars of the genre of the "revenge of the children" novel that has proliferated since the end of the 1960s.

In closing this essay, we want to reflect on two things: the kinds of assignments we asked of students and the conclusions we drew from the course. We had the students write a great deal in addition to doing the reading: several short papers and a seminar-length paper that focused on interpretation rather than research. The in-class discussions were challenging, both for their diversity of theme and for their great variety of texts and genres. The violence of the material shocked some students; others had difficulty expressing their ideas in class because of the challenges to modern liberal notions about the freedom of consenting adults. A law student was expected to read several books of *Paradise Lost*; an English or comparative literature graduate student was given pages of Supreme Court doctrine—but these modal differences were far less difficult for students to register than the sudden jolt of Sade or Carter or the sheer goofiness of 1970s feminism. We thought that students might feel more comfortable engaging with these texts in a paper than in class discussion, and this turned out to be true: it was the quieter students who wrote the riskier and more inquisitive essays. The chance to write through their doubts was essential. If that was the payoff for them (and several dissertations arose from this class), the payoff for us came at the end, when we turned to sources neither literary nor legal but shamelessly political.

For the final session we paired the Starr report on President Clinton's peccadillo (a text that Adam Gopnik has brilliantly satirized as a nineteenth-century novel)[4] with Jimmy Carter's infamous *Playboy* interview, in which he admitted to feeling lust in his heart. Its dazzling conjunction of political ambition (for such it was that led him to plan this interview); the use of biblical language to speak a seemingly forbidden desire; and its direct confrontation of media censorship, invasion of privacy, and the question of the traffic of desire, not to mention the misogyny at the heart of contemporary American culture, made all the issues of our course jump into bright relief. Is such a document law or literature? What kind of speech is it, and to whom does it speak? What, in such a moment of speaking desire and enacting repression, is the relation of the modern liberal subject to Puritanism (its secret twin) and libertinism (its secret double)? The chance to approach a question of such complexity, while working intensely with a group of very divergent students on so wide a range of texts, is to our mind the best justification of that final uneasy marriage, that of literature and law.

Notes

1. Readings on libertinism included Diderot's "Supplement to Bougainville's Voyage" and other texts in *The Libertine Reader* (Feher) and such troubling texts as the preface to *Les liaisons dangereuses* (Laclos). Our analysis of puritanism and the founding fathers' debate on religious liberty drew on Walzer's brilliant *The Revolution of the Saints*, a formative text on the complexities of puritanism; Locke's "A Letter concerning Toleration"; and Madison's "A Memorial and Remonstrance." The essays by Goldman included "The Hypocrisy of Puritanism," "The Tragedy of Women's Emancipation," and "Marriage and Love." We also read Bakunin's "Church and State" and Godwin's "Education through Desire." We read significant First Amendment cases, among them *Abrams v. United States*; the texts of the Alien and Sedition Acts of 1798 and the Sedition Act of 1918; free-speech cases through *Texas v. Johnson*; and Frankfurter's *Case of Sacco and Vanzetti*.

2. Among the essays by MacKinnon we read are "Desire and Power," "Andrea's Work and Linda's Life," and "The Sexual Politics of the First Amendment," all in *Feminism Unmodified*.

3. See Judy Syfers's "I Want a Wife" and Susan Edminston's "How to Write Your Own Marriage Contract," in Klagsbrun.

4. As Gopnik stunningly claimed, " 'The Report' is a classic story about adultery, in which the law and human affection are in tension, and it resolves itself in the usual way. When there's a choice between law and sympathy, the law may take the lovers but the lovers take the cake" (39).

Philip Auslander

"The Gollum Problem": Teaching Performance and/as Intellectual Property

To be protected under title 17 of the United States Code, otherwise known as the 1976 Copyright Act, a work must be "fixed in a tangible medium of expression" ("Subject Matter" 8) that renders it replicable (that is what *copy*right means, after all). Title 17 is implicitly a work of performance theory. Historically, copyright law has refused to grant to live performance the status of intellectual property. The copyright clause of the United States Constitution (article 1, section 8, clause 8) gives Congress the power to secure "to Authors . . . the exclusive Right to their respective Writings." Although over the years Congress and the courts have shown themselves willing to construe the concept of a "Writing" quite broadly as "any physical rendering of the fruits of creative, intellectual or aesthetic labor" (*Goldstein v. California* [1973], qtd. in Miller and Davis 304), they have never granted that status to intangible expression, which is to say performed expression. One can have a proprietary interest in a play text or a musical score but not in an actor's execution of a role, for instance.

I have taught material concerning the relation between performance and intellectual property law to students in theater and performance studies at both the undergraduate and graduate levels, also to my freshman writing students (Georgia Tech's freshman writing course is akin to what might elsewhere be called a freshman seminar). But the approach I outline here is applicable to a variety of student populations, including those in general education, because it draws on students' general knowledge of familiar cultural practices while assuming no prior knowledge of intellectual property law.

I find discussion of performance to be an effective heuristic for introducing students to intellectual property law, in part because the relation between them is more problematic than that between many other kinds of cultural production. Most of my students have at least a general idea of what copyright is and how it applies to books, movies, and of course music and other material downloaded from the Internet. The idea of thinking of performance as something that may or may not be copyrightable is new to them. Examining why performance per se is not copyrightable and raising the question of whether it should be therefore allow them to entertain questions about the ontological assumptions underlying both copyright and our ideas about performance. Are not actors the authors of their performances even when the characters they play usually speak someone else's words? Theatrical directors, too, are excluded, yet isn't their work of interpreting and staging a play arguably authorial? Are there ways of fixing these kinds of work to render them copyrightable? It is not difficult to persuade students to address such questions, and discussions frequently become energetic very quickly!

The model course (or course unit) I outline here emphasizes the dynamism of the legal status of cultural practices and the mutual influence of law, cultural production, and technological development. The course traces the changing status of performance under intellectual property law, then looks at the implications for existing legal concepts of cultural practices enabled by digital technologies. The first part of the course emphasizes three key legal concepts in relation to performance: copyright, right of publicity, and trademark. The second part shows how digital technologies may be complicating our understanding of these concepts.

An assignment I like to give, which is adaptable to any part of the material outlined below and to any level, is to ask students to write as if they were attorneys arguing for a particular outcome in a particular case. The document should take the form of a brief addressed to a trial judge. I use scenarios derived from recent civil suits, either resolved or ongoing, and let them argue either side. These arguments can also form the basis of class discussion or even a mock trial.

Traditionally, performance was considered to lie outside the purview of copyright. Writing in 1950, one appellate judge observed that "there is a line of cases which holds that what we may call generically by the French word *representation*,—which means to perform, act, impersonate, characterize, and is broader than the corresponding English word,—is not copyrightable" (*Supreme Records v. Decca Records* 909). The most often cited reason why copyright protection does not apply to performance is that to grant to a performer exclusive rights to particular performed gestures or intonations would severely limit the vocabulary of gestures and intonations available to other performers and thus "impede rather than promote the useful arts" (*Booth v. Colgate-Palmolive* [1973], qtd. in J. Gaines 124).

While it remains true that the work of actors, dancers, and other performers cannot be copyrighted, it is also true that intellectual property law has developed in the direction of making more and more aspects of performance ownable. The landmark 1988 case *Midler v. Ford Motor Company* led to an explicit effort to construct a novel legal theory that would protect performance and performers in ways not possible under copyright. The singer Bette Midler sued the automobile company and its advertising agency for using a singer who sounded exactly like her in a commercial. After Midler had declined to replicate her performance of "Do You Wanna Dance" for the commercial, the agency hired one of her former backup singers as a soundalike. Midler lost her initial case but won on appeal.

Judge John Noonan stated bluntly in the *Midler* decision that "a voice is not copyrightable. The sounds are not 'fixed'" (462). The decision was made, therefore, not on the basis of copyright but on the basis of a California statute enshrining what has come to be called the right of publicity—also known as the Celebrity Rights Act—originally designed to allow the estate of a deceased celebrity to continue to control the use of the name, voice, signature, photograph, and likeness of that celebrity ("Deceased Personality's Name"). Judge Noonan interpreted this statute as protecting a living celebrity's identity or personhood and found that Midler has a property right not in her voice or performance but in her identity, her self.

The central difference between copyright and the right of publicity is that while the former protects works of authorship, the latter protects personhood and therefore applies only to those whose persons have market value—to celebrities, in short. Authors do not have to be well known or even published to enjoy copyright protection for their work, but performers must be sufficiently famous so that someone else would seek to purchase their identity to enjoy protection of their performance under the right-of-publicity paradigm. Even then, that protection is not of the performance as a work but an extension of the performer's identity, which is construed as having value in itself.

The third signal case in the chain I am constructing is *Waits v. Frito Lay* (1992), which arose from circumstances very similar to those of *Midler*. The Frito Lay Company hired an advertising agency to develop a campaign for a new brand of corn chips. Inspired by one of Tom Waits's songs, the agency composed a similar song and asked Waits if he would perform it. He declined on the grounds that he is philosophically opposed to endorsing products. The agency therefore auditioned for a singer who could sound like Waits and found one who actually performed Waits's songs in Waits's style as part of his act. Waits sued successfully and the verdict held up on appeal.

The decision in *Waits* drew to a large extent on *Midler* and effectively reaffirmed the idea that a performer's voice is a protectable aspect of the person. More important, the court found that Waits's case could be considered not only in terms of right of publicity but also as an instance of false endorsement, as defined under the Lanham Act governing trademarks. The court found, in other words, that not only could Waits's voice be considered an aspect of his person, it could also be considered his intellectual property: his trademark as a business. Therefore, as stated in the decision on appeal, "the wrongful use of his professional trademark, his unique voice, would injure him commercially" (1110).

The idea that a performer's voice can serve as a trademark has important implications. The *Waits* decision may expand the right to protect at least the voice of performers who are not celebrities, since ownership of a trademark is not dependent on fame—in this respect, a trademark is more like a copyright than like the right of publicity. Unlike a copyright, however, which is in force for a limited period of time, a trademark exists for as long as it is in active use. Although copyright law is clearly based on assumptions about the nature of performance that specifically exclude performance, *Midler* and *Waits* represent a general legal trend toward making more and more aspects of performance into property through the interpretation of concepts in business law and intellectual property and the coinage of such new legal theories as right of publicity. This trend parallels recent legislation that extends the term of copyright protection (the Sonny Bono Act of 1998) and strengthens the force of copyright (the Digital Millenium Copyright Act, also enacted in 1998). Students can be invited to discuss the wisdom of such policies as well as their specific application to performance. Should performers enjoy property rights in their performances, as authors do in their products? Should such rights be granted only to celebrity performers (and, if so, how does one assess celebrity)? What are the differences between thinking of performance or performance style as a work of authorship, as a manifestation of the person, or as an identifying mark of a business? Which theory makes the most sense? Does it vary according to genre of performance?

As it has in so many other areas of social and cultural life, digitization has created new issues in the relation between performance and intellectual property law, issues that necessitate careful consideration of how we distinguish between performer and performance. In an article on video games worth quoting at length, Derek Burrill identifies such issues as aspects of what he calls "the Gollum problem":

> During the period of preemptive gossip leading up to the 2002 Academy Awards, a bustling debate erupted around Anthony Serkis' digitally enhanced portrayal of the subhuman character, Gollum, in the film *Lord of the Rings: The Two Towers*. Serkis' performance was digitally recorded using motion capture and CGI [computer-generated image] technologies that mapped his actions and facial movements (the actor's voice was not adjusted or enhanced) into a software program to which digital graphic elements were added. The ensuing performance was sufficiently hybridized that Serkis' status as live actor/referent seemed to fall into question, so much so that his inclusion as a possible nominee for Best Supporting Actor became a conundrum for the Academy. The debate circulated around whether Serkis' performance could be considered "live" (regardless of the long history of analog and digital editing and "adjusting" in film acting production). Was Serkis present enough in the performance? At what point is something too digitized? If something is partially digitized, what of its ontology, its presence? Can someone (or something) perform, in the traditional sense, in the digital? (492)

More than one commentator has proposed that we need a new name, and perhaps a new award category, for human performers who submit themselves to extensive digitization and for the resulting performances: the term "synthespian" for the digital performer has been proposed (Askwith), as has the somewhat more soberly descriptive "source-actor" for the underlying human subject (Anderson 170). It will be interesting to see what kinds of standards evolve over time for assessing creditworthiness and creativity in this kind of performance.

The primary question the synthespian raises for intellectual property law is directly connected to the ontological question that makes Gollum a problem for existing conceptions of acting: Whose performance is it, anyway? From the legal perspective, the Gollum problem is one of a series of interrelated scenarios in which digital information derived from a performer is used to create performances, and often performers, with varying degrees of independence from the source. Once created, a digital clone can undertake an infinite variety of performances the actual performer never executed; such performances can also be extrapolated from other forms of information, such as motion capture data. These data can be stored and used to produce performances that have been, in some sense, executed by the performer but without the performer's direct participation. One unresolved question that looms is, "[A]t what point does the actor who provides the raw movements, persona, and appearance to an image no longer count as a 'creator' to future manipulation of that image down the line?" (Pessino 99).

Some uses of digital clones are subject to a straightforward legal analysis that employs the three concepts I outlined. It seems fairly clear, for example, that using a digital clone of a famous person to endorse a product without the person's permission would run afoul of both the right of publicity and the Lanham Act's concept of false endorsement. It also seems clear that using a clone after an actor turns down a role would constitute unfair competition as well as an infringement of the right of publicity. Although one can imagine any number of futuristic scenarios in which unauthorized digital clones run amuck, the more immediate questions pertain largely to the permissible uses of authorized clones, questions that turn on definitional issues not entirely different from those the academy had to confront when considering the status of Serkis/Gollum.

For instance, a production company might decide to reuse the Gollum character in contexts that go beyond the original *Lord of the Rings* films and their immediate derivatives (e.g., DVDs, video games, books, etc.), and a future, unanticipated Gollum performance could be created from the data already obtained from Anthony Serkis, very possibly without the actor's participation or permission. Or a digital clone of an actor made for one production might be used in a different way in another. This second scenario is not hypothetical: "Actor Robert Patrick's digital clone performed as the liquid metal cyborg in *Terminator 2: Judgment Day*. That same clone was later devoured by a digital T-Rex in *Jurassic Park*" (Beard 5), apparently without Patrick's knowledge or permission. The question of whose rights are involved in such instances, and even of whether digital clones themselves have rights, are currently under consideration in legal scholarship. Because this is still a new development and has given rise to very little relevant case law, the discussions thus far are primarily anticipatory, and my purpose here is to point to issues on the horizon rather than engage in specific argument. It is obvious that these issues concern theater students directly, as they may affect their future employment. But I have found that all students, at both the undergraduate and graduate levels, are familiar with the films and techniques in question and eager to share ideas concerning the ownership of labor and the problem of creditworthiness in technologically enhanced performance. Since this is an emerging issue and there are no settled right or wrong answers, students have the sense of participating in a real debate.

To determine who legally owns and controls a synthespian and its underlying code, it is necessary to determine what a synthespian is in relation to existing categories in intellectual property and related law. Students can participate in this determination by analyzing performances with which they are familiar. For example, is a synthespian like Gollum a work of authorship? If so, it is subject to copyright. But who is the author? Unless the source-actor is also the producer, the normal assumption would be that the actor was working for hire and the copyright in the synthespian is the property of the producer. (Note that it is precisely because traditional performances are not considered works of authorship but extensions of the person that performers enjoy certain rights in them.)

The same question pertains to the data set from which the synthespian was constructed. Who, if anyone, should own the scan and motion capture data derived from a performer's body, movements, and facial expressions? This question, too, hinges on the matter of authorship. Can digital data of this kind be considered a work of authorship, and, if so, who is the author? Although I agree with Joseph J. Beard that data of this kind will come under copyright, simply because of the seemingly unstoppable expansion of copyright into new areas, there is also a persuasive argument suggested by him and others that scanned data do not constitute a work of authorship because they do not reflect even the minimum degree of creativity required for that category. In principle, they are meant to be purely a record, not a creative product, of a performer's appearance, movement, facial expression, and so on. As such, they are more akin to a medical X-ray than to a copyrightable photograph.[1]

If digital data of this kind are eventually judged copyrightable, the most likely outcome will be that producers will own the data as work for hire and be able to use it in any way they wish. As Anthony L. Pessino warns, "actors who commit to digital performances must be wary that they have very limited rights in that performance and its potentially unlimited derivative works" (109). Unless existing laws are interpreted, or even revised, in favor of performers, performers are well advised to retain ownership of the digital data they produce through contractual provisions, though such ownership is unlikely to be possible for any but the most famous and powerful, raising issues that parallel the applicability of right of publicity only to celebrities.

For the most part, legal scholars do not see synthespians and digital clones as copyrightable works of authorship. Joel Anderson explains:

> Virtual clones complicate traditional analysis because a copyrighted virtual clone represents not just one specific copyrightable performance; it literally contains all potential performances by its source-actor. This goes beyond the scope of copyright concerns because copyright law was generally meant to apply to only one original or derivative expression at a time, but a copyrighted virtual actor literally contains unlimited latent original expressions. Similarly, a typical right of publicity case involves possible infringement in only one work at a time. (189–90)

It is the synthespian's status as a performer capable of further performances that complicates matters. For Pessino, the synthespian is essentially a doppelgänger of the source-actor. As a version of "the [performer] himself" (108), the digital clone falls squarely within the purview of right of publicity (not copyright), which, Pessino argues, should be strengthened and further codified as legal doctrine to allow performers to protect their digital selves just as much as they are able to protect their voice and appearance as aspects of their real selves. Right of publicity would certainly need to be expanded to cover digital clones, since those clones need not possess the protected characteristics of the actor traditionally included under that doctrine (e.g., likeness and voice). In the case of Robert Patrick, the clone created to portray the metallic version of the T-1000 robot in *Terminator 2* was derived from his physical features yet did not resemble him.

Anderson takes a different approach: "a virtual clone can be defined as an inextricably intertwined combination of a person and that person's copyrightable expressions" (189). For Anderson, then, the clone is a hybrid of the performer as human being and the performances as works of authorship. His position derives from the analysis that the clone, produced in the first instance by the voice, appearance, and actions of a specific author-performer, can be used to generate an infinite variety of subsequent individual performances. This hybrid entity requires a hybrid legal status: "both right of publicity and copyright protection are inextricably intertwined in the hybrid virtual clone" (190). Beard also understands the digital clone to be a hybrid, but of a different kind: in his view, the clone is a combination of the person and a representation of the person. Beard's emphasis on representations rather than works of authorship implies that right of publicity rather than copyright will be the primary legal theory used in this area. Beard even goes so far as to ask whether digital performers may themselves possess rights of publicity. Although he quickly concludes that this right pertains only to human beings, the fact that he poses the question indicates another, future ramification of the Gollum problem.

However the status of synthespians and of the data sets on which they are based is worked out legally, one thing is clear: digital captures and clones are not primarily records of particular performances but matrices from which an infinite number of new performances may be produced; therefore digitization has made it inevitable that aspects of performance beyond the voice and face (e.g., expressions, movements) will be understood as proprietary and regulated by some combination of copyright, trademark, business law, and right of publicity.

It is extremely important that our students gain an understanding of intellectual property law, in part because it affects them on a daily basis, often without their knowing it. Although the question of fair use is perhaps the one that engages us most often today, I find that teaching intellectual property law through performance is a helpful way of getting at some of the basic principles before we move to such higher-order issues as fair use.

Here's a final test case that shows how deeply imbricated intellectual property law and performance are in our everyday lives. Ask your students (and yourself) whether or not royalties must be paid when a fraternity or sorority plays commercially recorded music at an outdoor party. We know that copyright law entitles the copyright holder the exclusive right to license public performances and also that both the musical compositions on the recordings and the recordings themselves are copyrighted objects. In legal terms, is playing recorded music on the lawn of the frat house considered a public performance? And if so, to whom are royalties being paid to license those performances, and who is paying them? Well, class, what do you think?[2]

Notes

This essay is adapted from my book *Liveness: Performance in a Mediatized Culture.*

1. The copyrightability of motion capture data may depend on the nature of the motion captured. As Beard indicates, "motion capture data would not be copyrightable to the extent that it reflects ordinary movement. If the dynamics captured are sufficiently creative as to constitute choreography, however, copyright would of course be implicated" (31), since choreography is explicitly considered a work of authorship under United States law.

2. Actually, only the musical compositions need to be licensed. Unlike most Western nations, the United States does not require that sound recordings be licensed for public performance. Playing recorded music on the lawn of a sorority house is indeed a public performance under the law, and royalties are due to the holders of the copyrights in the musical compositions. Those royalties generally are paid under blanket licensing agreements for most uses of music on campus between educational institutions and the organizations that police music copyright, including Broadcast Music Incorporated (BMI) and the American Society of Composers, Authors, and Publisher (ASCAP). The annual licensing fees are determined by the number of students registered at the university. Usually, the students pay the royalties tacitly through their student activities fees.

Simon Stern

Literary Evidence
and Legal Aesthetics

Course offerings in law and literature have become increasingly popular over the last two decades, but the premises and goals of this fusion vary widely depending on where the courses are housed. In English departments, the syllabus is likely to place conventionally literary materials next to legal opinions. Generally, these courses treat legal and literary writings as mutually constitutive productions of a particular historical period or, less frequently, as modes of engagement with psychic and social problems such as trauma and revenge, which may or may not be treated as historically specific. In either case, the concern is primarily with representation. For example, students might read Mark Twain's *Pudd'nhead Wilson* and *Plessy v. Ferguson* as parallel texts, looking at their metaphors of racial and political disfranchisement, their ways of speaking about intention, and their use of the language of hypothesis at certain narrative cruxes. By putting the two texts in dialogue, students may also see how they contributed to a larger conversation in which the terms of representation were open to revision.

In law schools, on the other hand, law and literature classes are most commonly treated as an opportunity for moral education, by means of a syllabus that relies primarily, and often exclusively, on literary readings, particularly fiction and drama. Students are encouraged to focus on details that provide a richer and more detailed rendering of the human problems that legal decisions are seen as resolving after the manner of bloodless technocrats. Given the primacy of ethical questions in these classes, the text's language will likely be viewed as offering relatively transparent access to the story's action, with the discussion centering on the morality of the characters' behavior.

What explains these divergent approaches to law and literature? Professors on both faculties are notorious—perhaps the most notorious in the whole academy—for their tendency to poach on other fields, enthusiastically selecting the material that seems to support their agenda and not much caring about debates in the other discipline that ought to qualify that enthusiasm. Among law professors, this habit may be explained by reference to the concept of institutional competence, promulgated by the legal-process scholars of the 1950s and 1960s. The legal system structures its rules of scrutiny and deference to take account of the different decision-making processes and kinds of expertise of courts, legislators, and administrative agencies, leaving each one in charge of the functions that it can best control. It is hardly controversial to suggest that academic specialists have—and seek to retain—their own expertise over particular subjects and methods. What comes of the interdisciplinary effort, however, depends on what competence is ascribed to the external field. In the case of law and literature, law professors evidently are in search of a humanistic balm and regard literature as its source and essence. On that view, it is emphatically the province of the literary to say what human nature is and how it should be portrayed. It does not matter what other skills English professors might claim for themselves, because the humanizing touch is the only one that answers a felt need. That is their competence, and that is what motivates the importation of literature in the first place.

For English professors, the disciplinary imperialism that prompts the turn to law comes out of the idea that all discursive practices generate their own texts. Law is seen not as the bearer of certain values or skills that cannot be had elsewhere but as one more cultural site for the production of meaning—although perhaps an especially inviting site because of the very public disputes that it manages and because its productions abound in literary features that are much more sparsely distributed in spheres such as medicine and architecture. Law professors might protest that this fixation on language ignores the many other considerations that inform legal analysis and scholarship—such as legitimacy, transparency, and jurisdictional authority—but unless these concerns are explicitly articulated or can be derived from a verbal formula, they hold much less interest for scholars who go to law in search of new vocabularies to amplify familiar texts.

These two approaches to law and literature may appear so divergent as to define two separate enterprises that only by happenstance share the same name. The differences between law schools and English departments are vast, but a course in law and literature offers some opportunities to close the distance instead of preserving it. In this essay, I describe more fully what goes on in each area and then suggest some ways of helping students in both fields understand each other's methods. Promoting cross-disciplinary discussion in this way may help develop a more truly interdisciplinary body of scholarship.

In law schools, courses in law and literature are often presented—sometimes in expressly spiritual terms—as an antidote to the barren, ossified, regimented, hidebound abstractions of doctrinal analysis, with its balancing tests, burdens of proof, inventories of elements, and unblinking hostility toward imprecision. Reading novels and plays about accusation and revenge, watching movies about trials, learning the backstory about the passions and struggles animating the parties in a famous case—all these activities are extolled as ways of reminding students to think about the place of justice in the legal system. If that lesson risks sounding too abstract, there is a second, more practical benefit that flows from luxuriating in narrative detail and reflecting on the ambiguity of human motivation: these opportunities help students to develop a keener awareness of the subtleties and muted inflections in the stories that clients tell and to cultivate a capacity for empathy that keeps zealous advocacy from turning into inflated or demeaning caricature.

Both of these goals are concerned with tempering the instinct to shunt people and their actions into doctrinal boxes, so that students may develop lawyering skills that reflect the importance of accommodating individual needs, emotions, and idiosyncrasy. When taken up in this way as an object of legal study, literary works may be appreciated for their intricate plots and their floating, hazy explorations of consciousness, but ultimately—like the appellate decisions that fill the casebooks—they are mined for their propositional content. How should Captain Vere have acted? What does Portia's performance in court tell us about the role of the advocate?

By the second year of law school, students have learned how to read an opinion strategically, extracting its holding and *ratio decidendi*, and they are encouraged to apply a similar protocol to literary works, with the difference that novels earn their place on the syllabus by virtue of their ability to deliver a moral lesson instead of setting out a legal rule. This is not to say that the lesson must announce itself explicitly—after all, students can hardly be expected to sharpen their sensitivities unless they get to test their peripheral hearing. But even if the readings require forms of attention and interpretive skills that are different from the ones on display in the Socratic classroom, the goal of the exercise remains similar in nature. The syllabus may consist of novels and plays, but students are still probing the text with an eye for normative conclusions.

That effect is apparent from the tendency, in law schools, to offer theme-based courses in law and literature. The common thread connecting the readings, and highlighted in the course's name, is usually a topic such as personal responsibility, access to justice, or the obligations of advocacy—topics that invite students to evaluate the moral status of actors and the legal system. The thematic approach focuses on how the readings advance certain values or promote reflection on certain dilemmas. All the participants may then take it for granted that discussion will proceed by looking at how the text defends or criticizes the positions of various characters. Details that cannot be made to yield such conclusions are understood to be irrelevant. That the discussion will be framed in this way is so intuitively obvious, by virtue of the thematic focus, that no one even needs to be told about the evidentiary rules, the rules of admissibility, that determine what will count as a contribution.

Questions about tradition, convention, allusion, literary movements, and generic form—questions that might take up most of the discussion in an English seminar—are unlikely to surface here except when they can readily be turned toward the normative ends that the discussion solicits. Any of those questions might carry a significant moral valence when the text is read as an allegory or as a means of tracing the fault lines of a contemporaneous debate, but such readings would require more immersion in literary and historical context than the class usually affords. Similarly, while the characters' and narrator's language may receive close attention, the conditions of representation are rarely scrutinized. Hence there is little time for questions such as why certain events are mentioned after the fact but not portrayed, or why a text struggles to enlist the reader's sympathy in some places but forgoes the effort in others. Even when the class includes students who were used to that kind of analysis in college, they generally accept that for present purposes, the focus is on making character and action directly legible in moral terms. Because of this focus, law

professors often assign works that rarely appear on English syllabi, such as
Harper Lee's *To Kill a Mockingbird* and Scott Turow's *Presumed Innocent*.
Paradoxically (at least to the mind of an English professor), the concern to
encourage subtlety and nuance extends only to a single dimension, attending to the fine-grained details of character and motive but generally accepting a very truncated view of the cultural framework embedding those
details and ignoring the literary framework altogether.

If literary narratives provide the legal academy with the means of liv-
ening up an unremitting diet of doctrinal gruel, in English departments
the law is often a singularly appealing object of analysis because of its ready
exercise of power and its manipulation of the tools of social control. These
operations are fascinating enough when performed unabashedly, but are
all the more intriguing when done by sleight of hand. Where law professors generally mean to add narrative (and not, for example, lyric poetry)
when they teach law and literature, for English professors the foreign part
of the conjunction almost invariably refers to opinions (not statutes, regulations, rules, or pleadings). The reasons for that choice have partly to do
with the comparative salience and legibility of opinions, partly with their
use of narrative.

The prominence of opinions like *Brown v. Board* and *Roe v. Wade*
leads nonlawyers to think immediately of that category when considering
what counts as legal writing. The Racketeer Influenced and Corrupt Organizations Act and the Environmental Protection Act may be just as well
known, but fewer have read any part of these statutes, and few who have
dipped into them would relish the thought of assigning more of the same
in an English course. Rules and pleadings are even less likely to engage the
interest of anyone who is not professionally required to read them. Further, anyone who has read an opinion might at least entertain the illusion
that the document is legible as an independent piece of writing, whereas
rules and statutes are usually hard to understand when taken in isolation.
To place them in a larger scheme requires not only more reading but also
the ability to know where to look and where to draw the line in adding
more material. Perhaps most important, opinions have the virtue of being
packed with narrative. They include factual narratives of the events leading up to the dispute—sometimes even dueling factual narratives when
there is a dissent—and they also conduct an analysis that takes a narrative
form itself as it applies the law and reasons its way to a conclusion. Thus
students may look not only at how the court wields its authority in manag-
ing the dispute but also at how the court uses narrative form to shape the
reader's perceptions and to command assent.

When legal opinions and novels are read as mutually illuminating efforts to exercise power through the operations of rhetoric and narrative, the resulting discussion will be very different from the one that occurs in the law school classroom. English professors often assign opinions that have no place in the law school curriculum. Where the law side favors novels like *To Kill a Mockingbird*, the English side traffics in eighteenth-century slavery decisions and Victorian divorce cases that few law students, or even law professors, have ever heard of. And just as those in the literary academy may be nonplussed by the moral-propositional approach often used by law professors, the law professors would be nonplussed by many of the readings produced in English departments. Only rarely do law students read an opinion in its entirety; the casebooks include only those parts deemed relevant by the editors. Such a cavalier attitude toward the text would be unthinkable in an English department, and it signals a very different view of the object of study. During their first year, law students learn that some of the most important questions have nothing to do with the language of the text. Movies about the rigors of law school frequently make this point by showing a professor badgering a student about the court's jurisdiction, the procedural status of the case, the way in which the cause of action has been framed, or the decision's place in a chain of precedent. While students in the English classroom are carefully parsing an opinion's rhetorical and narrative structures and inquiring into the cultural logic entailed, there is usually little understanding of issues that would be fundamental to any legal discussion. A critique that fails to engage them risks misunderstanding the opinion's legal significance, even if the analysis provides a sophisticated understanding of the cultural and intellectual energies at work.

So far my comparison has brought out several asymmetries. Whereas law professors usually rely entirely on readings imported as a corrective to the students' standard fare, English professors usually combine legal and literary materials and see few differences between the two forms of writing. For law students, the turn to literature is often prompted by a sense that their doctrinal classes are missing an essential ingredient, whereas students of literature generally read legal opinions not to quench a thirst for logic, rigor, or consequentialist analysis but to find coercion and power displayed in an unusually pure form. The material imported as fodder for the course is often peripheral to the interests of scholars in the other field. Nevertheless, courses in both venues turn out to share much the same view of what counts as law and literature—namely, opinions and narratives—even if the rationale for that focus differs according to the field. In both venues, the imported texts typically are read according to the protocols of the home discipline.

These observations may seem to lead to an impasse. The agenda on each side presupposes that something is gained by blending the two fields, but the approaches themselves appear to be immiscible. While much would be gained by helping students on each side understand the methods and habits of mind cultivated in the other discipline, a course in law and literature cannot and should not present itself as an opportunity to master a new field in one semester. One way to bridge the gap, and to give students a basic understanding of the tools and styles of analysis used in the other discipline, is to rely on tools internal to each discipline.

On the law side, students' training in evidence may help them learn to think in a more sophisticated way about strategies of representation. Law students are used to thinking about what makes evidence admissible—indeed, this is one of the first things they learn in the Socratic classroom, where some previously acceptable forms of evidence turn out to be illegitimate and new ones must be acquired. Perhaps the most frequently rehearsed insight among scholars of law and narrative is that a trial involves two competing stories and the victor is the one who can tell the more persuasive story. Conversely, we might say that every story is told from a situated perspective aimed at eliciting a certain response from the reader. Though admittedly reductive, this characterization may prod students to examine their reactions to characters, events, and narrative styles instead of simply taking those reactions for granted and relying on them as the basis for moral judgments. Once students are asked to defend their responses on evidentiary grounds, they may start to see how the text withholds information, lavishes its attention on certain characters, and shifts rhetorical gears at certain key moments.

This point may be developed not only by using classroom discussion to focus more attention on the question of evidence but also by assigning scholarly work in law and literature that shows how representation depends on forensic strategies. For example, in *Strong Representations* Alexander Welsh argues that Henry Fielding's narrator in *Tom Jones* constantly doles out or conceals evidence about Tom's character, all the while purporting to interpret the evidence or tacitly leading the reader to make questionable inferences. The narrator, Welsh explains, "is not an eyewitness but a manager of the evidence, analogous to a prosecutor or a judge and later to defense attorneys in a trial" (58). That is, the narrator manages the evidence from opposite sides—and while he may seem to be a special case because he is so present throughout the novel, the point can be developed with subtler examples once it has been made with the aid of such an intrusive figure.

As it turns out, there is a long and respectable genealogy for the idea that novels may contribute to our understanding of law of evidence and vice versa. James Ram, in one of the major nineteenth-century contributions to evidence law, *A Treatise on Facts as Subjects of Inquiry by a Jury*, relied heavily on literary examples—including more than thirty references to Shakespeare and more than twenty to Sir Walter Scott.[1] Ram uses these writers to illustrate evidentiary principles—for example, he draws on a scene from *Ivanhoe* to show that hearsay is a poor source of information, because a witness's faith in his memory is no measure of his accuracy (191). As in *Tom Jones*, one may take the example a step further to ask why Scott arranges matters in this fashion, opting for questionable hearsay evidence rather than describing the event directly. Charles C. Moore followed Ram's example a generation later in another leading study of evidence, *A Treatise on Facts; or, The Weight and Value of Evidence*, which draws on a wide array of writers including not only Shakespeare and Scott but also American authors such as Washington Irving and Edgar Allan Poe.[2] For these commentators, it was quite obvious that literary works abound in the same evidentiary problems that are more conventionally illustrated through the use of legal opinions. One of the pedagogical virtues of Ram's and Moore's treatises is that, in a form already familiar to law students, they make the art of novelistic representation seem a perfectly unremarkable subject for the analysis of evidence.

It may seem less plausible, on the English side, that familiar literary texts can help students appreciate the concerns of legal scholarship. However, the objection most frequently leveled at literary critical discussions of law—namely, that cases are read in isolation and hence out of doctrinal context—also touches on questions associated with the study of narrative. Ronald Dworkin offers a useful heuristic for exploring the analogy when he considers the chain novel as a model for the application of a precedent over time, as successive judges build on and modify the original judgment (*Law's Empire* 228–38). The narrative arc of a chain novel, in which each successive chapter is written by a new author, could be seen as involving a similar process of modification. Dworkin's analogy has been heavily criticized and may even reflect a misperception of how chain novels work, but it depends fundamentally on the idea of an unfolding narrative whose conclusion is neither predetermined nor unconstrained. Dworkin emphasizes the concept of narrative development to describe a line of cases instead of treating a single decision as an example of narrative, but at the same time, his analogy also raises questions about narrative closure in the individual instance. If we use his discussion to develop a pedagogical strategy, then, we see that it counsels in favor of teaching cases in sets, working to establish the legal context as well as the historical and discursive context of the readings.

Reading cases as part of a larger body of related decisions—as law students do—ensures that idiosyncrasies are not mistaken for paradigmatic indexes of the legal culture more generally, and conversely, it helps to bring out patterns of thought and analysis that might be missed or misunderstood when cases are read in isolation. Reading the cases individually and collectively with respect to the question of narrative closure helps students see how an opinion's persuasiveness in legal terms is bound up with its narrative structure. In addition to its factual narrative, any opinion must seek to provide a legally satisfying resolution to the doctrinal considerations it engages, including implicit or explicit concerns about its own future application. What is perhaps most significant about this connection between doctrinal analysis and narrative form is that the latter can be shown to entail concrete commitments with effects in the world. The study of opinions as narrative thus becomes a study of how aesthetic forms can have social consequences.

The legal question of evidence and the literary question of closure converge as aspects of legal aesthetics. To the legal mind, a successful conclusion is one properly supported by competent evidence; to the literary mind, closure can be analyzed by examining the narrative strategies that produce it. By presenting students with a basic understanding of these concepts as understood in their home disciplines, a class in law and literature can give students a more sophisticated interdisciplinary understanding of both narratives and legal opinions.

Notes

1. See his table of authors quoted (xi-xii) and table of works quoted (xii–xv). Among Shakespeare's plays, *Romeo and Juliet* proves to be Ram's favorite, with seven quotations, and among Scott's writings, *Rokeby* and *The Heart of Mid-Lothian* receive the most citations—four and three, respectively.

2. See especially C. Moore's "table of non-legal authors and works cited" (xlvii–xlviii).

Brook Thomas

An Introduction to Law and
Literature for English Majors

I teach legal documents and works of literature together in a variety of courses, from seminars for graduate students to a three-week unit in a team-taught general education humanities course for 1,300 freshmen. Topics include "The Law and Literature of Segregation," "The Law and Literature of Citizenship," and "Nineteenth-Century United States Literature and Civil Liberties." The course I describe here is one for twenty to twenty-five upper-division English majors that focuses on a particular way of understanding works of literature while also fulfilling students' writing requirement. Some students use the course to count for the humanities and law minor at the University of California, Irvine. It is called simply Law and Literature.

The course has three basic units, each on different ways in which the relatively autonomous disciplines of law and literature can overlap with and relate to each other. The units are on (1) a way in which the law can directly control the production of literature, (2) a literary representation of a legal event or issue, and (3) a close literary—that is, rhetorical—analysis of documents related to the law. If UCI were on a semester system, I would add a fourth unit, on a literary response to a legal controversy.

But we have ten-week quarters, so fitting in four units can be a bit of a stretch.

There are many ways to cover each unit. For instance, the first can be on either censorship or copyright. In the second, there are numerous works that represent a legal event or issue. Likewise, in theory, any legal case or legally related document can be analyzed rhetorically, although the analysis of some is more productive than others. Finally, a number of works respond to a particular legal controversy. But if each unit can be taught differently, the challenge is to make the various units cohere. I describe three of the most successful versions of the course, spending more time on the two I most often teach.

When we focus on copyright, we conduct a brief history of the law of copyright. We also read some nineteenth-century calls for an international copyright agreement, by authors like Mark Twain and Henry James. Finally, we read some important early cases, like *Pope v. Curll* (1741), involving Alexander Pope's letters (M. Rose). We then switch units 2 and 3 and conduct a close rhetorical analysis of Samuel Warren and Louis Brandeis's famous 1890 *Harvard Law Review* essay "The Right to Privacy." This unit follows from the first because Warren and Brandeis trace a tort right to privacy to various copyright cases. Our analysis concentrates on how the two lawyers define an "inviolate personality" and how they establish a common-law right to privacy by drawing on some of the cases we read in the first unit, such as *Pope v. Curll* (205, 211). We also spend a class on differences between a tort right to privacy and a constitutional right to privacy, looking briefly at key metaphors in *Griswold v. Connecticut* (1965) and *Roe v. Wade* (1973) as well as Justice Brandeis's dissent in *Olmstead v. United States* (1928). We spend another class on the right to publicity and how it was derived from the tort right to privacy. The literary unit is on a work concerned with the issues Warren and Brandeis identify, such as James's *The Aspern Papers* or *The Reverberator* or Heinrich Böll's *The Lost Honor of Katerina Blum*.

Current debates over intellectual property and students' concerns about privacy make this version of the course popular. Nonetheless, students are generally more interested in censorship than in copyright. A focus on censorship allows me to assign three works that every English major should read at some time or another: Plato's *Republic*, John Milton's "Aereopagitica," and John Stuart Mill's *On Liberty*. After examining the arguments for and against censorship in these three works, we read excerpts from some landmark free-speech and hate-speech cases, making sure that students have a basic understanding of doctrines such as "clear and present danger" and "fighting words." We then discuss differences between censoring political and artistic expression and end with a class devoted to Justice John Woolsey's decision in *United States v. One Book Called "Ulysses"* (1933).

In one version of the course starting with censorship, we turn to Twain's *Pudd'nhead Wilson*. Twain's novel is short enough for sustained attention, has a trial scene, represents some of the legal issues involved with slavery, and yet is published in 1894, only two years before segregation received constitutional sanction. Although the book is not itself about legal forms of censorship, there are important, if not obvious, connections between it and the previous unit. First, in a short lecture, I point out how the censorship of abolitionists, especially the notorious mob execution of the abolitionist editor Elijah Lovejoy, mobilized proponents of free speech in the antebellum period (Curtis 216–70). Perhaps more important, as we read Twain's novel, we pay attention to the ways in which the issue of race leads to communal and extralegal forms of silencing. Attention to such silencing opens up discussion of how the book portrays the complicated relation between communal opinion and the law. Is the law a reflection of communal opinion, as some argue, or does it play an important role in shaping it? One way to explore that relation in *Pudd'nhead Wilson* is through the book's portrayal of legal determinations of race, whereby Roxy and her biological son look white physically yet officially are black because of a minor portion of black blood.

Twain's complicated treatment of the legal and cultural determinations of race has received lots of attention, and I ask students to read some criticism. I divide the class into groups of five, and each person reports on an essay (Carton; Gillman; L. Mitchell; Sundquist; B. Thomas, "Twain"). Each group then discusses the different points of view and conveys its sense of the best argument to the class as a whole. As a class, we also analyze the book's final trial scene, especially Pudd'nhead's use of the technology of fingerprinting to solve the book's murder mystery. In successfully reversing the community's opinion of him by solving the crime, Pudd'nhead suggests that scientific evidence has the power to alter communal opinion, thus raising the hope that the law can be based on a solid foundation of scientific truth. At the same time, by having the murderer turn out to be someone with black blood, Twain's novel raises the possibility that scientific evidence can, as it did in the late nineteenth century, confirm rather than challenge racial prejudice. A colleague from our Department of Criminology, Law, and Society uses *Pudd'nhead Wilson* to explore the limits of the use of DNA in criminal cases (Cole). I share his argument with the class.

After this unit on *Pudd'nhead Wilson*, we turn to a sustained analysis of *Plessy v. Ferguson* (1896). A number of issues raised by Twain's novel reoccur in *Plessy*. For instance, Homer Plessy, like Roxy and her son, could pass as white, even though he was officially "colored." Thus both *Plessy* and *Pudd'nhead* raise questions about the legal determination of race in the age of segregation. They also allow students to explore whether racial distinctions are, as Justice Henry Billings Brown writing for the *Plessy* majority argues, "in the nature of things" (B. Thomas, "*Plessy*" 44) or, in Twain's words, the product of "a fiction of law and custom" (9). Likewise, when Justice Brown declares that a measure of a law's reasonableness is whether it conforms to "established usages, customs, and traditions of the people" (50), the *Plessy* majority, like Twain's novel, suggests connections between law and communal opinion.

In addition to examining issues that *Plessy* has in common with *Pudd'nhead Wilson*, we look closely at the logic, evidence, and metaphors used in both the majority opinion and the dissent by Justice John Marshall Harlan. The existence of a dissent is pedagogically helpful, as it lets students explore how judges come up with and then justify different positions, even though they are looking at the same legal issues. We devote considerable time to examining the strengths and weaknesses of both Justice Brown's majority decision and Justice Harlan's dissent. Before this discussion, students are required to read the introduction to the Bedford edition of *Plessy*, which provides a basic understanding of the legal issues involved (B. Thomas, "*Plessy*"). Even so, I do not expect them to have a full understanding of each legal case that both sides draw on to make their arguments. I do expect them to be able to evaluate appeals to nonlegal evidence. For instance, we discuss what type of evidence is implied by Justice Brown's appeal to the "nature of things." Similarly, because the crucial issue in the case, for the majority, is whether separate-but-equal laws are reasonable, we weigh different criteria for determining reasonableness. Then we turn to a consideration of metaphor, spending the most time on Justice Harlan's appeal to a "color-blind" Constitution (57). Still contested today, the metaphor of color blindness has two competing meanings. On the one hand, it implies that the Constitution, like traditional images of the blindfolded figure of Justice, is unbiased. On the other, it raises the possibility of myopia, a failure of the law to see how racial prejudice has traditionally disadvantaged people of color.

The Bedford edition has a discussion of the metaphor of color blindness, and students are required to read it. Indeed, that edition has a number of selections that I assign to provide contextual understanding of both *Pudd'nhead Wilson* and *Plessy*, including an 1896 essay summarizing scientific views of race at the time and conflicting views of the race problem by Booker T. Washington and W. E. B DuBois. There is also a speech, "The Courts and the Negro," by Charles W. Chesnutt, the first major African American novelist (B. Thomas, "*Plessy*" 146–60). Chesnutt, like Justice Harlan, compares *Plessy* with *Dred Scott* and then adds, "Unfortunately, it applies to a class of rights which do not make to the heart and conscience of the nation the same direct appeal as was made by slavery, and has not been nor is likely to produce any such revulsion of feeling" (157). If we had time for a fourth unit on a literary response to a legal controversy, we would read Chesnutt's *A Marrow of Tradition* (1901), in which Chesnutt responds to *Plessy* by trying to produce in his audience the same revulsion of feeling toward segregation that *Uncle Tom's Cabin* had produced toward slavery.

In a second version of the course starting with censorship, we read Herman Melville's *Billy Budd*. As with *Pudd'nhead Wilson*, I manage the transition from censorship by showing how our work of fiction portrays modes of silencing other than strictly legal ones. Given the order that eventually leads to his execution, Billy "in silence mechanically obeyed" (101), a poignant example of how effective the naval system of discipline is in keeping sailors from speaking out against figures of authority even in the face of injustice. Likewise, the narrator describes how authoritative naval histories "naturally abridge" accounts of mutinies in order to present a view of the past legitimating the existing political order (55).

Billy Budd is frequently taught in courses on law and literature. Some would say it is too frequently taught, but there are good reasons why it is so popular. Because it raises important questions about the nature of both justice and acts of judgment, it is well suited to an introductory course. In teaching it, I do not try anything fancy. Melville's language and range of allusions do not make for easy reading, even for upper-division English majors, so my first task is to be sure that everyone understands, as clearly as possible, what happens in the story. We place issues the book raises in historical context by turning to selections from the debate between Thomas

Paine and Edmund Burke over the French Revolution. Worthy of attention on its own for expressing conflicting views about tradition, custom, legal institutions, and the rights of man, this debate helps illuminate the philosophical foundations of Captain Vere's view of the law.

We also read Charles Sumner's defense of Commander Alexander Slidell Mackenzie, who in 1842 executed three sailors aboard the USS *Somers* accused of mutiny. Mentioned by Melville, the *Somers* incident is a recognized source for *Billy Budd*. Sumner's essay is especially worth reading because it shows how even a strong defender of rule by law like Sumner can justify a military commander's violation of the strict letter of the law when he feels his ship is threatened. In using a number of the metaphors used by Captain Vere and the narrator, Sumner's essay also demonstrates the role figurative language can play in seemingly logical arguments about guilt and innocence.

After reading this background material, we turn our attention to Captain Vere's judgment of Billy. To make sure that different points of view are raised in class, after students come up with preliminary judgments of their own, I use the same strategy I use with *Pudd'nhead Wilson* and have them read selected works of criticism and share their findings in groups of five (B. Johnson; Reich, "Tragedy"; Stern; B. Thomas, *"Billy Budd"*; Weisberg, *Failure*). We then come together as a class and debate the different positions put forward.

While *Billy Budd* explores the rights—or lack of rights—of sailors in wartime, our next unit is on the most famous civil liberties dispute of the American Civil War, the case of Clement L. Vallandigham. A peace Democrat from Ohio, Vallandigham was accused of expressing support for the South. A civilian, he was arrested by the military and tried and convicted in a military tribunal, even though civil courts were open (Klement). Declaring the government's actions unconstitutional, New York Democrats, including Melville's uncle, sent a letter of protest to President Lincoln. Lincoln, like Sumner, a great advocate of rule by law, responded by arguing that measures unconstitutional during peace were constitutional during wartime. In this time of national emergency, he argued, dealing with "insurgent sympathizers," who he defined as anyone who remained silent or equivocated in their support of the government, required both the use of military courts and preventive arrests, "not so much for what has been done, as for what probably would be done" ("Truth" 746–47). Not satisfied by this response, the New York Democrats wrote another letter of protest (Pruyn et al.).

We scrutinize the rhetorical strategies of all three documents. We also supplement our understanding of Lincoln's views on rule by law by reading his "House Divided" speech, the First and Second Inaugurals, and "The Gettysburg Address." Are there, we ask, connections or contradictions between Lincoln's utopian ideal of a government of the people, by the people, for the people and his rationale for cracking down on civil liberties during wartime?

Finally, we look at excerpts from *Ex parte Milligan* (1866), in which, after the Civil War was over, Justice David Davis, Lincoln's former campaign manager and friend, writing for the Court, declared unconstitutional the Lincoln administration's use of military tribunals to try civilians when civil courts were open. In our censorship unit we have already read Justice Robert Jackson's dissent in the 1949 free-speech case *Terminiello v. Chicago*. Disagreeing with the majority's decision to overturn the conviction of a right-wing, anti-Semitic, pro-Nazi priest whose speech had provoked a riot, Justice Jackson pointed out the danger of letting such people hide behind the constitutional protection of civil liberties as they set about to destroy democratic forms of government. "There is a danger," he warned, "that if the Court does not temper its doctrinaire logic with a little practical wisdom, it will convert the constitutional Bill of Rights into a suicide pact" (37). Almost a century earlier, one of Lambdin P. Milligan's attorneys had used the suicide metaphor to make a different point: "A violation of law on the pretense of saving such a government as ours is not a self-preservation, but suicide" (81). Students are asked to side either with Lincoln's claim that "I felt that measures, otherwise constitutional, might become lawful, by becoming indispensable to preservation of the constitution, through the preservation of the nation" (*Collected Works* 2: 281) or with Justice Davis's claim that "A country, preserved at the sacrifice of all the cardinal principles of liberty, is not worth the cost of preservation" (Ex parte Milligan 126).

In this version of the course there is time to include a short fourth unit on Edward Everett Hale's once famous, now neglected "The Man without a Country," written in support of Lincoln in the midst of the Vallandigham controversy. Nonetheless, even though Hale briefly alludes to Vallandigham, he does not directly dramatize the Copperhead's arrest and punishment (B. Thomas, *Civic Myths* 55–101). Students are asked how Hale's fictional story—about the exile of a young soldier for damning his country while being tried for his involvement in Aaron Burr's allegedly treasonous plot in 1805 to create a separate country in either Texas or the newly acquired Louisiana Territory—takes a stand on the Vallandigham incident.

Because the course fulfills UCI's upper-division writing requirement, the writing component is important. Students write three five-to-seven-page essays, including drafts and revisions. We spend class time working on revisions, both through peer-editing and by examining examples from our reading. For instance, Garry Wills has a brilliant analysis of Lincoln's revisions of the end of the First Inaugural (158–59). For the censorship unit, I describe a couple of controversial examples of censorship—including, if possible, current ones. Students choose one and take a stand that draws on the reading we have done. For the unit on works of literature, the topics focus on issues we have discussed and debated in class. For *Pudd'nhead Wilson,* students write on the book's representation of the power of communal opinion, the status of evidence, or legal determinations of identity. For *Billy Budd,* students are asked to judge Captain Vere's judgment, a simple assignment with no simple answer. Drafts and revisions are timed to coincide with group discussions of the book, so that student writing contributes to the ongoing debates in the class.

The writing assignment on the third unit is directly related to our rhetorical analysis of legal documents. Ideally, what students learn from that analysis should help them improve their prose. Elsewhere I have described writing exercises linked to a close reading of *Plessy v. Ferguson* and *Brown v. Board of Education* (B. Thomas, "Constitutional Literacy"). When we read *Plessy,* we draw on the strategies outlined in that essay. Similarly, the material related to the Vallandigham controversy is perfectly suited for teaching counterargument. Having examined how Lincoln responded to his critics and how his critics countered his response to them, students produce their own counterarguments, engaging one of the three documents we have already examined.

The biggest danger in teaching this course is the temptation to assign too much. Each of the units could be expanded into a course of its own. But to ask students to master too much overwhelms them and makes it hard for them to give careful attention to their reading. If one goal of an introductory courses is to introduce students to new material, another should be to instill in them the habits of mind necessary to do justice to the material they confront, not only in the course being taught but in the future. As a result, they should not be held responsible for more works than they can reasonably handle—especially in a course on law and literature, which involves not one discipline but two. Indeed, one measure of the course's success is whether students come to realize that interdisciplinary analysis of law and literature requires them to become not singly but doubly disciplined. I have tried to design a course that, in addressing some pressing issues of the day, trains students in some of the skills necessary to study law and literature in conjunction with each other.

Valerie Karno

Law and Literature as Cultural and Aesthetic Products: Studying Interdisciplinary Texts in Tandem

The syllabus I describe here is for an upper-division undergraduate course titled Law and Literature, which I teach in both the English department and the honors program at the University of Rhode Island. The course is cross-listed between the English major and the Law, Justice, and Society minor at the university. In addition to fulfilling a requirement for both those programs, the course can fulfill a general education requirement in letters. To help students understand how different disciplines approach and contribute to the dissemination of normative cultural ideas, the course studies a range of concepts central to our lived experience of law. It proceeds topically. After briefly reviewing the history of the field of law and literature, we think about how construing law as a cultural and aesthetic product influences the way we read not only cases but representations of law all around us. Rosemary Coombe's essay "Critical Cultural Legal Studies" is a launching point for our discussion as we consider how products, advertisements, and myriad visual representations subtly reproduce legal concepts for us every day. Instead of considering law a system of monolithic rules outside our lives, we explore the ways legal norms are implicitly distributed through many cultural forms we routinely distribute and participate in. Throughout the course, we also ask how distinct disciplines reinforce or undermine the tenets by which we live.

Using legal cases and essays alongside literary and philosophical narratives, we consider the question, What is madness and reason, and how do we know to recognize the two? Sherman Alexie's novel *Indian Killer* illustrates how what is reasonable to some seems mad to others. The categories of reason and madness, so often taken for granted in their meanings and implications, become matters of perspective in the novel: no character who believes himself or herself to be reasonable remains unscrutinized. The text refuses simple categorizations and insists on rethinking how we comprehend the reasonable and the mad.

We augment this discussion by reading selections from Michel Foucault's *Madness and Civilization* so that we can think about how notions of madness and reason have evolved. We also read Alexie's novel about Native American and white identities in conjunction with selections on identity from Mashpee Indian cases. We read the definitional conundrum that the legal system faced in deciding what constituted the Mashpee tribe, in *Mashpee v. New Seabury Corp.* If not a tribe, the Mashpees could not sue for land reclamation collectively.

Noting both that identity categorization is pivotal in the law—one needs an identity to file a lawsuit—and that the law struggles to understand and apply identity categories, we read essays by Jack Campisi and by Jo Carrillo ("Identity"), both anthropologists and legal scholars, to highlight the perplexity legal officials experience in deciding who is a member of which identity category. Each of these texts, coming from a different discipline, approaches the subject of tribal identity under the law in a different way. But when read together, they contribute to a dynamic picture of the ways disciplines grapple with figuring identity. Our identities have become fixed under the law over time—through educational tracking, behavior management, and our treatment as racialized and gendered subjects since birth. Students can connect the literary and legal narratives we read to their own experiences of being brought into managed legal identities.

In each section we study, I highlight the importance of context in reading interdisciplinarily. We note the chronology and geographic origin of all the texts we study; we consider the cultural parameters around which they have been written. Legal case decisions are often particularly helpful in this endeavor, as they frequently use the principle of stare decisis, citing the prior cases and doctrines that lead to more recent decisions.

Thus they create a chronology that students can trace, even though divergent legal opinions often cite divergent chronologies in establishing their arguments.

While encouraging historicity, I also think about how larger cultural concepts like discrimination operate repeatedly through particular rhetorical valences. The course materials explore the rhetoric of both racial and gender discrimination through the preoccupation with legal protection. We closely read case law regarding unpleasant bodies, in particular regarding the historically questionable right for women to work at the types of jobs they wish and during the hours they choose. We then turn to the relatively recent legal decision disallowing a volunteer-only provision for female jury service and insisting on a defendant's Sixth Amendment right to a jury chosen from a cross-section of the community (Taylor v. Louisiana). We read landmark slavery cases about African Americans' right to own their own bodies, to affirm their personhood. The discourse of protection appears in many instances of legal discrimination, so we also examine how protection is represented in literary and cinematic texts as aesthetic displeasure.[1] We look for similar links between protection and bodily discrimination in minority and marginalized groups.

In the course section on equal protection we read Tomas Rivera's novella about Mexican American immigrant life, . . . *and the Earth Did Not Devour Him*. We had already studied the 1848 Treaty of Guadalupe Hidalgo, a landmark treaty concerning Mexican American settlements in the United States, and its resonances and repercussions prove useful in establishing a historical context for Rivera's novella. Representing the difficult and often deplorable conditions of migrant laborers, Rivera comments on whom and how the law protects within United States borders. He shows how bodies are regulated both overtly and indirectly through legal norms, and the book is filled with migrant laborer bodies literally and metaphorically scarred by legal protection or the lack of it. In the vignette "The Little Burnt Victims," the Garcia children are burned in a blaze in their "chicken shack" while their parents work in the fields (120). Protection interacts with discrimination as the rhetoric of protection is deployed across legal and literary texts.

We also read key essays by Felix Cohen and by Karl Llewellyn, legal realists, who concern themselves with lived daily legal experience, and we listen to the Supreme Court oral argument in *San Antonio v. Rodriguez* debating the right to equal education. This material further contributes to the question already engaging students: What sort and degree of protection do legal normative concepts supply and owe to individuals in the United States? Considering the effect of law on routine life, Cohen argues that law should be thought of in terms of experience rather than "supernatural concepts" (214). Any legal concept's definition—like that of protection—must be based on its functional consequences (219). Llewellyn helps students think about the "area of contact between judicial (or official) behavior and the behavior of laymen" (56). In Rivera's novella, contact zones between judicial and layperson behaviors are abundant. Students can examine the varied interactions between the two, noting how narratives are generated around them both within and outside the text.

Because this class is about locating and challenging assumptions inherent in discourse (e.g., the language of protection), students are asked to write a series of reflection papers and a longer project. The reflection pieces are practice in the type of analysis we do in class: isolating an aspect of a text or class discussion found vexing or curious and exploring it further. I ask students not to write a formulaic essay but announce the issue they are addressing and then move through a detailed and thoughtful analysis of it. I respond with lengthy comments in the margins, engaging in an ongoing dialogue with their thinking process. I also supply an end comment designed to encourage them to continue in their deliberations, sometimes suggesting ways to refine their ideas, sometimes providing them with additional texts to read.

Students seem to appreciate the opportunity to explore a query of their choice in depth and have said that they grow from our written interactions in these reflection papers. There is no unified writing prompt for the entire class, only possibilities that grow organically out of our readings and discussion. In the course section "Whiteness, Citizenship, and Immigration," for instance, I have suggested that students reflect on how *white* is deployed in the legal cases *Takao Ozawa v. United States* and *United States v. Bhagat Singh Thind*, how the term is used differently in the two cases and how it is used in common parlance today. Doing an analysis of *white* led some students into their final papers, where they utilized their abilities to uncover the rhetorical strategies behind the use of other words. One student looked at the use of *tribe* in numerous sovereignty cases. Some students noticed a thread of interest among the reflections and wished to devote more time to it. A textiles student wrote how legal concepts could be seen in our appearance and went on to create a series of garments in which we could literally see legal elements woven into clothing.

Because the students in the course regularly come from other disciplines—political science, biology, textiles, English, sociology, business, economics, chemistry, history, journalism, art—the final project is always tailored to each one's interests. Some students identify themselves as prelaw and plan to attend law school after the University of Rhode Island; some take the course simply because the title intrigued them. Most have had little to no previous exposure to reading legal documents. Some therefore prefer the comfort and familiarity of a research essay devoid of legal cases, like those that have explored expert psychologists' roles in jury selection. Some students embrace analyzing legal opinions and have written essays on the constitutionality of gay marriage. Many decide to experiment with other disciplinary forms, often tailoring the project toward their major by applying the cultural work we have done to their main program of study.

The textiles major who designed a law clothing collection drafted drawings of her collection, bought the fabrics, created the garments, and had them modeled for the class during presentations of final projects while she explained how she had made her decisions. A neckline, for instance, might be a legal stranglehold on identity formation. A patchwork fabric might be emblematic of the inconsistency of how legal norms were applied. She wrote a paper describing each garment's relation to law. Another student created a photographic exhibit, *Where We Find Law*, coupled with a paper documenting the relation of images to legal norms. Another student directed, filmed, and produced a documentary on the No Child Left Behind program and explained how the images on film reflected suspect legal norms.

Student presentations of their final projects are performed the last day of class, and participants have remarked at how inventive, insightful, and analytic the projects have been. This last day has been tremendously rewarding for me as a professor, as I can see students integrating keen critical inquiry and thinking across their many disciplines. The skills they have acquired to detect the logical or irrational assumptions behind legal and literary texts are applied to a variety of fields as students demonstrate their ability to think interdisciplinarily.

Students consider the rhetoric of disciplines as cultural artifacts that mutually influence one another, and they see how legal and literary discourses are produced by and create the same ideas. The study of law and literature in this course thus not only enables a greater understanding of the motivations underlying our treatments of issues such as race and gender but also reveals the ongoing but invisible discursive forces operating on and through us in different disciplines.

Note

1. In Ann Petry's *The Street*, the super of the building, presiding over its maintenance, is represented as "a tall, gaunt man and he towered in the doorway, looking at her . . . his eyes had filled with a hunger so urgent that she was instantly afraid of him and afraid to show her fear" (10). The notion of being looked at uncomfortably arises as well in Tomas Rivera's . . . *and the Earth Did Not Devour Him*. Entering a school, an institutional structure normally designed to protect children by enhancing their lives, a boy remarks, "It's always the same in these schools in the north. Everybody just stares at you up and down . . ." (92).

Bridget M. Marshall

Literature and Law Lite: Approaches in Surveys and General Education Courses

Willem J. Witteveen explains, "Law and Literature forces awareness and criticism of the power of language to persuade, to perform, and to confuse" (158). This attention to language is a key goal of any undergraduate literature course, and one of the many ways to achieve it is through the law and literature approach. However, it's not always easy to get a new course approved by a department or university, and sometimes it's especially difficult for an interdisciplinary course to gain the necessary approval from more than one department. When preparing to develop, propose, or gain approval for such a course, instructors may find it useful to experiment with small-scale literature and law lessons in other courses. Students, too, benefit from and enjoy the addition of law to literary readings. I currently integrate legal issues, legal texts, and legal readings of literature into two courses, neither of which is named Literature and Law. One way for law and literature courses to gain a foothold in an institution is through regular catalog literary courses (surveys and general education courses) that have at their core an interdisciplinary approach.

I have used literature and law's highly productive interdisciplinary model to make literature surveys and general education courses more interesting and engaging for students, while improving their reading, writing, and thinking skills through challenging readings and classroom activities. The two courses—one an American literature survey required for English majors, the other an elective course that fulfills the university's general education requirement—have different goals, but students in both have benefited from the addition of legal texts and issues, in the depth of their understanding and in their enjoyment of the diverse approaches and materials.

Law in the American Literature Survey

The survey course on American literature from its beginnings to the Civil War is required for our English majors but is also open to other students to fulfill a general education requirement. The class is typically filled with sophomores and juniors who have enrolled somewhat reluctantly, since they don't imagine that early American literature, with all its Puritans, will be very interesting. While each version of this survey varies, most anthologies designed for it contain texts from colonial times through the Civil War era, a time period that has a wealth of legal history that in many cases is indispensable to the literary history. I want students to gain a working knowledge of major figures, texts, and movements in American literary history and an understanding of canon formation—how and why works are included (or not) in our literary history and in published anthologies. To this end, I teach both canonical and noncanonical texts. We also have regular conversations about what makes a piece of writing literature and why any given piece fits (or doesn't) into our ideas about American literature. Adding legal texts to the course does more than enhance students' understanding of the cultural, social, and political issues surrounding a particular piece of literature; it presses students to talk about what makes literature and how categories and genres function. In several tries at teaching this survey, I have found it productive to focus on three legal issues: colonial witch trials, women's rights, and slavery.

My students' favorite part of the study of the colonial period is the Salem witch hysteria. Most anthologies include several selections about Salem in the form of tracts about witchcraft and letters and journals from those participating in the trials. Standard texts are Samuel Deodat Lawson's "Brief and True Narrative" (1692), Governor William Phips's letters (1692–93), Cotton Mather's "The Wonders of the Invisible World" (1693), Robert Calef's "More Wonders of the Invisible World" (1700), and John Hale's "A Modest Inquiry into the Nature of Witchcraft" (1702).

I use original legal documents to supplement my students' understanding of the context for these diaries and letters. The most accessible place for students and scholars alike to find these legal documents is the University of Virginia's Electronic Text Center's *Salem Witch Trials: Documentary Archive and Transcription Project*, which provides full transcripts of all of the Salem witchcraft papers and links to images of some of the original documents (Boyer and Nissenbaum).

In "Wonders of the Invisible World," Mather recounts the trials of several women, including that of Martha Carrier. Along with his discussion of the trial, I assign portions of the original legal documents (indictments, summonses, examinations) and ask students to consider the differences in content, form, and style between Mather's version of the events and the transcript's depiction.[1] While the transcripts are far from neutral in their telling of the alleged bewitching, students are able to discover and explain some of the rhetorical strategies that Mather used to convince his readers (who needed little convincing to begin with) that an evil witchcraft was afoot in Salem. In the same assignment, they also read portions of Samuel Sewall's diary reflections on the Carrier trial. On 19 August 1692, Carrier's execution day, Sewall wrote, "Mr. Mather says they all died by a Righteous Sentence" (294). Through this constellation of texts, students can see the growing momentum in the community that doomed the women accused of witchcraft.

Because students show a great interest in and knowledge of the witch trials (the University of Massachusetts, Lowell, is located not far from the town of Salem, and most of our students come from Massachusetts high schools, where they have already read about the trials), I expand their understanding of the events in Salem by talking about the witchcraft trials throughout the colonies. Using a Web site that I helped create several years ago, we explore the case of Mary Parsons, an accused witch in Northampton, Massachusetts. The site, *The Goody Parsons Witchcraft Case: A Journey into Seventeenth-Century Northampton*, provides background information, original documents, and transcripts relating to the case. For an in-class activity, I bring in copies of the original documents and pass them out to the students. Working in pairs, and without any introductory information about the case, they attempt to figure out as much as they can from the documents. They struggle with the old handwriting and spelling and with the varying degrees of deterioration of the documents. They piece together the details of the case from the recorded testimony and verdict, sharing information with their classmates as they go. Reading and sharing information—such as the fact that Mary supposedly caused cows to die, yarn to tangle, and children to fall ill—they begin to see the many levels of interpretation at work in the study of witchcraft.

Reading the original documents, the students come to understand how historians piece together history from available documents and how early New Englanders interpreted the world around them. They also gain an understanding of the role of the courts in early American society and are often surprised to discover that people then were not only strongly religious but also quite litigious. This cultural background helps them with the other literary texts we read in this unit as well as with the many levels of interpretation involved in looking at historical legal cases. Many begin the unit on the colonial period thinking they know the story of witchcraft (often from the version they have seen in Arthur Miller's *The Crucible*), but looking at original legal documents gets them engaged in and curious about the beginnings of the legal system in the American colonies. Often it leads them to draw connections between these historical trials and contemporary legal issues.

The study of witch trials tends to focus the course on the role of women in early America. We continue this focus when we read emerging voices of women in the late-eighteenth and nineteenth centuries. In nineteenth-century women's writing, we find frequent references to legal issues. *The Heath Anthology* I most recently used contains Frances Osgood's 1848 poem "Lines (Suggested by the Announcement That 'A Bill for the Protection of the Property of Married Women Has Passed Both Houses' of Our State Legislature)," which makes explicit reference to a law, the New York's Married Women's Property Act of 1848 (Lauter [5th ed.] 2983–84). In addition to assigning the poem, I have students read the text of the law itself, which is available at the Law Library of Congress's Web site ("Married Women's Property Laws").[2] Elizabeth Cady Stanton's "Declaration of Sentiments," from the Seneca Falls Women's Rights Convention in 1848, helps students understand the struggle and the slow process of achieving women's equality in this period ([6th ed.] 2270–71). Another frequently anthologized piece, Fanny Fern's 1858 column "A Law More Nice than Just" is an excellent point of departure for discussing laws about women at the time (2262–63). Reading the text of various property laws provides essential context for the literary texts under study, but the reading and interpreting of these legal texts are also valuable: students find that they can apply their close-reading skills learned in their English classes to engage with other kinds of texts—texts more connected to the real world, as they say.

Students often voice surprise at being assigned to read a poem along with the text of a law; the styles and purposes of the writing seem so different to them. Comparing the text of a law, with its formal (and often oddly repetitive) language, numerical divisions, and specialized terminology, to Osgood's poem helps us talk about form and what makes a poem poetic. Reading the "Declaration of Sentiments" alongside the Declaration of Independence shows how the women's rights movement sought to build on the ideals of the founding fathers and how authors use, borrow, and revise the language and forms of their predecessors. We also compare the Declaration's legal language and form with that of Osgood's poem and Fern's humorous essay. This grouping of readings explores the boundaries of genre and the ways that literature and authors respond directly to other forms of culture and writing.

Following our exploration of the role of women's rights in literary, cultural, and legal history, we turn to the literature and legal issues concerning slavery in America.[3] Obviously, the Fugitive Slave Act of 1850 looms large in this period's study. While the title of the law itself is well known to students, few have actually read the text, which is available online at Yale Law School's *Avalon Project*. I add further context to the law by introducing earlier legal texts about fugitive slaves, including the Fugitive Slave Act of 1793; article 4, section 2, of the Constitution; and the Thirteenth Amendment. Students are surprised to learn that the Fugitive Slave Act of 1850 was actually a strengthening of the older 1793 law, not a brand-new concept. These legal texts are particularly illuminating when read alongside Harriet Beecher Stowe's *Uncle Tom's Cabin* (1852) or any of the fugitive slave narratives frequently included or excerpted in anthologies, such as Frederick Douglass's *My Bondage and My Freedom* (1855) and Harriet Jacobs's *Incidents in the Life of a Slave Girl* (1861). Since these texts make explicit reference to the effects of the Fugitive Slave Act, students find it interesting to know the details of the legislation, including the fact that it set fines for both governmental officials and regular citizens for aiding a fugitive slave in any way. It also set fees in payment for the various services that an officer or a citizen might render to help in the capture of a slave.

The contrast in form and voice in these texts—the cold legal language in the laws compared with the passionate argument and pathos in the novel and narratives—is another angle that students pursue in discussing this grouping of texts. Pairing literary texts with legal texts encourages a broader understanding of the cultural moment that produced both as well as deeper thinking about our expectations of genre and the purposes of different kinds of writing. Coming out of a literature-and-law-infused American literature survey, students are better prepared to make connections between the literary and legal movements in this time period and in their own world.

Law and Literature in General Education Courses

When teaching my general education course, The Horror Story, I sometimes turn to legal texts to supplement and enhance our reading of literature and to a classroom activity—a mock trial—to help students in their close reading (and enjoyment) of some stories. The students in this course are not generally English majors; they come from all disciplines across the university and are a mix of freshmen through seniors. Although they are often drawn by the specific topic of horror stories, they tend not to be avid readers or terribly interested in literature. In fact, many believe or at least hope that the course will involve just watching horror movies (they are sadly mistaken).

The course fulfills a general education requirement and may be one of the few in literature or writing our students will take outside of the required composition courses. With this in mind, I seek to find both texts and activities that will engage them and help them see both the joys and the value of studying literature. Since our time is limited and the range of horror stories quite broad, I spend most of the course focused on our selection of stories and novels. At several key points, I connect the texts with a variety of legal issues, including Cesare Lombroso's concept of the "criminal man" when we read Bram Stoker's *Dracula* (1897) and nineteenth-century American laws restricting women when we read Charlotte Perkins Gilman's "The Yellow Wall-Paper" (1892). These students I don't send off to read the specific laws or trial documents; instead, I create an overview or time line of an issue to provide the background necessary to understand the context of the story.

For *Dracula*, I provide a brief history of Lombroso's work, including the use of phrenology and physiognomy in criminal detection. Student discussion around this topic tends toward modern-day manifestations of our idea of what a criminal looks like; students recognize that some of Lombroso's methods and stereotypes are alive and well in current horror stories and the current media coverage of crime. For Gilman's story, I provide a time line of women's social status, including relevant legal decisions around the period when Gilman wrote. Students see connections with modern-day legal issues — not so much for women as for people with disabilities. Since Gilman's story portrays a woman who has been diagnosed with a nervous condition and is enduring a debilitating treatment for it, this turn from women's legal issues to questions of the legal status of the physically, mentally, or emotionally disabled helps them see the story as more related to their own time than they thought at first. I frequently find that the presence of a legal issue — whether a historical case or a question of legal status — in our discussion of a story connects it more with the real world, a connection students frequently complain is lacking in stories.

Throughout my courses, I try to train students in the practice of close reading, asking them to use textual evidence to support their claims, both in their writing and in class discussion. Running a few class discussions styled after courtroom trials, where we put a character on trial for a crime committed in the story, encourages close reading. The course typically includes at least a few students enrolled in our criminal justice program, and they are especially eager to use their developing expertise in legal terms. The general student population, well versed in *Law and Order* and other television shows about crimes and trials, are also eager to participate. This activity works quite well when we read William Faulkner's "A Rose for Emily" (1930) and Edgar Allan Poe's "The Black Cat" (1843).

We conduct in-class trials for protagonists, approaching the texts as sources for evidence to present to the classroom jury. Since both stories are missing many details and have unreliable narrators, these are challenging trials to mount. Dividing the class into a prosecution team and a defense team, I ask students first to work in pairs to answer three central questions: What crime or crimes did the protagonist commit? What was the motive and intention? What evidence is there in the story to support these claims? Both teams must use evidence found in the text. For instance, students working on the defense for both these stories frequently attempt an insanity plea, so they must find details — quotations, actions — that forward this claim. Both sides must also anticipate the position and evidence that the other side will present so that they can refute arguments in their rebuttal. This exercise encourages students to think beyond just their own task and consider an alternate perspective, something they also must do when writing their papers. The in-class trials ultimately help students write stronger essays because they have practiced how to make an argument and how to find and use textual evidence.

Literature and Law: Putting the Pieces Together

Literature and Law is unlikely to be a required course for either the general student population or English majors. One way to expose more students to a literature and law approach is to work it into existing courses. Doing so both engages interest and helps students develop skills of close reading and argument. Once they see the relevant and exciting connections between literature and law, they will be more inclined to take a course focused on literature and law. Thus what I call "literature and law lite" can be used to raise student interest in a new course offering, which is sometimes necessary for a new course to gain a department's approval.

Both survey and general education courses can provide opportunities for making literature and law connections. This approach can be pedagogically useful and also quite enjoyable for students and teachers alike. Jane B. Baron writes, "Literature, it is said, sheds light on law's gaps, rhetoric, and moral stance" ("Law" 1060). In my experience, the reverse is also true: the study of legal documents and processes helps readers discover the missing pieces, methods of argument, and moral positions of literature and leads to more thoughtful and engaged explorations of both texts and the world.

Notes

1. Transcripts of all the original documents relating to Martha Carrier's trial are grouped together in *The Salem Witchcraft Papers* (Boyer and Nissenbaum).

2. For a detailed explanation of the movement to pass the law and its effects, see Basch.

3. For the study of this area, I recommend Paul Finkelman's *Slavery in the Courtroom: An Annotated Bibliography of American Cases.*

Part III

Texts

Elliott Visconsi

Measure for Measure:
No Remedy

Shakespeare's two law plays, *The Merchant of Venice* and *Measure for Measure*, share an idiosyncratic and deeply secular attitude toward justice. Their world is one of inscrutable divine intentions, opaque or irrational human motivations, casual violence, and ambivalent moral norms. Justice is retribution in the service of civic therapy, intended to purify the city; the moral reclamation of the individual criminal is a second-order concern. That reclamation, when it comes, is often nakedly compulsory, taking the form of forced conversions and marriages in which the stubborn outsider is assimilated into the *nomos*, the normative universe, of the city.

On a law and literature syllabus, *The Merchant of Venice* is the usual choice for a Shakespeare play. The famous trial scene in which Portia orchestrates Shylock's ironic humiliation—that sour reversal in which we see the biter bit—poses engaging and accessible questions about mercy and revenge, belonging and exclusion. To what degree is Shylock's cruel rigor explained or mitigated by his suffering a lifetime of religious and ethnic contempt? Is Shylock's dogged insistence on the letter of the law merely a figure for the strict Mosaic law, and is his punishment a proxy for the supplemental remedy of the Gospel? Is his forced conversion excessive? Isn't

Portia's merciless close reading at least ironic and perhaps unjust? These are some of the questions expressed in that long and wrenching scene, if not in the play more broadly, for *The Merchant of Venice* compresses most of its legal thinking—its exfoliation of such problems of justice—into the trial scene. Moments elsewhere in the play gesture subtly toward a motive behind Shylock's malignancy, but Shakespeare never provides a potentially mitigating portrait of the inner life of his demonic Jew the way he does for, say, Richard III.

Measure for Measure, on the other hand, is a sustained piece of legal thinking, an anthropology of the rule of law in all its social, political, moral, and cultural dimensions. The play was the first of Shakespeare's efforts under the new regime of James I, who styled himself a philosopher-king, a theorist of sovereignty, and a divinely appointed judge of law and equity. The play is set in a decadent Vienna, a fallen, claustrophobic Continental dukedom, which is governed by a morally undistinguished prince and in which everyone is implicated in the acts, desires, and intentions of others. *Measure for Measure*, perhaps because of its address to the intellectual habits and obsessions of the new king, feels like a theoretical experiment in which Shakespeare poses a set of questions about the nature and extent of the rule of law, including the following: To what degree should law regulate sexual conduct? Is the prince directly responsible for, or even capable of, reforming the souls of his subjects? Is equity the soul of justice or merely a rationale for the unitary executive to operate above the law? Can an exemplary punishment prevent fallen creatures from sinning? Is the will of one man, however virtuous, a reasonable basis for the rule of law? Is mercy an act of political prudence or moral charity? Are there structures or institutions that might prevent the law from degrading into tyranny? Where do the claims of the polity surpass the rights of the individual?

To provide a pedagogical entry point for the play, I often begin with such a list of core questions about law, justice, and moral regulation as well as with a brief account of the historical and political background of the play. In such a preamble, I outline the political and religious characteristics of England in 1603 and its proximate past—the complete interpenetration of religion and government, James's well-stated preference for a theory of absolute sovereignty, the rising tide of Puritanism, the echo of the French wars of religion—in order to establish the view that *Measure for Measure* is intended to work in part as an intervention into contemporary debates about law, kingship, and subjecthood.[1] From such a position, it is easier for students to see not only that *Measure* is a play about ideas of law and justice but also that it is designed to do precisely the kind of cultural work it thematizes. In other words, just like the Duke of Vienna, Shakespeare tries to cultivate the judgment and reform the soul of his audience.

Measure for Measure, even in a reading directed at the play's view of the limits of the rule of law, works most effectively when paired with at least one tragedy, classical or early modern. *Antigone*, for instance, is an excellent precursor text.[2] In that play, the eponymous heroine weighs the competing claims of divine and human law and finds the cruelly imposed positive law of a tyrant insufficient; by honoring the gods and burying her brother, Antigone invites legal retribution. Her death by suicide begins the bloody purification of a polluted Thebes; the city benefits even as its princes suffer. Does *Measure for Measure* rewrite *Antigone* in a Christian idiom? Is it a play about the distance between divine (Christian) and human law? Is the strict virgin Isabella a second Antigone, tasked with a more excruciating decision? Is Vienna rehabilitated, freed from its pollution by the punishment of the corrupt or hard-hearted? These are some of the questions that spring from such a juxtaposition.

Unlike *Antigone, Measure for Measure* is a play deeply concerned with equity, that principle of flexible legal interpretation in which a judge looks beyond the letter to the spirit of a law, beyond an act to its intention. As Aristotle has written:

> It is equitable to pardon human weaknesses, and to look not to the law but to the legislator; not to the letter of the law but the intention of the legislator; not to the action itself, but to the moral purpose; not to the part, but to the whole; not to what a man is now, but to what he has been always or generally; to remember good rather than ill treatment, and benefits received rather than those conferred; to bear injury with patience; to be willing to appeal to the judgment of reason rather than to violence. (1.13.15–19)

It is only through equity that worldly justice is possible; without the ability to relax the rigor of the law, the innocent may be punished and the lawgiver's intention may be corrupted or misapplied. That Shakespeare had equity in mind in 1603 is no great surprise, for princely equity was at the heart of James I's theory of sovereignty. James figured the king in a godlike position, above the law, from which he might dispense equity and mercy, relaxing the stony rigor of the law to defend the innocent or pardoning the guilty for the benefit of the state or the criminal's soul. In 1599, James had outlined such a theory in the *True Law of Free Monarchies*.

> The King is above the law, as both the author and giver of strength thereto; yet a good king will not only delight to rule his subjects by the law, but even will conform himself in his own actions thereunto, always keeping that ground, that the health of the common-wealth be his chief law: And where he sees the law doubtsome or rigorous, he may interpret or mitigate the same, lest otherwise *summus ius* be *summum iniuria*: And therefore general laws, made publicly in parliament, may upon known respects to the King by his authority be mitigated, and suspended upon causes only known to him. (75)[3]

Without equity, the highest law (*summum ius*) may lead to the greatest injury (*summum iniuria*). So too the power to pardon is contained in the king's equitable prerogatives: unless a king sits above the law, his ability to suspend punishment can be restricted by other constitutional actors. It is not hard to see where this theory leads. Early modern English republicanism was mobilized around the fear of a unitary executive whose arbitrary will is law.

In a law and literature classroom, a reading of the play as a theoretical discussion of the nature and limits of equitable judgment has particular utility, for it looks backward to works like Aeschylus's *Eumenides* and forward to popular works such as Herman Melville's *Billy Budd* and Stanley Kubrick's *Paths of Glory*. *Measure for Measure* describes the profanation and possible redemption of the principle of princely equity. The corrupt Angelo betrays the Duke's commission, debasing his moral and political responsibility to judge with equity as he uses a rigorous interpretation of the law as sordid leverage over the chaste, almost-nun Isabella. Angelo is an unambiguous tyrant—a prince who tries to use public authority for his private pleasure—and his bad-faith manipulation of the law as sexual leverage is a conventional plot. The question of the play hangs on the potential redemption of equity: Is there an affirmative account of princely equity attached to the morally ambiguous Duke? Does his magisterial resolution of the play's action vindicate a theory in which the word of the prince has the force of law? I like to introduce this key question with a scriptural source such as Christ's utterance in Matthew 7.2, "For with what judgment ye judge, ye shall be judged: and with what measure ye mete, it shall be measured to you again" (King James vers.). I propose that Shakespeare may parse this utterance, translating each half into the figures of the Duke and Angelo—of wise judgment and wicked measure, respectively. To oppose that mechanical view of the play, I ask students to consider whether or not the scriptural utterance is far more monitory, a warning of inevitable retribution for sin. In such a darker view, the Duke is not a nearly godlike figure of insight and mercy but merely the instrument of symmetrical retaliation, a mode of retribution designed to satisfy the moral and emotional needs of the polity.[4]

Such a reading begins with an account of Angelo's profane and sordid misuse of his equitable prerogatives. When the Duke deputizes Angelo, he emphasizes first the personal basis of power: "in our remove be thou at full ourself; / Mortality and mercy in Vienna / Live in thy tongue and heart" (1.1.48–50). Even though Angelo is a substitute prince, his individual will is absolute. The Duke elaborates on the pairing of mortality and mercy, punishment, and forgiveness by admonishing Angelo that, as the Duke's deputy, his "scope is as mine own, / So to enforce or qualify the laws / As to your soul seems good" (64–66). To enforce or qualify the law, to deliver mortality or mercy—these are the twin functions of the absolute prince, and they are all the guidance Angelo receives from the Duke (except the company of the wise counselor Escalus).

Angelo's profound failure to be equitable is the narrative motor of *Measure for Measure*. In the Duke's absence, Angelo enforces but never qualifies the laws on the books, including the old law against adultery. His ambition is, at first, one of general deterrence: the criminals of Vienna have lost their fear of the law, and his brief is to restore its just terror. Claudio, the unlucky test case, is given a capital sentence; the mild Escalus submits to Angelo's severity, metronomically repeating that there is "no remedy" (2.1.281). This new juridical motto, "no remedy," pops up again in Angelo's first meeting with the supplicant virgin Isabella. A rule follower, she responds to Angelo's initial rebuff in a ludicrously servile way: "O just, but severe law! / I had a brother then. Heaven keep your honor" (2.2.41–42). But after some coaching, Isabella approaches the realization that there is only severity in Angelo's version of the law—deterrence trumps charity, mortality outweighs mercy. She pleas for mercy in surprisingly secular terms, but Angelo is resolute:

ISABELLA. Must needs he die?
ANGELO. Maiden, no remedy.
ISABELLA. Yes, I think that you might pardon him.
    And neither heaven nor man grieve at the mercy.
ANGELO. I will not do't.
ISABELLA. But can you if you would?
ANGELO. Look what I will not, that I cannot do.

ISABELLA. But might you do't, and do the world no wrong,
    If so your heart were touched with that remorse
    As mine is to him?
ANGELO. He's sentenced; 'tis too late
. . . .

ISABELLA. No ceremony that to great ones 'longs
    Not the king's crown, nor the deputed sword
    The marshal's truncheon, nor the judge's robe
    Become them with one half so good a grace
    As mercy does.
    If he had been you, and you as he,
    You would have slipped like him; but he, like you,
    Would not have been so stern.
ANGELO. Pray you, begone.   (48–66)

Isabella makes a two-pronged appeal; she offers conventional endorsements of princely mercy and asks Angelo to perform an act of imaginative substitution, putting himself in the place of the sanctioned Claudio. But Angelo retreats behind the impersonal letter of the law: "be you content, fair maid / It is the law, not I, condemn your brother. / Were he my kinsman, brother, or my son, / It should be thus with him. He must die tomorrow" (79–82). No remedy, indeed.

So far, Angelo is an uncomplicated literalist, a princely Shylock who refuses an equitable reading of the law to promote general deterrence. But Isabella's appeal softens him, and, seduced by her virtue, he becomes the very criminal he hopes to punish. Once a cold-blooded executor of the letter of the law, he is now an appetitive sinner, a tyrant who knowingly uses mercy as sexual leverage. Isabella has transformed him through her virtuous agency—the imaginative substitution she proposed has been effected. Angelo becomes a criminal tyrant; much of the rest of the play illustrates his wicked acts and intentions.

Indeed, the Duke's hasty departure from Vienna is at least partially a cover for a political experiment with Angelo as the chief subject:

DUKE. Lord Angelo is precise,
    Stands at a guard with envy, scarce confesses
    That his blood flows, or that his appetite
    Is more to bread than stone. Hence shall we see,
    If power change purpose, what our seemers be. (1.3.50–54)

Here we see the Duke unfolding his plan to weigh the souls of his subjects with nearly magical omniscience, an approach very close to James's political ambitions. The Duke sees all "like power divine" (5.1.367) and proposes an orthodox account of princely virtue: "He who the sword of heaven will bear / Should be as holy as severe; / Pattern in himself to know, / Grace to stand, and virtue go; / More nor less to others paying / Than by self-offences weighing (3.2.249–54). The prince must be self-governing and equitable; he must be able to imagine and judge with other people rather than from a position of sovereign elevation.

Having established Angelo's profane version of princely equity, I turn to the Duke himself, promoting the notion that he is at best an ambivalent exemplar of princely judgment and far from an affirmative case of an equitable prince in the style James I promoted. Shakespeare is deeply skeptical of princely omniscience, unsure that a regulatory state is a good idea and unconvinced that mercy is ever more than a political expedient. I describe him as a secular protoliberal rather than a flatterer of the new regime, whose anthropology of power and desire in *Measure for Measure* undermines the cozy absolutism and magical thinking at the core of James's political theory. Is the Duke really so equitable? Do we want him holding the sword of heaven? The Duke's absconding smacks of cowardice—he leaves Angelo to restore the rule of a law he let slip—and his nearly divine omniscience is the result of fraudulent priestcraft and the abuse of confidence. Angelo is plausibly understood as a demonic scapegoat, a sacrificial victim of the Duke's inability to bear full moral responsibility for a career of laxity. Even as an experimental subject, Angelo was a bad choice; the Duke is contaminated by the creation and the malfeasance of his corrupt deputy.

The cascade of pardons that ends the play undermines the potentially therapeutic work of mercy. The Duke pardons everyone in an orgy of forgiveness, consolidating his base and earning the love of his wayward subjects back again. Forgiving Claudio is, in fact, a source of sexual leverage once again, for the Duke explains his pardon to Isabella as partially done "for your lovely sake" (5.1.489). It is unclear, moreover, that the Duke has used his equitable prerogatives in the service of redemptive rehabilitation. Angelo exits the play craving "death more willingly than mercy / 'Tis my deserving, and I do entreat it" (474–75), and while he is forcibly married off, the Duke's pardon is mostly an ironic and bloodless way of punishing him. The ruined deputy is right—he does deserve death but wishes for it out of pride rather than penitence or Christian humility. Moreover, the Duke fails absolutely to reform the stubborn soul of the prisoner Barnardine; even so, the Duke pardons the drunk man in a spontaneous gesture of futile magnanimity. And forced marriages are hardly triumphs of equity. The Duke compels Angelo to honor his precontract with the ruined Mariana, forces Lucio to marry a punk, and strong-arms Isabella into his bed, all in the service of symmetrical retribution, meting out measure for measure. Angelo is punished for hypocrisy, Lucio for bold speaking, Isabella for her stubborn and futile retreat from sexuality and fallen life. In this reading, the Duke is a proto-Hobbesian absolutist: his will has the force of law, and his gestures of forgiveness are transparently punitive and instrumental.

From such a view, at the end of the play there is no one left standing in a position of moral authority, as an expression of justice. Angelo is clearly contaminated by his malevolent hypocrisy and the Duke by his sneaking authoritarianism. Even Isabella, the maiden who refuses to swap her virginity for her brother's life, is suspiciously rigorous; like Angelo, her blood is "snow broth" (1.4.58), and she practices an inflexible moral severity. Claudio protests for his life—"Sweet sister, let me live. / What sin you do to save a brother's life, / Nature dispenses with the deed so far / That it becomes a virtue" (3.1.132–35)—but she blasts him as a dissolute coward:

> Of faithless coward! O dishonest wretch!
> Wilt thou be made a man out of my vice?
> . . . .
>   Take my defiance!
> Die, perish. Might but my bending down
> Reprieve thee from thy fate, it should proceed.
> I'll pray a thousand prayers for thy death,
> No word to save thee.   (136–37, 142–44)

Isabella offers Claudio no remedy; in return, she is measured out a compulsory marriage and forced to confront the sexuality she seems to fear. Shakespeare's Vienna begins and ends as a *nomos* governed by will and retribution and reason of state; the remedies it proposes are instrumental rather than redemptive.

Measure for Measure, like many literary works deeply entangled with legal thinking, invites its audience to perform what Philip Sidney called "judicial comprehending," acts of deliberative judgment about justice, law, and morality (*Apologie* 90). The play may not describe an equitable prince in action, but nonetheless Shakespeare asks his audience to perform the work of equity, evaluating facts and norms, acts and intentions, crimes and remedies, circumstances and contexts, all from a position of ironic omniscience. Indeed, the play is an expression of the idea at the heart of the law and literature enterprise, a fundamentally humanist notion that literary fiction is unusually well suited to cultivating individual judgment or functioning as a "school of equity" (Nussbaum, "Equity" 95).

Notes

1. For discussion of a productive historical approach to the play and a brilliant reading of the play more broadly, see Shuger.

2. On the echoes of *Antigone* in *Measure for Measure*, see Lupton 127–57.

3. I have modernized spelling for the convenience of nonspecialist readers.

4. Important studies of the play are Gless; Shell; and K. Gross 68–101.

Kieran Dolin

_____

Bleak House and the Connections between Law and Literature

Simon Petch recently argued that Charles Dickens's *Bleak House* "exemplifies the Law and Literature agenda" (370). This was my experience when teaching the novel in my unit on literature and the law. The unit was taught to upper-level students in a bachelor of arts course and to a smaller number of students enrolled in a combined degree program (bachelor of arts and bachelor of laws). The smaller group were in many ways the ideal students of my curriculum, since they brought to the lectures and tutorials a familiarity with both legal concepts and analytic methods and the interpretative and critical practices of literary studies. The arts students had some initial anxiety about their lack of knowledge about the law but generally possessed more highly developed skills in the critical analysis of cultural texts and in the methods of ideology critique pursued in the unit. I stressed to all students that they would not be disadvantaged in their understanding of the texts by a lack of legal knowledge, that the unit would primarily explore the use of language in and about the law, narratives in the legal context, and strategies of representation in both literature and law. My text list was mainly legal trials, a mix of fictions centered on trials, a nonfiction novel about a celebrated case, and a small sample of legal judgments and court reportage. Thus *Bleak House* was taught along with other law and literature favorites, such as *The Merchant of Venice* and *Billy Budd*, but also with John Bryson's *Evil Angels*, an account of the Australian dingo baby case; *A Pin to See the Peepshow*, F. Tennyson Jesse's novel about the trial of Edith Thompson for murder; and the opinions of the British Court of Appeal in *Miller v. Jackson*.

Despite its preponderance of literary texts, the unit aimed to explore connections between literature and law and to consider the possible influence of each on the other. I took the founding principle of the law and literature movement as my starting point, that both fields structure reality through language and both have more or less formalized practices of reading and writing (Weisberg and Barricelli; J. White, *Heracles' Bow*). My approach was also shaped by Robert Cover's powerful intervention into this humanistic dialogue between the two disciplines. Cover argues that a vital distinction be made between law and literature, because law wields social power, including the privilege of legitimated state force. His work properly alerts scholars and students to the need to attend to the perspectives of those subjected to law as well as those who write or implement it. Above all, his insistence that the words of the law have material consequences in the world, physical effects ("Violence"), led me to consider ways of conveying how texts are written, read, and interpreted in a field of power. I therefore took from contemporary critical theory the idea that texts in both fields involve the inscription of cultural ideologies and that one of the aims of the interdisciplinary study of law and literature is to critique those effects (Leckie). My pedagogical practice sought to emphasize a contextual reading method, providing in lectures information about relevant legal and social history as well as offering critical readings of texts.

To increase students' comprehension of the real-world operation of the legal word, I organized a tour of a Victorian prison that has been preserved as a heritage precinct. From this tour and a reading from Michel Foucault, the students were able to get a sense of some of the mechanisms of legal coercion. Although not specifically referable to Dickens's novel, I hoped that the prison, with its Victorian architecture and its closed world of violence and regulation, would give students an intimation of the "bleak house" of Chancery. The next week, I assigned Oscar Wilde's prison poem "The Ballad of Reading Gaol." Both *Bleak House* and Wilde's poem exemplify how literature is a space in which alternative narratives to the dominant ones presented by law can be articulated (B. Thomas, *Cross-Examinations*).

During the course, some of the law-arts students became especially interested in the detail of the plots, treating the literary texts as real-life cases, and class discussion swung more toward legal doctrine than I had planned, which fed the anxieties of some nonlaw students. The difficulty of maintaining a focus on the area of intersection between two disciplines is one of the consequences of interdisciplinary study. To address it, I invited the students to adopt a double focus, on the context (including law) and on textuality, to think about both the texture of the language in what they read, the rhetoric or figuration, and the social issues and political implications of the texts.

This strategy worked well in our discussion of *Bleak House*, because the bravura opening of the novel immediately rewards such an approach. The symbolic representation of the Court of Chancery at the heart of the fog and the description of the chancellor "with a foggy glory round his head" is so overt and yet so strange that a close analysis of its manifold imagery, its bizarre juxtapositions and comparisons, is rewarding. The narrator, engaged in the act of literary representation, is foregrounded. Literal detail is used as the launching pad for metaphoric transformation, as the courtroom is represented as the site of a sham imitation of legal process, with lawyers "groping knee-deep in technicalities, running their goat-hair and horse-hair warded heads against walls of words, and making a pretence of equity with serious faces as players might" (14). Legal jargon functions only as an obstacle to justice, "walls of words." Metaphor relies on such analogies between apparently unlike objects. This mode, established from the opening page, radiates throughout the novel, not just in describing Chancery but also in proposing links among the worlds of law, fashion, and politics. The narrator's teasing question to the reader, "What connexion can there be, between the place in Lincolnshire, the house in town, the Mercury in Powder, and Jo the outlaw?" (256) can engage the student not only in the mystery inherent in the plot but also, as J. Hillis Miller pointed out, in the interpretation of the text (Introduction). His classic article provides a brilliant reading of the novel and highlights the common work of law and literature in producing and interpreting documents. Miller later supplemented his argument with a study of the performative nature of legal documents, such as the will and court orders in *Bleak House* ("Moments"). His revised approach reflects new developments in law and literature and offers a wonderful example of a reader revisiting a text and deepening his understanding of it. Setting Miller's pair of articles as secondary reading can work not only as a model of these approaches but also as a revelation of the nature of textual meaning in both law and literature.

In addition to its rhetorical flights, the opening of *Bleak House* makes many references to mid-Victorian legal London. I have therefore always taken time to sketch in a summary of equity, both in the original sense of a supplementary power to redress injustices caused by law and in the English tradition of a separate jurisdiction, the Court of Chancery. J. H. Baker, a legal historian, cites *Bleak House* to illustrate the wide gap between these two meanings of equity, and his summary captures not only the position of the Court but Dickens's attitude to it:

> It is the height of irony that the Court which originated to provide an escape from the defects of common law procedure should in its later history have developed procedural defects worse by far than those of the law. For two centuries before Dickens wrote *Bleak House*, the word "Chancery" had been synonymous with expense, delay and despair. (95)

Like a prosecutor opening a case, Dickens's narrator distills this tradition and expresses a general community outrage in a stern denunciation of the Court:

> This is the Court of Chancery; which has its decaying houses and its blighted lands in every shire; which has its worn-out lunatic in every madhouse, and its dead in every church-yard; . . . which so exhausts finances, courage, patience, hope; so overthrows the brain and breaks the heart; that there is not an honourable man among its practitioners who would not give — who does not often give — the warning, "Suffer any wrong that can be done you, rather than come here!" (15)

This catalog of ills will be fleshed out in the lives of the characters, but it is useful to give students an appreciation that these claims were not exaggerated or fanciful. Without wishing to diminish students' engagement with the stories of the financial and emotional costs of litigation as an issue of continuing social and legal importance, I stress that Dickens's passionate criticism was generated as part of a larger reform movement. The novelist aimed to bring about legal change. He and many other nineteenth-century novelists believed that literature was a political tool. The Victorian critic George Henry Lewes captured the spirit of Dickens's scathing portrait of the Dedlocks when he wrote, "[T]he pen, in our age, weighs heavier on the social stage than the sword of a Norman Baron" (qtd. in Lucas 71). For Dickens and his readers, fiction and journalism were closely connected, not only because the novels first appeared as serials in magazines but also because both were mass media with a traffic in ideas and images between them. The pioneering research of John Butt and Kathleen Tillotson remains a clear, succinct source for a contextual reading of *Bleak House* and the law:

> Dickens's indictment of Chancery . . . followed in almost every respect the charges already levelled in the columns of *The Times*. In both we read of houses in Chancery, and wards in Chancery, of dilatory and costly procedure, of wasted lives, and of legal obstructionism. (187)

Although drawing from the existing discourse of reform, *Bleak House* introduces new aspects to the literary representation of law through its innovations in form. The most noticeable of these is the use of two narrators, an omniscient voice and Esther Summerson, who writes in the first person. As a character, Esther does not meet with universal approbation in modern classrooms, being at once too self-deprecating and too censorious of others. But it can be a productive exercise to consider what this unusual combination of narrators brings to the novel. They form a contrast: masculine and feminine; a masterly wielder of inside knowledge of various social scenes and an illegitimate orphan outsider; one at the heart of the lawsuit and one on its fringe (Blain). While one narrator tells a story of obstructed justice, the other embodies and narrates a counterworld of practical charity.

Dickens uses the lawsuit of *Jarndyce and Jarndyce* as the hidden center of the many subplots formed around his characters' lives. In this way the effects of the case ramify throughout society, and it comes to represent attitudes and conflicts dominant in the society. This approach to the novel builds on narrative jurisprudence, especially cultural studies of famous trials. Robert A. Ferguson's statement that "the trials that grip the communal imagination tend to formalize ideological paradoxes" of their societies ("Becoming" 116) summarizes this way of reading trials and the narratives produced by them. Rosemary J. Coombe argues that "in important trials . . . the community itself is put on trial and reconstructs itself poetically" ("Is There a Cultural Studies" 48). This insight can be useful for the analysis both of artfully plotted fictional trials and of actual causes célèbres. Obviously in the fictional trials the scope of *poiesis*, or creative refashioning, is much greater. Such an approach builds on students' familiarity with famous trials in the media-dominated world of contemporary culture. The Chancery lawyers describe *Jarndyce* with complacent fondness as a "monument of Chancery practice" (33), but their notion of a classic case is rejected as the novel transforms it into an example of all that is wrong in the law and in the English body politic.

Bleak House is an unusual legal narrative: although one of the most famous fictional trials, it is characterized by inaction and void of the drama and judgment usually afforded by a substantive trial and verdict. Tied up in the intricacies of Chancery procedure, the case of *Jarndyce and Jarndyce* makes no progress for two generations. As John Jarndyce tells Esther, "the original merits of the case have long since disappeared from the face of the earth." Instead, the case has become "an infernal country dance of costs and fees and nonsense and corruption" (118). Rather than attempt to thread its way through this "labyrinth," *Bleak House* follows the lives of its characters outside the court, tracing their descent into poverty, ill health, and madness. (784). The plot traces a downward trajectory of disappointment and exhaustion. The late discovery of a new will, which promises to resolve the long-drawn-out question of entitlement to the Jarndyce estate, is rendered useless, and the legal question is suspended forever, when the legal costs exceed the value of the estate.

This discovery elicits only laughter from the lawyers in the novel. With this inversion of decorum and plot expectation, the travesty that is *Jarndyce and Jarndyce* is complete; *Bleak House* presents its insights into law through the medium of satire. The name of the case, with its echo of the word *jaundice*, and the caricatures of the lawyers—the secretive and malevolent Mr. Tulkinghorn, the vampiric Mr. Vholes, the voluble ideologue Conversation Kenge, and "the blue-nosed, bulbous-shoed old benchers in select port-wine committee" (17)—show Dickens's mastery of satiric exaggeration. The wigs of the advocates are fused with the Chancery practice of conglomeration, under which an entire estate, not just one disputed piece, was administered by the court, into "Wiglomeration," the "vastly ceremonious, wordy, unsatisfactory and expensive" process of the court (121). As well as describing this system, the satiric narrator analyses its underlying cause: "The one great principle of English law is, to make business for itself" (621). This accusation of self-interest attacks the mentality of the entire profession, not the actions of a few. Thus Kenge rejects reform on the grounds that it will harm Vholes; and the profession protects its privileges, making its primary aim to perpetuate the institution rather than promote the client's interest.

Dickens portrays a system that consumes vastly more than it produces, slowed down by an inefficient, wasteful multiplication of documents and court appearances. To underline this point, he includes a parodic copy of the Court, the rag-and-bone shop where papers are bought but never sold. Its proprietor, Krook, is known locally as the Lord Chancellor. As the real chancellor's grotesque double, Krook is illiterate, greedy, alcoholic, and suffering from a circulatory disease. In an inspired piece of comic fantasy, he dies "the death of all Lord Chancellors in all Courts, and of all authorities in all places . . . where false pretences are made, and injustice is done," the death that is "inborn, inbred, engendered in the corrupted humours of the vicious body itself, and that only—Spontaneous Combustion" (519). The death of the pseudo lord chancellor is presented as a prophetic warning to all who preside over and benefit from deadlocked systems.

The person who discovers this awful death is Kenge and Carboy's clerk, Guppy, one of those "out of the suit [whom] Jarndyce and Jarndyce has stretched forth its unwholesome hand to spoil and corrupt" (17). All Guppy's private communications are conducted in legal discourse, including his proposal of marriage to Esther. Failing to acknowledge the middle-class distinction between public and private life, Guppy is a prisoner of the language of the law, his subjectivity shaped entirely by its self-serving, self-saving terms. Abandoning his scheme to blackmail Lady Dedlock, without confessing to such, Guppy ends up "in a state little short of forensic lunacy" (637).

The novel's only alternative, set out in Esther's narrative, is domestic economy, exemplified in orderly but caring households presided over by such women as Esther and Mrs. Bagnet. While Chancery exacerbates rivalry among family members, Esther's story is based on the existence of a natural law of love between mothers and children, between siblings, and even between cousins. Resting implicitly on Victorian ideologies of femininity, Dickens allows even the unmothered, like Esther, Caddy Jellyby, and Charley, to be wonderful mothers. Maternal feeling breaks through the self-protective reserve of Lady Dedlock. Even the unsentimental detective Bucket accepts a kind of natural right in Esther to be the first to touch her mother's hand (915). The masculine public world is corrupted, and the private feminine world redemptive when properly managed by a woman. Two male characters straddle this public-private divide, John Jarndyce and Allan Woodcourt. Jarndyce, being independently wealthy, refuses to participate in the famous lawsuit that has ruined his family; he operates a private charitable fund from home. Likewise, the work of Woodcourt as a doctor ministering to the poor takes him into their homes and involves a personal sacrifice of fees. The private sphere, exemplified by idealized homes, becomes the novel's preferred space of ethical judgment and action, the vantage point from which Skimpole, Chadband, Mrs. Jellyby, the

Smallweeds, and others are condemned. And yet these homes are to an extent "bleak houses," because they are not impervious to the "east wind" of unhappiness, separation, mistrust, or poverty (84). Esther's narrative is distinguished from that of Chancery by its responsiveness to hardship, by its attempts to alleviate such experiences. In this respect, it is constructed as a feminine supplement to the masculine world of Chancery, just as Chancery was originally intended to supplement the law.

Bleak House was a text well suited to my course objectives. Both its narrators tell stories of law. Its vigorous satire is not so much antilegal as a spur to reform the law. It rejects John Jarndyce's strategy of leaving the law to go its own way. Rather, it demonstrates literature's close engagement with law—with narratives of personal right and social values, with acts of verbal representation, and with the necessity of interpretation. By combining extrinsic and intrinsic, contextual and figurative modes of analysis, students can learn through this text about literature's influence on law (J. Miller, "Moments" 50). Thus the novel's question, "What connexion can there be . . . ?" elicits yet another answer: The connection between literature and the law.

Florence Dore

Guilty Reading: Obscenity Law, American Modernism, and the Case for Teaching Theodore Dreiser's *Sister Carrie*

> *His touch is neither firm enough nor sufficiently delicate to depict without offense to the reader the continued illicit relations of the heroine. The long succession of chapters dealing with this important feature of the story begins to weary very quickly. Their very realism weakens and hinders the development of the plot. The final scenes in New York are stronger and better— But I cannot conceive of the book arousing the interest or inviting the attention, after the opening chapters, of the feminine readers who control the destinies of so many novels.*
>
> —Harper and Brothers

> *There is never any danger of corrupting an inexperienced girl. For where there is no knowledge of sexual processes even in the unconscious, no hysterical symptoms will arise; and where hysteria is found there can no longer be any question of "innocence of mind."*
>
> —Sigmund Freud, *Dora: An Analysis of a Case of Hysteria*

A study of censorship can enhance students' understanding of American modernism, but teaching this historical, legal aspect of literature along with its aesthetic dimension is not a simple task. In my book *The Novel and the Obscene: Sexual Subjects in American Modernism*, I argue that obscenity law in fact shaped the American modernist aesthetic, and in this essay I hope to demonstrate that close reading is the best way for students to grasp this fact. In my courses—graduate, undergraduate, lecture, and discussion—I have found that text-based analysis is crucial to showing students the reciprocal relation between obscenity law and American modernism.

Between 1868 and 1933, roughly the same years that spanned the rise of American modernism, obscenity law underwent a dramatic change. The students I teach have usually heard of the famous case that ended the ban on James Joyce's *Ulysses* (1921), *United States v. One Book Called "Ulysses"* (1933). This is not surprising: along with the end of Prohibition and the rise of the flapper, the legalization of Joyce's novel in United States courts has come to symbolize modern progressivism. Students are always interested to learn that in addition to its general cultural significance, the *Ulysses* case had actual legal impact. In particular, *One Book* significantly weakened American obscenity standards by dismantling the prevailing obscenity test, taken from the 1868 British case *Queen v. Hicklin*.[1] Alongside the *Ulysses* case, I teach *Hicklin*, which declared that any text would be obscene if it might "corrupt those whose minds are open to such immoral influences and into whose hands a publication of this sort may fall" (371). *One Book* loosened this standard, stipulating that any text exciting "lustful thoughts" in a "person of average sex instincts" would be obscene (184). The shift from *Hicklin*'s "open minds" to *One Book*'s "person of average sex instincts" participates in a general turn toward sexual frankness at this moment in American culture. In the classroom, the pairing of these contrasting legal standards vivifies the broader cultural turn.

Teaching law and literature obviously involves comparing legal cases with works of literature, and in a literature course that includes *One Book*, James Joyce's *Ulysses* (1922) might seem at first glance to be the obvious choice for such a comparison. An examination of Joyce's novel alongside *One Book*, we might suppose, would demonstrate to students the openness of the era: a study of those formerly obscene topics in Joyce's novel might seem to give specific contour to an American public that after 1933 could accommodate them. But I seek to teach students something deeper about the relation between law and literature, something that goes beyond the simple historical observation that the ban on *Ulysses* was lifted at the height of literary modernism. For this reason, I do not teach the novel that was the subject of the legal case in my American modernism and censorship course. Theodore Dreiser's *Sister Carrie* (1900) serves the purpose better.

Like *Ulysses*, *Sister Carrie* portrays women in unconventional, self-consciously modern sexual situations: Dreiser's Carrie Meeber has sexual liaisons but never marries, and the novel ends with a moral valorization of her—an emotionally dissatisfied young woman, to be sure, but one who ends up financially and sexually independent. Unlike *Ulysses*, *Sister Carrie* was never legally censored, and although some scholars believe the version of *Sister Carrie* that Dreiser eventually published was censored by its publishers, neither is its publication history what qualifies it as an appropriate text for a course on censorship law and literature.[2] In the end, the historical facts of a literary text's legality offers only a very limited view of literature, and hence it offers students a limited understanding of literature's relation to the law. Whereas *Ulysses* was banned in American courts, Dreiser's novel engages the cultural narrative that created the conditions for that historical banning. *Sister Carrie* reveals an intriguing narrative about the persistence of normative gender roles in American society, a narrative that also crucially underwrites American obscenity law. The legalization of Joyce's novel marks an important historical point in this narrative, but *Sister Carrie* unravels that point. By inserting its key features into a narrative drama, Dreiser's novel lays bare what I describe as a cultural logic, one that structured both the law and the literature. As we shall see, literary analysis makes the relation between censorship and literature accessible to students in a way that history alone cannot.

I begin my discussion of obscenity law and *Sister Carrie* with a look at the epigraphs to this essay: the first is taken from a letter from Harper and Brothers declining to publish *Sister Carrie*; the second is taken from Sigmund Freud's *Dora* (1905), a contemporaneous and quite influential analysis of feminine sexuality. The cultural logic I uncover in my close readings turns out to be sexually inflected, and these two epigraphs give students a simple view of modern definitions of feminine sexuality. The editors at Harper and Brothers turned down the first version of *Sister Carrie* in part because they worried that the "illicit relations of the heroine" might cause "offense" to "the reader" (Elias 2: 210). I point out to students that the editors' implicit endorsement of the belief that the "offended" reader is by definition feminine affirms a familiar belief about feminine vulnerability, one that Dreiser's Carrie does not fit. Obscenity law is in large part justified by this belief. Dreiser's Carrie seems unaffected by this idea of feminine sexual innocence, and so it is no wonder, as my students often notice, that Harper and Brothers rejected *Sister Carrie*. I then direct students to the second epigraph, explaining that Freud suggests that his patient is like Carrie, outside the mold. Freud asserts that the very possibility of hysteria rests upon an idea that contradicts feminine sexual innocence: there "can no longer be any question of innocence of mind . . . where hysteria is found" (*Dora* 42). I ask students to consider the idea that Carrie is a version of Dora and that censorship law relies on the definition of feminine sexuality that Carrie and Dora contradict.

In more advanced undergraduate courses and graduate seminars, I assign the full text of *Dora* to deepen students' understanding of the standard of feminine innocence that justified censorship law. Freud commenced his treatment of the "hysteric" Dora in the same year Dreiser wrote *Sister Carrie*, and both Dreiser and Freud, it turns out, depict reading as a crucial threat to that standard. Dora reads about sex in an encyclopedia, and Carrie reads bad novels. Both girls feel guilty about their objectionable reading, and in both texts, indeed, guilt indicates the presence of a Victorian standard of feminine sexual innocence. Freud conjectures that Dora feels guilty about her reading because of Victorian squeamishness about feminine sexuality, and in the scenes in which Carrie reads, as well, there is the suggestion of sexual guilt. Carrie's guilt is similar to Dora's, but instead of representing Carrie's guilt as deriving from Victorian prudery, Dreiser portrays it as a shame about her feminine stupidity. My close reading of *Sister Carrie* and obscenity law demonstrates to students that the trenchant cultural myth of feminine stupidity in fact derives from this sexual standard, and that in spite of Dreiser's intention to flout traditional gender norms, Carrie's stupidity reiterates them. This surprising reiteration of the Victorian standard even in the context of a renegade novel mirrors the prudery that emerges in *One Book*'s new, looser standard for obscenity as well. At first glance, the new legal definition seems to reflect the culture's more open attitude toward sexuality: the idea of "average instincts" appears to legitimate the idea that legal subjects are sexual. But as *Sister Carrie* clarifies, the assertion that "average sex instincts" should be the deciding factor in determinations of obscenity turns out to preserve key assumptions about suppressing sexuality expressed in the "open minds" standard.

Freud concludes, from Dora's familiarity with sexual terms, that illicit reading caused her physical symptoms. The landscape of her dream is, in his reading, a "symbolic geography of sex," and "anyone who employed such technical names . . . must have derived [her] knowledge from books, and not from popular ones either, but from anatomical text-books or from an encyclopedia" (91). Dora admits to reading about appendicitis in the medical encyclopedia, but Freud believes that an "occasion of more guilty reading had become associated with this one." In Freud's analysis, she has "punished" herself somatically for reading about sex in the encyclopedia (92, 94). She has punished herself, that is, for becoming sexually aroused by reading. She is a guilty reader, a sexual reader who has repudiated the arousal caused by reading. In Freud's assessment, the cause of her somatic "punishment" is sexual knowledge gained from reading. Hysteria is thus a version of censorship.

Early on in *Sister Carrie*, Carrie has been waiting for her lover, Drouet, and she has "amused herself with a walk, a book by Bertha M. Clay . . . and by changing her dress for the evening" (78). The book she reads is an actual novel, entitled *Dora Thorne*. Later, the character Bob Ames compares another popular novelist to Clay with the quip, "His stuff is nearly as bad as Dora Thorne." Carrie reacts with shame. At first, Freud's Dora (not to be confused with Clay's heroine) seems unlike Carrie; the hysteric is guilty of sexual arousal; Carrie is guilty of reading lowbrow novels. We will return to this question. First, however, I want to draw our attention again to the standard for obscenity to examine guilty reading from a legal point of view. Obscenity signifies a legal version of guilt, and the law too is defined in terms of a particular kind of reading. In *Hicklin*, recall, obscenity is that which might "deprave and corrupt those whose minds are open to immoral influences." As I have explained, the case concerns the legality of a pamphlet depicting the "open minds" of young girls in particular: *The Confessional Unmasked: Shewing the Depravity of the Romish Priesthood, the Iniquity of the Confessional, and the Questions Put to Females in Confession*. This legal standard thus emerges in response to a portrayal of feminine readers as sexually corrupted by reading. It involves the legality of a particular construal of "iniquity": sexual "questions" asked of "females," words that put "immorality" into them. In *Hicklin* as in Freud's text, obscenity is understood as an external "influence," an intrusion of "immorality" into an "open mind"—a female opening, here figured as the female mind.

In class discussions, I point out that the sexualized scene of corruption illustrated in the pamphlet is the basis for the obscenity regulation it inspires. The pamphlet in *Hicklin*, that is, depicts an instance of corruption that resembles the standard for obscenity it articulates. Like the "girl" in the "confessional," susceptible to the questions of the "depraved" priest, the reader's "mind" is "open to immoral influences." The obscenity, then, is like the priest—the man—and "readers" are like the "girls," "open" to the "depraving" influences of obscenity. Readers in *Hicklin* are "open" like girls; they are feminized, it seems, likened in their susceptibility to girls' openings. *Hicklin*'s construal of obscenity relies upon an idea of vulnerable bodily openness, and on this view, "immorality," like the priest, would seem to be a phallic intrusion. Guilty reading is thus a distinctly sexual scene. It protects an "innocence of mind," to return to Freud's words, that emerges here as an innocence of body—a body without the intrinsic possibility of sexual arousal, and thus a vulnerable body. *Hicklin,* which justified the censorship of actual texts between 1868 and 1933 in the United States, also expresses this more subtle prohibition, this insistence that to be a woman is to be asexual, and that to be asexual is to be a woman.

Dreiser represents Carrie as a guilty reader because at the turn of the twentieth century this figure necessarily inserts Carrie into a narrative of sexual corruption. It is by making Carrie a different kind of feminine reader, moreover, that he can alter the Victorian construal of femininity. In the moment of Carrie's guilty reading, Ames makes Carrie feel ashamed not for reading sexual matter but for indulging in a lowbrow novel:

> Carrie felt this as a personal reproof. She read "Dora Thorne," or had a great deal in the past. It seemed only fair to her, but she supposed that people thought it very fine. Now this clear-eyed, fine-headed youth, who looked something like a student to her, made fun of it. It was poor to him, not worth reading. She looked down, and for the first time she felt the pain of not understanding. (237)

Carrie's shame comes from intellectual inferiority here; as Dreiser's narrator describes it, it is "the pain of not understanding." Toward the end of *Sister Carrie,* we find Carrie reading again: "Carrie was reading at this time *Père Goriot*, which Ames had recommended to her. It was so strong, and Ames' mere recommendation had so aroused her interest, that she caught nearly the full sympathetic significance of it." In her second appearance as a reader, Dreiser again points to her lack of knowledge: she only "nearly" understands Balzac. The narrator explains her response to Ames as a sense that "her earlier reading, as a whole" has been "silly and worthless" (363). Like the "personal reproof" she feels at the earlier reading, Carrie feels shame here too. But Dreiser's character and Freud's patient seem to differ, since guilty reading is for Carrie a consequence of not "catching" the "significance" rather than a sign of damaged moral virtue. Carrie too is a sexual woman, but her shame is intellectual instead of sexual—a matter of "understanding" rather than of sexual corruption. Between Dora and Carrie, then, "the pain of not knowing" replaces "knowledge of sexual processes" as the cause of shame. We find out early on in *Sister Carrie* that intellectual inferiority is a basic tenet of Carrie's character: "She was no talker. She could never arrange her thoughts in a fluent order. It was always a matter of feeling with her, strong and deep" (88). Unlike the "hysteric," Carrie is not repressing a forbidden sexual arousal; she just lacks knowledge.

The idea that Carrie has managed to escape the idea of "feminine innocence" that snares Dora is echoed in the description of Carrie as a "new and different individual." With this phrase, Dreiser's narrator indicates the new kind of subject the author wants Carrie to be:

> She was so turned about in all of her earthly relationships that she might well have been a new and different individual. She looked into her glass and saw a prettier Carrie than she had seen before; she looked into her mind, a mirror prepared of her own and the world's opinions, and she saw a worse. Between these two images she wavered, hesitating which to believe. (70)

Carrie is "turned about," no longer vulnerable in *Hicklin*'s terms. Like the editors at Harper and Brothers, here "the world's opinion" is that Carrie's sexual liaisons make her "worse," but Carrie continually opts out of the actions that would conform to this opinion. The "worse" Carrie is like Dora, subject to an ideal of feminine purity, and her status as the "new individual" would seem to indicate that she has been liberated from this constraint. But there is more to the "new and different individual" than this. Indeed, there is skewed contrast between mirrors in this passage that suggests an entirely different reading. Notice that the mirroring does not indicate any simple idea of reflection. In fact, beyond the normal process of reflection, there is a doubling: a suggestion of two mirrors, two reflections, and two views of Carrie as "worse" and "pretty." We might conjecture that there are two mirrors here because Carrie does not simply see herself as "better" versus "worse." The double mirror suggests that Carrie has another option, another way to see herself. Rather than in a "mirror prepared of her own and the world's opinions," that is, Carrie, the "new and different individual," can now look into an actual "glass." This is Dreiser's way of indicating a shift from a moral to a physical view of Carrie, and what replaces the idea of Carrie as illicit (here "worse") is the physical reflection, her "pretty" face. "Pretty," it seems, is the "new and different" version of "worse." In the classroom, I have found it useful to point out that this is the neutral narrator for which naturalist authors are known. Dreiser, one of the most influential American naturalists, indicates that neutrality has been achieved in his portrayal of Carrie as pretty. Intriguingly, this creates the idea that feminine beauty is an objective quality.

But the "pretty" Carrie crucially repeats the "worse" Carrie, and the doubling turns out to be a reflection after all. One mirror, it seems, is a reflection of the other—"pretty" is a reflection of "worse." Carrie only appears "worse," recall, in a "mirror prepared of her own and the world's opinions," and the "world" here is a symbol of the obsolete moral view. When she seems "worse," it is because she is being held to the feminine in-nocence standard, and throughout *Sister Carrie* Dreiser attributes this view to something he calls the "world." The mirror passage appears in a chapter that in fact begins with such a claim: "In light of the world's atti-tude towards woman and her duties, the nature of Carrie's mental state de-serves consideration" (68). The narrator is cultivating a point of view here that resembles the glass. He is pointing to a more neutral view of Carrie— to a "consideration" of her "mental state"—and it is this view that will replace the moralizing of "the world's attitude towards woman and her duties." Like the pretty Carrie, her "mental state" appears outside of the "the world's" view that she is "worse." It is only where the world's view has been replaced by the physical view, in fact, that we can "see" Carrie's face as pretty, and the "pretty" Carrie—along with the "mental state" that ac-companies being pretty—would seem to be outside of "the world."

In the following exchange between Carrie and Ames, however, "the world" whose rejection has crucially enabled Carrie turns out rather to constitute her:

> "The world is always struggling to express itself," he went on. "Most people are not capable of voicing their feelings. They depend upon others. That's what genius is for. One man expresses their desires for them in music; another one in poetry; another one in a play. Some-times nature does it in a face—it makes the face representative of all desire. That's what has happened in your case."
>
> He looked at her with so much import of the thing in his eyes that she caught it. At least, she got the idea that her look was something which represented the world's longing. (356)

"The world," says Ames, "expresses itself" in Carrie's face, and here, her face emerges as utterly paradoxical. To be pretty she must exist outside of "the world," but what makes her pretty is that she "represents" the world, reflects it. It is for this reason that Carrie is an actress, a "mirror," as the narrator explains, of "the world" outside of her: "She was created with that passivity of soul which is always the world's mirror" (117). And it is not only Ames who confirms this aspect of Carrie; in the "world" of the novel, it is literally the "world's opinion" that Carrie is pretty—everyone agrees. In the novel's logic, this means that the moralistic view embodied in "the world" has been rejected. But in the exchange before us, being outside of the world turns out to be the condition, precisely, of being defined by the world, indeed as the world. For Carrie to exist outside of the world is to have it emerge on her face—it is to have it emerge, strangely, as her face. Pretty is not only the new "worse," then, it is also the new "good," and Carrie's face thus symbolizes the impossibility of the entirely objective view embodied in the physical mirror. Even in the new view of Carrie that Dreiser cultivates throughout the novel, Carrie remains, crucially, subject to the standard of feminine sexual innocence that Freud sees as debilitating Dora.

This emphasis on objectivity in the mirror passage turns out to characterize a broader cultural trend that we find in the author's aesthetic as well as in the new standard for obscenity. In a letter to Walter Hines Page, senior editor at Doubleday, Dreiser described *Sister Carrie* as "uncovering the rudeness and bitterness of life" (Elias 1: 62). In a 1903 editorial, "True Art Speaks Plainly," Dreiser declared that "the business of the author, as well as of other workers upon this earth, is to say what he knows to be true." And "truth," he argued, "is what is . . . the seeing of what is, the realization of truth. To express what we see honestly and without subterfuge: this is morality as well as art" (qtd. in G. Becker 155). The obscenity cases of the era demonstrate a similar perception of morality as truth. It was an idea of honesty, in fact, that governed the redefinition of the obscenity standard in the *Ulysses* decision. As we have seen, in the new standard, Judge John Woolsey writes that obscenity is that which might "arouse" a "person of average sex instincts." He argues, in particular, that Joyce's

> attempt sincerely and honestly to realize his objective has required him incidentally to use certain words which are generally considered dirty words and has led at times to what many think too poignant a preoccupation with sex in the thoughts of his characters.
> (US v. One Book 183)

Woolsey argues, moreover, that we should be able to read *Ulysses*, because Joyce has drawn a "true picture": "When such a great artist in words . . . seeks to draw a true picture . . . ought it be impossible for the American public legally to see that picture?" (184). It is in the interest of "sincerity" and "honesty," then, that a "person of average sex instincts" replaces *Hicklin*'s open "mind." Judge Woolsey acknowledges that this ideal entails a new view of women: the "words," he quipped, "which are criticized as dirty are old Saxon words known to almost all men and, I venture, to many women" (183–84).

The new standard for obscenity would thus seem both to reject feminine sexual innocence and to make way for the sexual arousal that *Hicklin* prohibited. This standard indeed appears to challenge the idea of feminine sexual purity as a justification for obscenity regulations to dissociate femininity from offense. But like Carrie's "pretty" face—sign of her entry into a world where she can be sexual—in the law, too, the "truth" of sex comes at a cost. In the novel, Carrie's move away from morality delivers her into a physical realm that reproduces feminine sexual innocence as innocence of mind. In the law, similarly, "average sex instincts" are prohibited from the person who has them. In the new standard a text is "obscene," that is, if it "arouses" a "person of average sex instincts." We might have "sex instincts," in other words, but if we are "aroused" by a text, that text will be "obscene," prohibited by law. The legal recognition of "sexual arousal," sign of a move away from *Hicklin*, thus refuses arousal, and this refusal is accomplished through the prohibition of its source, the "obscene" text. As soon as "sex" is removed from the moralizing prohibitions of *Hicklin*, then, it becomes reinscribed as "sex instinct," a truth that renders sex nothing, an absence. Like the view of Carrie as "worse" that emerges in her "pretty" face, *Hicklin*'s sexual purity appears as something new in *One Book*. *One Book* indeed challenges *Hicklin*'s feminizing ideal of sexual purity, in other words, but its prohibition of the very arousal it recognizes undoes that challenge, feminizing the guilty reader anew. This is the sexual logic that governs Dreiser's novel and obscenity law alike: the guarantee of an endlessly prohibited sexual body, in the place of which a feminine body, understood as asexual, fills in.

In his 1991 *Law and the Order of Culture*, the legal scholar Robert Post argued that law is not "something apart" from culture (vii). In addition to its more obvious operations, he argued, law makes meaning (vii). To make this point, Post relies on Robert Cover's idea of "jurisgenesis," what Cover calls the "creation of legal meaning" ("Foreword" 11) to suggest that law not only governs in the social world but also operates in a dimension that we might identify as more obviously associated with literature. The law not only imposes social order, that is, it also signifies, and this signification bears a relation to the social world that is distinct from direct governance. As Cover puts it, "jurisgenesis" occurs in "an essentially cultural medium" (11). Law, he suggests, makes meaning in relation to culture. An uncritical pairing of *One Book* with *Ulysses* suggests to students that there is no "jurisgenesis"—that the novel's censorship, a historical limit, constitutes an aesthetic limit as well. There are of course ways to combat this suggestion, and I am not arguing that Joyce's novel cannot be effectively taught with *One Book*. But the legal case does not ground the novel's literary meanings, and if we teach Joyce's novel with *One Book*, we need to take care not to perpetuate the illusion that it does. Teaching *One Book* alongside Dreiser's *Sister Carrie* leads more easily to the recognition that law operates in a cultural medium.

Notes

Sections of this essay are taken from my book *The Novel and the Obscene: Sexual Subjects in American Modernism*.

1. For a fuller discussion of *One Book*'s legal context, see Dore.

2. Because of the changes that Dreiser made to the manuscript after the initial rejection from Harper's, James West reissued *Sister Carrie* in what he claimed was its unexpurgated form in 1981. For an accurate and comprehensive account of *Sister Carrie*'s publication history, see Pizer; for convincing critiques of the claim to the superior literary quality of West's edition, see Brodhead.

Theodore Ziolkowski

Literature in Its
Legal Context: Kafka

Readings of classic works of literature and law that fail to take into account their historical legal context miss a fascinating and essential dimension. We do an injustice to the Sophoclean *Antigone* if we prioritize the righteousness of the heroine and fail to understand the work as a tragedy of *two* equal figures—Antigone and Creon—caught in the lively struggle in fifth-century BC Athens between *physis* and *nomos*, between church and state, between conservatism and progress. We do not grasp the full irony of *The Merchant of Venice* if we ignore the controversy in Shakespeare's day regarding strict liability and equity and overlook the deviousness of Portia's allegedly professional ethics when Portia plays fast and loose with the rules of court, Jew-baiting Shylock, subjecting Antonio to unnecessary mental torment, and exposing through the verdict the social and legal anomie of late-sixteenth-century England. Heinrich von Kleist's *Michael Kohlhaas*, along with his other stories and plays, exemplifies his disdain for the prevailing eighteenth-century theory of natural law, which Kleist regarded as an invitation to chaos, and his advocacy of the social order underlying the Prussian legal code (Allgemeines Landrecht) of 1794.

In the canon of literature and law, few works match the stature of Franz Kafka's *The Trial* (written 1914–15). Readers have long been aware of the centrality in Kafka's oeuvre of the law, which figures in many titles beyond *The Trial*: for instance, "The Judgment," "In the Penal Colony," and "Before the Law." For many years it was widely assumed that the law, whenever it occurs in Kafka's works, is no more than an image for concerns that are theological, metaphysical, psychological, or generally sociological in their meaning. Even readers with an informed interest in literature and law often forgot that Kafka was a trained lawyer who was involved professionally with the law for over twenty years and keenly aware of the legal debates of his day.

At the beginning of the twentieth century, the philosophy of law in Europe was experiencing its greatest crisis since the codification controversy surrounding the Code Napoléon and the Prussian legal code. The arguments anticipated the debate in the United States today between strict constructionists and those activists who regard the Constitution as a living organism that must be interpreted in the light of changing times. Nineteenth-century judicial thinking in Europe was dominated by a legal positivism that denied the existence of absolute standards of right and wrong or the relevance of moral norms of good and evil and focused its attention instead on the rational analysis of existing systems of law. Legal positivism eventually reached its extreme in the so-called pure law theory, according to which the law is autonomous, a formal pattern of logic distinct from political and social ideology. The excesses of legal positivism produced a counterreaction in the form of sociological approaches that sought to understand the law as an expression of society and its values — a movement associated in Europe with the name of Max Weber and in the United States with the legal realism of Oliver Wendell Holmes. Holmes famously opened his classic work *The Common Law* (1881) with the statement, "The life of the law has not been logic: it has been experience" (5). This tendency reached its extreme in the so-called free law school, whose adherents argued that the particular circumstances in any given case were more important than written legal norms and that judges should feel free to ignore positive law altogether or to fill its gaps by applying their own sense of right and wrong.

Austria was a leader in the development of modern criminal psychology — a fact exemplified by the interest of Sigmund Freud and other Viennese psychiatrists in the criminal mind. The Austrian legal thinkers were opposed to the classical school that prevailed in the German legal system, a system based on the assumption, stemming from Immanuel Kant's *Groundwork for the Metaphysics of Morals* (1797), that criminals are people who have freely decided to break the law; therefore they deserve the punishment specified for their crime, a punishment they were able to foresee. Kafka's professor Hans Gross, known as the father of criminal psychology, wrote the standard work on the subject (*Criminal Psychology* [1897]), arguing that psychology has a major role to play in the understanding of any criminal proceeding, not just the mental state of the criminal but also the psychology of the judge, experts, witnesses, jury—in short, of every agent in the judicial process.

The lively debate also engaged the general public in the Austro-Hungarian Empire, which was ruled by the oldest criminal code in force anywhere on the Continent, the Strafgesetz of 1852, which went back to the Constitutio Criminalis Theresiana of 1768. The urgent need for reform was obvious not only to jurists of the free law movements and the criminal psychologists but to the thoughtful laity as well. Accordingly the debate was reflected in works by leading Austrian writers: Karl Kraus's essays in *Morality and Criminal Justice* (1908), Hugo von Hofmannsthal's dramatic parable *Everyman* (1911), and Robert Musil's novel *The Man without Qualities* (1930). Kafka's *The Trial* belongs in the same category, reflecting as it does the legal situation in the Austro-Hungarian Empire at the turn of the century—not the more highly modernized system in Germany and certainly not the common-law system practiced in Great Britain and the United States.

That *The Trial* constitutes in one sense a burlesque of the legal procedures in which Kafka was himself skilled helps us understand why, when he read the first chapter of his novel to a group of friends, he laughed so hard that he could hardly continue. "The Trial" is actually a mistranslation of the German title. *Prozess* in German legal terminology designates the entire investigatory proceeding, which may or may not culminate in a formal trial (*Gerichtsverfahren*). The process begins when the state attorney notifies the examining magistrate that there is reason to believe that a crime has been committed and to suspect an individual of having committed it. The magistrate undertakes preliminary interviews with full powers of investigation. Only if his investigation concludes that the suspected individual is guilty does the magistrate recommend a formal indictment and turn his dossier over to the prosecuting attorney, whereupon the accused is indicted and the actual trial takes place. Up to this point the procedures are essentially secret. The suspect is permitted only limited access to an attorney since, according to the theory of justice underlying civil law, the examining magistrate in his inquisitorial role is interested not in proving the guilt of the suspect—hence he is not equivalent to an American prosecutor—but in establishing truth. (This role is sympathetically depicted in Franz Werfel's novel *The Class Reunion* [1928].)

When Josef K. learns that he has been arrested, the normal procedure to be anticipated in an Austrian legal proceeding would consist of four stages: investigation, accusation, defense, and verdict. But Josef K.'s "process" evolves quite differently. After his "arrest," he is left free to go about his business as usual. Several days later he is notified by phone that he must appear on the following Sunday for a preliminary investigation of his case, which takes place in a remote suburb and in the crowded attic rooms of a tenement house—an unruly occasion that suggests to K. a political assembly rather than a court hearing. He leaves the proceedings indignantly, telling the magistrate (who bears the official designation of "examining magistrate") that he wants nothing further to do with their hearings.

Though he receives no further summons, he returns the following Sunday, only to find the premises empty. He tries unsuccessfully to elicit information from the various people he finds there. Several weeks later, K.'s uncle takes K. to consult an old school friend, the lawyer Huld, who is reputed to be versed in the practices of the law but who actually knows nothing but court gossip. At the bank where he is employed, K. is asked one day to accompany a visitor to the cathedral. As he waits for the visitor, he hears from the pulpit a parable about a man from the country who spends his life before the door of the law without ever being admitted. K. falls into conversation with the preacher, who turns out to be the prison chaplain, from whom K. learns that his case has taken a turn for the worse—that he is considered guilty. Exactly a year after his arrest, K. is fetched from his room by two men, who take him to an abandoned quarry where they stab him to death with a butcher knife.

K. is fully aware of his rights under the law. He lives in a constitutional state where "all the laws [are] in force" (*Prozess* 12). He possesses all the requisite legal documents. One of his close friends is the state prosecuting attorney, and he himself is regarded as an expert in trade law. His clients at the bank consider him as "virtually a lawyer" (164). So K. is not legally naive and has every reason to expect that his case will proceed as specified in the 1873 Austrian code of criminal procedure.

But it rapidly becomes apparent that K. has been caught up in a different jurisdiction altogether—one that he does not understand. His lawyer explains the difference between "normal legal affairs" and "these legal affairs" (226). Yet it is unclear where this other law is actually written down: the alleged law books that K. sees in the interrogation rooms turn out to be pornographic novels, and even Huld admits that he has never actually read the law. All the self-proclaimed experts in the secret law know it only by hearsay.

The parallel existence of dual legal systems is not in itself unusual. As Kafka knew from his studies, Roman civil law functioned effectively alongside church canon law throughout centuries of European history (just as today in certain Muslim countries Koranic law and secular law coexist). He was also aware that the two systems, deriving as they did from a common source in Roman law, shared procedures that revealed their kinship. In his novel, accordingly, Kafka stresses the existence of the familiar legal system because the procedures of the paralegal court invariably depend for their effect on our knowledge of that system. In a few cases, familiar civil rights established by the constitution of 1867 are violated, as in the opening scene, when the basic article concerning the inviolability of the home (article 9) is infringed by the three men who invade K.'s bedroom to arrest him without a warrant (Heidsieck 12). Other incidents involve a violation of the prevailing Austrian code of civil procedure: the arresting officials give no reason for his arrest, as stipulated by the code, nor does the magistrate inform him of the nature of his crime, as required by another section, or warn that his refusal to participate in the hearing could deprive him of the grounds for defense.

In most cases, however, Kafka achieves his effect simply by alienating what is legally obvious. On the morning of his arrest, K. is instructed that the authorities are "attracted by guilt" (15). He tells them that he is unaware of that law, yet it is nothing more than routine procedure. When the state has reason to suspect a crime, it is required to instruct the magistrate to undertake an investigation; to this extent it is "attracted by guilt." The wardens joke that K. concedes he doesn't know the law and yet claims to be innocent. Again they are simply stating a principle inherent in all civilized law, as set forth in the Austrian criminal code of 1852 (§3): "No one can claim innocence on the basis of ignorance of the existing criminal law" (*Strafgesetz* [trans. mine]). Yet their behavior, along with K.'s astonished reaction, has the effect of making this fundamental legal principle seem somehow absurd.

The preliminary investigation amounts to a burlesque of any normal investigation as specified in the code of criminal procedure: the proceedings are not held at a normal hour in a official court building; they are not kept confidential; the accused never hears the accusation; K. consults various advocates and helpers, all of whom give him useless advice; the proceedings never move to a formal trial and verdict; the execution is summary and irregular. Kafka's constant implicit references to the code of criminal procedure provide the structure of the narrative (Robinson 137). The novel's title draws our attention to the legal proceedings and not to any such dramatic culmination as suggested by the English word *trial*. Yet despite its considerable procedural detail, the comic aspect does not hint at the substantive theoretical issues that generated the pressure for legal reform in Austria during the prewar years and that underlie Kafka's work.

It has often been noted that the duality of legal systems in the novel is reflected in Kafka's consistent use of the forms "laws" and "the law." The plural form clearly refers to the positive laws of the constitutional state; but whenever referring to the other system, which is based on tacit and implicit understanding, he uses the singular. Thus when K. is arrested, he is told simply, "That is the Law" (15). In this sense the novel suggests the struggle in fin de siècle Europe between the conservative values of the past, which cling to an unspecified yet generally acknowledged law, and progressive forces of modern society as represented by constitutional laws.

This interpretation is borne out by a careful reading of the first sentence: "Someone must have slandered [*verleumdet*] Josef K., for without his having done anything wrong [*Böses*], he was arrested one morning" (9). The sentence contains two concepts basic to Austrian law and unknown to the more progressive German law. The Austrian code (*Strafgesetz*, ch. 25, §§209–10) uses the word *Verleumdung* for slander in the technical sense of the false accusation of a crime, punishable by imprisonment from one to five years. Josef K. assumes therefore that someone has reported him to the authorities because of an imputed crime "without his having done anything wrong." The concept *Böses*—inadequately rendered by the word "wrong"—has a moral, not merely legal, implication of "evil." The first paragraph of the Austrian code defines crime according to an inner criterion: "evil intent" (*böser Vorsatz*). With Kafka's first sentence we are plunged into a moral universe that is absent in the German code or the "pure law" advocated by advanced jurisprudents.

Lawyers in the German tradition were trained to look at the criminal act and the facts of the case. Kafka's legal contemporaries in the Austro-Hungarian Empire, in contrast, were taught to concentrate more on the criminal and the "evil intent" than on the criminal act. As the Austrian code explains, "To have a crime it is not necessary that the deed be actually carried out" (*Strafgesetz* §8). Kafka has constructed an absurd paradigm of the legal system that believes in a theoretical guilt without illegality and that focuses on the criminal rather than on the criminal act. In the absence of any deed whose illegality can be determined, the procedure is restricted to the determination of the evil intent of the accused. This shift reflects the typical subjectivism of Austrian criminal law in contrast to the rational objectivism of the neo-Kantian German law.

Kafka's novel is of course more than a parodistic paradigm of fin de siècle legal controversies: it makes a moving statement about the nature of human guilt and responsibility—our tendency to deny the guilt into which we are inevitably plunged by existence and our reluctance to accept responsibility for the consequences of our actions. This guilt need not be understood in any narrowly legal sense; it can be read as theological, metaphysical, existential, or social guilt. At the same time, the organization and terminology of *The Trial* are indebted entirely to the legal system in which Kafka was trained and in which he functioned effectively as a lawyer; and implicit in its text is the legal controversy dominating the fin de siècle.

Kafka cannot be pinned down to a simple position. He recognizes the differences between Austrian traditionalism and Prussian modernism, but he characteristically takes an intermediate stand on the various legal issues. *The Trial* depicts the injustices of a subjective law as practiced in the Hapsburg fin de siècle and carried to its absurd extremes. At the same time, his account of the whimsicality of the examining magistrate implies a degree of discomfort regarding the free law movement that sought to liberate judges from the narrow constraints of the codified law. The opposition of the two systems suggests that Kafka, contemplating the shift from community to society, from *Kultur* to *Zivilisation*, in the modern bourgeois world—a shift that alarmed such contemporaries as Thomas Mann, C. G. Jung, and Martin Heidegger—was on the side of civil society with its codified laws and safeguards for the rights of the individual. At the same time, K.'s obsession with the vagaries of his guilt allows us to surmise that Kafka was less than sanguine about a legal system that conflated law and morality and that stressed subjective concerns with the doer over the objective definition of the deed. *The Trial* thus exemplifies the continuing process of evolution that has characterized the history of Western law since its earliest beginnings—a process evident only to readers who take the trouble to inform themselves about the historical legal context of the novel.

Note

This essay summarizes the general theme and chapter 11 of my book *The Mirror of Justice*. The translations of Kafka are mine.

Harriet Murav

Dostoevsky and the Law

Fyodor Dostoevsky's writings show an all-encompassing concern with the problem of law and justice. The depiction of transgression, crime, confession, trials, judgment, punishments, and prison fill the pages of his fiction and journalism — from his 1861 *Notes from the House of the Dead* (*Zapiski iz myortvogo doma*), his thinly fictionalized account of his own imprisonment in Siberia, to his last novel, *The Brothers Karamazov* (*Bratya Karamazovy*), which devotes an entire book to the trial of Dmitry. Dostoevsky's early optimism about the ability of courtroom trials to reveal the truth is evidenced in his journalism of the 1860s. The Dostoevsky brothers' journal *Time* (*Vremya*) published translations of sensational French criminal trials of an earlier period. In his preface to the trial of the thief and murderer Lacenaire, Dostoevsky compared the trial transcript to a "daguerreotype" and a "physiological sketch," suggesting that it was an accurate and true-to-life portrait of the criminal (*Polnoe sobranie* 19: 89–90). But soon after this, Dostoevsky grows increasingly skeptical about the forms and procedures of the legal world.

Porfiry Petrovich, the examining magistrate in *Crime and Punishment* (*Prestuplenie i nakazanie*), says that he will trap his suspect "psychologically" (6: 344). Ultimately Raskolnikov confesses to the murder of the old pawnbroker and her sister. But the confession does not bring the closure usually found in detective fiction. As Michael Holquist writes, closure is typically achieved when the detective learns what the criminal already knows. The crime is solved when the detective figures out the criminal's plot (78). In *Crime and Punishment*, the examining magistrate never attains the omniscience of a narrator. The criminal makes more than one confession; he confesses not only to Porfiry Petrovich but also to Sonya Marmeladova, to whom he gives more than one version of his motive. At first, Raskolnikov says that he committed the murders out of economic need and the desire to help his mother and sister. Then he describes the crime as a way of determining whether he is a superman for whom the laws of ordinary morality do not apply. Confession does not lead to the discovery of the truth about Raskolnikov; nor does it lead to a refutation of the truth that he seeks to preach, the Nietzschean transvaluation of morality. That Raskolnikov ends up in prison in Siberia does not diminish the force of his self-experimentation. His repentance and resurrection remain unexpressed, and his outrageous challenge to law and morality reverberate beyond the pages of the novel.

Crime and Punishment was written after the passage of the great legal reform in Russia of 1864, which introduced trial by jury in most criminal cases, replaced the inquisitorial principle with the adversary principle, established a professional bar and justices of the peace, and made what had been secret proceedings into open, public trials. The Russian public could, for the first time, visit courts in session and read accounts of ongoing jury trials in the daily newspapers. This legal reform had a profound effect on Dostoevsky's writing.

Among the outstanding trials of the time were those for the political crimes of such figures as Sergey Nechaev and Vera Zasulich. Nechaev, who had worked with Mikhail Bakunin, was the leader of a revolutionary group called the People's Will. Nechaev was convicted of ordering the group to murder one of its own members, allegedly as a way of cementing their bond by blood. The Nechaev affair became the basis for Dostoevsky's novel *The Devils* (*Besy*), first published serially in 1871–72. Dostoevsky's portrait of the radical group provoked heated controversy among liberal critics, some of whom charged that he had represented the entire younger generation as raving maniacs. According to one critic, Dostoevsky had simply taken "ready-made heroes" from the stenographic accounts of Nechaev's trial and forced them to commit acts of lunacy in his novel (Budanov and Fridlender 338). This reading of the novel is vastly oversimplified, yet it reveals how important the new jury courts were for the creation of Dostoevsky's works. The dominant realist aesthetic of the time called for a blurring of the boundary between art and life. Literary heroes were to be taken from life and also to serve as models for life. The public jury trial offered an opportunity to capture a dramatic turning point that could be used in an account of a fictional character. The stenographic record of the trial provided a verbal photograph—a "daguerreotype," as Dostoevsky himself said earlier, of the human personality (*Polnoe sobranie* 19: 89–90). He later wrote a remarkable short fiction "A Meek One" ("Krotkaya"), using the stenographic transcript of the confession as a device. The jury trial suggested a new technology that could enhance the practice of the realist aesthetic of the day.

In his *Writer's Diary* (*Dnevnik pisatelya*), which appeared first as a column in the conservative newspaper *The Citizen* (*Grazhdanin*) and then as a separate one-man journal, Dostoevsky is fascinated by the new jury trials and the new institution of the bar.[1] In this experimental work, which combined fiction, journalism, and autobiography, he seeks to influence his readers directly. Like other observers of his time, he is dismayed by the high number of acquittals and by the use of what were then fashionable new defense strategies, such as temporary insanity and the argument that a hostile social and economic environment was responsible for individual crimes. Dostoevsky is particularly upset by excesses of courtroom oratory, whereby a talented attorney could change the entire emphasis of a case, even representing a victim as a perpetrator, as happened in the Kronenberg trial of 1876—according to Dostoevsky. The defense attorney, the renowned Vladimir Spasovich, who defended Nechaev, transformed the victim, a seven-year-old girl viciously beaten by her father, into a laughing, red-cheeked thief with secret vices, thereby exonerating her father. As Dostoevsky points out, once the jury was convinced that the little girl was a criminal, the beating her father gave her no longer appeared excessive. Dostoevsky avoids writing about the great political cases of the time directly, but his legal commentary, focused on domestic violence, nonetheless addresses basic questions about order, authority, and legitimacy.

Dostoevsky used the child abuse cases he wrote about in his *Diary* in his last great work of fiction, *The Brothers Karamazov*. Ivan accumulates a catalog of abuses perpetrated by adults against children as evidence for his indictment of "God's world" and rejection of the possibility of redemption in ongoing historical reality (*Polnoe sobranie* 14: 214). Ivan "returns his entrance ticket" because the price of universal harmony—the suffering

of the innocent— is too high (223). From the pages of the daily newspapers comes one of the greatest challenges to theodicy. Raskolnikov attacks
the basis for human law and justice; Ivan goes a step farther and challenges
the idea of divine justice. There can be neither order nor justice based on the
torture of children. Ivan's philosophical despair and guilt over his possible
involvement in his father's murder lead to his breakdown at Dmitry's trial,
which Ivan dismisses as mere bread and circuses. Ivan's contention that
the trial is nothing more than a spectacle for the crowd is supported by the
description of the huge numbers of people who come to watch the trial,
especially the women, who believe in Dmitry's guilt but want an acquittal
to prove how liberal their town is.

Dostoevsky seems to contend in *The Brothers Karamazov* that the jury
court and the professional bar do not mean that justice will be done. Dmitry's trial leads neither to a restoration of order nor to the discovery of the
truth. Knowledge of the events that have transpired becomes uncertain.
The narrator confesses that he may not have reported the most important
aspects of Dmitry's trial to his readers. Neither the prosecution nor the
defense can tell Dmitry's story accurately, and both have been influenced
by Smerdyakov, whose own involvement with the murder remains hidden.
The defense argues that the prosecutor has been overcome by the need to
exercise the psychological gifts for which he is already famous in order to
create a "novel" about Dmitry (15: 365). In the notebooks to the novel,
the point is elaborated at greater length. The defense says:

> For you a character is created, like a novelist, like a storyteller, and you
> go and believe my novel. It's a game of artistry, psychology, eloquence.
> But because of this toy, a man can perish! Have we gathered to listen
> to the novel of a fashionable writer or to the fate of a man? A charac-
> ter is created, his thoughts and feelings are connected—all very well
> constructed. But what if it's something completely different? (*Polnoe
> sobranie* 15: 365)

A lawyer's skill in constructing an aesthetically pleasing story may cause a
jury to depart from the truth.

The argument about courtroom oratory as novelization cannot be
taken at face value; there is another side to the story. One of the most
important points Dostoevsky makes in *Notes from the House of the Dead* is
that crimes and punishments are incommensurable. The unique individuality of the criminal and the criminal's life circumstances mean that uniform penalties are inherently unjust, since the same punishment for the

same crime will have a vastly different effect on the different criminals who commit it. In his *Writer's Diary*, Dostoevsky is particularly concerned about the law's insensitivity to the individual's unique story. Using his artistic gifts to generate alternate stories, he destabilizes legal meaning and certainty and disaggregates the unity of the legal subject. In one outstanding trial of 1876, the Kornilova case, he helps secure the acquittal of an already convicted defendant—not challenging or undermining law but enhancing it, and his own stature, in the process.

Ekaterina Kornilova, a seamstress, was four months pregnant when she threw her seven-year-old stepdaughter out of a window. The child survived unharmed. Kornilova confessed to the police, telling them that she acted to take revenge on her husband, who compared her unfavorably with his first wife and did not permit her to visit her own family. She was convicted by a jury to hard labor in Siberia. Dostoevsky first discusses the trial in May 1876 and returns to it four more times: in October and December that year, in April and December of 1877.

Dostoevsky responds to the Kornilova case with horror and dismay. He writes a parody (*karikatura*) of what a clever lawyer could do for Kornilova in the way of a defense: describe the young wife's burdensome housekeeping and child care, her exhaustion and frustration. Imitating a lawyer, Dostoevsky writes that Kornilova "naturally had to hate this child . . . in a desperate moment, in an attack of insanity, beside herself, she grabbed the girl and . . . Gentlemen of the jury, who of you would not have done the same thing?" Dostoevsky quickly adds, however, that there is something "too strange" about what Kornilova did and that a "subtle and profound analysis" of the case would be required, which might lead to a softening of Kornilova's fate (23: 19).

Dostoevsky himself will provide the "subtle and profound analysis." In October 1876 he poses a question, "Here are the facts, what could be simpler, but nonetheless, there is much that is fantastic here, isn't that true?" (22: 263). The fantastic element is supplied by the psychological effect of Kornilova's pregnancy. Dostoevsky defends Kornilova accordingly: pregnant at the time of the crime, she might have been suffering from a special form of temporary insanity (*vremennyi affekt*). The examining physician determined that Kornilova acted "consciously" and that therefore legal incompetence could not be shown (23: 138). But even "lunatics" rarely perform actions "unconsciously." Dostoevsky asks his readers to consider the kinds of actions that might be performed consciously but without legal culpability. He recalls a story he heard in childhood about a lady in Moscow who developed a "passion for stealing" every time she became pregnant. Dostoevsky tells us, "It is well known that a woman at the time of pregnancy is very often subject to certain strange influences and impressions," which sometimes take on "extraordinary, abnormal, almost absurd forms" (138). Had Kornilova not been pregnant, she would perhaps have contemplated but not committed the crime. The very possibility that the pregnancy was a factor should have been enough to persuade the jury to act mercifully, Dostoevsky concludes.

In part through Dostoevsky's intervention, Kornilova's conviction is overturned. As Igor Volgin's research has shown, the writer's plea for mercy on Kornilova's behalf led to an appeal. The grounds for the appeal were based on a legal formality: the same individual had testified both in the capacity of witness and expert. At the subsequent retrial, a jury trial that Dostoevsky attended, Kornilova was acquitted, notwithstanding the prosecutor's instruction to the jury "not to yield to the influence of 'certain talented writers.'" The prosecutor uses "talent" here as a term of opprobrium with regard to Dostoevsky in the same way Dostoevsky had used it with regard to Spasovich.

Dostoevsky returns to the Kornilova case in the December 1877 issue of *A Writer's Diary*. Stung by an attack of his defense of Kornilova, published in *The Northern Messenger* (*Severnyi vestnik*), he ends up repeating some of the strategies that Spasovich used to depend Kronenberg—strategies that previously outraged Dostoevsky. As Dostoevsky reports it, *The Northern Messenger* argued that Kornilova "systematically beat" the child for a year. He replies that the child was indeed beaten, by both parents, but not out of "cruelty"; it was out of "ignorance" (26: 97). Kornilova had beaten her stepdaughter so hard on one occasion that welts were raised, but the beating was done to train the child not to wet her bed at night. Spasovich had used similar reasoning in his defense of Kronenberg: the father beat his daughter only to rid her of "secret vices" (*Polnoe sobranie* 22: 57); the expert testimony of the doctors, the precise description of the welts and bruises on the child's body, and the vagueness of the law itself, all taken together, showed that torture could not be proved. In the Kornilova case, Dostoevsky plays the role of doctor and lawyer and an authority on corporal punishment, its motivation and severity.

In *The Brothers Karamazov*, Dmitry Karamazov's defense attorney is based on Spasovich. The defense argues that Fyodor Karamazov did not act as a true father to his son, neglecting him entirely. The horrific charge of patricide is softened when the murdered man was a father in name only.

In the *Writer's Diary*, fatherhood is of prime importance. In his discussion of the Dzhunkovsky case, Dostoevsky stresses the need for strong families with fathers who inspire respect in their children. The parents were charged with having singled out three of their children for special ill-treatment. The children were not provided with adequate food (they ate from the servants' table); they were kept in unheated rooms; they were beaten ("with such cruelty that it was terrible to look at"); one of them was beaten especially severely by his mother because he brought his hungry sister a potato from the kitchen for her breakfast (25: 183). As in the Kronenberg case, the parents were acquitted.

The strategy of Dostoevsky is to speak from the position of the father and of the state. He remarks that when people are acquitted, sometimes the chairman of the court takes the opportunity to make comments of an edifying nature, in order that the accused may avoid trouble in the future (188). Dostoevsky will play the role of the chairman, who speaks "on behalf of all of society and on behalf of the government." In doing this, he is fulfilling his "obligation" to speak on behalf of society, the government, and the "fatherland" (192). In the Kronenberg case, the child was valorized; it is children who "humanize" adults by their mere presence among them. But here in the Dzhunkovsky case, Dostoevsky makes gods out of fathers, who must "always be spiritually on a mountain" for their children "as an object of love . . . respect . . . and imitation" (190). In the Kronenberg case, Dostoevsky rejected the argument that the state depends on strong families; in the Dzhunkovsky case, the child is subsumed to the state; children are the "future Russia" (192).

Having uttered his paternal and authoritative word in the Dzhunkovsky case in July-August 1877, Dostoevsky continues in the same vein in his final discussion of the Kornilova case in December 1877. He characterizes his intervention in the Kornilova case as "fatherly": "chopping off heads is easy according to the letter of the law, but understanding truthfully, humanely, and in a fatherly way is always harder" (26: 106).

Dostoevsky is not only fatherly toward Kornilova; he plays judge, teacher, and husband as well. The Kornilovs came to visit Dostoevsky after her release from prison. Mr. Kornilov told Dostoevsky that the first thing he did when his wife arrived home was read to her from the Gospels. Mr. Kornilov is a predictable type, Dostoevsky tells his readers in the December 1877 *Diary* and imagines Kornilova's reaction to the moral lesson. "Here is the person upon whom she depends, raising himself over her in the highest halo of a judge; he is merciless in her eyes because of the way that he too autocratically invaded her soul" (104). Note the political language, the parallel drawn between the power of the autocrat and the power of the husband. Yet Dostoevsky claims a similar power over Kornilova when he imagines her response to her husband. The words that he puts into her mouth resemble those he wrote for the hero of *The Devils*, Stavrogin, who says, "I hate spies and psychologists, at least those who climb into my soul" (11: 11).[2] To be known by another is invasive and threatening; to have this knowledge is to have a certain power.

Dostoevsky himself is guilty of such invasiveness. He has already given Kornilova her moral lesson. Her husband's version is an inept repetition of it. On the evening of her retrial, Dostoevsky went to teach her how to live in Siberia, should that be her fate. During that visit, he warned her against the temptation of prostitution. He describes the visit in the same December 1877 *Diary*. His Siberian experience provides him with a certain expertise. "Her marriage destroyed, in a foreign place, alone, defenseless, still attractive, and so young—how could she resist the temptation?" Kornilova's child will follow her mother's footsteps; "she will be *compelled* to inherit her mother's career" (26: 105).

Women—real, historical women—play roles in the *Diary* that Dostoevsky did not imagine in his fiction.[3] In the Kornilova case, he enters into a competition of sorts with the prosecution, defense lawyer, and the medical experts. This competition centers on who is most qualified to understand the behavior of the female defendant. But to understand and to interpret another's behavior, as Dostoevsky very well knows and as we have seen in *The Devils*, is to have power over the other. That power easily flows into controlling, disciplining, and finally authoring. In the same December 1877 issue that concludes the Kornilova case, Dostoevsky points with pride to the correspondents he has acquired over the course of the publication of the *Diary*. He considers them "collaborators" (126). He has begun to dispense advice. He has authored himself as diarist, authored his own reading audience, and fathered a community of like-minded readers who will become the new Russia.

Dostoevsky, witness to corporal punishment in Siberia and vicarious witness to the beating of the little girls in the Kronenberg and Kornilova cases, pronounces himself more knowledgeable about torture than the lawyers and medical experts and declares that in the first case the little girl suffered too much, in the second case hardly at all, even though her stepmother threw her out of a window. One can imagine another, younger Dostoevsky writing a very different story, from the perspective of the child. He moves from identification with the victim to identification with the executioner, speaking almost as a doctor who in the service of the state presides over the administration of corporal punishment or torture. Juxtaposed, Dostoevsky's responses to the two stories are irreconcilably contradictory. Sigmund Freud tells us that in the fantasy of "a child is being beaten," the beating is a punishment for the illicit love felt for the father ("Child" 171–201). The fantasizer gets what he wants but is punished for it, but the punishment is what he wants—this is a circular story that goes nowhere. Dostoevsky, however, untangles the knot. Out of the contradictions of wanting to be child and father simultaneously (and the child of and the father to Russia simultaneously) comes a coherent linear narrative. Out of suffering, criminality, pain, and violence, Dostoevsky negotiates an authoritative position for himself. Fictions of chaos become fictions of order.

Notes

All translations from Russian, unless otherwise indicated, are mine.

1. For a general discussion of the *Diary*, see Frank; Morson.

2. See Bakhtin's discussion of this and other similar passages in Dostoevsky (59–61).

3. For a discussion of women in the *Diary* and in Dostoevsky more generally, see Straus.

Chaya Halberstam

Law and Literature
of the Hebrew Bible

The biblical scholar Robert Alter, differentiating the ancient text of the Hebrew Bible from the modern book, writes:

> [T]he biblical term . . . *sefer* . . . can refer to anything written on a scroll—a letter, a relatively brief unit within a longer composition, or a book more or less in our sense. A scroll is not a text shut in between covers, and additional swathes of scroll can be stitched onto it, which seems to have been a very common biblical practice. (*Five Books* 9)

As scrolls were stitched one to another, great myths, genealogical lists, short narratives, and legal imperatives flowed effortlessly from one to the other, without hard covers to delimit spheres of knowledge. When these texts were later canonized by interpretive communities, sacred status was conferred equally on every word, ensuring that no section or subsection of the text would any longer be seen as less significant, less integral, less substantial. Profound sacred meaning would be derived from a list of place-names no less than from the story of Creation or the revelation of the Ten Commandments.

But at the advent of the modern era, the juxtaposition of such diverse biblical genres, and their indiscriminate treatment by commentators,

323

made scholars uncomfortable. The formulation of the documentary hypothesis—that four or more authors are represented in the first five books of the Bible (the Pentateuch) and beyond, though no claims to authorship are present in the text—has allowed for the creation of a variety of subdivisions in the biblical text, usually along the lines of genre and style, and the attribution of these newer, simpler, and more logical sections of text, having a unified vision, to one author. Such subdividing applied especially to the legal portions of the Pentateuch, which could now be neatly excised from their literary contexts and recontextualized—in the whole of Israelite law, in ancient Near Eastern legal thought and practice, in Israelite legal culture and history. As such, they have for the most part been studied as part of the field of ancient law: taxonomies of biblical law have been developed and then matched to the various forms of ancient legal writing. Biblical law has also been mined by ancient historians for the insights they provide into Israelite society. But the connections between biblical law and its immediate, literary context were largely neglected until the second half of the twentieth century.

Recently, biblical scholarship has turned its attention to reading biblical law in its narrative context, showing how each is illuminated by the other. The primary focus of this scholarship is the immediate context of most biblical law, the covenant narrative. I have used excerpts from Denis McCarthy's book *Treaty and Covenant* in the course I teach on this subject, Biblical Justice. I discuss with students both the benefits and drawbacks of this emphasis on covenant. One drawback is that the powerful covenant narrative, the ancient Israelite divine social contract, may reduce the legal stipulations themselves to a mere footnote. I propose that when it comes to the Hebrew Bible, the often bizarre and alienating content of the law must not be ignored (as it continues to be in many classrooms); instead, the distinct style and substance of biblical law may be understood as a unique form of ancient literature, one that lies on a continuum with biblical narrative and even poetry. Alter, a founder and champion of the literary approach to biblical texts, suggests that the literary study of biblical narrative cannot be segregated from the aims of the Bible as a whole; he "insist[s] on a complete interfusion of literary art with theological, moral, or historiosophical vision" (*Art* 19). I suggest that we add legal vision to Alter's list.

Raymond Westbrook's and James Watts's work helps us define the rhetorical style and generic features of biblical law by identifying the similarities it bears to other forms of biblical literature. Westbrook famously argues that biblical law should not be understood at all as a "law code" in the contemporary sense of the term, which would imply that it is systematic and thorough, but rather as a record of precedents that could "act as reference works for the royal judges in deciding difficult cases." Among its "secondary purposes," Westbrook lists biblical law's function as "part of a religio-historical narrative . . . where the deity replaces the king as the source of law" (258). Watts furthers Westbrook's insight that biblical law must not be read as a detached and hermetic law code. He argues, on the basis of pre-Aristotelian theories of rhetoric, that biblical persuasive strategies rely on the intertwining of narrative and legal lists and that such juxtapositions are omnipresent throughout the ancient world. For pre-Aristotelian orators, Watts maintains, "persuasion depend[ed] on the combination of list and story" (39). As for the Hebrew Bible, Watts concludes:

> Biblical law and narrative are two parts of a persuasive strategy that depends on both to make its case. Their mutual aim, persuasion, naturally causes them to influence each other's literary conventions. Neither, however, dominates the other. In other words, Pentateuchal law cannot be analyzed successfully as simply narrative, nor can biblical stories be reduced entirely to legal case studies. The strategy of persuasion requires that both, together with divine sanctions, function on their own terms to state the conditions of Israel's existence as a people (stories), the possibility of an ideal divine/human community (laws), and the consequences of the people's actions (sanctions). (88)

Watts's insights regarding the continuity of law and narrative in the Hebrew Bible ring true, but I am not certain that we need to locate it solely in the rhetorical goal of persuasion. The ideal vision on the one hand and concrete practice on the other are always, in Robert Cover's words, part of a "normative universe." If narrative and law influence each other, it is not always because they aim to persuade and exhort but rather because they are two sides of the same coin: "Every prescription is insistent in its demand to be located in discourse. . . . And every narrative is insistent in its demand for its prescriptive point, its moral" ("Nomos" 95). For both Watts and Cover the "vision" of narrative and "praxis" of law are perhaps still too segregated one from the other. Though I would never contend that law and narrative are indistinguishable, I might modify Watt's notion of mutual influence to one of mutual entwinement.

Perhaps modern law codes are indeed the anomaly,[1] aiming to provide pure imperatives washed in the language of objectivity and neutrality, segregated from narrativity and imagination.[2] Biblical legislation more naturally uses the features and devices of narrative to embed within it its vision of the future, of a better world. In general, according to Watts, biblical law employs features of narrative to exhort the reader, which he enumerates as repetition, variation, hortatory addresses, and motive clauses. But even beyond these isolated tropes, which again center on persuasion, much of biblical law can be seen to present mininarratives in order to motivate legal stipulations. There is much more in casuistic law than persuasion: in each, we find conflicts of motivation and point of view, situations fraught with tension, and gestures toward resolution—the very stuff of which drama is built.

One example of the narrativity of biblical law comes in the form of a kind of record of case law. Though we have no way of knowing whether such cases actually occurred (see, e.g., Carmichael) or—which is more likely—were developed for the sake of illustrating a biblical legal or moral imperative, such precedents lie on the border of law and narrative. For example, in the course I teach I invite students to discuss the case of the blasphemer:

> A man whose mother was an Israelite and whose father was an Egyptian came out among the people of Israel; and the Israelite woman's son and a certain Israelite began fighting in the camp. The Israelite woman's son blasphemed [God's] Name in a curse. And they brought him to Moses—now his mother's name was Shelomith, daughter of Dibri, of the tribe of Dan—and they put him in custody, until the decision of the LORD should be made clear to them. The LORD said to Moses, saying: Take the blasphemer outside the camp; and let all who were within hearing lay their hands on his head, and let the whole congregation stone him. And speak to the people of Israel, saying: Anyone who curses God shall bear the sin. One who blasphemes the name of the LORD shall be put to death; the whole congregation shall stone the blasphemer. Aliens as well as citizens, when they blaspheme the Name, shall be put to death. Anyone who kills a human being shall be put to death. . . . Moses spoke thus to the people of Israel; and they took the blasphemer outside the camp, and stoned him to death. The people of Israel did as the LORD had commanded Moses.
> (Lev. 24.10–17, 23)[3]

That this episode is inserted in the middle of a long list of legal prescriptions implies that its primary purpose is legal rather than narrative. However, when we begin reading, we get the sense of a story that gives details of characters and even some names, an immediate conflict, and suspense over how the conflict will be resolved. When the verdict is rendered, the narrative shifts back into legal mode — a list of laws are stipulated regarding the punishments for killing human beings and animals. But the story concludes in the indicative, telling us that Moses and the Israelites carried out the sentence as specified.

I challenge my students to explain why the biblical authors-editors felt it necessary to include the narrative illustration of this law. Is it merely to convey the development of Israelite law and to convince us of the authority of the divine lawgiver, as Watts would argue (104)? Students, encouraged to think closely about what effect the narrative has on them as readers, usually suggest that the use of narrative here allows them to enter into the conflict and horror of the case of the blasphemer in a way that no list of prescriptions could. It dangerously allows room for sympathy with the blasphemer, whose mother is named, yet nonetheless proceeds to its shocking and uncompromising conclusion. Readers must conquer their emotional responses and align themselves with the community of Israel as they absolve themselves from bloodguilt and subscribe to the idea of the equity of the law, or they must stand opposed to God and the congregation, insisting that such extreme punishment is neither equitable nor ethical. Instead of exhorting or persuading, the story and law of the blasphemer, like any good narrative, create a space, however small, for more than one hegemonic interpretation. They allow future shifts in normative vision and a transformation of Israel's normative world.

While the story of the blasphemer is usually considered a kind of case law or precedent — that is, belonging essentially in the legal genre — texts more often seen as exclusively literary (parable, poetry) may have juridical underpinnings or purposes. In other words, both law and narrative may offer us models of vision and praxis intertwined. The story of David's sin with Bathsheba is a familiar one. While the Israelites are at war, David, the king, remains in his palace and seduces and impregnates the married woman Bathsheba. When David cannot tempt her husband, Uriah, to return from the front and sleep with his wife, thus covering up Bathsheba's illegitimate pregnancy, he sends word to his general to have Uriah placed in a particularly vulnerable position among the troops, ensuring that he will be killed in battle. The plan works, and David then takes Bathsheba as his wife. Shortly afterward, Nathan, a prophet, comes before David but not immediately with words of divine judgment. Rather, Nathan tells David a story:

There were two men in a certain city, the one rich and the other poor. The rich man had very many flocks and herds; but the poor man had nothing but one little ewe lamb, which he had bought. He brought it up, and it grew up with him and with his children; it used to eat of his meager fare, and drink from his cup, and lie in his bosom, and it was like a daughter to him. Now there came a traveler to the rich man, and he was loath to take one of his own flock or herd to prepare for the wayfarer who had come to him, but he took the poor man's lamb, and prepared that for the guest who had come to him. (2 Sam. 12.1–4)

This narrative provokes an immediate response from David. He says, "As the LORD lives, the man who has done this deserves to die; he shall restore the lamb fourfold, because he did this thing, and because he had no compassion" (5–6). Nathan then tells David the true meaning of his story; as Alter puts it, "Nathan's rhetorical trap . . . now snap[s] shut" (*David Story* 258). Nathan tells David, "You are the man!," and continues by spelling out the divine judgment on him. David responds by acknowledging his guilt: "I have sinned against the LORD," he utters, without adding any words in his own defense (12.13).

Nathan's parable achieves more than a typical narrative—it compels a character in the story to recognize a responsibility to which he was previously blind. The biblical scholar Uriel Simon coins a term for the subgenre of narrative that this short narrative exemplifies: the "juridical parable." Simon formulates the definition of the juridical parable: "a realistic story about a violation of the law, related to someone who had committed a similar offence with the purpose of leading the unsuspecting hearer to pass judgment on himself" (220). Simon has been taken to task by scholars claiming that his idea confuses form (what the story must be about) with function (in what circumstances the story is used) (see Coats 371). Even if Simon's category does not stand up to critical scrutiny, I suggest his intuition is right. David's story may not be juridical because it crudely describes a violation of the law or because it literally is told in order to provoke a legally binding judgment. But I ask students to consider how it might be juridical after all, taking into account especially their reading of Cover's "Nomos and Narrative." In the ensuing discussion, it is often suggested that Nathan's parable is juridical, in the sense that Cover understands the *nomos* and describes law's purpose: "A *nomos*, as a world of law, entails the application of human will to an extant state of affairs as well as toward our visions of alternative futures. A *nomos* is a present world constituted by a system of tension between reality and vision" (Cover, "Nomos" 101). A juridical parable describes one reality in order to urge the listener to imagine an alternative and to act accordingly.

David's reaction to the story is instructive: David acknowledges the rich man's criminal and civil responsibilities. The man must die for his crime and pay back fourfold for his theft, because he had no compassion. David, like the rich man, is guilty. But instead of wallowing in shame, he is inspired to make amends, to repair his wrong. Nathan's parable does not seek to depict what is; rather, its purpose is to spur a vision of what should be. The rich man in the story clearly has the power to do what he wills, but the parable impels us to imagine a world in which those with power have compassion and act ethically. As Cover reveals, the bridge between these two states of affairs is law, the acceptance of responsibility and paying back what is owed.

Some of Simon's other examples of juridical parables do not fit his own criteria but do meet the criteria established here. He refers to the song of the vineyard in Isaiah:

> Let me sing for my beloved my love-song concerning his vineyard:
> My beloved had a vineyard on a very fertile hill.
> He dug it and cleared it of stones,
> and planted it with choice vines;
> he built a watchtower in the midst of it,
> and hewed out a wine vat in it;
> he expected it to yield grapes,
> but it yielded wild grapes.
> And now, inhabitants of Jerusalem and people of Judah,
> judge between me and my vineyard.
> What more was there to do for my vineyard that I have not done in it?
> When I expected it to yield grapes, why did it yield wild grapes? (5.1–4)

Simon includes this passage in his study because "Isaiah . . . sets his audience up as judges" (222). But this parable describes no violation of the law, unless one widens one's category to include a law of nature. Rather, it seeks to accomplish precisely what Nathan's parable does: to enjoin the reader to imagine an alternative to the bleak one described, and to accept responsibility for an injustice and work to correct it. The people of Judah are urged to see themselves as the wild grapes, tended to and cared for by God. If they recognize the injustice of their ways, they may reform themselves.

Isaiah's poetry aims to judge a current reality and transform it into something better, just as the legal case of the blasphemer does.[4] In fact, much of biblical poetry, placed in the mouths of Israel's prophets, has a manifest juridical undercurrent. As the prophets sought to convince the wayward Israelites that historical catastrophes such as military defeat were none other than a direct and proportional response to their crimes, the prophets developed a kind of rhetorical talion—a discursive instantiation of "an eye for an eye" (the law of retaliation, the *lex talionis*). Employing the medium of poetry, they used both linguistic and metrical correspondences to underscore the juridical logic they saw in Israel's ill-fated history. Patrick Miller exhaustively traces these correlations in prophetic texts. In class, we turn to his analysis of several passages from Hosea that conform most closely to the talionic ideal, in order to illustrate the category of prophetic juridical poetry.

Hosea's descriptions of God's retribution undoubtedly draw on a talionic sense of justice. The prophet writes, "Ephraim has become like a dove, silly and without sense; they call upon Egypt, they go to Assyria. As they go, I will cast my net over them; I will bring them down like birds of the air . . ." (7.11–12). The correspondence between sin and punishment, as Miller points out, here "depends entirely on figures of speech, metaphor, and simile. . . . The key clause in this regard is the beginning of verse 12, 'as they go' referring back to verse 11, 'they go to Assyria.' So even as Israel plays the fowl, then Yahweh will play the fowler" (16–17). This wordplay underscores the idea that God's defeat of Israel (at the hands of Assyria) corresponds in kind to Israel's sin. The equivalence in degree is also emphasized, as Israel's sin of abandoning God and placing their hope in foreign powers warrants God's abandonment of them to the hands of the foreign power. In every sense, the punishment fits the crime.

Another verse in Hosea describes a similar type of divine judgment. Only this time the priests, the very representatives of God in the community, are judged and promised punishment: "My people are destroyed for lack of knowledge; because you have rejected knowledge, I reject you from being a priest to me. And since you have forgotten the law of your God, I also will forget your children" (4.6). In this passage, Miller observes, "the prophet . . . announces a judgment against the priesthood which point for point matches the sin it has committed. The talionic emphasis is inescapable in such an extended correspondence as these verses contain" (14). The priests' direct rejection of knowledge leads to God's direct rejection of the priests. In the following phrase, the priests' rejection of God's issue (his teaching, Torah) leads to God's rejection of the priests' issue (their children).

In a third passage, Hosea says, hyperbolically, that the destruction of the entire earth will come about because of Israel's sins:

> Hear the word of the LORD, O people of Israel; for the LORD has an indictment against the inhabitants of the land. There is no faithfulness or loyalty, and no knowledge of God in the land. Swearing, lying, and murder, and stealing and adultery break out; bloodshed follows bloodshed. Therefore the land mourns, and all who live in it languish; together with the wild animals and the birds of the air, even the fish of the sea are perishing. (4.1–3)

Again we encounter "an excellent example of the correlation of sin and punishment," this time "centering upon the thematic word 'land'" (P. Miller 10). But it is not the use of this word, or even the locus of sin and punishment, that underlies the correspondence. The utter desolation of the earth comes only after the utter desecration of the land. The sheer magnitude of sin—no faith, loyalty, or acknowledgment of God, swearing, killing, robbing, committing adultery and murder—all these crimes, which in biblical theology pollute the land, when combined, earn the utter desolation God foretells. In all these passages, God's actions are entirely justified by the talionic notion of justice: the measure that Israel sows is the measure that Israel reaps. In emphasizing the utter predictability of natural and political disaster, Hosea provides the Israelites the means by which to avoid their fate: refraining from committing these crimes, changing their ways.

A course entitled Biblical Justice could cover the whole continuum of biblical literature, with one unit on law, one on narrative, and one on poetry. Students would be required to read, alongside the primary sources, key secondary texts on biblical law (such as Westbrook; Greenberg) and on law and narrative (Cover, "Nomos"; P. Brooks, "Narrativity"). Students may be challenged in one short paper per unit to analyze closely how one primary text weaves together vision and praxis, the image of a better world and the invocation of a practice that aims to achieve it. Certainly there are ajuridical and uninspiring texts throughout the Hebrew Bible, narratives that invite us to forget about our own lives for a while and be entertained, poetry that is hopeless and nihilistic, and legal lists that are terse and dry. But these need not dissuade us from teaching and studying the Hebrew Bible, a book that influences the lives of millions to this day, as an ancient paradigm of law and literature interfused. The Hebrew Bible aspires to have us fit its world into our lives—to transform our reality based on the visions its laws and narratives afford us.

Notes

1. I specify law *codes* here, because they are ones most lacking in narrative features. Much modern law does in fact partake in the rhetoric of narrative. See, e.g., P. Brooks, "Narrativity."

2. Bourdieu notes the particular character of juridical language as exhibiting a "predominance of passive and impersonal constructions . . . to mark the impersonality of normative utterance and to establish the speaker as universal subject, at once impartial and objective" ("Force" 821).

3. In this essay, all English translations of biblical texts are from the New Revised Standard Version, which strikes a balance between accuracy and readability. The edition of the Bible I urge students to buy is the *Harper Collins Study Bible*.

4. Having no information about any official enforcement of biblical law, we cannot know that a chief dividing line between law and narrative is the law's maintenance through the bodies of Israelite citizens. Moshe Greenberg notes that biblical law rarely if ever distinguishes between law that is enforceable and law that must remain rhetorical (11).

David H. Fisher

Law and Revenge Violence:
From Saga to Modern Fiction

With laws shall our land be built up but with lawlessness laid waste.

—Njals Saga

What is law but a partially realized promise to overcome disorder and aggression, tame and domesticate force, and subject action and instinct to reason and will?

—Austin Sarat and Thomas R. Kearns,
"Making Peace with Violence"

If there were a perfect satisfaction, we expect that it would put an end to matters. But we do not even know how to envisage perfection: what our anger wants may not be what our hate wants.

—William Ian Miller, *Eye for an Eye*

This essay introduces two texts, *Broken April* (Kadare) and *Njals Saga*, describing revenge violence cultures separated by geography (resp., Iceland and Albania) and a thousand years of history. Advocates of the rule of law in its modern sense, like Brian Tamanaha, often assume a Hobbesian position: absent a state monopoly on lethal violence backed by police and military power (accompanied by a system of rules constraining state power, by a formal legality, and by the notion of a "government of laws and not of men" [J. Adams, *Massachusetts Constitution*]), the result will be either a nasty state of nature or a tyrannical imposition of order without law (Schmitt) to bring an end to anarchy. In the worlds imagined by Ismail Kadare and by an anonymous Icelandic saga writer, there are indeed varieties of violence — physical, psychological, and structural — but it does not follow that there will be a "war of all against all."

In my experience teaching these texts together in courses that deal with literary representations of revenge violence in cross-cultural perspective over the past eight years, three points stand out, the first concerning law, the second literature, and the third revenge. First, both texts show that chronic social instability cannot be overcome by law alone. Customary law, seeking to endorse yet channel revenge in shame-honor cultures, can create mechanisms for feud abatement but cannot compensate for a lack of basic economic resources, nor can it provide the levels of security and predictability that come from a state monopoly on violence and rule of law in the modern sense. Second, figure-ground relations between physical violence and structural or psychological violence are well represented through irony (in *Njals Saga*) or allegory (in *Broken April*). Irony signals the potentially endless cycle of feud in shame-honor cultures, while allegory points to the process of displacement from consciously accepted (but disastrous) moral and social norms to manufactured memories of a time out of mind as the origin of such norms (Handwerk). Third, revenge, whether the product of desire (from anger, hatred, fear) or duty (to kin defined by custom), is as difficult to accomplish in fact as it is necessary to imagine in fiction. It is not true, as some Icelanders believed, that "everything is compensable." Some wrongs, some harms cannot be "made whole": consider Malvolio in Shakespeare's *Twelfth Night:* "I'll be revenged on the whole pack of you" (5.1.385; W. Miller, *Humiliation* 203–07). At the same time, the illusion of closure and the belief that closure is possible and final are necessary for social order.

Broken April and *Njals Saga* imagine worlds where customary law authorizes yet seeks to limit revenge violence, without the backing of a state monopoly on violence. Saga Iceland (c. 1000 AD) and northern Albania (during the rule of King Zog I [1928–39]) share features that separate them from rule-of-law cultures: minimal state apparatus, no state monopoly on violence, and no independent judiciary or professional advocates. Lay advocates, like Njal Thorgeirson in the saga, counsel and argue on behalf of disputed claims, and lay members of courts function as judge and jury but without enforcement powers. Self-help enforcement of judgments operates within shame-honor-based norms that accept blood vengeance as an option or sometimes a duty in response to homicide and other assaults on honor.[1]

Both worlds embody imperatives for action in response to attacks on honor. "It was by getting even that one established the inviolability of one's honor . . . honor involved a paradox, requiring equality among the players in the game at the same time that the object of the [zero sum] game was to undo the basis for equality" (W. Miller, *Bloodtaking* 302). Bergthora goads Skarp-Hedin into action in *Njals Saga* thus:

> "Gifts have been given to you, father and sons alike; and you would scarcely be men if you did not repay them."
>
> "What kind of gifts?" asked Skarp-Hedin.
>
> "You, my sons, share the one gift between you; you have all been nicknamed 'Little Dung-Beards,' and my husband has been nicknamed 'Old Beardless.'" (44)

In the Kanun, "A man who has been dishonored is considered dead according to the Kanun" and "Blood is never unavenged" (§§600, 917).

The story of Gudmund and Ofeig from the *Ljósvetninga Saga* illustrates the combination of humor and sensitivity about honor typical of Icelandic family sagas. Gudmund was a powerful *goðar* (chief), Ofeig a substantial *bondi* (farmer). At a feast given by a thingman of Gudmund he was given the seat of honor, and Ofeig was placed beside him:

> And when the tables were set, Ofeig put his fist on the table and said,
>
> "How big does that fist seem to you, Gudmund?"
>
> "Big enough," he said.
>
> "Do you suppose that there is any strength in it?" asked Ofeig.
>
> "I certainly do," said Gudmund.
>
> "Do you think it would deliver much of a blow?" asked Ofeig.
>
> "Quite a blow," Gudmund replied.
>
> "Do you think it might do any damage?" continued Ofeig.
>
> "Broken bones or a deathblow," Gudmund answered.
>
> "How would such an end appeal to you?" asked Ofeig.
>
> "Not much at all, and I wouldn't choose it," said Gudmund.
>
> Ofeig said, "Then don't sit in my place."

"As you wish," said Gudmund—and he sat to one side.

People had the impression that Ofeig wanted the greater place of honor, since he had occupied the high seat up to that time.

(W. Miller, *Bloodtaking* 30)

Read in the context of jurisprudence, these texts provide powerful, readable case illustrations of the costs and benefits of customary law in a shame-honor *nomos* and a minimalist state. Both saga Iceland and twentieth-century northern Albania were relatively poor in material resources and isolated—psychologically as well as geographically—from their larger cultural worlds. In both the imagined worlds of the texts and in actual history, customary law proved insufficient to maintain order, and in both texts extended feud violence leads to exhaustion and social dissolution.

The reconciliation of Flosi Thordarson, leader of the band that burns Njal and his family to death in an act of revenge, and his opponent, Kari Solmundarson, a survivor of the burning, occurs only at the conclusion of the saga, after a protracted feud and a large body count. In Icelandic history, the independent commonwealth begun in 930 dissolved itself in 1271, seeking protection from the king of Norway by treaty in response to the devastation of unchecked feud violence. The preordained death of Gjorg Berisha at the end of *Broken April* likewise occurs against a backdrop of villages decimated and impoverished by feud. An old woman explains to Bessian Vorpsi and his wife, Diana, that "my village is quite big, but most of the men are cloistered in the towers [places of refuge sanctioned by blood feud rules]. . . . Of the two hundred households of our village, only twenty are not involved in the blood feud" (172). Customary law, in both worlds, supplies incentives for feud, even as it seeks to mitigate the social, economic, and personal damage produced by it.

When teaching *Njals Saga* in undergraduate and graduate courses on revenge violence in cross-cultural perspective, I assigned chapters from Jesse Byock's *Viking Age Iceland* together with William Miller's more detailed descriptions in "Feud, Vengeance, and the Disputing Process," "Law and Legal Process," and "Peacemaking and Arbitration" (*Bloodtaking*, chs. 6–8), and recommended part 1 of David Cohen's *Law, Violence and Community in Classical Athens* (discussing the problem of stability and the rule of law in the agonistic, shame-honor society of ancient Athens) as collateral reading.[2] The juxtaposition of saga Iceland and classical Greece was helpful for those students who pursued it in discerning identities in difference in the feud process at different times and locations. Had it been available at the time, I would have added selections from Miller's *Eye for an Eye,* including "The Proper Price of Property in an Eye" (ch. 4), "Dismemberment and Price Lists" (ch. 8), and "Satisfaction Not Guaranteed" (ch. 10).[3] These would have added a perspective on Anglo-Saxon ideas of compensation to revenge norms in ancient Iceland and Greece.

There are clear analogies between Miller's work and Cohen's. Cohen, drawing on anthropological research about contemporary Mediterranean shame-honor societies (Herzfeld; Peristiany) for his analysis of classical Athenian legal texts, shows how ancient Greek law both enabled and contained feud. Miller's secondary sources include work on feud by anthropologists such as Jacob Black-Michaud, Christopher Boehm, Max Gluckman, and Michael Herzfeld as well as literary, historical, and legal sources on ancient Scandinavian culture. Although my rationale for assigning this material was to make explicit the workings of feud and feud arbitration in saga Iceland and northern Albanian cultures, the same material could be expanded to introduce a controversial topic in legal history and jurisprudence: the relevance of contemporary cultural anthropology for understanding ancient legal cultures. Both Miller and Cohen assume that anthropological work is applicable to an understanding of issues in ancient law and some contemporary legal issues. Miller, for example, makes suggestive comments about advocates of dignity as "priceless worth" and more "primitive" notions of blood price, at the conclusion of *Eye for an Eye* (190).

From a comparative literature perspective in preparation for *Broken April,* the classes read Ivo Andrić's *Bridge on the Drina* during the previous week. Andrić's depiction of relationships of hostility and hospitality between Muslim and Christian populations (separated by River Drina in Bosnia for over four hundred years) includes examples of dispute and dispute arbitration by customary law. This novel gave students a background understanding of how historical memory shapes thinking in and about events in contemporary Balkan life. Andrić's characters perceive one another's actions through the screen of inherited stories of violence at the hands of others, violence said (by those seeking political or social power) to require retaliation hundreds of years later. Students were then able to grasp how a feud whose precise origins had been forgotten could continue to activate violence (in *Broken April* and, to a far lesser degree, in *Njals Saga*). I also assigned selections from Boehm on Balkan feuds (*Blood Revenge*) during the week on *Broken April* to provide a level of critical analysis equivalent to that given by Miller for saga Iceland. I showed the

Macedonian director Milcho Manchevski's *Before the Rain* in an evening film series that accompanied the class. The film makes explicit the cyclic character of revenge violence and draws connections between the workings of revenge violence in places that are distant and considered savage (e.g., Macedonia) and those closer to home (contemporary London). I did not need to speak about the use and abuse of memory in the depiction of others and their legacies and in the current war of terror; my students spontaneously began making such connections after the readings and the film.

At a time when modern legal theory focuses on law's violence, critical reading of *Njals Saga* and *Broken April* also offers a comparative, cross-cultural perspective on revenge violence in relation to law. From 1991 to the present, Austin Sarat and others have developed a complex jurisprudence of violence at a time when legal theory has been dominated by debates between advocates of law as procedural justice and those who see law as a means of wealth maximization.[4] The image that emerges in the anthologies edited by Sarat is of law as itself a violent force. Sarat comments, "Cover was hopeful about law even in the shadow of violence. We are much less hopeful" (*Law, Violence* 50).

By Robert Cover's criteria, there is clearly a richness of *nomos* coexisting with a high degree of homogeneity in both *Njals Saga* and *Broken April*. Saga Icelanders clearly understood the difference between law and force. Unn in *Njals*, demanding help in recovering money from Gunnar, observes, "Hrut [who has her funds] relied on force rather than law." Njal later insists, "With laws shall our land be built up but with lawlessness laid waste" (§§ 21, 70). Njal's considerable legal skills are employed in efforts to mitigate, if not eliminate, physical violence. Njal is said to have been "so skilled in law that no one was considered his equal. He was a wise and prescient man. . . . He was a gentle man of great integrity: he remembered the past and discerned the future" (§ 20). Yet even his formidable skills are unable to prevent feud process from destroying his friend Gunnar, or himself and his family, in the end.

Broken April's world displays far less humor ("The Code is never a laughing matter, Diana remembered someone saying" [75]), and little display of *phronesis* like that of Njal, perhaps reflecting Kadare's understanding of the causes for a return of blood feuds in Albania in the 1990s.[5] Kadare is well known for his use of allegory to deal with issues under Enver Hoxha's repressive regime, and it is clear that *Broken April* displaces problems arising from a breakdown of law in Albania at the time of the

novel into an earlier period of Albanian history. There is a constant interplay between appearance and reality in the text, as in the cynical physician
assistant's remarks to Bessian Vorpsi:

> You are sure that my function here is to dress and cure wounds—isn't
> that so? . . . But I have nothing to do with things of that kind. . . .
> I am not here as a doctor but as an assistant to a judge. I count the
> wounds, classify them, and do nothing more. . . . In every aspect of the
> events that were discussed today, it was purely a question of settling a
> debt. . . . Blood, precious stones, cloth, it makes no difference. To me,
> it concerns a debt, and that is all. (191)

Instead of seeing rule of law as a progressive evolution from primitive, self-help, customary law societies to modern regimes, *Njals Saga* and
Broken April suggest that legal history may be less a matter of movement
from force to understanding than of different ways of coming to terms
with agonistic conflict. Miller observes:

> The Icelandic example reveals the force of law as a legitimating entity
> in a society in which legitimacy was not firmly fixed or complacently
> assumed. . . . The limits of law might well have been clearer to these
> people than they are to us because they would not have been tempted
> to confuse the category of law with the category of the state. . . .
> (*Bloodtaking* 307)

In the final chapter of his *Bloodtaking*, he sounds cautionary notes about
excessive admiration for the saga world.[6]

The nature of violence—physical, systemic, and interpretive—and
its representation are the primary normative and literary issues in these
texts. The world of *Njals Saga* will seem to casual American readers more
violent than ours, in part because the convention of narrative compres-
sion highlights moments of conflict while minimizing accounts of daily
farm chores that would have preoccupied most Icelandic lives. Sheep are
a subject of limited interest—unless they are stolen (Herzfeld 30–32).
The sense of excessive violence in both worlds may also be due to the fact
that "responsibility for actually doing acts of [physical] violence was more
evenly distributed than it is now, there being no state agents to delegate
the dirty work to, or to claim a monopoly on the dirty work" (W. Miller,
Bloodtaking 304).

Violence is a highly contested topic in recent interdisciplinary anthologies such as Manfred Steger and Nancy Lind's *Violence and Its Alternatives*

and Hent de Vries and Samuel Weber's *Violence, Identity, and Self-Determination.* In the course on revenge violence, following an introductory reading of Friedrich Nietzsche's *Genealogy* (in week 2), I assigned excerpts, from Steger and Lind, of Hannah Arendt's *On Violence,* Walter Benjamin's "Critique of Violence," and Derrida's "Force of Law: The 'Mystical Foundations of Authority.'" In retrospect, I would now substitute C. A. J. Coady's defense of a restricted, *OED* definition of violence ("The Idea of Violence") and Johan Galtung's argument for a wider view of structural violence ("Cultural Violence") from the Steger and Lind volume, for the Arendt, Benjamin, and Derrida material, given the difficulty experienced by my undergraduates in dealing with issues posed especially by Benjamin and by Derrida. Benjamin requires exposition of a tradition of European reflection on violence that extends at least from Edmund Burke and Hegel through Marx and Georges Sorel; Derrida's essay requires, in turn, a careful analytic reading of Benjamin. The contrast between narrow and expanded versions of violence articulated by Coady and Galtung, respectively, is more easily grasped by undergraduates than complex philosophical debates over force and violence.

The use of Coady's essay is also helpful when reading Cover's "Nomos and Narrative" in a course on the philosophy of law. Cover follows Elaine Scarry in "rendering violence as the painful infliction of physical force" supporting the "civilized contention that violence destroys from without" (Fitzpatrick, "Why the Law" 143–44). For Scarry physical pain produced by violence actively destroys or negates language, thereby "bringing about an immediate reversion to a state anterior to language, to the sounds and cries a human being makes before language is learned" (qtd. in Fitzpatrick, "Why the Law" 143). In *Njals Saga,* however, pain finds eloquent expression in language through conventions of irony, sarcasm, and dark humor. Contemporary readers of the saga were doubtless as aware of the improbability of an actual response to a lost leg in battle like Kol's observation ("That's my reward for not having my shield" [149]), just as readers of the *Iliad* understand the improbability of actual Bronze Age warriors addressing one another in Homeric couplets. The conventions of saga writing intensify physical pain rather than render it beyond saying.

Read as works on law, *Njals Saga* and *Broken April* support Derrida's observation that "[v]iolence is not exterior to the order of *droit*. It threatens it from within and we must recognize meaning in a violence that is not an accident arriving from outside the law" (qtd. in Fitzpatrick, "Why the

Law" 154). In both texts there is a constant tension between the physical violence authorized by the legal systems and elaborate formal mechanisms for arbitration designed to constrain it. The topic of law's violence and its relation to a comparative reading of *Njals Saga* and *Broken April* suggests a concluding observation.

One aim of the new jurisprudence of violence has been to restore linkages between law and justice. Adam Thurschwell, a leading exponent of the movement, having noted law's "impossible, necessary promise of justice" (329), attempts to articulate an understanding of law that resists a thoroughgoing identification of law with violence in his "Reading the Law," the final essay in *The Rhetoric of Law* (Sarat and Kearns). The problem with this search for connections between law and justice among advocates of a jurisprudence of violence is that, given the instrumentalist basis of critical legal studies, the quest for justice, especially justice for the marginalized and oppressed, is self-defeating. As Nancy Weston observes:

> [I]n the end, the pursuit of efficacy as the end of law, the seeing of no alternative to force as the substance and explanation of the world (and so of law) arise from and manifest the same underlying understanding that what is in being—what is "real"—is only power and its effects in force. (787)

This instrumental understanding of power and force is mirrored today in apologists such as Richard Posner (*Not a Suicide Pact*) and Alan Dershowitz (*Why Terrorism Works*) for the employment of extralegal expedients in dealing with the violence of global terrorism: establishment of legal black holes beyond the reach of ordinary law (Danner), rationalizations for torture (Greenberg and Dratel), and extreme rendition. In *Njals Saga* and *Broken April,* recourse to extralegal expedients was prevented by allowance for violence in law and the very mystical authority of law—*Grágás* or Kanun—said to have been demystified by Benjamin and subjected to deconstruction in the name of justice by Derrida.

This preventing was not done in blind faith, as *Njals Saga*'s ironic recounting of Njal's legal creativity or the physician's cynical account of the reality of exchanges beneath the Kanun shows. The texts honor the stability of law and at the same time applaud the inventiveness of those clever enough to find ways to bend the law to achieve their purposes—within limits established by custom. Tamanaha, at the conclusion of his recent criticism of legal instrumentalism fostered by realism and critical legal studies, offers an alternative. He cites the Marxist historian E. P. Thompson's claim that "[t]he essential precondition for the effectiveness of law in its function as ideology is that it shall display an independence from gross manipulation and shall seem to be just. It cannot seem to be so without . . . on occasion actually *being* just." Tamanaha adds:

> [E]ven recognizing that the law did not live up to its idealized characterizations, it is a grave error to dismiss traditional, non-instrumental views of law as mere rhetoric. . . . The most portentous development chronicles in these pages is the progressive deterioration of ideals fundamental to the system of law and government: that law is a principled preserver of justice, that law serves the public good, that legal rules are binding on government officials . . . and that judges must render decisions in an objective fashion based upon law." (*Law* 249)

Lacking a central state or an independent judiciary, the last of Tamanaha's four ideals do not apply to either the world of saga Iceland or northern Albanian under the Kanun. Yet there was widespread support in both for "our law" as something unique, in its combination of substantive and procedural justice. One could hardly characterize the Icelanders of *Njals Saga* or the northern Albanians of *Broken April* as naive idealists about the law. They did, however, understand the danger of dissolving all legal rhetoric into a play of power and force. As Njal wisely remarks, "With laws shall our land be built up but with lawlessness laid waste."

Notes

1. The manslaughter section of the *Grágás,* a written collection of early Icelandic law from the mid thirteenth century, authorizes revenge: "It is prescribed that a man on whom injury is inflicted has the right to avenge himself if he wants to up to the time of General Assembly at which he is required to bring a case for the injuries" (ch. 7). The Kanun, a set of laws developed by Lekë Dukagjini used in northern Albania and Kosovo from the fifteenth century until the twentieth (revived recently after the fall of the Communist regime in the early 1990s), provides the basis for events described in *Broken April. The Kanuni i Lekë Dukagjinit: The Code of Lekë Dukagjini* requires rather than merely permits acts of revenge under certain circumstances: "If you do not avenge the murder of your guest, even if the murderer is a fellow-villager, you may not participate in meetings of honorable men, because you remain dishonored for the rest of your life" (§ 651). Although Kanun and *Grágás* contain elaborate provisions for mediating disputes (descriptions of mediators in disputes and murders in *Kanun* [§§ 667–82, 851–53, 695–68] are paralleled by discussions of mediation in *Grágás* sections on homicide [§§ 86–112]), in the end there is a limit to the principle that "everything is com-

pensable" (W. Miller, *Eye* 131). Blood calls for blood, and justice means a settling of accounts, a repayment of debt, or a return for "gifts."

2. Chapters from Byock include "The Legislative and Judicial System," "Systems of Power: Advocates, Friendship, and Family Networks," and "Aspects of Blood Feud."

3. In chapter 4 of *An Eye for an Eye*, Miller draws a vivid example from *Guðmundar saga dýra* (the same example with which he begins *Bloodtaking and Peacemaking*) to show the difference between property and liability rule protection. "Property-rule protection means the entitlement is transferable only at a price the entitlement holder is willing to pay" (49). His discussion of King Æthelbert of Kent's (590–616) price list for various body parts as a schedule of evaluations in chapter 8 forms part of his argument against those whom he calls apples-and-oranges people (people who claim that human dignity has no price and that turning body parts into money equivalents shows a more primitive understanding of value) but is also valuable for understanding comments such as Snorri's response (in *Njals Saga* [139]) to Asgrim's request for assistance: "As soon as I estimate that you have killed off as many of them as you can afford to pay compensation for . . . I shall intervene with all my men to stop the fighting" (296). Finally, "Satisfaction Not Guaranteed" provides a useful discussion of the difference between the ideology of satisfactory revenge achieved and the difficulty of accomplishing it. The ideal is expressed in a citation from Christopher Boehm, who reports that a certain Savo Todorovic, a seventy-year-old man, "explained the spiritual meaning of ostveta (*vengeance*) thus: 'Osveta, that means . . . a kind of spiritual fulfillment. You have killed my son, so I killed yours; I have taken revenge for that, so I now sit peacefully in my chair. There you are'" (*Eye* 145). The reality, according to Miller, is that "there can be no perfect satisfaction" (157).

4. Sources of inspiration are the critical legal studies movement, the pioneering work of Robert Cover on law's violence, and Jacques Derrida's critical reading of Walter Benjamin's "Critique of Violence" in "Force of Law." For a provocative example of Derrida's influence on this movement, see Peter Fitzpatrick's *Modernism and the Grounds of Law* (70–84). For a review of several collaborative works by Sarat and Kearns, see Weston.

5. "Kadare says the resurgence of blood vengeance in Albania is less a return to the ways of the *kanun* than an angry reaction to the former communist regime: '[Blood vengeance] is a caricature of the *kanun*, a stigmatization of it. . . . Reaction to the communist form of communication resulted in the revival of the *kanun* as a form of nostalgia'" (Naegele).

6. Miller turns to possible reactions to the saga world from an imagined feminist, a libertarian, and a communitarian. Individual women characters in the sagas are often portrayed as strong, self-reliant (and to some extent as instigators of feud violence), and female virginity—a central concern of Mediterranean shame-honor cultures—was "a non-issue" (*Bloodtaking* 305). Nevertheless, the saga world was patriarchal, and women as a class were both dominated and oppressed. Libertarians "might have reason to be suspicious of a society that draws them like a siren," in part because the public-private dichotomy with which libertarians begin analysis has little relevance to a world of self-help law, in part because "it was not the [jealous,

resentful] have-nots who invented the state. . . . Early state formation tended to involve redistributions not from rich to poor, but from poor to rich, from weak to strong" (306). Miller concludes with the wry observation that "a significant portion of [saga character] charm is their absence, their distance in time," adding his belief that "it would have been my luck to have lived as poor Skaereing Hroaldsson did whom we met in the preface to this book: a minor cleric, for a while without hand, and finally without head" (308).

Susan Sage Heinzelman

Teaching Eighteenth-Century Law and Literature: *The Adventures of Rivella*

Rivella, the fictional autobiography of Delarivier Manley, is not an easy book to teach, and its difficulty is not confined to the complications of the plot, the elusive nature of its putative subject, Rivella, or the historical knowledge required of a modern reader. *Rivella* is difficult for all these reasons but also because it demands a nuanced response from the students to issues of literary and legal representation and to the relation between those two kinds of representation. Specifically, the text requires that we understand the "protean, diffuse, contradictory" embodiments of the protagonist, Rivella (Zelinsky 17), as representative of the historical and gendered complexity of the relation between law and literature in early-eighteenth-century England. In other words, Rivella is not just the fictional persona of the author, she also embodies the historically specific and gendered affiliation between the literary and the legal. In this sense, the eponymous heroine is an allegorical figure and has to be read as such. Reconceiving the connection between law and literature in this way is the reward for teaching this book. More, employing this pedagogical method can offer us a model for teaching law and literature in other historical periods.

I have successfully taught *Rivella* in upper-division honors seminars and graduate classes specializing in eighteenth-century English women writers—in both cases to students who were not familiar with the historical period or the work of Manley. These courses had not been designated as teaching law and literature, but I asked the students to focus their analysis on how these two discursive formations interacted with each other and how issues of gender complicated that interaction. I begin by suggesting that our modern understanding of the distinction between law and literature can be traced back to the early eighteenth century and to a cultural crisis over ways of representing the truth. I suggest that as religious truth slowly relinquished its claims to epistemological superiority, late-seventeenth- and early-eighteenth-century English culture turned to history (as articulated both conventionally and through the emerging form of the novel) and law (as articulated in black-letter law and the formalizing of evidentiary procedures) to stabilize its representations of truth telling.[1]

Although these two discourses were often represented as mutually contesting—most often through attacks on the dangerous fictionality of the novel, especially when a novel claimed to be a "true history"—in fact they worked together to produce a gendered and nationally identified citizen-subject, one who was male and English. This privileging of an apparently natural site of authority was reinforced both by the growing professionalization of lawyering in the eighteenth century (no more amateurs, especially female ones, like Rivella) and by the gradual elevation during the century of respectable novelistic narrative over the scandalous, female-authored, secret memoirs and romances (like *Rivella*) of the early eighteenth century (see W. Warner). Thus the original hybridity of the novel—its mixing of memoir, romance, travel narrative, criminal confession, of legal and literary discourse—had to be purified in order to privilege the specific form of the novel that would be defined, by the end of the eighteenth century, as the English novel. What also came into being during the course of the eighteenth century, partly as a result of this privileging of certain literary and legal institutions, are those early versions of the disciplines we now so confidently identify as literature and law.

So how best to teach this complicated cultural history? I divide this essay into three parts, following the general structure of my course: part 1 situates *Rivella* in the traditional history of the novel, part 2 analyzes the plot of the novel, and part 3 models a gendered and historical reading of the relation between law and literature.

Rivella: Novel, Memoir, or Romance?

Mary Delarivier Manley wrote and published her fictional autobiography in 1714 to preempt a hostile account of her life that had been commissioned by the publisher Edmund Curll, who hoped to exploit Manley's notoriety as a writer of scandalous secret memoirs and amatory fictions. (In 1709, Manley had been arrested and jailed for seditious libel, the consequence of writing a scurrilous, but very successful, political novel, *New Atalantis,* which attacked the Whig government by revealing their purported amorous adventures—*plus ça change.*) Manley was one of several women writers who flourished at the beginning of the eighteenth century and who, with Aphra Behn and Eliza Haywood, was frequently abused for the content of her novels as well as for the presumption that she, a woman, should set herself up as a writer.

It does not surprise students that women novelists and playwrights were vilified and spoken of as whores who publicly displayed their wares (works) for sale. Most are familiar with the long tradition of antifeminism and the marginalization of women writers through the centuries. What does come as somewhat of a shock, however, is just how long this tradition has continued—although the antagonism may not be voiced in the same virulent terms. Antagonism was replaced by bean counting (the idea that women were more profligate in their production of novels than men, their very productivity being the reason for their inferiority) or the erasure of women's critical contribution to the development of the novel.

A paradigmatic version of this literary history is Ian Watt's *The Rise of the Novel* (1957), which makes little mention of the contribution to the genre by women writers (except in terms of quantity and by invidious comparisons to Defoe, Richardson, and Fielding). For Watt, the "novel's mode of imitating reality may . . . be . . . summarised in terms of the procedures of another group of specialists in epistemology, the jury in a court of law. Their expectations, and those of the novel reader coincide in many ways . . ." (31). Further, Watt argues, "Of no fiction before Defoe's could Lamb have written: 'It is like reading evidence in a court of Justice'" (34). This epistemological analogy would seem to exclude women as official witnesses and judges of what counts as reality: there were no trained women lawyers, no woman judges, and no women on formal juries. Literary historical accounts of the novel have more or less endorsed Watt's version of early-eighteenth-century culture and his account of the relation between novelistic and legal representations as based on a shared sense of what constitutes the real and as privileging a legalistic sense of the truth.

One reason this gender prejudice seems impossible to overcome is that Watt's analogy results from retroactively defining the novel form, a definition that relies on several problematic premises. Let me isolate just two of these: first, Watt assumes that in the early eighteenth century the legal system in general and court testimony in particular could be clearly identified as a stable epistemological category against which an equally stable generic form, the novel, could be measured. The second assumption, which follows from the first, is that these two discursive formations—the literary and the legal—are discrete categories of knowledge and representation. In other words, the legal and the literary occupy separate cultural spaces and produce separate, although related, cultural representations. Watt, and those critics who accepted his demarcation of discursive regimes, would come to determine the excellence of a particular novel precisely on the grounds that it marked and enforced the boundaries between the fictional and the nonfictional, between the literary and the legal (or political or scientific), in ways that readers could agree on. Even the explicit revisions of Watt's argument from critics, like Michael McKeon (*Origins of the English Novel*), and the insistence of feminist critics (e.g., Ballaster; Craft-Fairchild; Gallagher; and Todd) that Behn, Haywood, and Manley made significant contributions to the generic development of the novel have done little to lessen the prejudice against women writers as less able than their male counterparts to offer a recognizable version of what would be defined, by the end of the eighteenth century, as the English novel. *Rivella* does not offer comfortable reading precisely because the reader cannot discern those epistemological distinctions and hierarchies that have come to define the order that novel reading should produce.

The first step, then, in adjusting the students' view of texts that do not fit conventional definitions of the novel is to ask students to identify what is difficult about reading *Rivella* in contrast to narratives that have a secure place in the history of the novel, like Daniel Defoe's *Robinson Crusoe,* which seems to draw a picture of a historically specific culture through the persona of a contemporary individual. One answer is bound to be that one cannot fix the character of Rivella or the details of the world she inhabits. The reality of *Rivella* does not seem to bear much relation to the real as we have come to understand it in the context of the history of the English novel. But that real is a retroactively produced version based, in part, on gendered premises about the relation between the novel and the law and the distinctions that mark their respective representational territories. Discomfort therefore is not a quality of the text but the reader's response to unfulfilled expectations.

Rivella: Mistress of the Art of Love and of Business

The title page of *Rivella* aligns the work with those very same generic categories from which the official version of the novel will eventually be distinguished: "The Adventures of *Rivella*; or, The History of the Author of *Atalantis:* With Secret *Memoirs* and *Characters* of Several Considerable Persons Her *Contemporaries*" (39). Mixing the adventures of the romance genre with the history of autobiography and memoirs, the narrative delivers portraits of the famous and the infamous in the manner of scandalous journalism. Moreover, all this is filtered through the point of view of Sir Charles Lovemore, Rivella's admirer and biographer, whose voice has in turn been preserved by the former amanuensis of and gentleman of the chamber to the chevalier D'Aumont, a young Frenchman. It is this original French version, claims the anonymous translator, that has been translated into English. It is hard to imagine more layers of transmission, more complicating frames, than those that preface this story. At once a reminder of the seventeenth-century amatory French romance and a parody of romance's deliberate distance from real and contemporaneous events, at once a Continental narrative and a claim to describe a still-living English celebrity, *Rivella* invokes a plurality of genres. Such plurality provides evidence of unsophistication and instability to those critics who would judge *Rivella* by the standards of the later novel. Yet it is precisely this instability that registers the complexity of the relation between law and literature at this particular historical moment.

Rivella begins with the chevalier D'Aumont's requesting that his companion, Sir Charles Lovemore, tell "as many particulars relating to [Rivella's] life and behaviour as [he] can possible recollect" (46). Long an admirer of Rivella, Lovemore proceeds to describe her person and her life, beginning with her birth, her early life as the daughter of the governor of the island of Jersey, Lovemore's unrequited passion for her as a young woman, her first love affair with a soldier under her father's command, and her bigamous marriage to her already married cousin, John Manley, followed by her social success and infamy as the author of the *New Atalantis*. Despite the drift of the narrative and the chevalier's interest in Rivella as a "mistress of love" (46), it is Rivella's involvement as mediator between the two parties to the Albemarle lawsuit—the duke of Montagu and the earl of Bath—that occupies a large part of the text (approximately a third).[2]

That legal business should occupy such a significant portion of a narrative about a woman writer who was infamous for her politically aggressive, amatory fiction reminds us that the two modes of representation and action—law and love—were mutually interwoven even (especially?) in the life of a woman. Indeed, Lovemore exclaims, "Behold Rivella in a new scene, that of business; in which however Love took care to save all his own immunities" (86). The final section of the narrative returns to the character of Rivella, the consequences of her political attacks on the Whig government, and her poor treatment by her political allies. It closes with Lovemore's judgment that her true brilliance lies not in her intervention in political affairs but in knowing "how to *live*" and in making "such noble discoveries in that passion [of love]" (114). Thus Lovemore tries one last time, as he has throughout his relationship with Rivella, to confine her to the private realm, to those amatory fictions she has written and that he has spun around her character. He even believes that he has persuaded her that "politicks is not the business of a woman, especially of one that can so well delight and entertain her readers with more gentle pleasuring theams" and that she has therefore turned "to write a tragedy for the stage" (112). The subject matter of this tragedy, *Lucius, the First Christian King of Britain* (1717), is not, however, "more gentle" than politics: the play intertwines the arts of politics and love in the same way that Rivella's own life has done. The tragedy engages both the military and amatory adventures of the hero, Lucius, as Richard Steele's prologue to the play makes clear:

> But the ambitious author of these scenes,
> With no low arts, to court your favour means;
> With her success, and disappointment, move,
> *On the just laws of empire, and of love.* (*Lucius*; emphasis added)

Manley's semifictional, semi-autobiographical adventure complicates discursive distinctions and offers us instead a narrative that is both allegorical and particular, both fictional and factual, one that is able to encompass both the *imitatio* of the novel and the *advocatio* of the law. Rivella is an accomplished author of memoirs and romances but also the mediator in a complicated legal property dispute. The boundary between the character who models an allegorical romance heroine and the skilful legal adviser to the aristocracy is fluid. By the end of the text, one comes to see both narratives as interchangeable, so fraught with issues of law and property is the heroine's condition as a single and married (and abandoned) woman and so limned with romance and desire is the legal battlefield on which the two lords skirmish.

A Lady Who Could So Well Give Laws to Others Yet Was Not Obliged to Keep Them Herself

The heroine is not just an autobiographical fiction; she also embodies a specific historical relation between the literary and the legal. That historical relation is defined, in part, by the instability of the generic categories that the narrative invokes—the amatory, the romance, the confessional, the journalistic, the legal—as well as by their essential interdependence. Thus the eponymous heroine is both a realistic representation and an allegorical one, both a re-presentation of Delarivier Manley and an allegorical account of how cultural representations perform their meaning through and about the body of a woman.

The questions of property that are played out in the Albemarle lawsuit between Montagu and Bath cannot be isolated from the questions of sexuality and desire that permeate the story of Rivella's life. Zelinsky argues:

> Equivocal itself, *Rivella* raises questions about its own truthfulness, obscuring clear distinctions between fact and fiction in its complex interplay of discrete discursive modes and practices—historical, juridical, romantic and otherwise—with which Manley constructs her self-portrait. (11)

Zelinsky is correct in her identification of the "complex interplay" among different discursive modes, but I would suggest that to describe those "modes and practices" as discrete is to impose on the text a reading that reflects our own sense of how disciplines have constructed the relation among discourses instead of inquiring into this text's historical circumstances. Although it is inevitable that we read through our own experiences as critics and readers, we should try to suspend the inclination to categorize according to already existing genres and allow the text to teach us how it might be read—which is, not accidentally, the manner by which allegorical narrative proceeds.

While it is true, as Zelinsky argues, that "Lovemore interweaves amatory and juridical strains, as Rivella's adventures in love recurrently turn on questions of guilt or innocence" (27), the narrative also demands that we recognize the amatory in the juridical and vice versa. The romance narrative that details Rivella's amatory adventures depends, as do all romances, for its affective power on both the positive and figurative presences of the law: Rivella steals from her father to enrich her lover, marries a man who is already married, and enters into an affair with a man who is married. All these amorous adventures are played out against the positive presence of legal restraints such as laws prohibiting bigamy and theft, but Lovemore's romance narrative is also internally constrained by the laws of love that figure as what one might call intimate juridical devices. Lovemore is forbidden from disclosing too much; he must represent Rivella's reputation and behavior as if he were an advocate. Moreover, Rivella herself is both literally and figuratively on trial throughout the narrative, exposing herself to public gaze even as she does when she is forced before the court on charges of seditious libel and when she seeks out her ex-husband, Manley, in the court of Westminster. By contrast, the body of a woman also privatizes the public space of the court, and thus a public yet intimate space emerges, one in which Rivella's personal and juridical self are inseparable.[3]

Just as the juridical shadows the amatory, the romance narrative, so does the amatory inhabit the juridical. Rivella becomes embroiled in the complicated Albermarle lawsuit only because of her attachment to an interested party. The account of the legal, political, and personal maneuverings of the parties is criss-crossed with desire and amorous adventures that profoundly alter the lawsuit's outcome. Marriage, seduction, and all the apparatus of the romance seep into its account: Montagu (one of the parties to the lawsuit) marries Elizabeth Cavendish (the inheritor of the Albemarle estate) in a suspiciously arranged ceremony, the bride seemingly unaware of the ceremony taking place; another party to the lawsuit has been tricked into marriage with the daughter of a poor merchant; Rivella's lover, Cleander, a supporter of Montagu, finds himself charged with corruption, and Rivella must intervene on his behalf with her ex-husband, John Manley, who is an advocate for Montagu's adversary in the lawsuit, Lord Bath; and so on. Law, it seems, is not only present in legal spaces (the courtroom, the prison, the bar, and the bench) or in legal texts (wills, confessions, testimonies, and legislation); it also permeates quotidian experience and its literary representations. In other words, there is law outside the law.

The disputed legal documents—the two versions of the duke of Albemarle's will—disappear from view as juridical text, appearing in the narrative only as the ghostly remainder-reminder of a dead man's imposition of his wishes on his widow. Thus the amatory and the juridical are inseparably intertwined and create an imaginary (but not therefore unreal) space that is neither public nor private, neither masculine nor feminine, a space that lies outside the jurisdiction of either literature or law.[4] This imaginary space should not be taken merely as that which stands opposed to reality, to the embodiment of experience. On the contrary, it is precisely where law (and reality) happens and where literature records the consequences.

What I hope this essay has suggested is that we should attend to the individual historical circumstances that govern the specific relation between law and literature at any given moment in time. Further, focusing on the representation of woman as the lens through which one examines this discursive relation discloses not only the gendered nature of that relation but also the historical roots of certain gender, genre, and disciplinary expectations.

Notes

All references to the text of *Rivella* are to the 1999 Broadview edition, edited by Katherine Zelinsky.

1. For a fuller discussion of this argument, see Heinzelman.

2. The lawsuit originates as a result of two wills left by Christopher Monck (1653–88), the second duke of Albermarle (Mr. Double in *Rivella*). He married Elizabeth Cavendish in 1669 and served as governor of Jamaica from 1686 to 1688. In his first will, made in 1675, Lord Albemarle made John Granville (1628–1701), first earl of Bath (Baron Meanwell in *Rivella*) and a cousin of his father, the primary beneficiary, as he, Albemarle, was in Bath's will should Bath die first. While in Jamaica, Albemarle was persuaded by his wife to make another will (1687) in order to revenge herself on Lord Bath, who had persuaded her husband to part with a house of which she was very fond. In this second will, Lord Bath's portion of the estate was bequeathed to Christopher Monck (1674–1701), who was the adopted son of the duke of Albemarle and thus assumed his father's name. The lawsuit between Bath and Monck is joined by Elizabeth Cavendish's second husband, the first duke Montagu (1638–1700) (Lord Crafty in *Rivella*), in 1691, and it lasted until 1698, when a compromise among the three parties was reached. Rivella acts as a mediator between Lord Crafty and Baron Meanwell.

3. For further discussion of the personal and the juridical, the private and the public, see Goodrich, *Law* (58).

4. For the concept of imaginary space, see Goodrich (citing Cornell, *Imaginary Domain*) in *Law* (61).

Nancy S. Marder

Law, Literature, and Feminism: Broadening the Canon with New Texts

For over a decade, I have taught a law school course entitled Law, Literature and Feminism. The course draws on cases, law review articles, newspaper articles, a short film, and four novels to trace the major developments in feminist legal theory and practice in the United States. The novels are Zora Neale Hurston's *Their Eyes Were Watching God*, Toni Morrison's *The Bluest Eye*, Gloria Naylor's *The Women of Brewster Place*, and Cristina García's *Dreaming in Cuban*. Each novel highlights a different development in feminist legal theory. Although cases and law review articles — the traditional readings in a law school course — chart this development, the four novels do so, quite memorably, from the perspectives of those who are outsiders to the legal system. The characters in these novels are outsiders on the basis of their gender, race, class, ethnicity, or sexual orientation. The novels, focusing on the most disadvantaged in society, provide powerful perspectives from which to explore and to understand major developments in feminist legal theory. They should become part of the traditional law and literature canon. These novels help law students think about how feminist theories and legal doctrines might play out among those who are the most vulnerable in society and who rarely have access to the protections of the law. Law students remember these novels long after the course has ended.

Early Proponents of Women's Equality

The first development in feminist legal theory in the United States grew out of struggles undertaken by proponents of women's equality. They argued that women should have the opportunity to perform the same jobs as men, whether as lawyers, laundry workers, or jurors. Cases such as *Bradwell v. State* (1873), *Muller v. Oregon* (1908), and *Hoyt v. Florida* (1961) chart this development. These cases are premised on equality, even though they do not always make an explicit equality argument. In *Bradwell*, Myra Bradwell argued that she should be admitted to the practice of law in Illinois because she had met all the qualifications that men had to meet. In *Muller*, the owner of a laundry, who was convicted of violating a state statute that limited the number of hours that female (but not male) employees could work, argued that such a statute violated an employee's right to contract. In *Hoyt*, Gwendolyn Hoyt, charged with the murder of her philandering husband, faced a jury consisting solely of male jurors. She argued that female jurors (who she thought would be more sympathetic to her situation) should not have to register affirmatively for jury service, as Florida then required, because Florida did not require male jurors to do so. In these early equality cases, the people making equality arguments were white middle-class women, or, as in *Muller*, a man who owned a business.

Their Eyes Were Watching God richly explores the demand for gender equality as Janie, a black woman, seeks equality in each of her marriages but finds it only in her third one. Only her third husband is willing to flout many of the conventions about men's and women's proper roles. Although the early cases discussed in my course explore equality for white women who are of the middle or working class, Hurston's novel explores equality for a black woman with little education and initially little money living in an all-black community in the South.

Janie's search for equality takes place through her marriages. Her first marriage to Logan Killicks was arranged by her grandmother, who viewed a husband as a means of protection and a source of property (30). Killicks viewed Janie much as he viewed his mule: they were both creatures who needed to be broken in and made to work (52). Janie escaped this marriage by running off with and marrying Jody Starks. Starks, a man of ideas and ambition, placed Janie on a pedestal (49). He "aimed tuh be uh big voice" (74) and became mayor of Eatonville, an all-black town; her role was to play the mayor's wife. Starks did not want others, including his wife, to express their own views (69). Although Janie stayed with Starks until his death, she had learned long before then to put aside her own thoughts because Starks did not want to hear any ideas other than his own (112).

Janie's third husband, Tea Cake, did not conform to Eatonville's idea of an appropriate husband, yet he provided Janie with a partnership that approached equality. The town had rejected Tea Cake as a suitor for her because he was young, poor, and transient, whereas Janie, by that point, was middle-aged and had status and property in the black community (169–70). However, she rejected the town's notion of an appropriate husband and married Tea Cake. He believed in her, even when she doubted herself. He taught her to play checkers, to fish, and to hunt so they could do these activities together. When they decided to seek their fortune in the Everglades, they eventually worked in the fields together during the day and prepared dinner together in the evening (199). The sharp demarcation between men's and women's roles that Janie had experienced in her other marriages vanished in her life with Tea Cake. Although their relationship had its dark moments (218), it was as close to an equal partnership as she could imagine. She never used the word *equality* but sought it intuitively in all her marriages and found it at last in her marriage to Tea Cake.

Tragically, Janie had to kill Tea Cake in self-defense, after he was bitten by a rabid dog. She appeared in court before an all-white, all-male jury to justify her actions in a highly abbreviated trial. She sensed that the courtroom setting and the legal procedures would not allow her to do justice to describing her relationship with Tea Cake. She would have preferred a jury that included women, even white women, because she thought that they were more likely than men to understand. Although the jurors acquitted her, they took only five minutes to deliberate. According to some in the black community, they acquitted her because she was an attractive black woman who had killed a black man.

Janie returned to Eatonville and told her story to Pheoby; in doing so, Janie explains it to the reader as well. She knew that Pheoby would be a sympathetic listener because they had "been kissin'-friends for twenty years" (19). Janie also taught Pheoby, who in turn will teach the rest of the town, the importance of having a marriage that is based on equality rather than property.

Equality or Special Treatment?

A second development in feminist legal theory arose from the commitment to fight for equality while grappling with the demand for special treatment. Arguments for equality succeeded in the courts, as exemplified by cases such as *Reed v. Reed* (1971) and *Frontiero v. Richardson* (1973), but they did not always succeed in the workplace. The equality cases of the 1970s were easy compared with the challenge presented by pregnant women in the workplace in cases brought in the 1980s. In *Reed*, for example, the United States Supreme Court held that the Idaho legislature's preference for men over women as administrators of estates merely to eliminate the need for additional hearings violated the equal protection clause of the Fourteenth Amendment (76). Similarly, in *Frontiero*, the Court held that the statutory requirement that a servicewoman had to show that her husband was dependent on her for over half his support in order to qualify for increased benefits, whereas a serviceman did not have to make such a showing as to his wife, violated the equal protection clause of the Fifth Amendment.

The conundrum for feminists was whether to pursue strict equality for pregnant women in the workplace so that they were treated as men who were temporarily disabled, as some legal academics, such as Wendy Williams and Ruth Bader Ginsburg, advocated, or whether to seek special treatment that accommodated the special needs of pregnant women in the workplace, as other legal academics, such as Linda Krieger and Patricia Cooney (Krieger and Cooney), urged.

One case that brought out this conflict among feminists was *California Federal Savings and Loan Assn. (Cal Fed) v. Guerra*. In this case, Lillian Garland took a pregnancy leave, and when she sought to return to her position as a receptionist at the bank, she was told it had already been filled. She argued that Cal Fed, her employer, had to reinstate her because there was a California statute that provided pregnant women with reinstatement. Cal Fed argued that the state statute violated the Pregnancy Discrimination Act (PDA), amending Title VII, because it provided different treatment in the workplace based on sex. Garland argued that the different treatment was designed to help rather than hurt women and to level the playing field so that women could compete in the workplace after years of discrimination, which is what Congress aimed to accomplish when it passed Title VII and amended it by the PDA.

Feminists were divided and submitted amicus briefs on both sides of the case. Equality proponents agreed with Cal Fed; special treatment proponents agreed with Garland. The Supreme Court sided with Garland, in that it upheld the validity of the California statute, but it also made use of the language of the strict equality proponents. The Court's opinion, written by Justice Thurgood Marshall, explained that the state statute, though providing preferential treatment for pregnant women in the workplace, was doing so not to be paternalistic, as earlier statutes had done, but to provide them with "equal employment opportunity" (289).

Once again, the theoretical debate (equality vs. special treatment) and the cases were based on middle-class women who held jobs in the workplace. What would happen if the focus were on the most marginalized in society? What would strict equality mean for a poor black girl? Morrison's *The Bluest Eye* focuses on Pecola, a young girl who is poor, black, and ugly (34–35) and who wants desperately to fit into the white world and to satisfy white norms of beauty. She does everything she can to transform herself. She drinks white milk from a Shirley Temple cup and stares longingly at the image of the cute Shirley Temple (22); she eats Mary Jane candies and feels momentary pleasure from the closeness of the image of a white Mary Jane (43). She hopes that white beauty can be absorbed by these actions. Finally, she goes to Soaphead Church, a charlatan who she hopes will provide her with the ultimate symbol of white beauty: blue eyes. In the end, she believes that she has been given blue eyes, but by this point she has gone mad. In her madness, she believes that others are ignoring her because they envy her blue eyes (151–52), not that they are ostracizing her because she was raped by her father and is carrying his child (147–48). Despite the crimes committed against Pecola, the law never affords her any of the protections it is supposed to provide to all citizens. She is among the most marginalized in society and beyond the protection of the law. Even the poor black community in which she lives has cast her off.

It may be that just as Pecola can never be beautiful according to white norms of beauty, pregnant women can never fit the norm of male workers in the workplace. *The Bluest Eye* illustrates, as few legal cases can, the conflict of wanting desperately to conform to the prevailing norm and the impossibility—including the physical impossibility—of doing so. Even as feminist writers such as Williams took the position that women and men should simply be considered "androgynous" workers in the workplace (363), as long as the workplace is designed for men rather than pregnant women, pregnant women will find it difficult to conform. Similarly, Pecola wants to be seen as beautiful in a white world but can never be seen in that way without white skin and blue eyes.

Dominance versus Difference

A third development among feminists arose in the 1980s from two competing theories: the difference theory of Carol Gilligan and the dominance theory of Catharine MacKinnon. In her groundbreaking book *In a Different Voice*, Gilligan interviewed women who faced a moral decision, such as whether to have an abortion (64–150). She recounted how they thought about and described their decision. She listened carefully to their language and found that they tended to focus on the ethics of care and responsibility (105, 126). In contrast, she noted that men and boys whom she interviewed in other studies tended to focus on hierarchy and rights (32). Gilligan was sensitive to the ways in which women spoke about their decision. She observed that women's approaches to moral reasoning did not fit neatly into the moral stages that had been defined by other psychologists because those psychologists had conducted their studies using only boys or men (18–19). By omitting women's experiences, they had defined human experience as male. Gilligan's book inspired academics in a number of fields, including law (Menkel-Meadow 39), to consider how women could contribute to their respective fields if their voices were heard and their approaches were incorporated.

One feminist who rejected this celebration of difference was MacKinnon. In her view, the voice celebrated as that of women was merely the voice of the victim. Until women had power, they could not speak in their own voice but only in the voice that men had left to them. Women were left with the voice of caring and compliance because that is what men valued in women. MacKinnon's approach, which she called dominance, focused on giving women power (40). In her view, the equality approach of the early feminists and the difference approach of Gilligan were variations on the same theme because each used men as the benchmark. Either women were to be treated the same as men under the equality approach, or they were to be appreciated for the ways in which they differed from men under the difference approach (36). According to either theory, women defined themselves in relation to men. Only the dominance approach focused on power. Only after women had secured power, so that they no longer had to live in fear of incest, rape, domestic violence, pornography, and other forms of male oppression (41), could they begin to define themselves and speak in their own voices (45).

MacKinnon's theory required recognizing that the world was constructed according to male dominance and female subordination. MacKinnon urged women to share their experiences with one another so that they could see that male domination was pervasive and systematic. Those women who thought they had avoided male domination suffered from false consciousness. If women engaged in consciousness-raising and shared their experiences of rape, incest, pornography, and other forms of male oppression, then they would find ways to challenge their subordination. The goal was for women to gain power so that they would no longer be subordinated. There was no guarantee that women would handle power any better than men, but at least they should have the opportunity to try.

Gilligan, unlike MacKinnon, did not believe that women were subordinated to men but that men had failed to listen to women, and therefore women's viewpoints, experiences, and perspectives had not been given sufficient attention—to the detriment of both men and women. Whereas MacKinnon argued for a shift in power—from men to women—even though there was no guarantee that women would handle power more responsibly than men, Gilligan believed in a transformation that would occur when men's and women's perspectives were incorporated into traditionally male-dominated fields. Like the young girl who wanted to play the game of neighbors and the young boy who wanted to play the game of pirates, when they combined their interests, they arrived at a new game of pirates who are neighbors (Marcus et al. 45). Gilligan holds out the hope of such a positive transformation in the future, whereas MacKinnon is far less sanguine.

Both Gilligan and MacKinnon recognized the importance of listening to women's experiences, but their theories led them in different directions. For Gilligan, women's experiences would transform fields that had traditionally been built on only men's point of view. A range of contributions would enrich these fields because they would reflect human experience. For MacKinnon, women's experiences would reveal male oppression. This was an important first step in challenging women's subordination. MacKinnon believed in listening to women's accounts of rape, incest, sexual harassment, and other forms of oppression. Until women could identify and put an end to every form of oppression, they would not be able to speak with an authentic, nonsubordinated voice. Only when men took "their foot off [women's] necks" could we "hear in what tongue women speak" (45).

Although these two theories of voice and power—difference and dominance—divided feminists into seemingly irreconcilable camps (Marcus et al. 75–76), Naylor's novel can be read as illustrating how these two theories could coexist. *The Women of Brewster Place* depicts a community of poor black women who illustrate MacKinnon's theory because they live in a world in which they are powerless; yet, the novel also illustrates Gilligan's theory because Naylor celebrates the characters' differences and perspectives.

The most obvious symbol of the women's powerlessness is the wall that divides Brewster Place from the rest of the community. The women of Brewster Place are cut off from commerce, jobs, and services available to the larger community. Again, the law does not enter their domain or provide them with even minimal protections. When one woman complains repeatedly to the police about the young men who loiter in the alley, smoke marijuana, and rob passersby, the police ignore her calls (140). The women live on a dead-end street, literally because it is separated from the rest of the community by a wall and figuratively because the women who live there have nowhere else to go (4). They have no resources other than the strength that they give to one another.

Although Naylor portrays these women as powerless, as MacKinnon would see them, she also celebrates their differences, as Gilligan would see them. Whereas MacKinnon would focus only on the women's powerlessness and poverty, Naylor also sees their rich diversity. Mattie is a homebody who was overprotective of her son (52); Etta Mae refuses to settle down and keeps looking for her next business opportunity, which she is sure will be a success (61); Sophie is a prying, narrow-minded homophobe (145); Theresa and Lorraine are a lesbian couple, one domineering and the other needy (134–35); and Ciel is a doting mother willing to have an abortion to hold on to an abusive boyfriend (95). Only Kiswana, who comes from a middle-class family, has a choice about living on Brewster Place. She stays because she wants to help the women to form a tenants' organization even though she is a dreamer and is often overwhelmed by living there (143). Although these women are poor and powerless, as MacKinnon would observe, they are also different from one another by dint of personality, attitude, and life experience, as Gilligan would note. Naylor weaves both strands into her novel and in doing so offers a rich and diverse portrayal of the women who live on Brewster Place.

Naylor highlights not only the diversity of these women but also the ways in which they support one another, bringing to life Gilligan's ethics of care and responsibility. For example, when Etta Mae returns late at night after having had sex with a minister who she thought was interested in marrying her but who only wanted a one-night stand, Mattie is there for her. Mattie has stayed up, awaiting her return. She has the light on in the apartment and Etta Mae's favorite blues playing in the background (74).

After the Antiessentialists

The next generation of feminists criticized MacKinnon and Gilligan for writing about women as if all women were white, middle-class, and heterosexual and for overlooking or obscuring all the ways in which women differed from one another by class, race, ethnicity, and sexual orientation. Writers such as Patricia Cain focused on a lesbian perspective because there were lessons to be learned from living in a community of women. Writers such as Angela Harris and Kimberle Crenshaw focused on the intersection of race and gender.

Crenshaw, for example, suggested that if one focused on the least advantaged and figured out how to raise their status, the status of all women would be raised. Crenshaw used the image of women in a house ("Demarginalizing" 151). The most disadvantaged women, who are poor and black, are standing in the basement. On their shoulders stand other women, who have more advantages by virtue of their race, class, or ethnicity. The women nearest to the hatch in the ceiling—from which they are able to escape from the basement and to enter the next level of the house—are white, upper-class, and educated. They most closely approximate men in the opportunities that they have.

Crenshaw criticized courts for the limited way in which plaintiffs seeking to bring discrimination claims are viewed (141–60). White women can bring claims of sex discrimination, and black men can bring claims of race discrimination, but when black women try to bring claims of sex and race discrimination, they are told they can bring one or the other but not both. Crenshaw argued that black women should not have to choose, because it is the intersection of race, gender, and other categories that affects how they are perceived and treated.

Crenshaw's shift in focus—from the most privileged to the most disadvantaged—is one that novelists can make more readily than judges or even writers of feminist theory. Judges look for broad categories and have trouble peeling away layers and offering more nuanced descriptions of plaintiffs or defendants as, for example, "black women" or "black lesbian women." Antiessentialists like Crenshaw and Harris are able to go further than judges and recognize that each person has multiple layers and should not be asked to choose one over another when all play a role in forming one's identity. The challenge posed by the antiessentialist critique is, Who can speak on behalf of women? Are women so divided by race, ethnicity, class, and sexual orientation, to name just a few categories, that the debate is at a standstill? Can women today speak only on behalf of themselves individually and whichever categories they personally represent? Do any commonalities in women's experience remain?

Although many of the writers of feminist theory seem to be stymied by the question of who can speak for all women without being labeled essentialist, novelists can portray myriad characters and show the ways that they differ from each other as well as the experiences they still have in common. García's *Dreaming in Cuban* offers the story of three generations of women. On one level, the women can all be described as Cuban or Cuban American, which is the level that the law would use, but in García's fictional world these women are deeply divided by temperament, political beliefs, and geography. Yet, as unlike one another as they are, they share experiences and connections that allow them occasionally to transcend, but not to obliterate, their differences.

Celia, the matriarch of the family, lives in Cuba and is devoted to the revolution. She idolizes Fidel Castro and has placed his photograph over that of her husband in frame that sits by her bed (217). She fulfills her patriotic duty by joining a brigade to cut sugar cane (44), by watching the horizon for Yankee invasions (3), and by serving as a judge in the local people's court (111–16). Her daughter, Lourdes, has emigrated to America and has taken her own daughter, Pilar, with her. Just as Celia is devoted to communism, Lourdes is committed to capitalism. Lourdes and her husband, Rufino, settled in New York City, where she opened a bakery, the Yankee Doodle Bakery, and thrived as an entrepreneur (73). Celia and Lourdes are at opposite ends of the political spectrum, and their political differences are heightened by their physical separation. Celia will not leave Cuba, even when her ailing husband, Jorge, goes to the United States for treatment (6), and Lourdes will not return to Cuba. Celia and Lourdes do not understand each other; so too Lourdes and Pilar do not understand each other (74). Whereas Lourdes has embraced all things American, Pilar aspires to be an artist and rebel and questions all things American. These women are separated by geographic distance, by ideologies, and by temperaments.

Yet across these chasms they manage to communicate in ways that magical realism permits. Celia is able to stay in touch with Pilar by speaking to her at night through her dreams. Celia has also written letters to a lost lover, none of which she has ever mailed, and she gives these letters to Pilar so that Pilar will understand Celia's passions and disappointments in life (235). Lourdes communicates with her father's spirit after her father,

Jorge, dies (73). As a spirit, Jorge confesses to Lourdes that he tried to break her mother's will and helps Lourdes to understand how hard Celia's life was so that Celia and Lourdes can be reconciled (195–97). Celia too sees a vision of her husband, Jorge, after he dies.

Although these three women are committed to different causes or pursuits—Celia to Castro, Lourdes to capitalism, and Pilar to painting—they all embrace them with great passion. Each is also a woman living in a world run by men, whether that world is Cuba or the United States. Lourdes was raped by a soldier in Cuba when Castro came to power (70–72). Only a few months earlier, she had lost the son she was carrying. She developed a deep-seated hatred for Castro's regime. Pilar, while walking in Central Park in New York City, was molested by a group of young boys (202). Celia was put into a mental institution by her husband because she still loved her Spanish lover (195). The law in this novel, as in *Brewster Place*, provides no protection to any of these women; they are left to respond on their own. Whereas Celia responded by never leaving her house by the beach and by writing letters that she never mailed, Lourdes and Pilar responded by taking journeys. Lourdes fled to America with her family, and Pilar traveled to Cuba with her mother.

Dreaming in Cuban points to the need for a long-term perspective and for recognizing that change comes about slowly and incrementally and may take several generations. The novel holds out the possibility of understanding but suggests that it may skip a generation. Celia and Lourdes do not reconcile, nor do Lourdes and Pilar ever see eye to eye, but Celia and Pilar do understand each other. Celia and Pilar intuitively grasp what the other needs even if each cannot always provide it for the other. Mothers and daughters have difficulty talking to each other, but grandmothers and granddaughters seem to have a special bond. There is hope for understanding across the generations.

All four of these novels illustrate significant developments in feminist legal theory. Their inclusion in the law and literature canon will help law students see how major developments in feminist legal theory affect those who are the most disadvantaged in society and whose needs are not addressed by courts.

The novels also can move law students in ways that cases and law review articles do not. A law school elective course that uses novels is likely to produce lively discussion. My students, most of whom are in their second or third year of law school—though there is an occasional graduate student in English literature or a foreign student pursuing a master's degree in law—must write four short papers in response to any of the course readings. These papers, submitted before class discussion of the readings, are ungraded. Their purpose is for students to write more freely about their reactions and to think more deeply about the readings in advance of the discussion. My goal in the course is for students to share their different perspectives with one another. At the end of the semester, their take-home exam is an essay, which they have a week or two to write. The essay requires thought and creativity but no outside research. The goal is for students to make connections among the novels and other course materials—cases, law review articles, and current newspaper and magazine articles—that were not made in class.

The novels challenge law students by introducing them to characters who are so marginalized that they are outside the protection of the law. A few students are a little overwhelmed by reading about characters who have so few opportunities and endure so many hardships. Most students, however, leave the course with greater empathy for those who are the most vulnerable in society. My hope is that they also leave the course with a commitment to using their legal skills to help those who are the most disadvantaged in society and most in need of the protection of the law.

Ravit Reichman

Neutrality in Law and Literature: Reading the Supreme Court with Joseph Conrad

Discussions of the connection between law and literature tend to approach the relation in complementary terms, viewing literary excess as a necessary addition to legal economy. As Martha Nussbaum (*Poetic Justice*) and others have suggested, literature edifies lawyers by teaching them how to feel—to sympathize or empathize. My courses on law and literature take a different tack: instead of seeing literature as helpful but ultimately secondary to law, they encourage students to consider how legal and literary texts make sense of similar emotions, ideas, situations, and people. One of the most productive ways to do this is through the concept of neutrality. Arguably the predominant legal attitude, neutrality appears as a mediating position through which to examine the legal-literary intersection. By discussing the notion of neutrality in legal and literary narratives, students come to think of it not just as an absence of feeling but as the site of competing claims, assumptions and desires in jurisprudence, literature, politics, and emotional life. With this in mind, my courses on law and literature ask students to relate two different texts on neutrality: the Supreme Court opinion *California v. Brown* (1987) and Joseph Conrad's story "The Tale" (1917). This essay provides a method and context for teaching these strikingly different texts together.

The task of relating the two narratives begins with the broader question of what neutrality is and how it functions in both legal and extralegal contexts. In its simplest iteration, neutrality figures as the purest and most widespread legal stance, one that modifies, moderates, and admits a range of emotions that, in and of themselves, are thought of as unfairly tilting the scales of justice. Other emotions appear in legal discourse, but when they do, they are necessarily tempered by a generous measure of neutrality; they are, in other words, neutralized. Thus vengeance, anger, fear, sympathy, or compassion goes through a process of neutralization in order to be rendered legally appropriate—and in order to be appropriated by law. This process, in *California v. Brown* and many opinions like it, asks individuals to sift through a messy emotional terrain, retaining only those feelings pertaining to a legal set of circumstances and discarding those that are extralegal—somewhat like panning for emotional gold.

Critics from across the disciplines—Thomas Kuhn, Ronald Dworkin, Hayden White, Stanley Fish (*Doing*), as well as a range of scholars in critical legal studies and critical race theory—have long understood neutrality to be little more than a cultural mirage, an impossibility and a pretense. Yet neutrality has yet to lose its hold as a juridical ideal: few among us want biased judges at the helm of our legal system. Even when we acknowledge the reality of judicial partisanship, we still expect our judges to appear neutral—a desire for the effect of neutrality that recalls the old axiom: it is not enough that justice be done; justice must be seen to be done. Pierre Bourdieu refers to this appearance as law's "neutralization effect," which he explains as the combined force of syntax such as passive and impersonal constructions, "designed to mark the impersonality of normative utterances and to establish the speaker as a universal subject, at once impartial and objective" ("Force" 820). Seen in this light, law's nonneutrality operates like an open secret, a truism best disregarded.

Neutrality's pride of place in jurisprudence has much to do with the way that emotions are often perceived in the legal system: as interferences and threats to the rule of law. Indeed, law and feeling are often imagined as adversaries. Writing against the commonplace that posits emotions as irrational distractions from the more grounded business of reason, Nussbaum proposes that emotions are, in fact, "intelligent responses to the perception of value" (*Upheavals* 1). Her contention, however, still tells us little about the complex course through which emotions are fitted in the contours of law. Neutrality offers a way to examine this process by illustrating how a feeling is made legally appropriate and how law appropriates emotion. What is adjudicated feeling? And what do we gain by trying—and failing—to feel neutral? The aim in reading *California v. Brown* alongside Conrad's "The Tale" is to arrive at a thick description of the cultural work that neutrality does, which means keeping the term as open as possible, recognizing its multiple contexts and harnessing its myriad valences.

California v. Brown

In 1986, a California jury found Albert Greenwood Brown, Jr., guilty of raping and murdering fifteen-year-old Susan J. During the penalty phase of the capital trial, the court advised the jury to consider the defendant's mitigating circumstances, cautioning jury members that they must not "be swayed by mere sentiment, conjecture, sympathy, passion, prejudice, public opinion or public feeling" (837). The jury sentenced Brown to death. On appeal, California's supreme court reversed the death sentence, maintaining that the jury instruction violated Brown's constitutional right to the sympathy factor. A year later, the case reached the Supreme Court, which had to consider whether the jury instruction violated the Eighth Amendment against cruel and unusual punishment or the Fourteenth Amendment guaranteeing due process under the law. In this case of life or death, the constitutional question hinged on the question of sympathy and specifically what it means to invoke sympathy in a criminal trial.

What one might imagine as an occasion to consider the place of emotions in the law, to weigh the rewards and risks of sympathetic judgment, became for the Rehnquist Court an exercise in semantics. The majority opinion, authored by William Rehnquist, reasoned as follows:

> By concentrating on the noun "sympathy," respondent ignores the crucial fact that the jury was instructed to avoid basing its decision on *mere* sympathy. Even a juror who insisted on focusing on this one phrase in the instruction would likely interpret the phrase as an admonition to ignore emotional responses that are not rooted in the aggravating and mitigating evidence introduced during the penalty phase. (840)

"[T]he noun 'sympathy,'" according to this logic, should be taken in its proper context—as a word modified by the adjective "mere" and embedded in a longer list of emotional states: conjecture, passion, prejudice, public opinion, and public feeling. Jurors who parse the instruction in this way will be able to discern "sympathy" from "mere sympathy." Convinced that a reasonable juror could not possibly understand the instructions in a way that would violate the Eighth and Fourteenth Amendments, the Supreme Court reversed the California supreme court's decision. Students, here, come to appreciate how the distinction that the trial court in California asked jurors to draw—which the Rehnquist Court ultimately upheld—amounted to a difference between law and life: between an ordinary feeling and a legal one. The trial court's commitment to neutrality does not amount to an insistence on emotionless judgment. Rather, *California v. Brown* suggests that neutrality is defined by the ability to tell the difference between two versions of the same emotion, one that is legally appropriate and one that is not. It is important, in this regard, that the Supreme Court opinion never in fact uses the word *neutrality*, even as the trial court's jury instructions outline a way to achieve it.

The majority opinion implies that the question of the relation between neutrality and feeling comes down to a question of reading: jurors are asked to be a certain kind of reader and to handle their emotions in a certain way. In addition to insisting that a reasonable juror (the only sort of juror that the Supreme Court admits) would understand the instruction not to rely on "mere sympathy" as a directive to weed out all sympathy not related to the case, the Supreme Court also maintains that to focus on sympathy alone would be to misread the court's instructions:

> We also think it highly unlikely that any *reasonable juror* would almost *perversely single out the word "sympathy"* from the other nouns which accompany it in the instruction: conjecture, passion, prejudice, public opinion, and public feeling. Reading the instruction as a whole, as we must, it is no more than a catalog of the kind of factors that could improperly influence a juror's decision to vote for or against the death penalty. The doctrine of noscitur a sociis [know it from its associates] is based on *common sense*, and a *rational juror* could hardly hear this instruction without concluding that it was meant to confine the jury's deliberations to considerations arising from the evidence presented, both aggravating and mitigating. (840; emphasis added)

In unpacking this passage, students tend to notice a vocabulary accruing around the notion of legal feeling, which emerges as a kind of subcategory of ordinary feeling and requires a particular kind of reader, the reasonable or rational juror: the law's version of a discerning reader—the sort of reader, indeed, students may themselves aspire to be. Legal feeling—something to take seriously but also to challenge—appears as reasonable, commonsensical, rational, as opposed to perverse and chaotic.

Unchecked emotion threatens to run wild, throwing impartial judgment off balance. To counter this tendency, legal feeling is actively fashioned through judicious reading and posited as the outcome of a process that neutralizes those parts of an emotion that would unfairly influence a sentence.

In a dissenting opinion, Justice William Brennan challenges the majority's ruling by responding in kind: if the Court insists on being technical, Brennan counters with his own painstaking exercise in semantics:

> In order for "mere" to be regarded as modifying "sympathy," as the Court contends, "mere" must be read to modify all the other terms in the instruction as well: conjecture, passion, prejudice, public opinion, or public feeling. By the Court's own logic, since "mere" serves to distinguish "tethered" from "untethered" sympathy, it also serves to distinguish "tethered" from "untethered" versions of all the other emotions listed. Yet surely no one could maintain, for instance, that some "tethered" form of prejudice relating to the case at hand could ever be appropriate in capital sentencing deliberations. (843)

One cannot but be struck by how much Brennan ends up sounding like a literary critic here. In a kind of reductio ad absurdum, he suggests that the jury instructions do indeed call for a suspension of sympathy, since it is inconceivable that the instruction could be interpreted as meaning that one should avoid using "mere prejudice" to judge, only legally appropriate prejudice. The more troubling problem, he maintains, arises when we assume that jury members would draw their emotional lines in the same way. An unanswerable question lies at the heart of his objection: How can we tell the difference between an emotion in its broadest sense and its legal variant? The range of answers generated by a class's discussion—and there is always a range—indicates just how thorny this problem can be and how generative it is of further questions: How can we be certain that one person's neutrality is the same as another's—or that a person who claims to be neutral is in fact neutral? Put differently, what does it mean not to be able to legislate emotions uniformly?

Conrad's "The Tale"

As Brennan's dissent points out, the majority opinion's sense of how sympathy can be distinguished from "mere sympathy" depends on a reading practice that assumes a stable and discrete binary between legally appropriate and legally inappropriate feeling. If *California v. Brown* illustrates the problem of neutrality in legal discourse, I want now to situate this problem in the historical context of war—that is, in a moment when neutrality is articulated explicitly as a nation's right not to be drawn into military conflict. I turn to Conrad's story "The Tale" to examine this position and also to illustrate how the study of literature can serve as a vital supplement to legal thought strictly conceived. Students are encouraged to think about what is at stake in this story: the tenability of neutrality; the difficulty, even the impossibility, of judging neutrally; and, finally, the absolute necessity of doing so nonetheless, even with the knowledge that one's actions may not yield a desirable—that is, a safe—outcome.

From a political standpoint, a nation's entitlement to keep its citizens out of harm's way—and the duty of belligerents to respect this decision—constitutes the rationale behind the sovereign right of neutrality. In approaching this right through Conrad's text, students may want to consider how an analogous right is claimed by writers: the sovereign right to literary neutrality. How is it possible to tell a story from a position of neutrality? What are the implications of invoking this right in narrative? And how can literature shed light on the experience of—as opposed to the declaration of—neutrality? In answering these questions, I look to "The Tale" as a narrative that grapples with the vicissitudes of neutrality in both its political and literary manifestations.

By reading "The Tale" as a story about the implications of neutrality in wartime, students engage it as a metanarrative about the role of storytelling as an extension of, or an analogy for, such neutrality. One of just two pieces that Conrad wrote during World War I, when he felt deeply conflicted about writing fiction in tragic times, "The Tale" betrays anxiety over the possibility of neutrality in both politics and stories. This anxiety is manifested not as a concern for how political bodies—nations or armies—assert a government's neutrality but as a story of how individuals negotiate the precariousness of taking or not taking a side.

The opening of "The Tale" is shot through with images of neutrality, beginning with its first sentence: "Outside the large single window the crepuscular light was dying out slowly in a great square gleam without colour, framed rigidly in the gathering shades of the room" (155). Neutrality proves the dominant feature of Conrad's story, from its generic title to the anonymity of its characters, including the man and woman who emerge from the shadowy room of the opening. In keeping with the narrative's overarching framework of generality, the nature of their relationship remains unspecified, although it is eventually revealed that the man is on five days' leave, and that the two were involved in some way before the war.

In this temporary, suspended time frame — at a distance from the war — the woman asks her lover to revive his talent for storytelling. He does so reluctantly, in the form of an allegory — "a tale not of this world" (158). The allegory is not terribly subtle. A British ship during wartime comes across a neutral ship in a cove. The neutral ship's captain, known only as the Northman, insists that his crew is lost. Despite a dense fog, the British Commanding Officer forces the Northman to leave the cove, giving him directions back to sea. These directions, however, prove disastrously wrong: the Northman's ship crashes, killing everyone on board. The Commanding Officer cannot answer the only question that would shed light on the incident: Was it in fact an enemy ship — in which case the English captain did the right thing? Or was the Northman telling the truth — that his crew was neutral and his vessel lost — in which case the English captain bears responsibility for the death of hundreds of innocent men?

That "The Tale" does not answer this question speaks to the fraught nature of political neutrality, which Conrad treats as a place neither here nor there, an indeterminate position that is grasped most meaningfully by depicting the collision between a nation's declared neutrality and the way that this declaration is experienced by individuals. But the individual experience unfolds from at least two perspectives. First, we can think of it as the treatment of neutrality from the subject position of the neutral individual: the Northman is a figure for any one of the neutral Scandinavian countries during the Great War. Second, we can approach the story as an examination of someone from a belligerent nation who is confronted with the difficult task of evaluating a claim of neutrality. Conrad's depiction of neutrality amounts ultimately to a practical problem of interpretation, a problem that must be solved in the context of individuals rather than nations or armies. The attempt at reading, understanding, and judging becomes painful and is often unsuccessful.

In Conrad's narrative, the sea proves a particularly apt place to think about these issues, not just because of its connection to submarine warfare but also because the conflict seems strangely distant on the ocean's glittering expanse. Unlike the brutal reality of the trenches, the narrator reflects, the sea "seemed to pretend that there was nothing the matter with the world" (167). In this context of incongruity, when what one sees does not correspond to what is, a stranger's words cannot be taken at face value. Like the surrounding waters, the Northman's story, from the English captain's perspective, must contain hidden depths. This submerged story, moreover, unfolds simultaneously with what the Northman says, making it impossible to believe — or, for that matter, to really hear — the account of his poverty, his family, and his anxiety about violating neutrality for financial gain.

> The Commanding Officer listened to the tale. It struck him as more plausible than simple truth is in the habit of being. But that, perhaps, was prejudice. All the time the Northman was speaking the Commanding officer had been aware of an inward voice, a grave murmur in the depth of his very own self, *telling another tale*, as if on purpose to keep alive in him his indignation and his anger with that baseness of greed or of mere outlook which lies often at the root of simple ideas.
> (188; emphasis added)

As one story begets another and the Northman's tale fuels the Commanding Officer's suspicion, it becomes increasingly harder to distinguish between truth and deception, neutrality and belligerence. Seized with the urgent need to decide, the Englishman orders the Northman to leave the cove. The choice proves disastrous: "That course would lead the Northman straight on a deadly ledge of rock. And the Commanding Officer gave it to him" (203).

Students may initially interpret this consequence as an illustration of the dangers of political neutrality. When pressed to apply this interpretation to the text's narrative structure, however, they tend to note how this straightforward political reading does not explain why Conrad cast the story as a framed tale. That is, the story of political or military neutrality ends with the shipwreck, but Conrad's text does not. After reporting the fate of the Northman's ship, the narrative takes one last turn and in the process questions literature's own neutrality. As the story draws to a close, the narrator reveals himself to be the Commanding Officer.

> He abandoned all pretence. "Yes, I gave that course to him. It seemed to me a supreme test. I believe — no, I don't believe. I don't know. At the time I was certain. They all went down; and I don't know whether I have done stern retribution — or murder; whether I have added to the corpses that litter the bed of the unreadable sea the bodies of men completely innocent or basely guilty. I don't know. I shall never know."
> (204)

The narrative frame collapses, exposing the story not as "a tale not of this world" but as the confession of a man haunted by the possibility — and indeterminacy—of his own guilt. Students might even connect the narrator and the Northman here: like the competing narrative of suspicion that unmoors the Northman's story of neutrality, the narrator's tale is undone by the parallel story of his complicity, which he had, until now, managed to conceal. "He abandoned all pretence": neutrality—like the sea that "seemed to pretend that there was nothing the matter with the world"—emerges here as a tragic form of self-deception that, even when exposed, yields no definitive answer. What the Commanding Officer saw as "a supreme test"—a trial of his intuition and of the Northman's neutrality—speaks to the wider test that Conrad's narrative stages. As a test in politics and literature, neutrality invariably fails, revealing its position as nothing more than pretense: a possibility in theory, but a catastrophe in practice.

Conrad's story also suggests something beyond this failure and self-deception of neutrality. As students discover when they discuss the emotional and psychological elements of the text, the narrator finds himself in an anguished state of not knowing. Neutrality in the California courtroom is a matter of distinction, of knowing one emotion from the other. Conrad, however, suggests that neutrality is about *not* being able to distinguish. This inability is experienced not as neutrality but as confusion, bewilderment, or agony.

The inconsolability of Conrad's narrator forms the unwritten story behind an opinion like *California v. Brown*. The subject of this anguish is, broadly speaking, any legal subject who may be asked to deny feeling in its widest sense and experience it only in its narrower, juridical incarnation—the juror, for example, who is asked to feel only a particular kind of sympathy. It is this sense of neutrality—not an absence of feeling but a state in which one does not know what one should feel—that disappears when we look only at the language of a legal opinion. What remains unseen is the life of feeling that exists in excess of this work of parsing appropriate and inappropriate emotions. Literature thus functions as a supplement to law, not because it adds to it in some ancillary way but because it offers a means of accessing the more complex, robust feelings beneath the surface of legal discourse.

Greg Pingree

How Rhetoric Shapes Cultural Legitimacy: Teaching Law Students the Moral Syllogism

What is healing, but a shift in perspective?
— Mark Doty, *Heaven's Coast: A Memoir*

Like many academics today, I have of necessity taught a variety of subjects (writing, rhetoric, literature, humanities, philosophy, and law) in a variety of institutional and disciplinary contexts (small colleges, universities, and law schools). Whatever and wherever I have taught, my study and teaching of texts have presented me with basic interpretive and epistemological tensions between legal and literary discourse—between legal hermeneutic ideals such as objectivity and neutrality, on the one hand, and humanistic (mainly postmodern) concerns such as the indeterminacy of language and the problem of autonomous subjectivity, on the other. From my varied pedagogical takes on this law-letters dichotomy, I have come to appreciate a rhetorical device that I consider crucial to the persuasiveness of texts and thus a worthy subject in the teaching of textual reading across disciplines: I call it the moral syllogism.

Identifying and analyzing this rhetorical device are especially useful in teaching law, because the moral syllogism is accessible to law students and illuminates their struggle to understand the basic thrust of judicial opinions, the complex, layered, often disjointed texts commonly used to teach them to "think like lawyers." Moreover, reading texts with the moral syllogism in mind helps upper-division law students gain perspective on the interpretive myopia of their first year, during which they are pushed to incorporate methodologically narrow and ideologically entrenched ways of reading texts. Thus in seminars like Jurisprudence, discussing how moral syllogisms operate—to shape texts and to drive textual purposes—provides a way for the law student to situate judicial opinions relative to other texts on a broad, interdisciplinary spectrum, an exercise in reading that helps demonstrate how acts of purposeful discourse are impelled, through rhetorical strategy, by a normative view of things. To teach this simple insight is profoundly worthwhile, for it enables students, by their own ascendant reading skills, to cross the conceptual border that separates merely inherited from thoughtfully chosen understandings of the hierarchical domain of law.[1] In essence, I teach the moral syllogism to demystify (though not to dishonor) the subject of law so that students can better grasp the rich paradox of high interpretive ideals and hard political realities that lies at the heart of American common-law jurisprudence.

In this essay, I discuss how I have taught law students in my Jurisprudence seminar to identify and analyze moral syllogisms in two kinds of texts that may seem to be pedagogically incongruous: judicial opinions and gay memoirs.[2] Judicial opinions, the meat and potatoes of legal education, operate according to ideals of reason and argument; gay memoirs, typically narratives of personal loss and identity struggle, operate according to conventional narrative devices such as concrete description, self-disclosure, and metaphor. Despite such obvious formal and methodological differences, both legal and literary texts can be read as rhetorical vehicles that rely on the moral syllogism to convey normative messages of real social consequence—moral visions of what constitutes cultural legitimacy, especially for traditionally marginalized individuals and groups.

To exemplify the pedagogical power of the moral syllogism, I consider two texts that address the subject of homosexuality, each according to a fundamentally different normative view of the cultural legitimacy of homosexuals: the Supreme Court majority opinion in *Bowers v. Hardwick* (1986) and the autobiographical essay "American Things" (1994), by the playwright Tony Kushner.[3]

First, I define my central concept. A moral syllogism is a version of the classic logical syllogism: a major premise, a minor premise, and a conclusion that must follow if the two premises have been accepted as accurate or true. (In many texts, including judicial opinions, moral syllogisms are conveyed enthymemically, one or both of the premises being implicit.) The term *moral* is arguably redundant, because all premises, even when presented as objectively factual assertions, carry some degree of normative direction. Yet precisely because all syllogisms lean in some moral direction, in that their normative assumptions imply something about right and wrong, I have found it useful to highlight and distinguish the foundational moral from the procedurally logical aspects of syllogisms. This ultimately artificial distinction helps make clear that all syllogisms contain one or more premises that make or rely on discernible value judgments.[4] That such value judgments are discernible does not mean that they are obvious to many readers, however. What in a judicial opinion often seems to be an unobjectionable premise will, by virtue of the limited scope of interpretive possibilities it establishes, lead with logical force to a particular moral conclusion. Most of the time, this rhetorical exercise of premise construction is manifest in how the court characterizes the "issue" of the case.

The most critical normative aspect of a judicial opinion, then, is not the conclusion or holding, which expresses the court's resolution of the matter before it, but rather the threshold decision of how the judge frames the basic issue, question, or problem to be addressed—the first among many rhetorical steps judges make in seeking to persuade their readers to accept a particular conclusion. This threshold step, however subtly or inconspicuously made, calls for our scrutiny if we are to understand the core thrust of the text. Indeed, we must determine the persuasiveness of this major premise. Is it what we might call fundamentalist—narrow and categorical in that it brooks no dissent and seeks only to reaffirm what it perceives to be the audience's established belief? Or is it what we might call literary—open-ended, presented as negotiable in the face of reasonable criticism, criticism that the authors themselves might acknowledge in order to strengthen the persuasiveness of their syllogism?[5]

In *Bowers*, the Supreme Court had to determine the constitutionality of a Georgia antisodomy statute, which was similar to antisodomy statutes on the books in roughly half the states at that time. Justice Byron White, authoring the majority opinion, deployed a moral syllogism to reach the conclusion that the Georgia statute was constitutionally permissible. White framed the *Bowers* opinion by adroitly precluding alternative threshold questions—alternative syllogistic premises—from the question on which he would base his reasoning:

This case does not require a judgment on whether laws against sodomy
between consenting adults in general, or between homosexuals in particular, are wise or desirable. It raises no question about the right or
propriety of state legislative decisions to repeal their laws that criminal-
ize homosexual sodomy, or of state-court decisions invalidating those
laws on state constitutional grounds. The issue presented is whether
the Federal Constitution confers a fundamental right upon homosexuals to engage in sodomy and hence invalidates the laws of the many
States that still make such conduct illegal and have done so for a very
long time. (190)

White reemphasized this threshold question in observing that "[p]recedent
aside, . . . respondent [Hardwick] would have us announce . . . a fundamental right to engage in homosexual sodomy" (191). Based on his own
announcement of the issue of the case, the major premise of White's moral
syllogism can be stated as a straightforward question: Does the Constitution provide homosexuals the fundamental right to engage in sodomy?

From here, White followed the logical momentum of this major premise. William Eskridge describes it as follows:

> *As narrowed in this way*, Hardwick's claim struck the Supreme Court
> as unlike those earlier privacy cases, which had arisen in the context of
> heterosexual intimacy. Key to the Court's analysis was its belief that
> the due process right of privacy could only be applied to protect those
> fundamental liberties "deeply rooted in this Nation's history and tradi-
> tion." Because "homosexual sodomy" had long been criminal in Anglo-
> American law, the Court held that there was no "deeply rooted" liberty
> Hardwick could claim. In the light of history, the Court majority found
> Hardwick's fundamental rights claim "at best, facetious." (150)

Eskridge identifies the minor premise of White's syllogism, which can be
stated in relation to the major premise like this: In order to enjoy the status of the fundamental constitutional right claimed here, the right must
protect behavior that is "deeply rooted in this Nation's history and tradition" (*Bowers* 192).

It takes little imagination to surmise what the Court's conclusion
would be to the question raised, in effect, by the combined premises of
Justice White's moral syllogism: Is consensual homosexual activity "deeply
rooted in this Nation's history and tradition"? It seems certain that in *no*
modern nation's "history and tradition" is homosexual activity "deeply
rooted." Accordingly, could the opinion logically proceed in any direction

other than it did, summarily concluding that private sex between consenting homosexual adults is not protected by the Constitution?

Justice White articulated another possible minor premise to accompany the presumably obvious requirement that the right claimed be "deeply rooted in this Nation's history and tradition." He reasoned that homosexual sodomy would have to be one of "those fundamental liberties that are 'implicit in the concept of ordered liberty,' such that 'neither liberty nor justice would exist if [they] were sacrificed'" (191–92; citing *Moore v. East Cleveland* [1977]). Although he quickly dispensed with this premise as well ("[i]t is obvious to us that neither of these formulations would extend a fundamental right to homosexuals to engage in acts of consensual sodomy" [192]), this latter formulation had the potential to produce a more literary, less fundamentalist analysis than its alternative (Scholes 219).

Unlike the "deeply rooted in . . . tradition" minor premise on which White actually relied (a premise that effectively deferred the constitutional question to the Judeo-Christian moral tradition), this "implicit in the concept of ordered liberty" formulation might have enabled him to leaven his judicial reasoning with greater nuance and thus to engage a broader audience. Indeed, the term "implicit in the concept of ordered liberty," combined with the admonition to consider whether "liberty" or "justice would exist if [the claimed right to engage in consensual homosexual sex] were sacrificed," would seem to open the discussion of homosexuality to a broad, culture-sensitive analysis. For example, "implicit in the concept of ordered liberty" is far more open to different and changing behavioral norms than is "deeply rooted in this Nation's history and tradition," which serves only to narrow the scope of analysis to the indisputable fact that the Judeo-Christian tradition has not, historically, been kind to homosexuals. Similarly, to ask whether "liberty" or "justice would exist" if the right of homosexuals to have private, consensual sex "were sacrificed" is a genuinely complex, open-ended question, at least for many in contemporary society. Thus both parts of this alternative premise would yield a more interpretively rich—and arguably a more socially legitimate—analysis of the behavior at issue in *Bowers* than the opinion itself demonstrates.

In the end, White's moral syllogism, certainly successful as a rhetorical strategy for affirming the mainstream view of homosexuality, yielded a remarkably narrow normative view of whether homosexuality could be culturally legitimate, for he resolved the controversy before the Court in a fundamentalist way, asking a seemingly neutral question from which only one answer could logically follow. His own pronouncement of the issue notwithstanding, he could have formulated other, more literary framing questions (i.e., major premises) or contemplated more culture- and context-sensitive minor premises and still have arrived at the same conclusion, but with the result that *Bowers* would have gained greater legitimacy, if not agreement, in both the legal community and the general population. This problem became increasingly clear in the light of the enduring criticism of the opinion (Eskridge 150), which culminated in *Lawrence v. Texas* (2003), in which the Court pointedly overruled *Bowers* (578).

Like White's majority opinion in *Bowers*, Kushner's autobiographical essay "American Things" conveys a normative message about the cultural legitimacy of homosexuals, though Kushner's rhetorical method is dramatically different from the exclusionary nature of White's syllogism. While the moral syllogism is perhaps more readily identified in *Bowers* because of the common role that logical constructions play in legal discourse, Kushner also forges one (albeit more sprawling and literary than White's narrow legal casuistry) by which to advance his message about the cultural legitimacy of homosexuals. White's syllogism proceeded from a fundamentalist major premise—that is, a rhetorical framing of the issue that invited no critical scrutiny and thus enabled the author to arrive at his conclusion with little or no interpretive friction. Kushner, by contrast, arrives at his conclusion in a literary fashion, by subverting—throwing wide open—the narrow but well-established normative premise that homosexuals, whether by deviant choice or inborn sickness, should be excluded from the legitimacy of mainstream American society.

Kushner achieves this subversion by transparently invoking a broad, inherently open-ended premise for his moral syllogism: that the American dream is founded on the idea of cultural inclusion. He illustrates this premise through a personal narrative that links the particularity of his childhood experience, the plight of homosexuals in our culture, and the American ideals that will legitimize his argument:

> On my seventh birthday, midsummer 1963, my mother decorated my cake with sparklers she'd saved from the Fourth of July. This, I thought, was extraordinary, fantastic, sparklers spitting and smoking, dangerous and beautiful atop my birthday cake. In one indelible, ecstatic instant my mother completed a circuit of identification for me, melding two iconographies, of self and liberty: of birthday cake, delicious confectionary emblem of maternal enthusiasm about my exis-

tence, which enthusiasm I shared; and of the nighttime fireworks of pyro-romantic Americana, fireworks-liberty-light which slashed across the evening sky, light which thrilled the heart, light which exclaimed loudly in the thick summer air, light which occasionally tore off fingers and burned houses, the fiery fierce explosive risky light of Independence, of Freedom.

Stonewall, the festival day of lesbian and gay liberation, is followed closely by the Fourth of July; they are exactly one summer week apart. The continuity of these two festivals of freedom is important, at least to me. Each adds piquancy and meaning to the other. In the years following my seventh birthday, I had lost some of my enthusiasm for my own existence, as most queer kids growing up in a hostile world will do. I'd certainly begun to realize how unenthusiastic others, even my parents, would be if they knew I was gay. Such joy in being alive as I can now lay claim to has been returned to me largely because of the successes of the political movement which began, more or less officially, twenty-five years ago on that June night in the Village. I've learned how absolutely essential to life freedom is.

Lesbian and gay freedom is the same freedom celebrated annually on the Fourth of July. Of this I have no doubt; my mother told me so, back in 1963, by putting sparklers on that cake. She couldn't have made her point more powerfully if she'd planted them on my head. Hers was a gesture we both understood, though at the time neither could have articulated it: "This fantastic fire is yours." Mothers and fathers should do that for their kids: give them fire, and link them proudly and durably to the world in which they live. (3–4)

Kushner here relies on an alchemy of deeply shared American ideals to draw together an audience (the American reading public) otherwise fractured by its views on homosexuality. Many Americans may recoil at the thought of two men holding hands, let alone kissing or having sex, but few would not relate to, and thus few would reject, the "two iconographies . . . of self and liberty" (3) that Kushner embeds in the image of a parent celebrating her child.[6]

By structuring his major premise in these ways, Kushner invites the reader to evaluate the larger moral syllogism that drives the memoir. (For example, does Kushner's personal narrative demonstrate, or at least persuade us seriously to consider, the premise that the American dream is anchored in the idea of cultural inclusion?) As a result, the ensuing steps of minor premise and conclusion will more likely be understood and accepted, if not embraced, for having been achieved by persuasion rather than by logical fiat (a loaded question asked and answered), as White's conclusion was in *Bowers*.

Joseph Singer, drawing on his experience teaching law students, has observed that the persuasion process turns on whether the speaker succeeds in moving the audience to recognize or discover common ground (e.g., shared values or experience) with a person or position that the audience initially does not support (2444). By recasting in personal and especially in patriotic terms the long-standing cultural premise that homosexuals are an undeserving minority, Kushner deploys two currencies in which, presumably, his audience is fluent: the universal currency of difficult personal experience in the struggle for identity and the currency of American patriotic values — freedom, autonomy, tolerance, and the prerequisite for those values, social and cultural inclusion. Creating such recognizable narrative currency has the effect of establishing common ground and thus opening avenues of persuasion (Singer 2444), of inviting, in this case, genuine narrative engagement in readers otherwise unfamiliar or uncomfortable with gay experience. This exercise in persuasion encourages his desired conclusion (that homosexuals deserve to be included in the American dream as much as anyone else) by eroding conventional barriers to public acceptance of, and cultural legitimacy for, homosexuals.

Kushner, the accomplished dramatist, knows how to put talent on stage and let it do its work. He invokes broadly appealing narratives of the American dream, then allows them to carry his argument forward. He has earned his conclusion, it seems to me, largely because he so persuasively marshals powerful, shared American identity metaphors to make what should seem, but is too seldom recognized as, a truly obvious patriotic argument for an equal place for gays in America. This argument is even stronger for its recognition, at least figuratively, of the real dangers and risks that come with accepting the major premise that legitimacy in America is about genuine inclusion in the fray of public discourse. Recall that the fireworks that thrilled the young Kushner with a sense of self-esteem and innate legitimacy "occasionally tore off fingers and burned houses, the fiery fierce explosive risky light of Independence, of Freedom" (4).

To teach law students that careful reading matters is not difficult; they learn quickly that their success depends on it. But to teach law students to read between the lines, with intertextual connections and interdisciplinary possibilities in mind, is more challenging, because legal education and the hierarchical system it serves imprint on their minds a kind of binary correctness: the overriding need to know the right rule, to identify the correct issue, to be on the winning side of the case. Yet law students must learn above all the process of advocacy, the success of which depends on much more than the copious memorization, the interpretive simplification, and the intellectual suffering that characterize the mythology of legal education. Indeed, successful advocacy requires creative thinking, rhetorical fluency, and sensitivity to the larger social and cultural implications of the case at hand. Thus law school is an excellent place to sophisticate one's reading capacity, not least because, in the face of a prevailing interpretive ethos that borders on hegemonic, it is a considerable accomplishment to learn to demystify judicial opinions and to situate them on a textual spectrum that includes all purposeful human discourse. Law does not happen in a vacuum, and learning to read for the moral syllogism enables students to discover or rediscover how and why law is part of a much larger world—and how law, for better or worse, plays a critical role in determining the legitimacy of those who live in that world.

Notes

1. The insight that law is political, more animated by dominant cultural values than it is constrained by neutral principles and impartial systemic standards, is not new, of course. In American jurisprudence, this paradigm shift began at least as far back as legal realism and has been foundational to critical legal studies, feminist legal theory, critical race theory, gay legal perspectives, postmodern legal theory, and cultural legal studies, to name some of the salient schools of thought that have emerged since the early twentieth century. Yet most contemporary law students arrive at law school without a clear understanding of—let alone an ability to articulate—this intuitively unassailable insight about the inherent relation that law bears to society, culture, politics, and so on. Hence the value of teaching reading methods that help students gain greater intellectual awareness of the contingent, embedded, and interdisciplinary nature of law.

2. For purposes of this discussion, I define *gay memoir* as any discursive attempt (including the standard book-length memoir, the essay, and the short story) to claim some kind of legitimate cultural identity for the gay author—and, more broadly and less uniformly, for the gay community.

3. As this discussion is meant to contribute fresh ideas to those who teach law and literature, I note here several other literary and judicial texts that address questions about homosexuality and are well suited to discussion of how moral syllogisms work to advance normative views regarding the cultural legitimacy of gay identity. Three pedagogically useful gay memoirs are Edmund White's "The Gay Philosopher," a seminal autobiographical essay and cultural critique written in 1969; Paul Monette's *Becoming a Man: Half a Life Story,* a book-length gay memoir and winner of the 1992 National Book Award; and Bernard Cooper's "A Hundred and One Ways to Cook Hamburger," a memoir in short story form

from his 1996 collection *Truth Serum: Memoirs.* Three Supreme Court cases that provide useful examples of the Court's varied approaches to homosexuality are *Romer v. Evans* (1996), ruling unconstitutional Colorado's Amendment 2, which sought to preclude gays and lesbians from the protection of antidiscrimination laws; *Boy Scouts of America v. Dale* (2000), determining that the Boy Scouts' decision to terminate a gay scout leader was constitutionally protected; and *Lawrence et al. v. Texas* (2003), in which the Court rejected *Bowers* and ruled that state laws criminalizing private, consensual homosexual sex were unconstitutional.

4. I often remind my students that law is a discipline more rhetorical than logical, in that legal rules and decisions depend on the enduring persuasiveness of the arguments that support them, arguments that in turn reflect social values and perceptions, the bases of all persuasion. (Among the values that drive these arguments are reverence for cultural tradition and deference to legal precedent, values that explain why many judicial opinions, like Justice White's in *Bowers*, are conservative rather than progressive.) Legal writers and readers do value the ideal of logical reasoning, but that ideal, like those of fairness, objectivity, consistency, and equality, is just one of many rhetorical means to persuade an audience. Were the law a purely logical system, like applied mathematics, then the same facts would always yield the same outcomes, a state of affairs that any trial lawyer knows does not exist. Because the facts are never exactly the same from case to case, the core work of judges is to decide in principled and thus legitimate ways how to draw meaningful distinctions and analogies — or, in the parlance of this essay, to decide how to frame the premises of the opinion's justifying syllogism or syllogisms in ways that both honor precedent and consider the realities of an ever-changing society.

5. For a fascinating discussion of this fundamentalist-literary dichotomy of reading, see Scholes 212–39.

6. "American Things" was first published in the 27 June 1994 issue of *Newsweek* magazine. Kushner, newly famous after the immense cultural impact of his two-part drama *Angels in America*, had been invited to write about the meaning of freedom on the occasion of the Fourth of July.

Nan Goodman

Roger Williams and the Law and Literature of Colonial New England

If it's fair to say that American authors like Herman Melville, James Fenimore Cooper, and Nathaniel Hawthorne have been favored by those working in the law and literature paradigm in recent years, it's equally fair to say that their predecessors—authors writing in the sixteenth through the early eighteenth centuries—have been the victims of sustained neglect. A quick survey of the scholarly monographs and college courses from the law and literature movement of the last fifteen to twenty years suggests that, with the exception of certain obvious texts like John Winthrop's "A Model of Christian Charity" (1630), the literary and legal connections of the early American period have been overlooked. Several reasons, familiar to literary scholars and historians of early America, present themselves—the earlier texts are less accessible to most readers; many have only recently come back into print—but a recent resurgence of literary and historical interest in the writings of the period makes these possibilities less than convincing (Clark).

In this essay I offer an explanation for the neglect of these earlier American texts and a remedy for it that finds its source not in the disciplines of literature or history but in the critical methodology of the law and literature movement itself. More specifically, through a reading of a number of works by Roger Williams, a seventeenth-century Puritan, I demonstrate that the interdisciplinary connections between law and literature in the early American period have remained unexamined because the reading practices that have come to dominate the field—largely as a result of its emphasis on later American authors—have blinded us to reading practices more appropriate to earlier authors. In particular, two assumptions central to these reading practices are to blame: that texts conducive to the law and literature approach share a thematic in which meaning revolves around the concept of the nation and that they share an aesthetic defined by a devotion to an abstract notion of the law and to classical notions of legal eloquence (Ferguson, *Law*).

Considered an upstart by most of his fellow Puritans, Williams took issue with many of the religious and secular shibboleths—about freedom of conscience, law, authority, and the appropriate treatment of the Indians—that governed the affairs of his day. Not surprisingly, his writings reveal the fragility of many of these standards and provide students with a revised understanding of how law and literature may have interacted in the New World. Through a number of his works, primarily *A Key into the Language of America* (1643), but also "Christenings Make Not Christians" (1645), *The Bloody Tenent of Persecution* (1643–44), "Mr. Cotton's Letter Examined and Answered" (1644), and *The Bloody Tenent Yet More Bloody* (1652), we can begin to see how an understanding of community that was in many ways far more complex than that of the nation served the early Americans as their theme and how a personal, as opposed to a public and classically informed, form of expression served for their aesthetic.

Written before the nation came into being, Williams's work rarely concerns itself with nation building, and yet the assumption that it, along with most texts from the colonial period, was protonationalist—that is, moving inexorably toward a notion of republican sovereignty—has been so widespread as to produce a disconnect between the reading practices commonly adopted by law and literature scholars and the textual evidence of the period. Far from being protonational, texts from the early period display a variety of theories about sovereignty—what several scholars have aptly called the period's "many legalities"—from a blind allegiance to the king, to a preference for church over state, to a belief in the primacy of an individual's private conscience (Tomlins and Mann). To set the stage for a reading of early American texts along these lines, one needs to make a rigorous effort to historicize and demythologize the period—to make it clear, for example, that the North American colonial settlements were divided by differing religious beliefs, degrees of affiliation to the mother country, and forms of ethnic creolization that suggest a society that was not nearly as homogeneous as we have been led to believe (M. Warner; Cressy). As they divest themselves of their preconceptions about the period, students come to a turning point in the realization that migration itself was not a one-way street, that for example some of the same people who traveled from England to New England traveled back again, claiming subject status and habitation in both places. Armed with these facts, students are able not only to revise their sense of colonial history but also to accept a more multifaceted conception of the law than a nationalist paradigm alone could provide.

Famous for challenging the religious constitution of the New England colonies, Williams's ideas are instrumental in complicating the nationalist paradigm, but his legacy alone does not do justice to the subtlety of his opinions. Only a close reading of his texts affords an accurate view. In "Christenings Make Not Christians" (1645; 7: 31–41), for example, Williams explains that it was not the censure leveled at him by the ministers that angered him; on the contrary, he believed that the ministers had every right to challenge him, even to excommunicate him, if it came to that. What irked him, rather, was the censure of the magistrates who according to Williams had no business involving themselves in church affairs. At the heart of this complaint were two related issues that were central to Williams's political and religious agenda: that the civil state was different from the church state and that the ministers of New England, in aligning the two, had misconstrued the nature of Christianity. In contrast to most ministers, Williams saw land, including the land of the New World colonies, as able to accommodate a diverse number of inhabitants. In keeping with this belief, he loathed the concept of Christendom, which held that where Christians lived was by definition a Christian place and, conversely, that everyone living in a Christian place was or should be a Christian. In fact, as soon as Christianity became associated with a specific place, which, Williams believed, occurred during the establishment of the Holy Roman Empire, it became impure. "Then began the great Mysterie of the Churches Wildernesse of National religion," he wrote, "and the World (under Constantine's dominion) to the most unchristian Christendom" (4: 442).

The tensions Williams saw in the nature of Christendom have their secular counterpart in his best-known work, *A Key into the Language of America*. In attending carefully to this text, students can begin to appreciate the ways in which Williams's antipathy toward the establishment of a Christian kingdom or nation carried over to his feelings about the colony itself. In *Key*, which is part English-Algonkian lexicon, part poetry, and part protoethnography, Williams calls into question the English seizure of Indian lands and the ostensibly protonationalist claims of the king.[1] Most famously, he writes:

> The Natives are very exact and punctual in the bounds of their Lands (even to a River or Brooke) & c. And I have known them make sale or bargain amongst themselves for a small piece, or quantity of Ground: notwithstanding a sinfull opinion amongst many that Christians have right to *Heathens* Lands. (1: 95)

From this statement we can infer that even if the Indians did not always fence in their land or cultivate it, they marked its boundaries in ways that were visible to those who wanted to see them. What is less apparent and yet far more important to a reading of Williams's work in the law and literature paradigm is that *Key*, too often read only in excerpts, offers an account of Indian property and personal relations that constitutes an alternative and viable form of nonnationalistic sovereignty.

Central to Williams's account of Indian sovereignty is his description of the Indians' language, which foregrounds the lexical aspects of *Key* and calls attention to the issue of translation, one of the most important and yet least understood conduits for legal and literary interaction in this period. Organized thematically around some of the ethnographic and cultural concerns of the Indians, like warfare and gaming, *Key* includes translations of relevant words and phrases—a kind of English-Algonkian Berlitz guide—that could be called on to facilitate communication between the two cultures. Although they occasionally mimic real speech (Williams called *Key* an "implicit dialogue" [29]), the phrases, if read in snatches, can seem disconnected, offering only rough equivalents between words that do not readily lend themselves to semantic coherence. Read as a whole, however, the lexical entries, arranged in facing columns, not only reveal certain cultural preoccupations but also tell stories about the Indian language and the process of oral communication.

To read these transcriptions, in fact, is to recognize the role played by oral language, another significant and yet completely overlooked aspect of the law and literature equation in the early American period. *Key* is a testament to Williams's understanding of the consequences of orality for the Indian and English notions of sovereignty and community (M. Cohen

92–98, 112–29). Specifically, through an emphasis on the figure of the Indian messenger who brings news to the various Indian communities, Williams gives voice to an alternative kind of community that is, though more provisional than that of the English community, also more vital. Entrusted with conveying crucial information about wars, peace, and trade, messengers, although they mediate communication between two parties who never come face to face, nevertheless compel face-to-face communication in the form of public assemblies. Williams notes how people gather at the first sign of their arrival. "Comming within a mile or two of the Court, or chiefe house," he writes, "he [the messenger] hollowes often and they that heare answer him untill by mutual hollering and answering hee is brought to the place of audience, whereby this meanes is gathered a great confluence of people to entertaine the newes" (60).

Although similar if far more erratic crowds were known to gather in Puritan towns when messengers, often bearing written communications, arrived, by the 1650s much of the population of English towns had dispersed to build houses and work farms that were increasingly distant from their metropolitan centers (Konig 49). The neighboring Indians, by contrast, though they moved frequently, tended to move in groups and continued to live in close proximity to one another; their public assemblies, not surprisingly, were long-lived and all-inclusive, and even the sick were sometimes brought out on makeshift beds to join the crowd. In the chapter "Of Discourse and News," Williams explains how a message from outside one community did not simply reinforce that community's parameters but also re-created it in another, admittedly contiguous, space:

> Obs. Their manner is upon any tidings to sit round double or treble or more, as their numbers be; I have seene neer a thousand a round, where English could not well neere halfe so many have sitten. (55)

That the English could and occasionally did assemble crowds of a thousand or more cannot be doubted, but when Williams says that the "English could not well neere . . . have sitten," he is not speaking of the Indian crowd's size but of their "manner" of sitting. Sitting in a "round," he seems to say, reconstitutes their community and links their presence on the land with their manner of speaking. When they assemble to hear a messenger, the Indians re-create a coherent space that is brought into being by speech.[2]

Key's depiction of the constitution of community through speech has consequences for both assumptions of the law and literature paradigm that have constrained the reading of early American texts. First, it figures as a way of complicating, perhaps even undoing, the thematic of the nation; it suggests the mutability, fragility, and intimacy of communities formed among the Indians and between the Indians and the early settlers, qualities normally not associated with the nation. Second, it rewrites the classical aesthetic. Seventeenth-century expression, among the different ethnic groups in the American colonies but also among the members of the white population, was not driven by the aesthetic common to writers in the eighteenth and nineteenth centuries, which assumed a single and uniform public sphere. Rather, documents intended for public consumption often contained a multitude of local, private, and personal expressions, examples of which are available in the carefully chosen translations in *Key*.

In this regard, *Key* is especially illuminating because it demonstrates the importance to early America not only of the provisional and personalized communication achievable only through speech but also of additional forms of oral and written expression. Alongside its lexical transcriptions, for example, *Key* includes poetry, protoethnographic description, and the occasional adage. Not surprisingly, scholars of *Key* typically examine its different forms of expression in isolation, but it is the generic diversity of the volume that contributes to our revised understanding of the aesthetic practices that drove legal and literary expression in the early period.[3] In mixing genres, in other words, Williams seems to reenact on a written level what he admires in the Indians' orality—their appeal to different audiences and to the composition of mixed communities on the basis of that appeal.

But if the shifting genres of *Key* hint at the emphasis Williams placed on tailoring forms of public address for the benefit of certain private audiences, his protracted pamphlet war with John Cotton brings that emphasis into focus. In *The Bloody Tenent* and *The Bloody Tenent Yet More Bloody*, he not only displays multiple sorts of eloquence but also invites an understanding of a public sphere that is rooted in a variety of individual experiences and rhetorical expressions.

The pamphlet war between Williams and Cotton concerned two interrelated issues: whether clerical or civil authorities had the right to persecute others for their thoughts and whether Williams should have been banished for raising that question among others.[4] Williams's basic position about persecution stemmed from his belief that the Christian church, in order to flourish, needed to allow dissent. This belief he took from Bible passages and from the history of the apostolic church in which different

Christian sects coexisted peacefully. His position on his banishment from the Massachusetts Bay Colony derived from his further conviction that even if he had committed a sin in advocating religious freedom—a point he did not concede—it was a religious offense for which he should have suffered a religious, not a civil, penalty. Cotton, by contrast, argued that the church had the right to impose its own sanctions for heresy and that Williams had unfairly skewed the biblical and historical evidence in his favor. More to the point, he argued that in Williams's case banishment was imposed not for a religious offense but for aggressively—that is to say, repeatedly, even after he had been admonished not to do so (*actum agere*)—publishing his opinions in such a way as to breach what Puritans often called the civil peace.

Williams, not surprisingly, denied both the religious and the civil charge; he argued that his opinions, though strong, were not expressed aggressively. The written record, however, which includes a host of provocative metaphors and personal accusations, suggests otherwise. A surrogate for the trial he never had, *The Bloody Tenent, The Bloody Tenent Yet More Bloody*, as well as "Mr. Cotton's Letter Examined and Answered," recall and counter each of Cotton's points and insist at every turn that Cotton not only take personal responsibility for his banishment but also understand the gravity of the punishment as if it had been meted out to him instead. "I conceive Mr. Cotton himself," Williams wrote, "were he seated in Old England againe, would not count it a mercy to be banished from the civil state" (1: 54 ["Mr. Cotton's Letter Lately Printed"]). More telling still are the countless occasions on which Williams does not appeal to logic to refute Cotton's accusations against him but asks rather that Cotton view his personal experience of banishment as sufficient proof of his good intentions. "But how could I possibly be ignorant (as he seemeth to charge me)," he writes of Cotton, "of [his parishioners'] state . . . when [I] suffered for such admonitions to them, the miserie of a Winters Banishment amongst the Barbarians" (1: 371).

If these statements reveal the kind of relentlessness that we associate with an aggressive writing style, they point even more significantly to an aggressive orientation toward writing as a whole. For Williams, written and spoken expression was intended as a way not merely to air his opinions but also to change the opinions of others. With this belief, he urged a redefinition of justice, one that stemmed not from some positive or predetermined legal authority but from the intersubjective expression of two or more individuals. Put another way, for Williams the public sphere was the result of an individual's sense of obligation not to an abstract notion of the law, a view promoted commonly in the late eighteenth and nineteenth centuries, but to the discursive production of that obligation, a view espoused by several seventeenth-century political philosophers (Grotius; Pufendorf). That Williams wished to ground the public sphere—the sphere in which his ostensible crimes against the state received their airing—in the idiosyncracies of his personal expression and personal experience also suggests how inextricable literary and legal aesthetics were for him. Writing was a matter of speaking publicly and privately at the same time and not, as is true of the law and literature paradigm applied to nineteenth-century texts, a matter of private individuals adopting a public voice.

The crucial component of this rhetorical operation was Williams's extension of private subjectivity to others, including Cotton. In statements that invite, sometimes beg, Cotton to put himself in Williams's shoes, Williams reveals how committed he was to turning his private experience into a communal or public one. "Had his soul been in my soul's case," he writes, "exposed to the miseries, poverties, necessities, wants, debts, hardships of sea and land, in a banished condition, he would, I presume, reach forth a more merciful cordial to the afflicted" (3: xxiv [*Bloody Tenent of Persecution*]). He makes clear here that his interest is in demonstrating a parity of words not only between people of different cultures, as was evident in *Key*, but also between people in the same culture who had assumed different subject positions. Banishment was not only unjust; it was also inappropriate, because it prevented people who held different opinions from living in the same community. Although he had removed himself from much of his society, by separating from a church he deemed impure, Williams did not consider himself severed entirely until he was banished. From a position outside the community, he is afforded a unique opportunity to argue for his reassimilation and for the reconstitution of the community as one that does not impose a notion of law on its inhabitants but grounds it in their diverse views. To this end he asks Cotton to consider his banishment as if Cotton himself had been banished and to read William's words as if Cotton had written them, making literary expression a source for a variable and responsive law—one that students can begin to associate with the early American period.

Notes

1. In a work now lost to us, Williams explicitly took issue with the legitimacy of the patent the king had granted to the Massachusetts Bay Company to

authorize their New World settlement. For Williams, the central problem was the patent's claim that the English might take as their own land that had not been worked up or fenced in by the Indians, of which there was, it was argued, an abundance (Leavenworth; Banner). That Williams's counterposition and the document he wrote in support of it were considered a direct threat to the constitution of the colony as a sovereign entity can be seen by some of his contemporaries' claims that "treason might lurk there" (Merriman 82).

2. This sitting "round" may also be linked to the Indians' preference for decision making by consensus. For a discussion of the political organization of northeastern tribes, see Bragdon 48–49.

3. For an examination of Williams's poetry in *Key*, for example, see Schweitzer 181–229.

4. See Cotton's "Letter of Mr. John Cotton" in volume 1 of Williams's *Complete Works*, "John Cotton's Answer to Roger Williams" in volume 2, and Cotton's *Bloody Tenent Washed and Made White in the Blood of the Lamb*.

Linda Myrsiades

Sangrado and the Cloven Foot: A Case in Teaching Eighteenth-Century Law

This essay describes a project in teaching law and literature through the interfaces of rhetoric, narrative, and culture. Teaching law and literature means that we accept that law begins and ends with a text. Law emerges from a culture, and it creates a text that informs that culture, the culture itself operating as a text, albeit written and read on a considerably larger scale. Interpreting its culture, law provides a text that must itself be interpreted. In the texts created by the law, narratives are embedded and perspectives maintained. At the same time, the culture of discourse enacted through law's rhetoric creates a community in the law as well as expresses a relation with communities outside the law. It is this series of recursive understandings that I share with students to disrupt their initial understanding of the law in isolation and to prod them to a recognition of how to place law in a more fluid, interactive, and complex context.

The Case

During the 1797 yellow fever epidemic in Philadelphia, William Cobbett, an English journalist, attacked Benjamin Rush, a prominent Philadelphia physician, and his followers for their practice of extreme, or heroic, bloodletting. Cobbett entered a controversy over treatments for yellow fever that had engaged the entire medical community and led to doctors' wars that compromised both medical authority and the confidence of the public in the medical profession. Cobbett was charged with libel by Rush in October 1797 but was not brought to trial until December 1799, two years and two months later.

Several backstories spun the *Rush v. Cobbett* libel trial, appearing in satire, poetry, and novels—among which were poetry by Philip Freneau on the Rush-Cobbett dispute; incendiary satires and poetry by Cobbett in his newspapers *Porcupine's Gazette* and *Rush-Light;* and a novel by Alain Rene LeSage, *Adventures of Gil Blas of Santillanes*, featuring the infamous bleeder Sangrado. That context, its rhetoric and narratives, affected public perceptions about the trial, tainted the jury pool, seeded arguments made by lawyers on both sides in the trial, and structured the way in which subsequent generations would think not only about the actors and issues that made up the trial but also about medicine and law in general and their place in eighteenth-century society.

Teaching

The material of this project is taught most fruitfully at the level of upper-class undergraduates, master's students, or entry-level law school students. Teaching it requires some sophistication on the part of students in analysis and the ability to work with primary sources, a complex cultural context, and an interdisciplinary methodology. Students would profit most from narrative, rhetorical, and cultural approaches before they become focused on a professional course of training that is narrowly disciplinary.

Teaching from primary sources—the trial report and period case law, novels, poetry, the defendant's newspaper publications, and the plaintiff's medical reports and medical school lectures—is an effective way to immerse students in the issues and period. Not only do the life of the times and the choices made by each of the trial participants—the judge, jury, plaintiff, defendant, the legal teams, and the courtroom crowd—come alive for the student, but students are also able to gain hands-on familiarity with period materials that are accessible in microform and on Web sites.[1]

My experience teaching this material comes from an English department undergraduate senior seminar. Students responded to a questionnaire at the end of the seminar to assess the pedagogy. They compared the seminar with ways of teaching and learning they had experienced in other classes; located it in the frame of the teacher-scholar model; and described their growth in the use of period sources, in interdisciplinary study, and in an understanding of law and medicine. At first they were shell-shocked by having to work with primary legal and medical reports, with no background in either field; by having to work with eighteenth-century sources (although they had considerable experience with textual analysis); and by having to apply an interdisciplinary methodology. Halfway through the semester they learned to become interdisciplinary by doing it, a task they found less daunting than Stanley Fish's warning "being interdisciplinary is so very hard to do" would suggest (*There's No Such Thing* 231–42). The medicolegal leap took them until the end of the semester and was never fully made, despite valiant efforts at mimicking the language and attitudes of the professions of medicine and law. They were most impressed by the teacher-scholar model: being treated in their research efforts as peers while the instructor, who embraced the role of a student in the field, encouraged them to strive for excellence. They also felt like independent scholars, from accessing primary materials before they were introduced to secondary materials. This excercise made them more critical of scholarly sources and inclined to developing their own positions on issues.

Student Interface with the Material

Freneau, Cobbett, and LeSage each present a picture of eighteenth-century medicine that involves at least three areas of law: freedom of the press, libel, and medical malpractice. Whether through satire, doggerel, or literature with aesthetic value, they provide expressive evidence of issues that arose related to the trial as reflections of middle-class values or popular perceptions.

But culture is both performative and interactive: it enacts, interferes, and embeds itself in a totality of events that operate as a single piece, all functioning in relation to one another to create a ground from which a figure emerges. Context is thus a text made up of texts, which not only can be read but also can read and write one another. In my teaching, therefore, literature is an active presence, interrupting the law, interrogating it, constituting it. Freneau's poetry and Cobbett's poetry and satires are not intended to provide amusement to their readers; they are constructions intended to change a culture's course. They are partisan players, agents of change, not as propaganda pieces but as positions taken in a gestalt that acts like a magnetic field in which each bit exerts a force on every other (see Bourdieu, *Outline*; Lyotard).

In the trial text, we find a comparable field of elements in interplay. Medicine and law are imbued with stories, rhetoric, and imagery; with themes of character and party; with frames of good and evil; with the contest between citizen and alien. Questions of libel are subsumed in morality and politics, so that cultural context trumps legal text in the jury verdict. This is a vision of the law that students find troubling. It disrupts their notions of fairness, justice, order, and legitimacy, their allegiance to legal doctrine, standards, and tests. It raises the prospect that law is not rule-based but malleable, not determinative but negotiable. The message in *Rush v. Cobbett* is not one that students anticipate, and it makes them doubt either the messenger or the profession. In any case, it does not leave them where they were when they enrolled for the seminar.

They have discovered not only that there are narratives embedded in the trial but also that the trial itself is a narrative. It tells the story of Cobbett—at the leading edge of doctors' wars, press commentary, and literary expression—flailing Rush in the press, a venue in which victim refuses to engage tormentor, just as Cobbett is later advised to flee the venue of the court. Cobbett uses the press to publicize the conflict and bring in outside allies. Rush's strong suit lies in using the court to control the conflict, preventing news of an assault on his reputation from getting out. Rush plays according to a strict set of insider rules. For Cobbett to win, the social norms of feuds and the open marketplace of ideas that privileges freedom of speech must prevail. For Rush to win, the closed court, professional voices, and formal rules must prevail. The alien foreigner profits from the former, the local son from the latter. Opposed in a contest of values that is magnified in the trial to threaten the very welfare of society, the satanic outlier must be marginalized and the citizen savior centered. If not, society, represented by the sitting jury, will be put at risk.

Where the press is figured as an exogenous force, the court will circle its wagons around its endogenous own. But the voice of the press cannot be silenced; it infiltrates the court both in the evidence of libel that is presented and in the legal rhetoric designed to ward off the poisons spewed by the press. The press in the marketplace plays out its own version of lawfulness and order. It champions those not given effective representation in the court, and it gives social conflict an outlet. When it inserts itself in the domain of the court, however, the press must conform to rules-based order of the type imposed by formal law. Shackled in a foreign terrain, it finds that the libel charge against Cobbett is played out anew, this time as a protected counterlibel: Rush can in effect publish his views without being called a quack, and slander can be spoken with impunity in Rush's defense.

The Culture

Cobbett's most memorable tactic in the dispute with Rush was to associate the physician with Sangrado, a figure that appeared in *Adventures of Gil Blas*—an inspired conflating of the medicine in LeSage's wildly popular novel with the yellow fever epidemic under whose conditions Rush practiced. The term *Sangrado* conjured up images of a quack bleeder responsible for the deaths of so many patients that his apprentice, Gil Blas, remarks that "in no less than six weeks we made more widows and orphans than the siege of Troy. By the number of burials, one would have thought that the plague was in Valladoid" (72). Under the pretext of amusing Rush and his student Dr. Caldwell, Cobbett provides an excerpt from Sangrado's apprentice in which the apprentice protests that he has followed his mentor's practice faithfully: "yet, nevertheless, *every one of my patients leaves me in the lurch*. It looks as if they took a pleasure in dying, thereby to bring our practice into discredit" (Cobbett, "To Drs. Rush").

The journalist-poet Freneau frames the Rush-Cobbett dispute in the medical confusion of the doctors' wars over bloodletting during the epidemic. He directs his caustic wit to Cobbett's claim that "lancet and calomel," the cures administered by Rush, rather than the epidemic, "slaughtered thousands." The blackguard Peter Porcupine, editor of *Porcupine's Gazette*, is advised to join the fallen hosts and subscribe to Doctor Rush's system to preserve Philadelphia from "the future exercise of canes." Adverting to the social norms of feuds and duels resorted to by physicians of the period, Freneau recalls in effect the attempt of Rush's son John to avenge the newspaper attacks on his father. The poet has a surer "cure": death, Freneau counsels, resolves both the physician's excess and the journalist's attacks, for "[n]o Doctor bleeds a man—when dead" ("To Peter Porcupine"; cf. Cobbett, "A Hard Case").

Deflecting accusations that his is a party press, Freneau is just as hard on the bleeders as on Cobbett. The warring physicians of Freneau's world are "a ghastley crew," "troops of butcher boys," each physicians defending his own whim "as if contending for a prize." The physician observed by the semiconscious patient is named "doctor Devil," and when one proposes a "cure by calomel" another "[s]wears 'tis the nearest road to hell." "Poor Florio," the patient, "frets,—as well he may," crying out, "Dear doctors! let me die in peace," and begging, "doctors! doctors! do not fight" ("No. XII"). Freneau plays on the providential explanations of yellow fever sermons justifying the plague as the "scourge of God" by reframing the archetypal struggle of God and Satan over the souls of the dying as a battle between patient and doctor in the secular world of Hamlet's soliloquy:

> And the angel Michael disputed with the Devil about the
> Body of Moses. *Ancient History.*
> To bleed or not to bleed—that is the question!
> Whether tis better in our beds to suffer
> The slights and snufflings of outrageous doctors,
> Or, by the *Lancet*—quit them. ("Book")

The debate over bleeding did not occur in a vacuum. This was a time of home medicine, when folk healers and herbalists were prevalent among practitioners, when ads for quacks and nostrums were widely publicized in handbills and newspapers, when home remedy books and medical manuals for the common people sold widely, and when doctors' squabbles appeared routinely in newspapers. Wading into the midst of the turmoil, Cobbett published a serial tale of bloodletting (*Porcupine's Works* 7: 164–65, 194–96, 201–03) that was later entered into evidence at the *Rush v. Cobbett* trial. Two characters, a tavern keeper and a hostler, are inspired by "the soporific essays with which our scribbling physicians and their hopeful pupils have so generously favoured the public" (164). The tavern keeper proposes to turn bleeder, a reasonable step inasmuch as medicine has become no more than a business. Reductionist thinking has simplified its practice, and disease has become a question of supply and demand, with considerable room for consumer choice. Providence appears to have provided an increased demand in the bleeding field, and the present shortage of bleeders offers the tavern keeper an opening. The epidemic may well have been pictured by divines as punishment for people's profligacy, but it also is an opportunity that the tavern keeper, and later the hostler, is prepared to exploit.

Capitalizing on the reciprocal relation of fiction and fact, Cobbett's tavern keepers are like Rush, who published instructions to the public "to take *his mercurial purges*" but without advertising a vendor, for they "may now be had with suitable directions at most of the apothecaries" (*Porcupine's Works* 11: 311).[2] The owners decide not to announce the taverns in which compounds may be had, for "[t]he superior merit of some, who sell stale porter, dead cider, etc. will be soon discovered by their respective patients." Readying his horse and carriage, the tavern keeper paints on its side the sign of a French hostler, "whose merits and *sang froid* in the use of the lancet, are, I believe, unrivalled; for I believe he was an *eleve* of Robespierre's." Cobbett thereby identifies bleeding with republicanism and the excesses of the French Revolution, even as he recalls his own ribbing of the bleeder Dr. Leib, who rose "from the dirt, into a one horse chair!" amid competition for horses and carriages that were "not to be got for certificates" (7: 185; see also Cobbett, "Equipage"). Paralleling Rush's training of poor black assistants to bleed his patients and subsequent charges that the assistants had charged excessive fees and pillaged property, the tavern keeper has hired nurses who "will never desert their patients, as I have engaged to supply them constantly with excellent gin; and have also promised them the pillage of such of my patients as may be determined to die" (196). In a reflection on doctors' feuds and scribblers' wars, the tavern keeper is disappointed that his hostler has deserted him to enter the medical wars himself, having become infected with the Latin disease "*cacoethes scribendi*" (an "incurable itch to write" [195]). The lack of licensing and regulation and the prevalence of quack practitioners will nevertheless keep both men in business, as will the ability to bury their mistakes; indeed, of all trades, the tavern keeper offers, "I prefer that of the lancet, because you know, Mr. P[orcupine], that *dead men never tell tales*" (195).

Cobbett's press attacks both preceded and succeeded the trial. Before the trial, they provided a socially validated venue to address conflicts that the law was not involved with or that the law had failed to resolve. The press here risked provoking the very disorder it intended to avoid, because its attacks were inflammatory and could influence participants in the court proceedings. After the trial, the press gave Cobbett the defense he felt he had been deprived of and retried the case before the public, whose verdict he considered of greater value than that of the court. Following the judgment against him for the then exorbitant sum of $5,000, he published the newspaper *Rush-Light,* in which he considered trial evidence, testimony, legal arguments, political bias, and the judge's charge to the jury. He expressed his disdain for American lawyers (the prosecutors Jared Ingersol and Joseph Hopkinson) and judges,[3] the American legal process, and the jury verdict delivered against him. Turning to a tragedy scene to argue his case before readers to whom metaphor constituted a higher form of un-

derstanding than legal talk, Cobbett transformed his defense into a soliloquy and has Sangrado speak it:

> Why for thyself construct the fun'ral fire?
> What though an Ingersol before thee stood,
> With dangling brush, to paint thee fair and good;
> A weeping Hopkinson, dear tender creature,
> Sobbing to wail the injuries of Nature;
> What though kind-hearted jurors press'd thee round,
> And philanthropic judges too were found;
> What though the gentle, just, and gen'rous crowd
> The verdict sanction'd with applauses loud. . . .
>
> (*Porcupine's Works* 11: 385–86)

In "Porcupine's Revenge" (11: 385), Cobbett has Rush intimate that
the jury was in his pocket all along;[4] Rush seeks advice from Porcupine on
how to reward "my twelve sov'reign men . . . now I no longer need them. . . ."
Porcupine counsels him, "Why bleed them, Rush, bleed them." The other
players in the trial should be rewarded as well: the judge, Rush's legal
team, even Cobbett's "[f]aithful counsel" (385), and the self-interested
physicians who "volunteered" to testify for Rush are all to be rewarded as
well: "Why *purge* them, Rush, *purge them*" (385).[5] In Cobbett's construction, the judge was a "[b]uffle-headed" rascal, the jury "a set of perjured
scoundrels" (*Letters* 35), the crowd in the court "base miscreants" who
hissed when defense counsel spoke (*Porcupine's Works* 11: 374, 383), and
the whole proceedings rife with "flagrant partiality" and "barefaced illegality" (*Letters* 25). The court, like the press, undermined order, in this
case the legal order supposed to rein in feuds, mob actions, and duels.

Framing the Trial

Cobbett's trial by press was met by Rush's legal team in court with a
counternarrative that reads like a political tract, a sermon, and a moral tale
rolled into one. The Rush story is in many ways the final act of the yellow
fever epidemic of 1793, an act in all its permutations—political, medical,
religious, social, and legal. It is also an archetypal narrative of the battle of
good and evil. Barely touching on the evidence and testimony on which
Cobbett was actually prosecuted, Rush's lawyers enacted each of Rush's
roles: father and husband in defense of home and family, physician-savior
in defense of neighbor and community, patriot and republican in defense
of country.

In line with the performative cast of the trial, Cobbett considered the role played by "the zealous Hopkinson," Rush's lead lawyer, to be "rare sport." Citing his adversary's depiction of Rush as one who *"in the service of his country . . . has added a fresh and blooming laurel to the head of American genius,"* he expresses surprise that Hopkinson did not carry laurel under his arm and brandish it before the jury (*Porcupine's Works* 11: 239). In Cobbett's construction, the trial is very much a tale of the death of a tyrant. Hopkinson mirrors Mark Antony's resurrection of the great Caesar (Rush) cut down at his height, this "ambitious" man whose words might once "have stood against the world" (*Julius Caesar* 3.2.119) but whose blood now flows through the wounds that Brutus (Cobbett) has made. Brutus's civic sacrifice is transformed into a self-interested act of rebellion, and the courtroom crowd is roused to a fever pitch against this "honorable man."

The Stories of Character and Politics

In line with the storying produced by Hopkinson, the prosecution team raised the level of struggle in *Rush v. Cobbett* from that of two mere mortals to a moral tale, a battle of good and evil that featured satanic motives and angelic acts of humanity. "Malice," said Ingersol, "adopts an equivocal ambiguous stile"; it attempts to elude the law "by artful and ingenious constructions" (Carpenter 61). The jury, he claimed, stands for the law and shall be the judge. It is perspicacious, and "if the 'clove foot' is discovered, if the veil is seen through, if the disguise is discovered, the law strips the sheep's clothing from the wolf, and exposes him to indignation in his own natural deformity" (61).

The prosecution's political tract poses a converging line of attack that declares Cobbett an alien. Moses Levy implicates him in the acts of an English agent undermining the city at a time when fever-ridden Philadelphia was "in a distressed state" (41). In Ingersol's rendition, Cobbett patiently waits for the city to become a patient itself, "stretched on his bed of sickness; physicians themselves at a loss how to relieve that distress" (64). By undermining confidence in Rush and the bleeders, the alien Cobbett would leave America bereft of care.

Against the subterfuges of Cobbett's satanic ambiguities and nuances, Ingersol cites Cobbett's depiction of Rush "as the exterminating Angel, going through the streets and heaping bodies on each other." Against the view of Cobbett insidiously polluting the city from within, Ingersol counterposes a heroic tale of the citizen-physician rescuing public health in a time of national crisis, the physician-savior who "like a saving *Angel*, arrested the arms of Death" (55).

Imaging the Trial

The prosecution's storying requires the support of a rhetoric whose metaphoric power is capable of running the range from the atavistic to the apocryphal, rising from the depths of the primordial to the heights of the heavenly. The story tells of a nation just born, unstable and still struggling with issues of unity and identity. It tells of separation anxiety as the political child severs itself from its birth parents, England and France. Hopkinson's opening for the prosecution puts before the jury the danger that Cobbett offers, thrown up on America's shores and seeking refuge from his troubles in England. Using imagery reminiscent of the slime, noxious odors, and rot associated with yellow fever, Hopkinson depicts Cobbett as a "vile source of falshood and pollution, [who] vomited forth the blackest venom of slander." Progeny of the nation, Rush is unresponsive to such vile attacks: "He did not even wipe away by contradiction the filth with which he was covered; determined that the hands of his country alone shall either cleanse him from these foul aspersions, or sink him deeper in disgrace." Rush is the American Hippocrates, a model of the immortal physician unfazed by the "besom of destruction" (Carpenter 11), which he must brave to perform the good works that will bring health to the nation and rescue it from the throes of disease. The rewards enjoyed by the Athenian were not, however, those accorded the Philadelphian Rush, who, tottering "into the infected chambers of the sick" and having himself "languished on the bed of sickness," was accosted by "contumely and defamation" (12).

The imagery of pollution and slander is converted in Ingersol's final words, summarizing the prosecution's case, into the worst of offenses an honest man has to fear: "*It is the PESTILENCE working in darkness, spreading CONTAGION far and wide. . . . It is the heart searching DAGGER of the dark ASSASSIN. . . . MURDER is its employment; INNOCENCE and MERIT its prey, and RUIN its SPORT*" (67). Assassination, infestation, and turbulence pour slander forth as a

> headlong torrent that rushes over the land — like a mighty water rolling from the mountain's top, it spreads and strengthens as it goes — the palace and the cottage are involved in its common ruin — nothing is so

> high that it cannot reach it, or so mean that it will not descend to it. . . .
> like death it comes to every man's door. (14)

Cobbett is swept up by this perverse image of a torrent as he exerts his "tyrannical jurisdiction over everything public or private" (14). A liberty of the press from which "flow the wholesome waters of Liberty" should not, Hopkinson warns, be confused with a press like Cobbett's, which "begins the poisoned torrent of Licentiousness" (15). Recalling images of the shining city on a hill, the serpent in the garden, the fall from grace, and providential punishment and redemption, Hopkinson contrasts Cobbett's free use of the press to the *"true liberty of the press* . . . as a lofty citadel" that will reward the worthy and destroy the ambitious (16) . Offering a patriot's sermon, Hopkinson argues that true lovers of liberty will preserve the citadel's beauty and elegance, its shining walls, and "let not its foundations be sapped by treacherous guardians, till its high walls totter and fall" (16). Unafraid of confounding religion, morals, law, government, and the press, he slides the slippery slope of rhetorical misrule to locate the cause of social anarchy in the lap of "licentious libels," for it is here that governments totter and social contracts burst, that religion and the morals of a people decay, with all "the consequent scenes of blood-shed, revolutions and warring chaos" (17).

Accessing the Law

Rooting its argument in ground that serves as the very foundation of order, of security in home and family, the prosecution's final act plays on the necessity of a free man's access to the law. Rush's only means of protecting his wife and sons becomes "the hope of justice" that the jury, his "guardian angel," will administer. His sons rage with indignation, driven "headlong to desperate deeds, accumulating woe on woe. With difficulty the prudential advice, the parental command of the father restrain their fury" (Carpenter 19). Government and the law fail to deliver on their "promised protection of our lives, property and reputation." Hopkinson warns, "An immediate, nay, a justifiable resort to private vengeance for private wrongs; an immediate and a necessary introduction of murder and assassination" must necessarily follow (19). He is joined by Ingersol, who raises the dreaded specter of dueling where one lives in "a state of nature" or lacks sufficient confidence in the law. Speaking in Rush's voice, Ingersol mimics the man who has lost the law. Should the "law allow me no remedy: then the bands of society are rent asunder—I am in a state of nature, let me seek my private revenge, and I am satisfied without the aid of courts" (62).

The remedy lies in the jury's performing the role of a deus ex machina, rescuing the injured by returning the court to a natural law and universal understanding that will defeat wickedness, outrage, and malignancy. As Hopkinson posits in his closing words, "Virtue, bleeding at every pore, calls for justice on her despoiler, and the anxious heart of every honest man pants with impatience to meet in you, THE DEFENDERS OF VIRTUE, AND THE SCOURGERS OF VICE" (19–20). The jury is entreated to act *parens patriae* on behalf of the nation and on behalf of Rush and his sons, to preserve the laws that provide for the father's legacy of reputation and economic well-being. Hopkinson calls on the jury to go beyond the mere legal doctrine and standards of evidence to which the court adheres. He inspires it to carry the burden of religious and secular law, of nature and society, to render a decision that will complete the nation building only begun by the war against England and that will extinguish the insidious alien presence that has infiltrated the heart of the republic. The jury is asked, in sum, to take up the burden of the citizen-patriot and finish the work Rush has set out to do as physician, moral guardian, and private prosecutor: to cull the ranks of the wicked, to raise up the afflicted, and to save the fatherland. Where moral tales, political tracts, and high rhetoric eclipsed legal evidence, and where popular prejudice and local preferences guided the verdict, the deciding factors in *Rush v. Cobbett* were questions of honor and saving grace under the assault of dark forces, of primordial evil against life-giving sources of good, morphing into a libation poured at the feet of a fallen hero.

Law and Literature

The task we face in teaching law and literature is to engage students in an enriched conversation about the law that expands their "horizon of expectations" (Jauss 28) beyond a ghettoized discourse to account for other kinds of texts and the tools by means of which they are studied. Literary texts that boundary-lope across the law, methodologies that construct the law, and the stories that we tell in the law offer us those texts and tools for our analysis. Not only do such approaches add to students' repertoires and restructure their thinking about the law—producing new legal frames as well as rhetorical, argumentative, and narrative strategies—but they also enable a legal pedagogy for teachers that allows for rediscovering the world of the law by stepping out of it (Amsterdam and Bruner 4–5; see also 110–216). Not only are students exposed by such methodologies to differential ways of using the law and understanding its political impact, but they are also brought to a fuller legal consciousness and self-identity as purveyors of the law (Binder and Weisberg 27, 200, 219; see 201–377). It is unlikely that academics will be much good, or indeed do much good, as teachers if they fail to break out of their individual disciplines and undertake productive boundary busting. Such teaching defies insularity and opens itself to a broader circle of interfaces that more accurately replicate the complexities we face in the world.

Notes

1. For area maps and buildings, see Webster; Snyder. Useful libraries are the Historical Society of Pennsylvania and Library Company of Philadelphia and the College of Physicians of Philadelphia. For Web sites, see *Accessible Archives* (a repository of eighteenth- and nineteenth-century periodicals) and *Library of Congress Online Catalog*. For microforms, see Early American Imprints, Early American Medical Imprints (1668–1820), Library of American Civilization, American Culture Series, and American Periodical Series (1800–50).

2. For a copy of Rush's instructions, see Rush, *Letters* 660.

3. State Supreme Court Chief Justice Thomas McKean used the grand jury to persecute Cobbett, and Supreme Court Justice Edward Shippen presided over the trial.

4. Reference is to a "struck" jury, one packed with jurors favoring Rush.

5. The judge is Shippen, who awaited a possible appointment as chief justice by McKean, newly elected governor of the state. Of the legal team, Moses Levy and William Lewis are cited in addition to Ingersol and Hopkinson. "Faithful counsel" refers to "the mob-courting [Robert Goodloe] Harper," who, Cobbett believed, had sold out his English client (385). The volunteering physicians are James Mease, John Coxe, and William Dewees.

Jacqueline O'Connor

Performing the Law in Contemporary Documentary Theater

In her discussion of the ritualistic elements that theater and trials share, Lucy Winner reminds us that "trials, like rituals, function as a way for the public to confront chaotic, painful, and contradictory social issues" (151). Beginning with Aeschylus's *Oresteia*, Western theater has operated as a place for acting out criminal and other judicial concerns, just as trials have served as a space for the re-creation and climax of some of our culture's most moving real-life tragedies. Indeed, the connections between artistic and legalistic performance events, particularly their shared purpose of airing different perspectives on an event and bringing participants to a better understanding of its complexities, have been well documented by analysts of both theater and law.

But a growing subgenre of twentieth-century drama called documentary theater has uniquely married stage and courtroom and thereby created a new and vital opportunity for exploring this association. Documentary theater reconfigures historical events through texts and performances that are partially or completely composed of court transcripts, interviews, newspaper reports, and other documents, and they frequently dramatize excerpts from trial records verbatim in their collage of information. In doing so, these plays transform legal texts into literary texts and legal

407

proceedings into theatrical performances. They demonstrate the ways that art can be constructed from previously existing nonartistic materials, and they highlight the performative aspects of the law.

The study of documentary theater can make a unique contribution to the law and literature classroom. Many documentary plays are created entirely from existing texts and thus represent a factual report of an incident, albeit one that makes no secret of its constructed nature, since parts of documents are selected and arranged so as to produce a dramatic narrative. In some cases the narrative imparts a particular point of view on the incident and explicitly employs the performance text to challenge a perceived wrong perpetuated by the justice system. More often, the point of view is diverse, even contradictory, requiring readers and audiences to reach for an unambiguous conclusion and frustrating that attempt. The staging of real trials in this manner turns viewers into gallery spectators, sometimes even enlisting the audience as judge and jury and thereby emphasizing the ordinary citizen's role in the process of judgment. In Emily Mann's play *Execution of Justice*, for example, a character in one of the opening scenes addresses the court and the spectators as "Your Honor, members of the jury—and you (*Takes in audience*) must be the judges now" (160).

The documentary theater genre has flourished as a way of reexamining key trials and tribunals of the twentieth century, from the 1924 Leopold-Loeb murder trial to the Senate confirmation hearings of Clarence Thomas in 1993.[1] By using existing materials to re-create courtroom proceedings onstage, these performance texts challenge their recorded, often collective history. They also investigate many of the issues central to the law and literature classroom: the role of storytelling in jurisprudence, the criminal justice system's treatment of people from underrepresented groups, how the media influence public opinion of well-publicized trials. As Michael Meyer claims, "the world as it is delineated by lawyers is indeed a text that like its literary counterparts sometimes blurs the distinction between fact and fiction as it attempts to define 'truth' and to establish criteria for 'impartial' justice" (viii).

This essay shows that documentary theater texts take legal texts and push them to ambiguous conclusions, that truth is multivocal and often contradictory, and that justice is largely elusive. Moreover, documentary theater bridges the two main strains of law and literature. Its texts are at once examples of law in literature—that is, they reflect cultural attitudes on truth and justice—and law as literature, because the inclusion of verbatim legal documents in a performance piece serves to highlight the literary qualities of the legal text.

Because my field is English, specifically American literature and drama, I teach documentary theater in courses on twentieth-century American drama and in American literature survey courses. The unit that I describe here could also fit nicely into an entire course on law and literature. Indeed, I taught a graduate course on this topic in the spring of 2008, and documentary theater was one of several genre-based units in the course. In the classroom, the focus on these texts is informed by my interest in dramatic texts as literature, by my interest in performance studies, and by my interest in American culture. Our class discussions follow a mixture of these approaches, and my students have opportunities to pursue one or more of these strains of inquiry through group presentations and individual written analyses. The study of documentary theater and the law takes three weeks in a fifteen-week semester. Because my department's curriculum is structured on a historical, chronological model and because the American documentary theater genre is recent, this unit comes at the end of the term, when students are already familiar with textual and theatrical analysis.

I begin the unit with *Zoot Suit* (1978), written by Luis Valdez and commissioned by the Mark Taper Forum in Los Angeles as part of its series New Theatre for Now. The play is a dramatization of the Sleepy Lagoon murder trial of 1942, in which a group of East Los Angeles Mexican Americans were convicted, imprisoned, and ultimately released on appeal for the murder of a young Latino male. Valdez intertwined events surrounding the trial with scenes and details from the 1943 Zoot Suit riots, a series of Los Angeles neighborhood turf wars that pitted city boys against servicemen. The play is quasi-documentary, blending trial transcripts and newspaper reports with a semifactual account of one of the defendants and his family.[2]

In the original production, a giant facsimile of a newspaper served as a drop curtain, and the play began as the character El Pachuco, an embodiment of the zoot-suited youths put on trial, cut through the newspaper with a switchblade. This opening provides a starting point for a class discussion of one of the play's primary themes: the role of the media in high-profile legal proceedings. The case became notorious in part for the way that several William Randolph Hearst–controlled Los Angeles newspapers used negative racial stereotypes of Mexican Americans to sway public opinion during the trial and during the riots that ensued in the months following the verdict.

Valdez makes clear that the play attempts to expose this racism and to indict the press and the prosecution for their collusion. In the first trial scene, the judge's bench is made from stacks of newspapers, and throughout the scene a character named the Press interjects opinions about the case. Because Valdez freely adapted the original source material he used to construct this performance text, it is important to point out to students his blending of fact and fiction and to introduce other views about the trial and the riots that followed. I show a clip from the film *Zoot Suit* (1981), which contains many features of the original production as well as much of the original cast, alongside the PBS American Experience documentary *Zoot Suit Riots* (2001). The documentary also provides important historical background on the racial tensions in Los Angeles during World War II, which is useful for expanding students' perspectives about the wartime period.

Two plays that make a nice pair for comparison are Mann's *Execution of Justice* and *Twilight: Los Angeles, 1992: On the Road: A Search for American Character* (1993), by Anna Deavere Smith. As the author's note explains, the words of Mann's play are taken entirely from trial transcripts, reportage, and interviews (149). Likewise, Smith's one-woman performance is constructed from selections of hundreds of verbatim interviews that Smith herself conducted. Smith's work in documentary theater is more widely known than Mann's, in part because both *Twilight* and another of her one-person shows, *Fires in the Mirror: Crown Heights, Brooklyn, and Other Identities*, were adapted for television and aired on PBS. But both playwrights have been noted for the advances they've made to what has become known as the theater of testimony.

Like *Zoot Suit*, these performance texts by Mann and by Smith concern trials whose controversial outcomes are linked to civil disturbances, and they emphasize the important role that legal proceedings can play in resolving—or failing to resolve—community differences. As is common to the documentary theater genre, the conflicts on which these plays are based have their origins in the race, class, and gender inequities that continue to divide American society; thus they challenge readers and audiences to confront their own prejudices even as they interrogate local and national attitudes about justice.

Mann's work dramatizes the trial of Dan White, a former San Francisco city supervisor, for the 1978 murders of Mayor George Moscone and Supervisor Harvey Milk. The killings and the trial that followed underscored the tensions between a city hall long controlled by relatively conservative Irish Catholics and the new voices of minorities and gays represented by Moscone and Milk. Despite White's admission of guilt, the defense dominated the proceedings, and White's attorney claimed that high levels of junk food contributed to his defendant's "diminished capacity" (thereafter known as the "Twinkie defense" ["Diminished Capacity"]). A conviction on the reduced charge of voluntary manslaughter, with a minimum sentence, shocked the public, many of whom perceived the crimes as calculated and cold-blooded. A mob of thousands stormed city hall after the verdict, smashing windows and burning police cars.

More recent events prompted the creation of *Twilight*: the trials that followed from the videotaped beating of suspect Glen "Rodney" King in March 1991 by four Los Angeles police officers, and the riots that rocked the city after the officers' acquittal. Unlike Mann's play, Smith does not stage the courtroom activity that is nonetheless a central topic for many of the people she embodies in her compelling shape-shifting style; rather, as part of her ongoing project of recording and reenacting the words and witnesses of contemporary history entitled "On the Road: A Search for American Character," her focus is on their memories and interpretations of what took place But law and justice are central to this play, for with her interviews Smith provides an inside look at incendiary events that affected Los Angelenos of every color and political persuasion and challenged the city's notion of diversity and equality.

Neither play seeks to resolve the issues it raises. Both Mann and Smith create ambiguously multivoiced dramas that prompt open-ended and often unusually honest dialogue, whether at a performance talk back or in a classroom. Mann's dramatic strategy has been noted for its evenhanded presentation of the White case. For example, Mel Gussow, in his review of the New York production of *Execution*, asserts that with the playwright "acting as investigative reporter, the play is not a polemic but a judicious assessment of a turbulent episode in recent American political history." In order to balance the perceived inequity of the original trial, Mann includes what she calls a "Chorus of Uncalled Witnesses," a collection of characters who mourn the passing of the deceased and question the trial transcript's reflection of White as a sympathetic defendant. Smith herself claimed in an interview that while her work is clearly theater, "it's also community work in some ways. It's a kind of low anthropology, low journalism; it's a bit documentary" ("Circle" 56). Jonathan Kalb argues that Smith and other documentary solo performers are "conduits for testimony that might otherwise never be heard and thus [possess] a certain 'secondary' authenticity as witnesses of witnesses" (19).

A play that particularly resonates with my students at Boise State University, because of its setting in the intermountain West, where many of them were raised, is *The Laramie Project* (2000). This documentary play was composed by Moisés Kaufman and members of his company, the Tectonic Theater Project, and it treats the aftermath of the 1998 murder of Matthew Shepard, a gay college student, and the trials of the two defendants, Russell Henderson and Aaron McKinney. Like the other plays discussed here, this text helps students make connections between discrimination and violence while exploring legal and literary narratives that perform our culture's conflicts as a means of moving toward understanding and tolerance.

In class, I compare a scene from the original play script, entitled "The Essential Facts," with the same scene, renamed "Statement of Facts," from the 2002 HBO film version of *The Laramie Project*. An examination of two versions of a scene serves to launch a discussion of how different representations of justice can radically affect our interpretations as well as our emotional responses. In the script, the scene lasts less than two minutes and does little more than provide information from the defendants' preliminary hearing about the facts of the case against them. In the television version, the scene lasts ten minutes and contains excerpts from interviews inserted from other sections of the text. It still informs the audience of the details of the case, but it does much more than that.

Opening with the television and radio reports of the upcoming hearing, the HBO version then cuts to close-ups of the town's array of residents as they hear the news and walk to the courthouse. From a legal standpoint, of course, this scene marks the official public charge against the defendants, heard here for the first time. But in the movie version the audience sees and hears not only a preliminary hearing but an entire range of testimony; it comes not from investigative proceedings but from interviews conducted by members of the Tectonic Theater Project. Thus are these interviews added to the judicial process, even though technically they are not part of the legal proceeding. As we see and hear them framed in a courtroom scene, however, they seem to be transformed from private exchange to evidence. While as interviews they are already testimony, this stylistic strategy transforms them into publicly aired statements that become, at least by implication, part of the legal record of the event. Our comparison of these scenes, which begins with a discussion of the differences between theater and television, often ends with a lively debate about the effects that law and order television shows and films have on our perceptions of the American justice system.

The final play I teach is *The Exonerated* (2002), composed primarily of interviews and other materials collected and compiled by Jessica Blank and Erik Jensen. Six former death-row inmates narrate their stories of arrest, conviction, imprisonment, and exoneration, while key episodes from their arrests and interrogations are acted out on a minimalist stage. The exonerated persons' narratives of their interrogations prove particularly useful in our investigation of the role that confession plays in the judicial process. As Peter Brooks claims, the "story of what goes on in that closed room, where interrogations lead to confessions, always leaves us uneasy, like so many modern narratives proffered by 'unreliable narrators,' narratives indeed that give us no basis for judging what 'reliability' might mean" (*Troubling Confessions* 32). In this text, we are witness to the characters' attempts to make sense of the conflicting narratives of their lives, for while all proclaim an innocence that has been belatedly upheld by the courts, several of them also acknowledge that at some point they confessed to the crimes in question.

A shocking testament to the fact that our system of justice sometimes not only fails to punish the guilty but also charges and convicts the innocent, *The Exonerated* is a sobering work. It serves as a powerful example of theater activism, for the play has been performed throughout the country both as an argument against the death penalty and as a fund-raiser for the Innocence Project, which in 2007 celebrated its two hundredth exoneration. It could be used in numerous ways in a law and literature classroom: to prompt a discussion of the death penalty or to act as an entry point to a case of an exonerated person that might become a research topic for students. Court TV produced a television version of this play in 2005, using many of the revolving cast of well-known actors who played the roles during the original New York production.

For those interested in teaching the texts discussed here, all are available in inexpensive paperback editions, and several contain useful introduction or production information that informs students about the historical context of the work and the composition process. Film versions of *Zoot Suit*, *The Laramie Project*, and *The Exonerated* are readily available on video for rent or purchase.

The range of topics and approaches an instructor might draw from these documentary plays will vary depending on the course subject matter and purpose, but using examples of this genre of performance text contributes greatly to a course on law and literature. The inclusion of actual trial documents into dramatic texts calls attention to connections between theater and the courtroom and emphasizes the literary elements of the legal text. As witness questioning becomes stage banter and closing remarks become soliloquy, the transformation underscores at once the eloquence and the banality, the clarity and the obscurity of legal speech. As narrative components of a court proceeding are dramatized as constructed stories of an event, we are reminded, as Robert Cover argues, that in our normative world, "prescription, even when embodied in a legal text, [cannot] escape its origins and its end in experience, in the narratives that are the trajectories plotted upon material reality by our imaginations" ("Foreword" 5). The texts discussed here, in taking as their subjects trials and legal proceedings that expose the political fissures in our culture, demonstrate the important role that both the justice system and the theater can play in community reconciliation and in our ongoing struggles to achieve equality under the law.

Notes

1. John Logan's *Never the Sinner* is a documentary play based on the Leopold and Loeb case, and Mame Hunt's *Unquestioned Integrity: The Hill-Thomas Hearings, Voicings* treats the Anita Hill testimony in the Clarence Thomas confirmation hearings. I do not include these plays in my discussion, because they have not been widely produced and are not readily accessible in print. But they do help indicate the extent to which major trials of the twentieth century have been transformed into documentary theater.

2. The Reynas of the play are based on the Leyvases of Los Angeles. The son, Henry Reyna, is (as Henry Leyvas was in life) the unofficial leader of the gang and the young man singled out for much of the action in *Zoot Suit*.

Richard Schur

"Fight the Power": Hip-Hop in the Law and Literature Classroom

At first glance, hip-hop may seem ill suited to the law and literature classroom. It is a relatively new cultural phenomenon, little more than thirty years old. While most scholars and critics agree that the movement began in New York during the 1970s, there are widespread debates about whether it is an African American or multicultural movement; whether graffiti, b-boying, deejaying, and rapping constitute one cultural formation or distinct movements; whether commercialization and its recent popularity with white suburbanites have ruined it; and whether it is inherently misogynistic. Moreover, the hip-hop canon has undergone nearly constant revision, and few artists achieve commercial or critical success for more than a few years. For all these reasons, someone new to hip-hop might conclude that it is easier to avoid these issues altogether and stick to more traditional law and literature texts. A brief review of hip-hop's history, however, suggests that hip-hop offers a compelling and contemporary iteration of some of the central concerns that animate law and literature studies.[1]

This essay examines how hip-hop can be used to introduce undergraduate students to the field of law and literature. By focusing on sampling, flow, and irony, I demonstrate how hip-hop's defining features can illustrate three central concerns of law and literature. First, hip-hop's use of sampling provides an excellent opportunity to explore the use of precedent in the fields of law and literature. Its reliance on sampling and the resulting copyright disputes illustrate how the legal use of past texts in making decisions, known as stare decisis, differs from literature's emphasis on intertextuality and allusion. Hip-hop provides insight into the boundaries and interrelations between law and culture. Second, I explore flow—a key musical technique of hip-hop—to consider how temporal disjunctions manifest themselves in the relation between law and literature. Third, hip-hop lyrics provide an effective way for teachers to introduce students to key concepts and themes of literary and cultural studies: for example, the cultural valences of irony; the difference between author and authorial voice or persona; and the complex, sometimes cooptative, relation between the marketplace and literary or cultural production.

Hip-hop blossomed in the South Bronx during the 1970s. Dancers, known as b-boys, claimed ownership over public spaces through competitive performances. Graffiti artists marked their presence on subways cars, alley walls, and any other available surface and transformed these objects and spaces into alternative art galleries, revealing both the hidden creativity and the simmering tensions and anxieties of disenfranchised youth of color. Through b-boying and graffiti, young people of color could demand social recognition amid New York's decaying infrastructure during the 1970s. Politicians ignored Brooklyn, the South Bronx, and other hip-hop hotspots; graffiti artists and b-boys, in response, asserted their right to participate in the reshaping of urban spaces. Rejecting the status quo, hip-hop culture sought new ways to rebuild community even if it lacked officially recognized ownership or authority over these public spaces and its proponents were not duly elected representatives.

Deejays, such as Kool Herc DJ, Afrika Bambaataa, and Grandmaster Flash, wove together increasingly diverse records into a seamless mix. Rappers shouted out rhymes over the new form of music that deejays created. Through their lyrics, rappers created personas that challenged other rappers, the police, and national politicians. From its earliest days, hip-hop intersected with law as police began a massive surveillance campaign over urban youth of color in the fight against drugs and gangs. In response, hip-hop challenged racial stereotypes that underwrote this surveillance even as the music, especially gangsta rap, adopted the trope of "keepin' it real," which frequently meant describing urban drug violence (see Ogbar 68–69). From these humble origins, hip-hop has become a lucrative genre in the national market and a global phenomenon, finding performers and audiences in Europe, Africa, Asia, and the Middle East.

Hip-hop's first appearance in a courtroom involved the question of the legality of sampling. The case explored whether hip-hop's use of sampling—the appropriation of existing sounds, texts, and images—constituted copyright infringement. In an infamous opinion, Judge Kevin Thomas Duffy tersely noted that hip-hop sampling did violate copyright. He wrote, "[T]his callous disregard for the law [by Biz Markie in his song "Alone Again"] and for the rights of others requires not only the preliminary injunction sought by the plaintiff but also sterner measures" (*Grand Upright Music* 188). The court seemed particularly troubled that Biz Markie suggested he "should be excused [for any infringing activities] because others in the 'rap music' business are also engaged in illegal activity" (188n2). The court disagreed that cultural practices ought to influence the application of seemingly neutral laws against theft and invoked biblical authority to assert the universality of this building block of the Western legal tradition. In particular, the court could not envision how Biz Markie or any other hip-hop artist might be appropriating mainstream texts to engage in cultural criticism.

Hip-hop's use of sampling provides an opportunity for teachers in undergraduate courses—either in literature classes or in the context of a general studies curriculum—to introduce students to the legal principle of stare decisis and the literary practice of intertextuality and to compare the two. Students may be shown how, according to stare decisis contracts, legal briefs, and case reports borrow or sample extensively from past legal decisions, sometimes clearly identifying their sources. Students learn that, in the teaching and practice of law in the United States, lawyers and judges commonly argue that the best legal advice or decision is the one that most fully and effectively incorporates existing case law. Similarly, though writers and literary scholars value originality and creativity (as does copyright law, which determines how the ownership rights in and profits from original works are distributed), they have long recognized that allusion and intertextual linkages are essential, if not indeed inextricable, elements of literary creativity. By the same token, writers, scholars, and judges alike face the challenge of negotiating with tradition or established canons of interpretation, while attending to the irreducible singularity of particular texts or cases. Judges, even the most restrained, sometimes must resolve questions for which there is no ready precedent or reevaluate settled doctrine as cultural practices and social mores change over time, as in *Grand Upright Music*.

Through sampling, hip-hop artists have demonstrated remarkable self-consciousness about their creative processes and implicitly questioned racial and generic boundaries in American music. Deejays have sampled from African American artists, such as James Brown and George Clinton, and many white artists, such as Eric Clapton, Billy Joel, AC/DC, and Steely Dan. Depending on the context, samples can either recognize a precursor's (e.g., James Brown's) or a genre's (e.g., funk's) importance or ridicule a song, an artist, or an entire form of music. During hip-hop's golden age, Public Enemy's "Caught, Can I Get a Witness!" and Ice Cube's "Jackin' for Beats" romanticize the producer's use of samples and rewrite that appropriation as a form of cultural resistance. More recently, DJ Danger Mouse released, on the Internet, his *Grey Album*, which is known as a mash-up because it blended the Beatles' *White Album* and Jay Z's *Black Album*. After receiving cease-and-desist letters, DJ Danger Mouse withdrew the album from the Internet.[2] Despite its potential illegality, sampling remains a central feature of hip-hop (Schloss, *Making* 177–80; Demers 97). Sampling has also influenced writers, probably most notably Alice Randall's *The Wind Done Gone* but also Paul Beatty's *White Boy Shuffle* and Colson Whitehead's *John Henry Days* and *Apex Hides the Hurt,* and artists, including Adrian Piper, Allison Saar, Michael Ray Charles, Kerry James Marshall, Eileen Gallagher, and Glenn Ligon. In each case, the writers and artists sample the material they seek to criticize or rework, thus making visible hidden racist attitudes or practices.[3]

For the undergraduate teacher as well as for teachers in law school settings, sampling's role in hip-hop can highlight the conceptual difficulties in distinguishing between legal rules and cultural practices. Copyright law regulates the ownership interests of imaginative texts. What counts as a valid or legitimate text, for the purposes of copyright and thus social and economic recognition, depends on legal analysis, not literary or cultural merit. Judges apply, consciously or unconsciously, cultural norms about textual production and meaning as they apply copyright law to new kinds of texts, especially as the Internet and globalization are creating new genres. As a result, the very nature and existence of a cultural practice gets shaped by law. In other words, hip-hop teaches us that cultural texts do not exist in a vacuum outside law; rather, they gain social recognition precisely to the extent to which law embeds them in a regime of rights. Artists, such as Public Enemy, Ice Cube, and DJ Danger Mouse, have used their music to question how courts have applied copyright law to sampling. Because they narrate their criticism of law in hip-hop songs, their ability to produce and distribute their messages frequently relies on courts to hold that a particular sample constitutes fair use or on copyright owners to permit sampling. Unlike other iterations of law and literature, hip-hop texts require teachers and students to examine how law shapes the texts that purport to criticize it.

Hip-hop's concept of flow provides an opportunity for students to build on their examination of sampling and develop a theoretically sophisticated understanding of the temporality of relations between law and works of literature. Early deejays sampled the breaks between verses, because those breaks had the best rhythms. This practice is known as flow. These deejays then blended them to make a potentially endless dance mix. Today, rappers build their reputations on the quality of their flow or ability to "ride the beat" (Alim 92–96). One critic has defined "the aim" of flow "to be fluid, liquid, protean in one's approach to sound . . . it is not a matter of strength, but finesse" (Cobb 87). Alien Ness, a former member of the seminal b-boy groups the New York City Breakers and the Rock Steady Crew, argues that flow is central to hip-hop dancing because it is the connective tissue that holds together the moves that compose a performance (Schloss, "Art" 28–29). Popping and locking, break-dancing moves that emphasize dancers' dexterity and the strength of their joints, serve as a foundational element of b-boying. According to Tricia Rose, "[I]n hip hop, visual, musical, and lyrical lines are set in motion, broken abruptly with sharp angular breaks, yet they sustain motion and energy through fluidity and flow" (38).

Hip-hop's emphasis on flow, which signals a deep concern with time and timing, also expresses itself in the creative exploration of rupture—that is, the intentional creation of temporal fissures or breaks for aesthetic and critical purposes. Although rarely discussed in such terms, law and literature typically adopts a spatial perspective for understanding the relation between the two discourses. Most commonly the field is organized by prepositions and conjunctions that signal a spatial reorganization of scholarly structures: law *and* literature, law *in* literature, and law *as* literature. By and large, these wordings suggest that spatial constraints impede the integration of legal and literary knowledge (law is subsumed by literature, literature is superimposed on law, the two fields are parallel but distant) or that academic or cultural geography has kept lawyers from learning about literary and cultural studies and literary scholars and artists from understanding law. As a result, scholars, judges, and teachers have sought to break down this discursive divide and read legal and literary texts together.

At the textual level, a focus on rhythmic flow and asymmetry might provide a tool or method for examining how specific legal decisions, novels, songs, and films represent temporal shifts in juridical and cultural thinking. Instead of deploying spatial logic to contrast legal and literary texts and theories, a temporal or rhythmic approach might consider how texts create the appearance of flow or rupture in disciplinary histories as part of their legal-cultural critiques. For example, legal decisions rely on stare decisis when explicating their reasoning. Does the decision's review of history flow, or are there ruptures, obvious or hidden—for example, because of race? Turning to literary texts, one might note that it is increasingly common to find Toni Morrison's *Beloved* and other neo-slave narratives from the post-civil-rights era, such as Gayl Jones's *Corregidora*, Randall's *The Wind Done Gone*, and Edward P. Jones's *The Known World*, included in law and literature classes. These texts present a temporal fissure, because the legal setting they describe, slavery, no longer exists.[4] Law and literature then must examine the novelist's purpose in treating a legal problem that now seems resolved. On the other hand, Charles Johnson's short story "Executive Decision" and Walter Mosley's "Equal Opportunity" (both from the mid-1990s) examine how affirmative action law, especially after *Bakke v. California* limited its potential reach, has failed to help many African Americans realize professional success. By focusing on the temporal parity or disparity between these stories and law, students can explore whether such stories respond to legal discourse, serve as a catalyst for new strategies, or both.

An examination of a literary text's account of legal history can be similarly analyzed. Students, for example, could examine the temporal flows and ruptures within and between the Fugitive Slave Act of 1850, Harriet Beecher Stowe's *Uncle Tom's Cabin*, and the Dred Scott decision.[5] Instead of assuming that literature criticizes legal discourse, such an exploration might find unrecognized similarities among these works or identify how their respective flows differ. Law and literature tend to share stereotypes, biases, and values. One might study the flow or rupture in the narratives of post-civil-rights-era life offered by Grandmaster Flash and the Furious Five's "The Message" or by Public Enemy's *Fear of a Black Planet* and the decision *United States v. Armstrong*, in which the Rehnquist Court considered whether the Drug Enforcement Agency's choice to investigate drug trafficking in predominantly African American neighborhoods constituted prosecutorial misconduct. A temporal comparison of these narratives might reveal some surprising commonalities and differences. Perhaps William Rehnquist, Grandmaster Flash, and Chuck D share attitudes about personal responsibility even if they differ on how law should promote it.

Hip-hop provides an example of the effectiveness—but also of the paradoxes and complexities—of irony as a rhetorical strategy for raising consciousness and cultivating the conditions necessary for the possibility of social justice. Darryl Dickson-Carr argues that African American literature, despite its interest in challenging injustice, has a long history of deploying irony as a method to "express . . . anger and aggression toward authority" (20). For Dickson-Carr, irony always depends on a specific cultural location for its meaning, and outsiders can easily mistake it for realism (24–25).[6] His analysis suggests that crucial to a text's meaning is whether the writer and reader share historical experiences and cultural knowledge. He also argues that ironic texts frequently cannot serve overtly political purposes, because their politics can be easily or universally determined.[7]

Hip-hop's rhetorical emphasis on keeping it real has caused some commentators to understand it as a form of realism. Robin Kelley, however, argues that "violent lyrics in rap music are rarely meant to be literal. Rather, they are often more than not metaphors to challenge competitors on the microphone" (38). Rose characterizes hip-hop as possessing a "hidden transcript" with "cloaked speech and disguised cultural codes." Irony allows it to "comment on and challenge aspects of current power inequalities" (100). A fairly basic example from the golden era of hip-hop would be Boogie Down Productions' "Dope Beat," in which KRS-One, the group's rapper, tells the audience numerous times that he has a "dope beat" as he raps over a sample from AC/DC's song "Back in Black." He also boasts about how he is the best rapper and that he can rap over any kind of music. The song is ironic, however, because the "dope beat" is not actually theirs and the words possess a layered and ironic meaning. KRS-One uses the words against the sample to suggest the irony in having a band of white Australians claim some sort of metaphoric blackness as they appropriate (without paying royalties) African-derived musical styles. I would also argue that much of the violence in hip-hop, especially that which is directed at police enforcement and legal institutions, is ironic, because the songs articulate claims for justice by describing putatively criminal acts. "Dope Beat," for example, was released on the album *Criminal Minded* not because they were encouraging criminal activity but because they sought to upset settled definitions of legality and criminality. Such a discussion can help students understand the symbolic and metaphoric role that law plays in literary and other cultural texts. This discussion can also lead to a productive consideration of the distinction between author and speaker.

Hip-hop frequently relies on misogynistic and homophobic language to describe people, situations, and stories. Nelson George notes that "hip hop's typical narrator is a young, angry, horny male" (185). Numerous commentators have examined the abundant sexism in hip-hop music and culture (Guevara; Kitwana 85–119; J. Morgan; I. Perry 156–90; T. Rose 146–82). Hip-hop's sexism and homophobia, while contested within the community, illustrates the limits of irony and the playful use of language. Many defenders will argue that hip-hop's critics have misunderstood sexist or homophobic comments as reflecting its attitude toward women or homosexuals when they were intended as criticisms about specific kinds of people or actions. The very realness that hip-hop demands has also created rhetorical excesses and tended to imagine heterosexual males as the primary agents for social criticism and change. For example, Public Enemy's song "Fight the Power" begins with a sample of Louis Farrakhan identifying black male homosexuals as traitors to the nation, who fail to fight racism. Similarly, Kanye West's "Gold Digger" modifies a Ray Charles song and suggests that the materialism of African American women has undermined African American men's chances at success and power.

Examining the history of women in hip-hop, Gwendolyn Pough concluded that hip-hop generation women have used their experiences and stories to counteract the "negative images and stereotypes that influence their lives" (101). Mary J. Blige and Lauryn Hill's lyrics provide an alternative to hip-hop's aggressive masculinity to show how some legal norms, especially those pertaining to domestic violence, are necessary and cannot be ignored simply because legal discourse and law enforcement have a history of racial discrimination. For Hill especially, the struggle for justice need not choose between the fight against racism and the fight against sexism or create a hierarchy between them. Rather, justice can be achieved only when people challenge racism and sexism with equal vigor.[8] For students in the law and literature classroom, womanist approaches to hip-hop, such as Pough's, offer a way to explore a central irony of the post-civil-rights era: the very tools and methods hip-hop offers for social and legal criticism are infected with many of the same biases and stereotypes as legal and literary discourses. Hip-hop's poetic and critical vision must be read somewhat ironically, or at least pragmatically, because its artists speak from specific cultural locations that reflect and embody dominant stereotypes and biases.

Perhaps the final irony of hip-hop is that it began in some of the poorest neighborhoods in the United States and has become commercialized and, in the words of Elizabeth Blair, "sanitized by the producers of the mass culture" (503; I. Perry 87). S. Craig Watkins has argued, on the other hand, that hip-hop's corporatization ironically provided previously disenfranchised youth an opportunity to develop a critique of the post-civil-rights America (571).[9] I cannot resolve this debate, but the law and literature classroom offers a unique location to ask such a question. The more that discourses of law and of literature explicitly regulate and authorize hip-hop's production through corporate investment in and academic scholarship of hip-hop music, graffiti art, and b-boy contests, the more the very meaning of the social practice changes, as does its ability to influence legal and political debate. It has been my experience that many students are quite aware of hip-hop's corporate image and think about how this image shapes and affects their own consumption of hip-hop. The law and literature field might help them confront their own habits, beliefs, practices, and values.

Hip-hop, I would argue, ought to be an essential component of an undergraduate course that introduces students to the field of law and literature. It offers students and teachers alike the opportunity to examine the role of precedent and the concept of intertextuality, the relation between law and culture, and the uses of irony from the perspective of historically marginalized voices. Because many of our students participate in deejaying, rapping, b-boying, or graffiti, studying hip-hop in the law and literature classroom may help students better connect with and understand what is at stake in academic debates, within and between disciplines, about the political significance of popular and mass culture.

Notes

1. In the past decade, a growing number of scholars have become interested in exploring the intersection between the field of law and literature and African American studies. For an example, see King and Schur.

2. According to both Joanne Demers (140) and Kembrew McLeod (154), more than one million people downloaded the album the day before DJ Danger Mouse was forced to withdraw it.

3. In *Parodies of Ownership* (2009), I analyze contemporary African American literature and art through the lens of intellectual property doctrines, such as

fair use, transformative use, and originality. The book argues that these writers and painters, building on the work of earlier African American writers and painters, deploy sampling techniques precisely to raise issues about who can or should own the symbols, logos, sounds, and neologisms that define the American cultural imagination. My research also reveals that hip-hop artists, in many ways, were the first to experience legal discourse's effort to regulate "cut and mix" or "rip, mix, and burn" artistry.

4. Although beyond the scope of this essay, the return of slavery as a subject for African American literature suggests overlap with critical race theory, especially as developed by legal scholars of color. As critical race theorists have explored how legal discourse has normalized and legitimized practices and doctrines with racially disparate effects, African American writers have returned to slavery in order to show that the existing language and structure of the law have not produced remedies adequate to the nature and scope of the traumatic experience of slavery and, more broadly, to the continuing experience of legally sanctioned oppression. Texts such as Morrison's are valuable for law and literature teachers because even as they make plain that the traumas of slavery have yet to be integrated, the act of representing and giving voice to traumatic experience itself participates in the cultural work of integration and healing. (For further analysis of temporal flows and ruptures in Morrison's fictional explorations of legal discourse, see Schur, "Subject" and "Locating.") The neo-slave narratives of Morrison and others could be used to illustrate the controversy surrounding legal reparations—a controversy that has many dimensions, among them the problem of seeking a remedy for a harm that was legal at the time it was committed.

5. B. Thomas (*Cross-Examinations*) and Ferguson (*Law*) provide a foundation for this exercise, but they typically revert to a more spatial approach.

6. Cobb argues that "irony is not at the center of the hip hop ethos" (24). I believe that Cobb has misunderstood irony, because he connects it more closely to the blues than to the broader literary history Dickson-Carr discusses (30). Later sections of his book actually illustrate Dickson-Carr's analysis of irony in African American texts (43, 61, and 114).

7. Some have mistakenly reduced irony to signifying. Dickson-Carr makes clear that the two are related but distinct linguistic practices (28).

8. In many ways, Hill and Blige both create music that illustrates the critical race theory concept of intersectionality, first articulated by Kimberle Crenshaw ("Mapping").

9. Gangsta rap, with its violent and misogynistic lyrics, came to dominate hip-hop music precisely when corporate interests began taking an interest in hip-hop. Some of the music's violence and sexism may reflect the interests of white audiences and the lengths to which record companies will go to sell music.

Lenora Ledwon

Ten Kinds of Law and Literature Texts You Haven't Read

What texts can law and literature teachers assign? Since I have taught law and literature courses in law schools for the past twelve years and edited an anthology of law and literature readings, this question is near and dear to my heart. The most recent survey of professors teaching in this field in law schools indicates that, despite some movement toward an opening up of the canon, the great books are alive and kicking. Law schools already tend to be bastions of tradition, allowing change only with great reluctance and at a glacial pace. The most frequently assigned texts still are stalwarts such as *Billy Budd*, *The Merchant of Venice*, *Measure for Measure*, and *The Stranger* (Gemmette 686). Consequently, the reading assignments tend to underrepresent works by women and minorities and underrepresent popular-culture texts.

I would encourage teachers not simply to substitute a different canon but to think expansively when selecting texts for class. By all means, assign *Bleak House* and your favorite Shakespeare play but also consider including something new and different. In this essay, I offer ten kinds of texts that work well in a law-lit classroom. The selections emphasize writings by women and minorities and cover a variety of different categories — Internet blogs, graphic novels, and children's literature, among others.

425

The advantages of making such additions are twofold. First, students are delighted when we use innovative, accessible texts. Second, these texts involve profoundly interesting legal themes and generate lively class discussion. With them, educators can create a richer, more meaningful experience for students.

I. Blawgs

Students preparing to enter law school used to read Scott Turow's *One L* or John Jay Osborn's *The Paper Chase* for insight into the horrors of the Socratic method and life as a first-year law student. Both are excellent books (*One L* is nonfiction and *The Paper Chase* is fiction). Each tells the story of a white male student during his first year at an elite law school. However, as noted by one of my friends, who happens to be a female, an African American, and a Harvard Law grad, "That may have been Scott Turow's experience of Harvard Law, but it sure wasn't my experience." Where do we look for stories of law student life that reflect the diversity of our students? Where are the stories about law students who are single mothers, or Asian, or working class, or transgendered, or devout Christians? Where are the stories about the experiences of law students at lower-ranked or bottom-tier law schools? The answer is, in blawgs.

A blog is an online journal, and a blawg is a law-related blog. Blawgs written by law students are a special category in the blogosphere. There are many blawgs about life during law school—for example, *Three Years of Hell to Become the Devil*, *Law School Barbie*, or A *Girl Walks into a Bar (Exam)*. One good starting index is *Blawg* (www.blawg.com). Although Web sites constantly change, other good sources are the American Bar Association's annual listing of the top hundred blawgs (www.abajournal.com) and a *Google* search for law student blogs (http://blogsearch.google.com). Blawgs help law students figure out their personal connections to the law. For students swimming in a big pool of anxiety, a blawg can be a life preserver. Blawgs also can help students reflect on their career choice, by discussing topics such as how to be happy and fulfilled as a lawyer. Finally, blawgs can help nontraditional students cope with a sense of alienation by confirming that other students have faced similar issues or challenges. In this respect, they are a form of survival literature. Teaching assignments might have students not only read selected blawgs but also (if you are brave) write one. For example, instead of asking students to keep a journal, ask them to write a blawg about their life as a law student. Caveat: advise them to refer to teachers only as Professor X or Professor Y, to keep from bruising their teachers' egos.

2. Graphic Novels

If, as many educators suspect, Gen X and Gen Y students are more visually oriented than older students, then why not tap into some of that visual skill by assigning a visual text? Graphic novels have the reputation of being comic books for adults, but they are much more than that. The best of them, such as Art Spiegelman's *Maus* or Marjane Satrapi's *Persepolis*, pack a double punch—a terrific voice combined with compelling pictures.

I have taught *Persepolis* in my law-lit course, under the topic "Picturing Injustice." *Persepolis* tells the story of the author's childhood in Iran during the time of the Islamic Revolution. Satrapi uses deceptively simple drawings in black and white to tell the story of her girlhood during a time of great political, cultural, and religious turbulence. Once the shah is overthrown and the Islamic republic comes into power, the ten-year-old Marjane struggles to understand the increasingly authoritarian nature of life.

A story about childhood often is a story of education, a bildungsroman. But education requires a movement from innocence to experience, and sometimes that new knowledge is acquired at a great price. In *Persepolis*, Marjane must learn bitter lessons about survival, lessons that she cannot always reconcile with her understanding of God or history or justice.

That children have a great sense of justice can be witnessed in any playground debate about what is fair in a game. But they also pick up on and may even imitate constant injustices in their world. Satrapi begins her story with a section titled "The Veil." Much commented on, it shows what it was like when suddenly all the girls at school were required to wear veils. The drawings show the schoolgirls at recess, turning their veils into toys. One girl is jumping rope with her veil; another, chanting, "Execution in the name of freedom," pretends to strangle a girl who is not wearing her veil (3). In play, the child is imitating the repression and violence of her world.

Graphic novels can be a wonderful addition to a law-lit class. Some of the best graphic novels featuring superheroes offer excellent opportunities for class discussion on themes such as vigilante justice, the nature of crime, and the role of punishment. I am thinking particularly of Alan Moore's groundbreaking *Watchmen* and Frank Miller's *Batman: The Dark Knight Returns*.

3. Mystery

Mystery novels almost inherently involve legal themes and issues. Uncovering a wrong and searching for justice are common themes. Ordinarily, my first choice of a mystery novel for a law-lit course would be *The Woman in White*, by that lawyer-turned-sensation-novelist Wilkie Collins. This nineteenth-century novel has a highly legalistic structure, as different eyewitnesses give their testimony concerning the strange story of the ghostly woman in white. Equally important, the novel is a delicious mystery story, populated with an over-the-top villain (a grossly fat Italian count who keeps little pet mice in his pockets), a beautiful persecuted heroine and her spirited "new woman" half-sister, and of course an ardent and handsome young drawing master. However, like many of those other loose, baggy monsters from the nineteenth century, Collins's novel is well over six hundred pages, and may be too much to cover if there are many other assignments. Therefore, let me suggest another (shorter) mystery written by a lawyer: Sarah Caudwell's *The Shortest Way to Hades*.

Sarah Cockburn, writing under the pseudonym Sarah Caudwell, was a barrister who worked in the legal section of Lloyds Bank Trust Division. Her wonderfully funny mysteries featured Hilary Tamar, a professor of medieval law whose gender is just one of the many mysteries in the books. (Hilary can be a name for a man or a woman, and Caudwell was careful never to use pronouns when referring to Professor Tamar, so the professor's gender is left up to the reader's imagination.) Professor Tamar joins forces with a group of former law students who are now practitioners and whose cases tend to embroil them all in legal mysteries.

What I find particularly appealing about Caudwell's books, aside from the fact that they feature a law professor as a hero, is that Caudwell humanizes her lawyers through gentle humor. Humanity is a precious characteristics in literary portraits of lawyers, and it is particularly important for law students. Every year, I see first-year law students who are defensive about their chosen profession. They have been bombarded with overwhelmingly negative popular-culture images of lawyers as sharks in suits. While Chaucer, Shakespeare, and Dickens had plenty of negative things to say about lawyers, they recognized some positive things about lawyers, too. It's worth remembering that Shakespeare's Dick the Butcher, who says. "The first thing we do, let's kill all the lawyers," is an anarchist who wants to overthrow the government (*2H6* 4.2.83–84). Shakespeare recognized that once lawyers go, any possibility for order and social justice goes, too. Caudwell pokes fun at her lawyer characters, but in doing so she humanizes rather than demonizes them. She is never mean or cruel as she describes their quirks and foibles. Her mysteries feature a very British, dry sense of humor, and it helps to read aloud passages to the class, preferably doing one's best imitation of Dame Maggie Smith or perhaps Dame Edna. It's refreshing to find a good mystery that also is humorous, since so many law-lit texts can be depressing (*Bleak House*, anyone?), and a whole semester of gloom can put students (and professors) off their feed.

4. Fantasy Literature

Military fantasy is a subgenre of fantasy literature with a long tradition. It typically features battles, military strategy, and the life of a good soldier in a futuristic setting. (It's usually shelved in with the science fiction books at bookstores. For a classic example of military science fiction, see Robert Heinlein's *Starship Troopers.*) This type of story opens up the topic of the jurisprudence of war. What are the rules of war? If might makes right, what happens if might restrains itself? And what role does law play during war?

An excellent contemporary fantasy novel that plays out and plays against the conventions of military fantasy is Laurie J. Marks's *Earth Logic*. While *Earth Logic* is a war novel in the long tradition of military fantasy, such a description is reductive. Like all the best war literature, *Earth Logic*, despite its violence, is a pacifist text.

War is ravaging the once prosperous land of Shaftal. The Shaftali have formed bands of fighters into a guerrilla army to resist the invading Sainnites. But what are the costs of victory? (Sadly, it seems every generation faces this question. It is urgent today, as the Iraq War rages.) How much will we change in order to prevail? Does winning come at the price of becoming like our enemies? Is there any other path? Some of the people of Shaftal are born with a special elemental power, corresponding to one of the four elements. Fire elementals have great powers of intuition. Air elementals are powerful truth finders and often act as judges. Water elementals can manipulate time. But the rarest and most powerful is the Earth elemental, someone whose healing powers extend not only to other people but to the land itself.

Earth Logic and its predecessor, *Fire Logic*, center around a small group of scholar-warriors and elementals who search for a path to peace that will not end with the transformation of the generous and free-spirited

Shaftali into a brutal and mean-spirited society. The price of survival is the theme. Can a people survive if their laws do not? How can a legal system operate in an occupied land? One air elemental, a kind of circuit-riding judge, is determined to use law to keep the social fabric intact: "she ceaselessly rewove and repaired the fabric of the law, which the Sainnites tore apart again, before and behind her" (*Fire Logic* 150).

Marks's central philosophical question is, How shall we live in the world, for good or for ill? As very different people join together and bond into a family, we learn both the true nature of community and the difference between the letter and spirit of the law. The spirit of community must infuse the letter of the law. What makes *Earth Logic* a natural for a law-lit course is its confidence in the power of the word. (Marks makes clear this is a power that can be used for good or for evil.) Lawyers, being wordsmiths and knowing the importance of words, understand why, in *Fire Logic*, a repressive government classifies a printing press as a dangerous weapon. Marks's books not only include legal themes but also treat gender, race, and class in interesting ways. To give one example, in her world, women commonly take on a number of traditionally masculine jobs (farmer, soldier, etc.), while men can be healers and nurturers. Sometimes speculative fiction makes its point by treating as ordinary something that would be extraordinary in the real world—something, for example, like equality.

5. Children's Picture Books

Children's literature is laden with law-related themes. Traditionally, much of it has had a didactic purpose. Rules (and the consequences of breaking them) abound in children's literature. Picture books in particular often present a story about right and wrong behavior. Such literature acts as a social indoctrination, telling a child how to live in the world. A good example from the enduring series of Little Golden Books is *The Poky Little Puppy*, by Janette Sebring Lowrey: a naughty dog incessantly breaks the rules and finally learns his lesson by missing dessert. Each semester, I ask students to bring in a children's book that involves legal themes and have them talk about why they chose it. Such themes may be crime and punishment, ideas of justice, or equal treatment under the law. The discussion is always lively.

My favorite contemporary children's picture book happens to have been written by a lawyer and involves the concept of labor negotiations. In

Doreen Cronin's *Click, Clack, Moo: Cows That Type*, Farmer Brown's dairy cows leave him a note with a request: since the barn is cold at night, they ask for electric blankets. Farmer Brown refuses to give them the blankets, so the cows go on strike and refuse to give milk. The situation escalates, in a humorous way, until both sides reach a compromise. The simple story is accompanied by charming illustrations. You could read a boatload of labor law cases to come to the same understanding a child gets from this book: negotiations must be carried out in good faith; and, when in doubt, put it in writing. The power of the written word is clear.

6. Young Adult Literature

Young adult literature often exists in a kind of limbo, sometimes shelved with children's literature, sometimes with adult literature, sometimes under a marginally helpful heading such as "Teens." But that a book is marketed as a young adult text does not mean that it lacks depth or sophistication. Case in point: the three books that make up Philip Pullman's *His Dark Materials* trilogy are among the best books I have ever read. The trilogy is an epic meditation on natural law. It is *Paradise Lost* retold from a child's point of view. It's also a marvelous adventure story, a fantasy, and a bildungsroman, all wrapped up with quantum physics and theology.

Lyra is the protagonist of the first book, *The Golden Compass*. She is a young girl living in an Oxford of another universe. Although her parents are alive, they have essentially abandoned her, and she is being raised by the scholars of Oxford. The theme of abandoned children is prevalent in the trilogy, until it begins to seem as if we all (readers included) are children abandoned by an indifferent universe. In Lyra's world, theologians take the place of scientists, and study dust, which is dark-matter particles. These particles seem attracted to adults but not to children, and the theologians believe that dust is something like original sin. This theory quickly takes on political implications, and Lyra becomes embroiled in an epic power struggle.

Pullman's imaginative scope is enormous, as witnessed by some of the characters Lyra encounters (a talking bear-king, beautiful witches, vampire-like specters, Gypsies who live their entire lives on the water). His intellectual scope is equally broad, as difficult issues surrounding choice, free will, and natural law become key to his theme of the developing of moral judgment. Children, like adults, must choose between good and evil. How

Lyra will choose at her moment of temptation, whether she will become a new Eve only to re-enact another Fall, and whether there could ever be a fortunate Fall are questions addressed in the trilogy. Lyra's journey toward the answers involves choices every step of the way, choices to follow old rules, to break existing rules, or to create new rules for living.

7. Comic Strips

Long-running comic strips can take on an epic quality. We follow the characters as they grow and change over the years and understand the complicated histories behind particular relationships. The richness of the imaginative world created by such comics is not unlike the depth of those worlds created by Victorian serial fiction writers or the addictive worlds of contemporary soap operas.

Alison Bechdel's *Dykes to Watch Out For* comic strip is not the only gay- or lesbian-themed one in existence, but it is certainly long-running (more than twenty years) and very evocative. The strip began in alternative newspapers and now is online. It also can be found in a series of paperback collections from Firebrand Press. It centers around the lives and loves of a group of lesbian friends. Legal and political issues abound, and one of the recurring characters is an environmental lawyer. Gay marriage, adoption rights, health insurance issues, gender and equal pay, race and voting rights are just a few of the law-related themes that appear. But Bechdel's humor and engaging drawings ensure that the strip never seems didactic.

Bechdel elegantly makes clear the bedrock connection between personal and political by focusing on the everyday lives of this group of friends. In a strip titled "Everything I Need to Know I Learned from My Four-Year-Old," the overworked Toni (a CPA) and Clarice (an attorney) are having a late dinner of cold pizza while discussing their son Raphael's behavior in preschool. Raphael hit his friend with a Tonka toy because his friend wouldn't share. The two moms, upset with Raffie's behavior, discuss what to do. They also talk about how overly full their days have become, and Toni mentions that she has to go to a Freedom to Marry Coalition meeting. Clarice asks, "So now you want to get married? Isn't our life oppressive enough?" Toni responds, "It's just not fair! Why should straight couples get all the legal perks?" Raffie chips in with, "They should share!," and Clarice tells him, "You should go down to the state capitol and tell them that, sport." "And take your Tonka truck," adds Toni (56).

In this short strip—eleven panels—there's more than enough material for a class discussion. Discussion topics can include not only constitutional issues such as equal protection and due process but also broad political and narrative questions such as, How can a minority group acquire the authority to tell a story of injustice? What are some possible rhetorical strategies for those seeking social justice? (For example, how does humor operate in this comic strip?) The movement toward social justice is an especially rich one for comic strips and graphic novels, which have not only written language but also visual representations to analyze.

8. Life Stories

Biographies, autobiographies, memoirs, and life stories all tend to be overshadowed in law-lit courses by works of straightforward fiction (novels, plays, poetry). But who is better qualified to give us a perspective on a law than the person whose body has been subjected to its harsh effects? Linda Brent (pen name for Harriet Jacobs) in her autobiographical *Incidents in the Life of a Slave Girl* describes firsthand the effects of slavery and the Fugitive Slave Act. Samuel Delany's essay and short memoir, *Times Square Red, Times Square Blue*, illustrates how New York City's zoning laws of the 1990s affected the lives of gay men who frequented the X-rated movies theaters of Times Square seeking companionship, sex, and sometimes love. It's amazing that a book essentially about zoning can be so sexy (but not prurient), so poignant, and so hard-hitting. (Delany is a science fiction writer, an African American, a gay man, and an English professor.)

9. Supreme Court Briefs

Ordinarily, legal briefs are not the first things that come to mind when I think of law-lit texts to assign. The law part is there, all right, but how can we talk about briefs as literature? Many briefs are dry, poorly written, and monological; the best (the most persuasive and most thoughtful), however, are dialogical. They create tensions, make utterances that anticipate the generation of other utterances and that are shaped by that anticipation. A brief that we can read as opening up, not closing down, the dialogic process is written for the church in the infamous animal sacrifice case decided by the Supreme Court in 1993, *Church of the Lukumi Babalu Aye v.*

City of Hialeah. In that case, a group that practiced animal sacrifice as part of its religion announced plans to open a church in the city of Hialeah, Florida. The city council quickly drafted several ordinances prohibiting the sacrifice of animals in the city, on grounds of animal cruelty, public safety, and public health. The Supreme Court held that the ordinances were an improper infringement on the church's First Amendment right of freedom of religion.

Sometimes focusing on how each side treats a particular word can suggest some of the subtleties and complexities at work in storytelling and the making of meaning in legal briefs. The key word in *Church of the Lukumi Babalu Aye* is *sacrifice*. The concept of animal sacrifice here is part of a dialogic exchange occurring on several levels at once. Each side has a particular meaning in mind, and both sides realize that the readers (the members of the Supreme Court) are unlikely to have had any previous knowledge of a minority religion whose practitioners conduct animal sacrifice. Take a look at the brilliant way the church handles the meaning of *sacrifice* in its brief. It essentially takes an uncanny, unfamiliar concept (animal sacrifice) and, by doing an etymological history of the word *sacrifice*, converts the uncanny to something familiar.

Legal briefs can be used to good effect in class, particularly when discussing the concept of storytelling in the law. A good (and free) source for Supreme Court briefs is the multivolume reference set *Landmark Briefs and Arguments of the Supreme Court of the United States* (Kurland and Casper). (Most law libraries carry this.) Online, in addition to *LexisNexis* and *Westlaw* (paid services that include links to the briefs), it is possible to find recent Supreme Court briefs at such sites as the Yale Law Library site (*United States Supreme Court Records and Briefs*).

10. Your Students' Original Works

Finally, don't forget the possibility of using original work by students in your law-lit class. I typically require a final research paper from my students. But, almost every semester I have at least one student who proposes something a little different. So, for example, I have happily read several law-themed short stories, a libretto for an opera, a couple of chapters from a proposed true-crime novel, and so on. One of my favorites was an unusual student project: a beautiful and challenging original oil painting illustrating the story of freedom of expression. This law student was an artist who had had gallery shows. He was going to write a research paper on the First Amendment and artistic expression, when we decided that a painting might be an even better idea.

The above suggestions are just a few ideas educators might want to consider when selecting new texts for a law-lit course. There are many more possibilities—Internet fan fiction, video games, online multiplayer gaming—all ripe with potential for law-lit analysis.

Zoe Trodd

American Blueprints: Alternative Declarations and Constitutions in the Protest Tradition

> *Literature was urged upon the law school with creative pluck. Af-*
> *ter the agenda made room for Homer and Melville, however, the*
> *audacity and openness stalled. . . . Where are the . . . equivalents*
> *in our practice to . . . "The Trickster Figure in Chicano and Black*
> *Literature" . . . ?*
>
> — Milner Ball, "Confessions"

> *We shall demonstrate once again that in this great, inventive land*
> *man's idlest dreams are but the blueprints and mockups of emerging*
> *realities.*
>
> — Ralph Ellison, *Juneteenth*

In January 1787, Thomas Jefferson declared that "a little rebellion, now and then, is a good thing." Rebellion, he continued, was "as necessary in the political world as storms in the physical" (Letter to James Madison). So too was rebellion on paper: delegates signed the United States Constitution in September that year, and Jefferson later explained that he wanted to "provide in our Constitution for its revision . . . so that it may be handed on, with periodical repairs, from generation to generation" (Letter to Samuel Kercheval 42).

Sure enough, rebellions little and large have repeatedly refreshed America's political world, and made repairs to its founding documents. As Ralph Ellison once observed, the Constitution and the Bill of Rights made up the acting script which future Americans would follow in the process of improvising the futuristic drama of American democracy" (*Collected Essays* 567). While we might be more familiar with attempts by conservatives to employ the language of the Declaration of Independence and the Constitution to make their political case, reformers and radicals have also improvised on that "acting script"—trying to reconcile the Declaration of Independence's ideals with the Constitution's acceptance of slavery and male-only suffrage. They have used the country's founding documents to call for change, to invoke the right of continuous revolution, and to preempt charges of un-Americanism by setting themselves in the mold of 1776 and 1787.

Sometimes this strategy meant rewriting both documents. In a series of little-studied alternative declarations and constitutions that were rooted in broader cultures of reform and canons of protest literature, activist writers adapted the country's very birth certificates for their own burgeoning protest movements. Living in a partially achieved nation and realizing that democracy was not inherited but achieved, they believed—as Ellison phrased it elsewhere—that "in this great, inventive land man's idlest dreams are but the blueprints and mockups of emerging realities" (*Juneteenth* 17). Protest writers saw in these blueprints a route to fulfilling the democratic experiment's failed promises.

Beyond, then, the study of law in literature or law as literature is the study of literature attempting to change the law by rewriting legal documents as new protest literature. "You can dehydrate soups and teas . . . all you need to do is add a drop of water and [they are] reconstituted into [their] real substance. Maybe, that's what those words in those great documents are," suggested the poet Lorenzo Thomas in 2002, of the Declaration and Constitution (345). Protest writers have offered their own words as the drops of water that might reconstitute a dehydrated social contract.

Teaching alternative declarations and constitutions opens up the possibility of connecting the processes of teaching and the products of protest writers. If protest literature has involved a series of reconstitutions, then perhaps the protest classroom can also reconstitute America's blueprints. If protest is a form of intellectual bricolage—ideas and language transformed by new contexts into a living protest legacy—then perhaps students might continue to debunk the myth of American history as a series of fresh starts, of America as a perpetual New World. In creating their own reconstitutions, students might enter the ongoing conversation with a palpable protest past.

Toward the Second American Revolution: Abolitionist Blueprints

The first voice in that palpable past is the Declaration of Independence. One of America's first great works of protest literature, it is judiciously alliterated ("British brethren," "common kindred," "connections and correspondence"), with a chiasmus ("Enemies in War, in Peace Friends") and a harmonious blend of short and long words in the penultimate paragraph (Jefferson et al. 18). The preamble's sentences begin with single-syllable words that progress toward concluding three- and four-syllable words, so that the paragraph's progression feels as inevitable ("necessary," as the preamble puts it) as independence itself (16). Carl Becker even called the last section of the document "perfection itself." He added:

> [It] was a sure sense that made Jefferson place "lives" first and "fortunes" second. How much weaker if he had written "our fortunes, our lives, and our sacred honor"! . . . Or suppose him to have omitted "sacred"! Consider the effect of omitting any of the words. . . . (197)

But if the document's concision and rhythms embodied the necessary revolution, the document nonetheless contained an important omission. Jefferson had originally drafted a denunciation of the slave trade, and its deletion left America's "original sin" (as James Madison once put it [qtd. in Ketcham 627]) lurking between the final document's lines. The abolitionist Wendell Phillips would later write to Frederick Douglass that "the fathers, in 1776, signed . . . with the halter about their necks" (12). The Constitution, Phillips said, meant there was "no single spot" where a "fugitive slave" was safe (12–13). Indeed, the Constitution quietly accepted slavery. It gestured at the existence of slaves in 1.2 ("all other persons"), legalized the "importation" of people until 1808 in 1.9, and announced that any "person held to service or labor in one State" who escaped into another would be "delivered up" in 4.2 (Constitution).

Abolitionists attempted to remove that "halter" and bring slavery out from the margins of both documents. William Lloyd Garrison's "No Union with Slaveholders" (1840) and Douglass's "A Nation in the Midst of a

Nation" (1853) echoed the Declaration to point out its silence on slavery. Other writers justified slave rebellion with reference to 1776. William Wells Brown's rebel slave George in *Clotel* (1853) exclaims, "You say your fathers fought for freedom—so did we" (224). Harriet Beecher Stowe's George in *Uncle Tom's Cabin* (1852) declares, "You say your fathers did it; if it was right for them, it is right for me!" (187). Douglass's Madison Washington in *The Heroic Slave* (1853) claims his freedom with the words, "We have done that which you applaud your fathers for doing, and if we are murderers, so were they" (235).

Abolitionists took up the Constitution as well. Gerrit Smith insisted that it was an antislavery document and simply required correct interpretation, while Garrison publicly burnt it as a proslavery document on 4 July, 1854. Douglass famously pronounced it a "most cunningly-devised and wicked compact" that demanded "the most constant and earnest efforts of the friends of righteous freedom for its complete overthrow" ("Constitution" 91). While not transforming its language into literature, as he did with the Declaration, Douglass proposed that the Constitution should be approached from the heart nonetheless. He explained in 1849:

> We cannot talk "lawyer like" about law, nor can we, in connection with such an ugly matter-of-fact looking thing as the United States Constitution, bring ourselves to split hairs about the alleged legal rule of interpretation. . . . The Constitution is not an abstraction. It is a living, breathing fact. (91–92)

It was the radical abolitionist John Brown who finally took Douglass at his word and interpreted the Constitution as so "living" that it might be transformed. In April 1858, Brown traveled to Chatham, Ontario. He carried with him a "Provisional Constitution" for the government of a slave-free nation, drafted during a recent two-week stay at Douglass's home in Rochester, New York. Complete with a three-branch government, Brown's document was a full imitation of the Constitution and opened with a ringing condemnation of slavery:

> Whereas slavery . . . is none other than a most barbarous, unprovoked, and unjustifiable war of one portion of its citizens upon another portion . . . in utter disregard and violation of those eternal and self-evident truths set forth in our Declaration of Independence: Therefore we, citizens of the United States, and the oppressed people . . . ordain and establish for ourselves the following Provisional Constitution and Ordinances, the better to protect our persons, property, lives, and liberties. (110)

Faced with the Declaration's ideal of equality and the Constitution's acceptance of slavery, Brown was trying to remove the contradiction (while emphasizing in article forty-six of the document that he looked "to no dissolution of the Union, but simply to Amendment and Repeal" [119]).

Seeking support, he organized a Provisional Constitutional Convention for 8–10 May 1858. Chatham had a large free black community, a number of whom attended. Douglass did not attend, though he kept a copy of Brown's constitution, and the forty-six delegates who attended were Brown's men. To those present, Brown outlined his plans to attack Harpers Ferry in western Virginia, arm slave rebels, march south, and establish a slave-free nation in the southern Appalachian Mountains under the convention's constitution. He suggested a separate state government in the Union, but the delegates objected that blacks were not equal under American law, approving instead a proposal for a new independent society. In their America, everyone would be free, equal, and enfranchised.

By the end of the first day, the convention had ratified a provisional constitution and elected Brown as commander in chief of the provisional forces and the paper government. On 10 May, Brown appointed a committee with full power to fill all the executive, legislative, judicial, and military offices named in the constitution. He also continued to plan his raid on Harpers Ferry throughout the days in Chatham, and the Provisional Constitution was ready for distribution when he attacked on 16 October 1859. Interviewers repeatedly questioned him about it after the raid.

But while the language of the Declaration and Constitution loomed large in the antebellum imagination, America's Second Revolution soon seemed as incomplete as its first. The Civil War, with its Emancipation Proclamation and three reconstruction amendments, might have produced what Eric Foner calls a "new American Constitution" (12), but for many reformers the amendments "became dead letters" (13). Taking up the abolitionist mantel, late-nineteenth-century protest writers tried to bring those letters to life.

Beyond the Second Revolution: Feminist and Labor Blueprints

Feminists were another group of nineteenth-century activists who echoed the Declaration in their fiction, poetry, and essays. They produced explicit rewrites as well; new declarations that, like the original document of 1776, achieve the level of literature. As early as 1848, Elizabeth Cady Stanton and others had produced the "Seneca Falls Declaration of Sentiments"

(Trodd 27–30). They kept the three-part structure of the 1776 Declaration but made additions in the preamble that brought women out from its margins. The women directly substituted the original eighteen grievances with eighteen new ones. Solutions followed as eleven resolutions.

Then, in 1876, Stanton and the National Woman Suffrage Association took up the country's founding documents with a new urgency, writing the "Declaration and Protest of the Women of the United States" (1876). Fighting to remove the word "male" from the Fourteenth Amendment and add "sex" to the Fifteenth's assurance that the right to vote could not be denied because of "race, color, or previous condition of servitude" (thereby laying the groundwork for the Nineteenth Amendment), Stanton included in the declaration a long list of solutions that adapted the United States Constitution. Again blending both documents, Victoria C. Woodhull wrote "A New Constitution for the United States of the World" (1872): a full rewrite of the Constitution, with nineteen constitutional articles, and a "Declaration of Independence" that insisted on the freedom and equality of all persons at birth.

Labor activists were still another group who offered their own interpretations of the Declaration and Constitution in literature (e.g., in numerous labor songs of the nineteenth century; in Edward Bellamy's *Looking Backward* [1888]; in Eugene Debs's 1918 speech to the Court, "Address to the Jury"). Like abolitionists and feminists, labor activists revised the founding documents. An early example came in December 1829, when George Evans published "The Working Men's Declaration of Independence" in New York's *Working Man's Advocate* and Philadelphia's *Mechanic's Free Press*. It concluded with a demand for "equal means to *obtain* equal moral happiness" (26)—changing "pursuit of happiness" (25), quoted in its opening, to achievement of happiness, so that the document itself seems to journey toward happiness in the movement between its opening and its close. Evans also wrote new grievances and made additions to the original Declaration: "'in the course of human events, it becomes necessary' for one class of a community to assert their natural and unalienable rights in opposition to other classes" (24); "'All experience hath shown, that mankind' in general, and we as a class in particular, 'are more disposed to suffer'" (25).

After the Civil War, adapting the abolitionists' rhetoric for their own protests against wage slavery, labor activists returned to the language of the Declaration. In 1895, the socialist Daniel De Leon examined "'76 in '95," as he phrased it in the introduction to his "Declaration of Interdependence." De Leon explained:

> [T]he American colonists . . . bequeathed to their descendents a na-
> tional fabric suited to their time and surroundings, but, as they be-
> lieved, readily adjustable to future conditions of progress. . . . Now . . .
> in imitation of their manly course, we, free-born men held in wage ser-
> vitude against natural law and social principles . . . hereby call upon our
> fellow sufferers to be one with us in the present class struggle.
> (qtd. in P. Foner, *We* 142)

His declaration lists grievances like the 1776 document, but in the second
paragraph he emphasizes that the situation in 1895 is even more desperate: "More truly can we say of our plutocracy than our forefathers did of
the British crown that 'its history is one of repeated injuries and usurpa-
tions'" (De Leon 38–39).

The populist and progressive eras, then the Depression, saw the publication of new declarations and constitutions: James West's *A Proposed New
Constitution for the United States* (1890); Frederick Adams's "A Majority Rule Constitution" (1896); Henry Morris's *Waiting for the Signal*
(1898); Eustace Reynolds's "Modified Constitution" (1915); "Declaration of Workers' and Farmers' Rights and Purposes," by the National Unemployed Leagues (1933); and Hugh Hamilton's *A Second Constitution
for the United States of America* (1938). Socialists continued to insist on
the need for "repairs," as Jefferson had put it, and Algie Simons declared
that the Constitution was "forced upon a disenfranchised people . . . in . . .
the interests of a small body of wealthy rulers" (123).

But while John Adams had acknowledged "the toil, and blood, and
treasure, that it will cost us to maintain this declaration" and concluded that
"posterity will triumph" (Letter 420), posterity had still not triumphed—
despite the efforts of radical reformers to "maintain this declaration." In
1920, Archibald Grimke returned to Adams's image of blood. "The muse
of history, dipping her iron pen in the generous blood of the Negro, has
written large across the page of that Preamble, and the face of the Declaration of Independence, the words, 'sham, hypocrisy,'" he proclaimed
(675).

Nor had "posterity" triumphed by 1963, when Martin Luther King,
Jr., called again on the Declaration's promise in his "I Have a Dream"
speech at the March on Washington. King said:

> When the architects of our republic wrote the magnificent words of the
> Constitution and the Declaration of Independence, they were signing
> a promissory note to which every American was to fall heir. This note
> was a promise that all men . . . would be guaranteed the unalienable

rights of life, liberty, and the pursuit of happiness. It is obvious today that America has defaulted on this promissory note insofar as her citizens of color are concerned. (217)

In fact, King's speech was part of a newly sustained attempt to redraw America's blueprints: at the centennial of America's Second Revolution came the civil rights and black power era.

A Third American Revolution: The Civil Rights and Black Power Blueprints

King continued to call on the Declaration in his speech "Declaration of Independence from the War in Vietnam" (1967), and other radicals went on to rewrite the Constitution: Leland D. Baldwin in "A Reformed Constitution" (1972) and Rexford G. Tugwell in "An Emerging Constitution" (1974). Yet the most infamous attempt of the 1960s to rewrite the Declaration and Constitution, and so draw up a new "promissory note," came from the Black Panther Party. Their "Ten Points" (1966) referenced the Constitution and quoted the Declaration of Independence ("Ten-Point Platform"). They used a bold font to make their own additions (through emphasis):

> Prudence, indeed, will dictate that governments long established should not be changed for light and transient causes. . . . But, when a long train of abuses and usurpations . . . evinces a design to reduce them under absolute despotism, it is their right, it is their duty, to throw off such government.

The rest of the platform was intended, as Reginald Major later explained, to complete "the work done by the revolution of 1776" (281–82).

In a speech of 19 June 1970, Huey Newton called for a convention like John Brown's—to write a new constitution: Newton said:

> The empty promise of the Constitution to "establish Justice" lies exposed to the world by the reality of Black Peoples' existence. The Constitution of the U.S.A. does not and never has protected our people or guaranteed to us those lofty ideals enshrined within it. (269).

He added:

> [T]he present structure of power and authority in the United States must be radically changed or we, as a people, must extricate ourselves. . . .

> If we are to remain a part of the United States, then we must have
> a new Constitution that will strictly guarantee our Human Rights to
> Life, Liberty and the Pursuit of Happiness. (270)

He emphasized as well:

> Black people are not the only group within America that stands in need
> of a new Constitution. Other oppressed ethnic groups, the youth of
> America, Women, young men who are slaughtered as cannon fodder
> in mad, avaricious wars of aggression, our neglected elderly people all
> have an interest. (271)

Between 10,000 and 15,000 people arrived at the Constitutional
Convention on the weekend of 5 September 1970 in Philadelphia. Some
delegates were from the American Indian Movement, Students for a Democratic Society, and the Gay Liberation Front. After a series of working-
group sessions, delegates presented their reports at a plenary session. The
documents proposed an international bill of rights, an end to the draft,
proportional representation for women and minorities, free decentralized
medical care, and a ban on the manufacture of genocidal weapons. The
Black Panther Party explained a week later that these reports as a whole
"provided a basis for one of the most progressive Constitutions in the
history of humankind." That constitution would guarantee the "right
of national self-determination . . . to all oppressed minorities," prohibit
"U.S. aggression and interference in the internal affairs of other nations,"
affirm sexual "self-determination for women and homosexuals," make
"[a]dequate housing, health care, and day care . . . Constitutional Rights,
not privileges" ("People"). The next step was to circulate the documents
to a continuance committee and gather again on 4 November in Washington, DC, to ratify a final document. The date was changed to 27 November but canceled at the last minute, just as several thousand delegates
reached DC.

The Black Panther Party achieved no third American revolution for a
post-civil-rights generation—not even those "repairs" envisaged by Jefferson. But their attempt to reconstitute, yet again, America's dehydrated
social contract—along with their repeated self-locations alongside Nat
Turner, John Brown, and radical abolitionism—placed them in a protest
tradition that has refused to discard history or participate in what D. H.
Lawrence terms "the true myth of America": the "sloughing of the old
skin, towards a new youth" (60). With its chosen and reshaped ancestry,
protest literature has challenged the particularly pervasive idea that radi-

cal reform movements are without memory, never putting down roots. "[T]he literature of America is above everything else a literature of protest and of rebellion," insisted Floyd Dell in 1920; "Debs and Haywood are as American as Franklin and Lincoln" (46). In the tradition of Douglass, Brown, Stanton, De Leon, King, and others, the Black Panther Party established a patriotic protest by redrawing America's blueprints.

Reconstituting Today: Student Blueprints for the Twenty-First Century

In 2002, Harvard launched a lecture course called American Protest Literature, from Tom Paine to Tupac. Each year since then, it has attracted between two hundred and three hunderd undergraduates, who explain their interest in the course as both academic and political: they take the course in order to understand the nature of protest and its literature and to find tools with which to further transform society. The course's journey from 1776 to the present day asserts that while "it is the present that calls us to activism, it is history that must nourish our choices and commitment" and that historical amnesia means "we cannot build on what has been done before because we do not even know it is there to build on" (Rich 152, 147).

The course is structured around two lectures and a discussion section each week. At the end of the course, students are offered the option of producing a work of creative protest instead of a final critical essay. Around ninety-five percent of all students take the creative route. The course frames protest literature as a genre that has deep historical memory, and students build on the activism that has gone before by creating their own protest pieces: poetry, short stories, drama, pamphlets, speeches, novellas, painting, photography, music, conceptual art, installation, sculpture, short films, fictionalized interviews, quilting, protest events, wood engravings, mock newspapers.

Students accompany these creative projects with a short analysis. They are asked to consider how their aesthetic choices support the protest message and to argue how their project is an effective work of protest today. They are also asked to make connections between their work and the reform movements we have studied; to analyze it in a formal and historical tradition; and to discuss how their work's structure, style, and devices build on and revise the narrative traditions we have encountered. Some examples of successful student projects have been a mural of the Last Supper protesting homophobia and its links to the Christian tradition (the student revised Leonardo da Vinci's *The Last Supper* to depict Christ and his disciples in erotic poses), a revision of "America the Beautiful" protesting the war in Iraq (the student wrote a cello piece that had unresolved tensions through dissonance), and a series of lithographs protesting homophobia (the student built on the poetry of Hart Crane and used bridges to symbolize the healing of cultural divides). The course includes an exhibition at the end of the semester. Students perform their plays, music, dances, and speeches and display their literature and visual art.

Students are asked in the last lecture to see that they have become protest artists themselves and that, as a new generation of activists, they might continue to seek out what is wrong in their society, reimagine that society, and do what they can to fix it. Reading the course literature and producing works of protest leave them with a further responsibility: to know that "[h]istorical responsibility has, after all, to do with action" (Rich 145).

Recommended Teaching Materials

Boyd, Stephen R., ed. *Alternative Constitutions for the United States: A Documentary History.* Westport: Greenwood, 1992.

Foner, Philip S., ed. *American Labor Songs of the Nineteenth Century.* Urbana: U of Illinois P, 1975.

———, ed. *We, the Other People: Alternative Declarations of Independence by Labor Groups, Farmers, Woman's Rights Advocates, Socialists, and Blacks, 1829-1975.* Urbana: U of Illinois P, 1976.

McCarthy, Timothy Patrick, and John McMillian, eds. *The Radical Reader: A Documentary History of the American Radical Tradition.* New York: New, 2003.

Ollman, Bertell, and Jonathan Birnbaum, eds. *The U.S. Constitution: 200 Years of Anti-federalist, Abolitionist, Feminist, Muckraker, Progressive, and Especially Socialist Criticism.* New York: New York UP, 1990.

Trodd, Zoe, ed. *American Protest Literature.* Cambridge: Harvard UP, 2006.

Notes on Contributors

Matthew Anderson is associate professor and chair of the Department of English and Language Studies at the University of New England. He co-edited, with Austin Sarat and Cathrine Frank, *Law and the Humanities: An Introduction*.

Philip Auslander is professor in the School of Literature, Communication, and Culture at Georgia Institute of Technology. He is the author of *Liveness: Performance in a Mediatized Culture* and *Performing Glam Rock: Gender and Theatricality in Popular Music*. He is also a freelance art writer.

Ayelet Ben-Yishai is lecturer at the University of Haifa. She is currently writing "Common Precedents: The Presentness of the Past in Victorian Fiction and Law," a book on the impact of precedent in the nineteenth century, from law to the culture at large.

Mary Flowers Braswell is professor of English at the University of Alabama, Birmingham. She is the author of *The Medieval Sinner* and *Chaucer's "Legal Fiction": Reading the Records* and the coeditor, with John Bugge, of *The Arthurian Tradition: Essays in Convergence*. Her current book project is "The Chaucer Scholarship of Mary Eliza Haweis."

Peter Brooks is Andrew W. Mellon Foundation Scholar in the University Center for Human Values and the Department of Comparative Literature at Princeton University. He is the author of *Henry James Goes to Paris* and *Troubling Confessions: Speaking Guilt in Law and Literature*.

Kieran Dolin is associate professor of English and cultural studies at the University of Western Australia. He is the author of *Fiction and the Law: Legal Discourse in Victorian and Modernist Fiction* and is currently studying the significance of property law, especially of native title and Aboriginal land rights, in Australian literature.

Florence Dore has joined the faculty of the English and Comparative Literature Department at the University of North Carolina, Chapel Hill. The author of *The Novel and the Obscene: Sexual Subjects in American Modernism*, she is completing a new book on postwar Southern fiction and privacy law.

Alex Feerst is a fellow at the Center for Internet and Society at Stanford Law School, specializing in intellectual property and constitutional law.

David H. Fisher is professor of philosophy at North Central College. Among his current interests are revenge violence narratives in cross-cultural perspective, Paul Ricoeur, and ancient Athenian law.

Cathrine O. Frank is associate professor of English at the University of New England. She is author of *Law, Literature, and the Transmission of Culture in England, 1837–1925* and, with Austin Sarat and Matthew Anderson, of *Law and the Humanities: An Introduction.*

Nan Goodman is associate professor at the University of Colorado, Boulder, and has been a visiting professor of law and humanities at Georgetown Law Center. She is the author of *Shifting the Blame* and the coeditor of *The Turn around Religion in America.* Her book "Banish'd: Common Law and the Rhetoric of Social Exclusion in Early America," is forthcoming.

Chaya Halberstam is assistant professor of religious studies at King's University College, University of Western Ontario. She is the author of *Law and Truth in Biblical and Rabbinic Literature.* Among her interests are questions of justice, legal authority, and divine command in ancient Judaism.

Susan Sage Heinzelman is associate professor of English and director of the Center for Women's and Gender Studies at the University of Texas, Austin. She coedited, with Zipporah Batshaw Wiseman, the anthology *Representing Women in Law and Literature.* She is the author of *Riding the Black Ram: Law, Literature, and Gender.*

Peter C. Herman is professor of English literature at San Diego State University. He is the author of *Royal Poetrie: Monarchic Verse and the Political Imaginary of Early Modern England* and *Destabilizing Milton:* Paradise Lost *and the Poetics of Incertitude.*

Diane Hoeveler is professor of English at Marquette University. She is the author of *Gothic Riffs: Secularizing the Uncanny in the European Imaginary, 1780–1820, Romantic Androgyny: The Women Within,* and *Gothic Feminism: The Professionalization of Gender from Charlotte Smith to the Brontës.*

Harold Joseph is president of the Hopi Conservation District. He works to promote awareness of natural resource concerns on Indian lands, to recover the environment that has been destroyed by fast development and mining companies, and to preserve Hopi cultural ceremonies.

Valerie Karno is associate professor of English at the University of Rhode Island. She has written about film, animation and the animate, vengeance and forgiveness, treaties with Native Americans, and small-claims-court shows on television.

Lenora Ledwon is professor of law at the Saint Thomas University School of Law. She is the author of *Law and Literature: Text and Theory* and, with several other authors, *Law and Popular Culture: Text, Notes, and Questions.* Her current project is the use of graphic novels to teach visual persuasion.

Nancy S. Marder is professor of law at the Chicago-Kent College of Law in the Illinois Institute of Technology. She is the author of *The Jury Process.* She teaches statutory interpretation and a course on law, literature, and feminism.

Bridget M. Marshall is assistant professor at the University of Massachusetts, Lowell. She is the author of *The Transatlantic Gothic Novel and the Law, 1790–1860*. Among her interests are disability in literature and the witch-craft trials.

Alyce Miller is professor of English at Indiana University, Bloomington, and a fiction writer, essayist, and poet. Her book *Water* is winner of the Mary McCarthy Prize. She teaches creative writing, literature, and special-topics courses and leads a double life as an attorney specializing in animal rights and family law.

D. Quentin Miller is associate professor of English at Suffolk University. He is the author of *Prose and Cons: New Essays on Contemporary U.S. Prison Literature* and *Reviewing James Baldwin: Things Not Seen*. He is currently preparing a monograph on James Baldwin and the law.

Harriet Murav is professor of Slavic languages and literatures at the University of Illinois. She is the author of *Music on a Speeding Train: Soviet Yiddish and Russian-Jewish Literature of the Twentieth Century*, *Russia's Legal Fictions*, and *Holy Foolishness: Dostoevsky's Novels and the Poetics of Cultural Critique*.

Victoria Myers is professor of English at Pepperdine University. She coedited, with Robert M. Maniquis, *Godwinian Moments: From Enlightenment to Romanticism*. Among her interests are the Restoration and eighteenth-century drama.

Linda Myrsiades is professor of English and comparative literature at West Chester University. She is the author of *Medical Culture in Revolutionary America: Feuds, Duels, and a Court Martial* and *Splitting the Baby: A Cultural Study of Abortion in Literature and Law, Rhetoric and Cartoon*.

Jacqueline O'Connor is professor of English at Boise State University. She is the author of *Dramatizing Dementia: Madness in the Plays of Tennessee Williams*. Among her interests is documentary theater.

Julie Stone Peters is professor of English and comparative literature at Columbia University. She is the author of *Theatre of the Book: Print, Text, and Performance in Europe, 1480–1880*. She is currently working on a book on legal performance.

Greg Pingree is professor of law at the Florida Coastal School of Law. He is the author of *Narrative, Argument, and Persuasion in American Public Discourse*. Among his interests are legal and cultural narratives of Mormon polygamy in nineteenth-century America and of homosexuality in contemporary America.

Ravit Reichman is associate professor of English at Brown University. She is the author of *The Affective Life: Legal Modernism and the Literary Imagination*. Among her interests are literary responses to war.

Lisa Rodensky is associate professor of English at Wellesley College. She is the author of *The Crime in Mind* and the editor of *Decadent Poetry from Wilde to Naidu*. She is currently writing a monograph on critical terms in the nineteenth- and twentieth-century novel review.

Austin Sarat is William Nelson Cromwell Professor of Jurisprudence and Political Science at Amherst College. He is the author of *The Road to Abolition? The Future of Capital Punishment in the United States* and *When Government Breaks the Law* and is currently writing "Hollywood's Law: What Movies Do for Democracy."

Hilary Schor is professor of English, comparative literature, gender studies, and law in USC College at the University of Southern California. She is the author of *Dickens and the Daughter of the House* and *Scheherezade in the Marketplace: Elizabeth Gaskell and the Victorian Novel*.

Richard Schur is associate professor at Drury University. He is the author of *Parodies of Ownership: Hip-Hop Aesthetics and Intellectual Property Law* and the coeditor, with Lovalerie King, of *African American Culture and Legal Discourse*.

Caleb Smith is associate professor of English and American studies at Yale University. He is the author of *The Prison and the American Imagination* and is currently working on "The Oracle and the Curse: A Poetics of Justice, 1765–1865."

Cristine Soliz is assistant professor of English and director of Liberal Studies at Fort Valley State University. She is interested in cultural studies and Chicano discourse in its dialectic with indigenous and American discourse and is currently writing a monograph on the Aztecs.

Simon Stern is assistant professor of law and English at the University of Toronto. He has written on eighteenth-century fiction, literary fraud, copyright law, and criminal procedure. His current research includes the origins of the "reasonable person" standard in the common law and the rise of the analytical method in Anglo-American law.

Nomi Stolzenberg is Nathan and Lilly Shapell Professor of Law at the University of Southern California Law School. She is interested in the modern liberal secular state and currently writing a book, with David N. Myers, about the Satmar community of Kiryas Joel.

Brook Thomas is chancellor's professor of English at the University of California, Irvine. He is the author of *Civic Myths: A Law and Literature Approach to Citizenship* and *American Literary Realism and the Failed Promise of Contract*. His current project is the literary economies of Reconstruction.

Zoe Trodd teaches English and African American studies at Columbia University. Her books include *Modern Slavery, To Plead Our Own Cause, American Protest Literature,* and *Meteor of War: The John Brown Story.* She is currently working on a book about historical memory in African American protest literature.

Elliott Visconsi is associate professor of English at the University of Notre Dame. He is the author of *Lines of Equity: Literature and the Origins of Law in Later Stuart England* and is currently working on "The Invention of Civil Religion: Church and State in Postrevolutionary England and America."

Patricia D. Watkins is associate professor of English at California State University, Northridge. She has published in the area of African American literature and the law.

Richard H. Weisberg is Walter Floersheimer Professor of Constitutional Law at Cardozo School of Law, Yeshiva University. He is the author of *The Failure of the Word, Poethics: And Other Strategies of Law and Literature,* and *When Lawyers Write.* He represented plaintiffs in Vichy-related litigation for the restitution of stolen banking assets.

Robert Weisberg is Edwin E. Huddleson, Jr., Professor of Law and codirector of the Stanford Criminal Justice Center. He is the author, with Guyora Binder, of *Literary Criticisms of Law.* His current project is a study of causes and implications of mass incarceration in the United States.

Robin West is professor of law and dean for research and academic programs at the Georgetown University Law Center. She is the author of *Marriage, Sexuality, and Gender, Re-imagining Justice,* and *Progressive Constitutionalism.*

James Boyd White is Hart Wright Professor of Law emeritus and professor of English emeritus at the University of Michigan. He is the author of *Living Speech: Resisting the Empire of Force, Justice as Translation: An Essay in Cultural and Legal Criticism,* and *The Legal Imagination: Studies in the Nature of Legal Thought and Expression.*

Theodore Ziolkowski is professor emeritus of German and comparative literature at Princeton University. He is the author of *Dresdner Romantik, Die Welt im Gedicht: Rilkes Sonette an Orpheus II.4* and *Scandal on Stage.* One of his current projects is the reception of *Gilgamesh* in the twentieth century.

Works Cited

Abraham, Kenneth S. "Statutory Interpretation and Literary Theory: Some Common Concerns of an Unlikely Pair." *Rutgers Law Review* 32 (1980): 676–94. Print.

Abrams v. US. 250 US 616. Supreme Court of the US. 1919. *Supreme Court Collection*. Legal Information Inst., Cornell U Law School, n.d. Web. 17 Feb. 2010.

Abu-Jamal, Mumia. *Live from Death Row*. New York: Addison, 1995. Print.

Ackroyd, Peter. *The Life of Thomas More*. New York: Doubleday, 1988. Print.

Adams, Carol J. *The Sexual Politics of Meat: A Feminist-Vegetarian Critical Theory*. London: Continuum, 1999. Print.

Adams, Frederick Upham. "A Majority Rule Constitution." Boyd 92–106.

Adams, John. Letter from John Adams to Abigail Adams. 3 July 1776. *The Works of John Adams: Second President of the United States*. 1856. Ed. Charles Francis Adams. Vol. 9. New York: AMS, 1971. 419–20. Print.

———. *Massachusetts Constitution*. 2 Mar. 1780. *The Founders' Constitution*. Ed. Phillip Kurland and Ralph Lerner. U of Chicago P; Liberty Fund. Web. 14 Dec. 2009.

Aeschylus. *Oresteia*. Ed. and trans. Michael Ewans. London: Dent, 1995. Print.

Aesop. *Aesop's Fables*. Trans. Laura Gibbs. New York: Oxford UP, 2003. Print.

Alexie, Sherman. *Indian Killer*. New York: Warner, 1998. Print.

Alien and Sedition Acts (1798). Our Documents, n.d. Web. 5 Oct. 2009.

Alim, H. Samy. *Roc the Mic Right: The Language of Hip Hop Culture*. New York: Routledge, 2006. Print.

Allen, Stephen. *Observations on Penitentiary Discipline: Addressed to William Roscoe, Esq., of Liverpool, England*. New York: Totten, 1827. Print.

Allott, Antony. *Essays in African Law: With Special Reference to the Law of Ghana*. London: Butterworth, 1960. Print.

Alter, Robert. *The Art of Biblical Narrative*. New York: Basic, 1981. Print.

———. *The David Story*. New York: Norton, 1999. Print.

———. *The Five Books of Moses*. New York: Norton, 2004. Print.

Amsterdam, Anthony, and Jerome Bruner. *Minding the Law*. Cambridge: Harvard UP, 2000. Print.

Anderson, Joel. "Note and Comment: What's Wrong with This Picture? Dead or Alive: Protecting Actors in the Age of Virtual Reanimation." *Loyola of Los Angeles Entertainment Law Review* 25 (2004–05): 155–201. Print.

Andrić, Ivo. *The Bridge on the Drina*. Chicago: U of Chicago P, 1977. Print.

Angel, Marina. "Susan Glaspell's *Trifles* and a 'Jury of Her Peers': Woman Abuse in a Literary and Legal Context." *Buffalo Law Review* 45 (1997): 779–837. Print.

The Animated Skeleton. 1798. Chicago: Valancourt, 2005. Print.

Annan, Kofi A. *We the Peoples: The Role of the United Nations in the Twenty-First Century*. United Nations Millennium Declaration. United Nations, Mar. 2000. Web. 23 Feb. 2010.

Ardener, Shirley. "The Comparative Study of Rotating Credit Associations." *Journal of the Royal Anthropological Institute of Great Britain and Ireland* 94.2 (1964): 202–29. Print.

Aristotle. *Art of Rhetoric*. Trans. J. H. Freese. Cambridge: Harvard UP, 1926. Print.

Arnold, Matthew. *Culture and Anarchy*. 1869. Ed. J. Dover Wilson. Cambridge: Cambridge UP, 1990. Print.

———. "Dover Beach." *Norton Anthology of English Literature*. Ed. M. H. Abrams. 6th ed. Vol. 2. New York: Norton, 1993. 1366–67. Print.

Askwith, Ivan. "Gollum: Dissed by the Oscars?" *Salon*. Salon Media Group, 18 Feb. 2003. Web. 17 Feb. 2010.

Auslander, Philip. *Liveness: Performance in a Mediatized Culture*. 2nd ed. London: Routledge, 2008. Print.

Auster, Paul. *Timbuktu*. New York: Picador, 2000. Print.

Ayer, John D. "The Very Idea of 'Law and Literature.'" *Michigan Law Review* 88 (1987): 1559–612. Print.

Babe. Dir. Christopher Noonan. Kennedy Miller Productions, 1995. Film.

Baillie, Joanna. *De Monfort*. Baillie, *Plays* 299–388.

———. "Introductory Discourse." Baillie, *Plays* 67–114.

———. *Plays on the Passions*. 1798. Ed. Peter Duthie. Ontario: Broadview, 2001. Print.

Baker, John Hamilton. *An Introduction to English Legal History*. 1979. 3rd ed. London: Butterworth, 1990. Print.

Bakhtin, Mikhail. *Problems of Dostoevsky's Poetics*. Trans. Caryl Emerson. Minneapolis: U of Minnesota P, 1984. Print.

Bakke v. Regents of Univ. of California. S.F. no. 23311. 553 P. 2nd 1152. Supreme Court of California. 1976. *Pacific Reporter*. 2nd ser. Vol. 553. 1976. 1152–91. *LexisNexis*. Web. 6 Aug. 2010 Cal. LEXIS 336.

Bakunin, Mikhail. "Church and State." *No Gods, No Masters: An Anthology of Anarchism*. Ed. Daniel Guérin. Trans. Paul Sharkey. Oakland: AK, 2005. 170–76. Print.

Balcombe, Jonathan. *Pleasurable Kingdom: Animals and the Nature of Feeling Good*. New York: Palgrave, 2006. Print.

Baldwin, James. *If Beale Street Could Talk*. New York: Dell, 1964. Print.

———. *Notes of a Native Son*. 1955. Boston: Beacon, 1984. Print.

Baldwin, Leland D. "A Reformed Constitution." Boyd 206–45.

Ball, Milner S. "Confessions." *Cardozo Studies in Law and Literature* 1.2 (1989): 185–97. Print.

———. *The Word and the Law*. Chicago: U of Chicago P, 1995. Print.

Ballaster, Rosalind. *Seductive Forms: Women's Amatory Fiction from 1684–1740*. Oxford: Clarendon, 1992. Print.

Balzac, Honoré de. *Le colonel Chabert*. Paris: Livre de Poche Classique, 1973. Print.

———. *Père Goriot*. Paris: Livre de Poche Classique, 2007. Print.

Banner, Stuart. *How the Indians Lost Their Land: Law and Power on the Frontier*. Cambridge: Harvard UP, 2005. Print.

Barber, Greg. "The Birmingham Church Bombing." "Pursuing the Past: A Mississippi Newspaper Investigates Crimes of the Civil Rights Era." *Online News-Hour*. MacNeil/Lehrer Productions, n.d. Television, Web. 17 Feb. 2010.

Barfield, Owen. *Poetic Diction: A Study in Meaning.* Middletown: Wesleyan UP, 1973. Print.

Baron, Jane B. "Interdisciplinary Legal Scholarship as Guilty Pleasure: The Case of Law and Literature." Freeman and Lewis 21–45.

———."Law, Literature, and the Problems of Interdisciplinarity." *Yale Law Journal* 108 (1999): 1059–85. Print.

Barthes, Roland. "The Old Rhetoric: An Aide-Memoire." *The Semiotic Challenge.* Trans. Richard Howard. New York: Hill, 1988. 11–94. Print.

Basch, Norma. "For Good or for Evil: The 1848 Statute." *In the Eyes of the Law: Women, Marriage, and Property in Nineteenth-Century New York.* Ithaca: Cornell UP, 1982. 136–61. Print.

Beard, Joseph J. "Clones, Bones, and Twilight Zones: Protecting the Digital Persona of the Quick, the Dead, and the Imaginary." *Berkeley Technology Law Journal* 16.3 (2001): 1–111. Print.

Beatty, Paul. *The White Boy Shuffle.* New York: Picador, 1996. Print.

Beaumont, Gustave de, and Alexis de Tocqueville. *On the Penitentiary System in the United States and Its Application in France.* 1833. Trans. Francis Lieber. Carbondale: Southern Illinois UP, 1964. Print.

Bechdel, Alison. *Split-Level Dykes to Watch Out For.* Ithaca: Firebrand, 1998. Print.

Becker, Carl. *The Declaration of Independence.* New York: Knopf, 1942. Print.

Becker, George, ed. *Documents of Literary Realism.* Princeton: Princeton UP, 1963. Print.

Before the Rain. Dir. Milcho Manchevski. Aim, 1994. Film.

Bekoff, Marc. *The Emotional Lives of Animals.* Novato: New World Lib., 2007. Print.

Bell, Derrick. "Racial Realism—After We're Gone: Prudent Speculations on America in a Post-racial Epoch." Delgado, *Critical Race Theory* 2–8.

Bellamy, Edward. *Looking Backward, 2000–1887.* Boston: Ticknor, 1888. Print.

Ben. Dir. Phil Karlson. Bing Crosby Productions, 1972. Film.

Benjamin, Walter. "Critique of Violence." *Reflections: Essays, Aphorisms, Autobiographical Writings.* Trans. Edmund Jephcott. New York: Schocken, 1978. 277–300. Print.

Bentham, Jeremy. *An Introduction to the Principles of Morals and Legislation.* 1823. Facsim. rpt. Introd. Laurence J. LaFleur. New York: Hafner, 1948. Print.

Binder, Guyora. "Representing Nazism: Advocacy and Identity at the Trial of Klaus Barbie." *Yale Law Journal* 98 (1989): 1321–83. Print.

Binder, Guyora, and Robert Weisberg. *Literary Criticisms of Law.* Princeton: Princeton UP, 2000. Print.

Birus, Hendrik. "Nietzsche's Concept of Interpretation." *Revue de critique et de théorie littéraire* 3 (1984): 78–82. Print.

Blackstone, William. *Commentaries on the Laws of England.* Introd. Thomas A. Green. 4 vols. Chicago: U of Chicago P, 1979. Print. Facsim. of the first ed. 1765–69.

Blain, Virginia. "Double Vision and Double Standard in *Bleak House*: A Feminist Perspective." Tambling 65–86.

Blair, M. Elizabeth. "Commercialization of Rap Music Youth Subculture." Forman and Neal 497–504.

Blank, Jessica, and Erik Jensen. *The Exonerated.* New York: Faber, 2004. Print.

Bloom, Harold. *Jesus and Yahweh.* New York: Riverhead, 2005. Print.

Boehm, Christopher. *Blood Revenge: The Anthropology of Feuding in Montenegro and Other Tribal Societies.* Lawrence: UP of Kansas, 1984. Print.

Bolt, Robert. *A Man for All Seasons.* New York: Vintage, 1960. Print.

Boogie Down Productions. "Dope Beat." *Criminal Minded.* B-Boy Records, 1987. Audio CD.

Bourdieu, Pierre. "The Force of Law: Toward a Sociology of the Juridical Field." Trans. Richard Terdiman. *Hastings Law Journal* 38 (1987): 805–50. Print.

———. *Outline of a Theory of Practice.* Trans. Richard Nice. Cambridge: Cambridge UP, 1977. Print.

Bouvier, John. *Institutes of American Law.* Philadelphia: Peterson, 1851. Print.

Bowers v. Hardwick. 478 US 186. Supreme Court of the US. 1986. *Supreme Court Collection.* Legal Information Inst., Cornell U Law School, n.d. Web. 18 Feb. 2010.

Boyd, Stephen R., ed. *Alternative Constitutions for the United States: A Documentary History.* Westport: Greenwood, 1992. Print.

Boyer, Paul. "Should Expediency Always Trump Tradition? AIHEC/NSF Project Develops Indigenous Evaluation Methods." *Tribal College Journal* 18.2 (2006): 12–15. Print.

Boyer, Paul, and Stephen Nissenbaum, eds. *The Salem Witchcraft Papers.* New York: Da Capo, 1977. *Salem Witch Trials: Documentary Archive and Transcription Project.* Ed. Benjamin C. Ray. U of Virginia. Web. 12 Aug. 2009.

Boyer, Peter J. "Big Men on Campus: The Lacrosse Furor and Duke's Divided Culture." *New Yorker* 4 Sept. 2006. Condé Nast Digital, n.d. Web. 18 Feb. 2010.

Boy Scouts of Amer. v. Dale. 530 US 640. Supreme Court of the US. 2000. *Supreme Court Collection.* Legal Information Inst., Cornell U Law School, n.d. Web. 18 Feb. 2010.

Bradwell v. State. 83 US 130. Supreme Court of the US. 1873. *US Supreme Court Center.* Justia, n.d. Web. 18 Feb. 2010.

Brady, Kristin. "Tess and Alec: Rape or Seduction." *Thomas Hardy Annual.* No. 4. Ed. Norman Page. Basingstoke: Macmillan, 1986. 126–47. Print.

Bragdon, Kathleen J. *Native People of Southern New England, 1500–1650.* Norman: U of Oklahoma P, 1996. Print.

Braswell, Mary Flowers. *Chaucer's "Legal Fiction": Reading the Records.* Madison: Assoc. UPs, 2001. Print.

Braudel, Ferdinand. *The Structures of Everyday Life: Civilization and Capitalism, 15th–18th Century.* Vol. 1. Berkeley: U of California P, 1992. Print.

Brent, Linda. *See* Jacobs, Harriet.

Brodhead, Richard. "The 'New' *Sister Carrie*." *Yale Review* 71.4 (1982): 597–600. Print.

Brooks, Cleanth. "The Heresy of Paraphrase." *The Well Wrought Urn.* New York: Harcourt, 1947. 192–214. Print.

Brooks, Peter. "Law and Literature in Dialogue." Letter. *PMLA* 120.5 (2005): 1645–46. Print.

———. "The Law as Narrative and Rhetoric." Brooks and Gewirtz 14–24.

———. "Narrativity of the Law." *Cardozo Studies in Law and Literature* 14 (2002): 1–10. Print.

————. "The Plain Meaning of Torture? Literary Deconstruction and the Bush Administration's Legal Reasoning." *Slate*. 9 Feb. 2005. Washington Post, n.d. Web. 18 Feb. 2010.

————. *Troubling Confessions: Speaking Guilt in Law and Literature*. Chicago: U of Chicago P, 2000. Print.

Brooks, Peter, and Paul Gewirtz, eds. *Law's Stories: Narrative and Rhetoric in the Law*. New Haven: Yale UP, 1996. Print.

Brown, John. "Provisional Constitution." Trodd and Stauffer 110–20.

Brown, William Wells. *Clotel*. London: Partridge, 1853. Print.

Brown v. Board of Educ. of Topeka, Kansas. 349 US 294. Supreme Court of the US. 1955. *Supreme Court Collection*. Legal Information Inst., Cornell U Law School, n.d. Web. 18 Feb. 2010.

Budanov, A. F., and G. M. Fridlender, eds. *Letopis' zhizni i tvorchestva F. M. Dostoevskogo, 1821–1881*. Vol. 2. Saint Petersburg: Akademicheskii proekt, 1994. Print.

Buell, Lawrence. "Introduction: In Pursuit of Ethics." *PMLA* 114.1 (1999): 7–19. Print.

Bulfinch, Thomas. *Bulfinch's Mythology*. New York: Modern Lib, 1943. Print.

Bulosan, Carlos. *America Is in the Heart*. Seattle: U of Washington P, 1973. Print.

Burrill, Derek Alexander. "Out of the Box: Performance, Drama, and Interactive Software." *Modern Drama* 48.3 (2005): 492–511. Print.

Burton, Steven J. *An Introduction to Law and Legal Reasoning*. Boston: Little, 1985. Print.

Butler, Octavia. *Parable of the Sower*. New York: Four Walls Eight Windows, 1993. Print.

Butt, John, and Kathleen Tillotson. "The Topicality of *Bleak House*." *Dickens at Work*. London: Methuen, 1957. 177–200. Print.

Bybee, Jay S. "Memorandum for Alberto R. Gonzales, Counsel to the President, Re: Standards of Conduct for Interrogation under 18 U.S.C. §§ 2340–2340A." Greenberg and Dratel 81–117.

Byock, Jesse. *Viking Age Iceland*. London: Penguin, 2001. Print.

Byrd, Mike. "Written Documentation at a Crime Scene." *Crime Scene Investigation Network*. Crime Scene Resources, n.d. Web. 18 Feb. 2010.

Byron, George Gordon. *The Two Foscari*. *LION* [1898 ed., ed. E. H. Coleridge]. Web. 15 Aug. 2010.

Cahan, Abraham. *The Rise of David Levinsky*. New York: Penguin, 1993. Print.

Cain, Patricia A. "Feminist Jurisprudence: Grounding the Theories." *Berkeley Women's Law Journal* 4 (1989–90): 191–214. Print.

California Federal Savings and Loan Assn. v. Guerra. 479 US 272. Supreme Court of the US. 1987. *US Supreme Court Opinions*. FindLaw, n.d. Web. 18 Feb. 2010.

California v. Brown. 479 US 538. Supreme Court of the US. 1987. *US Supreme Court Opinions*. FindLaw, n.d. Web. 18 Feb. 2010.

Callahan, S. Alice. *Wynema: A Child of the Forest*. 1891. Ed. A. Lavonne Brown Ruoff. Lincoln: U of Nebraska P, 1997. Print.

Campbell, Angela. "Could a Chimpanzee or Bonobo Take the Stand?" *Animal Law Review* 8 (2002): 243–57. Print.

Campbell, Lily B. *Shakespeare's "Histories": Mirrors of Elizabethan Policy*. San Marino: Huntington Lib., 1947. Print.

Campisi, Jack. "The Mashpee Indians: Tribe on Trial." Carrillo, *Readings* 32–42.

Canassatego. "Last Day of the Lancaster Treaty Council." Ed. Nicolas W. Proctor. Simpson Coll., n.d. Web. 18 Feb. 2010.

Capote, Truman. *In Cold Blood*. New York: Random, 1965. Print.

Cardozo, Benjamin N. *"Law and Literature" and Other Essays and Addresses*. New York: Harcourt, 1931. Print.

———. *Selected Writings*. Ed. Margaret E. Hall. New York: Bender, 1947. Print.

Carew, Thomas, and Inigo Jones. *Coelum Britannicum: The Poems of Thomas Carew*. Ed. Rhodes Dunlap. Oxford: Clarendon, 1949. Print.

Carmichael, Calum. *The Origins of Biblical Law*. Ithaca: Cornell UP, 1992. Print.

Carnegie, Andrew. "Autobiography of Andrew Carnegie." Hutner 56–68.

Carpenter, T. *A Report of an Action for a Libel Brought by Dr. Benjamin Rush against William Cobbett, in the Supreme Court of Pennsylvania, December Term, 1799, for Certain Defamatory Publications in a News-paper Entitled* Porcupine's Gazette, *of Which the Said William Cobbett Was Editor*. Philadelphia: Woodward, 1800. Print.

Carrillo, Jo. "Identity as Idiom: *Mashpee* Reconsidered." Carrillo, *Readings* 43–59.

———, ed. *Readings in American Indian Law*. Philadelphia: Temple UP, 1998. Print.

Carroll, Lewis. *Through the Looking-Glass and What Alice Found There*. London: Macmillan, 1899. Electronic Text Center, U of Virginia Lib., Mar. 1999. Web. 9 Mar. 2010.

Carroll, William C. "Theories of Kingship in Shakespeare's England." *A Companion to Shakespeare's Works: The Histories*. Ed. Richard Dutton and Jean E. Howard. Vol. 2. Malden: Blackwell, 2003. 125–45. Print.

Carter, Angela. *The Sadeian Woman and the Ideology of Pornography*. New York: Harper, 1978. Print.

Carter, Jimmy. Interview by Robert Scheer. *Playboy* Nov. 1976: 63–86. Print.

Carter, Stephen L. *The Emperor of Ocean Park*. New York: Knopf, 2002. Print.

Carton, Evan. "Pudd'nhead Wilson and the Fiction of Law and Custom." *American Realism: New Essays*. Ed. Eric J. Sundquist. Baltimore: Johns Hopkins UP, 1982. 82–94. Print.

Cat People. Dir. Paul Schrader. RKO Pictures, 1982. Film.

Caudwell, Sarah. *The Shortest Way to Hades*. New York: Penguin, 1984. Print.

Chafee, Zecharia. "The Disorderly Conduct of Words." *Columbia Law Review* 41.3 (1941): 381–404. Print.

Chapman, George. *Bussy D'Ambois. The Stuart Period*. Ed. Russell A. Fraser and Norman Rabkin. New York: Macmillan, 1976. 271–301. Print. Vol. 2 of *Drama of the English Renaissance*.

Chaucer, Geoffrey. *The Riverside Chaucer*. Gen. ed. Larry D. Benson. Boston: Houghton, 1987. Print.

Chaucer Life-Records. Ed. Martin M. Crow and Clair C. Olsen. Austin: U of Texas P, 1966. Print.

Cheever, John. *Falconer*. New York: Knopf, 1977. Print.

Chesnutt, Charles W. *The Marrow of Tradition*. New York: Penguin, 1993. Print. Penguin Classics.

Chevigny, Bell Gale, ed. *Doing Time: Twenty-Five Years of Prison Writing*. New York: Arcade, 1999. Print.

Cheyfitz, Eric. "The (Post) Colonial Construction of Indian Country." *The Columbia Guide to American Indian Literatures*. Ed. Cheyfitz. New York: Columbia UP, 2006: 1–124. Print.

Christianson, Scott. *Bodies of Evidence: Forensic Science and Crime*. Guilford: Lyons, 2006. Print.

Church of the Lukumi Babalu Aye v. City of Hialeah. 508 US 520. Supreme Court of the US. 1993. *US Supreme Court Center*. Justia, n.d. Web. 18 Feb. 2010.

Cicero. "In Support of the Manilian Law: On the Command of CNS Pampas." *Selected Political Speeches of Cicero*. Trans. Michael Grant. London: Penguin, 1969. 33–70. Print.

"The Civil Rights Act of 1875." *Citizen Source*. Citizen Source, 2009. Web. 18 Feb. 2010.

"Civil Rights Cases, 109 US 3 (1883)." *US Supreme Court Opinions*. FindLaw, n.d. Web. 18 Feb. 2010.

Clark, Michael P. "Teaching the Text of Early American Literature." *A Companion to the Literatures of Colonial America*. Ed. Susan Castillo and Ivy Schweitzer. Malden: Blackwell, 2005. 94–109. Print.

"Cloture." *Senate Glossary*. US Senate, n.d. Web. 18 Feb. 2010.

Coady, C. A. J. "The Idea of Violence." Steger and Lind 23–38.

Coats, George W. "Parable, Fable, and Anecdote: Storytelling in the Succession Narrative." *Interpretation* 35.4 (1981): 368–82. Print.

Cobb, William Jelani. *To the Break of Dawn: A Freestyle on Hip Hop Aesthetics*. New York: New York UP, 2007. Print.

Cobbett, William. "Equipage of Death." *Porcupine's Gazette* 5 Oct. 1797: n. pag. Print.

———. "A Hard Case." *Porcupine's Gazette* 26 Oct. 1797: n. pag. Print.

———. *Letters from William Cobbett to Edward Thornton Written in the Years 1797 to 1800*. Ed. G. D. H. Cole. London: Oxford UP, 1937. Print.

———. *Porcupine's Works; Containing Various Writings and Selections, Exhibiting a Faithful Picture of the United States of America; of Their Governments, Laws, Politics, and Resources; of the Characters of Their Presidents, Governors, Legislators, Magistrates, and Military Men; and of the Customs, Manners, Morals, Religion, Virtues and Vices of the People*. 12 vols. London: Cobbett, 1801. Print.

———. "To Drs. Rush and Caldwell." *Porcupine's Gazette* 21 Oct. 1797: n. pag. Print.

Coetzee, J. M. *Disgrace*. New York: Penguin, 2000. Print.

———. *Elizabeth Costello*. New York: Penguin, 2004. Print.

———. *The Lives of Animals*. Princeton: Princeton UP, 1999. Print.

Cohen, David. *Law, Violence and Community in Classical Athens*. Cambridge: Cambridge UP, 1995. Print.

Cohen, Felix. "Transcendental Nonsense and the Functional Approach." Fisher, Horwitz, and Reed 212–27.

Cohen, Matt. *The Networked Wilderness: Communicating in Early New England*. Minneapolis: U of Minnesota P, 2010. Print.

Coke, Edward. Preface to *The Fourth Part of the Reports of Edward Coke. The Selected Writings of Sir Edward Coke*. Ed. Steve Sheppard. Vol. 1. Indianapolis: Liberty Fund, 2005. 94–105. Print.

Coker v. Georgia. 433 US 584. Supreme Court of the US. 1977. *US Supreme Court Center*. Justia.com, n.d. Web. 31 Jan. 2011.

Cole, Simon A. "Twins, Twain, Galton, and Gilman: Fingerprinting, Individualization, Brotherhood, and Race in *Pudd'nhead Wilson*." *Configurations* 15.3 (2007): 227–65. Print.

Coleridge, Samuel Taylor. *Biographia Literaria*. Ed. James Engell and W. Jackson Bate. 2 vols. Princeton: Princeton UP, 1983. Print.

———. *Remorse: A Tragedy in Five Acts*. Cox and Gamer 165–204.

Collins, Wilkie. *The Woman in White*. 1860. Oxford: Oxford UP, 1973. Print.

Colvin, Sydney. Rev. of *Middlemarch. George Eliot: The Critical Heritage*. Ed. David Carroll. New York: Barnes, 1971. 331–38. Print.

Comprehensive Immigration Reform Act of 2007. THOMAS, Lib. of Congress, n.d. Web. 28 Mar. 2010.

Conrad, Joseph. "The Tale." *Tales of Hearsay*. London: Unwin, 1924. 155–205. Print.

Constitution of the United States. 1787. Our Documents, n.d. Web. 23 Feb. 2010.

Coombe, Rosemary J. "Critical Cultural Legal Studies." *Yale Journal of Law and the Humanities* 10 (1998): 463–86. Print.

———. "Is There a Cultural Studies of Law?" *A Companion to Cultural Studies*. Ed. Toby Miller. Oxford: Blackwell, 2001. 36–62. Print.

Cooper, Bernard. "A Hundred and One Ways to Cook Hamburger." *Truth Serum: Memoirs*. Boston: Houghton, 1996. 3–14. Print.

Cooper v. Aaron. 358 US 1. Supreme Court of the US. 1958. *US Supreme Court Center*. Justia, n.d. Web. 18 Feb. 2010.

Cormack, Bradin. "Strange Love; or, Holding Lands." *Law and Humanities* 1.2 (2007): 31–48. Print.

Cornell, Drucilla. *The Imaginary Domain: Abortion, Pornography, and Sexual Harassment*. New York: Routledge, 1995. Print.

Cornell, Drucilla, Michel Rosenfeld, and David Gray Carlson, eds. *Deconstruction and the Possibility of Justice*. New York: Routledge, 1992. Print.

Cotton, John. *Bloody Tenent Washed and Made White in the Blood of the Lamb*. Whitefish: Kessinger, 2003. Print.

Couch, Cullen. "Teaching the Narrative Power of the Law." *UVA Lawyer*. U of Virginia School of Law, fall 2005. Web. 14 June 2007.

Coughlin, Anne. "Regulating the Self: Autobiographical Performances in Outsider Scholarship." *Virginia Law Review* 81 (1995): 1229–340. Print.

The Court Baron: Being Precedents for Use in Seignoral and Other Local Courts, together with Select Pleas from the Bishop of Ely's Court of Littleport. Ed. Frederic William Maitland and William P. Baildon. Vol. 4. London: Quaritch, 1891. Print.

Cover, Robert. "Foreword: Nomos and Narrative." *Harvard Law Review* 97.1 (1983): 4–68. Print.

———. "Nomos and Narrative." Minow, Ryan, and Sarat 95–172.

———. "Violence and the Word." *Yale Law Journal* 95 (1986): 1609–21. Rpt. in Minow, Ryan, and Sarat 203–38.

Cox, Jeffrey, and Michael Gamer, eds. *The Broadview Anthology of Romantic Drama*. Ontario: Broadview, 2003. Print.

Craft-Fairchild, Catherine. *Masquerade and Gender*. University Park: Pennsylvania State UP, 1993. Print.

Craig, Richard B. *The Bracero Program*. Austin: U of Texas P, 1971. Print.

Crenshaw, Kimberle. "Demarginalizing the Intersection of Race and Sex: A Black Feminist Critique of Antidiscrimination Doctrine, Feminist Theory, and Antiracist Politics." *University of Chicago Legal Forum* (1989): 139–67. Print.

———."Mapping the Margins: Intersectionality, Identity Politics, and Violence against Women of Color." *Stanford Law Review* 43 (1991): 1241–99. Print.

Cressy, David. *Coming Over: Migration and Communication between England and New England in the Seventeenth Century*. Cambridge: Cambridge UP, 1987. Print.

Cronin, Doreen. *Click, Clack, Moo: Cows That Type*. New York: Simon, 2000. Print.

Curtis, Michael Kent. *Free Speech, "The People's Darling Privilege": Struggles for Freedom of Expression in American History*. Durham: Duke UP, 2000. Print.

Cuvier, Georges Leopold. "Varieties of the Human Species." *Animal Kingdom: Arranged according to Its Organization*. 1797. Trans. H. M. C. Murtrie. 1834. *Internet Archive*. Web. 18 Feb. 2010.

Danner, Mark. "Torture and Truth." *New York Review of Books*. New York Rev. of Books, 10 June 2004. Web. 18 Feb. 2010.

Danzig, Richard, and Richard Weisberg. "Reading List on Law and Literature." *Humanities* 7.3 (1977): 6–7. Print.

Davidowicz, Lucy S. *The War against the Jews, 1933–1945*. New York: Holt, 1975. Print.

Davies, Alan. *The Native Speaker: Myth and Reality*. Clevedon: Multilingual Matters, 2003. Print.

Davis, Rebecca Harding. Life in the Iron Mills *and Other Stories*. Ed. Tillie Olsen. New York: Feminist, 1993. Print.

Davis, William A., Jr. "The Rape of Tess: Hardy, English Law, and the Case for Sexual Assault." *Nineteenth Century Literature* 52 (1997): 221–31. Print.

Dayan, Joan. "Poe, Persons, and Property." *American Literary History* 11.3 (1999): 405–25. Print.

Debs, Eugene. "Address to the Jury." *Writings and Speeches of Eugene V. Debs*. Ed. Arthur M. Schlesinger. New York: Hermitage, 1948. 433–37. Print.

"Deceased Personality's Name, Voice, Signature, Photograph, or Likeness in Advertising or Soliciting." California Civil Code, Section 990, 1988. *Practitioner's Guide to California Right of Publicity Law*, by Amy Hogue. FindLaw, n.d. Web. 18 Feb. 2010.

Declaration of Independence. Charters of Freedom. Natl. Archives, n.d. Web. 12 Aug. 2009.

Dekker, Thomas. "Thomas Dekker's *The Shoemaker's Holiday*." *The Theatrical City: Culture, Theater and Politics in London, 1576–1649*. Ed. David L. Smith, Richard Strier, and David Bevington. Cambridge: Cambridge UP, 1995. 87–116. Print.

Delany, Samuel. *Times Square Red, Times Square Blue*. New York: New York UP, 2001. Print.

De Leon, Daniel. "Declaration of Interdependence by the Socialist Labor Party."
    Trodd 38–41.

Delgado, Richard, ed. *Critical Race Theory: The Cutting Edge*. Philadelphia: Temple
    UP, 1995. Print.

———. "Storytelling for Oppositionists and Others: A Plea for Narrative."
    Michigan Law Review 87.8 (1989): 2411–41. Print.

Dell, Floyd. "Our America." *Liberator* 3 (1920): 44–46. Print.

Deloney, Thomas. *Jack of Newbury. The Novels of Thomas Deloney*. Ed. Merritt E.
    Lawlis. Westport: Greenwood, 1978. 1–88. Print.

Deloria, Vine, Jr. *God Is Red: A Native View of Religion*. 30th anniversary ed.
    Golden: Fulcrum, 2003. Print.

de Man, Paul. *Allegories of Reading*. New Haven: Yale UP, 1979. Print.

———. "The Return to Philology." *The Resistance to Theory*. Minneapolis: U of
    Minnesota P, 1986. 21–53. Print.

Demers, Joanna. *Steal This Music: How Intellectual Property Law Affects Musical
    Creativity*. Athens: U of Georgia P, 2006. Print.

d'Errico, Peter. "The Law Is Terror Put into Words: A Humanist's Analysis of
    the Increasing Separation between Concerns of Law and Concerns of Justice."
    Learning and the Law 2.3 (1975): 38–58. Print.

Derrida, Jacques. "Force de loi: Le fondement mystique de l'autorité." *Cardozo
    Law Review* 11.5-6 (1990): 920–1036. Print.

———. "Force of Law: The 'Mystical Foundation of Authority.'" *Cardozo Law
    Review* 11.5-6 (1990): 921–1045. Cornell, Rosenfeld, and Carlson 3–67. *Acts
    of Religion*. Ed. Gil Anidjar. London: Routledge, 2002. 228–98. Print.

———. *Spurs: Nietzsche's Styles*. Trans. Barbara Harlow. Chicago: U of Chicago P,
    1979. Trans. of *Éperons: Les styles de Nietzsche*. Paris: Flammarion, 1978. Print.

Dershowitz, Alan. "Life Is Not a Dramatic Narrative." Brooks and Gewirtz 99–113.

———. *Why Terrorism Works: Understanding the Threat, Responding to the
    Challenge*. New Haven: Yale UP, 2003. Print.

DeStafano, John M., III. "On Literature as Legal Authority." *Arizona Law Review*
    49 (2007): 521–52. Print.

"Detroit Race Riots, 1943." People and Events. *The American Experience*. PBS
    Online, n.d. Web. 18 Feb. 2010.

De Vries, Hent, and Samuel Weber, eds. *Violence, Identity, and Self-Determination*.
    Stanford: Stanford UP, 1997. Print.

Dickens, Charles. *Bleak House*. 1853. Ed. Nicola Bradbury. London: Penguin,
    1996. Print.

———. *Oliver Twist*. 1838. Ed. Kathleen Tillotson. Oxford: Clarendon, 1966.
    Print.

———. "Philadelphia, and Its Solitary Prison." *American Notes and Pictures from
    Italy*. London: Macmillan, 1903. 84–96. Print.

Dickey, James. "The Sheep Child." *The Norton Anthology of Modern Poetry*. 2nd
    ed. Ed. Richard Ellmann and Robert O'Clair. New York: Norton, 1988. 1084.
    Print.

Dickinson, Emily. *Complete Poems*. Ed. Thomas H. Johnson. Boston: Little, 1961.
    Print.

Dickson-Carr, Darryl. *African American Satire: The Sacredly Profane Novel.* Columbia: U of Missouri P, 2001. Print.

di Donato, Pietro. *Christ in Concrete.* New York: Signet, 1993. Print.

"Diminshed Capacity." *Wex.* Legal Information Inst., Cornell U Law School, 19 Aug. 2010. Web. 7 Oct. 2010.

Dolin, Kieran. *Fiction and the Law: Legal Discourse in Victorian and Modernist Literature.* Cambridge: Cambridge UP, 1999. Print.

Dollimore, Jonathan. "Introduction: Shakespeare, Cultural Materialism, and the New Historicism." *Political Shakespeare: New Essays in Cultural Materialism.* Ed. Dollimore and Alan Sinfield. Ithaca: Cornell UP, 1994. 2–17. Print.

Dore, Florence. *The Novel and the Obscene: Sexual Subjects in American Modernism.* Stanford: Stanford UP, 2005. Print.

Dostoevsky, Fyodor. *Polnoe sobranie sochinenii v tridtsati tomakh.* 30 vols. Leningrad: Nauka, 1972. Print.

———. *A Writer's Diary, 1837–76.* Trans. Kenneth Lantz. Evanston: Northwestern UP, 1993. Print.

Douglass, Frederick. "The Constitution and Slavery." Ollman and Birnbaum 91–95.

———. *The Heroic Slave. Autographs for Freedom.* Boston: John P. Jewett, 1853. 174–239. Print.

———. *My Bondage and My Freedom.* 1855. Gates, *Douglass Autobiographies* 103–452.

———. *Narrative of the Life of Frederick Douglass, an American Slave.* 1845. New York: Signet, 1997. Print.

———. "A Nation in the Midst of a Nation." *The Frederick Douglas Papers.* Ser. 1, vol. 2. Ed. John W. Blassingame. New Haven: Yale UP, 1982. 423–40. Print.

Drapac, Vesna. *War and Religion: Catholics in the Churches of Occupied Paris.* Washington: Catholic U of Amer. P, 1998. Print.

Dreiser, Theodore. Sister Carrie*: An Authoritative Text, Backgounds and Sources, Criticism.* Ed. Donald Pizer. Norton Critical Ed. New York: Norton, 1991. Print.

DuBois, W. E. B. "Criteria of Negro Art." 1926. *The Norton Anthology of Theory and Criticism.* Ed. Vincent B. Litchi. New York: Norton, 2001. 980–87. Print.

Dumm, Thomas. *Democracy and Punishment: Disciplinary Origins of the United States.* Madison: U of Wisconsin P, 1987. Print.

Duncan, Ian. "The End of the Astrologer: *Guy Mannering.*" *Modern Romance and Transformations of the Novel: The Gothic, Scott, Dickens.* Cambridge: Cambridge UP, 1992. 111–34. Print.

Dworkin, Ronald. "Law as Interpretation." *Critical Inquiry* 9.1 (1982): 179–200. Print.

———. *Law's Empire.* Cambridge: Harvard UP, 1986. Print.

———. *A Matter of Principle.* Cambridge: Harvard UP, 1985. Print.

Edwards, Harry T. "The Growing Disjunction between Legal Education and the Legal Profession." *Michigan Law Review* 91 (1992): 34–78. Print.

Eggers, Dave. "After I Was Thrown in the River and Before I Drowned." *How We Are Hungry.* New York: Vintage, 2005. 211–18. Print.

Eigen, Joel Peter. *Witnessing Insanity: Madness and Mad-Doctors in the English Court.* Fwd. Nigel Walker. New Haven: Yale UP, 1995. Print.

Elias, Robert H., ed. *Letters of Theodore Dreiser.* 2 vols. Philadelphia: U of Pennsylvania P, 1959. Print.

Eliot, George. *Middlemarch.* Ed. Peter Carroll. Oxford: Clarendon, 1986. Print.

———. *The Mill on the Floss.* Ed. Gordon S. Haight. Oxford: Clarendon, 2008. Print.

———. *Quarry for Middlemarch.* Ed. Anna Theresa Kitchel. Berkeley: U of California P, 1950. Print.

———. "Silly Novels by Lady Novelists." *Westminster Review* 10 (1856): 442–61. Print.

Eliot, T. S. *After Strange Gods: A Primer of Modern Heresy.* London: Faber, 1934. Print.

———. *Notes toward the Definition of Culture.* London: Faber, 1948. Print.

Ellison, Ralph. *The Collected Essays of Ralph Ellison.* Ed. John F. Callahan. New York: Modern Lib., 2003. Print.

———. *Juneteenth.* New York: Vintage, 1999. Print.

Elyot, Thomas. *The Boke Named the Governour.* London: Dent, 1907. Print.

L'enfant sauvage. Dir. François Truffaut. Les Filmes du Carrosse, 1970. Film.

Engel, Marian. *Bear.* Boston: Godine, 2002. Print.

Erickson, Amy Louise. "Common Law versus Common Practice: The Use of Marriage Settlements in Early Modern England." *Economic History Review* 43 (1990): 21–39. Print.

Erskine, Thomas. *The Speeches of the Right Hon. Lord Erskine, When at the Bar.* Ed. James Ridgway. 3rd ed. 4 vols. London, n.d. Print.

Eskridge, William N., Jr. *Gaylaw: Challenging the Apartheid of the Closet.* Cambridge: Harvard UP, 1999. Print.

Euripides. "The Medea." *Euripides 1.* Ed. David Grene and Richard Lattimore. Chicago: U of Chicago P, 1955. Print.

Evans, E. P. *The Criminal Prosecution and Capital Punishment of Animals.* 1906. Whitefish: Kessinger, 2006. Print.

Evans, George. "The Working Men's Party Declaration of Independence." 1829. Trodd 24–26.

Executive Order 8802: Prohibition of Discrimination in the Defense Industry. 25 June 1941. Our Documents, n.d. Web. 19 Feb. 2010.

Executive Order 9066: The President Authorizes Japanese Relocation. 19 Feb. 1942. *History Matters.* Amer. Social History Productions, n.d. Web. 19 Feb. 2010.

Ex parte Milligan. 71 US 2. Supreme Court of the US. 1866. *US Supreme Court Opinions.* FindLaw, n.d. Web. 19 Feb. 2010.

Farber, Daniel, and Suzanna Sherry. *Beyond All Reason: The Radical Assault on Truth in American Law.* New York: Oxford UP, 1997. Print.

Faulkner, William. *Intruder in the Dust.* 1948. New York: Vintage Intl., 1991. Print.

———. "A Rose for Emily." Oates 182–90.

Favre, David. "Equitable Self-Ownership for Animals." *Duke Law Journal* 50 (2000): 473–502. Print.

Feher, Michel, ed. *The Libertine Reader: Eroticism and Enlightenment in Eighteenth-Century France*. New York: Zone, 1997. Print.

Ferguson, Robert. "Becoming American: High Treason and Low Invective in the Republic of Laws." Sarat and Kearns 103–33.

———. *Law and Letters in American Culture*. Cambridge: Harvard UP, 1984. Print.

———. *Reading the Early Republic*. Cambridge: Harvard UP, 2004. Print.

———. "Story and Transcription in the Trial of John Brown." *Yale Journal of Law and the Humanities* 6 (1994): 37–74. Print.

Fifteenth Amendment to the U.S. Constitution: Voting Rights. 3 Feb. 1870. Our Documents, n.d. Web. 23 Feb. 2010.

Finkelman, Paul. *Slavery in the Courtroom: An Annotated Bibliography of American Cases*. Washington: Lib. of Cong., 1985. Print.

Fish, Stanley. *Doing What Comes Naturally: Change, Rhetoric, and the Practice of Theory in Literary and Legal Studies*. Durham: Duke UP, 1999. Print.

———. "Holocaust Denial and Academic Freedom." *Valparaiso Law Review* 35 (2001): 499–524. Print.

———. *Is There a Text in This Class? The Authority of Interpretive Communities*. Cambridge: Harvard UP, 1980. Print.

———. *There's No Such Thing as Free Speech . . . and It's a Good Thing Too*. New York: Oxford UP, 1994. Print.

Fisher, William, III., Morton Horwitz, and Thomas Reed, eds. *American Legal Realism*. New York: Oxford UP, 1993. Print.

Fiss, Owen M. "Objectivity and Interpretation." *Stanford Law Review* 34 (1982): 739–64. Print.

Fitzpatrick, Peter. *Modernism and the Grounds of Law*. Cambridge: Cambridge UP, 2001. Print.

———. "Why the Law Is Also Nonviolent." Sarat 142–73.

Fleta*: Volume 2, Prologue, Books 1–2*. Ed. and trans. H. G. Richardson and G. O. Sayles. London: Quaritch, 1955. Print.

The Fly. Dir. David Cronenberg. Brooks Films, 1986. Film.

Foner, Eric. "The Second American Revolution." *In These Times* 16–22 Sept. 1987: 12–13. Print.

Foner, Philip S., ed. *American Labor Songs of the Nineteenth Century*. Urbana: U of Illinois P, 1975. Print.

———, ed. *The Black Panthers Speak*. New York: Da Capo, 1995. Print.

———, ed. *We, the Other People: Alternative Declarations of Independence by Labor Groups, Farmers, Woman's Rights Advocates, Socialists, and Blacks, 1829–1975*. Urbana: U of Illinois P, 1976. Print.

Fortescue, John. *On the Laws and Governance of England*. Ed. Shelley Lockwood. Cambridge: Cambridge UP, 1997. Print.

Foucault, Michel. *Discipline and Punish*. 1975. Trans. Alan Sheridan. New York: Vintage, 1977. Print.

———. *Madness and Civilization*. New York: Vintage, 1988. Print.

———. *The Order of Things: An Archaeology of the Human Sciences*. New York: Vintage, 1994. Print.

Fourteenth Amendment to the Constitution of the United States. *Charters of Freedom.* Natl. Archives, n.d. Web. 12 Aug. 2009.

Francione, Gary. *Introduction to Animal Rights: Your Child or Your Dog?* Philadelphia: Temple UP, 2000. Print.

Frank, Joseph. Introduction. *The Diary of a Writer.* By F. M. Dostoevsky. Trans. Boris Brasol. Santa Barbara: Smith, 1979. Print.

Frankfurter, Felix. *The Case of Sacco and Vanzetti: A Critical Analysis for Lawyers and Laymen.* Boston: Little, 1927. Print.

Franklin, H. Bruce, ed. *Prison Writing in Twentieth-Century America.* New York: Penguin, 1998. Print.

Fraser, David. *The Jews of the Channel Islands and the Rule of Law.* Brighton: Sussex Academic, 2000. Print.

———. *Law after Auschwitz.* Durham: Academic, 2005. Print.

Freeman, Michael, and Andrew D. E. Lewis, eds. *Law and Literature.* Oxford: Oxford UP, 1999. Print.

Freidel, Frank, ed. *Union Pamphlets of the Civil War.* Vol. 2. Cambridge: Belknap, 1967. Print.

Freneau, Philip. "The Book of Odes." Hiltner 601.

———. "No. XII. To the Philadelphia Doctors." Hiltner 602–04.

———. *The Poems of Philip Freneau: Poet of the American Revolution.* Ed. Fred Lewis Pattee. 3 vols. New York: Russell, 1963. Print.

———. "To Peter Porcupine." *Time-Piece* 25 Oct. 1797: n. pag. Print.

Freud, Esther. *Hideous Kinky.* New York: Harper-Perennial, 1999. Print.

Freud, Sigmund. "A Child Is Being Beaten." Trans. Joan Riviere. Freud, *Collected Papers* 2: 117–201.

———. *Collected Papers.* Trans. Alix Strachey and James Strachey. 5 vols. New York: Basic, 1959. Print.

———. *Dora: An Analysis of a Case of Hysteria.* 1905. Ed. Philip Reiff. New York: Touchstone, 1997. Print.

Frontiero v. Richardson. 411 US 677. Supreme Court of the US. 1973. *US Supreme Court Opinions.* FindLaw, n.d. Web. 19 Feb. 2010.

Frye, Northrop. *Anatomy of Criticism.* New York: Antheneum, 1957. Print.

Fugitive Slave Act of 1793. *Africans in America.* PBS Online, n.d. Web. 19 Feb. 2010.

Fugitive Slave Act of 1850. *Avalon Project: Documents in Law, History, and Diplomacy.* Yale Law School. Lilian Goldman Law Lib., n.d. Web. 19 Feb. 2010.

Gaakeer, Jeanne. "Law and Literature" *IVR Encyclopedia of Jurisprudence, Legal Theory, and Philosophy of Law.* Intl. Assn. of Philosophy of Law and Social Philosophy, 25 Jan. 2010. Web. 19 Feb. 2010.

Gaines, Ernest. "The Sky Is Gray." *Bloodline.* New York: Vintage, 1997. 83–120. Print.

Gaines, Jane. *Contested Culture: The Image, the Voice, and the Law.* Chapel Hill: U of North Carolina P, 1991. Print.

Gallagher, Catherine. *Nobody's Story: The Vanishing Acts of Women Writers in the Marketplace, 1670–1820.* Berkeley: U of California P, 1994. Print.

Galtung, Johan. "Cultural Violence." Steger and Lind 39–56.

Galway, Margaret. "Geoffrey Chaucer, JP and MP." *Modern Language Review* 36 (1941): 23–24. Print.

Ganz, Melissa. "Binding the Will: George Eliot and the Practice of Promising." *ELH* 75.3 (2008): 565–602. Print.

Garber, Marjorie. "Discipline Envy." *Academic Instincts*. Princeton: Princeton UP, 2001. 53–96. Print.

García, Cristina. *Dreaming in Cuban*. New York: Ballantine, 1992. Print.

Garrison, William Lloyd. "No Union with Slaveholders." *Selections from the Writings and Speeches of William Lloyd Garrison*. Boston: R. F. Wallcut, 1852. 136–42. Print.

Gaskell, Elizabeth. *North and South*. 1854–55. London: Penguin, 1995. Print. Penguin Classics.

Gates, Henry Louis, Jr., ed. *Douglass Autobiographies*. New York: Lib. of Amer., 1996. Print.

———. "Let Them Talk: Why Civil Liberties Pose No Threat to Civil Rights." *New Republic* 20 Sept. 1993: 37–49. Print.

Geertz, Clifford. "The Rotating Credit Association: A 'Middle Rung' in Development." *Economic Development and Cultural Change* 10.3 (1962). Print.

Gemmette, Elizabeth. "Law and Literature: Joining the Class Action." *Valparaiso University Law Review* 29 (1995): 665–859. Print.

Gengembre, Gerard. "Balzac, ou comment mettre le droit en fiction." *Actes du colloque de la cour de cassation*. Paris: Michalon, forthcoming.

George, Nelson. *Hip Hop America*. New York: Penguin, 1998. Print.

George (a Slave) v. State of Mississippi. 39 Miss. 570. Supreme Court of Mississippi. 1860. 570–92. *LexisNexis*. Web. 6 Aug. 2010. 1860 Miss. LEXIS 89.

Gerard, Alexander. *An Essay on Taste, together with Observations concerning the Imitative Nature of Poetry*. 1780. Introd. Walter J. Hipple, Jr. Delmar: Scholars' Facsims., 1978. Print. Facsim. of 3rd ed.

Gibson, Walker. "Literary Minds and Judicial Style." *New York University Law Review* 36 (1961): 915–30. Print.

Gilbert, Geoffrey. *The Law of Evidence*. Considerably enlarged by Capel Lofft. 4 vols. London, 1791–96. Print.

Gilligan, Carol. *In a Different Voice: Psychological Theory and Women's Development*. Cambridge: Harvard UP, 1982. Print.

Gillman, Susan. "'Sure Identifiers': Race, Science, and the Law in *Pudd'nhead Wilson*." Gillman and Robinson 86–104.

Gillman, Susan, and Forest G. Robinson, eds. *Mark Twain's* Pudd'nhead Wilson*: Race, Conflict, and Culture*. Durham: Duke UP, 1990. Print.

Gilman, Charlotte Perkins. *The Yellow Wallpaper*. Ed. Dale M. Bauer. Boston: Bedford, 1998. Print.

Gilmore, Myron P. *Humanists and Jurists: Six Studies in the Renaissance*. Cambridge: Harvard UP, 1963. Print.

Ginsburg, Ruth Bader. "Gender and the Constitution." *University of Cincinnati Law Review* 44 (1975): 1–42. Print.

Girard, René. *Deceit, Desire, and the Novel*. Trans. Yvonne Freccero. Baltimore: Johns Hopkins UP, 1965. Print.

Glaspell, Susan. "A Jury of Her Peers." *Every Week* 15 Mar. 1917: n. pag. Print.

Gless, Darryl. *Measure for Measure, the Law, and the Convent.* Princeton: Princeton UP, 1979. Print.

Godwin, William. *Caleb Williams.* London: Penguin, 1988. Print. Penguin Classics.

Goffman, Erving. *Asylums: Essays on the Social Situation of Mental Patients and Other Inmates.* New York: Anchor, 1961. Print.

Goldman, Emma. *Red Emma Speaks: An Emma Goldman Reader.* Ed. Alix Kates Shulman. Atlantic Highlands: Humanities, 1996. Print.

Goodall, Jane. *My Life with the Chimpanzees.* New York: Simon, 1996. Print.

Goodrich, Peter. *Law in the Courts of Love.* New York: Routledge, 1996. Print.

———. "Of Law and Forgetting." *Arachne* 1 (1994): 198–230. Print.

———. "Response to [Brook] Thomas." *Arachne* 1 (1994): 224–26. Print.

The Goody Parsons Witchcraft Case: A Journey into Seventeenth-Century Northampton. Ed. Bridget M. Marshall, Victoria Getis, and Matthew Mattingley. Historic Northampton Museum and Educ. Center; Center for Computer-Based Instructional Technology, n.d. Web. 12 Aug. 2009.

Gopen, George. "Rhyme and Reason: Why the Study of Poetry Is the Best Preparation for the Study of Law." *College English* 46 (1984): 333–47. Print.

Gopnik, Adam. "American Studies." *New Yorker* 28 Sept. 1998: 39–42. Print.

Gordon, Robert Ellis, ed. *The Funhouse Mirror: Reflections on Prison.* Pullman: Washington State UP, 2000. Print.

———. "The Legal Profession." *Looking Back at Law's Century.* Ed. Austin Sarat, Bryant Garth, and Robert Kagan. Ithaca: Cornell UP, 2002. 287–336. Print.

Grágás: Laws of Early Iceland. Trans. Andrew Dennis, Peter Foote, and Richard Perkins. Winnipeg: U of Manitoba P, 1980. Print.

Grandison (a Slave) v. State. 21 Tenn. 451. Supreme Court of Tennessee. 1841. 451–52. *LexisNexis.* Web. 6 Aug. 2010. 1841 Tenn. LEXIS 44.

Grand Upright Music v. Warner Brothers. 780 F. Supp. 182. Southern District New York. 1991. *Copyright Infringement Project.* UCLA Law and Columbia Law School, n.d. Web. 19 Feb. 2010.

Greenberg, Karen J., and Joshua L. Dratel, eds. *The Torture Papers: The Road to Abu Ghraib.* Cambridge: Cambridge UP, 2006. Print.

Greenberg, Moshe. "Some Postulates of Biblical Criminal Law." *The Jewish Expression.* Ed. Judah Goldin. New Haven: Yale UP, 1976. 5–28. Print.

Greville, Fulke. "A Dedication to Sir Philip Sidney." *The Prose Works of Fulke Greville, Lord Brooke.* Ed. John Gouws. Oxford: Oxford UP, 1986. 3–136. Print.

———. *Mustapha. Poems and Dramas of Fulke Greville First Lord Brooke.* Ed. Geoffrey Bullough. Vol. 2. Edinburgh: Oliver, 1939. Print.

Grimke, Archibald. "The Shame of America." 1920. *Negro Orators and Their Orations.* Ed. Carter Woodson. Washington: Assoc., 1925. 671–89. Print.

Grimsley, Jim. *Winter Birds.* New York: Touchstone, 1997. Print.

Griswold v. Connecticut. 381 US 479. Supreme Court of the US. 1965. *US Supreme Court Opinions.* FindLaw, n.d. Web. 19 Feb. 2010.

Gross, Hans. *A Manual for Judges, Practitioners, and Students.* Trans. Horace M. Kallen. Boston: Little, 1911. Print. Trans. of *Kriminal-Psychologie.* 1905.

Gross, Kenneth. *Shakespeare's Noise.* Chicago: U of Chicago P, 2001. Print.

Grossman, Jonathan. *The Art of the Alibi: English Law Courts and the Novel.* Baltimore: Johns Hopkins UP, 2002. Print.

Grotius, Hugo. *On the Law of War and Peace*. 1625. Whitefish: Kessinger, 2004. Print.

Guevara, Nancy. "Women Writin' Rappin' Breakin'." *Droppin' Science: Critical Essays on Rap Music and Hip Hop Culture*. Ed. William Eric Perkins. Philadelphia: Temple UP, 1996. 49–62. Print.

Gussow, Mel. "Stage: Emily Mann's 'Execution of Justice.'" Rev. of *Execution of Justice*, dir. Emily Mann. *New York Times* 14 Mar. 1986, late ed.: C3. Print.

Habermas, Jürgen. "Modernity: An Unfinished Project." *Habermas and the Unfinished Project of Modernity: Critical Essays on the Philosophical Discourse of Modernity*. Ed. Maurizio Passerin d'Entreves and Seyla Benhabib. Cambridge: MIT P, 1997. 38–56. Print.

———. "The Public Sphere: An Encyclopedia Article." *New German Critique* 3 (1974): 49–55. Print.

Hale, Edward Everett. "The Man without a Country." *Atlantic Monthly* 7 (1863): 665–79. Print.

Hall, Edward. *Hall's Chronicle*. Ed. Henry Ellis. London: Johnson, 1809. Print.

Halperin, Jean-Louis. *The French Civil Code*. Trans. Tony Weir. London: Univ. Coll. London, 2006. Print.

Hamilton, Donna B. "The State of Law in *Richard II*." *Shakespeare Quarterly* 34.1 (1983): 5–17. Print.

Hamilton, Hugh. *A Second Constitution for the United States of America*. Richmond: Garrett, 1938. Print.

Handwerk, Gary. *Irony and Ethics in Narrative from Schlegel to Lacan*. New Haven: Yale UP, 1985. Print.

Haraway, Donna. *When Species Meet*. Minneapolis: U of Minnesota P, 2007. Print.

Hardy, Thomas. *Tess of the D'Urbervilles*. Oxford: Oxford UP, 1998. Print.

———. *Thomas Hardy: Interviews and Recollections*. Ed. James Gibson. New York: Basingstoke, 1999. Print.

Harper, Frances E. W. *Iola Leroy; or, Shadows Uplifted*. 1892. Boston: Beacon, 1999. Print.

The Harper Collins Study Bible: Fully Revised and Updated. Ed. Harold W. Attridge. New York: Harper, 2006. Print.

Harper v. Virginia State Board of Elections. 383 US 663. Supreme Court of the US. 1966. *US Supreme Court Opinions*. FindLaw, n.d. Web. 19 Feb. 2010.

Harris, Angela P. "Race and Essentialism in Feminist Legal Theory." *Stanford Law Review* 42 (1990): 581–616. Print.

Hart, H. L. A. *The Concept of Law*. 2nd ed. Oxford: Clarendon, 1994. Print.

Hart, Henry M., Jr., and Albert M. Sacks. *The Legal Process: Basic Problems in the Making and Application of Law*. Westbury: Foundation, 1994. Print.

Hartman, Geoffrey. *The Fateful Question of Culture*. New York: Columbia UP, 1997. Print.

———. "Is an Aesthetic Ethos Possible? Night Thoughts after Auschwitz." *Cardozo Studies in Law and Literature* 6 (1994): 135–55. Print.

———. *The Longest Shadow*. Bloomington: Indiana UP, 1996. Print.

———. *Minor Prophecies*. Cambridge: Harvard UP, 1991. Print.

———. "The Question of Our Speech." Hartman and O'Hara 321–46.

Hartman, Geoffrey, and Daniel O'Hara, eds. *The Geoffrey Hartman Reader*. New York: Fordham UP, 2004. Print.

Hassine, Victor, Robert Johnson, and Ania Dobrzanska, eds. *"The Crying Wall" and Other Prison Stories*. West Conshohocken: Infinity, 2005. Print.

Hawthorne, Nathaniel. *The Scarlet Letter*. 1850. New York: Penguin, 1986. Print.

Hayden v. Pataki. 449 F. 3rd 305. US Court of Appeals, 2nd Circuit. 2006. *Open Jurist*. Open Jurist, n.d. Web. 19 Feb. 2010.

Hayman, Robert L., Jr., and Nancy Levit. "The Tales of White Folk: Doctrine, Narrative, and the Reconstruction of Racial Reality." *California Law Review* 84 (1996): 377–440. Print.

Hayward, John. *The First and Second Parts of John Hayward's* The Life and Raigne of King Henrie IIII. Ed. John J. Manning. Vol. 42. London: Royal Historical Soc., 1991. Print.

Hearne, Vicki. *Animal Happiness: A Moving Exploration of Animals and Their Emotions*. New York: Skyhorse, 2007. Print.

Heidsieck, Arnold. *The Intellectual Contexts of Kafka's Fiction: Philosophy, Law, Religion*. Columbia: Camden, 1994. Print.

Heilbrun, Carolyn, and Judith Resnik. "Convergences: Law, Literature, and Feminism." *Yale Law Journal* 99.8 (1990): 1912–56. Print.

Heinlein, Robert. *Starship Troopers*. 1959. New York: Ace, 1987. Print.

Heinzelman, Susan Sage. "Black Letters and Black Rams: Fictionalizing Law and Legalizing Literature in Enlightenment England." *Law Text Culture* 5.2 (2002): 377–406. Print.

Helgerson, Richard. *Forms of Nationhood: The Elizabethan Writing of England*. Chicago: U of Chicago P, 1992. Print.

Hempel, Amy, and Jim Shepard, eds. *Unleashed: Poems by Writers' Dogs*. New York: Three Rivers, 1999. Print.

Herman, Peter C. *Destabilizing Milton: Paradise Lost and the Poetics of Incertitude*. New York: Palgrave, 2005. Print.

———. "*Macbeth*: Absolutism, the Ancient Constitution, and the Aporia of Politics." *The Law in Shakespeare*. Ed. Constance Jordan and Karen Cunningham. New York: Palgrave, 2007. 208–32. Print.

———. "Rastell's *Pastyme of People*: Monarchy and the Law in Early Modern Historiography." *Journal of Medieval and Early Modern Studies* 30.2 (2000): 275–308. Print.

Herzfeld, Michael. *The Poetics of Manhood: Contest and Identity in a Cretan Mountain Village*. Princeton: Princeton UP, 1985. Print.

Heywood, Thomas. *The First and Second Parts of King Edward IV*. Ed. Richard Rowland. Manchester: Manchester UP, 2005. Print.

Higginbotham, A. Leon, Jr. *In the Matter of Color: Race and the American Legal Process: The Colonial Period*. Oxford: Oxford UP, 1980. Print.

Hilaire, J. *Histoire des institutions publiques et des faits sociaux XIe – XIXe siècles*. 8th ed. Paris: Dalloz, 1999. Print.

Hiltner, Judith R., ed. *Newspaper Verse of Philip Freneau: An Edition and Bibliography*. Troy: Whitson, 1986. Print.

Himes, Chester. *If He Hollers Let Him Go*. 1945. New York: Thunder Mouth, 1986. Print.

Hoagland, Edward. "Circus Music: For Clowns, Lions, and Solo Trapeze." *Harper's* Feb. 2002: 31–38. Print.

———. "Personal History: Calliope Times (A Life in the Circus)." *New Yorker* 22 May 2000: 36–45. Print.

Hofmannsthal, Hugo von. *Everyman.* 1911. San Francisco: Robertson, 1917. Print.

Holdheim, Wolfgang. *Der Justizirrtum als literarische Problematik.* Berlin: de Gruyter, 1969. Print.

Holinshed's Chronicles of England, Scotland and Ireland. Ed. Henry Ellis et al. 6 vols. London: Rivington, 1807–08. Print.

Holmes, Oliver Wendell. *The Common Law.* Ed. Mark DeWolfe Howe. Boston: Little, 1963. Print.

Holquist, Michael. *Dostoevsky and the Novel.* Evanston: Northwestern UP, 1977. Print.

Holub, Robert C. "Reading Nietzsche as Postmodernist." *Why Literature Matters.* Ed. Ruediger Ahrens and Lorenz Volkmann. Heidelberg: Heidelberg UP, 1996. 247–63. Print.

Home, Henry [Lord Kames]. *Elements of Criticism.* 1762. 3 vols. New York: Johnson Rpt., 1970. Print.

Homily on Obedience. Renaissance Electronic Texts. Ed. Ian Lancashire. U of Toronto English Lib. Web. 23 May 2007.

Hone, William. *The First Trial of William Hone, on an Ex-Officio Information.* London, 1818. Print.

Howells, William Dean. *The Rise of Silas Lapham.* 1885. Ed. Kermit Vanderbilt. New York: Penguin, 1983. Print.

Hoyt v. Florida. 368 US 57. Supreme Court of the US. 1961. *US Supreme Court Opinions.* FindLaw, n.d. Web. 19 Feb. 2010.

Hughes, Carl Milton. *The Negro Novelist.* 1953. New York: Citadel, 1967. Print.

Hume, David. "Of National Characters." 1742. *The Philosophical Works of David Hume.* Essay 21. Boston: Little, 1854. *Internet Archive.* Web. 1 June 2009.

Hunt, Mame. *Unquestioned Integrity: The Hill-Thomas Hearings, Voicings: Ten Plays from the Documentary Theater.* Ed. and introd. Attilio Favorini. Ecco: Hopewell, 1995. Print.

Hurston, Zora Neale. *Their Eyes Were Watching God.* Urbana: U of Illinois P, 1978. Print.

Hutner, Gordon, ed. *Immigrant Voices.* New York: Signet, 1999 Print.

Illegal Immigration Relief Act. Ordinance 2006–18. 21 Sept. 2006. Small Town Defenders, n.d. Web. 19 Feb. 2010.

Jacobs, Harriet [Linda Brent]. *Incidents in the Life of a Slave Girl.* 1861. New York: Harcourt, 1973. Print.

James VI and I. *Political Writings.* Ed. Johann P. Sommerville. Cambridge: Cambridge UP, 1994. Print.

———. *The Trew Law of Free Monarchies.* 1599. *Political Writings.* Ed. J. P. Somerville. New York: Cambridge UP, 1999. 62–84. Print.

Jameson, Frederic. *The Political Unconscious.* London: Routledge, 2002. Print. Routledge Classics.

Jauss, Hans Robert. "Literary History as Challenge." *Toward an Aesthetic of Reception.* Trans. T. Bahti. Minneapolis: U of Minnesota P, 1982. 3–45. Print.

Jefferson, Thomas. Letter to Samuel Kercheval. 12 July 1816. *The Writings of Thomas Jefferson*. Vol. 15. Washington: Thomas Jefferson Memorial Assn., 1903. 32–44. Print.

———. Letter to James Madison. 30 Jan. 1787. *Political Writings*. Ed. Merrill D. Peterson. Chapel Hill: U of North Carolina P, 1993. 79–80. Print.

———. *Notes on the State of Virginia*. Philadelphia: Prichard, 1788. *Documenting the American South*. Univ. Lib., U of North Carolina, Chapel Hill, n.d. Web. 19 Feb. 2010.

Jefferson, Thomas, et al. "The Declaration of Independence." 1776. Trodd 16–18.

Jocks, Christopher Ronwanien:te. "Spirituality for Sale: Sacred Knowledge in the Consumer Age." *American Indian Quarterly* 20.3-4 (1996): 415–31. *JSTOR*. Web. 19 Feb. 2010.

Johnson, Barbara. "Melville's Fist: The Execution of Billy Budd." *Studies in Romanticism* 18 (1979): 567–99. Print.

Johnson, Charles. "Executive Decision." *"Dr. King's Refrigerator" and Other Stories*. New York: Scribner's, 2005. 55–75. Print.

Johnson, Samuel. Preface to *The Plays of William Shakespeare*. *The Oxford Authors: Samuel Johnson*. Ed. Donald Greene. Oxford: Oxford UP, 1986. 419–66. Print.

Johnson, Wayne. "Harvest from the Sea." *New York Times* 21 May 1999: A27+. Print.

Jones, Edward P. *The Known World*. New York: Harper, 2004. Print.

Jones, Gayl. *Corregidora*. New York: Random, 1975. Print.

Jonson, Ben. *Catiline*. Ed. W. F. Bolton and Jane F. Gardner. London: Arnold, 1972. Print.

Jordan, Constance. *Shakespeare's Monarchies: Ruler and Subject in the Romances*. Ithaca: Cornell UP, 1997. Print.

Julius, Anthony. Introduction. Freeman and Lewis xi–xxvi.

Kadare, Ismail. *Broken April*. New York: New Amsterdam, 1990. Print.

Kafka, Franz. "Before the Law." Kafka, *"Transformation"* 165–66.

———. *In the Penal Colony*. New York: Schocken, 1971. Print.

———. "The Judgment." Kafka, *"Transformation"* 37–47.

———. *Der Prozess*. 5th ed. New York: Schocken, 1946. Print.

———. *The Metamorphosis*. New York: Bantam, 1972. Print.

———. *"The Transformation" and Other Stories: Works Published in Kafka's Lifetime*. Trans. and ed. Malcolm Pasley. New York: Penguin, 1992. Print.

Kahn, Paul W. *The Cultural Study of Law*. Chicago: U of Chicago P, 1999. Print.

Kalb, Jonathan. "Documentary Solo Performance: The Politics of the Mirrored Self." *Theater* 31.3 (2001): 13–29. Print.

Kant, Immanuel. *Groundwork for the Metaphysics of Morals*. 1797. Trans. Allen W. Wood. Ed. J. B. Schneewind and Wood. New Haven: Yale UP, 2002. Print.

———. "On National Characteristics, so far as They Depend upon the Distinct Feeling of the Beautiful and the Sublime." 1764. *Race and the Enlightenment: A Reader*. Ed. Emmanuel Chukwudi Eze. Cambridge: Blackwell, 1997. 49–57. Print.

Kanuni i Lekë Dukaginit: The Code of Lekë Dukagjini. Trans. Leonard Fox. Ed. Shtjefën Gjeçov. New York: Glonlekaj, 1989. Print.

Kastan, David Scott. "*Macbeth* and the 'Name of King.'" *Shakespeare after Theory.* New York: Routledge, 1999. 165–82. Print.

Kaufman, Moisés. *The Laramie Project.* New York: Vintage, 2001. Print.

Kelley, Donald R. *Historians and the Law in Postrevolutionary France.* Princeton: Princeton UP, 1984. Print.

Kelley, Robin. *Yo' Mama's Disfunktional! Fighting the Culture Wars in Urban America.* Boston: Beacon, 1997. Print.

Kenan, Randall. *A Visitation of Spirits: A Novel.* New York: Grove, 1989. Print.

Kennedy, Randall. *Race, Crime, and the Law.* New York: Pantheon, 1997. Print.

Ketcham, Ralph. *James Madison: A Biography.* Charlottesville: UP of Virginia, 1990. Print.

Kimball, Roger. "Geoffrey Hartman Reconstructs Paul de Man." *New Criterion* 6 (1988): 36–43. Print.

Kincaid, Jamaica. *Lucy.* New York: Farrar, 2002. Print.

King, Lovalerie, and Richard Schur, eds. *African-American Culture and Legal Discourse.* New York: Palgrave-Macmillan, forthcoming.

King, Martin Luther, Jr. "Declaration of Independence from the War in Vietnam." 5 Apr. 1967. *Ramparts* 5.11 (1967): 32–37. Print.

———. "I Have a Dream." 28 Aug. 1963. *Testament of Hope: The Essential Writings and Speeches of Martin Luther King, Jr.* San Francisco: Harper, 1991. 217–20. Print.

———. "Letter from Birmingham Jail." *Why We Can't Wait.* 1963. New York: Signet, 2000. Print.

Kitwana, Bakari. *The Hip Hop Generation: Young Blacks and the Crisis in African-American Culture.* New York: Basic, 2002. Print.

Kiyama, Henry. *The Four Immigrants Manga.* Trans. Frederik L. Schodt. Berkeley: Stone Bridge, 1998. Print.

Klagsbrun, Francine, ed. *The First* Ms. *Reader.* New York: Warner, 1973. Print.

Klement, Frank L. *The Limits of Dissent: Clement L. Vallandigham and the Civil War.* Lexington: UP of Kentucky, 1972. Print.

Knapp, Carolyn. *Pack of Two: The Intricate Bond between People and Dogs.* New York: Delta, 1999. Print.

Knox v. Massachusetts SPCA. 425 N.E. 2nd 393. Massachusetts Appeals Court. 1981. *North Eastern Reporter.* 2nd ser. Vol. 425. Eagen: West, 1982. 393–96. Print.

Konig, David Thomas. *Law and Society in Puritan Massachusetts: Essex County, 1629–1692.* Chapel Hill: U of North Carolina P, 1979. Print.

Konkle, Maureen. *Writing Indian Nations: Native Intellectuals and the Politics of Historiography, 1827–1863.* Chapel Hill: U of North Carolina P, 2004. Print.

Korematsu v. US. 323 US 214. Supreme Court of the US. 1944. *US Supreme Court Opinions.* FindLaw, n.d. Web. 19 Feb. 2010.

Kornstein, Daniel. "He Knew More: Balzac and the Law." *Pace Law Review* 21 (2000): 1–102. Print.

Kraker, Daniel. "Desert Rock, Coal and Climate Change." Burnham, NM. 30 May 2007. Radio.

Kraus, Karl. *Sittlichkeit und Kriminalität* [Morality and Criminal Justice]. 1908. Frankfurt am Main: Suhrkamp, 1987. Print.

Kretschman, Karen L., and Richard Weisberg. "Wigmore's 'Legal Novels' Expanded: A Collaborative Effort." *Maryland Law Review* 7.2 (1977): 94–103. Print.

Krieger, Linda J., and Patricia N. Cooney. "The Miller-Wohl Controversy: Equal Treatment, Positive Action, and the Meaning of Women's Equality." *Golden Gate University Law Review* 13 (1983): 513–72. Print.

Kuhn, Thomas. *The Structure of Scientific Revolutions.* Chicago: U of Chicago P, 1962. Print.

Kurland, Philip, and Gerhard Casper, eds. *Landmark Briefs and Arguments of the Supreme Court of the United States.* Arlington: UPs of Amer., 1975. *LexisNexis.* Web. 19 Feb. 2010.

Kushner, Tony. "American Things." *Thinking about the Longstanding Problems of Virtue and Happiness: Essays, a Play, Two Poems and a Prayer.* New York: TheatreCommunications Group, 1995. 3–12. Print.

———. *Angels in America: A Gay Fantasia on National Themes: Part One: Millennium Approaches; Part Two: Perestroika.* New York: Theatre Communications Group, 1992. Print.

Laclos, Pierre Choderlos de. "Editor's Preface." *Les Liaisons Dangereuses.* Trans. P. W. K. Stone. New York: Penguin, 1961. 19–22. Print.

Lai, Him Mark, Genny Lim, and Judy Yung. *Island: Poetry and History of Chinese Immigrants on Angel Island, 1910–1940.* Seattle: U of Washington P, 1980. Print.

Lamb, Wally, ed. *Couldn't Keep It to Myself.* New York: Harper, 2003. Print.

La Porte v. Assoc. Independents Inc. 163 So. 2nd 267. Supreme Court of Florida. 1964. *Animal Legal and Historical Center.* Michigan State U Coll. of Law, n.d. Web. 20 Feb. 2010.

The Laramie Project. Dir. Moises Kaufman. HBO, 2002. Television.

Lawrence, D. H. *Studies in Classic American Literature.* 1923. New York: Penguin, 1977. Print.

Lawrence et al. v. Texas. 539 US 558 (Thomas, J., dissenting). Supreme Court of the US. 2003. *US Supreme Court Opinions.* FindLaw, n.d. Web. 20 Feb. 2010

Leavenworth, Peter. "'The Best Title That Indians Can Claime': Native Agency and Consent in the Transferal of Penacook-Pawtucket Land in the Seventeenth Century." *New England Quarterly* 72.2 (1999): 275–300. Print.

Leckie, Barbara. "The Force of Law and Literature: Critiques of Ideology in Derrida and Bourdieu." *Mosaic* 28 (1995): 109–36. Print.

Lee, Chang-Rae. *Native Speaker.* New York: Riverhead, 1995. Print.

Lee, Harper. *To Kill a Mockingbird.* New York: Harper, 1960. Print.

Leet Jurisdiction in the City of Norwich during the Eighteenth and Nineteenth Centuries, with a Short Notice of Its Later History and Decline, from Rolls in the Possession of the Corporation. Ed. William Hudson. London: Quaritch, 1892. Print. Pub. of the Selden Soc. 5.

Lemon, Rebecca. *Treason by Words: Literature, Law, and Rebellion in Shakespeare's England.* Ithaca: Cornell UP, 2006. Print.

Leocal v. Ashcroft. 125 S. Ct. 377. Supreme Court of the US. 2004. *Supreme Court Reporter.* Vol. 125. Eagen: West, 2004. 377–84. Print.

LeSage, Alain Rene. *Adventures of Gil Blas of Santillane.* Trans. Tobias Smollett. Philadelphia: Horn, 1749. Print.

Levi, Edward H. *An Introduction to Legal Reasoning.* Chicago: U of Chicago P, 1949. Print.

Levine, George. *The Realistic Imagination: English Fiction from* Frankenstein *to* Lady Chatterley. Chicago: U of Chicago P, 1981. Print.

Levinson, Sanford. "Law as Literature." *Texas Law Review* 60.3 (1982): 373–414. Print.

Levinson, Sanford, and Steven Mailloux, eds. *Interpreting Law and Literature: A Hermeneutic Reader.* Evanston: Northwestern UP, 1998. Print.

Lincoln, Abraham. *The Collected Works of Abraham Lincoln.* 9 vols. Ed. Roy P. Basler and Lloyd A. Dunlap. New Brunswick: Rutgers UP, 1953. Print.

———. "The Truth from an Honest Man." Freidel 739–51.

Linzey, Andrew. *Animal Gospel.* Louisville: Westminster, 2004. Print.

———. *Animal Theology.* Urbana: U of Illinois P, 1995. Print.

Littell, Franklin H. *The Crucifixion of the Jews.* New York: Harper, 1975. Print.

Llewellyn, Karl. "A Realistic Jurisprudence—the Next Step." Fisher, Horwitz, and Reed 53–58.

Locke, John. *A Letter concerning Toleration.* 1689. Indianapolis: Hackett, 1983. Print.

Loesberg, Jonathan. "Aesthetics, Ethics, and Unreadable Acts in George Eliot." *Knowing the Victorians.* Ed. Suzy Anger. Ithaca: Cornell UP, 2001. 121–47. Print.

Logan, George M. *The Meaning of More's* Utopia. Princeton: Princeton UP, 1983. Print.

Logan, John. *Never the Sinner.* Woodstock: Overlook, 1999. Print.

Lombroso, Cesare. *Criminal Man.* Trans. and ed. Mary Gibson. Durham: Duke UP, 2006. Print.

London, Ephraim, ed. *The Law as Literature.* New York: Simon, 1960. Print.

———, ed. *The World of the Law: A Treasury of Great Writing about and in the Law, Short Stories, Plays, Essays, Accounts, Letters, Opinions, Pleas, Transcripts of Testimony; from Biblical Times to the Present.* 2 vols. New York: Simon, 1960. Print.

London, Jack. "Bâtard." The Call of the Wild, White Fang, *and Other Stories.* New York: Penguin, 1993. 293–307. Print.

Loving v. Virginia. 388 US 1. Supreme Court of the US. 1967. *US Supreme Court Opinions.* FindLaw, n.d. Web. 20 Feb. 2010.

Low, A. *A Bibliographical Survey of Rotating Savings and Credit Associations.* Oxford: Oxfam; Centre for Cross-cultural Research on Women at Queen Elizabeth House, 1995. Print.

Lowe, Lisa. *Immigrant Acts.* Durham: Duke UP, 1996. Print.

Lowrey, Janette Sebring. *The Poky Little Puppy.* Illus. Gustaf Tenggren. New York: Random, 2002. Print. A Little Golden Book.

Lozano v. City of Hazleton. 496 F. Supp. 2nd 477. Middle District Pennsylvania. 2007. *Federal Supplement.* 2nd ser. Vol. 496. Eagen: West, 2007. 477–562. Print.

Luban, David. *Legal Modernism*. Ann Arbor: U of Michigan P, 1997. Print.

Lucas, John. *Dickens: The Major Novels*. Harmondsworth: Penguin, 1992. Print.

Lujan v. Defenders of Wildlife. 504 US 555. Supreme Court of the US. 1992. *US Supreme Court Opinions*. FindLaw, n.d. Web. 20 Feb. 2010.

Lupton, Julia Reinhard. *Citizen-Saints: Shakespeare and Political Theology*. Chicago: U of Chicago P, 2005. Print.

Lynch v. Donnelly. 465 US 668. Supreme Court of the US. 1984. *US Supreme Court Opinions*. FindLaw, n.d. Web. 20 Feb. 2010.

Lyotard, Jean François. *The Differend: Phrases in Dispute*. Trans. G. Van Den Abbeele. Minneapolis: U of Minnesota P, 1988. Print.

MacKinnon, Catharine A. *Feminism Unmodified: Discourses on Life and Law*. Cambridge: Harvard UP, 1987. Print.

Madison, James. "A Memorial and Remonstrance." 1785. *Church and State in American History*. Ed. John Wilson and Donald Drakeman. Boulder: Westview, 2003. 63–68. Print.

Mailer, Norman. *The Executioner's Song*. Boston: Little, 1979. Print.

Maine, Henry Sumner. *Ancient Law, Its Connection with the Early History of Society and Its Relation to Modern Ideas, by Sir Henry Sumner Maine . . . with Introduction and Notes by the Right Hon. Sir Frederic Pollock, Bart*. 1861. London: Murray, 1930. Print.

Major, Reginald. *A Panther Is a Black Cat*. New York: Morrow, 1971. Print.

Malamud, Bernard. *The Fixer*. New York: Farrar, 1966. Print.

Manley, Mary Delarivier. *The Adventures of Rivella*. Ed. Katherine Zelinsky. Peterborough: Broadview, 1999. Print.

———. *Lucius, the First Christian King of Britain: A Tragedy*. U of Virginia Lib., n.d. Web. 22 Jan. 2011.

Mann, Emily. *Execution of Justice. Testimonies: Four Plays*. New York: Theatre Communications Group, 1997. 133–246. Print.

Mann, Thomas. "A Man and His Dog." *"Death in Venice" and Seven Other Stories*. Trans. H. T. Lowe-Porter. New York: Vintage, 1989. 215–87. Print.

Manning, John J. Introduction. Hayward 1–57.

Manza, Jeff, and Christopher Uggen. *Locked Out: Felon Disenfranchisement and American Democracy*. Oxford: Oxford UP, 2007. Print.

Marbury v. Madison. 5 US 137. Supreme Court of the US. 1803. *Supreme Court Collection*. Legal Information Inst., Cornell U Law School, n.d. Web. 17 Feb. 2010.

Marcus, Isabel, et al. "The 1984 James McCormick Mitchell Lecture: Feminist Discourse, Moral Values, and the Law—a Conversation." *Buffalo Law Review* 34 (1985): 11–87. Print.

Marks, Laurie. *Earth Logic*. New York: Doherty, 2004. Print.

———. *Fire Logic*. New York: Doherty, 2002. Print.

Marlowe, Christopher. *Tamburlaine the Great: Part One. English Renaissance Drama: A Norton Anthology*. Ed. David Bevington et al. New York: Norton, 2002. 183–243. Print.

"Married Women's Property Laws." *American Women*. Law Lib. of Congress, n.d. Web. 17 Apr. 2010.

Martin, David A., and Peter H. Schuck, eds. *Immigration Stories*. New York: Foundation, 2005. Print.

Marvell, Andrew. "An Horation Ode upon Cromwell's Return from Ireland." *The Oxford Authors: Andrew Marvell*. Ed. Frank Kermode and Keith Walker. Oxford: Oxford UP, 1990. 82–85. Print.

Mashpee v. New Seabury Corporation. 592 F. 2nd 575. US Court of Appeals, 1st Circuit. 1979. *Open Jurist*. Open Jurist, n.d. Web 16 Feb. 2010.

Maturin, Charles Robert. *Melmoth the Wanderer*. Ed. Douglas Grant. Oxford: Oxford UP, 1989. Print.

McCarran Internal Security Act. 1950. 50 USC. *History Central.com*. Multi-Educator, n.d. Web. 10 Aug. 2010.

McCarthy, Denis. *Treaty and Covenant*. Rome: Biblical Inst., 1978. Print.

McCorkle, Jill. *Creatures of Habit*. Chapel Hill: Algonquin, 2003. Print.

McDonald, Russ, ed. *The Bedford Companion to Shakespeare*. Boston: Bedford, 1996. Print.

McKeon, Michael. *The Origins of the English Novel, 1600–1740*. Baltimore: Johns Hopkins UP, 1987. Print.

McLeod, Kembrew. *Freedom of Expression: Resistance and Repression in the Age of Intellectual Property*. Minneapolis: U of Minnesota P, 2007. Print.

McNair, Wesley. "The Puppy." Sage 2.

Melville, Herman. "Bartleby, the Scrivener: A Story of Wall-Street." *Great Short Works of Herman Melville*. New York: Harper, 2004. 39–74. Print.

———. *Billy Budd, Sailor (An Inside Narrative)*. Chicago: U of Chicago P, 1962. Print.

Menkel-Meadow, Carrie. "Portia in a Different Voice: Speculations on a Women's Lawyering Process." *Berkeley Women's Law Journal* 1 (1985): 39–63. Print.

Merriman, Titus Mooney. *The Pilgrims, Puritans and Roger Williams Vindicated: And His Sentence of Banishment Ought to Be Revoked*. 1892. Whitefish: Kessinger, 2008. Print.

Merryman, John Henry. *The Civil Law Tradition*. Stanford: Stanford UP, 1969. Print.

Meyer, Michael J., ed. *Literature and Law*. Amsterdam: Rodopi, 2004. Print.

Mezey, Naomi. "Law as Culture." *Yale Journal of Law and the Humanities* 13 (2001): 35–67. Print.

Mezey, Naomi, and Mark C. Niles. "Screening the Law: Ideology and Law in American Popular Culture." *Columbia Journal of Law and Arts* 28 (2005): 91–185. Print.

Michelman, Frank. "Traces of Self-Government." *Harvard Law Review* 100 (1986): 3–77. Print.

Midler v. Ford Motor Company. 849 F. 2nd 460. US Court of Appeals, 9th Circuit. 1988. *Open Jurist*. Open Jurist, n.d. Web 16 Feb. 2010.

Mill, John Stuart. On Liberty *and Other Writings*. Ed. Stefan Collini. Cambridge: Cambridge UP, 1989. Print.

———. "The Subjection of Women." Mill, On Liberty 117–217.

Miller, Arthur. *The Crucible*. New York: Penguin, 2003. Print.

Miller, Arthur R., and Michael H. Davis. *Intellectual Property: Patents, Trademarks, and Copyright in a Nutshell*. 2nd ed. Saint Paul: West, 1990. Print.

Miller, D. A. "Cage aux Folles: Sensation and Gender in Wilke Collins's *The Woman in White*." *The Novel and the Police*. Berkeley: U of California P, 1988. 146–91. Print.

Miller, D. Quentin. "Behind the Wall: On Teaching Prison Literature." *Heath Anthology Newsletter* 29 (2005): 4–6. Print.

———, ed. *Prose and Cons: Essays on Prison Literature in the United States.* Jefferson: McFarland, 2006. Print.

Miller, Frank. *Batman: The Dark Knight Returns.* 1986. New York: DC Comics, 2002. Print.

Miller, J. Hillis. Introduction. *Bleak House.* By Charles Dickens. Ed. Norman Page. Harmondsworth: Penguin, 1971. 11–34. Print.

———. "Moments of Decision in *Bleak House.*" *The Cambridge Companion to Charles Dickens.* Ed. John O. Jordan. Cambridge: Cambridge UP, 2001. 49–63. Print.

Miller, Patrick D. *Sin and Judgment in the Prophets.* Chico: Scholars, 1982. Print.

Miller, William Ian. *Bloodtaking and Peacemaking: Feud, Law, and Society in Saga Iceland.* Chicago: U of Chicago P, 1990. Print.

———. *Eye for an Eye.* Cambridge: Cambridge UP, 2006. Print.

———. *Humiliation.* Ithaca: Cornell UP, 1993. Print.

Milton, John. *The Doctrine and Discipline of Divorce. Milton Reading Room.* Trustees of Dartmouth Coll., n.d. Web. 4 Oct. 2010.

———. *Paradise Lost.* Milton, *Riverside Milton* 297–710.

———. *The Readie and Easie Way to Establish a Free Commonwealth.* Milton, *Riverside Milton* 1134–49.

———. *The Riverside Milton.* Ed. Roy Flannagan. Boston: Houghton, 1998. Print.

———. *The Tenure of Kings and Magistrates.* Milton, *Riverside Milton* 1057–75.

Minow, Martha, Michael Ryan, and Austin Sarat, eds. *Narrative, Violence, and the Law: The Essays of Robert Cover.* Ann Arbor: U of Michigan P, 1993. Print.

Mirror for Magistrates. Ed. Lily B. Campbell. New York: Barnes, 1960. Print.

Mitchell, Lee Clark. "'De Nigger in You': Race or Training in *Pudd'nhead Wilson.*" *Nineteenth-Century Literature* 42 (1987): 295–312. Print.

Mitchell, W. J. T. "Editor's Introduction: The Politics of Interpretation." *Critical Inquiry* 9.1 (1982): iii–viii. Print.

Monette, Paul. *Becoming a Man: Half a Life Story.* New York: Harper, 1992. Print.

Moore, Alan. *Watchmen.* New York: Warner, 1987. Print.

Moore, Charles C. *A Treatise on Facts; or, The Weight and Value of Evidence.* 2 vols. New York: Thompson, 1908. Print.

Moore v. City of East Cleveland. 431 US 494. Supreme Court of the US. 1977. *Supreme Court Collection.* Legal Information Inst., Cornell U Law School, n.d. Web. 22 Feb. 2010.

Moran, Leslie J. "Law and the Gothic Imagination." *The Gothic.* Ed. Fred Botting. Cambridge: Brewer, 2001. Print.

More, Thomas. The History of King Richard III *and Selections from the English and Latin Poems.* Ed. Richard S. Sylvester. New Haven: Yale UP, 1976. Print.

———. *Utopia.* 1516. Ed. and trans. Edward Surtz. New Haven: Yale UP, 1964. Print.

Morgan, Joan. *When Chickenheads Come Home to Roost: A Hip Hop Feminist Breaks It Down.* New York: Simon, 1999. Print.

Morris, Henry. *Waiting for the Signal.* Chicago: Schulte, 1897. Print.

Morrison, Toni. *Beloved*. New York: Vintage, 2004. Print.

———. *The Bluest Eye*. New York: Washington Square, 1972. Print.

———. *Conversations with Toni Morrison*. Ed. Danille Taylor-Guthrie. Jackson: UP of Mississippi, 1994. Print.

———. "The Language Must Not Sweat: A Conversation with Toni Morrison." Interview with Thomas LeClair. 1981. Morrison, *Conversations* 119–28.

———. "The One out of Sequence." Interview by Anne Koenen. 1980. Morrison, *Conversations* 67–83.

———. *Playing in the Dark: Whiteness and the Literary Imagination*. Cambridge: Harvard UP, 1992. Print.

———. *Song of Solomon*. New York: Vintage, 2004. Print.

Morson, Gary Saul. "Introductory Study: Dostoevsky's Great Experiment." *A Writer's Diary*. By Fyodor Dostoevsky. Trans. and ed. Kenneth Lantz. Evanston: Northwestern UP, 1993. 1–117. Print.

Mosley, Walter. "Equal Opportunity." *Always Outnumbered, Always Outgunned*. New York: Washington Square, 1998. 63–78. Print.

Mueller, Ian. *Hitler's Justice*. Cambridge: Harvard UP, 1991. Print.

Muller v. Oregon. 208 US 412. Supreme Court of the US. 1908. *Supreme Court Collection*. Legal Information Inst., Cornell U Law School, n.d. Web. 22 Feb. 2010.

Musil, Robert. *The Man without Qualities*. 1930. New York: Vintage, 1996. Print.

Myers, Victoria. "Blasphemy Trials and *The Cenci*: Parody as Performative." *Spheres of Action: Speech and Performance in Romantic Culture*. Ed. Alexander Dick and Angela Esterhammer. Toronto: U of Toronto P, 2009. 100–23. Print.

———. "Joanna Baillie and the Emergence of Medico-legal Discourse." *European Romantic Review* 18.3 (2007): 339–59. Print.

———. "Justice and Indeterminacy: Wordsworth's *The Borderers* and the Trials of the 1790's." *Studies in Romanticism* 40.3 (2001): 427–57. Print.

Naegele, Jolyon. "Albania: Blood Feuds—'Blood for Blood' (Part 1)." *Radio Free Europe / Radio Liberty*. Radio Free Europe / Radio Liberty, 12 Oct. 2001. Web. 22 Feb. 2010.

National Unemployed League. "Declaration of Workers' and Farmers' Rights and Purposes." 1933. P. Foner, *We* 159–62.

Naylor, Gloria. *The Women of Brewster Place*. New York: Penguin, 1982. Print.

Newton, Huey. "Call for Revolutionary People's Constitutional Convention." P. Foner, *Black Panthers* 267–71.

Nietzsche, Friedrich. *Zur Genealogie der Moral*. Vol. 76. Stuttgart: Kroener, 1964. Print.

Nixon, Richard. "302: Statement on Signing Bill Repealing the Emergency Detention Act of 1950." 25 Sept. 1971. *The American Presidency Project*. Ed. John Woolley and Gerhard Peters. U of California, Santa Barbara, n.d. Web. 22 Feb. 2010.

Njal's Saga. Trans. Magnus Magnusson and Hermann Pálsson. London: Penguin, 1960. Print.

Norbrook, David. "'A Liberal Tongue': Language and Rebellion in *Richard II*." *Shakespeare's Universe: Renaissance Ideas and Conventions: Essays in Honour of W. R. Elton*. Ed. John M. Mucciolo. Aldershot: Scolar, 1996. 37–51. Print.

Norris, Christopher. *Paul de Man: Deconstruction and the Critique of Aesthetic Ideology.* New York: Routledge, 1988. Print.

Nussbaum, Martha. "Cultivating Humanity in Legal Education." *University of Chicago Law Review* 70 (2002): 265–79. Print.

——. "Equity and Mercy." *Philosophy and Public Affairs* 22 (1993): 83–125. Print.

——. *Poetic Justice: The Literary Imagination and Public Life.* Boston: Beacon, 1997. Print.

——. *Upheavals of Thought: The Intelligence of Emotions.* Cambridge: Cambridge UP, 2001. Print.

Oates, Joyce Carol, ed. *American Gothic Tales.* New York: Penguin, 1996. Print.

Ogbar, Jeffrey. *Hip Hop Revolution: The Culture and Politics of Rap.* Lawrence: UP of Kansas, 2009. Print.

Old Chief v. US. 519 US 172. Supreme Court of the US. 1997. *Supreme Court Collection.* Legal Information Inst., Cornell U Law School, n.d. Web. 22 Feb. 2010.

Ollman, Bertell, and Jonathan Birnbaum, eds. *The U. S. Constitution: Two Hundred Years of Anti-federalist, Abolitionist, Feminist, Muckraker, Progressive, and Especially Socialist Criticism.* New York: New York UP, 1990. Print.

Olmsted, Wendy. "The Uses of Rhetoric: Indeterminacy in Legal Reasoning, Practical Thinking, and the Interpretation of Literary Figures." *Rhetoric and Hermeneutics in Our Time: A Reader.* Ed. Walter Jost and Michael J. Hyde. New Haven: Yale UP, 1997. 235–53. Print.

Olmstead v. US. 277 US 438. Supreme Court of the US. 1928. *Supreme Court Collection.* Legal Information Inst., Cornell U Law School, n.d. Web. 22 Feb. 2010.

One Hundred and One Dalmatians. Dir. Clyde Geronimi. Walt Disney Productions, 1961. Film.

Orwell, George. *Animal Farm.* New York: Plume, 2003. Print.

Osborn, John Jay. *The Paper Chase.* New York: Warner, 1983. Print.

Osgood, Frances. "Lines (Suggested by the Announcement That 'A Bill for the Protection of Married Women Has Passed Both Houses' of Our State Legislature." *Early Nineteenth Century, 1800–1865.* Ed. Paul Lauter. 5th ed. Boston: Houghton, 2006. 2883–84. Print. Vol. B of *The Heath Anthology of American Literature.*

Oyama v. California. 332 US 633. Supreme Court of the US. 1948. *US Supreme Court Opinions.* FindLaw, n.d. Web. 22 Feb. 2010.

Paikeday, Thomas M. *The Native Speaker Is Dead!* New York: Paikeday, 1985. Print.

Paine, Thomas. *Common Sense.* 1791. Rights of Man *and* Common Sense. New York: Knopf, 1994. 249–91. Print.

Paral, Rob. *The Growth and Reach of Immigration: New Census Bureau Data Underscore Importance of Immigrants in the U.S. Labor Force.* Immigration Policy Center, 1 Aug. 2006. Web. 22 Sept. 2010.

Patterson, Annabel. *Reading* Holinshed's Chronicles. Chicago: U of Chicago P, 1994. Print.

Patterson, Orlando. *Slavery and Social Death: A Comparative Study.* Cambridge: Harvard UP, 1982. Print.

Peller, Gary. "The Metaphysics of American Law." *California Law Review* 73 (1985): 1151–290. Print.

Peltier, Leonard. *Prison Writings: My Life Is My Sun Dance.* New York: St. Martin's, 1999. Print.

"The People and the People Alone Were the Motive Power in the Making of the History of the People's Revolutionary Constitutional Convention Plenary Session!" *Black Panther* 12 Sept. 1970: 3. Print.

Pérez, Ramón "Tianguis." *Diary of an Undocumented Immigrant.* Trans. Dick J. Reavis. Houston: Arte Publico, 1991. Print.

Peristiany, J. G. *Honor and Shame: The Values of Mediterranean Society.* London: Weidenfeld, 1965. Print.

Perry, Curtis. *Literature and Favoritism in Early Modern England.* Cambridge: Cambridge UP, 2006. Print.

Perry, Imani. *Prophets of the Hood: Politics and Poetics in Hip Hop.* Durham: Duke UP, 2004. Print.

Pessino, Anthony L. "Mistaken Identity: A Call to Strengthen Publicity Rights for Digital Personas." *Virginia Sports and Entertainment Law Journal* 4 (2004): 86–118. Print.

Petch, Simon. "Law, Literature, and Victorian Studies." *Victorian Literature and Culture* 35 (2007): 361–84. Print.

Peters, Julie Stone. "Law, Literature, and the Vanishing Real: On the Future of an Interdisciplinary Illusion." *PMLA* 120.2 (2005): 442–53. *LexisNexis.* Web. 23 Feb. 2011.

———. " 'Literature,' the 'Rights of Man,' and Narratives of Atrocity: Historical Backgrounds to the Culture of Testimony." *Yale Journal of Law and the Humanities* 17.2 (2005): 253–81. Print.

Petry, Ann. *The Street.* 1946. New York: Mariner, 1998. Print.

———. *Tituba of Salem Village.* 1964. New York: Harper, 1991. Print.

Phayer, Michael. *The Catholic Church and the Holocaust, 1930–1965.* Bloomington: Indiana UP, 2000. Print.

Phillips, Wendell. Letter to Frederick Douglass. 22 Apr. 1845. Gates, *Douglass Autobiographies* 11–13.

Pizer, Donald. "Self-Censorship and Textual Editing." *Textual Criticism and Literary Interpretation.* Ed. Jerome McGann. Chicago: U of Chicago P, 1985. 144–62. Print.

Plessy v. Ferguson. 163 US 537. Supreme Court of the US. 1896. *US Supreme Court Opinions.* FindLaw, n.d. Web. 22 Feb. 2010.

Pocock, J. G. A. *The Ancient Constitution and the Feudal Law: A Study of English Historical Thought in the Seventeenth Century.* Cambridge: Cambridge UP, 1987. Print.

———. *The Machiavellian Moment: Florentine Political Thought and the Atlantic Republican Tradition.* Princeton: Princeton UP, 1975. Print.

Poe, Edgar Allan. "The Black Cat." Oates 78–86.

———. *Complete Tales and Poems.* New York: Vintage, 1975. Print.

———. "The Murders in the Rue Morgue." *The Murders in the Rue Morgue: The Dupin Tales.* New York: Modern Lib., 2006. 3–36. Print.

Posner, Richard. "The Deprofessionalization of Legal Teaching and Scholarship." *Michigan Law Review* 91 (1993): 1921–28. Print.

———. *Law and Literature: A Misunderstood Relation*. Cambridge: Harvard UP, 1988. Print.

———. *Not a Suicide Pact: The Constitution in a Time of National Emergency*. Oxford: Oxford UP, 2006. Print.

Post, Robert C., ed. *Law and the Order of Culture*. Berkeley: U of California P, 1991. Print.

Pough, Gwendolyn. *Check It While I Wreck It: Black Womanhood, Hip-Hop Culture, and the Public Sphere*. Boston: Northeastern UP, 2004. Print.

Preface. *Supreme Court Review* 1 (1960): frontispiece. Print.

Prendergast, Christopher. "Balzac: Narrative Contracts." *The Order of Mimesis: Balzac, Stendhal, Nerval, Flaubert*. Cambridge: Cambridge UP, 1986. 83–118. Print.

Price, Hiram. *Rules Governing the Court of Indian Offenses*. 30 Mar. 1883. Office of Robert N. Clinton, n.d. Web. 19 Jan. 2011.

"Proceedings on the Trial of Daniel Isaac Eaton for Blasphemous Libel." *A Complete Collection of State Trials and Proceedings for High Treason and Other Crimes and Misdemeanors from the Earliest Period to the Year 1783*. Comp. T. B. Howell and Thomas Jones Howell. Vol. 31. Hansard, 1823. Cols. 927–58. Print.

Pruyn, John V. L., et al. "Reply to President Lincoln." Freidel 752–65.

Public Enemy. "Fight the Power." *Fear of a Black Planet*. Def Jam, 1990. Audio CD.

Pufendorf, Samuel. *On the Duty of Man and Citizen according to Natural Law*. Cambridge: Cambridge UP, 1991. Print.

Pullman, Philip. *The Golden Compass*. New York: Ballantine, 1995. Print.

Punter, David. *Gothic Pathologies: The Text, the Body, and the Law*. Basingstoke: Macmillan, 1998. Print.

Pupin, Michael. "From Immigrant to Inventor." Hutner 254–78.

"The Putney Debates." Wootton 285–317.

Queen (Regina) v. Hicklin. LR 3 QB 360, 371. Queen's Bench, 1868. London: William Clowes and Sons, 1868. Print. Printed for *The Council of Law Reporting*.

R. v. Coney, Gilliam, and Tully. 8 QBD 534–70. Queen's Bench Division. London: William Clowes and Sons, 1882. Print. Printed for *The Council of Law Reporting*.

R. v. Young. 14 Cox's Criminal Law Cases 114–15. 1878. London: Horace Cox, 1882. Print.

Radcliffe, Ann. *The Italian*. Ed. Frederick Garber. Oxford: Oxford UP, 1970. Print.

———. *The Mysteries of Udolpho*. 1794. Ed. Bonamy Dobree. Oxford: Oxford UP, 1998. Print.

———. *The Romance of the Forest*. 1791. Ed. Chloe Chard. Oxford: Oxford UP, 2009. Print.

———. *A Sicilian Romance*. Ed. Alison Milbank. Oxford: Oxford UP, 1993. Print.

Radzinowicz, Leon. *A History of English Criminal Law and Its Administration*. Vol. 1. New York: Macmillan, 1948. Print.

Ram, James. *A Treatise on Facts as Subjects of Inquiry by a Jury*. New York: Baker, 1870. Print.

Randall, Alice. *The Wind Done Gone*. Boston: Houghton, 2001. Print.

Rawls, John. *A Theory of Justice*. Cambridge: Harvard UP, 1971. Print.

Raz, Joseph. *The Authority of Law: Essays on Law and Morality*. Oxford: Clarendon, 1983. Print.

Reed v. Reed. 404 US 71. Supreme Court of the US. 1971. *Supreme Court Collection*. Legal Information Inst., Cornell U Law School, n.d. Web. 22 Feb. 2010.

Reeve, Clara. *The Old English Baron*. 1778. *Seven Masterpieces of Gothic Horror*. Ed. Robert D. Spector. New York: Bantam, 1963. 103–236. Print.

Regents of the Univ. of California v. Bakke. 438 US 265. Supreme Court of the US. 1978. *Supreme Court Collection*. Legal Information Inst., Cornell U Law School, n.d. Web. 22 Feb. 2010.

Reich, Charles A. "Toward the Humanistic Study of Law." *Yale Law Journal* 74.6 (1965): 1402–08. Print.

———. "The Tragedy of Justice in *Billy Budd*." *Yale Review* 56 (1967): 368–89. Print.

Reid, Thomas. *Essays on the Active Powers of Man*. Edinburgh, 1788. Charlottesville: Ibis, n.d. Print. Facsim. rpt.

Reitman, Janet. "Sex and Scandal at Duke: Lacrosse Players, Sorority Girls, and the Booze-Fueled Culture of the Never-Ending Hookup on the Nation's Most Embattled College Campus." *Rolling Stone Magazine*. 15 June 2006: 70–109. Print.

Rex. v. Murphy. 6 C&P 103–04. Carrington and Payne. 1833. ER 172. *English Reports*. London: Stevens, 1928. Print.

Reynolds, Eustace. "Modified Constitution." 1915. Boyd 129–50.

Rich, Adrienne. "Resisting Amnesia: History and Personal Life." *Blood, Bread, and Poetry: Selected Prose, 1979–85*. New York: Norton, 1986. 133–55. Print.

Richards, I. A. *Coleridge on Imagination*. New York: Harcourt, 1935. Print.

Richetti, John. "The Public Sphere and the Eighteenth-Century Novel: Social Criticism and Narrative Enactment." *Eighteenth-Century Life* 16 (1992): 114–29. Print.

Ricoeur, Paul. *Freud and Philosophy: An Essay on Interpretation*. New Haven: Yale UP, 1970. Print.

Rivera, Tomas. *. . . and the Earth Did Not Devour Him*. Houston: Arte Publico, 1992. Print.

Robinson, Martha S. "The Law of the State in Kafka's *The Trial*." *ALSA Forum* 6 (1982): 127–47. Print.

Rodensky, Lisa. *The Crime in Mind: Criminal Responsibility and the Victorian Novel*. Oxford: Oxford UP, 2003. Print.

Roe v. Wade. 410 US 113. Supreme Court of the US. 1973. *Supreme Court Collection*. Legal Information Inst., Cornell U Law School, n.d. Web. 22 Feb. 2010.

Romer v. Evans. 517 US 620. Supreme Court of the US. 1996. *Supreme Court Collection*. Legal Information Inst., Cornell U Law School, n.d. Web. 22 Feb. 2010.

Rooney, Ellen. "'A Little More than Persuading': Tess and the Subject of Sexual Violence." *Rape and Representation*. Ed. Lynn A. Higgins and Brenda R. Silver. New York: Columbia UP, 1991. 87–114. Print.

Roscoe, William. *Observations on Penal Jurisprudence and the Reformation of Criminals: Part 3*. London: M'Creery, 1825. Print.

Rose, Mark. "The Author in Court: Pope v. Curll (1741)." *The Construction of Authorship: Textual Appropriation in Law and Literature.* Ed. Martha Woodmansee and Peter Jazzi. Durham: Duke UP, 1994. 211–30. Print.

Rose, Tricia. *Black Noise: Rap Music and Black Culture in Contemporary America.* Middleton: Wesleyan UP, 1994. Print.

Roth, Philip. *The Dying Animal.* New York: Vintage, 2006. Print.

Rothman, David. *The Discovery of the Asylum: Social Order and Disorder in the New Republic.* Boston: Little, 1971. Print.

———. "Perfecting the Prison: The United States, 1789–1865." *The Oxford History of the Prison: The Practice of Punishment in Western Society.* Ed. Norval Morris and Rothman. Oxford: Oxford UP, 1998. 100–16. Print.

Rousseau, Jean-Jacques. *A Discourse on Inequality.* 1754. Trans. Maurice Cranston. London: Penguin, 1984. Print.

Ruckelshaus, William D. "Toward a Sustainable World." *Scientific American* Sept. 1989: 166–75. Print.

Rush, Benjamin. *Essays: Literary, Moral, and Philosophical.* Ed. Michael Meranze. Schenectady: Union Coll., 1988. Print.

———. *Letters of Benjamin Rush.* Ed. L. H. Butterfield. Vol. 2. Princeton: Princeton UP, 1951. Print.

Rusk v. State of Maryland. 406 A. 2nd 624. Court of Special Appeals of Maryland. 1979. *Atlantic Reporter.* 2nd ser. Vol. 406. St. Paul: West, 1980. 624–36. Print.

Sacks, David Harris. "Political Culture." *A Companion to Shakespeare.* Ed. David Scott Kastan. Oxford: Blackwell, 1999. 117–38. Print.

Sage, C. J., ed. *And We the Creatures: Fifty-One Contemporary American Poets on Animal Rights and Appreciation.* Aptos: Dream Horse, 2003. Print.

Said, Edward. "Opponents, Audiences, Constituencies, and Community." *Critical Inquiry* 9.1 (1982): 1–27. Print.

Salzman, Mark. *True Notebooks: A Writer's Year at Juvenile Hall.* New York: Vintage, 2003. Print.

San Antonio Independent School District v. Rodriguez. 411 US 1. Supreme Court of the US. 1973. *Supreme Court Collection.* Legal Information Inst., Cornell U Law School, n.d. Web. 16 Apr. 2010.

Sarat, Austin, ed. *Law, Violence, and the Possibility of Justice.* Princeton: Princeton UP, 2001. Print.

Sarat, Austin, Matthew Anderson, and Cathrine O. Frank. "Introduction: On the Origins and Prospects of the Humanistic Study of Law." *Law and the Humanities: An Introduction.* Ed. Sarat, Anderson, and Frank. Cambridge: Cambridge UP, 2010. 1–46. Print.

Sarat, Austin, and Thomas R. Kearns, eds. *The Rhetoric of Law.* Ann Arbor: U of Michigan P, 1994. Print.

Satrapi, Marjane. *Persepolis: The Story of a Childhood.* New York: Pantheon, 2003. Print.

Saunders, Marshall. *Beautiful Joe.* Middlesex: Echo Lib., 2006. Print.

Sawada, Mitziko. *Tokyo Life, New York Dreams: Urban Japanese Visions of America, 1890–1924.* Berkeley: U of California P, 1996. Print.

Scalia, Antonin. *A Matter of Interpretation: Federal Courts and the Law.* Princeton: Princeton UP, 1998. Print.

Scarry, Elaine. "The Made-Up and the Made-Real." *Field Work: Sites in Literary and Cultural Studies*. Ed. Marjorie Garber, Paul B. Franklin, and Rebecca L. Walkowitz. New York: Routledge, 1996. 214–24. Print.

———. "War and the Social Contract: Nuclear Policy, Distribution, and the Right to Bear Arms." *University of Pennsylvania Law Review* 139 (1991): 1257–316. Print.

Scheffler, Judith, ed. *Wall Tappings: An Anthology of Writings by Women Prisoners*. Boston: Northeastern UP, 1989. Print.

Scheppele, Kim Lane. "Foreword: Telling Stories." *Michigan Law Review* 87.8 (1989): 2073–98. Print.

Schine, Cathleen. "Dog Trouble." *Best American Essays, 1995*. New York: Mariner, 1995. 181–94. Print.

Schloss, Joseph. "The Art of the Battle: An Interview with Zulu King Alien Ness." *Total Chaos: The Art and Aesthetics of Hip Hop*. Ed. Jeff Chang. New York: Basic, 2007. 27–32. Print.

———. *Making Beats: The Art of Sample-Based Hip-Hop*. Middletown: Wesleyan UP, 2004. Print.

Schlosser, Eric. "The Prison-Industrial Complex." *Atlantic Magazine*. Atlantic Monthly Group, Dec. 1998. Web. 18 Mar. 2010.

Schmidgen, Wolfram. *Eighteenth-Century Fiction and the Law of Property*. Cambridge: Cambridge UP, 2002. Print.

Schmitt, Carl. *Concept of the Political*. Trans. George Schwab. Chicago: U of Chicago P, 1996. Print.

Scholes, Robert. *The Crafty Reader*. New Haven: Yale UP, 2001. Print.

Schramm, Jan-Melissa. *Testimony and Advocacy in Victorian Law, Literature, and Theology*. Cambridge: Cambridge UP, 2000. Print.

Schur, Richard. "Locating Paradise in the Post-Civil Rights Era: Toni Morrison and Critical Race Theory." *Contemporary Literature* 45.2 (2004): 276–99. Print.

———. *Parodies of Ownership: Hip Hop Aesthetics and Intellectual Property*. Ann Arbor: U of Michigan P, 2009. Print.

———. "The Subject of Law: Toni Morrison, Critical Race Theory, and the Narration of Cultural Criticism." *Forty-Ninth Parallel: An Interdisciplinary Journal of North American Studies* 6 (2000): n. pag. Web. 11 Nov. 2009.

Schweitzer, Ivy. *The Work of Self-Representation: Lyric Poetry in Colonial New England*. Chapel Hill: U of North Carolina P, 1991. Print.

Scott, Walter. *Guy Mannering*. 1815. Ed. P. D. Garside. London: Penguin, 2003. Print.

———. *The Heart of Mid-Lothian*. 1818. Ed. Tony Inglis. New York: Penguin, 1994. Print.

———. *Rokeby: A Poem*. Edinburgh: Ballantyne, 1813. Print.

Scott v. Sandford. 60 US 393. Supreme Court of the US. 1857. *Supreme Court Collection*. Legal Information Inst., Cornell U Law School, n.d. Web. 22 Feb. 2010.

Scrivener, Michael. "Trials in Romantic-Era Writing: Modernity, Guilt, and the Scene of Justice." *The Wordsworth Circle* 35 (2004): 128–33. Print.

"Secret Information concerning Black American Troops." "Documents of the War." Comp. W. E. Burghardt DuBois. *The Crisis* 18.1 (1919): 16–18. *Google Books*. Web. 10 Aug. 2010.

Sei Fujii v. State of California. L. A. no. 21149. 38 Cal. 2nd 718. Supreme Court of California. 1952. *West's California Reporter.* 2nd ser. Vol. 38. 1952. 718–70. *LexisNexis.* Web. 6 Aug. 2010. 1952 Cal. LEXIS 221.

Selden, John. *Table Talk of John Selden.* Ed. Frederick Pollock. London: Selden Soc., 1927. Print.

Sewall, Samuel. *The Diary of Samuel Sewall, 1674–1729.* Ed. M. Halsey Thomas. New York: Farrar, 1973. Print.

Shakespeare, William. *The Life of Henry the Fifth.* Shakespeare, *Riverside Shakespeare* 1: 935–75.

———. *Measure for Measure.* Ed. Jonathan Crewe. New York: Penguin, 2000. Print.

———. *The Riverside Shakespeare.* Ed. G. Blakemore Evans et al. 2 vols. Boston: Houghton, 1974. Print.

———. *The Second Part of Henry the Fourth.* Shakespeare, *Riverside Shakespeare* 1: 886–929.

———. *The Second Part of Henry the Sixth.* Shakespeare, *Riverside Shakespeare* 1: 630–70.

———. *The Tragedy of Julius Caesar.* Shakespeare, *Riverside Shakespeare* 2: 1100–34.

———. *The Tragedy of King Richard the Second.* Shakespeare, *Riverside Shakespeare* 1: 805–41.

Shapiro, Barbara J. *"Beyond Reasonable Doubt" and "Probable Cause": Historical Perspectives on the Anglo-American Law of Evidence.* Berkeley: U of California P, 1991. Print.

Sharp, Andrew, ed. *The English Levellers.* Cambridge: Cambridge UP, 1998. Print.

Sharpe, J. A. *Crime in Early Modern England, 1550–1750.* London: Longman, 1984. Print.

Shell, Marc. *The End of Kinship:* Measure for Measure, *Incest, and the Ideal of Universal Siblinghood.* Stanford: Stanford UP, 1988. Print.

Shelley, Mary. *Frankenstein.* 1818. Ed. Maurice Hindle. London: Penguin, 1992. Print.

Shelley, Percy Bysshe. *The Cenci: A Tragedy in Five Acts.* Cox and Gamer 221–59.

———. "A Philosophical View of Reform." *Shelley's Prose; or, The Trumpet of a Prophecy.* Ed. David Lee Clark. Pref. Harold Bloom. Chicago: New Amsterdam, 1988. 230–61. Print.

———. *Zastrozzi.* 1810. London: Hesperus, 2002. Print.

Shelley v. Kraemer. 334 US 1. Supreme Court of the US. 1948. *Supreme Court Collection.* Legal Information Inst., Cornell U Law School, n.d. Web. 22 Feb. 2010.

Sherman Anti-Trust Act. 2 July 1890. Our Documents, n.d. Web. 5 Oct. 2009.

Sherwin, Richard K. "Law and Popular Culture: Nomos and Cinema." *UCLA Law Review* 48 (2001): 1519–43. Print.

Shirley, James. *The Triumph of Peace. The Dramatic Works and Poems of James Shirley.* Vol. 6. Ed. William Gifford. London: Murray, 1833. 253–85. Print.

Shuger, Debora. *Political Theologies in Shakespeare's England: The Sacred and the State in* Measure for Measure. New York: Palgrave, 2001. Print.

Shulman, Alix Kates. *Memoirs of an Ex-Prom Queen.* New York: Farrar, 2007. Print.

Sickelmore, Richard. *Edgar; or, The Phantom of the Castle.* 1798. Ed. James D. Jenkins. Chicago: Valancourt, 2005. Print.

Sidney, Philip. *An Apologie for Poetry.* Ed. Geoffrey Shepherd. Manchester: Manchester UP, 2002. Print.

———. *The Old Arcadia.* Ed. Katherine Duncan Jones. Oxford: Oxford UP, 1985. Print.

Silence of the Lambs. Dir. Jonathan Demme. Orion, 1991. Film.

Silko, Leslie Marmon. *Almanac of the Dead.* New York: Penguin, 1992. Print.

———. "America's Debt to the Indian Nations." *Cultural Conversations.* Ed. Stephen Dilks et al. Boston: Bedford, 2001. 616–19. Print.

Simon, Uriel. "The Poor Man's Ewe-Lamb: An Example of a Juridical Parable." *Biblica* 48 (1967): 207–42. Print.

Simonin, Anne. "'Make the Unorthodox Orthodox': John Henry Wigmore et la naissance de l'intérêt du droit pour la littèrature." *Actes du colloque de la cour de cassation.* Ed. Antoine Garapon and Denis Salas. Paris: Michalon, forthcoming.

Simons, Algie. "Social Forces and the Constitution." 1911. Ollman and Birnbaum 16–124.

Singer, Joseph William. "Persuasion." *Michigan Law Review* 87 (1989): 2442–48. Print.

Singer, Peter. *Animal Liberation: A New Ethics for Our Treatment of Animals.* New York: Random, 1975. Print.

Smith, Anna Deavere. "The Circle of Confusion: A Conversation with Anna Deavere Smith." Interview by Barbara Lewis. *Kenyon Review* 15.4 (1993): 54–64. Print.

———. *Fires in the Mirror: Crown Heights, Brooklyn, and Other Identities.* New York: Anchor, 1998. Print.

———. *Twilight: Los Angeles, 1992: On the Road: A Search for American Character.* New York: Anchor, 1994. Print.

Smith, Gerrit. "Speech on the Nebraska Bill." 6 Apr. 1854. *Speeches of Gerrit Smith in Congress.* New York: Mason Brothers, 1855. 113–215. Print.

Smith, J. Allen. "Aspects of Law and Literature: The Revival and Search for Doctrine." *University of Hartford Studies in Literature* 9 (1977): 213–22. Print.

———. "The Coming Renaissance in Law and Literature." *Maryland Law Forum* 7.2 (1977): 84–92. Print.

Smith, Thomas. *De Republica Anglorum.* Ed. Mary Dewar. Cambridge: Cambridge UP, 1982. Print.

Snyder, Martin P. *City of Independence: Views of Philadelphia before 1800.* New York: Praeger, 1975. Print.

Sophocles. *Antigone. Antigone, Oedipus the King, Electra.* Ed. Edith Hall. Trans. H. D. F. Kitto. Oxford: Oxford UP, 1994. 1–46. Print. Oxford World's Classics.

Spiegelman, Art. *Maus: A Survivor's Tale.* New York: Pantheon, 1973. Print.

Stanton, Domna C. "Foreword: ANDs, INs, and BUTs." The Humanities in Human Rights: Critique, Language, Politics. *PMLA* 121.5 (2006): 1518–25. Print.

Stanton, Elizabeth Cady. "Declaration of Sentiments." P. Foner, *We* 78–83.

State of Maryland v. Rusk. 289 Md. 230. Court of Appeals of Maryland. 1981. *Maryland Reporter.* Vol. 289. 230–66. *LexisNexis.* Web. 6 Aug. 2010. 1981 Md. LEXIS 265.

State of Missouri v. Celia, a Slave. File 4496, Callaway County Court, Oct. Term. 1855. *State of Missouri vs. Celia, A Slave: Trial Record, Selected Links, and Bibliography.* By Kathleen Hall. *Famous Trials,* by Douglas O. Linder. U of Missouri, Kansas City, School of Law, n.d. Web. 20 Jan. 2011. <http://www .law.umkc.edu/faculty/projects/ftrials/celialinks.html>.

Steger, Manfred B., and Nancy S. Lind, eds. *Violence and Its Alternatives: An Interdisciplinary Reader.* New York: St. Martin's, 1999. Print.

Steinbeck, John. *The Red Pony.* New York: Penguin, 2001. Print.

Stendhal. *The Red and the Black.* Trans. Catharine Slater. New York: Oxford UP, 1991. Print.

Stern, Milton R. Introduction. *Billy Budd.* By Herman Melville. Indianapolis: Bobbs, 1975. vii–xliv. Print.

Stoker, Bram. *Dracula.* Ed. Glennis Byron. Peterborough: Broadview, 1998. Print.

Stowe, Harriet Beecher. *Uncle Tom's Cabin.* 1852. New York: Penguin, 1986. Print.

Strafgesetz vom 27. Mai 1852. Ed. Hans Hoyer. Vienna: Manz, 1944. Print.

Straus, Nina Pelikan. *Dostoevsky and the Woman Question: Rereadings at the End of the Century.* New York: St. Martin's, 1994. Print.

"Subject Matter of Copyright: In General." 17 USC. Sec. 102. 5 Jan. 2009. *U.S. Code.* Legal Information Inst., Cornell U Law School, n.d. Web. 23 Feb. 2010.

Sumner, Charles. "The Mutiny on the *Somers.*" *North American Review* 107 (1843): 95–241. Print.

Sundquist, Eric J. "Mark Twain and Homer Plessy." Gillman and Robinson 46–72.

Sunstein, Cass. "Beyond the Republican Revival." *Yale Law Journal* 97 (1988): 1539–90. Print.

Supreme Records v. Decca Records. 90 F. Supp. 904. US District Court for the Southern District of California. 1950. *Federal Supplement.* Vol. 90. St. Paul: West, 1950. 904–24. Print.

Suretsky, Harold. "Search for a Theory: An Annotated Bibliography of Writings on the Relation of Law to Literature and the Humanities." *Rutgers Law Review* 32 (1979): 727–40. Print.

Sutherland, John. *Can Jane Eyre Be Happy?* Oxford: Oxford UP, 2000. Print.

Swan, Beth. "Radcliffe's Inquisition and Eighteenth-Century English Legal Practice." *Eighteenth-Century Novel* 3 (2003): 195–216. Print.

"Symposium: The Nuremberg Trials: A Reappraisal and Their Legacy." *Cardozo Law Review* 27 (2006): 1549–738. Print.

Takao Ozawa v. US. 260 US 178. Supreme Court of the US. 1922. *US Supreme Court Opinions.* FindLaw, n.d. Web. 22 Feb. 2010.

Talbot, Steve. "Spiritual Genocide: The Denial of American Indian Religious Freedom, from Conquest to 1934." *Wicazo Sa Review* 21.2 (2006): 7–33. Print.

Tamanaha, Brian Z. *Law as a Means to an End: Threat to the Rule of Law.* Cambridge: Cambridge UP, 2006. Print.

———. *On the Rule of Law: History, Politics, Theory.* Cambridge: Cambridge UP, 2004. Print.

Tambling, Jeremy, ed. Bleak House: *New Casebooks.* London: Macmillan, 1998. Print.

Tanner, Tony. *Adultery and the Novel: Contract and Transgression.* Baltimore: Johns Hopkins UP, 1981. Print.

Taylor v. Louisiana. 419 US 522. Supreme Court of the US. 1975. *Supreme Court Collection.* Legal Information Inst., Cornell U Law School, n.d. Web. 23 Feb. 2010.

Temple, Kathryn. "Gender and Juridical Space in the Gothic Novel." *Illicit Sex: Identity Politics in Early Modern Culture.* Ed. Thomas DiPiero and Pat Gill. Athens: U of Georgia P, 1997. 68–85. Print.

Tennyson, G. B., ed. *A Barfield Reader.* Hanover: UP of New England, 1999. Print.

"The Ten-Point Platform and Program of the Black Panther Party." P. Foner, *Black Panthers* 78–80.

Terminiello v. Chicago. 337 US 934. Supreme Court of the US. 1949. Hearing denied (337 US 934). *US Supreme Court Center.* Justia, n.d. Web. 23 Feb. 2010.

Texas v. Johnson. 491 US 397. Supreme Court of the US. 1989. *Supreme Court Collection.* Legal Information Inst., Cornell U Law School, n.d. Web. 23 Feb. 2010.

That Darn Cat! Dir. Robert Stevenson. Walt Disney Productions, 1965. Film.

Thirteenth Amendment to the U.S. Constitution: Abolition of Slavery. 1865. Our Documents, n.d. Web. 23 Feb. 2010.

Thomas, Brook. *American Literary Realism and the Failed Promise of Contract.* Berkeley: U of California P, 1997. Print.

———. "*Billy Budd* and the Judgment of Silence." *Literature and Ideology.* Ed. Harry R. Garvin. Lewisburg: Bucknell UP, 1982. 51–78. Print.

———. *Civic Myths: A Law and Literature Approach to Citizenship.* Chapel Hill: U of North Carolina P, 2007. Print.

———. "Constitutional Literacy: Plessy and Brown in the Writing Class." *College English* 58 (1996): 637–53. Print.

———. *Cross-Examinations of Law and Literature: Cooper, Hawthorne, Stowe, and Melville.* Cambridge: Cambridge UP, 1987. Print.

———, ed. *"Plessy v. Ferguson": A Brief History with Documents.* Boston: Bedford, 1997. Print.

———. "*The Rise of Silas Lapham* and the Hazards of Realistic Development." B. Thomas, *American Literary Realism* 122–55.

———. "Twain, Tourgée, and the Logic of 'Separate but Equal.'" B. Thomas, *American Literary Realism* 191–230.

Thomas, Lorenzo. "How to See through Poetry: Myth Perception and History." 2002. *Civil Disobediences: Poetics and Politics in Action.* Ed. Anne Waldman and Lisa Birman. Minneapolis: Coffee House, 2004. 338–56. Print.

Thomas, Piri. *Down These Mean Streets.* New York: Vintage, 1973. Print.

———."Piri's Journey from Prison to Freedom." *The World of Piri Thomas.* Cheverote Productions, n.d. Web. 23 Feb. 2010.

Thomas of Woodstock; or, Richard the Second, Part One. Ed. Peter Corbin and Douglas Sedge. Manchester: Manchester UP, 2002. Print.

Thoreau, Henry David. "Civil Disobedience." *Collected Essays and Poems.* Ed. Elizabeth Hall Witherell. New York: Lib. of Amer., 2001. 203–24. Print.

Thurschwell, Adam. "Reading the Law." Sarat and Kearns 275–332.

Tillyard, E. M. W. *The Elizabethan World Picture*. 1943. Harmondsworth: Penguin, 1975. Print.

Tocqueville, Alexis de. *Democracy in America*. Trans. George Lawrence. New York: Harper, 1988. Print.

Todd, Janet. *The Sign of Angellica: Women, Writing, and Fiction, 1660–1800*. New York: Columbia UP, 1989. Print.

Tolstoy, Leo. "The Kreutzer Sonata." *"The Death of Ivan Ilych" and Other Stories*. Trans. Aylmer Maude. New York: Signet, 2003. 153–234. Print.

Tomlins, Christopher L., and Bruce H. Mann, eds. *The Many Legalities of Early America*. Chapel Hill: U of North Carolina P, 2001. Print.

Treaty of Guadalupe Hidalgo. 2 Feb. 1848. Our Documents, n.d. Web. 23 Feb. 2010.

Tribal Colleges: An Introduction. Amer. Indian Higher Educ. Consortium, Feb. 1999. Web. 14 June 2007.

Trilling, Lionel. *The Liberal Imagination: Essays on Literature and Society*. New York: Scribner's, 1976. Print.

Tritter, Dan. "Preface to the Symposium: A Lusty Voice." *Cardozo Studies in Law and Literature* 1 (1989): iv–v. Print.

Trodd, Zoe, ed. *American Protest Literature*. Cambridge: Harvard UP, 2006. Print.

Trodd, Zoe, and John Stauffer, eds. *Meteor of War: The John Brown Story*. New York: Blackwell, 2004. Print.

Tucker, Irene. *A Probable State: The Novel, the Contract, and the Jews*. Chicago: U of Chicago P, 2000. Print.

Tugwell, Rexford G. "An Emerging Constitution." 1974. Boyd 246–86.

Turow, Scott. *One L: The Turbulent True Story of a First Year at Harvard Law School*. 1977. New York: Warner, 1997. Print.

Twain, Mark. *Pudd'nhead Wilson, and Those Extraordinary Twins*. Ed. Sidney Berger. New York: Norton, 1980. Print.

Twenty-Fourth Amendment to the Constitution of the United States. *Charters of Freedom*. Natl. Archives, n.d. Web. 12 Aug. 2009.

US v. Armstrong. 517 US 456. Supreme Court of the US. 1996. *US Supreme Court Opinions*. FindLaw, n.d. Web. 23 Feb. 2010.

US v. Bhagat Singh Thind. 261 US 204. Supreme Court of the US. 1923. *US Supreme Court Opinions*. FindLaw, n.d. Web. 23 Feb. 2010.

US v. One Book Called *Ulysses*. 5 F. Supp. 182. US District Court for the Southern District of New York. 1933. *Federal Supplement*. Vol. 5. St. Paul: West, 1934. 182–85. Print.

Valdez, Luis. Zoot Suit *and Other Plays*. Houston: Arte Publico, 1992. Print.

Vattel, Emerich. "Of Nations Considered in Themselves." *The Law of Nations*. Constitution Soc., 1999. Web. 23 Feb. 2010.

Volgin, Igor. "Pis'ma chitatelei k F. M. Dostoevskom." *Voprosy literatury* 9 (1971): 196. Print.

Voting Rights Act. 6 Aug. 1965. Our Documents, n.d. Web. 23 Feb. 2010.

Waits v. Frito Lay. 978 F. 2nd 1093. US Court of Appeals, 9th Circuit. 1992. *Open Jurist*. Open Jurist, n.d. Web. 16 Feb. 2010.

Waldron, Jeremy "Dead to the Law: Paul's Antinomianism." *Cardozo Law Review* 28 (2006): 301–32. Print.

Walker, Alice. "Am I Blue?" *Living by the Word: Selected Writings, 1973–1987.* San Diego: Harcourt, 1988. 3–8. Print.

Walpole, Horace. *The Castle of Otranto.* 1764. Ed. W. S. Lewis. Oxford: Oxford UP, 1982. Print.

Walzer, Michael, ed. *Regicide and Revolution: Speeches at the Trial of Louis XVI.* Trans. Marian Rothstein. New York: Columbia UP, 1992. Print.

———. *The Revolution of the Saints: A Study in the Origins of Radical Politics.* Cambridge: Harvard UP, 1982. Print.

War Department General Order 143: Creation of the U.S. Colored Troops. 22 May 1863. Our Documents, n.d. Web. 31 Mar. 2010.

Warner, Michael. "What's Colonial about Colonial America?" *Possible Pasts: Becoming Colonial in Early America.* Ed. Robert Blair St. George. Ithaca: Cornell UP, 2000. 49–70. Print.

Warner, William B. *Licensing Entertainment: The Elevation of Novel Reading in Britain, 1684–1750.* Berkeley: U of California P, 1998. Print.

Warren, Samuel, and Louis Brandeis. "The Right to Privacy." *Harvard Law Review* 4 (1890): 193–220. Print.

Waters, Michael. "Commerce." *Gettysburg Review* 15 (2002): 446–47. Print.

Watkins, S. Craig. "Black Youth and the Ironies of Capitalism." Forman and Neal 557–78.

Watson, Brad. *Last Days of the Dog-Men: Stories.* New York: Norton, 2002. Print.

Watt, Ian. *The Rise of the Novel: Studies in Defoe, Richardson, and Fielding.* Berkeley: U of California P, 1957. Print.

Watt, James. *Contesting the Gothic: Fiction, Genre, and Cultural Conflict, 1764–1832.* Cambridge: Cambridge UP, 1999. Print.

Watts, James W. *Reading Law: The Rhetorical Shaping of the Pentateuch.* Sheffield: Sheffield Academic, 1999. Print.

Webb, Charles Harper. "Tormenting the Cat." Sage 9.

Weber, Samuel. "In the Name of the Law." Cornell, Rosenfeld, and Carlson 232–57.

Webster, Richard. *Philadelphia Preserved: Catalog of the Historic American Buildings Survey.* Philadelphia: Temple UP, 1976. Print.

Wein, Toni. "Legal Fictions, Legitimate Desires: The Law of Representation in *The Romance of the Forest.*" *Genre* 30 (1997): 289–310. Print.

Weisberg, Richard H. "De Man Missing Nietzsche: 'Hinzugedichtet' Revisited." *Nietzsche as Postmodernist.* Ed. C. Koelb. Albany: State U of New York P, 1990. 111–24. Print.

———. "Differing Ways of Reading: Differing Views of the Law: The Catholic Church and Its Treatment of the Jewish Question during Vichy." *Remembering for the Future: The Holocaust in an Age of Genocide.* Ed. Margot Levy. Vol. 2. London: Palgrave, 2001. 509–30. Print.

———. *The Failure of the Word: The Protagonist as Lawyer in Modern Fiction.* New Haven: Yale UP, 1984. Print.

———. "Fish Takes the Bait." *Critical Quarterly* 43 (2001): 19–27. Print.

————. "How Judges Speak: Some Lessons on Adjudication in *Billy Budd, Sailor* with an Application to Justice Rehnquist." *New York University Law Review* 57 (1982): 1–69. Print.

————. "Law and Literature in Dialogue." Letter. *PMLA* 121.2 (2006): 546–47. Print.

————. "Law in and as Literature: Self-Generated Meaning in the 'Procedural Novel.'" *The Comparative Perspective on Literature.* Ed. C. Koelb and S. Noakes. Ithaca: Cornell UP, 1988. 224–32. Print.

————. Rev. of *The Legal Imagination*, by James B. White. *Columbia Law Review* 74 (1974): 327–37. Print.

————. "Literature's Twenty-Year Crossing into the Domain of Law: Continuing Trespass or Right by Adverse Possession?" Freeman and Lewis 47–61.

————. "Nietzsche's Hermeneutics: Good and Bad Interpreters of Texts." *Nietzsche and Legal Theory.* Ed. Peter Goodrich and Mariana Valverde. New York: Routledge, 2005. 149–64. Print.

————. "Paul, Pomo, and the Legitimacy of Choice post-9/11." *Cardozo Law Review* 24 (2003): 1615–19. Print.

————. *Poethics and Other Strategies of Law and Literature.* New York: Columbia UP, 1992. Print.

————. "Text into Theory: A Literary Approach to the Constitution." *Georgia Law Review* 20 (1986): 939–94. Print.

————. "Twenty Years (or Two Thousand?) of Story-telling on the Law: Is Justice Detectable?" *Cardozo Law Review* 26 (2005): 2223–46. Print.

————. *Vichy Law and the Holocaust in France.* New York: New York UP, 1996. Print.

————. "'The Verdict' Is In: The Civic Implications of Civil Trials." *DePaul Law Review* 50 (2000): 525–33. Print.

————. "Wigmore's 'Legal Novels' Revisited: New Resources for the Expansive Lawyer." *Northwestern Law Review* 71 (1976): 17–28. Print.

Weisberg, Richard, and Jean-Pierre Barricelli. "Literature and Law." *Interrelations of Literature.* Ed. Barricelli and Joseph Gibaldi. New York: MLA, 1982. 150–75. Print.

Welch, James. *The Indian Lawyer.* New York: Penguin, 1991. Print.

Wells, Robin. "The Fortunes of Tillyard: Twentieth-Century Critical Debate on Shakespeare's History Plays." *English Studies* 66.5 (1985): 391–403. Print.

Wells, Rosemary. *Lassie Come-Home: Eric Knight's Original 1938 Classic.* New York: Henry Holt, 2000. Print.

Welsh, Alexander. "Stories of Things Not Seen." Welsh, *Strong Representations* 1–42.

————. *Strong Representations: Narrative and Circumstantial Evidence in England.* Baltimore: Johns Hopkins UP, 1992. Print.

Werfel, Franz. *The Class Reunion.* Trans. Whittaker Chambers. New York: Simon, 1929. Print. Trans. of *Der Abitürientag: Die Geschichte einer Jugendschuld.* Berlin: Zsolnay, 1928.

West, James. *A Proposed New Constitution for the United States.* 1890. Boyd 68–92.

West, Kanye. "Gold Digger." *Late Registration.* Roc-A-Fella Records, 2005. Audio CD.

West, Robin. "Adjudication Is Not Interpretation: Some Reservations about the Law-as-Literature Movement." *Tennessee Law Review* 54 (1987): 203–78. Print.

———. "Are There Nothing but Texts in This Class? Interpreting the Interpretive Turns in Legal Thought." *Chicago-Kent Law Review* 76 (2000): 1125–65. Print.

———. "Authority, Autonomy, and Choice: The Role of Consent in the Moral and Political Visions of Franz Kafka and Richard Posner." *Harvard Law Review* 99 (1985): 384–428. Print.

———. *Caring for Justice*. New York: New York UP, 1999. Print.

———. *Narrative, Authority, and Law*. Ann Arbor: U of Michigan P, 1993. Print.

Westbrook, Raymond. "Biblical and Cuneiform Law Codes." *Revue biblique* 92.2 (1985): 247–64. Print.

Weston, Nancy A. "The Fate, Violence, and Rhetoric of Contemporary Legal Thought: Reflections on the Amherst Series, the Loss of Truth, and Law." *Law and Social Inquiry* 22 (1997): 733–808. Print.

White, Edmund. "The Gay Philosopher." *The Burning Library: Essays*. Ed. David Bergman. New York: Vintage, 1995. 3–19. Print.

White, Hayden. *The Content of the Form*. Baltimore: Johns Hopkins UP, 1992. Print.

White, James B. *From Expectation to Experience: Essays on Law and Legal Education*. Ann Arbor: U of Michigan P, 1999. Print.

———. *Heracles' Bow: Essays on the Rhetoric and Poetics of Law*. Madison: U of Wisconsin P, 1985. Print.

———. *Justice as Translation: An Essay in Cultural and Legal Criticism*. Chicago: U of Chicago P, 1990. Print.

———. "Law as Rhetoric, Rhetoric as Law: The Arts of Cultural and Communal Life." *University of Chicago Law Review* 52 (1985): 684–702. Print.

———. *The Legal Imagination: Studies in the Nature of Legal Thought and Expression*. Boston: Little, 1973. Print.

———. "Making Sense of What We Do: The Criminal Law as a System of Meaning." J. White, *Heracles' Bow* 192–214.

———. "What Can a Lawyer Learn from Literature?" Rev. of *Law and Literature: A Misunderstood Relation*, by Richard A. Posner. *Harvard Law Review* 102 (1989): 2014–47. Print.

———. *When Words Lose Their Meaning*. Chicago: U of Chicago P, 1984. Print.

Whitehead, Colson. *Apex Hides the Hurt*. New York: Anchor, 2007. Print.

———. *John Henry Days*. New York: Doubleday, 2001. Print.

Wideman, John Edgar. *Brothers and Keepers*. New York: Holt, Rinehart, 1984. Print.

Wigmore, John H. "A List of Legal Novels." *Illinois Law Review* 2 (1908): 574–93. Print.

———. "A List of One Hundred Legal Novels." *Illinois Law Review* 17 (1922): 26–42. Print.

Willard. Dir. Daniel Mann. Bing Crosby Productions, 1971. Film.

Williams, John A. *The Man Who Cried I Am*. 1967. Boston: Little, 2004. Print.

Williams, Joy. "Hawk." *Ill Nature*. New York: Vintage, 2002. 159–62. Print.

Williams, Melanie. "'Is Alec a Rapist?': Cultural Connotations of 'Rape' and 'Seduction': A Reply to Professor Sutherland." *Feminist Legal Studies* 7 (1999): 299–316. Print.

———. "'Sensitive as Gossamer': Law and Sexual Encounter in *Tess of the D'Urbervilles.*" *Thomas Hardy Journal* 17 (2001): 54–60. Print.

Williams, Patricia J. "Spirit-Murdering the Messenger: The Discourse of Finger-pointing as the Law's Response to Racism." *University of Miami Law Review* 42 (1987): 127–57. Print.

Williams, Roger. *The Complete Writings of Roger Williams.* 7 vols. Ed. Perry Miller. Paris: Baptist Standard Bearer, 2005. Print.

Williams, Wendy W. "Equality's Riddle: Pregnancy and the Equal Treatment / Special Treatment Debate." *Review of Law and Social Change* 13 (1984–85): 325–80. Print.

Wills, Garry. *Lincoln at Gettysburg: The Words that Remade America.* New York: Touchstone, 1992. Print.

Wimsatt, William. "What to Say about a Poem." *Hateful Contraries.* Lexington: U of Kentucky P, 1965. 215–44. Print.

Winner, Lucy. "Democratic Acts: Theatre of Public Trials." *Theatre Topics* 15.2 (2005): 149–69. Print.

Winstanley, Gerrard. *"The Law of Freedom" and Other Writings.* Ed. Christopher Hill. Cambridge: Cambridge UP, 1973. Print.

Winthrop, John. "A Model of Christian Charity." *Puritan and Political Ideas, 1558–1793.* Ed. Edmund S. Morgan. Indianapolis: Bobbs, 2003. 75–93. Print.

Wise, Steven. *Rattling the Cage: Toward Legal Rights for Animals.* New York: Perseus, 2001. Print.

Witherspoon, Gary. *Language and Art in the Navajo Universe.* Ann Arbor: U of Michigan P, 1977. Print.

Witteveen, Willem J. "Law and Literature: Expanding, Contracting, Emerging." *Cardozo Studies in Law and Literature* 10.2 (1998): 155–60. Print.

Wolfe, Cary. *Animal Rites: American Culture, the Discourse of Species, and Posthumanist Theory.* Chicago: U of Chicago P, 2003. Print.

Wolfe, Tom. *I Am Charlotte Simmons.* New York: Picador, 2004. Print.

Wollstonecraft, Mary. *A Vindication of the Rights of Woman. The Feminist Papers: from Adams to de Beauvoir.* Ed. Alice S. Rossi. Boston: Northeastern UP, 1988. 40–85. Print.

Woodhull, Victoria C. "A New Constitution for the United States of the World." P. Foner, *We* 177–201.

Woolf, Virginia. "A Room of One's Own" *Cultural Conversations: The Presence of the Past.* Ed. Stephen Dilks et al. Boston: Bedford–St. Martin's, 2001. 564–69. Print.

Wootton, David, ed. *Divine Right and Democracy: An Anthology of Political Writing in Stuart England.* Harmondsworth: Penguin, 1986. Print.

Worden, Blair. "Milton's Republicanism and the Tyranny of Heaven." *Machiavelli and Republicanism.* Ed. Gisela Bock, Quentin Skinner, and Maurizio Viroli. Cambridge: Cambridge UP, 1990. 225–46. Print.

Wordsworth, William. *The Borderers.* Ed. Robert Osborn. Ithaca: Cornell UP, 1982. *LION* [1849–50 ed. of *Poetical Works*, ed. Edward Moxon]. Print, Web. 15 Aug. 2010.

———. *The Prelude*. Ed. Jonathan Wordsworth, M. H. Abrams, and Stephen Gill. New York: Norton, 1979.

Wroth, Lawrence C. "The Indian Treaty as Literature." *Literature of the American Indians*. Ed. Abraham Chapman. New York: New Amer. Lib., 1975. 324–37. Print.

Yava, Albert. "We Want to Tell You Something." 1894. *Cultural Conversations: The Presence of the Past*. Ed. Stephen Dilks et al. Boston: Bedford–St. Martin's, 2001. 564–69. Print.

Youngs, Raymond. *English, French and German Comparative Law*. 2nd ed. London: Routledge, 2007. Print.

Zelinsky, Katherine. Introduction. Manley 9–34.

Ziolkowski, Theodore. *The Mirror of Justice: Literary Reflections of Legal Crises*. Princeton: Princeton UP, 1997. Print.

Zoot Suit. Dir. Luis Valdez. Universal, 1982. Film.

"Zoot Suit Riots." *The American Experience*. PBS. WGBH, Boston. Mar. 2001. Television.

Index

Modern Language Association of America
Options for Teaching

Teaching Law and Literature. Ed. Austin Sarat, Cathrine O. Frank, and Matthew Anderson. 2011.

Teaching British Women Playwrights of the Restoration and Eighteenth Century. Ed. Bonnie Nelson and Catherine Burroughs. 2010.

Teaching Narrative Theory. Ed. David Herman, Brian McHale, and James Phelan. 2010.

Teaching Early Modern English Prose. Ed. Susannah Brietz Monta and Margaret W. Ferguson. 2010.

Teaching Italian American Literature, Film, and Popular Culture. Ed. Edvige Giunta and Kathleen Zamboni McCormick. 2010.

Teaching the Graphic Novel. Ed. Stephen E. Tabachnick. 2009.

Teaching Literature and Language Online. Ed. Ian Lancashire. 2009.

Teaching the African Novel. Ed. Gaurav Desai. 2009.

Teaching World Literature. Ed. David Damrosch. 2009.

Teaching North American Environmental Literature. Ed. Laird Christensen, Mark C. Long, and Fred Waage. 2008.

Teaching Life Writing Texts. Ed. Miriam Fuchs and Craig Howes. 2007.

Teaching Nineteenth-Century American Poetry. Ed. Paula Bernat Bennett, Karen L. Kilcup, and Philipp Schweighauser. 2007.

Teaching Representations of the Spanish Civil War. Ed. Noël Valis. 2006.

Teaching the Representation of the Holocaust. Ed. Marianne Hirsch and Irene Kacandes. 2004.

Teaching Tudor and Stuart Women Writers. Ed. Susanne Woods and Margaret P. Hannay. 2000.

Teaching Literature and Medicine. Ed. Anne Hunsaker Hawkins and Marilyn Chandler McEntyre. 1999.

Teaching the Literatures of Early America. Ed. Carla Mulford. 1999.

Teaching Shakespeare through Performance. Ed. Milla C. Riggio. 1999.

Teaching Oral Traditions. Ed. John Miles Foley. 1998.

Teaching Contemporary Theory to Undergraduates. Ed. Dianne F. Sadoff and William E. Cain. 1994.

Teaching Children's Literature: Issues, Pedagogy, Resources. Ed. Glenn Edward Sadler. 1992.

Teaching Literature and Other Arts. Ed. Jean-Pierre Barricelli, Joseph Gibaldi, and Estella Lauter. 1990.

New Methods in College Writing Programs: Theories in Practice. Ed. Paul Connolly and Teresa Vilardi. 1986.

School-College Collaborative Programs in English. Ed. Ron Fortune. 1986.

Teaching Environmental Literature: Materials, Methods, Resources. Ed. Frederick O. Waage. 1985.

Part-Time Academic Employment in the Humanities: A Sourcebook for Just Policy. Ed. Elizabeth M. Wallace. 1984.

Film Study in the Undergraduate Curriculum. Ed. Barry K. Grant. 1983.

The Teaching Apprentice Program in Language and Literature. Ed. Joseph Gibaldi and James V. Mirollo. 1981.

Options for Undergraduate Foreign Language Programs: Four-Year and Two-Year Colleges. Ed. Renate A. Schulz. 1979.

Options for the Teaching of English: Freshman Composition. Ed. Jasper P. Neel. 1978.

Options for the Teaching of English: The Undergraduate Curriculum. Ed. Elizabeth Wooten Cowan. 1975.